The Condition of Education 2018

Joel McFarland
Bill Hussar
National Center for Education Statistics

Xiaolei Wang
Jijun Zhang
Ke Wang
Amy Rathbun
American Institutes for Research

Amy Barmer
Emily Forrest
Cataldi Farrah
Bullock Mann
RTI International

Thomas Nachazel
Senior Editor
Wyatt Smith
Mark Ossolinski
Editors
American Institutes for Research

U.S. Department of Education
Betsy DeVos
Secretary

Institute of Education Sciences
Mark Schneider
Director

National Center for Education Statistics
James L. Woodworth
Commissioner

The National Center for Education Statistics (NCES) is the primary federal entity for collecting, analyzing, and reporting data related to education in the United States and other nations. It fulfills a congressional mandate to collect, collate, analyze, and report full and complete statistics on the condition of education in the United States; conduct and publish reports and specialized analyses of the meaning and significance of such statistics; assist state and local education agencies in improving their statistical systems; and review and report on education activities in foreign countries.

NCES activities are designed to address high-priority education data needs; provide consistent, reliable, complete, and accurate indicators of education status and trends; and report timely, useful, and high-quality data to the U.S. Department of Education, the Congress, the states, other education policymakers, practitioners, data users, and the general public. Unless specifically noted, all information contained herein is in the public domain.

The NCES Home Page address is http://nces.ed.gov. The NCES Publications and Products address is http://nces.ed.gov/pubsearch.

This report was prepared with assistance from the American Institutes for Research under Contract No. ED-IES-12-D-0002. Mention of trade names, commercial products, or organizations does not imply endorsement by the U.S. Government.

Suggested Citation
McFarland, J., Hussar, B., Wang, X., Zhang, J., Wang, K., Rathbun, A., Barmer, A., Forrest Cataldi, E., and Bullock Mann, F. (2018). *The Condition of Education 2018* (NCES 2018-144). U.S. Department of Education. Washington, DC: National Center for Education Statistics. Retrieved [date] from https://nces.ed.gov/pubsearch/pubsinfo.asp?pubid=2018144.

Content Contact
Joel McFarland
(312) 778-0167
Joel.McFarland@ed.gov

ISBN: 978-1-64143-387-7

A Letter From the

Commissioner of the National Center for Education Statistics

On behalf of the National Center for Education Statistics (NCES), I am pleased to present *The Condition of Education 2018*, a congressionally mandated annual report summarizing the latest data on education in the United States. This report is designed to help policymakers and the public monitor educational progress. This year's report includes 47 indicators on topics ranging from prekindergarten through postsecondary education, as well as labor force outcomes and international comparisons.

In addition to the regularly updated annual indicators, this year's spotlight indicators highlight new findings from recent NCES surveys:

The first spotlight indicator examines the choices and costs that families face as they select early childhood care arrangements. Drawing on data from the NCES National Household Education Survey, the indicator finds that early childhood care expenses were higher in 2016 than in 2001. For example, families' average hourly out-of-pocket expenses for center-based care were 72 percent higher in 2016 ($7.60) than in 2001 ($4.42), in constant 2016–17 dollars. The indicator also finds that in 2016, some 57 percent of children under the age of 6 had parents who reported there were good choices for child care where they lived. Among children whose parents reported difficulty finding child care in 2016, some 32 percent cited cost as the primary reason. The complete indicator, Early Childhood Care Arrangements: Choices and Costs, contains more information about how these findings varied by family income, race/ethnicity, locale (urban, suburban, town, or rural), and children's age.

The second spotlight describes the characteristics of teachers who entered the teaching profession through an alternative route to certification program. Compared to those who entered through a traditional route, higher percentages of alternative route teachers in 2015–16 were Black (13 vs. 5 percent), Hispanic (15 vs. 8 percent), of Two or more races (2 vs. 1 percent), and male (32 vs. 22 percent), and lower percentages were White (66 vs. 83 percent). Overall, 18 percent of public school teachers in 2015–16 had entered teaching through an alternative route to certification program. The percentages were higher among those who taught career or technical education (37 percent), natural sciences (28 percent), foreign languages (26 percent), English as a second language (24 percent), math and computer science (22 percent), and special education (20 percent). The analysis also examines how the prevalence of alternative route teachers varies between charter schools and traditional public schools, between high- and low-poverty schools, and between schools that enroll high or low percentages of racial/ethnic minority students. For more findings from this analysis of data from the National Teacher and Principal Survey, see the complete indicator, Characteristics of Public School Teachers Who Completed Alternative Route to Certification Programs.

The third spotlight presents data on average student loan balances for students completing graduate degrees. Using data from the National Postsecondary Student Aid Study, this indicator examines how average student loan balances changed between 1999–2000 and 2015–16, and how those trends varied by degree type. Among graduate school completers who had student loans for undergraduate or graduate studies, average student loan balances increased for all degree types (in constant 2016–17 dollars). For example, average student loan balances for students who completed research doctorate degrees, such as a Ph.D., doubled during this time period, from $53,500 to $108,400 (an increase of 103 percent). Average student loan balances increased by 90 percent for those who completed professional doctorate degrees, such as medical doctorates and law degrees (from $98,200 to $186,600). The complete indicator, Trends in Student Loan Debt for Graduate School Completers, also describes how average student loan balances varied among specific degree programs, such as medical doctorates, law degrees, and master's degrees in business administration.

The Condition includes an At a Glance section, which allows readers to quickly make comparisons within and across indicators, and a Highlights section, which captures key findings from each indicator. The report contains a Reader's Guide, a Glossary, and a Guide to Sources that provide additional background information. Each indicator provides links to the source data tables used to produce the analyses.

As new data are released throughout the year, indicators will be updated and made available on *The Condition of Education* website. In addition, NCES produces a wide range of reports and datasets designed to help inform policymakers and the public. For more information on our latest activities and releases, please visit our website or follow us on Twitter, Facebook, and LinkedIn.

James L. Woodworth
Commissioner
National Center for Education Statistics

Reader's Guide

The Condition of Education contains indicators on the state of education in the United States, from prekindergarten through postsecondary education, as well as labor force outcomes and international comparisons. Readers can browse the full report online through the HTML site or download PDFs of the full report or individual indicators. In both the PDF and HTML versions, indicators are hyperlinked to tables in the *Digest of Education Statistics*. These tables contain the source data used in the most recent edition of *The Condition of Education*.

Data Sources and Estimates

The data in these indicators were obtained from many different sources—including students and teachers, state education agencies, local elementary and secondary schools, and colleges and universities—using surveys and compilations of administrative records. Users should be cautious when comparing data from different sources. Differences in aspects such as procedures, timing, question phrasing, and interviewer training can affect the comparability of results across data sources.

Most indicators in *The Condition of Education* summarize data from surveys conducted by the National Center for Education Statistics (NCES) or by the U.S. Census Bureau with support from NCES. Brief descriptions of the major NCES surveys used in these indicators can be found in the Guide to Sources. More detailed descriptions can be obtained on the NCES website under "Surveys and Programs."

The Guide to Sources also includes information on non-NCES sources used to develop indicators, such as the Census Bureau's American Community Survey (ACS) and Current Population Survey (CPS). For further details on the ACS, see https://www.census.gov/programs-surveys/acs/. For further details on the CPS, see http://www.census.gov/cps/.

Data for *The Condition of Education* indicators are obtained from two types of surveys: universe surveys and sample surveys. In universe surveys, information is collected from every member of the population. For example, in a survey regarding expenditures of public elementary and secondary schools, data would be obtained from each school district in the United States. When data from an entire population are available, estimates of the total population or a subpopulation are made by simply summing the units in the population or subpopulation. As a result, there is no sampling error, and observed differences are reported as true.

Since universe surveys are often expensive and time consuming, many surveys collect data from a sample of the population of interest (sample survey). For example, the National Assessment of Educational Progress (NAEP) assesses a representative sample of students rather than the entire population of students. When a sample survey is used, statistical uncertainty is introduced because the data come from only a portion of the entire population. This statistical uncertainty must be considered when reporting estimates and making comparisons. For more information, please see the section on standard errors below.

Various types of statistics derived from universe and sample surveys are reported in *The Condition of Education*. Many indicators report the size of a population or subpopulation, and the size of a subpopulation is often expressed as a percentage of the total population. In addition, the average (or *mean*) value of some characteristic of the population or subpopulation may be reported. The average is obtained by summing the values for all members of the population and dividing the sum by the size of the population. An example is the annual average salaries of full-time instructional faculty at degree-granting postsecondary institutions. Another measure that is sometimes used is the *median*. The median is the midpoint value of a characteristic at or above which 50 percent of the population is estimated to fall, and at or below which 50 percent of the population is estimated to fall. An example is the median annual earnings of young adults who are full-time, full-year wage and salary workers.

Standard Errors

Using estimates calculated from data based on a sample of the population requires consideration of several factors before the estimates become meaningful. When using data from a sample, some *margin of error* will always be present in estimations of characteristics of the total population or subpopulation because the data are available from only a portion of the total population. Consequently, data from samples can provide only an approximation of the true or actual value. The margin of error of an estimate, or the range of potential true or actual values, depends on several factors, such as the amount of variation in the responses, the size and representativeness of the sample, and the size of the subgroup for which the estimate is computed. The magnitude of this margin of error is measured by what statisticians call the "standard error" of an estimate. Larger standard errors typically mean that the estimate is less precise, while smaller standard errors typically indicate that the estimate is more precise.

When data from sample surveys are reported, the standard error is calculated for each estimate. The standard errors for all estimated totals, means, medians, or percentages are reported in the reference tables.

In order to caution the reader when interpreting findings in the indicators, estimates from sample surveys are flagged with a "!" when the standard error is between 30 and 50 percent of the estimate, and suppressed and replaced with a "‡" when the standard error is 50 percent of the estimate or greater.

Data Analysis and Interpretation

When estimates are from a sample, caution is warranted when drawing conclusions about whether one estimate is different in comparison to another; about whether a time series of estimates is increasing, decreasing, or staying the same; or about whether two variables are associated. Although one estimate may appear to be larger than another, a statistical test may find that the apparent difference between them is not measurable due to the uncertainty around the estimates. In this case, the estimates will be described as having *no measurable difference*, meaning the difference between them is not statistically significant.

Whether differences in means or percentages are statistically significant can be determined using the standard errors of the estimates. In the indicators in *The Condition of Education* and other NCES reports, when differences are statistically significant, the probability that the difference occurred by chance is less than 5 percent, according to NCES standards.

For all indicators that report estimates based on samples, differences between estimates (including increases and decreases) are stated only when they are statistically significant. To determine whether differences reported are statistically significant, most indicators use two-tailed *t* tests at the .05 level. The *t* test formula for determining statistical significance is adjusted when the samples being compared are dependent. The analyses are not adjusted for multiple comparisons, with the exception of indicators that use NAEP data. All analyses in the NAEP indicators are conducted using the NAEP Data Explorer, which makes adjustments for comparisons involving a variable with more than two categories. The NAEP Data Explorer makes such adjustments using the Benjamini-Hochberg False Discovery Rate. When the variables to be tested are postulated to form a trend over time, the relationship may be tested using linear regression or ANOVA trend analyses instead of a series of *t* tests. Indicators that use other methods of statistical comparison include a separate technical notes section. For more information on data analysis, please see the NCES Statistical Standards, Standard 5-1, available at http://nces.ed.gov/statprog/2012/pdf/Chapter5.pdf.

Multivariate analyses, such as ordinary least squares (OLS) regression models, provide information on whether the relationship between an independent variable and an outcome measure (such as group differences in the outcome measure) persists after taking into account other variables (such as student, family, and school characteristics). For COE indicators that include a regression analysis, multiple categorical or continuous independent variables are entered simultaneously. A significant regression coefficient indicates an association between the dependent (outcome) variable and the independent variable, after controlling for other independent variables included in the regression model.

Data presented in the indicators typically do not investigate more complex hypotheses or support causal inferences. We encourage readers who are interested in more complex questions and in-depth analysis to explore other NCES resources, including publications, online data tools, and public- and restricted-use datasets at http://nces.ed.gov.

A number of considerations influence the ultimate selection of the data years to feature in the indicators. To make analyses as timely as possible, the latest year of available data is shown. The choice of comparison years is often also based on the need to show the earliest available survey year, as in the case of the NAEP and the international assessment surveys. In the case of surveys with long time frames, such as surveys measuring enrollment, a decade's beginning year (e.g., 1990 or 2000) often starts the trend line. In the figures and tables of the indicators, intervening years are selected in increments in order to show the general trend. The narrative for the indicators typically compares the most current year's data with those from the initial year and then with those from a more recent period. Where applicable, the narrative may also note years in which the data begin to diverge from previous trends.

Rounding and Other Considerations

All calculations within the indicators in this report are based on unrounded estimates. Therefore, the reader may find that a calculation cited in the text or figure, such as a difference or a percentage change, may not be identical to the calculation obtained by using the rounded values shown in the accompanying tables. Although values reported in the reference tables are generally rounded to one decimal place (e.g., 76.5 percent), values reported in each indicator are generally rounded to whole numbers (with any value of 0.50 or above rounded to the next highest whole number). Due to rounding, cumulative percentages may sometimes equal 99 or 101 percent rather than 100 percent. While the data labels on the figures have been rounded to whole numbers, the graphical presentation of these data is based on the unrounded estimates.

Race and Ethnicity

The Office of Management and Budget (OMB) is responsible for the standards that govern the categories used to collect and present federal data on race and ethnicity. The OMB revised the guidelines on racial/ethnic categories used by the federal government in October 1997, with a January 2003 deadline for implementation. The revised standards require a minimum of these five categories for data on race:

American Indian or Alaska Native, Asian, Black or African American, Native Hawaiian or Other Pacific Islander, and White. The standards also require the collection of data on ethnicity categories: at a minimum, Hispanic or Latino and Not Hispanic or Latino. It is important to note that Hispanic origin is an ethnicity rather than a race, and therefore persons of Hispanic origin may be of any race. Origin can be viewed as the heritage, nationality group, lineage, or country of birth of the person or the person's parents or ancestors before their arrival in the United States. The race categories White, Black, Asian, Native Hawaiian or Other Pacific Islander, and American Indian or Alaska Native, as presented in these indicators, exclude persons of Hispanic origin unless noted otherwise.

The categories are defined as follows:

- *American Indian or Alaska Native:* A person having origins in any of the original peoples of North and South America (including Central America) and maintaining tribal affiliation or community attachment.

- *Asian:* A person having origins in any of the original peoples of the Far East, Southeast Asia, or the Indian subcontinent, including, for example, Cambodia, China, India, Japan, Korea, Malaysia, Pakistan, the Philippine Islands, Thailand, and Vietnam.

- *Black or African American:* A person having origins in any of the black racial groups of Africa.

- *Native Hawaiian or Other Pacific Islander:* A person having origins in any of the original peoples of Hawaii, Guam, Samoa, or other Pacific Islands.

- *White:* A person having origins in any of the original peoples of Europe, the Middle East, or North Africa.

- *Hispanic or Latino:* A person of Mexican, Puerto Rican, Cuban, South or Central American, or other Spanish culture or origin, regardless of race.

Within these indicators, some of the category labels have been shortened in the text, tables, and figures for ease of reference. American Indian or Alaska Native is denoted as American Indian/Alaska Native (except when separate estimates are available for American Indians alone or Alaska Natives alone); Black or African American is shortened to Black; and Hispanic or Latino is shortened to Hispanic. Native Hawaiian or Other Pacific Islander is shortened to Pacific Islander.

The indicators in this report draw from a number of different data sources. Many are federal surveys that collect data using the OMB standards for racial/ethnic classification described above; however, some sources have not fully adopted the standards, and some indicators include data collected prior to the adoption of the standards. This report focuses on the six categories that are the most common among the various data sources used: White, Black, Hispanic, Asian, Pacific Islander, and American Indian/Alaska Native. Asians and Pacific Islanders are combined into one category in indicators for which the data were not collected separately for the two groups.

Some of the surveys from which data are presented in these indicators give respondents the option of selecting either an "other" race category, a "Two or more races" or "multiracial" category, or both. Where possible, indicators present data on the "Two or more races" category; in some cases, however, this category may not be separately shown because the information was not collected or due to other data issues. In general, the "other" category is not separately shown. Any comparisons made between persons of one racial/ethnic group to "all other racial/ethnic groups" include only the racial/ethnic groups shown in the indicator. In some surveys, respondents are not given the option to select more than one race. In these surveys, respondents of Two or more races must select a single race category. Any comparisons between data from surveys that give the option to select more than one race and surveys that do not offer such an option should take into account the fact that there is a potential for bias if members of one racial group are more likely than members of the others to identify themselves as "Two or more races."[1] For postsecondary data, foreign students are counted separately and are therefore not included in any racial/ethnic category.

More detailed information on racial/ethnic groups, including data for specific Asian and Hispanic ancestry subgroups (such as Mexican, Puerto Rican, Chinese, or Vietnamese) can be found in the *Status and Trends in the Education of Racial and Ethnic Groups* report.

Limitations of the Data

The relatively small sizes of the American Indian/Alaska Native and Pacific Islander populations pose many measurement difficulties when conducting statistical analyses. Even in larger surveys, the numbers of American Indians/Alaska Natives and Pacific Islanders included in a sample are often small. Researchers studying data on these two populations often face small sample sizes that reduce the reliability of results. Survey data for American Indians/Alaska Natives and Pacific Islanders often have somewhat higher standard errors than data for other racial/ethnic groups. Due to large standard errors, differences that seem substantial are often not statistically significant and, therefore, not cited in the text.

---

[1] See Parker, J., Schenker, N., Ingram, D.D., Weed, J.A., Heck, K.E., and Madans, J.H. (2004). Bridging Between Two Standards for Collecting Information on Race and Ethnicity: An Application to Census 2000 and Vital Rates. *Public Health Reports, 119*(2): 192–205. Retrieved April 25, 2017, from http://journals.sagepub.com/doi/pdf/10.1177/003335490411900213.

Data on American Indians/Alaska Natives are often subject to inconsistencies in how respondents identify their race/ethnicity. According to research on the collection of race/ethnicity data conducted by the Bureau of Labor Statistics in 1995, the categorization of American Indian and Alaska Native is the least stable self-identification. The racial/ethnic categories presented to a respondent, and the way in which the question is asked, can influence the response, especially for individuals who consider themselves as being of mixed race or ethnicity.

As mentioned above, Asians and Pacific Islanders are combined into one category in indicators for which the data were not collected separately for the two groups. The combined category can sometimes mask significant differences between subgroups. For example, prior to 2011, the NAEP collected data that did not allow for separate reporting of estimates for Asians and Pacific Islanders. Information from *Digest of Education Statistics 2017* (table 101.20), based on the Census Bureau Current Population Reports, indicates that 96 percent of all Asian/Pacific Islander 5- to 24-year-olds are Asian. This combined category for Asians/Pacific Islanders is more representative of Asians than Pacific Islanders.

Symbols

In accordance with the NCES Statistical Standards, many tables in this volume use a series of symbols to alert the reader to special statistical notes. These symbols, and their meanings, are as follows:

— Not available.

† Not applicable.

Rounds to zero.

! Interpret data with caution. The coefficient of variation (CV) for this estimate is between 30 and 50 percent.

‡ Reporting standards not met. Either there are too few cases for a reliable estimate or the coefficient of variation (CV) for this estimate is 50 percent or greater.

* $p < .05$ significance level.

Contents

Contents

Elementary and Secondary Enrollment

Schools

Teachers and Staff

Assessments

Postsecondary Institutions

Programs, Courses, and Completions

Finances and Resources

Economic Outcomes

Assessments

Finances

Attainment

This page intentionally left blank.

The Condition of Education 2018 At a Glance

More information is available at nces.ed.gov/programs/coe.

Preprimary, Elementary, and Secondary Education

Characteristics of Children's Families	2015	2016	Change between years
Highest level of education attained by parents of children under age 18			
Percentage whose parents' highest level of education was less than high school	10.5%	10.4%	
Percentage whose parents' highest level of education was a bachelor's or higher degree	39.0%	39.7%	▲
Percentage of children under age 18 living in mother-only households	27.0%	26.7%	▼
Percentage of children under age 18 in families living in poverty	20.3%	19.1%	▼

Children's Access to and Use of the Internet	2013	2015	
Percentage of children ages 3 to 18 who use the Internet from home			
3- and 4-year-olds	31%	39%	▲
5- to 10-year-olds	50%	54%	▲
11- to 14-year-olds	65%	65%	
15- to 18-year-olds	77%	76%	

Preschool and Kindergarten Enrollment	2015	2016	
Percentage of children enrolled in preprimary education			
3-year-olds	38%	42%	
4-year-olds	67%	66%	
5-year-olds	87%	86%	

Elementary and Secondary Enrollment	Fall 2014	Fall 2015	
Number of students enrolled in public schools	50.31 million	50.44 million	▲
Prekindergarten through 8th grade	35.37 million	35.39 million	▲
9th through 12th grade	14.94 million	15.05 million	▲

Public Charter School Enrollment	Fall 2014	Fall 2015	
Number of students enrolled in public charter schools	2.7 million	2.8 million	▲
Percentage of public school students enrolled in charter schools	5.4%	5.7%	▲
Number of public charter schools	6,750	6,860	▲
Percentage of public schools that are charter schools	6.9%	7.0%	▲

Private School Enrollment	Fall 2013	Fall 2015	
Total number of students enrolled in private schools (prekindergarten through 12th grade)	5.4 million	5.8 million	▲
Prekindergarten through 8th grade	4.1 million	4.3 million	▲
9th through 12th grade	1.3 million	1.4 million	▲
Percentage of all students enrolled in private schools (prekindergarten through 12th grade)	9.7%	10.2%	▲

See notes at end of table.

LEGEND: ▲ = Higher, ▼ = Lower, Blank = Not measurably different

			Change between years
English Language Learners in Public Schools	**Fall 2014**	**Fall 2015**	
Percentage of public school students who are English language learners	9.3%	9.5%	▲
Children and Youth With Disabilities	**2014–15**	**2015–16**	
Number of public school students ages 3–21 receiving special education services	6.6 million	6.7 million	▲
Percentage of public school students ages 3–21 receiving special education services	13.0%	13.2%	▲
Characteristics of Traditional Public Schools and Public Charter Schools	**2014–15**	**2015–16**	
Traditional public schools			
Total number of traditional public schools	91,430	91,420	▼
Percentage of traditional public schools			
With more than 50% White enrollment	59.0%	58.2%	▼
With more than 50% Black enrollment	9.0%	8.9%	▼
With more than 50% Hispanic enrollment	15.7%	16.0%	▲
Public charter schools			
Total number of public charter schools	6,750	6,860	▲
Percentage of public charter schools			
With more than 50% White enrollment	35.7%	34.4%	▼
With more than 50% Black enrollment	23.6%	23.4%	▼
With more than 50% Hispanic enrollment	23.9%	25.2%	▲
Concentration of Public School Students Eligible for Free or Reduced-Price Lunch	**2014–15**	**2015–16**	
Percentage of students attending public low-poverty schools[1]	20.4%	19.7%	▼
Percentage of students attending public high-poverty schools[1]	24.3%	24.4%	▲
School Crime and Safety	**2015**	**2016**	
Nonfatal victimization rate per 1,000 students			
Victimization occurred at school	33	29	
Victimization occurred away from school	21	24	
Characteristics of Public School Teachers	**1999–2000**	**2015–16**	
Total number of public school teachers	3.0 million	3.8 million	▲
In elementary schools	1.6 million	1.9 million	▲
In secondary schools	1.4 million	1.9 million	▲
Percentage of public school teachers			
Who are female	75%	77%	▲
Who are male	25%	23%	▼
Who held a postbaccalaureate degree	47%	57%	▲
Who held a regular teaching certificate	87%	90%	▲
	2011–12	**2015–16**	
Annual base salary of public school teachers[2]	$56,590	$56,140	

See notes at end of table.

LEGEND: ▲ = Higher, ▼ = Lower, Blank = Not measurably different

Reading Performance	2015	2017	Change between years
Percentage of students who scored at or above *Proficient*[3]			
4th-grade students	36%	37%	
8th-grade students	34%	36%	▲
	2013	**2015**	
12th-grade students	38%	37%	

Mathematics Performance	2015	2017	
Percentage of students who scored at or above *Proficient*[3]			
4th-grade students	40%	40%	
8th-grade students	33%	34%	
	2013	**2015**	
12th-grade students	26%	25%	

Science Performance	2009	2015	
Percentage of students who scored at or above *Proficient*[3]			
4th-grade students	34%	38%	▲
12th-grade students	21%	22%	
	2011	**2015**	
8th-grade students	32%	34%	

Public High School Graduation Rates	2014–15	2015–16	
Adjusted Cohort Graduation Rate (ACGR)[4]	83%	84%	▲

Status Dropout Rates	2015	2016	
Percentage of 16- to 24-year-olds not enrolled in school who have not completed high school	5.9%	6.1%	

Public School Revenue Sources[2]	2013–14	2014–15	
Total revenues	$644.1 billion	$664.0 billion	▲
Federal sources	$56.3 billion	$56.4 billion	▲
State sources	$298.1 billion	$309.1 billion	▲
Local sources	$289.7 billion	$298.5 billion	▲

Public School Expenditures[2]	2013–14	2014–15	
Total expenditures	$645 billion	$668 billion	▲
Current expenditures per student	$11,429	$11,734	▲

Postsecondary Education

Immediate College Enrollment Rate	2015	2016	Change between years
Percentage of recent high school graduates enrolled in college	69%	70%	
2-year institutions	25%	24%	
4-year institutions	44%	46%	

See notes at end of table.

LEGEND: ▲ = Higher, ▼ = Lower, Blank = Not measurably different

College Enrollment Rates	2015	2016	Change between years
College participation rates for 18- to 24-year-olds			
Total, all students	40%	41%	
Male	38%	39%	
Female	43%	44%	
White	42%	42%	
Black	35%	36%	
Hispanic	37%	39%	
Asian	63%	58%	
Pacific Islander	24%	21%	
American Indian/Alaska Native	23%	19%	
Two or more races	38%	42%	

Undergraduate Enrollment	Fall 2015	Fall 2016	
Total enrollment	17.0 million	16.9 million	▼
Full-time enrollment	10.6 million	10.4 million	▼
Part-time enrollment	6.4 million	6.4 million	▼ [5]
Percentage enrolled in any distance education course	29%	31%	▲
Percentage enrolled exclusively in distance education	12%	13%	▲

Postbaccalaureate Enrollment	Fall 2015	Fall 2016	
Total enrollment	2.9 million	3.0 million	▲
Full-time enrollment	1.7 million	1.7 million	▲ [5]
Part-time enrollment	1.3 million	1.3 million	▲ [5]
Percentage enrolled in any distance education course	34%	37%	▲
Percentage enrolled exclusively in distance education	26%	28%	▲

Characteristics of Postsecondary Students	2015–16	2016–17	
Total enrollment	20.0 million	19.8 million	▼
Undergraduate enrollment	17.0 million	16.9 million	▼
White	9.3 million	9.1 million	▼
Black	2.3 million	2.2 million	▼
Hispanic	3.0 million	3.2 million	▲
Asian	1.0 million	1.1 million	▲
Pacific Islander	49,500	47,100	▼
American Indian/Alaska Native	132,300	128,600	▼
Two or more races	592,200	595,700	▲
Nonresident alien	565,800	570,300	▲
Postbaccalaureate enrollment	2.9 million	3.0 million	▲
White	1.6 million	1.6 million	▼
Black	364,300	362,900	▼
Hispanic	242,600	259,600	▲
Asian	194,400	200,200	▲
Pacific Islander	6,000	6,100	▲
American Indian/Alaska Native	13,900	13,700	▼
Two or more races	67,400	70,700	▲
Nonresident alien	417,300	427,800	▲

See notes at end of table.

LEGEND: ▲ = Higher, ▼ = Lower, Blank = Not measurably different

Characteristics of Degree-Granting Postsecondary Institutions	2015–16	2016–17	Change between years
Total number of degree-granting institutions with first-year undergraduates	4,147	3,895	▼
Number of 4-year institutions with first-year undergraduates	2,584	2,395	▼
Number of 2-year institutions with first-year undergraduates	1,563	1,500	▼

Characteristics of Postsecondary Faculty	Fall 2015	Fall 2016	
Number of full-time instructional faculty[6]	807,000	816,000	▲
Number of part-time instructional faculty	745,000	733,000	▼

Undergraduate Degree Fields	2014–15	2015–16	
Number of bachelor's degrees awarded			
Business	364,000	372,000	▲
Health professions and related programs	216,000	229,000	▲
Social sciences and history	167,000	161,000	▼

Graduate Degree Fields	2014–15	2015–16	
Number of master's degrees awarded			
Business	185,000	187,000	▲
Education	147,000	146,000	▼
Health professions and related programs	103,000	110,000	▲

Undergraduate Retention and Graduation Rates	2014–15	2015–16	
4-year institutions			
Retention rate of first-time undergraduates	80.7%	80.8%	▲
Graduation rate (within 6 years of starting program) of first-time, full-time undergraduates	59.4%	59.8%	▲
2-year institutions			
Retention rate of first-time undergraduates	61.3%	62.3%	▲
Graduation rate (within 3 years of starting program) of first-time, full-time undergraduates	29.0%	30.3%	▲

Postsecondary Certificates and Degrees Conferred	2014–15	2015–16	
Number of degrees/certificates conferred by postsecondary institutions			
Certificates below associate's degrees	961,000	939,000	▼
Associate's degrees	1,014,000	1,008,000	▼
Bachelor's degrees	1,895,000	1,921,000	▲
Master's degrees	759,000	786,000	▲
Doctor's degrees	179,000	178,000	▼

Price of Attending an Undergraduate Institution[2]	2014–15	2015–16	
Average net price at 4-year institutions for first-time, full-time undergraduate students			
Public, in-state or in-district[7]	$13,300	$13,500	▲
Private nonprofit	$25,900	$26,200	▲
Private for-profit	$21,800	$22,300	▲

See notes at end of table.

LEGEND: ▲ = Higher, ▼ = Lower, Blank = Not measurably different

Loans for Undergraduate Students[2]	2014–15	2015–16	Change between year
Average tuition and fees	$11,780	$12,080	▲
Average student loan amount	$7,100	$7,120	▲

Sources of Financial Aid	2014–15	2015–16	
Percentage of students receiving any financial aid at 4-year institutions	86%	85%	▼
Percentage of students receiving any financial aid at 2-year institutions	79%	78%	▼

Postsecondary Institution Revenues[2]	2014–15	2015–16	
Revenue from tuition and fees per full-time-equivalent (FTE) student			
Public institutions	$7,091	$7,380	▲
Private nonprofit institutions	$21,125	$21,394	▲
Private for-profit institutions	$15,357	$15,806	▼

Postsecondary Institution Expenses[2]	2014–15	2015–16	
Instruction expenses per full-time-equivalent (FTE) student			
Public institutions	$10,156	$10,422	▲
Private nonprofit institutions	$17,690	$17,860	▲
Private for-profit institutions	$4,265	$4,378	▲

Population Characteristics and Economic Outcomes

Educational Attainment of Young Adults	2016	2017	Change between years
Percentage of 25- to 29-year-olds with selected levels of educational attainment			
High school completion or higher	92%	92%	
Associate's or higher degree	46%	46%	
Bachelor's or higher degree	36%	36%	
Master's or higher degree	9%	9%	

Youth Neither Enrolled in School nor Working	2015	2016	
Percentage of 20- to 24-year-olds neither enrolled in school nor working			
Total	17%	17%	
With less than high school completion	41%	42%	
High school completion	28%	26%	
Some college, no bachelor's degree	9%	9%	
Bachelor's or higher degree	8%	8%	

Annual Earnings of Young Adults	2015	2016	
Median annual earnings for 25- to 34-year-olds[2]			
Total	$40,400	$40,000	
With less than high school completion	$25,300	$25,400	
Who completed high school as highest level	$30,900	$31,800	
Who completed some college but did not attain a degree	$35,100	$34,900	
Who attained an associate's degree	$37,400	$38,000	
Who attained a bachelor's or higher degree	$54,500	$54,800	
Who attained a bachelor's degree	$50,600	$50,000	▼
Who attained a master's or higher degree	$60,800	$64,100	

See notes at end of table.

LEGEND: ▲ = Higher, ▼ = Lower, Blank = Not measurably different

Employment and Unemployment Rates by Educational Attainment	2016	2017	Change between years
Employment rates of 25- to 34-year-olds			
Total	77%	78%	▲
With less than high school completion	59%	57%	
Who completed high school as highest level	70%	72%	
Who attained a bachelor's or higher degree	86%	86%	
Unemployment rates of 25- to 34-year-olds			
Total	6%	5%	▼
With less than high school completion	13%	13%	
Who completed high school as highest level	9%	7%	▼
Who attained a bachelor's or higher degree	2%	3%	

International Comparisons

International Comparisons: Reading Literacy at Grade 4 (2016)	U.S. average score	International average score	Difference between the U.S. average and the international average
Progress in International Reading Literacy Study (PIRLS)			
Average reading literacy scores of 4th-grade students	549	500	▲
Average online informational reading score of 4th-grade students	557	500	▲

International Comparisons: U.S. 4th-, 8th-, and 12th-Graders' Mathematics and Science Achievement (2015)	U.S. average score	TIMSS scale center-point	Difference between the U.S. average and the TIMSS scale center-point
Trends in International Mathematics and Science Study (TIMSS)			
Mathematics scores of 4th-grade students	539	500	▲
Mathematics scores of 8th-grade students	518	500	▲
Science scores of 4th-grade students	546	500	▲
Science scores of 8th-grade students	530	500	▲
TIMSS Advanced			
Advanced mathematics scores of 12th-grade students	485	500	▼
Physics scores of 12th-grade students	437	500	▼

See notes at end of table.

LEGEND: ▲ = Higher, ▼ = Lower, Blank = Not measurably different

International Comparisons: Science, Reading, and Mathematics Literacy of 15-Year-Old Students (2015)	U.S. average score	OECD average score	Difference between the U.S. average and the OECD average
Program for International Student Assessment (PISA)			
Science literacy scores of 15-year-old students	496	493	
Reading literacy scores of 15-year-old students	497	493	
Mathematics literacy scores of 15-year-old students	470	490	▼

Education Expenditures by Country (2014)[8]	U.S.	OECD	Difference between the U.S. and OECD
Expenditure per full-time-equivalent (FTE) student			
Elementary and secondary education	$12,300	$9,600	▲
Postsecondary education	$29,700	$16,400	▲

International Educational Attainment	2015	2016	Change between years
Percentage of the population 25 to 34 years old who completed high school			
United States	90.5%	91.5%	▲
Organization for Economic Cooperation and Development (OECD) countries	83.6%	84.1%	▲
Percentage of the population 25 to 34 years old who attained a postsecondary degree			
United States	46.5%	47.5%	
OECD countries	41.8%	43.1%	▲

[1] Low-poverty schools are defined as public schools where 25 percent or less of the students are eligible for free or reduced-price lunch (FRPL). A high-poverty school is defined as a public school where more than 75 percent of the students are eligible for FRPL.

[2] Data are reported in constant 2016–17 dollars, based on the Consumer Price Index (CPI).

[3] *Proficient* indicates demonstrated competency in challenging subject matter.

[4] The Adjusted Cohort Graduation Rate (ACGR) is the number of students who graduate in 4 years with a regular high school diploma divided by the number of students who form the adjusted cohort for the graduating class. From the beginning of 9th grade (or the earliest high school grade), students who enter that grade for the first time form a cohort that is "adjusted" by adding any students who subsequently transfer into the cohort and subtracting any students who subsequently transfer out, emigrate to another country, or die.

[5] Data are measurably different, although they round to the same number.

[6] Data are for full-time instructional faculty on 9-month contracts at degree-granting postsecondary institutions.

[7] The average net price at public 4-year institutions uses the lower of in-district or in-state average net price.

[8] Data are reported in constant 2016 dollars based on the OECD's National Consumer Price Index.

NOTE: All calculations within the At a Glance are based on unrounded numbers. Race categories exclude persons of Hispanic ethnicity.

SOURCE: *The Condition of Education 2018.*

LEGEND: ▲ = Higher, ▼ = Lower, Blank = Not measurably different

Highlights From *The Condition of Education 2018*

Spotlights

Early Childhood Care Arrangements: Choices and Costs

Child care costs have changed over time for children under the age of 6 who are not yet enrolled in kindergarten. In 2016, the average hourly out-of-pocket expense for families of children in center-based care was 72 percent higher than in 2001 ($7.60 vs. $4.42, in constant 2016–17 dollars), the expense for families of children in nonrelative care was 48 percent higher than in 2001 ($6.54 vs. $4.42), and the expense for families of children in relative care was 79 percent higher than in 2001 ($4.99 vs. $2.78).

Characteristics of Public School Teachers Who Completed Alternative Route to Certification Programs

Approximately 18 percent of public school teachers in 2015–16 had entered teaching through an alternative route to certification program. Compared to those who entered through a traditional route, a higher percentage of alternative route teachers were Black (13 vs. 5 percent), Hispanic (15 vs. 8 percent), of Two or more races (2 vs. 1 percent), and male (32 vs. 22 percent).

Trends in Student Loan Debt for Graduate School Completers

Average loan balances for students who completed a research or professional doctorate increased between 1999–2000 and 2015–16 for all degree programs for which data were available (in constant 2016–17 dollars). Average loan balances approximately doubled for those who completed medical doctorates (from $124,700 to $246,000, an increase of 97 percent), Ph.D.'s outside the field of education (from $48,400 to $98,800, an increase of 104 percent), and other non-Ph.D. doctorates (from $64,500 to $132,200, an increase of 105 percent).

Preprimary, Elementary, and Secondary Education

 FAMILY CHARACTERISTICS

Characteristics of Children's Families

In 2016, some 10 percent of children under the age of 18 lived in households without a parent who had completed high school, 27 percent lived in mother-only households, 8 percent lived in father-only households, and 19 percent lived in poverty.

Children's Access to and Use of the Internet

In 2015, about 71 percent of children ages 3 to 18 used the Internet. Among these children, 86 percent used the Internet at home; 65 percent used it at school; 31 percent used it at someone else's home; 27 percent used it at a library, community center, or other public place; and 14 percent used it at a coffee shop or other business offering internet access. In addition, 27 percent of these children used the Internet while traveling between places.

 PREPRIMARY EDUCATION

Preschool and Kindergarten Enrollment

In 2016, the percentage of 3- to 5-year-olds enrolled in preschool programs was higher for those children whose parents had a graduate or professional degree (54 percent) than for those whose parents had a bachelor's degree (41 percent), an associate's degree (35 percent), some college but no degree (37 percent), a high school credential (33 percent), and less than a high school credential (30 percent).

ELEMENTARY AND SECONDARY ENROLLMENT

Elementary and Secondary Enrollment

Between fall 2015 and fall 2027, total public school enrollment in prekindergarten through grade 12 is projected to increase by 3 percent (from 50.4 million to 52.1 million students), with changes across states ranging from an increase of 28 percent in the District of Columbia to a decrease of 12 percent in Connecticut.

Public Charter School Enrollment

Between fall 2000 and fall 2015, overall public charter school enrollment increased from 0.4 million to 2.8 million. During this period, the percentage of public school students who attended charter schools increased from 1 to 6 percent.

Private School Enrollment

In fall 2015, some 5.8 million students (10.2 percent of all elementary and secondary students) were enrolled in private elementary and secondary schools. Thirty-six percent of private school students were enrolled in Catholic schools, 39 percent were enrolled in other religiously affiliated schools, and 24 percent were enrolled in nonsectarian schools.

English Language Learners in Public Schools

The percentage of public school students in the United States who were English language learners (ELLs) was higher in fall 2015 (9.5 percent, or 4.8 million students) than in fall 2000 (8.1 percent, or 3.8 million students). In fall 2015, the percentage of public school students who were ELLs ranged from 1.0 percent in West Virginia to 21.0 percent in California.

Children and Youth With Disabilities

In 2015–16, the number of students ages 3–21 receiving special education services was 6.7 million, or 13 percent of all public school students. Among students receiving special education services, 34 percent had specific learning disabilities.

 ## SCHOOLS

Characteristics of Traditional Public Schools and Public Charter Schools

In 2015–16, some 57 percent of public charter schools were located in cities, compared to 25 percent of traditional public schools. A higher percentage of public charter schools than of traditional public schools had more than 50 percent Black enrollment (23 vs. 9 percent), and more than 50 percent Hispanic enrollment (25 vs. 16 percent). A lower percentage of public charter schools than of traditional public schools had more than 50 percent White enrollment (34 vs. 58 percent).

Concentration of Public School Students Eligible for Free or Reduced-Price Lunch

Higher percentages of Hispanic (45 percent), Black (45 percent), American Indian/Alaska Native (37 percent), and Pacific Islander (25 percent) students attended high-poverty schools than of White students (8 percent) in school year 2015–16. The percentages of students of Two or more races (18 percent) and Asian students (15 percent) in high-poverty schools were higher than the percentage for White students but lower than the national average (24 percent).

School Crime and Safety

Between 2000 and 2016, the rates of nonfatal victimization both at school and away from school declined for students ages 12–18. The rate of victimization at school declined 65 percent, and the rate of victimization away from school declined 72 percent.

TEACHERS AND STAFF

Characteristics of Public School Teachers

The percentage of public school teachers who held a postbaccalaureate degree (i.e., a master's, education specialist, or doctor's degree) was higher in 2015–16 (57 percent) than in 1999–2000 (47 percent). In both school years, a lower percentage of elementary school teachers than secondary school teachers held a postbaccalaureate degree.

 ASSESSMENTS

Reading Performance

The average 4th-grade reading score in 2017 (222) was higher than the average score in 1992 (217), but not measurably different from the average score in 2015, when the assessment was last administered. At the 8th-grade level, the average reading score in 2017 (267) was higher than the scores in both 1992 (260) and 2015 (265).

Mathematics Performance

The average 4th-grade mathematics score in 2017 (240) was higher than the average score in 1990 (213), but not measurably different from the average score in 2015, when the assessment was last administered. Similarly, the average 8th-grade mathematics score was higher in 2017 (283) than in 1990 (263), but not measurably different from the average score in 2015.

Science Performance

The percentage of 4th-grade students scoring at or above the *Proficient* level was higher in 2015 (38 percent) than in 2009 (34 percent), according to data from the National Assessment of Educational Progress. In addition, the percentage of 8th-grade students scoring at or above the *Proficient* level was higher in 2015 (34 percent) than in 2009 (30 percent). The percentage of 12th-grade students scoring at or above the *Proficient* level in 2015 (22 percent) was not measurably different from the percentage in 2009.

 HIGH SCHOOL COMPLETION

Public High School Graduation Rates

In school year 2015–16, the adjusted cohort graduation rate (ACGR) for public high school students was 84 percent, the highest it has been since the rate was first measured in 2010–11. In other words, more than four out of five students graduated with a regular high school diploma within 4 years of starting 9th grade. Asian/Pacific Islander students had the highest ACGR (91 percent), followed by White (88 percent), Hispanic (79 percent), Black (76 percent), and American Indian/Alaska Native (72 percent) students.

Status Dropout Rates

The overall status dropout rate decreased from 10.9 percent in 2000 to 6.1 percent in 2016. During this time, the Hispanic status dropout rate decreased by 19.2 percentage points, while the Black and White status dropout rates decreased by 6.9 and 1.7 percentage points, respectively. Nevertheless, in 2016 the Hispanic status dropout rate (8.6 percent) remained higher than the Black (6.2 percent) and White (5.2 percent) status dropout rates.

 FINANCES

Public School Revenue Sources

In school year 2014–15, elementary and secondary public school revenues totaled $664 billion in constant 2016–17 dollars. Of this total, 8 percent of revenues were from federal sources, 47 percent were from state sources, and 45 percent were from local sources.

Public School Expenditures

In 2014–15, public schools spent $11,734 per student on current expenditures, a category that includes salaries, employee benefits, purchased services, and supplies. Current expenditures per student were 15 percent higher in 2014–15 than in 2000–01, after adjusting for inflation. During this period, current expenditures per student peaked in 2008–09 at $11,914, and fluctuated between 2008–09 and 2014–15.

Postsecondary Education

POSTSECONDARY STUDENTS

Immediate College Enrollment Rate

The immediate college enrollment rate for high school completers increased from 63 percent in 2000 to 70 percent in 2016. The enrollment rate for those from high-income families (83 percent) was higher than the rate for those from low-income (67 percent) and middle-income families (64 percent) in 2016. The gap in enrollment rates between low- and high-income students narrowed from 30 percentage points in 2000 to 16 percentage points in 2016. The gap between low- and middle-income students was 12 percentage points in 2000, but there was no measurable gap between low- and middle-income students in 2016.

College Enrollment Rates

The overall college enrollment rate for young adults increased from 35 percent in 2000 to 41 percent in 2016. During this time period, the enrollment rate increased by 3 percentage points for White young adults, 6 percentage points for Black young adults, and 17 percentage points for Hispanic young adults. In 2016, the rate for White young adults (42 percent) was higher than the rate for Black young adults (36 percent), but not measurably different from the rate for Hispanic young adults (39 percent).

Undergraduate Enrollment

Between 2000 and 2016, total undergraduate enrollment in degree-granting postsecondary institutions increased by 28 percent (from 13.2 million to 16.9 million students). By 2027, total undergraduate enrollment is projected to increase to 17.4 million students.

Postbaccalaureate Enrollment

Between 2000 and 2016, total postbaccalaureate enrollment increased by 38 percent (from 2.2 million to 3.0 million students). By 2027, postbaccalaureate enrollment is projected to increase to 3.1 million students.

Characteristics of Postsecondary Students

In fall 2015, some 77 percent of the 10.5 million undergraduate students at 4-year institutions were enrolled full time, compared with 39 percent of the 6.5 million undergraduate students at 2-year institutions.

POSTSECONDARY INSTITUTIONS

Characteristics of Degree-Granting Postsecondary Institutions

In academic year 2016–17, some 27 percent of 4-year institutions had open admissions policies (accepted all applicants), an additional 27 percent accepted three-quarters or more of their applicants, 32 percent accepted from one-half to less than three-quarters of their applicants, and 14 percent accepted less than one-half of their applicants.

Characteristics of Postsecondary Faculty

From fall 1999 to fall 2016, the number of faculty in degree-granting postsecondary institutions increased by 51 percent (from 1.0 to 1.5 million). The number of full-time faculty increased by 38 percent over this period, while the number of part-time faculty increased by 74 percent between 1999 and 2011, and then decreased by 4 percent between 2011 and 2016.

PROGRAMS, COURSES, AND COMPLETIONS

Undergraduate Degree Fields

In 2015–16, over two-thirds of the 1.0 million associate's degrees conferred by postsecondary institutions were concentrated in three fields of study: liberal arts and sciences, general studies, and humanities (381,000 degrees); health professions and related programs (191,000 degrees); and business (128,000 degrees). Of the 1.9 million bachelor's degrees conferred in 2015–16, over half were concentrated in six fields of study: business (372,000 degrees), health professions and related programs (229,000 degrees), social sciences and history (161,000 degrees), psychology (117,000 degrees), biological and biomedical sciences (114,000 degrees), and engineering (107,000 degrees).

Graduate Degree Fields

In 2015–16, over half of the 786,000 master's degrees conferred were concentrated in three fields of study: business (187,000 degrees), education (146,000 degrees), and health professions and related programs (110,000 degrees). Of the 178,000 doctor's degrees conferred, almost two-thirds were concentrated in two fields: health professions and related programs (73,700 degrees) and legal professions and studies (37,000).

Undergraduate Retention and Graduation Rates

About 60 percent of students who began seeking a bachelor's degree at a 4-year institution in fall 2010 completed that degree within 6 years; the 6-year graduation rate was higher for females than for males (63 vs. 57 percent).

Postsecondary Certificates and Degrees Conferred

The number of postsecondary certificates and degrees conferred at each award level increased between 2000–01 and 2015–16. The number of certificates below the associate's level conferred during this period increased by 70 percent. The number of degrees conferred during this period increased by 74 percent at the associate's level, by 54 percent at the bachelor's level, by 66 percent at the master's level, and by 49 percent at the doctor's level.

 FINANCES AND RESOURCES

Price of Attending an Undergraduate Institution

In 2015–16, the average net price of attendance (total cost minus grant and scholarship aid) at 4-year institutions for first-time, full-time undergraduate students at public institutions was $13,400, compared with $26,200 at private nonprofit institutions and $22,300 at private for-profit institutions (in constant 2016–17 dollars).

Loans for Undergraduate Students

In 2015–16, the average annual undergraduate student loan amount of $7,100 was 2 percent lower than the 2010–11 average of $7,300 (in constant 2016–17 dollars). Less than half (46 percent) of first-time, full-time undergraduate students were awarded loan aid in 2015–16, a 4 percentage point decrease from 2010–11 (50 percent).

Sources of Financial Aid

The percentage of first-time, full-time degree/certificate-seeking undergraduate students at 4-year postsecondary institutions who were awarded financial aid was higher in 2015–16 (85 percent) than in 2000–01 (75 percent).

Postsecondary Institution Revenues

Between 2010–11 and 2015–16, revenues from tuition and fees per full-time-equivalent (FTE) student increased by 23 percent at public institutions (from $6,003 to $7,380 in constant 2016–17 dollars) and by 7 percent at private nonprofit institutions (from $20,071 to $21,394). At private for-profit institutions, revenues from tuition and fees per FTE student were 5 percent lower in 2015–16 than in 2010–11 ($15,806 vs. $16,698).

Postsecondary Institution Expenses

In 2015–16, instruction expenses per full-time-equivalent (FTE) student (in constant 2016–17 dollars) was the largest expense category at public institutions ($10,422) and private nonprofit institutions ($17,860). At private for-profit institutions, the combined category of student services, academic support, and institutional support expenses per FTE student was the largest expense category ($10,398).

Population Characteristics and Economic Outcomes

 POPULATION CHARACTERISTICS

Educational Attainment of Young Adults

Educational attainment rates for 25- to 29-year-olds increased at all levels between 2000 and 2017. During this time, the percentage who had completed high school increased from 88 to 92 percent, the percentage with an associate's or higher degree increased from 38 to 46 percent, the percentage with a bachelor's or higher degree increased from 29 to 36 percent, and the percentage with a master's or higher degree increased from 5 to 9 percent.

Youth Neither Enrolled in School nor Working

In 2016, some 17 percent of 20- to 24-year-olds were neither enrolled in school nor working, compared to 12 percent of 18- and 19-year-olds and 5 percent of 16- and 17-year-olds. In each age group, the percentage who were neither in school nor working was higher for those in poor households than for those in nonpoor households. For example, among 20- to 24-year-olds in 2016, some 31 percent of those in poor households were neither in school nor working, compared to 13 percent of those in nonpoor households.

 ECONOMIC OUTCOMES

Annual Earnings of Young Adults

In 2016, the median earnings of young adults with a bachelor's degree ($50,000) were 57 percent higher than those of young adult high school completers ($31,800). The median earnings of young adult high school completers were 26 percent higher than those of young adults who did not complete high school ($25,400).

Employment and Unemployment Rates by Educational Attainment

In 2017, the employment rate was higher for young adults with higher levels of educational attainment than for those with lower levels of educational attainment. For example, the employment rate was 86 percent for young adults with a bachelor's or higher degree and 57 percent for those who had not completed high school.

International Comparisons

ASSESSMENTS

International Comparisons: Reading Literacy at Grade 4

In 2016, the United States, along with 15 other education systems, participated in the new ePIRLS assessment of students' comprehension of online information. The average online informational reading score for fourth-grade students in the United States (557) was higher than the ePIRLS scale centerpoint (500). Only three education systems (Singapore, Norway, and Ireland) scored higher than the United States.

International Comparisons: U.S. 4th-, 8th-, and 12th-Graders' Mathematics and Science Achievement

According to the 2015 Trends in International Mathematics and Science Study (TIMSS), the United States was among the top 15 educations systems in science (out of 54) at grade 4 and among the top 17 education systems in science (out of 43) at grade 8. In mathematics, the United States was among the top 20 education systems at grade 4 and top 19 education systems at grade 8.

International Comparisons: Science, Reading, and Mathematics Literacy of 15-Year-Old Students

In 2015, there were 18 education systems with higher average science literacy scores for 15-year-olds than the United States, 14 with higher reading literacy scores, and 36 with higher mathematics literacy scores.

 FINANCES

Education Expenditures by Country

In 2014, the United States spent $12,300 per full-time-equivalent (FTE) student on elementary and secondary education, which was 29 percent higher than the OECD average of $9,600. At the postsecondary level, the United States spent $29,700 per FTE student, which was 81 percent higher than the OECD average of $16,400.

 ATTAINMENT

International Educational Attainment

Across OECD countries, the average percentage of the adult population with any postsecondary degree was 36 percent in 2016, an increase of 14 percentage points from 2000. During the same period, the percentage of U.S. adults with any postsecondary degree increased 9 percentage points to 46 percent.

The spotlight indicators in this chapter of *The Condition of Education* examine selected topics in greater detail. These indicators feature innovative data collections and analyses from across the National Center for Education Statistics.

This chapter's indicators, as well as spotlight indicators and special analyses from previous editions, are available at *The Condition of Education* website: http://nces.ed.gov/programs/coe.

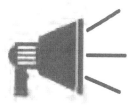

Spotlights

Early Childhood Care Arrangements: Choices and Costs

Child care costs have changed over time for children under the age of 6 who are not yet enrolled in kindergarten. In 2016, the average hourly out-of-pocket expense for families of children in center-based care was 72 percent higher than in 2001 ($7.60 vs. $4.42, in constant 2016–17 dollars), the expense for families of children in nonrelative care was 48 percent higher than in 2001 ($6.54 vs. $4.42), and the expense for families of children in relative care was 79 percent higher than in 2001 ($4.99 vs. $2.78).

Child care arrangements are influential in children's early education; children often learn skills in child care settings that not only are important for kindergarten entry but also can have a lasting impact on their development into adulthood.[1,2] In 2016, about 60 percent of the 21.4 million children under 6 years old who were not yet enrolled in kindergarten were in some type of nonparental care arrangement on a regular basis. Newly released data from the 2016 Early Childhood Program Participation survey (ECPP), a part of the National Household Education Surveys (NHES) Program, provide new insights about children's participation in nonparental care arrangements, including relative care, nonrelative care, and center-based care arrangements.

This spotlight uses ECPP survey data to explore whether children's parents report that there are good choices for child care or early childhood programs (also referred to as "child care" in this indicator) where they live; how much difficulty they have finding the type of child care they want for their children; what the primary reason is for the difficulty finding child care; and what the average out-of-pocket costs are for child care arrangements. Findings are presented overall, as well as by children's age, race/ethnicity, household income, and geographic locale (urban, suburban, town, or rural).

Figure 1.   Percentage distribution of children by whether their parents/guardians felt there were good choices for child care or early childhood programs where they live, by selected child and family characteristics: 2016

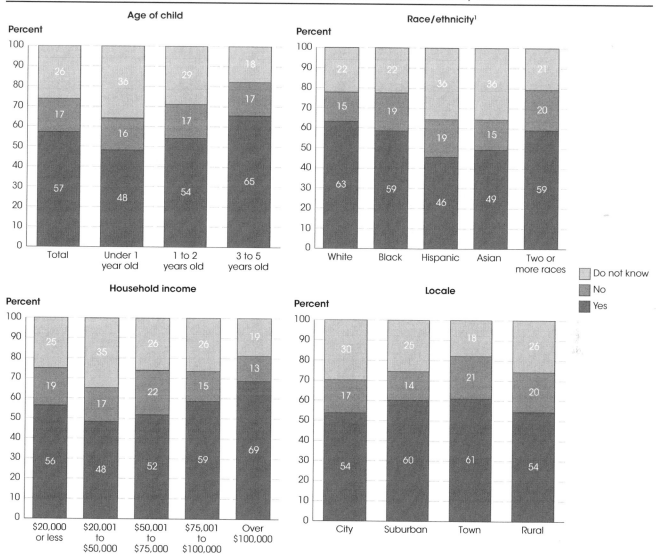

[1] Reporting standards for Pacific Islanders and American Indians/Alaska Natives were not met; therefore, data for these groups are not shown in the figure. Race categories exclude persons of Hispanic ethnicity.
NOTE: Data represent children who were under 6 years old and were not yet in kindergarten. Detail may not sum to totals because of rounding.
SOURCE: U.S. Department of Education, National Center for Education Statistics, Early Childhood Program Participation Survey of the National Household Education Surveys Program (ECPP-NHES:2016). See *Digest of Education Statistics 2017*, table 202.30b.

In 2016, some 57 percent of children under 6 years old[3] had parents[4] who reported that they felt there were good choices for child care where they lived. About 17 percent of children had parents who did not feel there were good choices, and the remaining 26 percent did not know whether there were good choices where they lived. These percentages were not measurably different from the corresponding percentages in 2012. In 2016, the percentage of children whose parents felt there were good choices for child care was highest for children 3 to 5 years old (65 percent), next highest for children 1 to 2 years old (54 percent), and lowest for children under 1 year old (48 percent).[5] The percentages of children under age 6 whose parents felt there were good choices for child care were higher for White children (63 percent), children of Two or more races (59 percent), and Black children (59 percent) than for Asian (49 percent) and Hispanic children (46 percent).

In 2016, the percentage of children under 6 years old whose parents reported that they felt there were good choices for child care was highest in households with incomes of over $100,000. Specifically, 69 percent of children in households with incomes of over $100,000 had parents who felt there were good choices for child care, compared with 59 percent for children in households with incomes of $75,001 to $100,000, 56 percent for children in households with incomes of $20,000 or less, 52 percent for children in households with incomes of $50,001 to $75,000, and 48 percent for children in households with incomes of $20,001 to $50,000. In addition, the percentage of children whose parents felt there were good choices for child care was higher for children in households with incomes of $75,001 to $100,000 than for children in households with incomes of $20,001 to $50,000 and incomes of $50,001 to $75,000. However, the percentage of children whose parents felt there were good choices for child care was higher for children in households with incomes of $20,000 or less than for children in households with incomes of $20,001 to $50,000.

With respect to the location of the home, the percentage of children under 6 years old whose parents felt there were good choices for child care was higher for children living in towns (61 percent) and suburban areas (60 percent) than for children in cities (54 percent) in 2016. In addition, the percentage of children whose parents felt there were good choices for child care was higher for children living in suburban areas than in rural areas (54 percent).

Figure 2.   Percentage distribution of children by their parents/guardians' reported level of difficulty finding the type of child care or early childhood program they wanted, by selected child and family characteristics: 2016

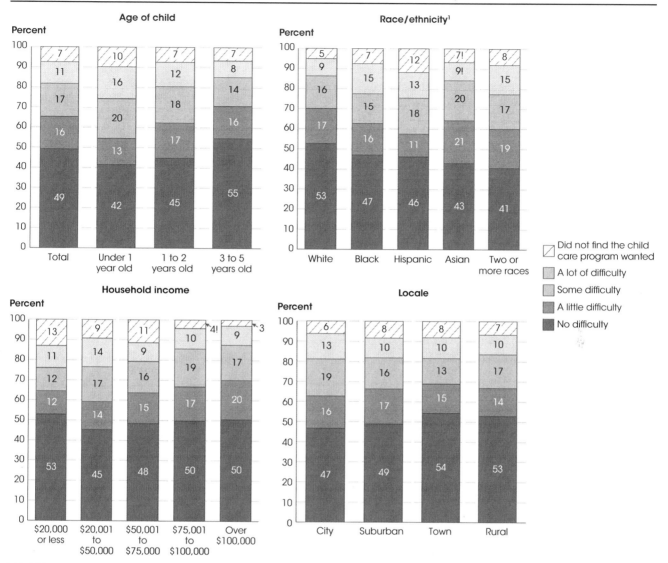

! Interpret data with caution. The coefficient of variation (CV) for this estimate is between 30 and 50 percent.
[1] Reporting standards for Pacific Islanders and American Indians/Alaska Natives were not met; therefore, data for these groups are not shown in the figure. Race categories exclude persons of Hispanic ethnicity.
NOTE: Data represent children who were under 6 years old and were not yet in kindergarten. Data exclude children whose parents/guardians did not try to find care. Detail may not sum to totals because of rounding.
SOURCE: U.S. Department of Education, National Center for Education Statistics, Early Childhood Program Participation Survey of the National Household Education Surveys Program (ECPP-NHES:2016). See *Digest of Education Statistics 2017*, table 202.30b.

Of children whose parents reported that they tried to find child care for them, 49 percent had parents who had "no difficulty" finding the type of care they wanted in 2016, which was higher than the corresponding percentage in 2012 (42 percent). In 2016, some 16 percent of children had parents who had "a little difficulty" finding the type of care they wanted, and 17 percent had parents who had "some difficulty" in doing so; both percentages were lower than their corresponding percentages in 2012 (19 and 22 percent, respectively). The percentage of children whose parents reported having "a lot of difficulty" finding the type of care they wanted in 2016 (11 percent) was not measurably different from the corresponding percentage in 2012. The percentage of children whose parents "did not find the type of care they wanted" in 2016 (7 percent) was higher than the corresponding percentage in 2012 (5 percent).

Whether parents reported having difficulty finding the type of child care they wanted in 2016 varied according to their children's age. For children whose parents reported that they tried to find child care for their children, 55 percent of 3- to 5-year-olds had parents who had no difficulty finding the care they wanted. This percentage was higher than the corresponding percentages for children 1 to 2 years old (45 percent) and for those under 1 year old (42 percent). When the data are examined by race/ethnicity, a higher percentage of White children (53 percent) had parents who had no difficulty finding the type of care they wanted, compared with the percentages of Asian children (43 percent) and children of Two or more races (41 percent). No measurable differences by household income or locale were observed in the percentages of children whose parents reported no difficulty finding the type of care they wanted.

Figure 3. Percentage distribution of children by their parents/guardians' primary reason for difficulty finding child care or an early childhood program, by selected child and family characteristics: 2016

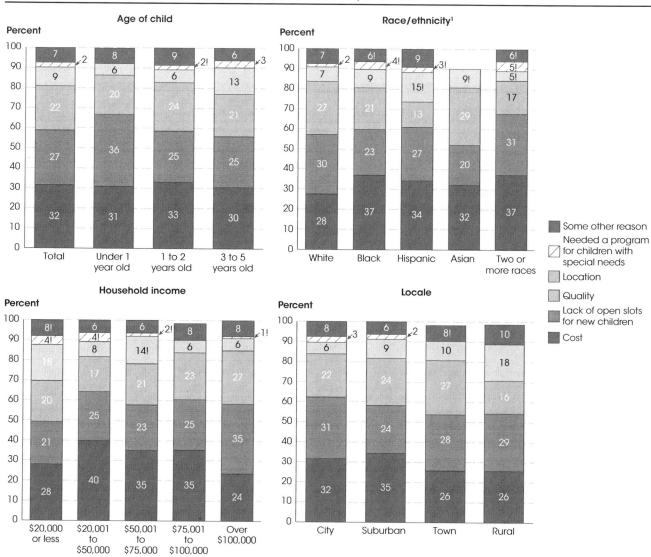

! Interpret data with caution. The coefficient of variation (CV) for this estimate is between 30 and 50 percent.
[1] Reporting standards for Pacific Islanders and American Indians/Alaska Natives were not met; therefore, data for these groups are not shown in the figure. Race categories exclude persons of Hispanic ethnicity.
NOTE: Data represent children who were under 6 years old and were not yet in kindergarten. Estimates exclude children whose parent/guardian reported either "have not tried to find care" or "no difficulty" finding the type of child care or early childhood program wanted. In addition, estimates also excluded nine cases whose parent/guardian reported "not applicable, did not look for care" in the open-ended response of "some other reason." Categories not shown in the figure have been suppressed because reporting standards were not met; either there are too few cases for a reliable estimate or the coefficient of variation (CV) is 50 percent or greater. Detail may not sum to totals because of rounding and suppressed data.
SOURCE: U.S. Department of Education, National Center for Education Statistics, Early Childhood Program Participation Survey of the National Household Education Surveys Program (ECPP-NHES:2016). See *Digest of Education Statistics 2017*, table 202.30a.

Among children whose parents reported difficulty finding child care in 2016, some 32 percent had parents who cited cost as the primary reason. Lower percentages of children had parents who cited the following as their primary reason for difficulty finding child care: lack of open slots for new children (27 percent), quality (22 percent), and location (9 percent). In addition, 2 percent of children had parents who reported that needing a program for children with special needs was the primary reason for difficulty finding care, and 7 percent had parents who reported other reasons.[6]

Among children whose parents reported difficulty finding child care in 2016, the percentage whose parents reported a lack of open slots for new children or location as the primary reason for the difficulty varied by children's age. A higher percentage of children under 1 year old (36 percent) than children 1 to 2 years old and 3 to 5 years old (25 percent each) had parents who reported that a lack of open slots was the primary reason for the difficulty finding care. Also, the percentage of children whose parents reported that location was the primary reason for the difficulty finding care was higher for children 3 to 5 years old (13 percent) than for children under 1 year old and children 1 to 2 years old (6 percent each).

When the data are examined by race/ethnicity, in 2016 a lower percentage of Asian children (20 percent) than White children (30 percent) had parents who reported a lack of open slots for new children as the primary reason for difficulty finding care. The percentage of children whose parents reported that quality was the primary reason for difficulty finding care was lower for Hispanic children (13 percent) than for Black (21 percent), White (27 percent), and Asian children (29 percent). In addition, a lower percentage of children of Two of more races (17 percent) than White and Asian children had parents who reported quality as the primary reason.

When the data are examined by household income level, in 2016 the percentage of children whose parents reported cost as the primary reason for difficulty finding care was lower for children in households with incomes over $100,000 (24 percent) than for children with household incomes of $50,001 to $75,000 (35 percent), $75,001 to $100,000 (35 percent), and $20,001 to $50,000 (40 percent). In comparison, the percentage of children whose parents reported a lack of open slots for new children as the primary reason for the difficulty was higher for children in households with incomes over $100,000 (35 percent) than for children in households with lower income levels (ranging from 21 to 25 percent). The percentage of children whose parents reported that location was the primary reason for the difficulty finding child care was higher for children in households with incomes of $20,000 or less (18 percent) than for children in households with incomes of $20,001 to $50,000 (8 percent), $75,000 to $100,000 (6 percent), and over $100,000 (6 percent).

When the data are examined by geographic locale, in 2016 a higher percentage of children in suburban areas (35 percent) than in rural areas (26 percent) had parents who cited cost as the primary reason for the difficulty finding care, and a higher percentage of children in cities (31 percent) than in suburban areas (24 percent) had parents who cited a lack of open slots for new children as the primary reason for difficulty. Quality was more commonly cited as the primary reason for difficulty finding care among the parents of children in suburban areas (24 percent) than of those in rural areas (16 percent), and location was more commonly cited as the primary obstacle for parents of children in rural areas (18 percent) than for parents of children in towns (10 percent), suburban areas (9 percent), and cities (6 percent).

Figure 4.   Average hourly out-of-pocket child care expense for children under 6 years old and not yet in kindergarten whose families paid for child care, by primary type of child care arrangement: 2001 and 2016

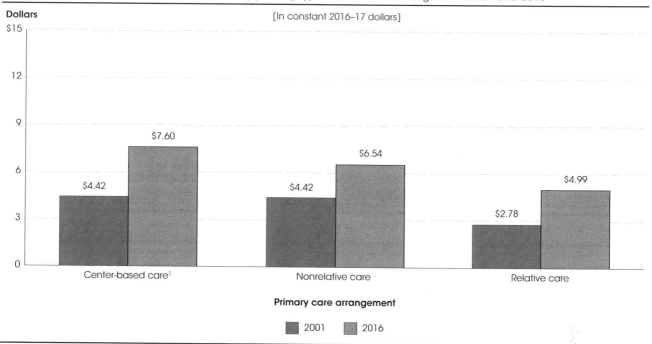

[1] Center-based arrangements include day care centers, Head Start programs, preschools, prekindergartens, and childhood programs.
NOTE: Average hourly expenses are reported in constant 2016–17 dollars, adjusted using the Consumer Price Index (CPI). Estimates include only those children whose families paid at least part of the cost out of pocket for their child to receive nonparental care at least weekly. Children for whom no fee was charged, or for whom another source paid the entire fee, are excluded from the estimates. A child's primary arrangement is the regular nonparental care arrangement or early childhood education program in which the child spent the most time per week. In 2001, National Household Education Surveys Program (NHES) surveys were administered via telephone with an interviewer. For NHES:2016, initial contact with all respondents was by mail, and the majority of respondents received paper-and-pencil questionnaires. However, as an experiment with web use, a small sample of NHES:2016 respondents received mailed invitations to complete the survey online.
SOURCE: U.S. Department of Education, National Center for Education Statistics, Early Childhood Program Participation Survey of the National Household Education Surveys Program (ECPP-NHES: 2001 and 2016). See *Digest of Education Statistics 2017*, table 202.30c.

The NHES Early Childhood Program Participation survey also asked parents about hourly out-of-pocket expenses for their children's primary child care arrangements. In 2016, the average hourly out-of-pocket expense was $7.60 for children in center-based programs, $6.54 for children in nonrelative care, and $4.99 for children in relative care. For all three child care types, the average hourly out-of-pocket expense in 2016 was higher than in 2001 (in constant 2016–17 dollars). The average hourly out-of-pocket expense for families of children in center-based care in 2016 was 72 percent higher than in 2001 ($7.60 vs. $4.42), the expense for families of children in nonrelative care was 48 percent higher than in 2001 ($6.54 vs. $4.42), and the expense for families of children in relative care was 79 percent higher than in 2001 ($4.99 vs. $2.78).

Figure 5.   Average hourly out-of-pocket child care expense for children under 6 years old and not yet in kindergarten whose families paid for child care, by primary type of child care arrangement and race/ethnicity: 2016

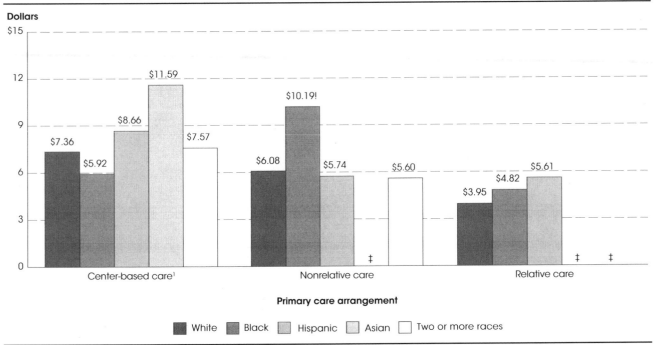

! Interpret data with caution. The coefficient of variation (CV) for this estimate is between 30 and 50 percent.
‡ Reporting standards not met. Either there are too few cases for a reliable estimate or the coefficient of variation (CV) is 50 percent or greater.
[1] Center-based arrangements include day care centers, Head Start programs, preschools, prekindergartens, and childhood programs.
NOTE: Reporting standards for Pacific Islanders and American Indians/Alaska Natives were not met; therefore, data for these groups are not shown in the figure. Estimates include only those children whose families paid at least part of the cost out of pocket for their child to receive nonparental care at least weekly. Children for whom no fee was charged, or for whom another source paid the entire fee, are excluded from the estimates. A child's primary arrangement is the regular nonparental care arrangement or early childhood education program in which the child spent the most time per week. Race categories exclude persons of Hispanic ethnicity.
SOURCE: U.S. Department of Education, National Center for Education Statistics, Early Childhood Program Participation Survey of the National Household Education Surveys Program (ECPP-NHES: 2016). See *Digest of Education Statistics 2017*, table 202.30c.

In 2016, there was no measurable variation across children's age groups in the average hourly out-of-pocket expenses for children in center-based care, nonrelative care, and relative care. In addition, no measurable differences were observed across children's racial/ethnic groups in families' out-of-pocket expenses for nonrelative care or relative care. However, the average hourly out-of-pocket expense in 2016 for center-based care for families of Asian children ($11.59) was higher than the expenses for families of children of Two or more races ($7.57), families of White children ($7.36), and families of Black children ($5.92).

Figure 6. Average hourly out-of-pocket child care expense for children under 6 years old and not yet in kindergarten whose families paid for child care, by primary type of child care arrangement and household income: 2016

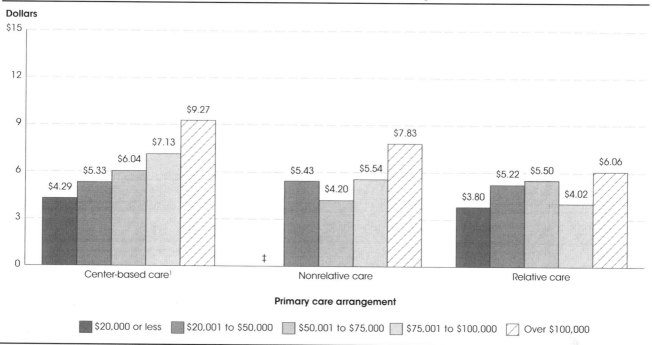

‡ Reporting standards not met. Either there are too few cases for a reliable estimate or the coefficient of variation (CV) is 50 percent or greater.
[1] Center-based arrangements include day care centers, Head Start programs, preschools, prekindergartens, and childhood programs.
NOTE: Estimates include only those children whose families paid at least part of the cost out of pocket for their child to receive nonparental care at least weekly. Children for whom no fee was charged, or for whom another source paid the entire fee, are excluded from the estimates. A child's primary arrangement is the regular nonparental care arrangement or early childhood education program in which the child spent the most time per week.
SOURCE: U.S. Department of Education, National Center for Education Statistics, Early Childhood Program Participation Survey of the National Household Education Surveys Program (ECPP-NHES: 2016). See *Digest of Education Statistics 2017*, table 202.30c.

In 2016, families at the highest income level tended to have a higher hourly out-of-pocket expense for center-based and nonrelative child care, on average, than families at lower income levels. Specifically, families with household incomes over $100,000 had a higher hourly out-of-pocket expense ($9.27) for center-based care, compared with families with lower household incomes. In addition, the average hourly out-of-pocket expense for children who were in center-based care was higher for families with household incomes of $75,000 to $100,000 ($7.13) than for families with household incomes of $20,001 to $50,000 ($5.33) and $20,000 or less ($4.29). And the average hourly out-of-pocket expense for children in center-based care was higher for families with

household incomes of $50,001 to $75,000 ($6.04) than for families with household incomes of $20,000 or less.

The average hourly out-of-pocket expense for children in nonrelative care was higher for families with household incomes of over $100,000 ($7.83) than for families with household incomes of $75,000 to $100,000 ($5.54), $20,001 to $50,000 ($5.43), and $50,001 to $75,000 ($4.20). The average hourly out-of-pocket expense for relative care was higher for children in families with household incomes of over $100,000 ($6.06) than in families with household incomes of $20,000 or less ($3.80), but there were no other measurable differences in relative care expenses by household income in 2016.

Figure 7. Average hourly out-of-pocket child care expense for children under 6 years old and not yet in kindergarten whose families paid for child care, by primary type of child care arrangement and locale: 2016

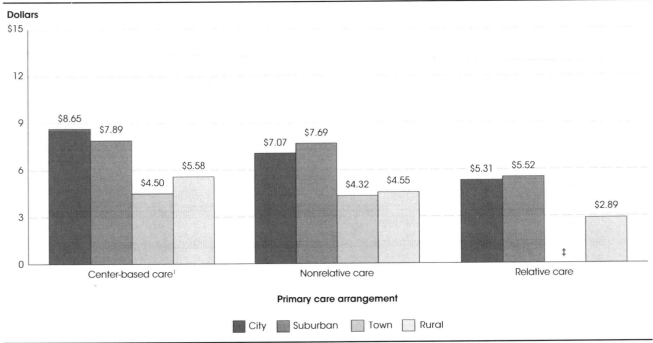

‡ Reporting standards not met. Either there are too few cases for a reliable estimate or the coefficient of variation (CV) is 50 percent or greater.
[1] Center-based arrangements include day care centers, Head Start programs, preschools, prekindergartens, and childhood programs.
NOTE: Estimates include only those children whose families paid at least part of the cost out of pocket for their child to receive nonparental care at least weekly. Children for whom no fee was charged, or for whom another source paid the entire fee, are excluded from the estimates. A child's primary arrangement is the regular nonparental care arrangement or early childhood education program in which the child spent the most time per week.
SOURCE: U.S. Department of Education, National Center for Education Statistics, Early Childhood Program Participation Survey of the National Household Education Surveys Program (ECPP-NHES:2016). See *Digest of Education Statistics 2017*, table 202.30c.

The families of children living in cities and suburban areas tended to have a higher average hourly out-of-pocket expense for child care than the families of children living in rural areas and towns. For example, the expense for families of children in center-based care was higher in cities ($8.65) and suburban areas ($7.89) than in rural areas ($5.58) and towns ($4.50). Similarly, the out-of-pocket expense for families of children in nonrelative care was higher in cities ($7.07) and suburban areas ($7.69) than in rural areas ($4.55) and towns ($4.32). Also, the expense for families of children in relative care was higher in cities ($5.31) and suburban areas ($5.52) than in rural areas ($2.89).

Endnotes:

[1] Flanagan, K.D., and McPhee, C. (2009). *The Children Born in 2001 at Kindergarten Entry: First Findings From the Kindergarten Data Collections of the Early Childhood Longitudinal Study, Birth Cohort (ECLS-B)* (NCES 2010-005). U.S. Department of Education. Washington, DC: National Center for Education Statistics. Retrieved May 1, 2018, from https://nces.ed.gov/pubsearch/pubsinfo.asp?pubid=2010005.
[2] Heckman, J.J., Moon, S.H., Pinto, R., Savelyev, P.A., and Yavitz, A. (2010). The Rate of Return to the HighScope Perry Preschool Program. *Journal of Public Economics, 94*(1): 114–128. Retrieved February 16, 2018, from https://www.sciencedirect.com/science/article/pii/S0047272709001418.
[3] In the remainder of the indicator, reference to "children under 6 years old" excludes children who are already enrolled in kindergarten or above.

[4] In this indicator, parents refer to parents or guardians.
[5] In comparison, the percentage of children whose parents did not know whether there were good choices for child care was highest for children under 1 year old (36 percent), followed by those who were 1 to 2 years old (29 percent), and was lowest for children 3 to 5 years old (18 percent).
[6] Due to unstable estimates or unmet reporting standards, the primary reasons of "needing a program for children with special needs" and "some other reason" are not discussed across the selected child and family characteristics.

Reference tables: *Digest of Education Statistics 2017*, tables 202.30, 202.30a, 202.30b, and 202.30c

Related indicators and resources: Early Childcare and Education Arrangements [*Status and Trends in the Education of Racial and Ethnic Groups*]; Preschool and Kindergarten Enrollment; *Primary Early Care and Education Arrangements and Achievement at Kindergarten Entry*

Glossary: Household, Racial/ethnic group

This page intentionally left blank.

Characteristics of Public School Teachers Who Completed Alternative Route to Certification Programs

Approximately 18 percent of public school teachers in 2015–16 had entered teaching through an alternative route to certification program. Compared to those who entered through a traditional route, a higher percentage of alternative route teachers were Black (13 vs. 5 percent), Hispanic (15 vs. 8 percent), of Two or more races (2 vs. 1 percent), and male (32 vs. 22 percent).

Of the 3.8 million public school teachers working in school year 2015–16, approximately 676,000 (18 percent) had entered teaching through an alternative route to certification program.[1] While the traditional route to certification typically requires the completion of a postsecondary degree in education, many alternative route programs are designed for individuals who have already completed a degree in a different field without teacher education courses.[2] These alternative pathways into the teaching profession may have important implications for the supply of teachers in the labor market, especially in the context of the declining number of bachelor's and master's degrees awarded in education[3] and persistent teacher shortages in certain subjects and categories of schools.[4]

The National Teacher and Principal Survey (NTPS) from the National Center for Education Statistics provides new insights about alternative route teachers in public elementary and secondary schools. This spotlight indicator uses NTPS data to examine the characteristics of teachers who entered teaching through alternative route to certification programs and compares them to those who entered through traditional routes. The indicator also describes the percentage of teachers in various academic subjects and categories of schools who entered teaching through an alternative route.

Figure 1. Percentage distribution of public elementary and secondary school teachers, by route to certification and race/
ethnicity: 2015–16

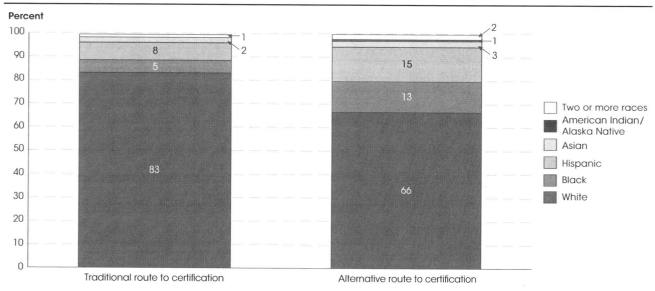

NOTE: Teachers were asked whether they entered teaching through an alternative route to certification program, which is a program that was designed to expedite the transition of nonteachers to a teaching career (for example, a state, district, or university alternative route to certification program). Data are based on a head count of full-time and part-time teachers rather than on the number of full-time-equivalent teachers. Detail may not sum to totals because of rounding. Race categories exclude persons of Hispanic ethnicity. Data for American Indian/Alaska Native teachers who entered teaching through a traditional route and Pacific Islander teachers who entered teaching through traditional and alternative routes round to zero and are not displayed.
SOURCE: U.S. Department of Education, National Center for Education Statistics, National Teacher and Principal Survey (NTPS), "Public School Teacher Data File," 2015–16. See *Digest of Education Statistics 2017*, table 209.24.

In 2015–16, the percentage of public school teachers who were members of racial/ethnic minority groups was generally higher among those who had entered teaching through an alternative route to certification than among those who entered through a traditional route. The percentages of alternative route teachers who were Hispanic (15 percent), Black (13 percent), of Two or more races (2 percent), and American Indian/Alaska Native (1 percent) were higher than the percentages for traditional route teachers (8 percent, 5 percent, 1 percent, and less than one-half of 1 percent, respectively). In

contrast, the percentage of teachers who were White was lower among alternative route teachers (66 percent) than among traditional route teachers (83 percent). The percentage of alternative route teachers who were Asian (3 percent) was not measurably different from the percentage of traditional route teachers who were Asian (2 percent). The percentages of teachers who were Pacific Islander and American Indian/Alaska Native were 1 percent or less among both alternative and traditional route teachers.

Figure 2.   Percentage distribution of public elementary and secondary school teachers, by route to certification and sex: 2015–16

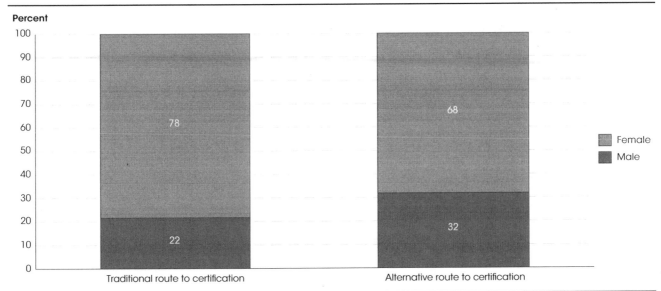

NOTE: Teachers were asked whether they entered teaching through an alternative route to certification program, which is a program that was designed to expedite the transition of nonteachers to a teaching career (for example, a state, district, or university alternative route to certification program). Data are based on a head count of full-time and part-time teachers rather than on the number of full-time-equivalent teachers.
SOURCE: U.S. Department of Education, National Center for Education Statistics, National Teacher and Principal Survey (NTPS), "Public School Teacher Data File," 2015–16. See *Digest of Education Statistics 2017*, table 209.24.

The distribution of teachers by sex also differed between alternative and traditional route teachers in 2015–16. The percentage of teachers who were male was higher among alternative route teachers (32 percent) than among traditional route teachers (22 percent).

Figure 3. Percentage distribution of public elementary and secondary school teachers, by route to certification and main activity the year before teaching: 2015-16

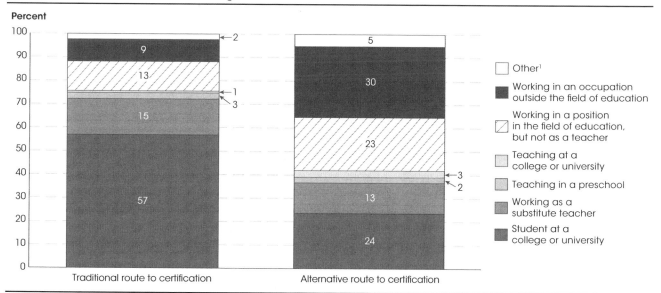

¹ Other includes caring for other family members, military service, unemployed and seeking work, and retired from another job.
NOTE: Includes only those teachers whose first year of teaching was between 2011-12 and 2015-16. Teachers were asked whether they entered teaching through an alternative route to certification program, which is a program that was designed to expedite the transition of nonteachers to a teaching career (for example, a state, district, or university alternative route to certification program). Data are based on a head count of full-time and part-time teachers rather than on the number of full-time-equivalent teachers.
SOURCE: U.S. Department of Education, National Center for Education Statistics, National Teacher and Principal Survey (NTPS), "Public School Teacher Data File," 2015-16. See *Digest of Education Statistics 2017*, table 209.24.

Public school teachers' prior work experiences also differed between those who entered teaching through an alternative route to certification program and those who entered through a traditional route. For teachers whose first year of teaching was between school years 2011–12 and 2015–16, NTPS collected data on their main activity the year before they started teaching. Over half (57 percent) of traditional route teachers were students at a college or university the year before they began teaching, compared to 24 percent of alternative route teachers. A greater percentage of traditional route teachers also reported that they were substitute teachers prior to their first year of teaching (15 percent) than did alternative route teachers (13 percent). In contrast, the following activities were more commonly reported among alternative route teachers than among traditional route teachers: working in a field outside of education (30 vs. 9 percent), working in education but not as a teacher (23 vs. 13 percent), and teaching at a college or university (3 vs. 1 percent). There was no measurable difference between alternative and traditional route teachers in the percentage who reported teaching in a preschool the year before they began teaching at the K–12 level (2 and 3 percent, respectively). Two percent of traditional route teachers and 5 percent of alternative route teachers reported that their main activity the year before teaching was caring for family members, serving in the military, seeking work while unemployed, or being retired from another job (these four activities are combined as "other" in figure 2).

Figure 4. Percentage of public elementary and secondary school teachers who had entered teaching through an
         alternative route to certification program, by main teaching assignment: 2015–16

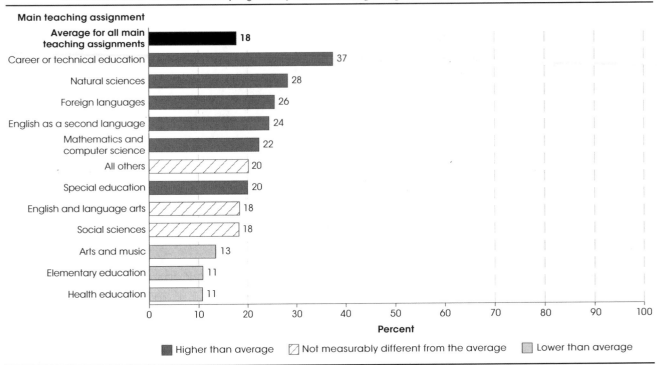

NOTE: Teachers were asked whether they entered teaching through an alternative route to certification program, which is a program that was designed to expedite the transition of nonteachers to a teaching career (for example, a state, district, or university alternative route to certification program). Data are based on a head count of full-time and part-time teachers rather than on the number of full-time-equivalent teachers.
SOURCE: U.S. Department of Education, National Center for Education Statistics, National Teacher and Principal Survey (NTPS), "Public School Teacher Data File," 2015–16. See *Digest of Education Statistics 2017*, table 209.24.

Data from NTPS can also be used to examine how the percentage of alternative route teachers varies by subject taught and school characteristics. On average, 18 percent of all public school teachers in 2015–16 reported that they had entered the teaching profession through an alternative route to certification program. The percentage of teachers who entered through an alternative route was higher than average for teachers whose main teaching assignment was career or technical education (37 percent), natural sciences (28 percent), foreign languages (26 percent),

English as a second language (24 percent), mathematics and computer science (22 percent), and special education (20 percent). The percentage of teachers who entered through an alternative route was lower than average for teachers whose main teaching assignment was arts and music (13 percent), elementary education (11 percent), and health education (11 percent). The percentages of English/language arts and social sciences teachers (both 18 percent) who entered through an alternative route were not measurably different from the average.

Figure 5. Percentage of public elementary and secondary school teachers who had entered teaching through an alternative route to certification program, by school classification and level: 2015–16

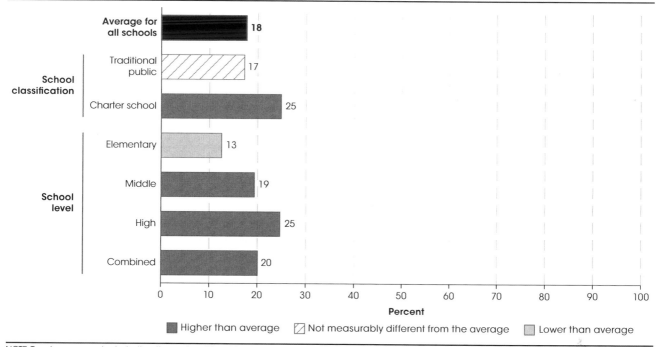

NOTE: Teachers were asked whether they entered teaching through an alternative route to certification program, which is a program that was designed to expedite the transition of nonteachers to a teaching career (for example, a state, district, or university alternative route to certification program). Data are based on a head count of full-time and part-time teachers rather than on the number of full-time-equivalent teachers.
SOURCE: U.S. Department of Education, National Center for Education Statistics, National Teacher and Principal Survey (NTPS), "Public School Teacher Data File," 2015–16. See *Digest of Education Statistics 2017*, table 209.24.

In 2015–16, the prevalence of alternative route teachers also varied between charter schools and traditional public schools and among elementary, middle, secondary, and combined schools. The percentage of public school teachers who entered teaching through an alternative route to certification program was higher for charter schools (25 percent) than for traditional public schools (17 percent). By school level, the percentage of teachers who entered through an alternative route was highest for high schools (25 percent). Lower percentages of teachers at combined elementary and secondary schools (20 percent), middle schools (19 percent), and elementary schools (13 percent) entered through an alternative route to certification program.

Figure 6. Percentage of public elementary and secondary school teachers who had entered teaching through an alternative route to certification program, by percentage of racial/ethnic minority students in school: 2015-16

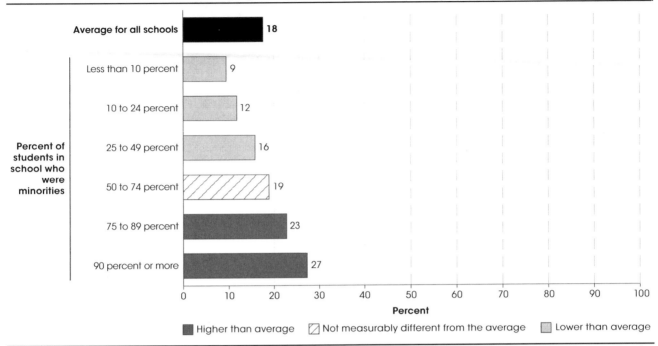

NOTE: Excludes the 7 percent of teachers for whom the percentage of racial/ethnic minority enrollment in the school was not available. Minority enrollment is the combined enrollment of students who are Black, Hispanic, Asian, Pacific Islander, American Indian/Alaska Native, and of Two or more races. Teachers were asked whether they entered teaching through an alternative route to certification program, which is a program that was designed to expedite the transition of nonteachers to a teaching career (for example, a state, district, or university alternative route to certification program). Data are based on a head count of full-time and part-time teachers rather than on the number of full-time-equivalent teachers.
SOURCE: U.S. Department of Education, National Center for Education Statistics, National Teacher and Principal Survey (NTPS), "Public School Teacher Data File," 2015-16. See *Digest of Education Statistics 2017*, table 209.24.

In 2015–16, public schools in which at least three-quarters of students were racial/ethnic minorities had percentages of alternative route teachers that were higher than the national average of 18 percent. Among schools with 75 to 89 percent minority enrollment, 23 percent of teachers had entered teaching through an alternative route to certification program. Among schools with 90 percent or more minority enrollment, 27 percent of teachers had entered teaching through an alternative route. In contrast, the percentages of alternative route teachers were lower than average in schools where less than half of students were minorities, including schools with less than 10 percent minority enrollment (9 percent alternative route teachers), schools with 10 to 24 percent minority enrollment (12 percent alternative route teachers), and schools with 25 to 49 percent minority enrollment (16 percent alternative route teachers).

Figure 7. Percentage of public elementary and secondary school teachers who had entered teaching through an alternative route to certification program, by percentage of students in school who were eligible for free or reduced-price lunch: 2015–16

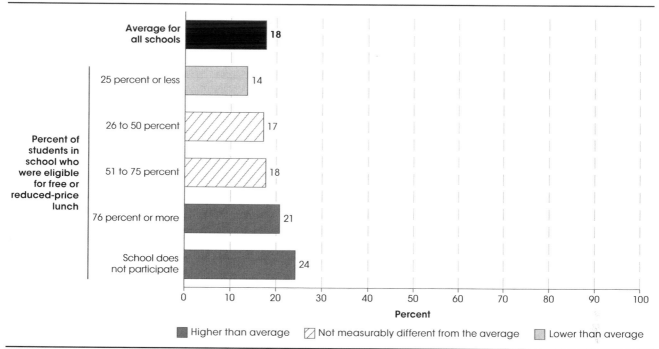

NOTE: For more information on free or reduced-price lunch eligibility and its relationship to poverty, see the *Forum Guide to Alternative Measures of Socioeconomic Status in Education Data Systems*. Teachers were asked whether they entered teaching through an alternative route to certification program, which is a program that was designed to expedite the transition of nonteachers to a teaching career (for example, a state, district, or university alternative route to certification program). Data are based on a head count of full-time and part-time teachers rather than on the number of full-time-equivalent teachers.
SOURCE: U.S. Department of Education, National Center for Education Statistics, National Teacher and Principal Survey (NTPS), "Public School Teacher Data File," 2015–16. See *Digest of Education Statistics 2017*, table 209.24.

The percentage of alternative route teachers also varied by school poverty level, as measured using the percentage of students in the school who were eligible for free or reduced-price lunch (FRPL) under the National School Lunch Program. While the FRPL data have a number of limitations, they are a widely used proxy for student poverty.[5] In this indicator, high-poverty schools are defined as public schools where 76 percent or more of the students are eligible for FRPL, and low-poverty schools

are defined as public schools where 25 percent or less of the students are eligible for FRPL. In 2015–16, high-poverty schools had a higher than average percentage of alternative route teachers (21 percent), and low-poverty schools had a lower than average percentage of alternative route teachers (14 percent). Schools that did not participate in the free or reduced-price lunch program also had a higher than average percentage of alternative route teachers (24 percent).

Endnotes:

[1] Data are based on a head count of full-time and part-time teachers rather than on the number of full-time-equivalent teachers. All states except Alaska offered alternative route to certification programs in 2015. Program providers varied widely from state to state, including school districts, colleges and universities, and nonprofit and for-profit organizations. For more information, see National Council on Teacher Quality. (2015). State Policy Yearbook Database: 2015. Washington, DC: Author. Retrieved February 13, 2018, from https://www.nctq.org/yearbook/home.
[2] Woods, J.R. (2016). *Mitigating Teacher Shortages: Alternative Teacher Certification* (Teacher Shortage Series Policy Brief). Denver, CO: Education Commission of the States. Retrieved

February 13, 2018, from https://www.ecs.org/mitigating-teacher-shortages-alternative-teacher-certification/.
[3] For more information on the number of degrees awarded in the field of education, see indicators Undergraduate Degree Fields and Graduate Degree Fields.
[4] Aragon, S. (2016). *Teacher Shortages: What We Know* (Teacher Shortage Series Policy Brief). Denver, CO: Education Commission of the States. Retrieved February 13, 2018, https://www.ecs.org/teacher-shortages/.
[5] For more information on eligibility for free or reduced-price lunch and its relationship to poverty, see the *Forum Guide to Alternative Measures of Socioeconomic Status in Education Data Systems*.

Reference tables: *Digest of Education Statistics 2017*, table 209.24

Related indicators and resources: Characteristics of Public School Teachers; Teacher Turnover: Stayers, Movers, and Leavers [*web-only*]

Glossary: Combined school, Elementary school, Free or reduced-price lunch, National School Lunch Program, Public school or institution, Racial/ethnic group, Secondary school

Trends in Student Loan Debt for Graduate School Completers

Average loan balances for students who completed a research or professional doctorate increased between 1999–2000 and 2015–16 for all degree programs for which data were available (in constant 2016–17 dollars). Average loan balances approximately doubled for those who completed medical doctorates (from $124,700 to $246,000, an increase of 97 percent), Ph.D.'s outside the field of education (from $48,400 to $98,800, an increase of 104 percent), and other non-Ph.D. doctorates (from $64,500 to $132,200, an increase of 105 percent).

Recently released data from the National Postsecondary Student Aid Survey (NPSAS)[1] shed new light on how the student loan burden of graduate school completers has changed over time. This spotlight analysis uses NPSAS data to describe the percentage of graduate school completers who hold student loans from undergraduate or graduate education and, for those who have student loans, the average combined balance for undergraduate and graduate school loans. Specifically, the analysis examines how trends in student loan debt vary by the following characteristics:

- broad degree type (postbaccalaureate certificate,[2] master's degree,[3] research doctorate,[4] or professional doctorate[5]),

- specific degree program (for example, law, medicine, or business administration), and

- institutional control (public, private nonprofit, or private for-profit).

This indicator uses data on the combined balance of undergraduate and graduate student loans to examine the total student loan debt burden that a typical graduate school completer faces as he or she enters the workforce. The data represent the principal balance (excluding interest) as of June 30th of the survey year. For example, the 2015–16 data represent balances as of June 30, 2016. The data include federal and private student loans, but exclude Parent PLUS loans.[6] Data on graduate student loans only (separate from undergraduate loans) are available in *Digest of Education Statistics 2017, table 332.45*. All dollar amounts are expressed in constant 2016–17 dollars.

Figure 1. Percentage of graduate school completers with student loans, by degree type: 2015–16

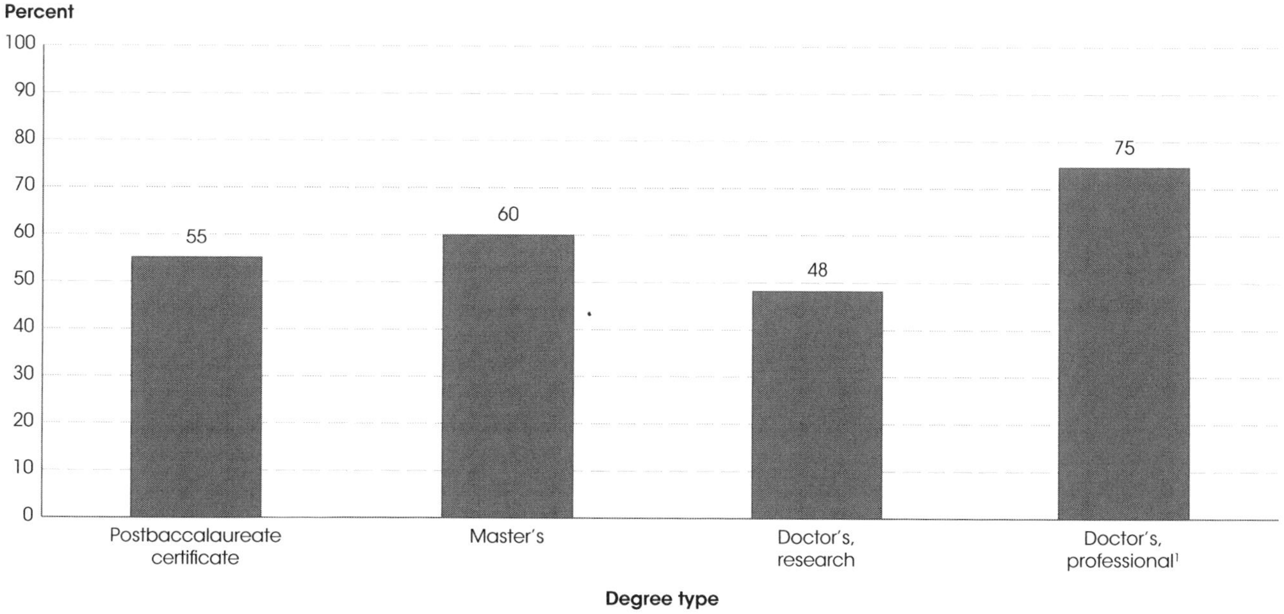

Percent

Degree type

¹ Includes chiropractic, dentistry, law, medicine, optometry, pharmacy, podiatry, and veterinary medicine.
NOTE: Data refer to students who completed graduate degrees in 2015–16. Includes student loans for undergraduate and graduate studies.
SOURCE: U.S. Department of Education, National Center for Education Statistics, 2015–16 National Postsecondary Student Aid Study (NPSAS:16). See *Digest of Education Statistics 2017*, table 332.45.

In 2015–16, a higher percentage of students who completed professional doctorates (such as a medical doctorate or law degree) had student loans (75 percent) than those who completed master's degrees (60 percent), postbaccalaureate certificates (55 percent), and research doctorates (48 percent). The percentage of master's degree completers with student loans was higher in 2015–16 than in 1999–2000 (60 vs. 47 percent). For other degree types, the percentage of completers with student loans in 2015–16 was not measurably different from the percentage with student loans in 1999–2000.

Figure 2.   Average cumulative student loan balance for graduate school completers, by degree type: Selected years, 1999–2000 through 2015–16

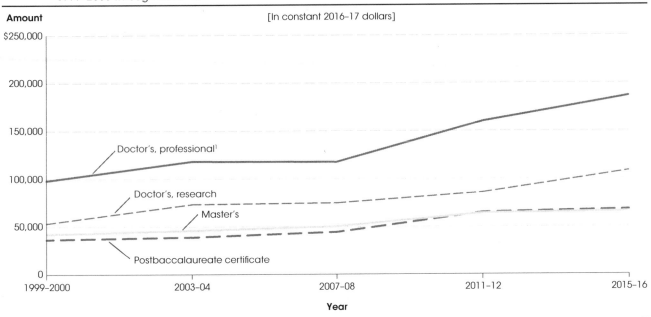

[1] Includes chiropractic, dentistry, law, medicine, optometry, pharmacy, podiatry, and veterinary medicine.
NOTE: Data refer to students who completed graduate degrees in the academic years indicated. Includes student loans for undergraduate and graduate studies. Average excludes students with no student loans. Constant dollars are based on the Consumer Price Index, prepared by the Bureau of Labor Statistics, U.S. Department of Labor, adjusted to an academic-year basis.
SOURCE: U.S. Department of Education, National Center for Education Statistics, 1999–2000, 2003–04, 2007–08, 2011–12, and 2015–16 National Postsecondary Student Aid Study (NPSAS:2000, NPSAS:04, NPSAS:08, NPSAS:12, and NPSAS:16). See *Digest of Education Statistics 2017*, table 332.45.

Among graduate school completers who had student loans for undergraduate or graduate studies, the average cumulative loan balance in 2015–16 was highest for those completing a professional doctorate ($186,600). The average loan balance for students who completed research doctorate degrees, such as Ph.D.'s or education doctorates, was $108,400; this balance was higher than the average loan balances for those who completed postbaccalaureate certificates ($67,800) and master's degrees ($66,000).

Between 1999–2000 and 2015–16, average student loan balances for graduate school completers increased for all degree types (in constant 2016–17 dollars). Average student loan balances for those who completed research doctorate degrees roughly doubled during this time period, from $53,500 to $108,400 (an increase of 103 percent). Average student loan balances increased by 90 percent for those who completed professional doctorate degrees (from $98,200 to $186,600), by 85 percent for those who completed postbaccalaureate certificates (from $36,600 to $67,800), and by 57 percent for those who completed master's degrees (from $42,100 to $66,000).

Figure 3.   Percentage of master's degree completers with student loans, by degree program: 2015–16

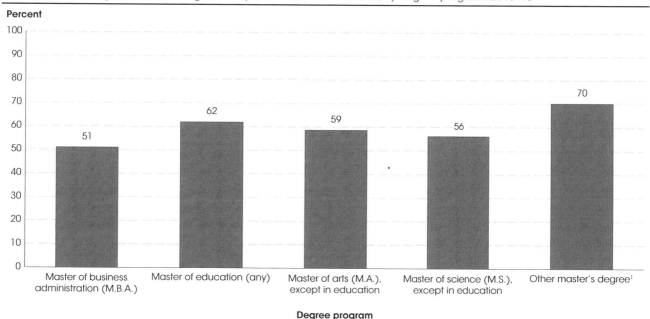

¹ Includes public administration or policy, social work, fine arts, public health, and other.
NOTE: Data refer to students who completed graduate degrees in 2015–16. Includes student loans for undergraduate and graduate studies.
SOURCE: U.S. Department of Education, National Center for Education Statistics, 2015–16 National Postsecondary Student Aid Study (NPSAS:16). See *Digest of Education Statistics 2017*, table 332.45.

Among students who completed a master's degree in 2015–16, the percentage with student loans varied by degree program. The percentage who had student loans was highest (70 percent) for those completing master's degrees in the "other" category, which includes public administration or policy, social work, fine arts, public health, and other fields. In comparison, the percentage of master's degree completers who had student loans was lower for students who completed a master of education degree (62 percent), master of arts degree[7] (59 percent), master of science degree[8] (56 percent), or master of business administration degree (51 percent). In addition, the percentage of students with loans was higher for those completing a master of education degree than for those completing a master of business administration degree.

The percentage of master's degree completers with student loans was higher in 2015–16 than in 1999–2000 for those completing a master's degree in an "other" field (70 vs. 58 percent), a master of education degree (62 vs. 46 percent), a master of science degree (56 vs. 42 percent), or a master of business administration degree (51 vs. 41 percent). For those completing a master of arts degree, there was no measurable difference between 1999–2000 and 2015–16 in the percentage with student loans.

Figure 4.   Average cumulative student loan balance for master's degree completers, by degree program: Selected years, 1999–2000 through 2015–16

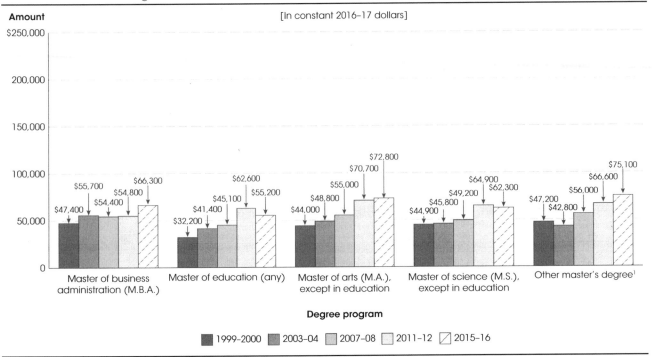

[1] Includes public administration or policy, social work, fine arts, public health, and other.
NOTE: Data refer to students who completed graduate degrees in the academic years indicated. Includes student loans for undergraduate and graduate studies. Average excludes students with no student loans. Constant dollars are based on the Consumer Price Index, prepared by the Bureau of Labor Statistics, U.S. Department of Labor, adjusted to an academic-year basis.
SOURCE: U.S. Department of Education, National Center for Education Statistics, 1999–2000, 2003–04, 2007–08, 2011–12, and 2015–16 National Postsecondary Student Aid Study (NPSAS:2000, NPSAS:04, NPSAS:08, NPSAS:12, and NPSAS:16). See *Digest of Education Statistics 2017*, table 332.45.

Among students who completed a master's degree in 2015–16 and had student loans, the average student loan balance varied by degree program. The average student loan balance for those completing a master's degree in the "other" category ($75,100) was higher than the average student loan balances for those completing master of science degrees ($62,300) and master of education degrees ($55,200). In addition, average student loan balances for those completing master of arts degrees ($72,800) and master of business administration degrees ($66,300) were also higher than the average balance for those completing a master of education degree.

Average student loan balances (in constant 2016–17 dollars) were higher in 2015–16 than in 1999–2000

for all master's degree fields. During this time, average loan balances increased by 71 percent (from $32,200 to $55,200) for completers of master of education degrees, by 65 percent for master of arts degree completers (from $44,000 to $72,800), by 59 percent for "other" master's degree completers (from $47,200 to $75,100), and by 39 percent for master of science degree completers (from $44,900 to $62,300). The average loan balance for master of business administration completers was 40 percent higher in 2015–16 ($66,300) than in 1999–2000 ($47,400), but showed no clear trend during this period.

Figure 5.   Percentage of doctorate degree completers with student loans, by degree program: 2015–16

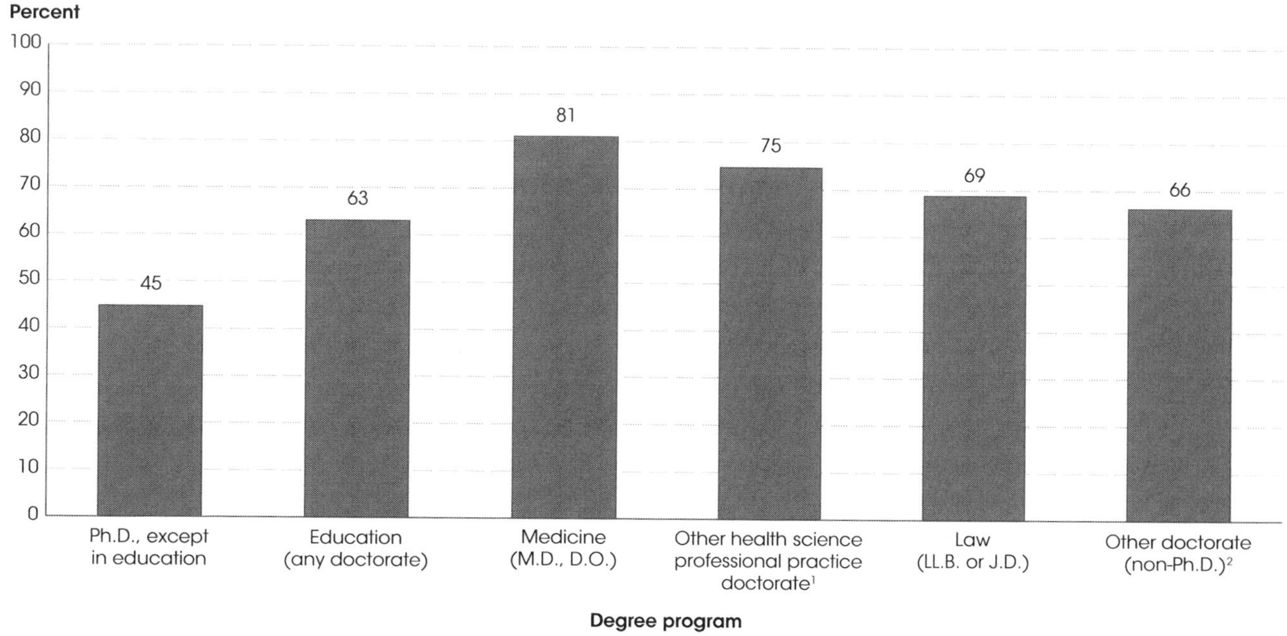

Percent

Degree program

[1] Includes chiropractic, dentistry, optometry, pharmacy, podiatry, and veterinary medicine.
[2] Includes science or engineering, psychology, business or public administration, fine arts, theology, and other.
NOTE: Data refer to students who completed graduate degrees in 2015–16. Includes student loans for undergraduate and graduate studies.
SOURCE: U.S. Department of Education, National Center for Education Statistics, 2015–16 National Postsecondary Student Aid Study (NPSAS:16). See *Digest of Education Statistics 2017*, table 332.45.

Among students who completed research or professional doctoral degrees in 2015–16, the percentage with student loans was lowest for those completing Ph.D.'s in fields other than education (45 percent). In comparison, the percentage of graduate completers with loans was 63 percent for those who completed education doctorates, 66 percent for doctorate completers in the "other" (non-Ph.D.) category,[9] 69 percent for law degree completers, 75 percent for other health science doctorate completers,[10] and 81 percent for medical doctorate

completers. The percentage of graduate completers with student loans was higher in 2015–16 than in 1999–2000 for students who completed education doctorates (63 vs. 33 percent), but lower in 2015–16 than in 1999–2000 for students who completed law degrees (69 vs. 85 percent). For completers in all other research and professional doctoral program categories, there was no measurable difference between 1999–2000 and 2015–16 in the percentages who had student loans.

Figure 6.   Average cumulative student loan balance for doctorate degree completers, by degree program: Selected years, 1999–2000 through 2015–16

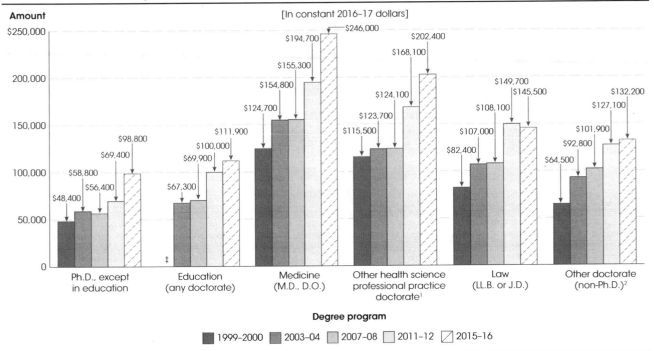

‡ Reporting standards not met. Either there are too few cases for a reliable estimate or the coefficient of variation (CV) is 50 percent or greater.
[1] Includes chiropractic, dentistry, optometry, pharmacy, podiatry, and veterinary medicine.
[2] Includes science or engineering, psychology, business or public administration, fine arts, theology, and other.
NOTE: Data refer to students who completed graduate degrees in the academic years indicated. Includes student loans for undergraduate and graduate studies. Average excludes students with no student loans. Constant dollars are based on the Consumer Price Index, prepared by the Bureau of Labor Statistics, U.S. Department of Labor, adjusted to an academic-year basis.
SOURCE: U.S. Department of Education, National Center for Education Statistics, 1999–2000, 2003–04, 2007–08, 2011–12, and 2015–16 National Postsecondary Student Aid Study (NPSAS:2000, NPSAS:04, NPSAS:08, NPSAS:12, and NPSAS:16). See *Digest of Education Statistics 2017*, table 332.45.

Among students who completed doctorates in 2015–16 and had student loans, average loan balances were highest for those completing medical doctorates ($246,000) and other health science doctorates ($202,400). In comparison, average loan balances were $145,500 for law degree completers, $132,200 for completers of doctorates in an "other" (non-Ph.D.) field, $111,900 for education doctorate completers, and $98,800 for those who completed Ph.D.'s (excluding those who completed Ph.D.'s in education).

Average loan balances (in constant 2016–17 dollars) for students who completed a research or professional doctorate increased between 1999–2000 and 2015–16 for

all degree programs for which reporting standards were met in both years.[11] Average loan balances approximately doubled for completers of "other" (non-Ph.D.) doctorates (from $64,500 to $132,200, an increase of 105 percent), Ph.D.'s outside the field of education (from $48,400 to $98,800 an increase of 104 percent), and medical doctorates (from $124,700 to $246,000, an increase of 97 percent). In addition, average loan balances increased by 77 percent for law degree completers (from $82,400 to $145,500) and by 75 percent for other health science doctorate completers (from $115,500 to $202,400). The average loan balance for education doctorate completers in 2015–16 ($111,900) was 66 percent higher than in 2003–04 ($67,300).

Figure 7.   Percentage of graduate school completers with student loans, by degree type and control of institution: 2015–16

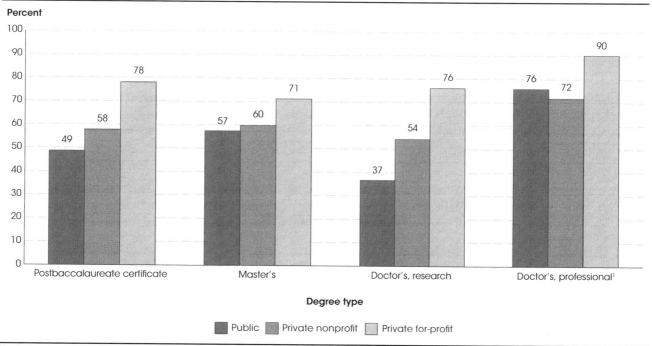

[1] Includes chiropractic, dentistry, law, medicine, optometry, pharmacy, podiatry, and veterinary medicine.
NOTE: Data refer to students who completed graduate degrees in 2015–16. Includes student loans for undergraduate and graduate studies. Although rounded numbers are displayed, the figures are based on unrounded estimates.
SOURCE: U.S. Department of Education, National Center for Education Statistics, 2015–16 National Postsecondary Student Aid Study (NPSAS:16). See *Digest of Education Statistics 2017*, table 332.45.

NPSAS data also shed light on how the student loan debt of graduate school completers varied by the control of the institution (public, private nonprofit, or private for-profit) attended.[12] For students who completed a postbaccalaureate certificate in 2015–16, the percentage who had student loans was higher for those who attended private for-profit institutions (78 percent) than for those who attended private nonprofit (58 percent) and public (49 percent) institutions. Similarly, the percentage of master's degree completers who had student loans was higher for those who attended private for-profit institutions (71 percent) than for those who attended private nonprofit (60 percent) and public (57 percent) institutions. Among students who completed a research doctorate, the percentage who had student loans was higher for those who attended private for-profit institutions (76 percent) than for those who attended private nonprofit institutions (54 percent), and both percentages, in turn, were higher than the percentage for those who attended public institutions (37 percent). Among students who completed a professional doctorate,

the percentage who had student loans was higher for those who attended private for-profit institutions (90 percent) than for those who attended public (76 percent) and private nonprofit (72 percent) institutions.

The percentage of master's degree completers who had student loans was higher in 2015–16 than in 1999–2000 for those who attended public institutions (57 vs. 44 percent) and private nonprofit institutions (60 vs. 51 percent), but not measurably different for those who attended private for-profit institutions. For the other degree types (postbaccalaureate certificate, research doctorate, and professional doctorate), there were no measurable differences between the percentages of students at public or private nonprofit institutions who had student loans in 2015–16 and the percentages who had student loans in 1999–2000. For private for-profit institutions, the complete time series data for completers of postbaccalaureate certificates, research doctorates, and professional doctorates did not meet reporting standards.

Figure 8.   Average cumulative loan balance for graduate school completers, by degree type and control of institution: 2015–16

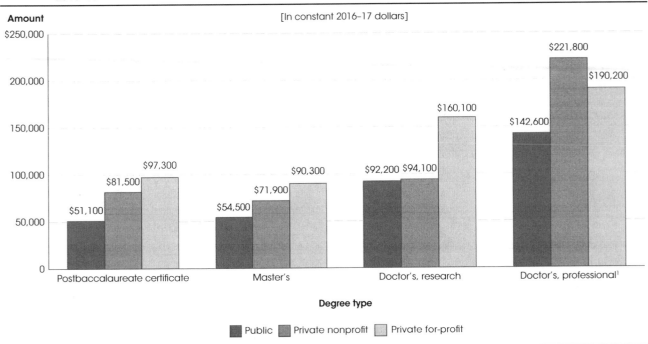

¹ Includes chiropractic, dentistry, law, medicine, optometry, pharmacy, podiatry, and veterinary medicine.
NOTE: Data refer to students who completed graduate degrees in 2015–16. Includes student loans for undergraduate and graduate studies. Average excludes students with no student loans. Constant dollars are based on the Consumer Price Index, prepared by the Bureau of Labor Statistics, U.S. Department of Labor, adjusted to an academic-year basis.
SOURCE: U.S. Department of Education, National Center for Education Statistics, 2015–16 National Postsecondary Student Aid Study (NPSAS:16). See *Digest of Education Statistics 2017*, table 332.45.

Among postbaccalaureate certificate completers in 2015–16 who had student loans, the average balance was higher for those who attended private for-profit institutions ($97,300) than for those who attended public institutions ($51,100), but neither was measurably different from the average balance for those who attended private nonprofit institutions ($81,500). Among master's degree completers who had student loans, the average balance was higher for those who attended private for-profit institutions ($90,300) than for those who attended private nonprofit institutions ($71,900), and both were higher than the average balance for those who attended public institutions ($54,500). For students who completed a research doctorate and had student loans, the average balance was higher for those who attended private for-profit institutions ($160,100) than for those who attended private nonprofit ($94,100) and public ($92,200) institutions. For students who completed a professional doctorate and had student loans, the average balances for those who attended private nonprofit ($221,800) and private for-profit ($190,200) institutions were not measurably different, but both were higher than the average student loan balance for those who attended public institutions ($142,600).

Average student loan balances were 57 percent higher in 2015–16 than in 1999–2000 for postbaccalaureate

certificate completers who attended public institutions ($51,100 vs. $32,600, in constant 2016–17 dollars), but trend data for those who attended private nonprofit and private for-profit institutions did not meet reporting standards. For master's degree completers who had student loans, average loan balances in 2015–16 were higher than in 1999–2000 for those who attended private for-profit institutions (54 percent higher, or $90,300 vs. $58,700), private nonprofit institutions (53 percent higher, or $71,900 vs. $46,900), and public institutions (49 percent higher, or $54,500 vs. $36,700). Among students who completed a research doctorate and had student loans, the average balance was 103 percent higher in 2015–16 than in 1999–2000 for those who attended public institutions ($92,200 vs. $45,500), but there was no measurable difference between average balances in 1999–2000 and 2015–16 for those who attended private nonprofit institutions. Among students who completed a professional doctorate and had student loans, the average balance was 107 percent higher in 2015–16 than in 1999–2000 for those who attended private nonprofit institutions ($221,800 vs. $107,000) and 64 percent higher in 2015–16 than in 1999–2000 for those who attended public institutions ($142,600 vs. $87,200). Trend data on average student loan balances for those who completed research doctorates and professional doctorates at private for-profit institutions did not meet reporting standards.

Endnotes:

[1] NPSAS is a nationally representative survey administered every 4 years by the National Center for Education Statistics. This analysis uses data from the 1999–2000, 2003–04, 2007–08, 2011–12, and 2015–16 NPSAS data collections.

[2] An award that requires completion of an organized program of study beyond a bachelor's degree. It is designed for persons who have completed a baccalaureate degree, but does not meet the requirements of a master's degree. Even though teacher preparation certificate programs may require a bachelor's degree for admission, they are considered subbaccalaureate undergraduate programs, and students in these programs are undergraduate students.

[3] A degree awarded for successful completion of a program generally requiring 1 or 2 years of full-time college-level study beyond the bachelor's degree. One type of master's degree, including the master of arts degree, or M.A., and the master of science degree, or M.S., is awarded in the liberal arts and sciences for advanced scholarship in a subject field or discipline and demonstrated ability to perform scholarly research. A second type of master's degree is awarded for the completion of a professionally oriented program, for example, an M.Ed. in education, an M.B.A. in business administration, an M.F.A. in fine arts, an M.M. in music, an M.S.W. in social work, and an M.P.A. in public administration. Some master's degrees—such as divinity degrees (M.Div. or M.H.L./Rav), which were formerly classified as "first-professional"—may require more than 2 years of full-time study beyond the bachelor's degree.

[4] A Ph.D. or other doctor's degree that requires advanced work beyond the master's level, including the preparation and defense of a dissertation based on original research, or the planning and execution of an original project demonstrating substantial artistic or scholarly achievement. Examples of this type of degree may include the following and others, as designated by the awarding institution: the Ed.D. (in education), D.M.A. (in musical arts), D.B.A. (in business administration), D.Sc. (in science), D.A. (in arts), or D.M. (in medicine).

[5] A doctor's degree that is conferred upon completion of a program providing the knowledge and skills for the recognition, credential, or license required for professional practice. The degree is awarded after a period of study such that the total time to the degree, including both preprofessional and professional preparation, equals at least 6 full-time-equivalent academic years. Some doctor's degrees of this type were formerly classified as first-professional degrees. Examples of this type of degree may include the following and others, as designated by the awarding institution: the D.C. or D.C.M. (in chiropractic); D.D.S. or D.M.D. (in dentistry); L.L.B. or J.D. (in law); M.D. (in medicine); O.D. (in optometry); D.O. (in osteopathic medicine); Pharm.D. (in pharmacy); D.P.M., Pod.D., or D.P. (in podiatry); or D.V.M. (in veterinary medicine).

[6] When comparing graduate student loan debt over time, it is important to note that Direct Subsidized Loans for graduate students were discontinued after academic year 2011–12.

[7] Excludes master of arts in education degrees.

[8] Excludes master of science in education degrees.

[9] Other doctorate (non-Ph.D.) includes science or engineering, psychology, business or public administration, fine arts, theology, and other.

[10] Other health science doctorates include chiropractic, dentistry, optometry, pharmacy, podiatry, and veterinary medicine.

[11] Data for education doctorates in 1999–2000 did not meet reporting standards.

[12] Data by institutional control (public, private nonprofit, or private for-profit) exclude individuals who attended more than one institution for graduate studies.

Reference tables: *Digest of Education Statistics 2017*, table 332.45

Related indicators and resources: Graduate Degree Fields; Loans for Undergraduate Students; Postsecondary Certificates and Degrees Conferred

Glossary: College, Constant dollars, Consumer Price Index (CPI), Control of institutions, Doctor's degree—professional practice, Doctor's degree—research/scholarship, Master's degree, Postbaccalaureate certificate, Private institution, Public school or institution

The indicators in this chapter of *The Condition of Education* describe aspects of preprimary, elementary, and secondary education in the United States. The indicators examine enrollment, school characteristics and climate; principals, teachers, and staff; school financial resources; student assessments; and other measures of students' progress as they move through the education system, such as graduation rates. In addition, this chapter contains indicators on key demographic characteristics, such as poverty and access to the Internet.

This chapter gives particular attention to how various subgroups in the population proceed through school and attain different levels of education. The indicators on student achievement illustrate how students perform on assessments in reading, mathematics, and science. Other indicators describe aspects of the context of learning in elementary and secondary schools.

Chapter 1
Preprimary, Elementary, and Secondary Education

Characteristics of Children's Families

In 2016, some 10 percent of children under the age of 18 lived in households without a parent who had completed high school, 27 percent lived in mother-only households, 8 percent lived in father-only households, and 19 percent lived in poverty.

Characteristics of children's families are associated with children's educational experiences and their academic achievement. Prior research found that the risk factors of living in a household without a parent who has completed high school, living in a single-parent household, and living in poverty are associated with poor educational outcomes, including low achievement scores, having to repeat a grade, and dropping out of high school.[1,2] In 2016, some 10 percent of children under the age of 18 lived in households without a parent who had completed

high school,[3] 27 percent lived in mother-only households, 8 percent lived in father-only households, and 19 percent were in families living in poverty. This indicator examines the prevalence of these risk factors among racial/ethnic groups and, for poverty status, among states. For more information on associations of risk factors with early learning, please see *The Condition of Education 2017* Spotlight indicator Risk Factors and Academic Outcomes in Kindergarten Through Third Grade.

Figure 1. Percentage distribution of children under age 18, by child's race/ethnicity and parents' highest level of educational attainment: 2016

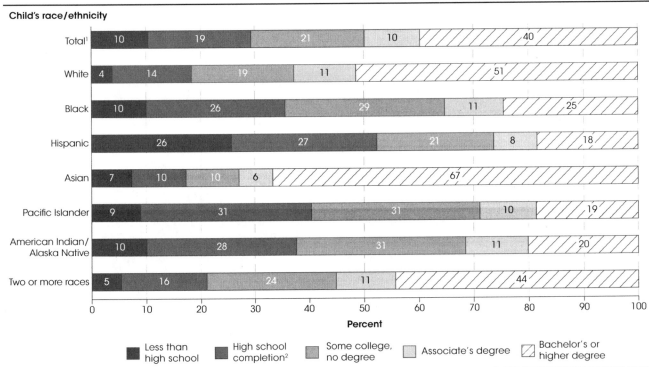

[1] Total includes races/ethnicities not reported separately.
[2] Includes parents who completed high school through equivalency programs, such as a GED program.
NOTE: Includes only children under age 18 who resided with at least one of their parents (including an adoptive or stepparent). Parents' highest level of educational attainment is the highest level of education attained by any parent residing in the same household as the child. Parents include adoptive and stepparents but exclude parents not residing in the same household as their child. Race categories exclude persons of Hispanic ethnicity. Detail may not sum to totals because of rounding.
SOURCE: U.S. Department of Commerce, Census Bureau, American Community Survey (ACS), 2016. See *Digest of Education Statistics 2017*, table 104.70.

In 2016, some 40 percent of children under age 18 lived in households where at least one parent's highest level of educational attainment was a bachelor's or higher degree: 22 percent lived in households where the highest level of education attained by either parent was a bachelor's degree, 13 percent lived in households where the highest level of education attained by either parent was a master's degree, and 5 percent had at least one parent whose highest level of educational attainment was a doctor's degree.[4] In addition, 10 percent of children lived in households without a parent who had completed high school, 19 percent lived in households where the highest level of education attained by either parent was high school completion,[5] 21 percent lived in households where the highest level of education attained by either parent was attending some college but not receiving a degree, and 10 percent lived in households where the highest level of education attained by either parent was an associate's degree. The percentages of children with at least one parent who completed an associate's degree or a bachelor's or higher degree were greater in 2016 than in 2010. In contrast, the percentages of children in households without a parent who had completed high school, where the highest level of education attained by either parent

was high school completion, and where the highest level of education attained by either parent was attending some college but not receiving a degree were lower in 2016 than in 2010.

The percentage distribution of children under age 18 by the highest level of education either parent in their household achieved varied across racial/ethnic groups in 2016. For example, the percentage of children with at least one parent who completed a bachelor's or higher degree was highest for Asian children (67 percent), followed by children who were White (51 percent), of Two or more races (44 percent), and Black (25 percent), and lowest for those who were American Indian/Alaska Native (20 percent), Pacific Islander (19 percent), and Hispanic (18 percent).

In contrast, in 2016 the percentage of children who lived in households without a parent who had completed high school was higher for Hispanic children (26 percent), than for those who were Black or American Indian/Alaska Native (10 percent each), Pacific Islander (9 percent), Asian (7 percent), of Two or more races (5 percent), or White (4 percent).

Figure 2. Percentage of children under age 18, by child's race/ethnicity and family structure: 2016

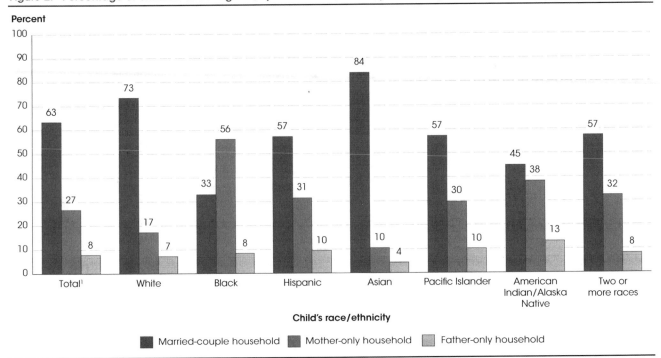

Percent

Child's race/ethnicity

■ Married-couple household ■ Mother-only household □ Father-only household

¹ Total includes races/ethnicities not reported separately.
NOTE: Data do not include foster children, children in unrelated subfamilies, children living in group quarters, and children who were reported as the householder or spouse of the householder. A "mother-only household" has a female householder, with no spouse present (i.e., the householder is unmarried or their spouse is not in the household), while a "father-only household" has a male householder, with no spouse present. Includes all children who live either with their parent(s) or with a householder to whom they are related by birth, marriage, or adoption (except a child who is the spouse of the householder). Children are classified by their parents' marital status or, if no parents are present in the household, by the marital status of the householder who is related to the children. The householder is the person (or one of the people) who owns or rents (maintains) the housing unit. Race categories exclude persons of Hispanic ethnicity. Although rounded numbers are displayed, the figures are based on unrounded estimates.
SOURCE: U.S. Department of Commerce, Census Bureau, American Community Survey (ACS), 2016. See *Digest of Education Statistics 2017*, table 102.20.

In 2016, some 63 percent of children under age 18 lived in married-couple households, 27 percent lived in mother-only households, and 8 percent lived in father-only households.[6] This pattern of a higher percentage of children living in married-couple households than in mother- and father-only households was seen for children across all racial/ethnic groups, except for Black children. Some 56 percent of Black children lived in mother-only households, compared with 33 percent who lived in married-couple households and 8 percent who lived in father-only households.

Figure 3.   Percentage of children under age 18 in families living in poverty, by child's race/ethnicity: 2010 and 2016

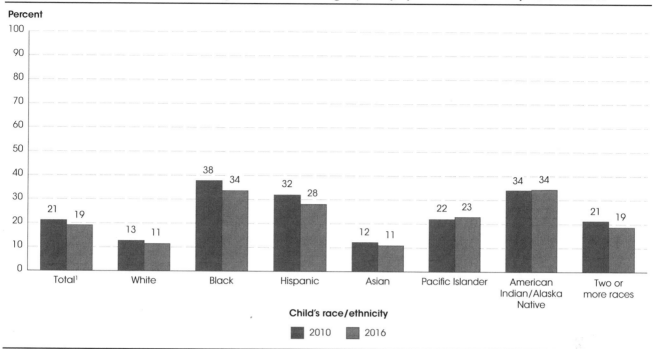

¹ Total includes races/ethnicities not reported separately.
NOTE: The measure of child poverty includes all children who are related to the householder by birth, marriage, or adoption (except a child who is the spouse of the householder). The householder is the person (or one of the people) who owns or rents (maintains) the housing unit. For additional information about poverty status, see https://www.census.gov/topics/income-poverty/poverty/guidance/poverty-measures.html. Race categories exclude persons of Hispanic ethnicity. Although rounded numbers are displayed, the figures are based on unrounded estimates.
SOURCE: U.S. Department of Commerce, Census Bureau, American Community Survey (ACS), 2010 and 2016. See *Digest of Education Statistics 2017,* table 102.60.

In 2016, approximately 13.7 million children under age 18 were in families living in poverty.[7] The poverty rate for children in 2016 (19 percent) was lower than in 2010 (21 percent). This pattern was observed for children who were White, Black, Hispanic, Asian, and of Two or more races. For example, 28 percent of Hispanic children lived in poverty in 2016, compared with 32 percent in 2010. The 2016 poverty rates for American Indian/Alaska Native and Pacific Islander children were not measurably different than the rates in 2010.

The poverty rate for children under age 18 varied across racial/ethnic groups. In 2016, the poverty rate was highest among Black and American Indian/Alaska Native children (34 percent each), followed by Hispanic (28 percent) and Pacific Islander children (23 percent). Additionally, the rate for children of Two or more races (19 percent) was higher than the rates for White and Asian children (11 percent each). Black, American Indian/Alaska Native, and Hispanic children had higher poverty rates than the national average (19 percent), and White and Asian children had lower rates than the national average. The poverty rates for Pacific Islander children and children of Two or more races were not measurably different from the national average. For additional information about poverty rates and racial/ethnic subgroups, please refer to the *Status and Trends in the Education of Racial and Ethnic Groups* report.

Figure 4. Percentage of children under age 18 in families living in poverty, by child's race/ethnicity and parents' highest level of educational attainment: 2016

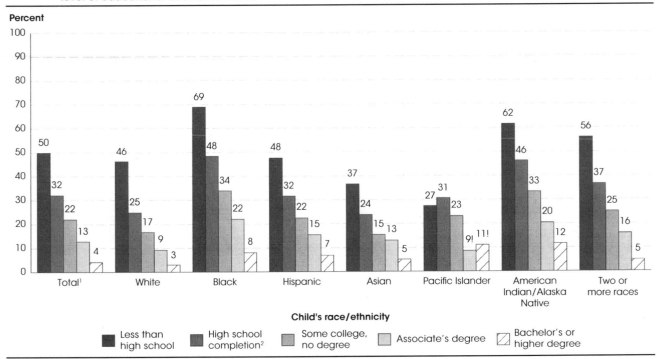

! Interpret data with caution. The coefficient of variation (CV) for this estimate is between 30 and 50 percent.
[1] Total includes races/ethnicities not reported separately.
[2] Includes parents who completed high school through equivalency programs, such as a GED program.
NOTE: Parents' highest level of educational attainment is the highest level of education attained by any parent residing in the same household as the child. Parents include adoptive and stepparents but exclude parents not residing in the same household as their child. The measure of child poverty includes all children who are related to the householder by birth, marriage, or adoption (except a child who is the spouse of the householder). The householder is the person (or one of the people) who owns or rents (maintains) the housing unit. For additional information about poverty status, see https://www.census.gov/topics/income-poverty/poverty/guidance/poverty-measures.html. Race categories exclude persons of Hispanic ethnicity. Although rounded numbers are displayed, the figures are based on unrounded estimates.
SOURCE: U.S. Department of Commerce, Census Bureau, American Community Survey (ACS), 2016. See *Digest of Education Statistics 2017*, table 102.62.

In 2016, the poverty rate for children under age 18 was highest for those in households without a parent who had completed high school and lowest for those in households where at least one parent attained a bachelor's or higher degree, both overall (50 vs. 4 percent) and within most racial/ethnic groups. For example, the poverty rate among American Indian/Alaska Native children was highest for those in households without a parent who had completed high school (62 percent) and lowest for those in households where at least one parent attained a bachelor's or higher degree (12 percent).

Figure 5.   Percentage of children under age 18 in families living in poverty, by child's race/ethnicity and family structure: 2016

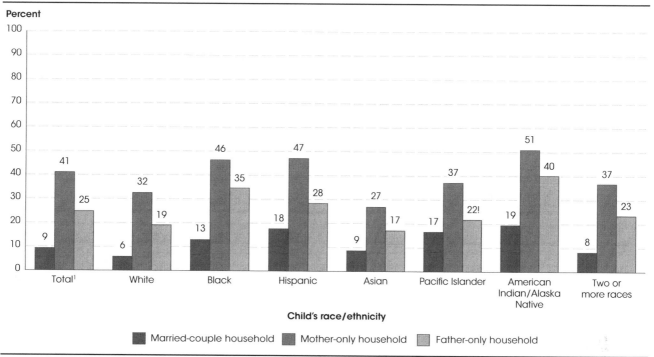

! Interpret data with caution. The coefficient of variation (CV) for this estimate is between 30 and 50 percent.
[1] Total includes races/ethnicities not reported separately.
NOTE: A "mother-only household" has a female householder, with no spouse present (i.e., the householder is unmarried or their spouse is not in the household), while a "father-only household" has a male householder, with no spouse present. Includes all children who live either with their parent(s) or with a householder to whom they are related by birth, marriage, or adoption (except a child who is the spouse of the householder). Children are classified by their parents' marital status or, if no parents are present in the household, by the marital status of the householder who is related to the children. The householder is the person (or one of the people) who owns or rents (maintains) the housing unit. For additional information about poverty status, see https://www.census.gov/topics/income-poverty/poverty/guidance/poverty-measures.html. Race categories exclude persons of Hispanic ethnicity. Although rounded numbers are displayed, the figures are based on unrounded estimates.
SOURCE: U.S. Department of Commerce, Census Bureau, American Community Survey (ACS), 2016. See *Digest of Education Statistics 2017*, table 102.60.

Among children under age 18, those living in mother-only households had the highest poverty rate (41 percent) and those living in father-only households had the next-highest rate (25 percent) in 2016. Children living in married-couple households had the lowest poverty rate, at 9 percent. This pattern of children living in married-couple households having the lowest poverty rate was generally observed across racial/ethnic groups. For example, among Black children the poverty rates were 46 percent for those living in mother-only households, 35 percent for those living in father-only households, and 13 percent for those living in married-couple households.

Figure 6.   Percentage of children under age 18 in families living in poverty, by state: 2016

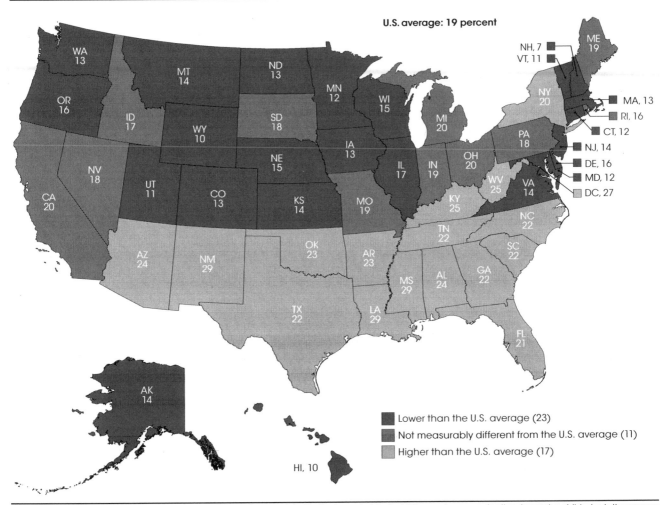

NOTE: The measure of child poverty includes all children who are related to the householder by birth, marriage, or adoption (except a child who is the spouse of the householder). The householder is the person (or one of the people) who owns or rents (maintains) the housing unit. For additional information about poverty status, see https://www.census.gov/topics/income-poverty/poverty/guidance/poverty-measures.html.
SOURCE: U.S. Department of Commerce, Census Bureau, American Community Survey (ACS), 2016. See *Digest of Education Statistics 2017*, table 102.40.

While the national average poverty rate for children under age 18 was 19 percent in 2016, the poverty rates among states ranged from 7 percent in New Hampshire to 29 percent in Louisiana, Mississippi, and New Mexico. Twenty-three states had poverty rates for children that were lower than the national average, 16 states and the District of Columbia had rates that were higher than the national average, and 11 states had rates that were not measurably different from the national average. Of the 17 jurisdictions (16 states and the District of Columbia) that had poverty rates higher than the national average, the majority (14) were located in the South. In 28 states, the poverty rates were lower in 2016 than in 2010. In the remaining 22 states and the District of Columbia, there was no measurable difference between the poverty rates in 2010 and 2016.

Endnotes:

[1] Pungello, E., Kainz, K., Burchinal, M., Wasik, B., Sparling, J.J., Ramey, C.T., and Campbell, F.A. (2010, January). Early Educational Intervention, Early Cumulative Risk, and the Early Home Environment as Predictors of Young Adult Outcomes Within a High-Risk Sample. *Child Development, 81*(1): 410–426. Retrieved March 25, 2018, from http://onlinelibrary.wiley.com/doi/10.1111/j.1467-8624.2009.01403.x/full.

[2] Ross, T., Kena, G., Rathbun, A., KewalRamani, A., Zhang, J., Kristapovich, P., and Manning, E. (2012). *Higher Education: Gaps in Access and Persistence Study* (NCES 2012-046). U.S. Department of Education. Washington, DC: National Center for Education Statistics. Retrieved March 25, 2018, from https://nces.ed.gov/pubsearch/pubsinfo.asp?pubid=2012046.

[3] In this indicator, "parents' highest level of educational attainment" is the highest level of education attained by either parent residing in the same household as the child.

[4] Includes parents who had completed professional degrees.

[5] Includes parents who completed high school through equivalency programs, such as a GED program.

[6] A "mother-only household" has a female householder, with no spouse present (i.e., the householder is unmarried or their spouse is not in the household) while a "father-only household" has a male householder, with no spouse present. Includes all children who live either with their parent(s) or with a householder to whom they are related by birth, marriage, or adoption (except a child who is the spouse of the householder). Children are classified by their parents' marital status or, if no parents are present in the household, by the marital status of the householder who is related to the children. The householder is the person (or one of the people) who owns or rents (maintains) the housing unit. Foster children, children in unrelated subfamilies, children living in group quarters, and children who were reported as the householder or spouse of the householder are not included in this analysis.

[7] In this indicator, data on household income and the number of people living in the household are combined with the poverty threshold, published by the Census Bureau, to determine the poverty status of children. A household includes all families in which children are related to the householder by birth or adoption, or through marriage. The householder is the person (or one of the people) who owns or rents (maintains) the housing unit. In 2016, the poverty threshold for a family of four with two related children under 18 years old was $24,339. For a more detailed breakdown of the 2016 poverty rate, refer to this table.

Reference tables: *Digest of Education Statistics 2017*, tables 102.20, 102.40, 102.60, 102.62, and 104.70

Related indicators and resources: Children Living in Poverty [*Status and Trends in the Education of Racial and Ethnic Groups*]; Children's Living Arrangements [*Status and Trends in the Education of Racial and Ethnic Groups*]; Concentration of Public School Students Eligible for Free or Reduced-Price Lunch; Disparities in Educational Outcomes Among Male Youth [*The Condition of Education 2015 Spotlight*]; Risk Factors and Academic Outcomes in Kindergarten Through Third Grade [*The Condition of Education 2017 Spotlight*]; Snapshot: Children Living in Poverty for Racial/Ethnic Subgroups [*Status and Trends in the Education of Racial and Ethnic Groups*]

Glossary: Associate's degree, Bachelor's degree, College, Doctor's degree, Educational attainment, High school completer, Household, Master's degree, Poverty (official measure), Racial/ethnic group

Children's Access to and Use of the Internet

In 2015, about 71 percent of children ages 3 to 18 used the Internet. Among these children, 86 percent used the Internet at home; 65 percent used it at school; 31 percent used it at someone else's home; 27 percent used it at a library, community center, or other public place; and 14 percent used it at a coffee shop or other business offering internet access. In addition, 27 percent of these children used the Internet while traveling between places.

Studies have shown that differences in internet access exist among students with different demographic characteristics. For instance, households with members who are racial or ethnic minorities or have low levels of educational attainment or income have lower levels of computer use and internet access.[1,2,3] Using data from the Current Population Survey (CPS), this indicator first describes the percentages of children between the ages of 3 and 18 who used the Internet from home in 2015, as well as changes from the corresponding percentages in 2010.[4] The indicator also describes, among children who used the Internet anywhere, the percentages of children who accessed the Internet in specific settings (e.g., home, school, library, etc.).

Figure 1. Percentage of children ages 3 to 18 who used the Internet from home, by selected child and family characteristics: 2010 and 2015

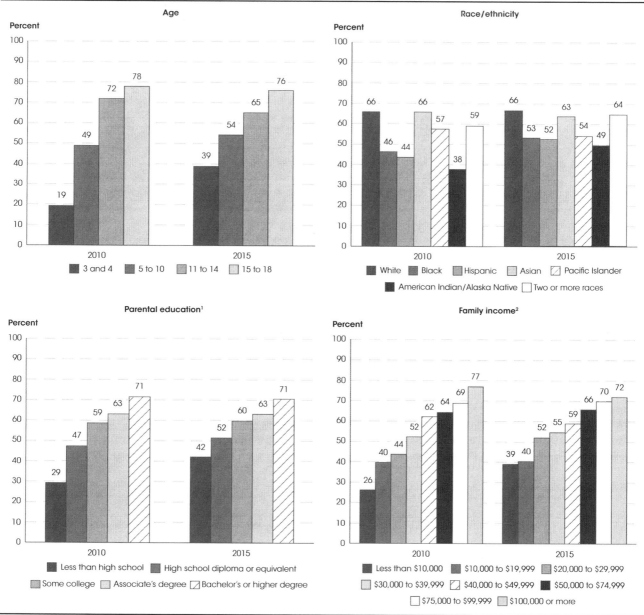

[1] Highest education level of any parent residing with the child (including an adoptive or stepparent). Includes only children who resided with at least one of their parents.

[2] In current dollars.

NOTE: Race categories exclude persons of Hispanic ethnicity. Data exclude children living in institutions (e.g., prisons or nursing facilities). Data for 2015 were collected in the July supplement to the Current Population Survey (CPS), while data for 2010 were collected in the October supplement. The 2015 July supplement consisted solely of questions about computer and internet use. In contrast, the 2010 October supplement focused on school enrollment, although it also included questions about computer and internet use. Measurable differences in estimates across years could reflect actual changes in the population; however, differences could also reflect seasonal variations in data collection or differences between the content of the July and October supplements. Therefore, caution should be used when making year-to-year comparisons.

SOURCE: U.S. Department of Commerce, Census Bureau, Current Population Survey (CPS), October 2010 and July 2015. See *Digest of Education Statistics 2016*, table 702.15.

In the years between 2010 and 2015,[5] it was more common for older children than for younger children to use the Internet from home. In 2015, the percentage of all children using the Internet from home was highest among 15- to 18-year-olds (76 percent), followed by 11- to 14-year-olds (65 percent), 5- to 10-year-olds (54 percent), and 3- and 4-year-olds (39 percent). A higher percentage of children used the Internet at home in 2015 than in

2010 (61 vs. 58 percent). However, this pattern was not consistently observed for children from different age groups. During this period, the percentage of children using the Internet from home was higher in 2015 than in 2010 for children ages 3 and 4 (39 vs. 19 percent) and 5 to 10 (54 vs. 49 percent); in contrast, the percentage was lower in 2015 than in 2010 for children ages 11 to 14 (65 v. 72 percent) and 15 to 18 (76 vs. 78 percent).

In the years between 2010 and 2015,[5] the percentage of children ages 3 to 18 using the Internet from home was higher for children who were White, Asian, and of Two or more races than for those who were Black, Hispanic, and American Indian/Alaska Native. In 2015, higher percentages of children who were White (66 percent), of Two or more races (64 percent), and Asian (63 percent) used the Internet from home than did Black (53 percent), Hispanic (52 percent), and American Indian/Alaska Native children (49 percent). The percentage of Pacific Islander children (54 percent) was not measurably different from that of any other racial/ethnic group. The percentage of children using the Internet from home was higher in 2015 than in 2010 for Black (53 vs. 46 percent) and Hispanic children (52 vs. 44 percent), but was not measurably different for children from other racial/ethnic groups. As a result, the White-Black and White-Hispanic gaps in home internet use narrowed between 2010 and 2015. The White-Black gap narrowed from 19 percentage points in 2010 to 13 percentage points in 2015, and the White-Hispanic gap narrowed from 22 percentage points in 2010 to 14 percentage points in 2015.

In general, the percentage of children ages 3 to 18 using the Internet from home was higher for children whose parents had attained higher levels of education. For instance, 71 percent of children whose parents had attained a bachelor's or higher degree used the Internet from home in 2015, compared with 42 percent of children whose parents had not completed high school and 52 percent of children whose parents had completed high school only. The percentage of children using the

Internet from home was higher in 2015 than in 2010 for children whose parents had not completed high school (42 vs. 29 percent) and those who had completed high school only (52 vs. 47 percent), but was not measurably different for those whose parents had at least some college education. Consequently, from 2010 to 2015, the gap in home internet use between children whose parents had attained a bachelor's or higher degree and children whose parents had not completed high school narrowed from 42 to 28 percentage points, and the gap between children whose parents had a bachelor's or higher degree and children whose parents had completed high school narrowed from 24 to 19 percentage points.

The percentage of children ages 3 to 18 using the Internet from home was also generally higher for children with higher family income. In 2015, about 72 percent of children with a family income of $100,000 or more and 70 percent of children with a family income between $75,000 and $99,999 used the Internet from home, compared with 39 percent of children with a family income of less than $10,000 and 40 percent of children with a family income between $10,000 and $19,999. The percentage of children using the Internet from home was higher in 2015 than in 2010 for children with a family income of less than $10,000 (39 vs. 26 percent), but it was lower in 2015 than in 2010 for children with a family income of $100,000 or more (72 vs. 77 percent). As a result, the home internet use gap between children in these two groups narrowed from 51 percentage points in 2010 to 33 percentage points in 2015.

Figure 2. Among those who used the Internet anywhere, percentage of children ages 3 to 18 using it in various locations: 2015

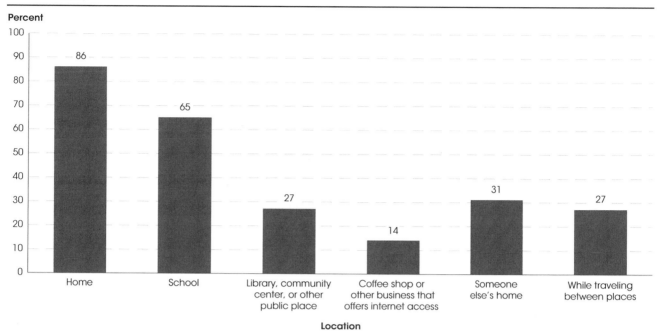

NOTE: Data exclude children living in institutions (e.g., prisons or nursing facilities). Percentages sum to more than 100 because a child could have used the Internet in more than one location.
SOURCE: U.S. Department of Commerce, Census Bureau, Current Population Survey (CPS), July 2015. See *Digest of Education Statistics 2016,* table 702.20.

Children access the Internet from a wide range of settings. In 2015, about 71 percent of children ages 3 to 18 used the Internet anywhere. Among these children, 86 percent used the Internet at home; 65 percent used it at school; 31 percent used it at someone else's home; 27 percent used it at a library, community center, or other public place; and 14 percent used it at a coffee shop or other business offering internet access. In addition, 27 percent of these children used the Internet while traveling between places.

Figure 3. Among those who used the Internet anywhere, percentage of children ages 3 to 18 who used the Internet at home and at school, by selected child and family characteristics: 2015

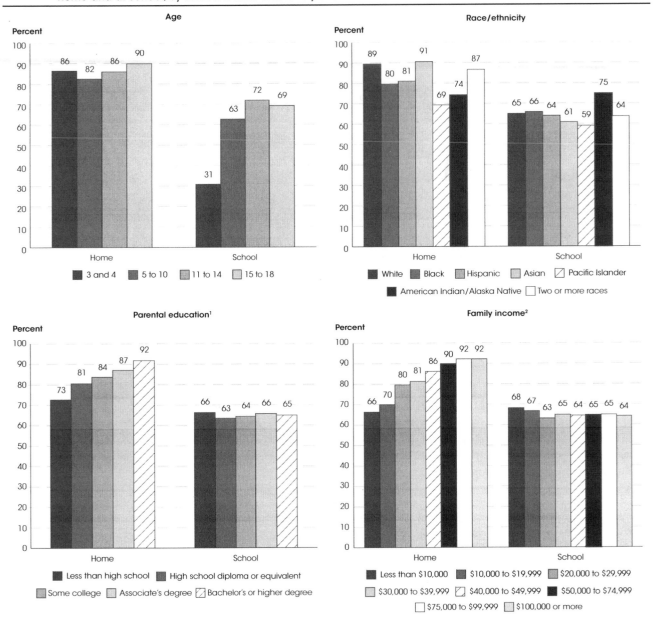

[1] Highest education level of any parent residing with the child (including an adoptive or stepparent). Includes only children who resided with at least one of their parents.
[2] In current dollars.
NOTE: Race categories exclude persons of Hispanic ethnicity. Data exclude children living in institutions (e.g., prisons or nursing facilities).
SOURCE: U.S. Department of Commerce, Census Bureau, Current Population Survey (CPS), July 2015. See *Digest of Education Statistics 2016*, table 702.20.

Among children ages 3 to 18 who used the Internet anywhere, there were differences in children's internet access at home across various child and family characteristics. For instance, among children who used the Internet anywhere in 2015, the percentage using it at home was higher for children who were Asian (91 percent), White (89 percent), and of Two or more races (87 percent) than for those who were Hispanic (81 percent), Black (80 percent), and American Indian/Alaska Native (74 percent). The percentage of children who used the Internet at home was also generally higher for older children, children whose parents had higher levels of educational attainment, and children with higher family incomes.

Compared to children's internet use at home, fewer differences by child and family characteristics were observed for children's internet use at school. In 2015, among children ages 3 to 18 who used the Internet anywhere, a higher percentage of American Indian/Alaska Native children (75 percent) used it at school than did children who were White (65 percent), Hispanic (64 percent), of Two or more races (64 percent), and Asian (61 percent); additionally, the percentage for White children was higher than for Asian children. There was no measurable difference in internet use at school among children who were White, Black, Hispanic, and of Two or more races. The percentage of children who used the Internet at school was generally higher for older children than for younger children. The only exception was that a higher percentage of children ages 11 to 14 than children ages 15 to 18 (72 vs. 69 percent) used the Internet at school. There were no measurable differences in the percentages of children using the Internet at school by family income or by highest level of education attained by either parent.

Children's internet use at libraries, community centers, or other public places[6] also varied by child and family characteristics. For instance, among children ages 3 to 18 who used the Internet anywhere in 2015, the percentage using it at a library, community center, or other public place was higher for children who were Pacific Islander (46 percent), Black (34 percent), of Two or more races (34 percent), Asian (32 percent), and Hispanic (29 percent) than for White children (23 percent); additionally, it was higher for Black children than for Hispanic children and higher for Pacific Islander children than for American Indian/Alaska Native children (25 percent).

Furthermore, the percentage of children ages 3 to 18 who used the Internet at a library, community center, or other public place was lower for children whose parents had completed high school only (24 percent) than for those whose parents had not completed high school (30 percent), had some college education (28 percent), and had attained a bachelor's or higher degree (27 percent). The percentage of children who used the Internet at a library, community center, or other public place was higher for children with family incomes of less than $20,000 than for children with family incomes of $40,000 or higher. For example, among children who used the Internet anywhere, 32 percent of children with a family income of less than $10,000 and 33 percent of children with a family income between $10,000 and $19,999 used the Internet at a library, community center, or other public place, while 25 percent of children with a family income between $75,000 and $99,999 and 26 percent of children with a family income of $100,000 or more did so.

Endnotes:

[1] DeBell, M., and Chapman, C. (2006). *Computer and Internet Use by Students in 2003* (NCES 2006-065). U.S. Department of Education. Washington, DC: National Center for Education Statistics. Retrieved February 17, 2017, from http://nces.ed.gov/pubs2006/2006065.pdf.

[2] File, T., and Ryan, C. (2014). *Computer and Internet Use in the United States: 2013* (ACS-28). U.S. Department of Commerce. Washington, DC: Census Bureau. Retrieved February 17, 2017, from https://www.census.gov/history/pdf/2013computeruse.pdf.

[3] Horrigan, J.B., and Duggan, M. (2015). *Home Broadband 2015*. Washington, DC: Pew Research Center. Retrieved February 17, 2017, from http://www.pewinternet.org/files/2015/12/Broadband-adoption-full.pdf.

[4] Data for 2015 were collected in the July supplement to the CPS, while data for 2010 were collected in the October supplement. Measurable differences in estimates across years could reflect actual changes in the population; however, differences could also reflect seasonal variations in data collection or differences between the content of the July and October supplements. Therefore, caution should be used when making year-to-year comparisons.

[5] Includes 2010, 2011, 2012, 2013, and 2015. Data for 2014 were unavailable.

[6] Excludes coffee shops and other businesses that offer internet access.

Reference tables: *Digest of Education Statistics 2016*, tables 702.15 and 702.20

Related indicators and resources: Technology and Engineering Literacy

Glossary: Bachelor's degree, College, Educational attainment (Current Population Survey), Gap, High school completer, Racial/ethnic group

Preschool and Kindergarten Enrollment

In 2016, the percentage of 3- to 5-year-olds enrolled in preschool programs was higher for those children whose parents had a graduate or professional degree (54 percent) than for those whose parents had a bachelor's degree (41 percent), an associate's degree (35 percent), some college but no degree (37 percent), a high school credential (33 percent), and less than a high school credential (30 percent).

Preprimary programs are groups or classes that are organized to provide educational experiences for children, including kindergarten and preschool programs.[1] Child care programs that are not primarily designed to provide educational experiences, such as daycare programs, are not included in preprimary programs.

Figure 1.   Percentage of 3-, 4-, and 5-year-old children enrolled in preprimary programs: 2000 through 2016

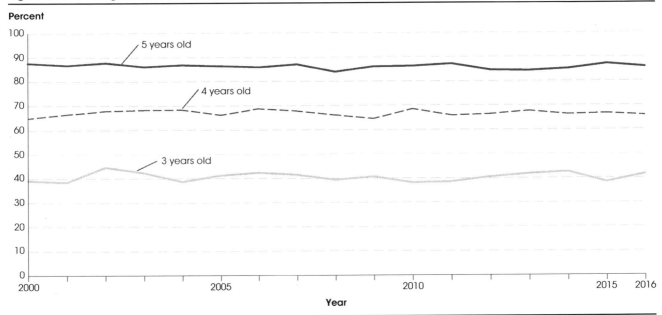

NOTE: "Preprimary programs" are groups or classes that are organized to provide educational experiences for children and include kindergarten, preschool, and nursery school programs. Enrollment data for 5-year-olds include only those students in preprimary programs and do not include those enrolled in primary programs. Data are based on sample surveys of the civilian noninstitutional population.
SOURCE: U.S. Department of Commerce, Census Bureau, Current Population Survey (CPS), October 2000 through 2016. See *Digest of Education Statistics 2006*, table 41; *Digest of Education Statistics 2009*, table 43; *Digest of Education Statistics 2011*, table 53; and *Digest of Education Statistics 2013, 2015, 2016*, and *2017*, table 202.10.

In 2016, some 42 percent of 3-year-olds, 66 percent of 4-year-olds, and 86 percent of 5-year-olds were enrolled in preprimary programs, which were not measurably different from the percentages enrolled in 2000. In 2016, the percentage of children enrolled in preprimary programs was higher for 5-year-olds than for 4-year-olds, and higher for 4-year-olds than for 3-year-olds.

Figure 2. Percentage of 3- to 5-year-old children in preprimary programs attending full-day programs, by program type: 2000 through 2016

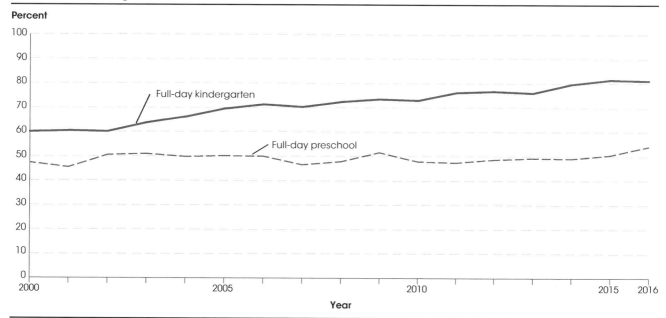

NOTE: "Preprimary programs" are groups or classes that are organized to provide educational experiences for children and include kindergarten, preschool, and nursery school programs. Enrollment data for 5-year-olds include only those students in preprimary programs and do not include those enrolled in primary programs. Data are based on sample surveys of the civilian noninstitutional population.
SOURCE: U.S. Department of Commerce, Census Bureau, Current Population Survey (CPS), October 2000 through 2016. See *Digest of Education Statistics 2006*, table 41; *Digest of Education Statistics 2009*, table 43; *Digest of Education Statistics 2011*, table 53; and *Digest of Education Statistics 2013, 2015, 2016*, and *2017*, table 202.10.

Among 3- to 5-year-olds who were enrolled in preschool programs in 2016, some 54 percent attended full-day programs, which was higher than the percentage who attended full-day programs in 2000 (47 percent). Among 3- to 5-year-olds attending kindergarten, the percentage attending full-day programs increased from 60 percent in 2000 to 81 percent in 2016. In every year from 2000 to 2016, the percentage of 3- to 5-year-old kindergarten students enrolled in full-day programs was higher than the percentage of 3- to 5-year-old preschool students enrolled in full-day programs.

Figure 3. Percentage of 3- to 5-year-old children enrolled in preschool programs, by race/ethnicity and attendance status: October 2016

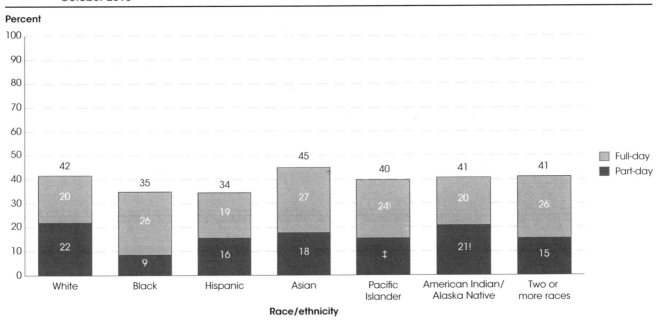

! Interpret data with caution. The coefficient of variation (CV) for this estimate is between 30 and 50 percent.
‡ Reporting standards not met. Either there are too few cases for a reliable estimate or the coefficient of variation (CV) is 50 percent or greater.
NOTE: Data shown are based on unrounded estimates. Race categories exclude persons of Hispanic ethnicity. Enrollment data include only those children in preschool programs and do not include those enrolled in kindergarten or primary programs. Data are based on sample surveys of the civilian noninstitutional population. Detail may not sum to totals because of rounding.
SOURCE: U.S. Department of Commerce, Census Bureau, Current Population Survey (CPS), October 2016. See *Digest of Education Statistics 2017*, table 202.20.

In 2016, the percentage of 3- to 5-year-olds enrolled in preschool programs was lower for Black (35 percent) and Hispanic (34 percent) children than for Asian (45 percent) and White (42 percent) children. The preschool enrollment rates of 3- to 5-year olds who were Pacific Islander (40 percent), American Indian/Alaska Native (41 percent), and of Two or more races (41 percent) were not measurably different from the preschool enrollment rates of children from other racial/ethnic groups.

In terms of attendance status, a higher percentage of Black 3- to 5-year-olds attended full-day than part-day preschool programs (26 vs. 9 percent) in 2016. Similar patterns were observed for Asian children (27 vs. 18 percent) and

children of Two or more races (26 vs. 15 percent). For children in the other racial/ethnic groups, there were no measurable differences in the percentages enrolled in full-day compared to part-day programs. Enrollment in full-day preschool programs was higher for Asian (27 percent) and Black (26 percent) children than for White (20 percent) and Hispanic (19 percent) children. The full-day preschool enrollment rates of 3- to 5-year-olds who were of Two or more races (26 percent), Pacific Islander (24 percent), and American Indian/Alaska Native (20 percent) were not measurably different from the full-day preschool enrollment rates of children who were White, Black, Hispanic, and Asian.

Figure 4. Percentage of 3- to 5-year-old children enrolled in preschool programs, by parents' highest level of education and attendance status: October 2016

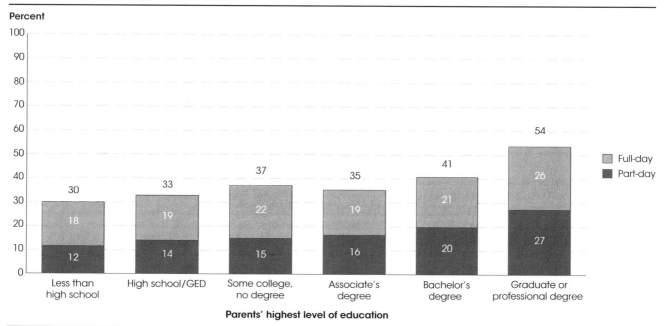

NOTE: Enrollment data include only those children in preschool programs and do not include those enrolled in kindergarten or primary programs. "Parents' highest level of education" is defined as the highest level of education attained by either parent in the child's household. Data are based on sample surveys of the civilian noninstitutional population. Detail may not sum to totals because of rounding.
SOURCE: U.S. Department of Commerce, Census Bureau, Current Population Survey (CPS), October 2016. See *Digest of Education Statistics 2017*, table 202.20.

Enrollment in preschool programs varied by parents' highest level of education, defined as the highest level of education attained by either parent in the child's household. In 2016, the percentage of 3- to 5-year-olds enrolled in preschool programs was higher for those children whose parents had a graduate or professional degree (54 percent) than for those whose parents had a bachelor's degree (41 percent), an associate's degree (35 percent), some college but no degree (37 percent), a high school credential (33 percent), and less than a high school credential (30 percent). The preschool enrollment percentage was also higher for those children whose parents had a bachelor's degree than for those whose parents had a high school credential and less than a high school credential.

The percentage of 3- to 5-year-olds enrolled in part-day and full-day preschool programs also varied by parents' highest level of education. In 2016, the percentage of 3- to 5-year-olds enrolled in full-day preschool programs was higher for those children whose parents had a graduate or professional degree (26 percent) than for those children whose parents had a bachelor's degree (21 percent), an associate's degree (19 percent), a high school credential (19 percent), and less than a high school credential (18 percent).

For the following groups, the percentage of 3- to 5-year-olds who were enrolled in full-day preschool programs was greater than the percentage enrolled in part-day preschool programs: children whose parents had less than a high school credential (18 vs. 12 percent), children whose parents had a high school credential (19 vs. 14 percent), and children whose parents had some college but no degree (22 vs. 15 percent). Among children whose parents had higher levels of educational attainment (i.e., an associate's degree, bachelor's degree, and graduate or professional degree), there were no measurable differences between the percentages of children enrolled in full-day and part-day programs.

Figure 5. Percentage of 3- and 4-year-old children enrolled in school, by OECD country: 2015

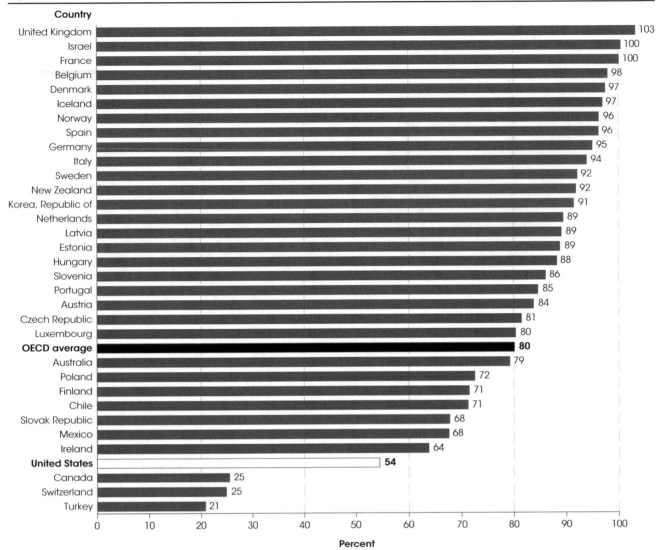

NOTE: Data shown are based on unrounded estimates. The enrollment rate is calculated as the number of persons in each age group who are enrolled in that country as a percentage of that country's total population in the specified age group. However, some of a country's population may be enrolled in a different country, and some persons enrolled in the country may be residents of a different country. If a country enrolls many residents of other countries, the country's total population in the specified age group can be smaller than the total number enrolled, resulting in enrollment estimates exceeding 100 percent. "OECD average" refers to the mean of the data values for all reporting Organization for Economic Cooperation and Development (OECD) countries, to which each country reporting data contributes equally.
SOURCE: Organization for Economic Cooperation and Development (OECD), Online Education Database. See *Digest of Education Statistics 2017*, table 601.35.

In 2015, some 54 percent of 3- and 4-year-olds in the United States were enrolled in school,[2] compared to the average enrollment of 80 percent for the Organization for Economic Cooperation and Development (OECD) countries. The OECD is an organization of 35 countries whose purpose is to promote trade and economic growth. The OECD also serves as a statistical agency, collecting and publishing an array of data on its member countries. Among the 33 OECD countries reporting data in 2015, the percentages of 3- and 4-year-olds enrolled in school ranged from 25 percent or less in Turkey, Switzerland, and Canada to 95 percent or more in Germany, Spain, Norway, Iceland, Denmark, Belgium, France, Israel, and the United Kingdom.

Endnotes:

[1] Preschool programs are also known as nursery school programs.

[2] The international data represent 3- and 4-year-olds enrolled in school at any level, rather than specifically in preprimary or preschool programs. The distinctions between preprimary, preschool, and elementary schools may vary by country.

Reference tables: *Digest of Education Statistics 2006,* table 41; *Digest of Education Statistics 2009,* table 43; *Digest of Education Statistics 2011,* table 53; *Digest of Education Statistics 2013, 2015, 2016,* and *2017,* table 202.10; *Digest of Education Statistics 2017,* tables 202.20 and 601.35

Related indicators and resources: Early Childcare and Education Arrangements [*Status and Trends in the Education of Racial and Ethnic Groups*]; Early Childhood Care Arrangements: Choices and Costs [*The Condition of Education 2018 Spotlight*]; Elementary and Secondary Enrollment; Kindergarten Entry Status: On-Time, Delayed-Entry, Repeating Kindergartners [*The Condition of Education 2013 Spotlight*]; Kindergartners' Approaches to Learning Behaviors and Academic Outcomes [*The Condition of Education 2015 Spotlight*]; Kindergartners' Approaches to Learning, Family Socioeconomic Status, and Early Academic Gains [*The Condition of Education 2016 Spotlight*]; Private School Enrollment; Risk Factors and Academic Outcomes in Kindergarten Through Third Grade [*The Condition of Education 2017 Spotlight*]

Glossary terms: Associate's degree, Bachelor's degree, College, Educational attainment (Current Population Survey), Enrollment, High school completer, Organization for Economic Cooperation and Development (OECD), Preschool, Racial/ethnic group

Indicator 1.4

Elementary and Secondary Enrollment

Between fall 2015 and fall 2027, total public school enrollment in prekindergarten through grade 12 is projected to increase by 3 percent (from 50.4 million to 52.1 million students), with changes across states ranging from an increase of 28 percent in the District of Columbia to a decrease of 12 percent in Connecticut.

This indicator discusses changes in the overall enrollment rate at schools of any type (including traditional public, public charter, parochial, and other private schools) as well as changes in the number of students enrolled in public schools specifically (including both traditional public schools and public charter schools). Overall enrollment rates are calculated using data from the Current Population Survey (CPS); public school enrollment is calculated using data from the Common Core of Data (CCD).

Figure 1. Percentage of the population ages 3–19 enrolled in any type of elementary or secondary school, by age group: October 2000 to October 2016

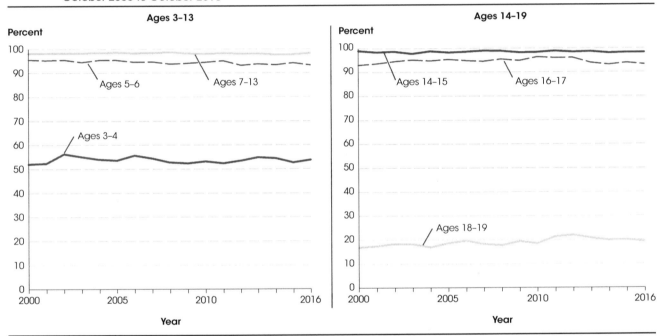

NOTE: This figure includes enrollment in traditional public, public charter, parochial, and other private schools, including nursery schools, kindergartens, and elementary and secondary schools.
SOURCE: U.S. Department of Commerce, Census Bureau, Current Population Survey (CPS), October Supplement, 2000 through 2016. See *Digest of Education Statistics 2017*, table 103.20.

Between October 2000 and October 2016, the enrollment rate for students ages 5–6, who are typically enrolled in kindergarten or grade 1, decreased from 96 to 93 percent. In contrast, the enrollment rate increased during this period for students ages 18–19 in secondary education (from 16 to 19 percent) and did not change measurably for students ages 3–4, 7–13, 14–15, and 16–17.

Figure 2. Actual and projected public school enrollment, by level: Fall 2000 through fall 2027

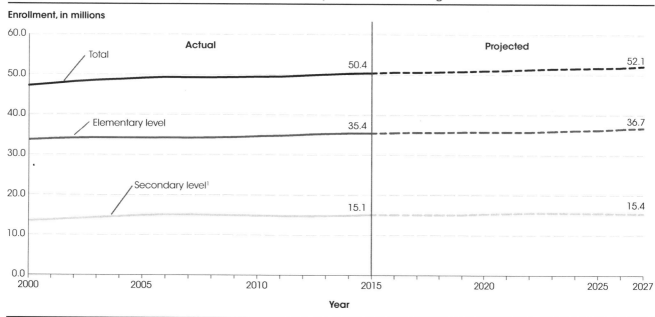

[1] Includes students reported as being enrolled in grade 13.
NOTE: The total ungraded counts of students were prorated to the elementary level (prekindergarten through grade 8) and the secondary level (grades 9 through 12). Prekindergarten enrollment for California and Oregon were imputed for fall 2015. Detail may not sum to totals because of rounding.
SOURCE: U.S. Department of Education, National Center for Education Statistics, Common Core of Data (CCD), "State Nonfiscal Survey of Public Elementary/ Secondary Education," 2000–01 through 2015–16; and National Elementary and Secondary Enrollment Projection Model, 1972 through 2027. See *Digest of Education Statistics 2017*, table 203.10.

Between fall 2000 and fall 2015, total enrollment in public elementary and secondary schools (prekindergarten [preK] through grade 12)[1] increased by 7 percent, reaching 50.4 million students. Of those 50.4 million students enrolled, 70 percent were enrolled in preK through grade 8, and the remaining 30 percent were enrolled in grades 9 through 12. Enrollment in preK through grade 8 increased by 5 percent from fall 2000 to fall 2015, reaching 35.4 million students. Enrollment in grades 9 through 12 increased by 12 percent between fall 2000 and fall 2007, to 15.1 million students, and remained at 15.1 million students in fall 2015.

Total public school enrollment is projected to continue increasing through fall 2027 (the last year for which projected data are available). From fall 2015 to fall 2027, total public school enrollment is projected to increase by 3 percent to 52.1 million students. During this period, public school enrollment in preK through grade 8 is projected to increase by 4 percent to 36.7 million students. Enrollment in grades 9 through 12 is projected to increase by 4 percent to 15.6 million students between fall 2015 and fall 2023 and then decline by 1 percent to 15.4 million students in fall 2027.

Figure 3. Percentage change in public elementary and secondary school enrollment, by state: Fall 2000 to fall 2015

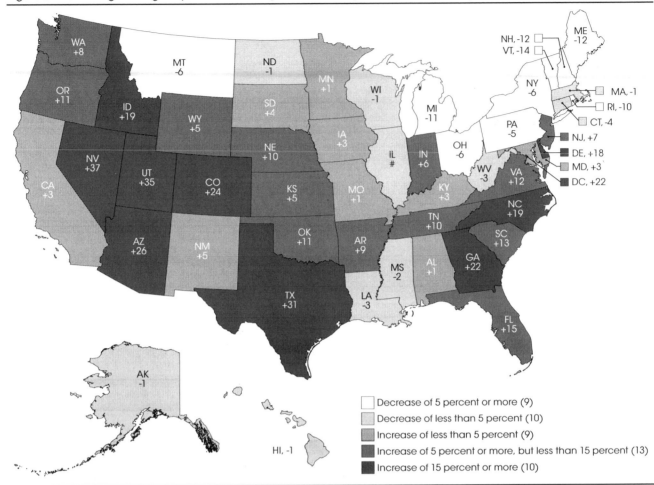

Decrease of 5 percent or more (9)
Decrease of less than 5 percent (10)
Increase of less than 5 percent (9)
Increase of 5 percent or more, but less than 15 percent (13)
Increase of 15 percent or more (10)

Rounds to zero.
NOTE: Categorizations are based on unrounded percentages. Prekindergarten enrollment for California and Oregon were imputed for fall 2015.
SOURCE: U.S. Department of Education, National Center for Education Statistics, Common Core of Data (CCD), "State Nonfiscal Survey of Public Elementary/ Secondary Education," 2000–01 through 2015–16. See *Digest of Education Statistics 2017*, table 203.20.

Changes in public elementary and secondary school enrollment varied by state. Total public school enrollment in preK through grade 12 was higher in fall 2015 than in fall 2000 for 31 states and the District of Columbia, with increases of 15 percent or more occurring in the District of Columbia and nine states (Delaware, Idaho, North Carolina, Georgia, Colorado, Arizona, Texas, Utah, and Nevada). Total public school enrollment in preK through grade 12 was lower in fall 2015 than in fall 2000 for the other 19 states, with decreases of 10 percent or more occurring in four states (Michigan, Maine, New Hampshire, and Vermont).

Figure 4. Projected percentage change in public elementary and secondary school enrollment, by state: Fall 2015 to fall 2027

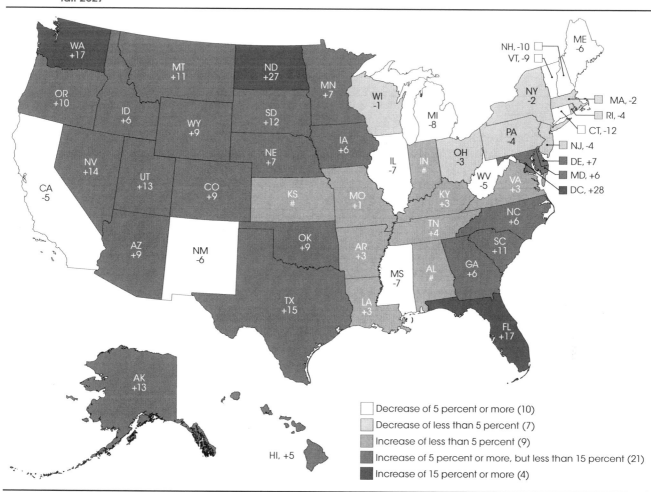

Decrease of 5 percent or more (10)
Decrease of less than 5 percent (7)
Increase of less than 5 percent (9)
Increase of 5 percent or more, but less than 15 percent (21)
Increase of 15 percent or more (4)

Rounds to zero.
NOTE: Categorizations are based on unrounded percentages. Prekindergarten enrollment for California and Oregon were imputed for fall 2015.
SOURCE: U.S. Department of Education, National Center for Education Statistics, Common Core of Data (CCD), "State Nonfiscal Survey of Public Elementary/ Secondary Education," 2015–16; and State Public Elementary and Secondary Enrollment Projection Model, 1972 through 2027. See *Digest of Education Statistics 2017*, table 203.20.

Total public school enrollment is projected to be higher in fall 2027 than in fall 2015 in the District of Columbia and 33 states, all of which are located in the South, the West, or the Midwest. Total public school enrollment is projected to be lower in fall 2027 than in fall 2015 in the other 17 states, most of which are located in the Northeast. During this period, the District of Columbia is projected to have the largest increase (28 percent) in total enrollment, while the state with the largest projected increase is North Dakota (27 percent). Connecticut and New Hampshire are projected to have the largest decreases in total public school enrollment (12 and 10 percent, respectively). In fall 2015, total public school enrollment ranged from fewer than 100,000 students in the District of Columbia (84,024), Vermont (87,866 students), and Wyoming (94,717 students), to 5.2 million students in Texas and 6.3 million students in California. In fall 2027, only Vermont (79,716 students) is projected to have fewer than 100,000 students. Texas is projected to have the largest total public school enrollment in fall 2027 (6.1 million students), followed by California (6.0 million students).

Reflecting the projected total public school enrollment increase between fall 2015 and fall 2027, some 28 states and the District of Columbia are projected to have enrollment increases in both preK through grade 8 and grades 9 through 12. However, 17 other states are projected to have enrollment decreases in both grade ranges. Alabama, Indiana, Kansas, Missouri, and Tennessee are projected to have enrollment increases in preK through grade 8 but enrollment decreases in grades 9 through 12. Enrollment in preK through grade 8 is projected to be at least 15 percent higher in fall 2027 than in fall 2015 in the District of Columbia and three states (Florida, Washington, and North Dakota), while enrollment is projected to be 11 percent lower in fall 2027 than in fall 2015 in Connecticut. During the same time period, enrollment in grades 9 through 12 is projected to be at least 15 percent higher in the District of Columbia and six states (Utah, Texas, Washington, Florida, Nevada, and North Dakota) but is projected to be at least 10 percent lower in six states (Maine, West Virginia, Vermont, Michigan, New Hampshire, and Connecticut).

Endnotes:

[1] Throughout the rest of the indicator, public elementary and secondary enrollment includes ungraded students for all years. This also includes a small number of students reported as being enrolled in grade 13, who were counted as enrolled in grades 9 through 12. Prekindergarten enrollment for California and Oregon were imputed for fall 2015.

Reference tables: *Digest of Education Statistics 2017,* tables 103.20, 203.10, 203.20, 203.25, and 203.30

Related indicators and resources: Characteristics of Traditional Public Schools and Public Charter Schools; Children and Youth With Disabilities; Elementary and Secondary Enrollment [*Status and Trends in the Education of Racial and Ethnic Groups*]; English Language Learners in Public Schools; Homeless Children and Youth in Public Schools [*The Condition of Education 2017 Spotlight*]; Private School Enrollment; Public Charter School Enrollment

Glossary: Elementary school, Enrollment, Prekindergarten, Public school or institution, Secondary school

This page intentionally left blank.

Public Charter School Enrollment

Between fall 2000 and fall 2015, overall public charter school enrollment increased from 0.4 million to 2.8 million. During this period, the percentage of public school students who attended charter schools increased from 1 to 6 percent.

A *public charter school* is a publicly funded school that is typically governed by a group or organization under a legislative contract (or charter) with the state, district, or other entity. The charter exempts the school from certain state or local rules and regulations. In return for flexibility and autonomy, the charter school must meet

the accountability standards outlined in its charter. A school's charter is reviewed periodically by the entity that granted it and can be revoked if guidelines on curriculum and management are not followed or if the accountability standards are not met.[1]

Figure 1. Percentage distribution of public charter schools, by enrollment size: School years 2000–01 and 2015–16

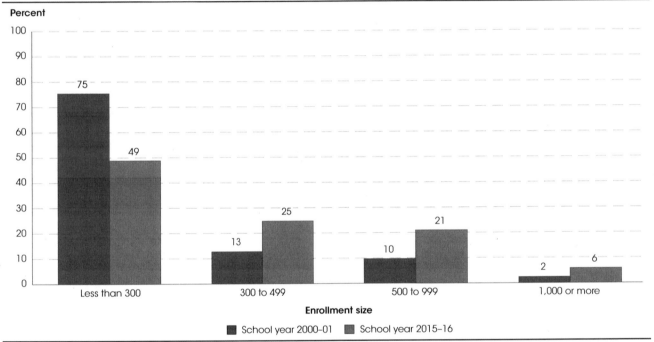

NOTE: Detail may not sum to totals because of rounding.
SOURCE: U.S. Department of Education, National Center for Education Statistics, Common Core of Data (CCD), "Public Elementary/Secondary School Universe Survey," 2000–01 and 2015–16. See *Digest of Education Statistics 2017*, table 216.30.

Between school years 2000–01 and 2015–16, the percentage of all public schools that were charter schools increased from 2 to 7 percent, and the total number of charter schools increased from 2,000 to 6,900. In addition to increasing in number, public charter schools have also

generally increased in enrollment size over this period: from 2000–01 to 2015–16, the percentages of public charter schools with 300–499, 500–999, and 1,000 or more students each increased, while the percentage of charter schools with fewer than 300 students decreased.

Figure 2.   Public charter school enrollment, by school level: Selected years, fall 2000 through fall 2015

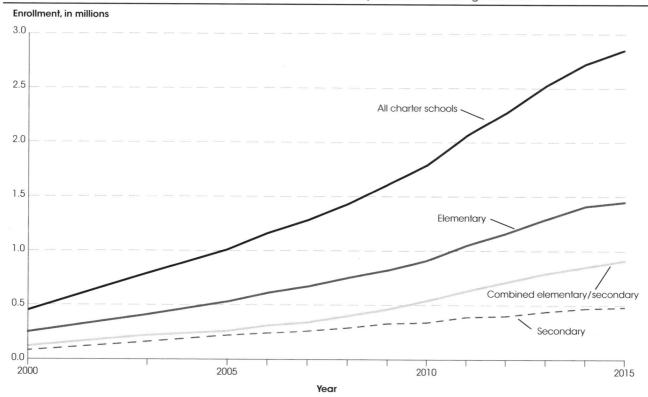

NOTE: "Elementary" includes schools beginning with grade 6 or below and with no grade higher than 8. "Secondary" includes schools with no grade lower than 7. "Combined elementary/secondary" includes schools beginning with grade 6 or below and ending with grade 9 or above. Other schools not classified by grade span are included in the "All charter schools" count but are not presented separately in the figure.
SOURCE: U.S. Department of Education, National Center for Education Statistics, Common Core of Data (CCD), "Public Elementary/Secondary School Universe Survey," 2000–01 through 2015–16. *See Digest of Education Statistics 2016* and *2017,* table 216.20.

The percentage of all public school students who attended public charter schools increased from 1 to 6 percent between fall 2000 and fall 2015. During this period, public charter school enrollment increased steadily, from 0.4 million students in fall 2000 to 2.8 million students in fall 2015, an overall increase of 2.4 million students. In contrast, the number of students attending traditional public schools increased by 1.3 million between fall 2000 and fall 2005, and then decreased by 0.6 million between fall 2005 and fall 2015 (see indicator Elementary and Secondary Enrollment). In each year from fall 2000 to fall 2015, larger numbers of public charter school students were enrolled in elementary schools than in any of the other types of charter schools: secondary, combined, and other types that were not classified by grade span.

Figure 3. Percentage of all public school students enrolled in public charter schools, by state: Fall 2015

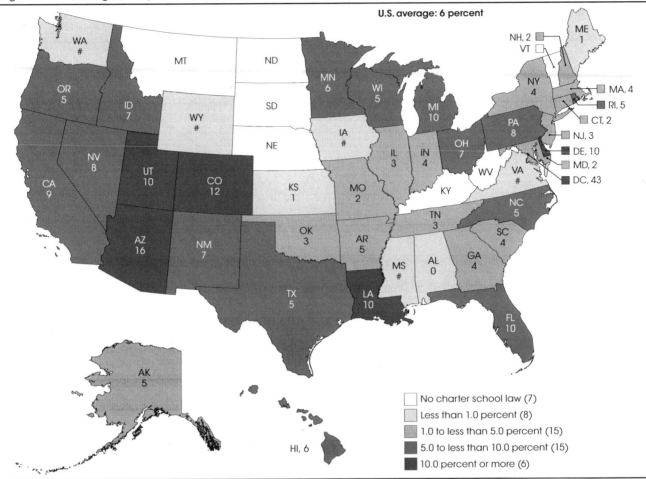

U.S. average: 6 percent

No charter school law (7)
Less than 1.0 percent (8)
1.0 to less than 5.0 percent (15)
5.0 to less than 10.0 percent (15)
10.0 percent or more (6)

Rounds to zero.
NOTE: Categorizations are based on unrounded percentages.
SOURCE: U.S. Department of Education, National Center for Education Statistics, Common Core of Data (CCD), "Public Elementary/Secondary School Universe Survey," 2015–16. See *Digest of Education Statistics 2017*, table 216.90.

The first law allowing the establishment of public charter schools was passed in Minnesota in 1991.[2] As of fall 2015, charter school legislation had been passed in 43 states and the District of Columbia.[3] The states in which public charter school legislation had not been passed by that time were Kentucky, Montana, Nebraska, North Dakota, South Dakota, Vermont, and West Virginia.

Of the 44 jurisdictions with legislative approval for public charter schools as of fall 2015, California had the largest number of students enrolled in charter schools (568,800, representing 9 percent of all public school students in the state), and the District of Columbia had the highest percentage of public school students enrolled in charter schools (43 percent, representing 35,800 students). After the District of Columbia, Arizona had the next highest percentage of public school students enrolled in charter schools (16 percent, representing 176,900 students). In contrast, eight states had less than 1 percent of their public school students enrolled in public charter schools in fall 2015: Alabama,[3] Iowa, Kansas, Maine, Mississippi, Virginia, Washington, and Wyoming.

Figure 4. Percentage distribution of public charter school students, by race/ethnicity: Fall 2000 and fall 2015

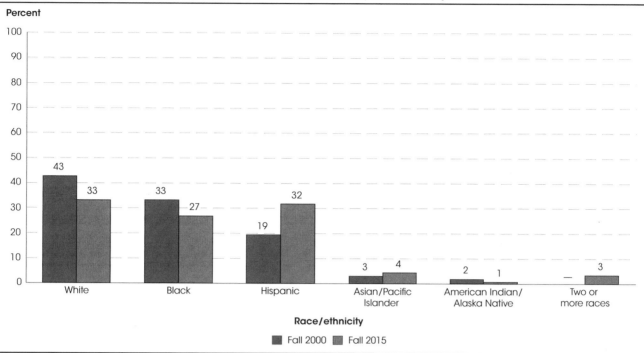

— Not available.
NOTE: Data for the "Two or more races" category were not available prior to 2009–10. Race categories exclude persons of Hispanic ethnicity.
SOURCE: U.S. Department of Education, National Center for Education Statistics, Common Core of Data (CCD), "Public Elementary/Secondary School Universe Survey," 2000–01 and 2015–16. See *Digest of Education Statistics 2017,* table 216.30.

Between fall 2000 and fall 2015, public charter schools experienced changes in their demographic composition similar to those seen in public schools overall. (For more information on racial/ethnic enrollment in public schools, please see the report *Status and Trends in the Education of Racial and Ethnic Groups.*) The percentage of public charter school students who were Hispanic increased (from 19 to 32 percent), as did the percentage who were Asian/Pacific Islander (from 3 to 4 percent). In contrast, the percentage of public charter school students who were White decreased (from 43 to 33 percent), as did the percentages who were Black (from 33 to 27 percent) and American Indian/Alaska Native (from 2 to 1 percent). Beginning in fall 2009, data were collected on students

of Two or more races attending public charter schools. Students of Two or more races accounted for 3 percent of public charter school students in fall 2015.

In fall 2015, the percentage of students attending high-poverty schools—schools in which more than 75 percent of students qualify for free or reduced-price lunch (FRPL) under the National School Lunch Program—was higher for public charter school students (33 percent) than for traditional public school students (24 percent). In the same year, 22 percent of public charter school students and 20 percent of traditional public school students attended low-poverty schools—those in which 25 percent or less of students qualify for FRPL.[4]

Endnotes:

[1] Thomsen, J. (2016). *50-State Comparison: Charter School Policies.* Denver, CO: Education Commission of the States. Retrieved September 18, 2017, from http://www.ecs.org/charter-school-policies/.
[2] Finnigan, K., Adelman, N., Anderson, L., Cotton, L., Donnelly, M., and Price, T. (2004). *Evaluation of the Public Charter Schools Program: Final Report.* U.S. Department of Education, Office of the Deputy Secretary. Washington, DC: Policy and Program Studies Service. Retrieved September 15, 2017, from https://www2.ed.gov/rschstat/eval/choice/pcsp-final/finalreport.pdf.

[3] Despite legislative approval for public charter schools in Alabama, none were operating in this state in fall 2015. For more information on charter school status in Alabama, please refer to https://www.publiccharters.org/publications/model-law-supporting-growth-high-quality-public-charter-schools.
[4] In fall 2015, some 9 percent of public charter school students and 2 percent of traditional public school students attended schools which did not participate in FRPL or had missing data.

Reference tables: *Digest of Education Statistics 2017,* tables 216.20, 216.30, and 216.90
Related indicators and resources: Characteristics of Traditional Public Schools and Public Charter Schools; Elementary and Secondary Enrollment; Elementary and Secondary Enrollment [*Status and Trends in the Education of Racial and Ethnic Groups*]; Private School Enrollment

Glossary: Combined school, Elementary school, Enrollment, Free or reduced-price lunch, National School Lunch Program, Public charter school, Public school or institution, Racial/ethnic group, Secondary school, Student membership, Traditional public school

Private School Enrollment

In fall 2015, some 5.8 million students (10.2 percent of all elementary and secondary students) were enrolled in private elementary and secondary schools. Thirty-six percent of private school students were enrolled in Catholic schools, 39 percent were enrolled in other religiously affiliated schools, and 24 percent were enrolled in nonsectarian schools.

Private elementary and secondary schools are educational institutions that are not primarily supported by public funds.[1] In this indicator, private schools are grouped into the following categories: Catholic, other religious, and nonsectarian (not religiously affiliated). Catholic schools include parochial, diocesan, and private Catholic schools. The other religious category includes conservative Christian schools, schools that are affiliated with other denominations, and religious schools that are not affiliated with any specific denomination.

Figure 1. Percentage of elementary and secondary students enrolled in private schools: Fall 1999 through fall 2015

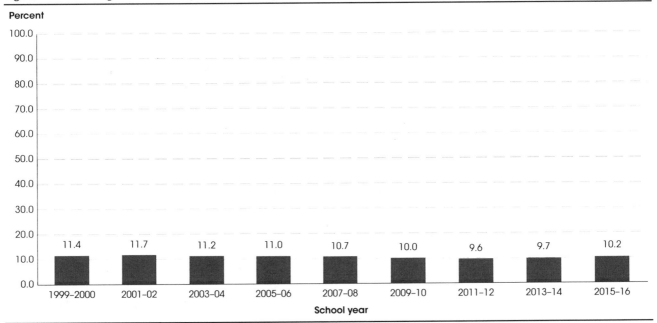

NOTE: Excludes prekindergarten students not enrolled in schools that offer kindergarten or higher grades.
SOURCE: U.S. Department of Education, National Center for Education Statistics, Private School Universe Survey (PSS), biennial, 1999–2000 through 2015–16; Common Core of Data (CCD), "State Nonfiscal Survey of Public Elementary and Secondary Education," 1999–2000 through 2015–16. See *Digest of Education Statistics 2016*, tables 105.30 and 205.20; *Digest of Education Statistics 2017*, table 203.40.

Between fall 1999 and fall 2015, the percentage of all elementary and secondary students who were enrolled in private schools fluctuated between 9.6 percent and 11.7 percent. During this time, the percentage of all elementary and secondary students who were enrolled in private schools decreased from 11.4 percent in fall 1999 to 9.6 percent in fall 2011. In 2015, the percentage of students enrolled in private schools (10.2 percent) was higher than in 2011.

Figure 2. Private school enrollment in prekindergarten (preK) through grade 12, by grade level: Fall 1999 through fall 2015

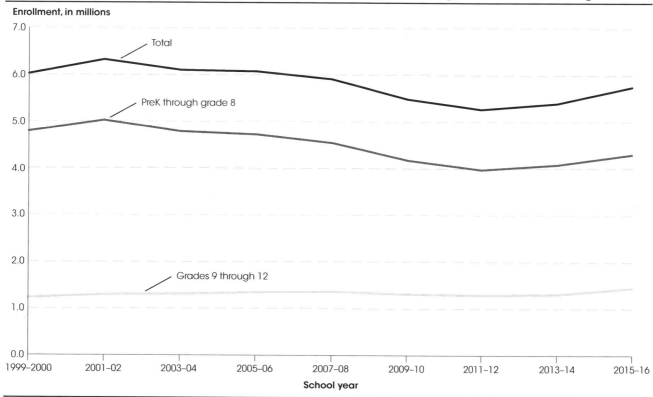

NOTE: Excludes prekindergarten students not enrolled in schools that offer kindergarten or higher grades. Ungraded students are prorated into prekindergarten through grade 8 and grades 9 through 12.
SOURCE: U.S. Department of Education, National Center for Education Statistics, Private School Universe Survey (PSS), biennial, 1999–2000 through 2015–16. See *Digest of Education Statistics 2016*, table 205.20.

Private school enrollment in prekindergarten (preK) through grade 12 was lower in fall 2015 (5.8 million students) than in fall 1999 (6.0 million students). During this time, private school enrollment was highest in fall 2001, at 6.3 million students, and decreased to 5.3 million in fall 2011. Private school enrollment then increased in each of the most recent years for which data are available, to 5.4 million students in fall 2013 and 5.8 million students in fall 2015.

Private school enrollment in preK through grade 8 followed a similar pattern during this time period,

peaking at 5.0 million students in fall 2001, decreasing to 4.0 million students in fall 2011, and increasing in each of the two most recent years for which data are available (to 4.1 million students in fall 2013 and to 4.3 million students in fall 2015). Private school enrollment in grades 9 through 12 was higher in fall 2015 (1.4 million students) than in fall 1999 (1.2 million students), but showed no clear trend during this period.

Figure 3. Private school enrollment in prekindergarten (preK) through grade 12, by school orientation: Fall 1999 through fall 2015

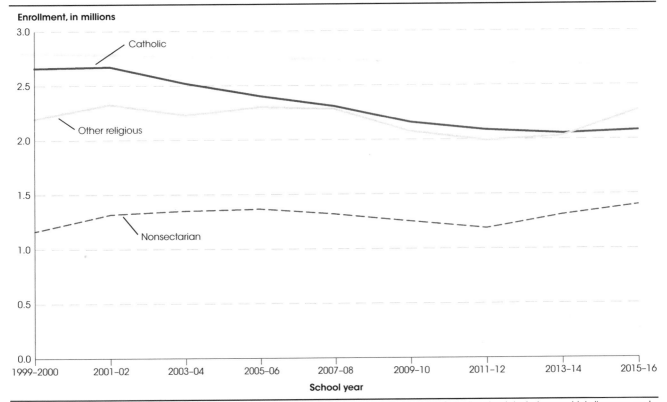

NOTE: Excludes prekindergarten students not enrolled in schools that offer kindergarten or higher grades. Catholic schools include parochial, diocesan, and private Catholic schools. Other religious schools include conservative Christian, affiliated religious, and unaffiliated religious schools. Nonsectarian schools do not have a religious orientation or religious purpose.
SOURCE: U.S. Department of Education, National Center for Education Statistics, Private School Universe Survey (PSS), biennial, 1999–2000 through 2015–16. See *Digest of Education Statistics 2016*, table 205.20.

In fall 2015, some 36 percent of all private school students were enrolled in Catholic schools, while 39 percent were enrolled in other religious private schools, and 24 percent of students were enrolled in nonsectarian private schools. The number of private school students enrolled in Catholic schools decreased from 2.7 million in fall 1999 to 2.1 million in fall 2015. This decrease was primarily due to a decline in the number of students enrolled in Catholic parochial schools (1.4 million in fall 1999 compared to 716,000 in fall 2015). The number of students enrolled in other religious schools in fall 2015 (2.3 million students) was not measurably different from the number enrolled in fall 1999 (2.2 million students). The number of students enrolled in nonsectarian schools was higher in fall 2015 (1.4 million students) than in fall 1999 (1.2 million students).

Figure 4. Percentage distribution of private school enrollment in prekindergarten (preK) through grade 12, by school orientation and level: Fall 2015

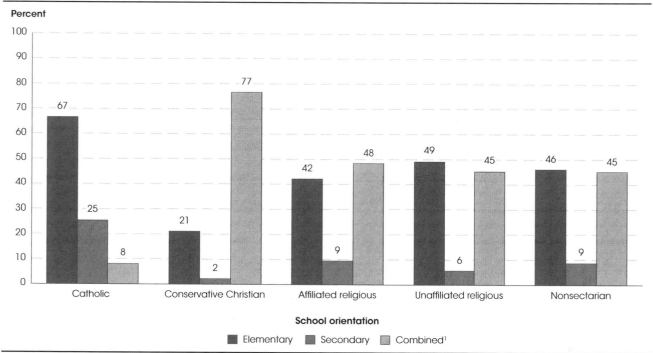

[1] Combined schools are those that have grades lower than 7 and higher than 8, as well as those that do not classify students by grade level.
NOTE: Excludes prekindergarten students not enrolled in schools that offer kindergarten or higher grades. Elementary schools are classified by state and local practice and are composed of any span of grades not above grade 8. Secondary schools have no grade lower than 7. Both junior high schools and senior high schools are included. Catholic schools include parochial, diocesan, and private Catholic schools. Affiliated religious schools belong to associations of schools with a specific religious orientation other than Catholic or conservative Christian. Unaffiliated religious schools have a religious orientation or purpose but are not classified as Catholic, conservative Christian, or affiliated religious. Nonsectarian schools do not have a religious orientation or religious purpose. Detail may not sum to totals because of rounding.
SOURCE: U.S. Department of Education, National Center for Education Statistics, Private School Universe Survey (PSS), 2015–16. See *Digest of Education Statistics 2016*, table 205.30.

In fall 2015, half of all private school students (50 percent) were at elementary schools, 13 percent were at secondary schools, and 36 percent were at combined elementary and secondary schools. The share of private school students at elementary schools was highest at Catholic schools (67 percent) and lowest at conservative Christian schools (21 percent). A quarter of Catholic school students (25 percent) attended secondary schools, while 9 percent or less of students at any other private school orientation did so. The share of private school students at combined schools was lowest at Catholic schools (8 percent) and highest at conservative Christian schools (77 percent).

Figure 5. Percentage distribution of private school enrollment in prekindergarten (preK) through grade 12, by school orientation and race/ethnicity: Fall 2015

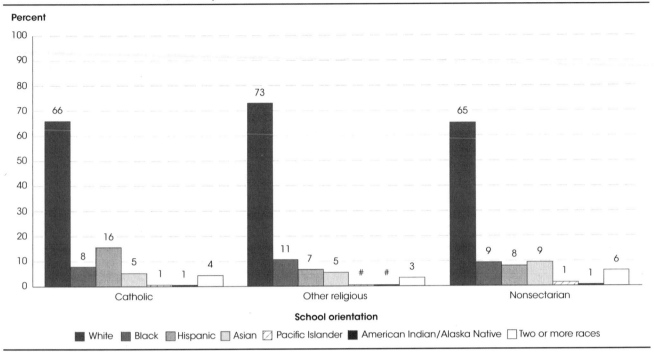

Rounds to zero.
NOTE: Prekindergarten students who are enrolled in private schools that do not offer kindergarten or higher grades are not included in this analysis. Catholic schools include parochial, diocesan, and private Catholic schools. Other religious schools include conservative Christian, affiliated religious, and unaffiliated religious schools. Nonsectarian schools do not have a religious orientation or religious purpose. Race categories exclude persons of Hispanic ethnicity. Percentage distribution is based on the students for whom race/ethnicity was reported. Although rounded numbers are displayed, the figures are based on unrounded estimates. Detail may not sum to totals because of rounding.
SOURCE: U.S. Department of Education, National Center for Education Statistics, Private School Universe Survey (PSS), 2015–16. See *Digest of Education Statistics 2016*, table 205.30.

White students constituted the largest share of enrollment among Catholic (66 percent), other religious (73 percent), and nonsectarian schools (65 percent) in fall 2015. Black students made up the second-largest share of enrollment in other religious schools (11 percent), and Hispanic students made up the second-largest share of enrollment at Catholic schools (16 percent). A larger percentage of students were Asian at nonsectarian schools (9 percent) than at Catholic and other religious schools (5 percent each). Similarly, the percentage of students who were of Two or more races was larger at nonsectarian schools (6 percent) than at Catholic schools (4 percent) and other religious schools (3 percent). Pacific Islander and American Indian/Alaska Native students constituted 1 percent or less of enrollment at Catholic, other religious, and nonsectarian schools.

Endnotes:
[1] For the purposes of this indicator, private schools exclude organizations or institutions that provide support for homeschooling.

Reference tables: *Digest of Education Statistics 2016*, tables 205.20 and 205.30

Related indicators and resources: Elementary and Secondary Enrollment; Elementary and Secondary Enrollment [*Status and Trends in the Education of Racial and Ethnic Groups*]; Public Charter School Enrollment

Glossary: Catholic school, Combined school, Elementary school, Enrollment, Nonsectarian school, Other religious school, Prekindergarten, Private school, Racial/ethnic group, Secondary school

This page intentionally left blank.

English Language Learners in Public Schools

The percentage of public school students in the United States who were English language learners (ELLs) was higher in fall 2015 (9.5 percent, or 4.8 million students) than in fall 2000 (8.1 percent, or 3.8 million students). In fall 2015, the percentage of public school students who were ELLs ranged from 1.0 percent in West Virginia to 21.0 percent in California.

Students who are identified as English language learners (ELLs) can participate in language assistance programs to help ensure that they attain English proficiency and meet the same academic content and achievement standards that all students are expected to meet. Participation in these types of programs can improve students' English language proficiency, which in turn has been associated with improved educational outcomes.[1] The percentage of public school students in the United States who were ELLs was higher in fall 2015 (9.5 percent, or 4.8 million students) than in fall 2000 (8.1 percent, or 3.8 million students).[2]

Figure 1. Percentage of public school students who were English language learners, by state: Fall 2015

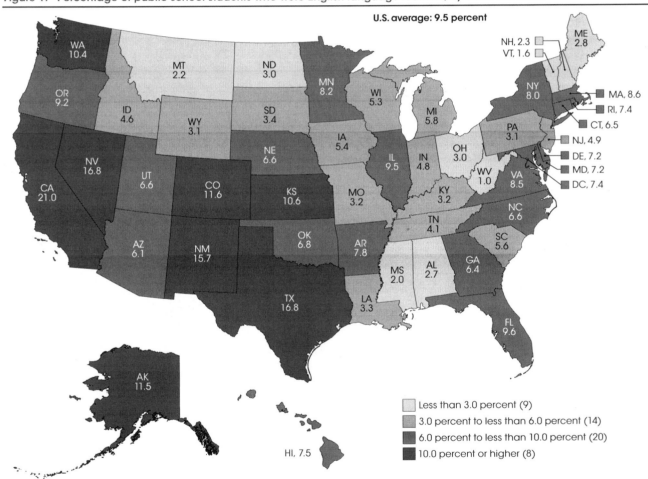

U.S. average: 9.5 percent

NH, 2.3
VT, 1.6
ME 2.8
WA 10.4
MT 2.2
ND 3.0
MN 8.2
WI 5.3
NY 8.0
MA, 8.6
RI, 7.4
OR 9.2
ID 4.6
WY 3.1
SD 3.4
IA 5.4
MI 5.8
PA 3.1
CT, 6.5
NJ, 4.9
OH 3.0
IN 4.8
WV 1.0
VA 8.5
DE, 7.2
MD, 7.2
DC, 7.4
NV 16.8
UT 6.6
CO 11.6
NE 6.6
IL 9.5
KY 3.2
NC 6.6
CA 21.0
KS 10.6
MO 3.2
TN 4.1
SC 5.6
AZ 6.1
NM 15.7
OK 6.8
AR 7.8
MS 2.0
AL 2.7
GA 6.4
TX 16.8
LA 3.3
FL 9.6
AK 11.5
HI, 7.5

Less than 3.0 percent (9)
3.0 percent to less than 6.0 percent (14)
6.0 percent to less than 10.0 percent (20)
10.0 percent or higher (8)

NOTE: Categorizations are based on unrounded percentages.
SOURCE: U.S. Department of Education, National Center for Education Statistics, Common Core of Data (CCD), "Local Education Agency Universe Survey," 2015–16. See *Digest of Education Statistics 2017*, table 204.20.

In fall 2015, the percentage of public school students who were ELLs was 10.0 percent or more in eight states. These states, most of which are located in the West, were Alaska, California, Colorado, Kansas, Nevada, New Mexico, Texas, and Washington. California reported the highest percentage of ELLs among its public school students, at 21.0 percent, followed by Texas and Nevada, each at 16.8 percent. Nineteen states and the District of Columbia had percentages of ELL students that were 6.0 percent or higher but less than 10.0 percent, and 14 states had percentages that were 3.0 percent or higher but less than 6.0 percent. The percentage of students who were ELLs was less than 3.0 percent in nine states, with Mississippi (2.0 percent), Vermont (1.6 percent), and West Virginia (1.0 percent) having the lowest percentages.

The percentage of public school students who were ELLs was higher in fall 2015 than in fall 2000 for all but eight states and the District of Columbia, with the largest percentage-point increase occurring in Kansas (7.5 percentage points) and the largest percentage-point decrease occurring in Arizona (9.0 percentage points). More recently, the percentage of public school students who were ELLs was lower in fall 2015 than in fall 2010 in 14 states, with the largest decrease occurring in Nevada (4.1 percentage points). In contrast, the percentage of public school students who were ELLs was higher in fall 2015 than in fall 2010 in 36 states and the District of Columbia, with the largest increase occurring in Massachusetts (3.0 percentage points).

Figure 2.   Percentage of public school students who were English language learners, by locale: Fall 2015

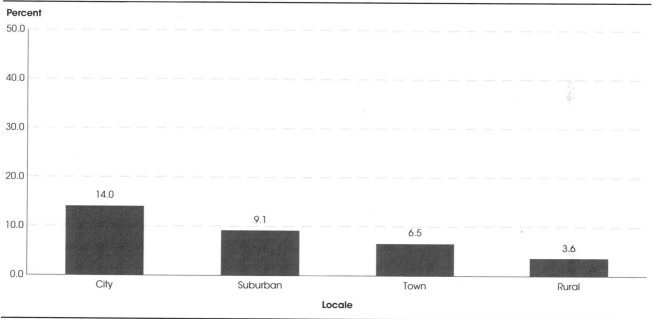

NOTE: Data are based on locales of school districts.
SOURCE: U.S. Department of Education, National Center for Education Statistics, Common Core of Data (CCD), "Local Education Agency Universe Survey," 2015–16. See *Digest of Education Statistics 2017*, table 214.40.

In fall 2015, the percentage of students who were ELLs was higher for school districts in more urbanized areas than for those in less urbanized areas. ELL students constituted an average of 14.0 percent of total public school enrollment in cities, 9.1 percent in suburban areas, 6.5 percent in towns, and 3.6 percent in rural areas.

Figure 3. Percentage of public K–12 students who were English language learners, by grade level: Fall 2015

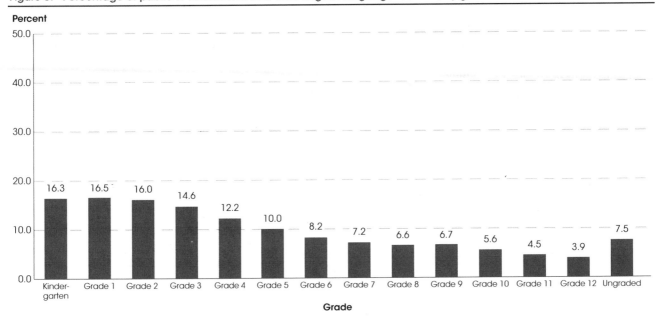

SOURCE: U.S. Department of Education, National Center for Education Statistics, ED*Facts* file 141, Data Group 678, extracted July 21, 2017; and Common Core of Data (CCD), "State Nonfiscal Survey of Public Elementary and Secondary Education," 2015–16. See *Digest of Education Statistics 2017*, table 204.27.

In fall 2015, a greater percentage of public school students in lower grades than of those in upper grades were ELL students. For example, 16.3 percent of kindergarteners were ELL students, compared to 8.2 percent of 6th-graders and 6.6 percent of 8th-graders. Among 12th-graders, only 3.9 percent of students were ELL students. This pattern is driven, in part, by students who are identified as ELLs when they enter elementary school but obtain English language proficiency before reaching upper grades.[3]

Table 1. Number and percentage distribution of English language learner (ELL) students and number of ELL students as a percent of total enrollment, by the 11 most commonly reported home languages of ELL students: Fall 2015

Home language	Number of ELL students	Percentage distribution of ELL students[1]	Number of ELL students as a percent of total enrollment
Spanish, Castilian	3,741,066	77.1	7.6
Arabic	114,371	2.4	0.2
Chinese	101,347	2.1	0.2
Vietnamese	81,157	1.7	0.2
English[2]	80,333	1.7	0.2
Somali	34,813	0.7	0.1
Hmong	34,813	0.7	0.1
Russian	33,057	0.7	0.1
Haitian, Haitian Creole	30,231	0.6	0.1
Tagalog	27,277	0.6	0.1
Korean	27,268	0.6	0.1

[1] Detail does not sum to 100 percent because not all categories are reported.
[2] Examples of situations in which English might be reported as an ELL student's home language include students who live in multilingual households and students adopted from other countries who speak English at home but also have been raised speaking another language.
SOURCE: U.S. Department of Education, National Center for Education Statistics, ED*Facts* file 141, Data Group 678, extracted July 21, 2017; and Common Core of Data (CCD), "State Nonfiscal Survey of Public Elementary and Secondary Education," 2015–16. See *Digest of Education Statistics 2017*, table 204.27.

Spanish was the home language of 3.7 million ELL students in fall 2015, representing 77.1 percent of all ELL students and 7.6 percent of all public K–12 students. Arabic, Chinese, and Vietnamese were the next most common home languages (spoken by approximately 114,400; 101,300; and 81,200 students, respectively). English was the fifth most commonly reported home language for ELL students (80,300 students), which may reflect students who live in multilingual households or students adopted from other countries who were raised speaking another language but currently live in households where English is spoken. Somali (36,000 students), Hmong (34,800 students), Russian (33,100 students), Haitian (30,200 students), Tagalog (27,300 students), and Korean (27,300 students) were the next most commonly reported home languages of ELL students in fall 2015. The 30 most commonly reported home languages also include several whose prevalence has increased rapidly in recent years. For example, the number of ELLs who reported that their home language was Nepali or a Karen language[4] more than quadrupled between fall 2008 and fall 2015 (from 3,200 to 14,100 students for Nepali and from 3,000 to 12,800 students for Karen languages).[5]

In fall 2015, there were about 3.8 million Hispanic ELL students, which constituted over three-quarters (77.7 percent) of ELL student enrollment overall. Asian students were the next largest racial/ethnic group among ELLs, with 512,000 students (10.5 percent of ELL students). In addition, there were 295,000 White ELL students (6.1 percent of ELL students) and 178,000 Black ELL students (3.7 percent of ELL students). In each of the other racial/ethnic groups for which data were collected (Pacific Islanders, American Indians/Alaska Natives, and individuals of Two or more races), fewer than 40,000 students were identified as ELLs.

The U.S. Department of Education's EDFacts data collection also sheds light on the population of ELL students who have disabilities. In fall 2015, some 713,000 ELL students were identified as students with disabilities, representing 14.7 percent of the total ELL population enrolled in U.S. public elementary and secondary schools.[6]

Endnotes:

[1] Ross, T., Kena, G., Rathbun, A., KewalRamani, A., Zhang, J., Kristapovich, P., and Manning, E. (2012). *Higher Education: Gaps in Access and Persistence Study* (NCES 2012-046). U.S. Department of Education. Washington, DC: National Center for Education Statistics. Retrieved September 28, 2017, from https://nces.ed.gov/pubsearch/pubsinfo.asp?pubid=2012046.

[2] For 2014 and earlier years, data on the total number of ELLs enrolled in public schools and on the percentage of public school students who were ELLs include only those ELL students who participated in ELL programs. Starting with 2015, data include all ELL students, regardless of program participation. Due to this change in definition, comparisons between 2015 and earlier years should be interpreted with caution. For all years, data do not include students who were formerly identified as ELLs but later obtained English language proficiency.

[3] Saunders, W.M., and Marcelletti, D.J. (2013). The Gap That Can't Go Away: The Catch-22 of Reclassification in Monitoring the Progress of English Learners. *Educational Evaluation and Policy Analysis, 35*(2): 139–156. Retrieved September 28, 2017, from http://journals.sagepub.com/doi/full/10.3102/0162373712461849.

[4] Includes several languages spoken by the Karen ethnic groups of Burma and by individuals of Karen descent in the United States.

[5] Fall 2008 data include all ELL students enrolled at any time during the 2008–09 school year, except data for California that reflect ELL students enrolled on a single date. All other data in this indicator include only ELL students enrolled on October 1 of the corresponding year.

[6] Includes only students with disabilities who were served under the Individuals with Disabilities Education Act (IDEA).

Reference tables: *Digest of Education Statistics 2017*, tables 204.20, 204.27, and 214.40

Related indicators and resources: Children and Youth With Disabilities; Elementary and Secondary Enrollment; English Language Learners [*Status and Trends in the Education of Racial and Ethnic Groups*]; Mathematics Performance; *Programs and Services for High School English Learners in Public School Districts*; Reading Performance; Science Performance; Technology and Engineering Literacy

Glossary: Disabilities, children with; English language learner (ELL); Enrollment; Geographic region; Household; Locale codes; Public school or institution; Racial/ethnic group; School district

Children and Youth With Disabilities

In 2015–16, the number of students ages 3–21 receiving special education services was 6.7 million, or 13 percent of all public school students. Among students receiving special education services, 34 percent had specific learning disabilities.

Enacted in 1975, the Individuals with Disabilities Education Act (IDEA), formerly known as the Education for All Handicapped Children Act, mandates the provision of a free and appropriate public school education for eligible students ages 3–21. Eligible students are those identified by a team of professionals as having a disability that adversely affects academic performance and as being in need of special education and related services. Data collection activities to monitor compliance with IDEA began in 1976.

From school year 2000–01 through 2004–05, the number of students ages 3–21 who received special education services increased from 6.3 million, or 13 percent of total public school enrollment, to 6.7 million, or 14 percent of total public school enrollment.[1] Both the number and percentage of students served under IDEA declined from 2004–05 through 2011–12. Between 2011–12 and 2015–16, the number of students served increased from 6.4 million to 6.7 million, while the percentage served remained at 13 percent of total public school enrollment.

Figure 1. Percentage distribution of students ages 3–21 served under the Individuals with Disabilities Education Act (IDEA), Part B, by disability type: School year 2015–16

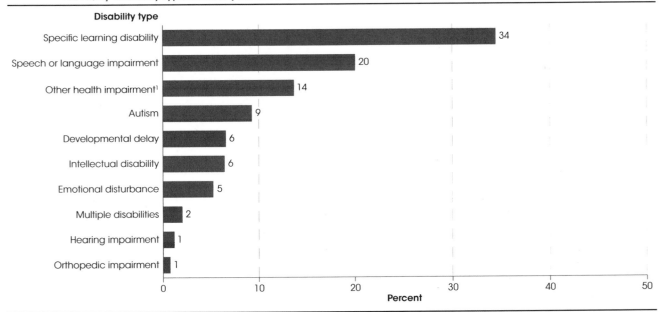

[1] Other health impairments include having limited strength, vitality, or alertness due to chronic or acute health problems such as a heart condition, tuberculosis, rheumatic fever, nephritis, asthma, sickle cell anemia, hemophilia, epilepsy, lead poisoning, leukemia, or diabetes.
NOTE: Deaf-blindness, traumatic brain injury, and visual impairment are not shown because they each account for less than 0.5 percent of students served under IDEA. Due to categories not shown, detail does not sum to 100 percent. Although rounded numbers are displayed, the figures are based on unrounded estimates.
SOURCE: U.S. Department of Education, Office of Special Education Programs, Individuals with Disabilities Education Act (IDEA) database, retrieved July 10, 2017, from https://www2.ed.gov/programs/osepidea/618-data/state-level-data-files/index.html#bcc. See *Digest of Education Statistics 2017*, table 204.30.

In school year 2015–16, a higher percentage of students ages 3–21 received special education services under IDEA for specific learning disabilities than for any other type of disability. A specific learning disability is a disorder in one or more of the basic psychological processes involved in understanding or using language, spoken or written, that may manifest itself in an imperfect ability to listen, think, speak, read, write, spell, or do mathematical calculations. In 2015–16, some 34 percent of all students receiving special education services had specific learning disabilities, 20 percent had speech or language impairments, and 14 percent had other health

impairments (including having limited strength, vitality, or alertness due to chronic or acute health problems such as a heart condition, tuberculosis, rheumatic fever, nephritis, asthma, sickle cell anemia, hemophilia, epilepsy, lead poisoning, leukemia, or diabetes). Students with autism, intellectual disabilities, developmental delays, and emotional disturbances each accounted for between 5 and 9 percent of students served under IDEA. Students with multiple disabilities, hearing impairments, orthopedic impairments, visual impairments, traumatic brain injuries, and deaf-blindness each accounted for 2 percent or less of those served under IDEA.

Figure 2. Percentage of students ages 3–21 served under the Individuals with Disabilities Education Act (IDEA), Part B, by race/ethnicity: School year 2015–16

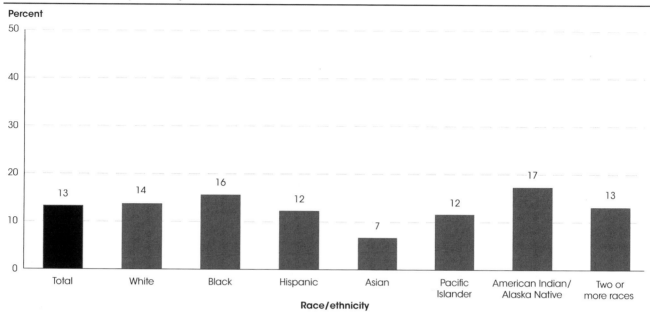

NOTE: Based on the total enrollment in public schools, prekindergarten through 12th grade. Race categories exclude persons of Hispanic ethnicity. Although rounded numbers are displayed, the figures are based on unrounded estimates.
SOURCE: U.S. Department of Education, Office of Special Education Programs, Individuals with Disabilities Education Act (IDEA) database, retrieved July 10, 2017, from http://www2.ed.gov/programs/osepidea/618-data/state-level-data-files/index.html#bcc; and National Center for Education Statistics, Common Core of Data (CCD), "State Nonfiscal Survey of Public Elementary/Secondary Education," 2015–16. See *Digest of Education Statistics 2017*, table 204.50.

In school year 2015–16, the percentage (out of total public school enrollment) of students ages 3–21 served under IDEA differed by race/ethnicity. The percentage of students served under IDEA was highest for those who were American Indian/Alaska Native (17 percent), followed by those who were Black (16 percent), White (14 percent), of Two or more races (13 percent), Hispanic and Pacific Islander (both at 12 percent), and Asian (7 percent).

In each racial/ethnic group except for Asian, the percentage of students receiving services for specific learning disabilities combined with the percentage receiving services for speech or language impairments accounted for over 50 percent of students served under IDEA. The percentage distribution of various types of special education services received by students ages 3–21 in 2015–16 differed by race/ethnicity. For example, the percentage of students with disabilities receiving services under IDEA for specific learning disabilities was lower among Asian students (21 percent), students of Two or more races (30 percent), and White students (31 percent) than among students overall (34 percent). However, the percentage of students with disabilities receiving services under IDEA for autism was higher among Asian students (21 percent), students of Two or more races (10 percent), and White students (10 percent) than among students

overall (9 percent). Additionally, among students who were served under IDEA, 7 percent of Black students and 7 percent of students of Two or more races received services for emotional disturbances. In comparison, 5 percent of all students served under IDEA received services for emotional disturbances. Among students who received services under IDEA, each racial/ethnic group other than Hispanic (5 percent) had a higher percentage of students receiving services for developmental delays than the overall percentage of students receiving services for developmental delays (6 percent).

Separate data on special education services for males and females are available only for students ages 6–21, rather than ages 3–21. Among those 6- to 21-year-old students enrolled in public schools in 2015–16, a higher percentage of males (17 percent) than of females (9 percent) received special education services under IDEA. The percentage distribution of students who received various types of special education services in 2015–16 differed by sex. For example, the percentage of students served under IDEA who received services for specific learning disabilities was higher among female students (44 percent) than among male students (35 percent), while the percentage served under IDEA who received services for autism was higher among male students (12 percent) than among female students (4 percent).

Figure 3. Percentage of students ages 6–21 served under the Individuals with Disabilities Education Act (IDEA), Part B, by amount of time spent inside general classes: Selected school years, 2000–01 through 2015–16

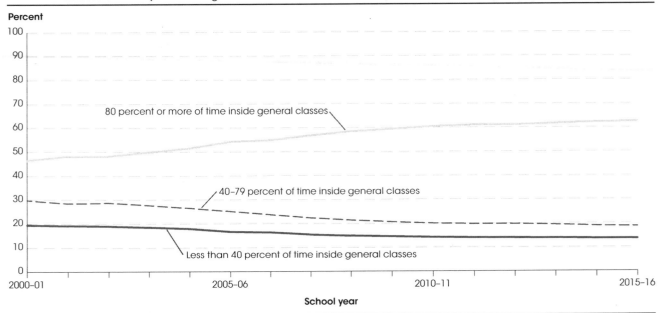

SOURCE: U.S. Department of Education, Office of Special Education Programs, Individuals with Disabilities Education Act (IDEA) database, retrieved July 15, 2017, from http://www2.ed.gov/programs/osepidea/618-data/state-level-data-files/index.html#bcc. See *Digest of Education Statistics 2017*, table 204.60.

Educational environment data are also available for students ages 6–21 served under IDEA. About 95 percent of students ages 6–21 served under IDEA in fall 2015 were enrolled in regular schools. Some 3 percent of students served under IDEA were enrolled in separate schools (public or private) for students with disabilities; 1 percent were placed by their parents in regular private schools; and less than 1 percent each were homebound or in hospitals, in separate residential facilities (public or private), or in correctional facilities. Among all students ages 6–21 served under IDEA, the percentage who spent most of the school day (i.e., 80 percent or more of their time) in general classes in regular schools increased from 47 percent in fall 2000 to 63 percent in fall 2015. In contrast, during the same period, the percentage of those who spent 40 to 79 percent of the school day in general classes declined from 30 to 19 percent, and the percentage of those who spent less than 40 percent of their time inside general classes also declined, from 20 to 14 percent. In fall 2015, the percentage of students served

under IDEA who spent most of the school day in general classes was highest for students with speech or language impairments (87 percent). Approximately two-thirds of students with specific learning disabilities (70 percent), visual impairments (67 percent), other health impairments (65 percent), and developmental delays (64 percent) spent most of the school day in general classes. In contrast, 16 percent of students with intellectual disabilities and 13 percent of students with multiple disabilities spent most of the school day in general classes.

Data are also available for students ages 14–21 served under IDEA who exited school during school year 2014–15, including exit reason.[2] Approximately 395,000 students ages 14–21 who received special education services under IDEA exited school in 2014–15: about two-thirds (69 percent) graduated with a regular high school diploma, 18 percent dropped out, 11 percent received an alternative certificate,[3] 1 percent reached maximum age, and less than one-half of 1 percent died.

Figure 4. Percentage of students ages 14-21 served under the Individuals with Disabilities Education Act (IDEA), Part B, who exited school, by selected exit reason and race/ethnicity: School year 2014-15

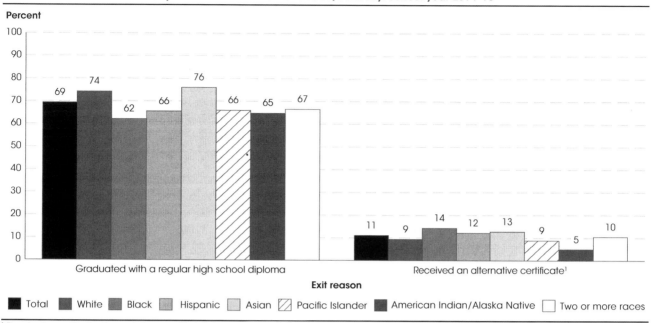

[1] Received a certificate of completion, modified diploma, or some similar document, but did not meet the same standards for graduation as those for students without disabilities.
NOTE: Data in this figure are for the 50 states, the District of Columbia, the Bureau of Indian Education, American Samoa, the Federated States of Micronesia, Guam, the Northern Marianas, Puerto Rico, the Republic of Palau, the Republic of the Marshall Islands, and the U.S. Virgin Islands. Data for all other figures in this indicator are for the 50 states and the District of Columbia only. Race categories exclude persons of Hispanic ethnicity.
SOURCE: U.S. Department of Education, Office of Special Education Programs, Individuals with Disabilities Education Act (IDEA) Section 618 Data Products: State Level Data Files. Retrieved July 14, 2017, from http://www2.ed.gov/programs/osepidea/618-data/state-level-data-files/index.html. See *Digest of Education Statistics 2017*, table 219.90.

Of the students ages 14–21 served under IDEA who exited school in 2014–15, the percentages who graduated with a regular high school diploma, received an alternative certificate, and dropped out differed by race/ethnicity. The percentage of exiting students who graduated with a regular high school diploma was highest among Asian students (76 percent) and lowest among Black students (62 percent). The percentage of exiting students who received an alternative certificate was highest among Black students (14 percent) and lowest among American Indian/Alaska Native students (5 percent). The percentage of exiting students who dropped out in 2014–15 was highest among American Indian/Alaska Native students (29 percent) and lowest among Asian students (7 percent).

Of the students ages 14–21 served under IDEA who exited school in 2014–15, the percentages who graduated

with a regular high school diploma, received an alternative certificate, and dropped out also differed by type of disability. The percentage of exiting students who graduated with a regular high school diploma was highest among students with visual impairments (82 percent) and lowest among those with intellectual disabilities (42 percent). The percentage of exiting students who received an alternative certificate was highest among students with intellectual disabilities (34 percent) and lowest among students with speech or language impairments (5 percent). The percentage of exiting students who dropped out in 2014–15 was highest among students with emotional disturbances (35 percent) and lowest among those with autism and visual impairments (both at 7 percent).

Endnotes:

[1] Data for students ages 3–21 and 6–21 served under IDEA are for the 50 states and the District of Columbia only.
[2] Data for students ages 14–21 served under IDEA who exited school are for the 50 states, the District of Columbia, the Bureau of Indian Education, American Samoa, the Federated States of Micronesia, Guam, the Northern Marianas, Puerto Rico, the

Republic of Palau, the Republic of the Marshall Islands, and the U.S. Virgin Islands.
[3] Received a certificate of completion, modified diploma, or some similar document, but did not meet the same standards for graduation as those for students without disabilities.

Reference tables: *Digest of Education Statistics 2017*, tables 204.30, 204.50, 204.60, and 219.90; *Digest of Education Statistics 2015*, table 204.30
Related indicators and resources: Disability Rates and Employment Status by Educational Attainment [*The Condition of Education 2017 Spotlight*]; English Language Learners in Public Schools; Students with Disabilities [*Status and Trends in the Education of Racial and Ethnic Groups*]

Glossary: Disabilities, children with; Enrollment; High school completer; High school diploma; Individuals with Disabilities Education Act (IDEA); Private school; Public school or institution; Racial/ethnic group; Regular school

Characteristics of Traditional Public Schools and Public Charter Schools

In 2015–16, some 57 percent of public charter schools were located in cities, compared to 25 percent of traditional public schools. A higher percentage of public charter schools than of traditional public schools had more than 50 percent Black enrollment (23 vs. 9 percent), and more than 50 percent Hispanic enrollment (25 vs. 16 percent). A lower percentage of public charter schools than of traditional public schools had more than 50 percent White enrollment (34 vs. 58 percent).

In school year 2015–16, there were 98,280 public schools in the United States, consisting of 91,420 traditional public schools and 6,860 public charter schools. The total number of public schools was higher in 2015–16 than in 2000–01, when there was a total of 93,270 public schools—91,280 traditional public schools and 1,990 public charter schools. Between school years 2000–01 and 2015–16, the percentage of all public schools that were traditional public schools decreased from 98 to 93 percent, while the percentage that were charter schools increased from 2 to 7 percent. See indicator Public Charter School Enrollment for additional information about charter schools and charter school legislation.

Figure 1. Percentage distribution of traditional public schools and public charter schools, by school level: School year 2015–16

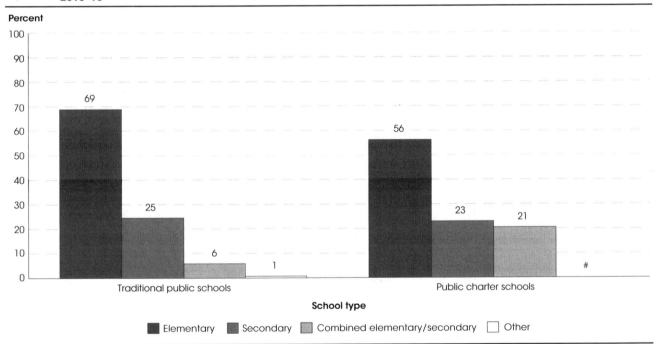

Rounds to zero.
NOTE: "Elementary" includes schools beginning with grade 6 or below and with no grade higher than 8. "Secondary" includes schools with no grade lower than 7. "Combined elementary/secondary" includes schools beginning with grade 6 or below and ending with grade 9 or above. "Other" includes schools not classified by grade span. Detail may not sum to 100 percent because of rounding.
SOURCE: U.S. Department of Education, National Center for Education Statistics, Common Core of Data (CCD), "Public Elementary/Secondary School Universe Survey," 2015–16. See *Digest of Education Statistics 2017*, table 216.30.

In school year 2015–16, over two-thirds of traditional public schools (69 percent) were elementary schools, compared to 56 percent of public charter schools. The percentages of traditional public and public charter schools that were secondary schools were similar (25 and 23 percent, respectively). In contrast, 6 percent of traditional public schools were combined elementary/ secondary schools,[1] compared with 21 percent of public charter schools.

Figure 2. Percentage of traditional public schools and public charter schools, by racial/ethnic concentration: School years 2000–01 and 2015–16

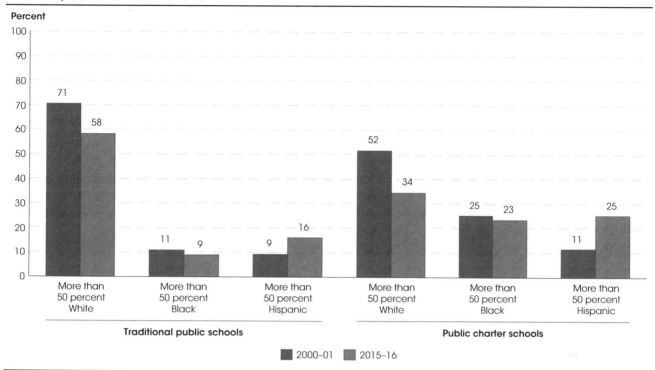

NOTE: Race categories exclude persons of Hispanic ethnicity.
SOURCE: U.S. Department of Education, National Center for Education Statistics, Common Core of Data (CCD), "Public Elementary/Secondary School Universe Survey," 2000–01 and 2015–16. See *Digest of Education Statistics 2017*, table 216.30.

In school year 2015–16, a lower percentage of public charter schools (34 percent) than of traditional public schools (58 percent) had more than 50 percent White enrollment. In contrast, a higher percentage of public charter schools (23 percent) than of traditional public schools (9 percent) had more than 50 percent Black enrollment, and a higher percentage of public charter schools (25 percent) than of traditional public schools (16 percent) had more than 50 percent Hispanic enrollment. For both traditional public and public charter schools, the percentages of schools that had more than 50 percent White enrollment and more than 50 percent

Black enrollment were lower in 2015–16 than in 2000–01, while the percentage of schools that had more than 50 percent Hispanic enrollment was higher in 2015–16 than in 2000–01. These shifts reflect, in part, general changes in the school-age population. Between 2000 and 2015, the percentage of children ages 5 to 17 who were White decreased from 62 to 52 percent, the percentage who were Black decreased from 15 to 14 percent, and the percentage who were Hispanic increased from 16 to 24 percent (see *Digest of Education Statistics 2017*, table 101.20).

Figure 3. Percentage of traditional public schools and public charter schools, by percentage of students eligible for free or reduced-price lunch: School year 2015–16

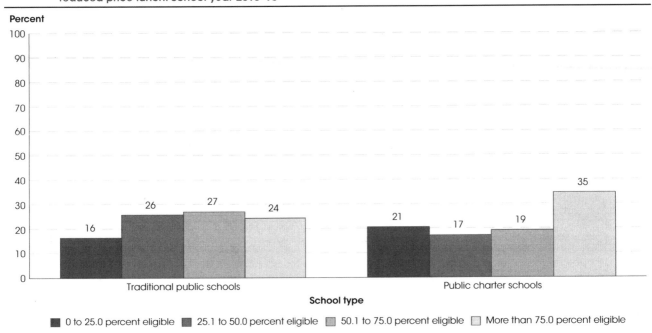

Percent

Legend:
- 0 to 25.0 percent eligible
- 25.1 to 50.0 percent eligible
- 50.1 to 75.0 percent eligible
- More than 75.0 percent eligible

NOTE: The National School Lunch Program is a federally assisted meal program. To be eligible for free lunch under the program, a student must be from a household with an income at or below 130 percent of the poverty threshold; to be eligible for reduced-price lunch, a student must be from a household with an income between 130 percent and 185 percent of the poverty threshold. The category "missing/school does not participate" is not included in this figure; thus, the sum of the free or reduced-price lunch eligible categories does not equal 100 percent.
SOURCE: U.S. Department of Education, National Center for Education Statistics, Common Core of Data (CCD), "Public Elementary/Secondary School Universe Survey," 2015–16. See *Digest of Education Statistics 2017*, table 216.30.

In school year 2015–16, some 35 percent of public charter schools were high-poverty schools, defined as those in which more than three-quarters of students were eligible for free or reduced-price lunch (FRPL). In the same year, 24 percent of traditional public schools were high-poverty schools. The percentage of schools that were low poverty (up to one-quarter of students were FRPL eligible) was also higher among public charter schools (21 percent) than among traditional public schools (16 percent). In contrast, the percentages of schools in the middle poverty categories (one-quarter to one-half FRPL eligible and one-half to three-quarters FRPL eligible) were higher among traditional public schools (26 percent and 27 percent, respectively) than among public charter schools (17 percent and 19 percent, respectively).[2]

Figure 4.   Percentage distribution of traditional public schools and public charter schools, by school locale: School year
2015–16

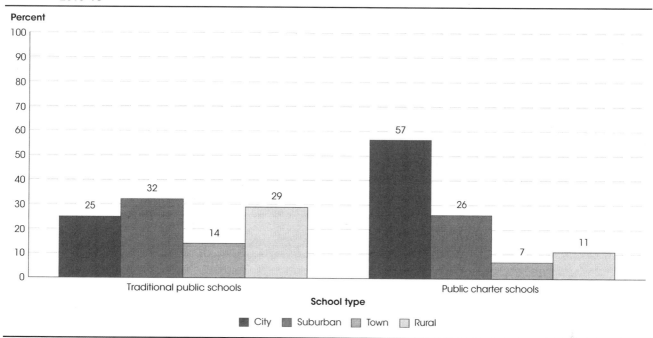

NOTE: Detail may not sum to totals due to rounding.
SOURCE: U.S. Department of Education, National Center for Education Statistics, Common Core of Data (CCD), "Public Elementary/Secondary School Universe Survey," 2015–16. See *Digest of Education Statistics 2017*, table 216.30.

Compared to traditional public schools, a higher percentage of public charter schools were located in cities and a lower percentage were located in all other locales in school year 2015–16. Some 57 percent of public charter schools were located in cities, compared to 25 percent of traditional public schools. In contrast, 11 percent of public charter schools were located in rural areas, compared to 29 percent of traditional public schools.

Endnotes:

[1] Combined elementary/secondary schools are schools beginning with grade 6 or below and ending with grade 9 or above.
[2] In school year 2015–16, some 9 percent of public charter school students and 2 percent of traditional public school students attended schools that did not participate in FRPL or had missing data.

Reference tables: *Digest of Education Statistics 2017*, tables 101.20 and 216.30

Related indicators and resources: Concentration of Public School Students Eligible for Free or Reduced-Price Lunch; Elementary and Secondary Enrollment; Public Charter School Enrollment

Glossary: Combined school, Elementary school, Enrollment, Free or reduced-price lunch, Locale codes, National School Lunch Program, Private school, Public charter school, Public school or institution, Racial/ethnic group, Secondary school, Traditional public school

Concentration of Public School Students Eligible for Free or Reduced-Price Lunch

Higher percentages of Hispanic (45 percent), Black (45 percent), American Indian/Alaska Native (37 percent), and Pacific Islander (25 percent) students attended high-poverty schools than of White students (8 percent) in school year 2015–16. The percentages of students of Two or more races (18 percent) and Asian students (15 percent) in high-poverty schools were higher than the percentage for White students but lower than the national average (24 percent).

The percentage of students eligible for free or reduced-price lunch (FRPL) under the National School Lunch Program provides a proxy measure for the concentration of low-income students within a school.[1] In this indicator, public schools[2] (including both traditional and charter) are divided into categories by FRPL eligibility. High-poverty schools are defined as public schools where more than 75.0 percent of the students are eligible for FRPL, and mid-high poverty schools as those where 50.1 to

75.0 percent of the students are eligible for FRPL. Low-poverty schools are defined as public schools where 25.0 percent or less of the students are eligible for FRPL, and mid-low poverty schools as those where 25.1 to 50.0 percent of the students are eligible for FRPL. In school year 2015–16, some 20 percent of public school students attended low-poverty schools, and 24 percent of public school students attended high-poverty schools.

Figure 1. Percentage distribution of public school students, by student race/ethnicity and school poverty level: School year 2015–16

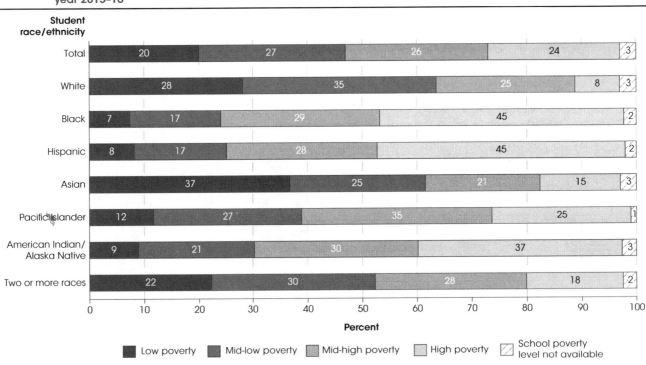

NOTE: Low-poverty schools are defined as public schools where 25.0 percent or less of the students are eligible for free or reduced-price lunch (FRPL), and mid-low poverty schools are those schools where 25.1 to 50.0 percent of the students are eligible for FRPL. High-poverty schools are defined as public schools where more than 75.0 percent of the students are eligible for FRPL, and mid-high poverty schools are those schools where 50.1 to 75.0 percent of the students are eligible for FRPL. "School poverty level not available" includes schools for which information on FRPL is missing and schools that did not participate in the National School Lunch Program. For more information on eligibility for FRPL and its relationship to poverty, see NCES blog post "Free or reduced price lunch: A proxy for poverty?" Race categories exclude persons of Hispanic ethnicity. Detail may not sum to 100 percent because of rounding.
SOURCE: U.S. Department of Education, National Center for Education Statistics, Common Core of Data (CCD), "Public Elementary/Secondary School Universe Survey," 2015–16. See *Digest of Education Statistics 2017*, table 216.60.

While the overall percentages of public school students in low- and high-poverty schools were similar (20 and 24 percent, respectively), they varied by race/ethnicity. In school year 2015–16, the percentages of Asian students (37 percent), White students (28 percent), and students of Two or more races (22 percent) who attended low-poverty schools were greater than the national average (20 percent), while the percentages of Pacific Islander (12 percent), American Indian/Alaska Native (9 percent), Hispanic (8 percent), and Black (7 percent) students who attended low-poverty schools were less than the national average. In contrast, the percentages of Hispanic (45 percent), Black (45 percent), American Indian/Alaska Native (37 percent), and Pacific Islander students (25 percent) who attended high-poverty schools were greater than the national average (24 percent), while the percentages of students of Two or more races (18 percent), Asian students (15 percent), and White students (8 percent) who attended high-poverty schools were less than the national average.

Figure 2. Percentage distribution of public school students, by school locale and school poverty level: School year 2015–16

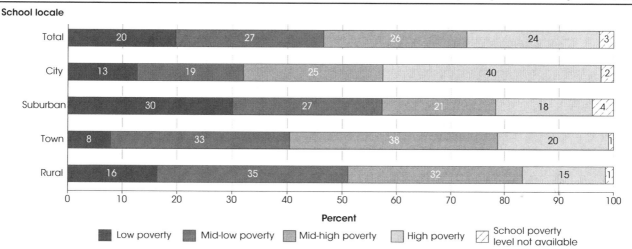

NOTE: Low-poverty schools are defined as public schools where 25.0 percent or less of the students are eligible for free or reduced-price lunch (FRPL), and mid-low poverty schools are those schools where 25.1 to 50.0 percent of the students are eligible for FRPL. High-poverty schools are defined as public schools where more than 75.0 percent of the students are eligible for FRPL, and mid-high poverty schools are those schools where 50.1 to 75.0 percent of the students are eligible for FRPL. "School poverty level not available" includes schools for which information on FRPL is missing and schools that did not participate in the National School Lunch Program. For more information on eligibility for FRPL and its relationship to poverty, see NCES blog post "Free or reduced price lunch: A proxy for poverty?" Detail may not sum to 100 percent because of rounding.
SOURCE: U.S. Department of Education, National Center for Education Statistics, Common Core of Data (CCD), "Public Elementary/Secondary School Universe Survey," 2015–16. See *Digest of Education Statistics 2017*, table 216.60.

The percentage of students attending public schools with different poverty concentrations varied by school locale (i.e., city, suburb, town, or rural). In school year 2015–16, some 40 percent of students attending city schools were in a high-poverty school, compared with 20 percent of students attending town schools, 18 percent of students attending suburban schools, and 15 percent of students attending rural schools. In contrast, the percentage of students attending suburban schools who were in a low-poverty school (30 percent) was nearly four times as large as the corresponding percentage for students attending town schools (8 percent). The percentage of students attending suburban schools who were in a low-poverty school was also greater than the corresponding percentages of students attending rural and city schools (16 and 13 percent, respectively).

Endnotes:

[1] For more information on eligibility for free or reduced-price lunch and its relationship to poverty, see NCES blog post "Free or reduced price lunch: A proxy for poverty?"

[2] In 2015–16, information on school poverty level is not available for 3 percent of public school students. This includes schools for which information on FRPL is missing and schools that did not participate in the National School Lunch Program.

Reference tables: *Digest of Education Statistics 2017*, table 216.60
Related indicators and resources: Characteristics of Children's Families; Mathematics Performance; Reading Performance

Glossary: Free or reduced-price lunch, Locale codes, National School Lunch Program, Public school or institution, Racial/ethnic group

School Crime and Safety

Between 2000 and 2016, the rates of nonfatal victimization both at school and away from school declined for students ages 12–18. The rate of victimization at school declined 65 percent, and the rate of victimization away from school declined 72 percent.

In 2016, students ages 12–18 reported 749,000 nonfatal victimizations at school[1] and 601,000 nonfatal victimizations away from school. Nonfatal victimizations include theft and all violent crime. Violent crime includes serious violent crime (rape, sexual assault, robbery, and aggravated assault) and simple assault. These figures translate to a total rate of victimization at school of 29 victimizations per 1,000 students and a total rate of victimization away from school of 24 per 1,000 students; the apparent difference between these two rates was not measurable.

Figure 1. Rate of nonfatal victimization per 1,000 students ages 12–18, by type of victimization and location: 2000 through 2016

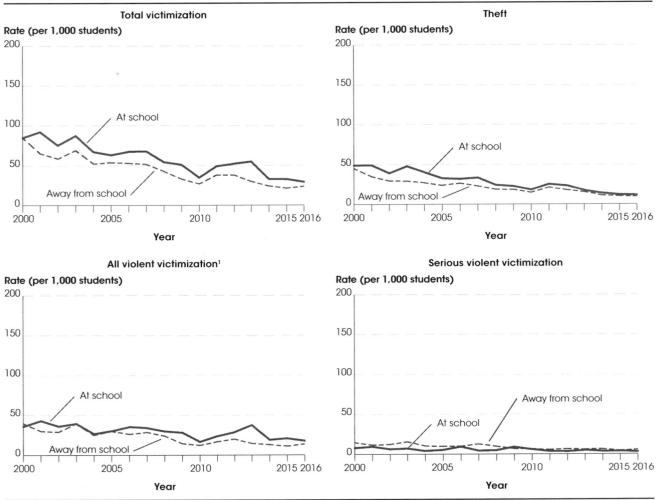

¹ Violent victimization includes serious violent victimization.
NOTE: "Total victimization" includes theft and violent crimes. "Theft" includes attempted and completed purse-snatching, completed pickpocketing, and all attempted and completed thefts, with the exception of motor vehicle thefts. Theft does not include robbery, which involves the threat or use of force and is classified as a serious violent crime. "All violent victimization" includes serious violent crimes as well as simple assault. "Serious violent victimization" includes the crimes of rape, sexual assault, robbery, and aggravated assault. "At school" includes inside the school building, on school property, on a school bus, and going to or from school. The survey sample was redesigned in 2006 and 2016 to reflect changes in the population; consequently, use caution when comparing data from 2006 through 2015 to earlier years, and when comparing data from 2016 to other years. For more information, see *Criminal Victimization, 2016* (available at https://www.bjs.gov/index.cfm?ty=pbse&sid=6).
SOURCE: U.S. Department of Justice, Bureau of Justice Statistics, National Crime Victimization Survey (NCVS), 2000 through 2016. See *Digest of Education Statistics 2017*, table 228.20.

Between 2000 and 2016, the total rates of nonfatal victimization both at school and away from school declined for 12- to 18-year-old students. The total rate of victimization at school declined 65 percent, and the total rate of victimization away from school declined 72 percent.

The rates of specific types of victimization—thefts, violent victimizations, and serious violent victimizations—both at school and away from school all declined between 2000 and 2016.

Figure 2. Percentage of public schools that used selected safety and security measures: School years 1999–2000, 2013–14, and 2015–16

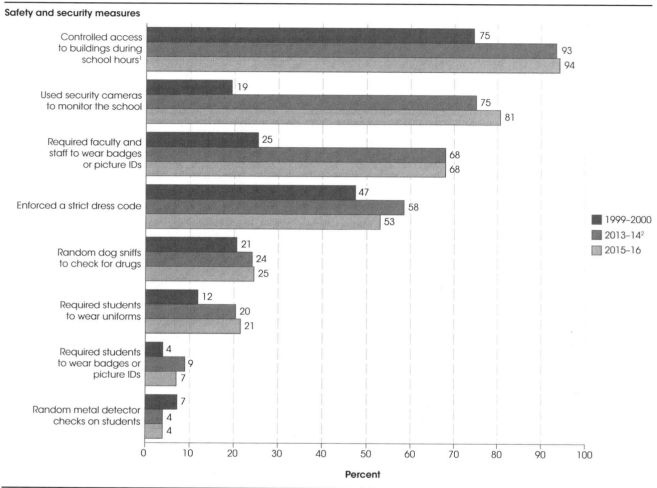

Safety and security measures

Controlled access to buildings during school hours[1]
- 1999–2000: 75
- 2013–14: 93
- 2015–16: 94

Used security cameras to monitor the school
- 1999–2000: 19
- 2013–14: 75
- 2015–16: 81

Required faculty and staff to wear badges or picture IDs
- 1999–2000: 25
- 2013–14: 68
- 2015–16: 68

Enforced a strict dress code
- 1999–2000: 47
- 2013–14: 58
- 2015–16: 53

Random dog sniffs to check for drugs
- 1999–2000: 21
- 2013–14: 24
- 2015–16: 25

Required students to wear uniforms
- 1999–2000: 12
- 2013–14: 20
- 2015–16: 21

Required students to wear badges or picture IDs
- 1999–2000: 4
- 2013–14: 9
- 2015–16: 7

Random metal detector checks on students
- 1999–2000: 7
- 2013–14: 4
- 2015–16: 4

Legend: ■ 1999–2000 ■ 2013–14[2] ■ 2015–16

Percent

[1] For example, locked or monitored doors.
[2] Data for 2013–14 were collected using the Fast Response Survey System (FRSS), while data for all other years were collected using the School Survey on Crime and Safety (SSOCS). The 2013–14 FRSS survey was designed to allow comparisons with SSOCS data. However, respondents to the 2013–14 survey could choose either to complete the survey on paper (and mail it back) or to complete the survey online, whereas respondents to SSOCS did not have the option of completing the survey online. The 2013–14 survey also relied on a smaller sample. The smaller sample size and difference in survey administration may have impacted the 2013–14 results.
NOTE: Responses were provided by the principal or the person most knowledgeable about crime and safety issues at the school.
SOURCE: U.S. Department of Education, National Center for Education Statistics, 1999–2000 and 2015–16 School Survey on Crime and Safety (SSOCS), 2000 and 2016; Fast Response Survey System (FRSS), "School Safety and Discipline: 2013–14," FRSS 106, 2014. See Digest of Education Statistics 2017, table 233.50.

Some security practices, such as locking or monitoring doors and gates, are intended to limit or control access to school campuses, while others, such as the use of metal detectors and security cameras, are intended to monitor or restrict students' and visitors' behavior on campus. The percentages of public schools reporting the use of various safety and security measures tended to be higher in 2015–16 than in prior years. For example, the percentage of public schools reporting the use of security cameras increased from 19 percent in 1999–2000 to 81 percent

in 2015–16, and the percentage of public schools reporting that they controlled access to school buildings increased from 75 percent to 94 percent during this time. Additionally, the percentage of schools reporting that they enforced a strict dress code increased from 47 percent in 1999–2000 to 58 percent in 2013–14, although the percentage in 2015–16 (53 percent) was lower than the percentage in 2013–14. From 1999–2000 to 2015–16, use of the following safety and security measures also increased: requiring faculty and staff to wear badges or picture IDs, using random dog sniffs, requiring school uniforms, and requiring students to wear badges or picture IDs. Conversely, the percentage of schools that reported

using random metal detector checks decreased from 7 percent in 1999–2000 to 4 percent in 2015–16.

Figure 3. Percentage of public schools with one or more security staff present at least once a week, by school level: School years 2005–06 and 2015–16

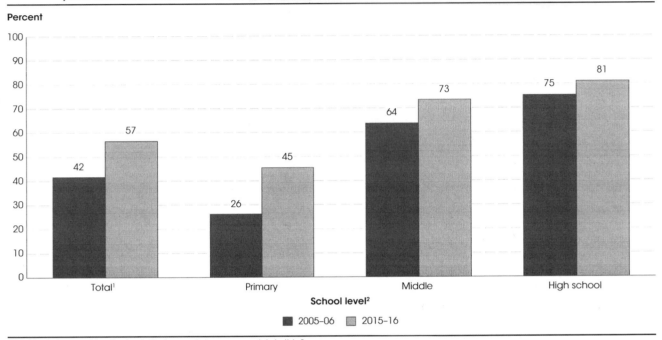

Percent

Legend: ■ 2005-06   ▢ 2015-16

School level[2]

[1] Total includes combined schools that are not shown separately in this figure.
[2] Primary schools are defined as schools in which the lowest grade is not higher than grade 3 and the highest grade is not higher than grade 8. Middle schools are defined as schools in which the lowest grade is not lower than grade 4 and the highest grade is not higher than grade 9. High schools are defined as schools in which the lowest grade is not lower than grade 9 and the highest grade is not higher than grade 12.
NOTE: Security staff include security guards, security personnel, school resource officers (SROs), and sworn law enforcement officers who are not SROs. SROs include all career law enforcement officers with arrest authority who have specialized training and are assigned to work in collaboration with school organizations. Responses were provided by the principal or the person most knowledgeable about crime and safety issues at the school.
SOURCE: U.S. Department of Education, National Center for Education Statistics, 2005–06 and 2015–16 School Survey on Crime and Safety (SSOCS), 2006 and 2016. See *Digest of Education Statistics 2017*, table 233.70.

In the 2015–16 school year, 57 percent of public schools reported the presence of one or more security staff at their school at least once a week during the school year.[2] The percentage of public schools reporting the presence of any security staff was higher in 2015–16 than in 2005–06. This same pattern of a higher percentage of public schools overall reporting the presence of any security staff in 2015–16 than in 2005–06 was observed for primary,

middle, and high schools. The percentage point change from 2005–06 to 2015–16 was larger for primary schools (19 percentage points) than for middle schools (10 percentage points) or high schools (6 percentage points). Despite these changes, the percentage of primary schools reporting the presence of any security staff in 2015–16 (45 percent) remained lower than the percentage of middle schools (73 percent) or high schools (81 percent).

Figure 4. Percentage of public schools with a written plan for procedures to be performed in selected scenarios: School year 2015–16

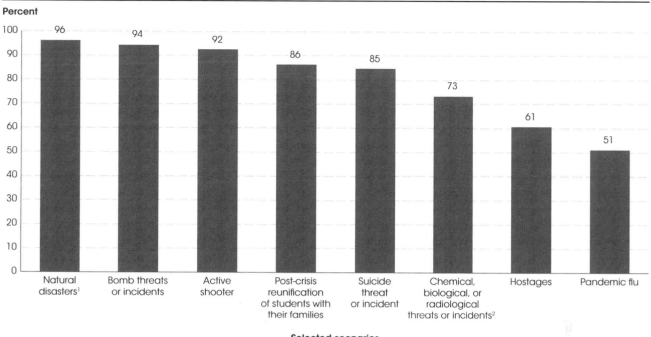

Percent

¹ For example, earthquakes or tornadoes.
² For example, release of mustard gas, anthrax, smallpox, or radioactive materials.
NOTE: Responses were provided by the principal or the person most knowledgeable about crime and safety issues at the school.
SOURCE: U.S. Department of Education, National Center for Education Statistics, 2015–16 School Survey on Crime and Safety (SSOCS), 2016. See *Digest of Education Statistics 2017*, table 233.65.

Schools use a variety of practices and procedures to promote the safety of students, faculty, and staff. One aspect of school safety and security is ensuring that plans are in place to be carried out in the event of specific scenarios. In 2015–16, about 96 percent of public schools reported they had a written plan for procedures to be performed in the event of a natural disaster, 94 percent of public schools reported they had a plan for procedures to

be performed in the event of bomb threats or incidents, and 92 percent reported they had a plan in place for procedures to be performed in the event of an active shooter. The percentage of schools reporting that they had a plan for procedures to be performed in response to other events included in the survey questionnaire ranged from 86 percent for post-crisis reunification of students with their families to 51 percent for a pandemic flu.

Endnotes:
¹ At school includes inside the school building, on school property, or on the way to or from school.
² Security staff include security guards, security personnel, school resource officers (SROs), and sworn law enforcement officers who are not SROs. "Security guards" and "security personnel"

do not include law enforcement. SROs include all career law enforcement officers with arrest authority who have specialized training and are assigned to work in collaboration with school organizations.

Reference tables: *Digest of Education Statistics 2017,* tables 228.20, 233.50, 233.65, and 233.70

Related indicators and resources: *Indicators of School Crime and Safety*; Safety at School [*Status and Trends in the Education of Racial and Ethnic Groups*]

Glossary: Public school or institution

Characteristics of Public School Teachers

The percentage of public school teachers who held a postbaccalaureate degree (i.e., a master's, education specialist, or doctor's degree) was higher in 2015–16 (57 percent) than in 1999–2000 (47 percent). In both school years, a lower percentage of elementary school teachers than secondary school teachers held a postbaccalaureate degree.

In the 2015–16 school year, there were 3.8 million full- and part-time public school teachers, including 1.9 million elementary school teachers and 1.9 million secondary school teachers. Overall, the number of public school teachers in 2015–16 was 27 percent higher than in 1999–2000 (3.0 million). These changes were accompanied by a 7 percent increase in public school enrollment in kindergarten through 12th grade, from 45.9 million students in fall 2000 to 49.0 million students in fall 2015. At the elementary school level, the number of teachers was 19 percent higher in 2015–16 than in 1999–2000 (1.6 million), while at the secondary school level the number of teachers was 37 percent higher in 2015–16 than in 1999–2000 (1.4 million).

Figure 1. Percentage distribution of teachers in public elementary and secondary schools, by instructional level and sex: School years 1999–2000 and 2015–16

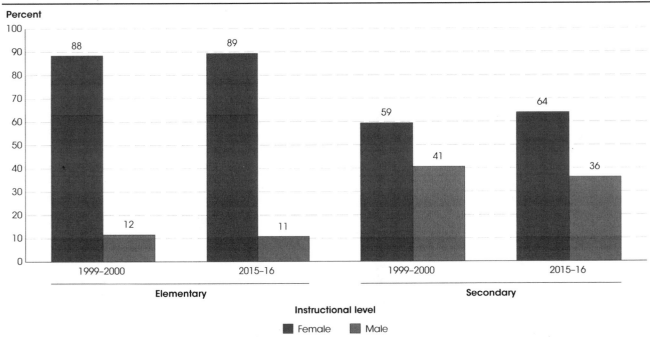

NOTE: Data are based on a head count of full-time and part-time teachers rather than on the number of full-time-equivalent teachers. Teachers were classified as elementary or secondary on the basis of the grades they taught, rather than on the level of the school in which they taught. In general, elementary teachers include those teaching prekindergarten through grade 6 and those teaching multiple grades, with a preponderance of grades taught being kindergarten through grade 6. In general, secondary teachers include those teaching any of grades 7 through 12 and those teaching multiple grades, with a preponderance of grades taught being grades 7 through 12 and usually with no grade taught being lower than grade 5.
SOURCE: U.S. Department of Education, National Center for Education Statistics, Schools and Staffing Survey (SASS), "Public School Teacher Data File," "Charter School Teacher Data File," "Public School Data File," and "Charter School Data File," 1999–2000; and National Teacher and Principal Survey (NTPS), "Public School Teacher Data File," 2015–16. See *Digest of Education Statistics 2017*, table 209.22.

About 77 percent of public school teachers were female and 23 percent were male in 2015–16, with a lower percentage of male teachers at the elementary school level (11 percent) than at the secondary school level (36 percent). Overall, the percentage of public school teachers who were male was 2 percentage points lower in 2015–16 than in 1999–2000.

At the elementary school level, the percentage of male teachers was 1 percentage point lower in 2015–16 than in 1999–2000. By comparison, at the secondary school level, the percentage of male teachers was 5 percentage points lower in 2015–16 than in 1999–2000.

Figure 2. Percentage distribution of teachers in public elementary and secondary schools, by race/ethnicity: School years 1999-2000 and 2015-16

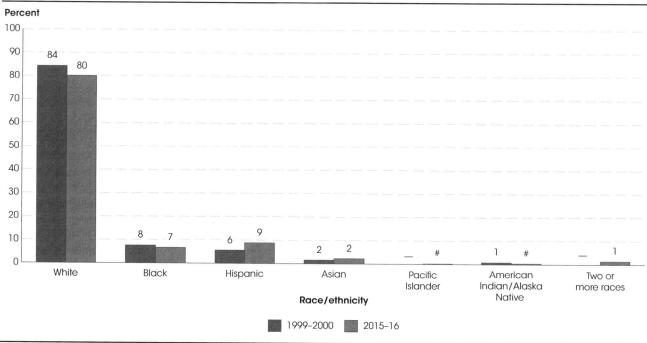

— Not available.
Rounds to zero.
NOTE: Data are based on a head count of full-time and part-time teachers rather than on the number of full-time-equivalent teachers. Data for 1999–2000 are only roughly comparable to data for 2015–16; in 1999–2000, data for teachers of Two or more races were not collected as a separate category and the Asian category included Pacific Islanders. Race categories exclude persons of Hispanic ethnicity. Although rounded numbers are displayed, the figures are based on unrounded estimates. Detail may not sum to totals due to rounding.
SOURCE: U.S. Department of Education, National Center for Education Statistics, Schools and Staffing Survey (SASS), "Public School Teacher Data File," "Charter School Teacher Data File," "Public School Data File," and "Charter School Data File," 1999–2000; and National Teacher and Principal Survey (NTPS), "Public School Teacher Data File," 2015–16. See *Digest of Education Statistics 2017*, table 209.22.

In 2015–16, about 80 percent of public school teachers were White, 9 percent were Hispanic, 7 percent were Black, 2 percent were Asian, and 1 percent were of Two or more races; additionally, those who were American Indian/Alaska Native and those who were Pacific Islander each made up less than 1 percent of public school teachers.

The percentages of public school teachers who were White and Black were lower in 2015–16 than in 1999–2000, when 84 percent were White and 8 percent were Black.[1] In contrast, the percentage who were Hispanic was higher in 2015–16 than in 1999–2000, when 6 percent were Hispanic.

Figure 3. Percentage of public school teachers who held a postbaccalaureate degree and percentage who held a regular or standard state teaching certificate or advanced professional certificate, by instructional level: School years 1999-2000 and 2015-16

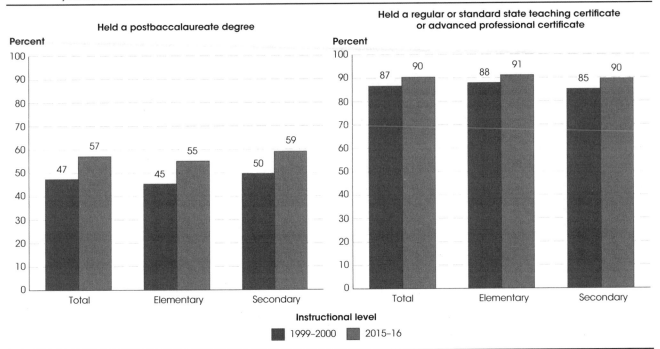

NOTE: Data are based on a head count of full-time and part-time teachers rather than on the number of full-time-equivalent teachers. Postbaccalaureate degree recipients include teachers who held a master's, education specialist, or doctor's degree. Education specialist degrees or certificates are generally awarded for 1 year's work beyond the master's level, including a certificate of advanced graduate studies. Doctor's degrees include Ph.D., Ed.D., and comparable degrees at the doctoral level, as well as first-professional degrees, such as M.D., D.D.S., and J.D. degrees. Teachers were classified as elementary or secondary on the basis of the grades they taught, rather than on the level of the school in which they taught. In general, elementary teachers include those teaching prekindergarten through grade 6 and those teaching multiple grades, with a preponderance of grades taught being kindergarten through grade 6. In general, secondary teachers include those teaching any of grades 7 through 12 and those teaching multiple grades, with a preponderance of grades taught being grades 7 through 12 and usually with no grade taught being lower than grade 5.
SOURCE: U.S. Department of Education, National Center for Education Statistics, Schools and Staffing Survey (SASS), "Public School Teacher Data File," "Charter School Teacher Data File," "Public School Data File," and "Charter School Data File," 1999–2000; and National Teacher and Principal Survey (NTPS), "Public School Teacher Data File," 2015–16. See *Digest of Education Statistics 2017*, table 209.22.

The percentage of public school teachers who held a postbaccalaureate degree (i.e., a master's, education specialist, or doctor's degree)[2] was higher in 2015–16 (57 percent) than in 1999–2000 (47 percent). This pattern was observed at both the elementary and secondary levels. Some 55 percent of elementary school teachers and 59 percent of secondary school teachers held a postbaccalaureate degree in 2015–16, whereas 45 and 50 percent, respectively, held a postbaccalaureate degree in 1999–2000. In both school years, a lower percentage of elementary school teachers than secondary school teachers held a postbaccalaureate degree.

In 2015–16, some 90 percent of public school teachers held a regular or standard state teaching certificate or advanced professional certificate, 4 percent held a provisional or temporary certificate, 3 percent held a probationary certificate, 1 percent held no certification, and 1 percent held a waiver/emergency certificate. A higher percentage of teachers in 2015–16 than in 1999–2000 held a regular certificate (90 vs. 87 percent). In both school years, a higher percentage of elementary than secondary school teachers held a regular certificate (88 vs. 85 percent in 1999–2000; 91 vs. 90 percent in 2015–16).

Figure 4. Percentage distribution of teachers in public elementary and secondary schools, by years of teaching experience: School years 1999–2000 and 2015–16

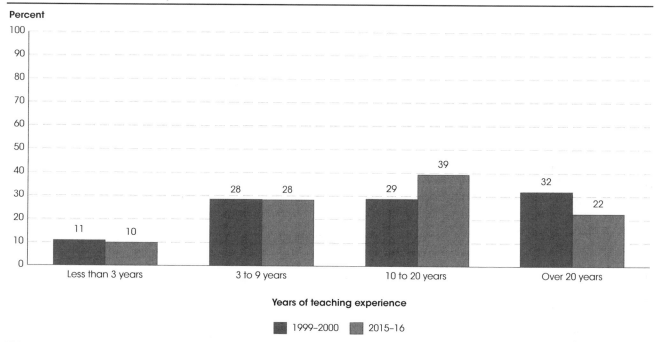

NOTE: Data are based on a head count of full-time and part-time teachers rather than on the number of full-time-equivalent teachers. Detail may not sum to totals due to rounding.
SOURCE: U.S. Department of Education, National Center for Education Statistics, Schools and Staffing Survey (SASS), "Public School Teacher Data File," "Charter School Teacher Data File," "Public School Data File," and "Charter School Data File," 1999–2000; and National Teacher and Principal Survey (NTPS), "Public School Teacher Data File," 2015–16. See Digest of Education Statistics 2017, table 209.22.

In 2015–16, about 10 percent of public school teachers had less than 3 years of teaching experience, 28 percent had 3 to 9 years of experience, 39 percent had 10 to 20 years of experience, and 22 percent had more than 20 years of experience. Lower percentages of teachers in 2015–16 than in 1999–2000 had less than 3 years of experience (10 vs. 11 percent) and over 20 years of

experience (22 vs. 32 percent). However, the percentage who had 10 to 20 years of experience was higher in 2015–16 than in 1999–2000 (39 vs. 29 percent). There was no measurable difference between 1999–2000 and 2015–16 in the percentage of teachers with 3 to 9 years of experience.

Figure 5. Average base salary for full-time teachers in public elementary and secondary schools, by years of full- and part-time teaching experience: 2015–16

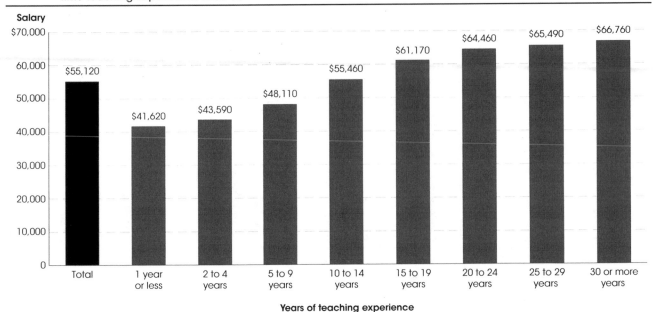

NOTE: Amounts presented in current 2015–16 dollars. Estimates are for regular full-time teachers only; they exclude other staff even when they have full-time teaching duties (regular part-time teachers, itinerant teachers, long-term substitutes, administrators, library media specialists, other professional staff, and support staff).
SOURCE: U.S. Department of Education, National Center for Education Statistics, National Teacher and Principal Survey (NTPS), "Public School Teacher Data File," 2015–16. See *Digest of Education Statistics 2017*, table 211.10.

Earlier sections of this indicator explore characteristics of all full-time and part-time public school teachers. Teacher salary information is also available, but only for regular full-time teachers in public schools.[3] In 2015–16, the average base salary (in current 2015–16 dollars) for full-time public school teachers was $55,120. Average salaries for full-time public school teachers in 2015–16 tended to increase with years of full- and part-time teaching

experience, with the exception that average salaries for teachers with 25 to 29 years of experience were not measurably different from those for teachers with 20 to 24 years of experience or those for teachers with 30 or more years of experience. Average base salaries, in current 2015–16 dollars, ranged from $41,620 for teachers with 1 year or less of experience to $66,760 for teachers with 30 or more years of experience.

Figure 6. Average base salary for full-time teachers in public elementary and secondary schools, by highest degree earned: 2015–16

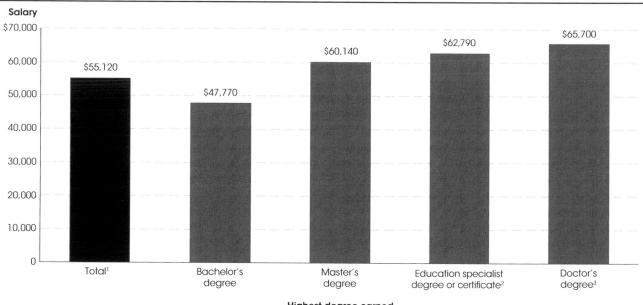

Highest degree earned

[1] Includes teachers with levels of education below the bachelor's degree (not shown separately).
[2] Education specialist degrees or certificates are generally awarded for 1 year's work beyond the master's level, including a certificate of advanced graduate studies.
[3] Doctor's degrees include Ph.D., Ed.D., and comparable degrees at the doctoral level, as well as first-professional degrees, such as M.D., D.D.S., and J.D. degrees.
NOTE: Amounts presented in current 2015–16 dollars. Estimates are for regular full-time teachers only; they exclude other staff even when they have full-time teaching duties (regular part-time teachers, itinerant teachers, long-term substitutes, administrators, library media specialists, other professional staff, and support staff).
SOURCE: U.S. Department of Education, National Center for Education Statistics, National Teacher and Principal Survey (NTPS), "Public School Teacher Data File," 2015–16. See *Digest of Education Statistics 2017*, table 211.10.

Higher educational attainment was associated with higher average base salaries for full-time public school teachers who held at least a bachelor's degree. For example, in 2015–16 the average salary for teachers with a doctor's degree ($65,700) was 38 percent higher than the salary of teachers with a bachelor's degree ($47,770), 9 percent higher than the salary of teachers with a master's degree ($60,140), and 5 percent higher than the salary of teachers with an education specialist degree or certificate ($62,790).

In 2015–16, the average base salary (in current 2015–16 dollars) for full-time public school teachers was lower for elementary school teachers ($54,020) than for secondary school teachers ($56,180). Female teachers had a lower average base salary than male teachers ($54,560 vs. $56,920).

Average salaries were higher for Asian ($61,350), Pacific Islander ($59,900), and Hispanic teachers ($56,240) than for White teachers ($55,120), teachers of Two or more races ($52,750), and Black teachers ($52,420), and were lowest for American Indian/Alaska Native teachers ($48,600). In addition, average salaries were higher for Asian than for Hispanic teachers and were higher for White teachers than for Black teachers and teachers of Two or more races.

Trends in average full-time public school teacher salaries can be explored using constant 2016–17 dollars.[4] From 1999–2000 to 2015–16, the average base salary for full-time public school teachers declined from $57,190 to $56,140.

Endnotes:

[1] Data for 1999–2000 are only roughly comparable to data for 2015–16; in 1999–2000, data for teachers of Two or more races were not collected as a separate category, and the Asian category included Pacific Islanders.

[2] Education specialist degrees or certificates are generally awarded for 1 year's work beyond the master's level, including a certificate of advanced graduate studies. Doctor's degrees include Ph.D., Ed.D., and comparable degrees at the doctoral level, as well as first-professional degrees, such as M.D., D.D.S., and J.D. degrees.

[3] Salary data are available for regular, full-time public school teachers only; the data exclude other staff even when they have full-time teaching duties (regular part-time teachers, itinerant teachers, long-term substitutes, administrators, library media specialists, other professional staff, and support staff).

[4] Constant dollar estimates are based on the Consumer Price Index, prepared by the Bureau of Labor Statistics, U.S. Department of Labor, adjusted to a school-year basis.

Reference tables: *Digest of Education Statistics 2017*, tables 209.22, 211.10, and 211.20; *Digest of Education Statistics 2016*, table 203.10

Related indicators and resources: Characteristics of Public School Teachers Who Completed Alternative Route to Certification Programs [*The Condition of Education 2018 Spotlight*]; Teacher Turnover: Stayers, Movers, and Leavers

Glossary: Bachelor's degree, Doctor's degree, Education specialist/professional diploma, Elementary school, Master's degree, Public school or institution, Secondary school

This page intentionally left blank.

Reading Performance

The average 4th-grade reading score in 2017 (222) was higher than the average score in 1992 (217), but not measurably different from the average score in 2015, when the assessment was last administered. At the 8th-grade level, the average reading score in 2017 (267) was higher than the scores in both 1992 (260) and 2015 (265).

The National Assessment of Educational Progress (NAEP) assesses student performance in reading at grades 4, 8, and 12 in both public and private schools across the nation. NAEP reading scale scores range from 0 to 500 for all grade levels. NAEP achievement levels define what students should know and be able to do: *Basic* indicates partial mastery of fundamental skills, *Proficient* indicates

demonstrated competency over challenging subject matter, and *Advanced* indicates superior performance beyond proficient. NAEP reading assessments have been administered periodically since 1992, more frequently in grades 4 and 8 than in grade 12.[1] The most recent reading assessments were conducted in 2017 for grades 4 and 8 and in 2015 for grade 12.[2]

Figure 1. Average National Assessment of Educational Progress (NAEP) reading scale scores of 4th-, 8th-, and 12th-grade students: Selected years, 1992–2017

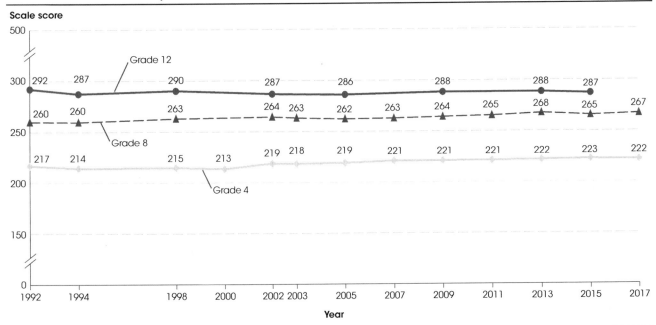

NOTE: Includes public and private schools. The reading scale scores range from 0 to 500. Assessment was not conducted for grade 8 in 2000 or for grade 12 in 2000, 2003, 2007, 2011, and 2017. Testing accommodations (e.g., extended time, small group testing) for children with disabilities and English language learners were not permitted in 1992 and 1994.
SOURCE: U.S. Department of Education, National Center for Education Statistics, National Assessment of Educational Progress (NAEP), selected years, 1992–2017 Reading Assessments, NAEP Data Explorer. See *Digest of Education Statistics 2017*, table 221.10.

The average reading score for 4th-grade students in 2017 (222) was not measurably different from the score in 2015, but it was higher than the score in 1992 (217). For 8th-grade students, the average reading score in 2017 (267) was higher than the scores in both 2015 and 1992 (265

and 260, respectively). The average reading score for 12th-grade students in 2015 (287) was not measurably different from the score in 2013, but it was lower than the score in 1992 (292).

NAEP also reports scores at five selected percentiles to show the progress made by lower- (10th and 25th percentiles), middle- (50th percentile), and higher- (75th and 90th percentiles) performing students.[3] At grade 4, the reading scores for students at the 10th and 25th percentiles in 2017 were lower than the corresponding scores in 2015. In comparison to 1992, however, reading scores were higher in 2017 for students at each selected percentile, with one exception: the score for lower-performing students at the 10th percentile was not significantly different from the score in 1992. At grade 8, students at the 50th, 75th, and 90th percentiles

scored higher in 2017 than in 2015. In comparison to 1992, however, the 8th-grade reading scores in 2017 were higher at all the selected percentiles. At grade 12, students at the 10th and 25th percentiles had lower scores in 2015 than in 2013. In addition, 12th-grade students at the 90th percentile scored higher in 2015 than in 2013. In comparison to 1992, only the highest-performing students (those at the 90th percentile) had a higher score in 2015. Lower- and middle-performing 12th-grade students at the 10th, 25th, and 50th percentiles had lower scores in 2017 than in 1992.

Figure 2. Percentage distribution of 4th-, 8th-, and 12th-grade students, by National Assessment of Educational Progress (NAEP) reading achievement level: Selected years, 1992–2017

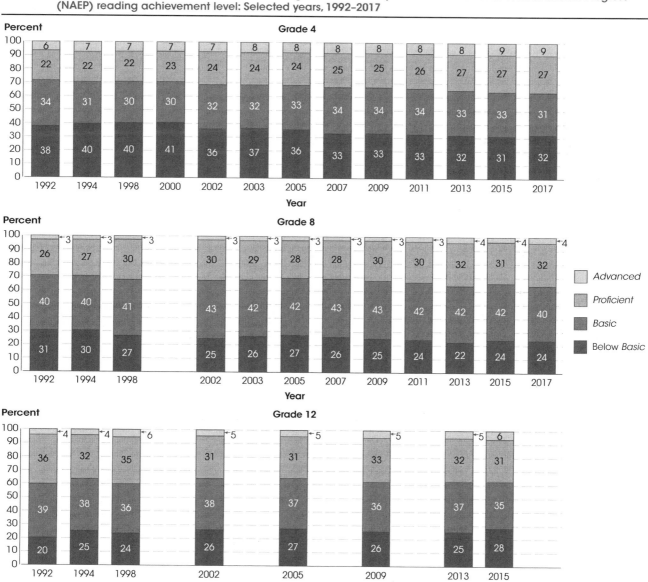

NOTE: Includes public and private schools. Achievement levels define what students should know and be able to do: *Basic* indicates partial mastery of fundamental skills, *Proficient* indicates demonstrated competency over challenging subject matter, and *Advanced* indicates superior performance beyond proficient. Assessment was not conducted for grade 8 in 2000 or for grade 12 in 2000, 2003, 2007, 2011, and 2017. Testing accommodations (e.g., extended time, small group testing) for children with disabilities and English language learners were not permitted in 1992 and 1994. Although rounded numbers are displayed, the figures are based on unrounded estimates. Detail may not sum to totals because of rounding.
SOURCE: U.S. Department of Education, National Center for Education Statistics, National Assessment of Educational Progress (NAEP), selected years, 1992–2017 Reading Assessments, NAEP Data Explorer. See *Digest of Education Statistics 2017*, table 221.12.

In 2017, some 68 percent of 4th-grade students performed at or above the *Basic* achievement level in reading, 37 percent performed at or above the *Proficient* level, and 9 percent performed at the *Advanced* level. The percentage of 4th-grade students who performed at or above *Basic* in 2017 was not measurably different from the percentage in 2015, but it was higher than the percentage in 1992 (62 percent). In addition, the percentage of 4th-grade students who performed at or above *Proficient* in 2017 was not measurably different from the percentage in 2015, but it was higher than the percentage in 1992 (29 percent). Similarly, the percentage of 4th-grade students who performed at the *Advanced* achievement level in 2017 was not measurably different from the percentage in 2015, but it was higher than the percentage in 1992 (6 percent).

In 2017, some 76 percent of 8th-grade students performed at or above *Basic* in reading, 36 percent performed at or above *Proficient*, and 4 percent performed at the *Advanced* level. The percentage of 8th-grade students who performed at or above *Basic* in 2017 was not measurably different from the percentage in 2015, but it was higher than the percentage in 1992 (69 percent). A higher percentage of 8th-grade students performed at or above *Proficient* in 2017 than in both 2015 and 1992 (34 and 29 percent, respectively). The percentage of 8th-grade students who performed at the *Advanced* level was higher in 2017 than in 1992 (3 percent). In addition, a higher percentage of 8th-grade students performed at the *Advanced* level in 2017 than in 2015, although in both years the percentage rounded to 4 percent (3.6 percent in 2015 and 4.3 percent in 2017).

In 2015, some 72 percent of 12th-grade students performed at or above *Basic* in reading, 37 percent performed at or above *Proficient*, and 6 percent performed at the *Advanced* level. A lower percentage of 12th-grade students performed at or above *Basic* in 2015 than in 2013 (75 percent) and 1992 (80 percent). The percentage of 12th-graders who performed at or above *Proficient* in 2015 (37 percent) was not measurably different from the percentage in 2013, but it was lower than the percentage in 1992 (40 percent). A higher percentage of 12th-grade students performed at the *Advanced* level in 2015 (6 percent) than in 2013 and 1992 (5 and 4 percent, respectively).

Figure 3. Average National Assessment of Educational Progress (NAEP) reading scale scores of 4th-grade students, by selected characteristics: Selected years, 1992–2017

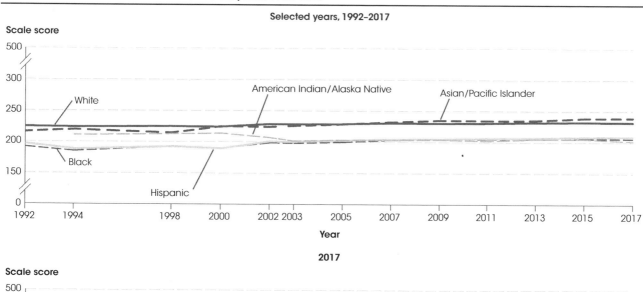

Selected years, 1992–2017

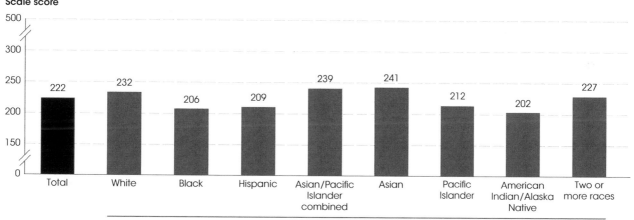

2017

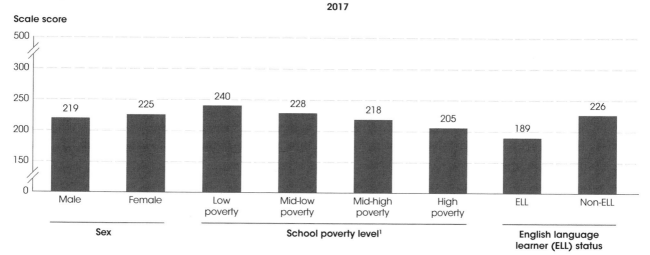

2017

[1] High-poverty schools are defined as schools where 76 to 100 percent of the students are eligible for free or reduced-price lunch (FRPL). Mid-high poverty schools are those schools where 51 to 75 percent of the students are eligible for FRPL, and mid-low poverty schools are those schools where 26 to 50 percent of the students are eligible for FRPL. Low-poverty schools are defined as schools where 25 percent or less of the students are eligible for FRPL. For more information on eligibility for FRPL and its relationship to poverty, see NCES blog post "Free or reduced price lunch: A proxy for poverty?"
NOTE: Includes public and private schools. The reading scale scores range from 0 to 500. Scale scores for American Indian/Alaska Native students were suppressed in 1992 and 1998 because reporting standards were not met (too few cases for a reliable estimate). Testing accommodations (e.g., extended time, small group testing) for children with disabilities and English language learners were not permitted in 1992 and 1994. Race categories exclude persons of Hispanic ethnicity.
SOURCE: U.S. Department of Education, National Center for Education Statistics, National Assessment of Educational Progress (NAEP), selected years, 1992–2017 Reading Assessments, NAEP Data Explorer. See *Digest of Education Statistics 2017*, tables 221.10 and 221.12.

At grade 4, the average 2017 reading scores for White (232), Black (206), Hispanic (209), and Asian/Pacific Islander students (239) were not measurably different from the corresponding scores in 2015, but the average reading score for each group was higher in 2017 than in 1992 (224, 192, 197, and 216, respectively). In 2017, the average score for American Indian/Alaska Native 4th-graders (202) was not measurably different from the scores in 2015 and 1994 (1994 was the first year data were available for 4th-grade American Indian/Alaska Native students). In 2011, NAEP began reporting separate data for Asian students, Pacific Islander students, and students of Two or more races.[4] The 2017 average 4th-grade reading scores for Pacific Islander students (212) and students of Two or more races (227) were not measurably different from their respective scores in 2015 and 2011. The 2017 average reading score for Asian students (241) was not measurably different from the score in 2015, but it was higher than the score in 2011 (236).

From 1992 through 2017, the average reading score for White 4th-graders was higher than those of their Black and Hispanic peers. Although the White-Black and White-Hispanic achievement gaps did not change measurably from 2015 to 2017, the White-Black gap narrowed from 32 points in 1992 to 26 points in 2017.

The White-Hispanic gap in 2017 (23 points) was not measurably different from the White-Hispanic gap in 1992.

At grade 4, the average reading scores for male (219) and female (225) students in 2017 were not measurably different from those in 2015 but were higher than those in 1992 (213 and 221, respectively). In each year since 1992, female students have scored higher than male students at grade 4. The 2017 achievement gap between male and female 4th-grade students (6 points) was not measurably different from the male-female gaps in 2015 and 1992.

NAEP also disaggregates scores by students' English language learner (ELL) status and by the poverty level of the school they attended. In 2017, the average reading score for 4th-grade ELL students (189) was 37 points lower than the average score for their non-ELL peers (226).[5] In 2017, the average reading score for 4th-grade students in high-poverty schools (205) was lower than the average scores for 4th-grade students in mid-high poverty schools (218), mid-low poverty schools (228), and low-poverty schools (240). At grade 4, the 2017 achievement gap between students at high-poverty and low-poverty schools (35 points) was not measurably different from the corresponding achievement gaps in 2005 and 2015.

Figure 4. Average National Assessment of Educational Progress (NAEP) reading scale scores of 8th-grade students, by selected characteristics: Selected years, 1992–2017

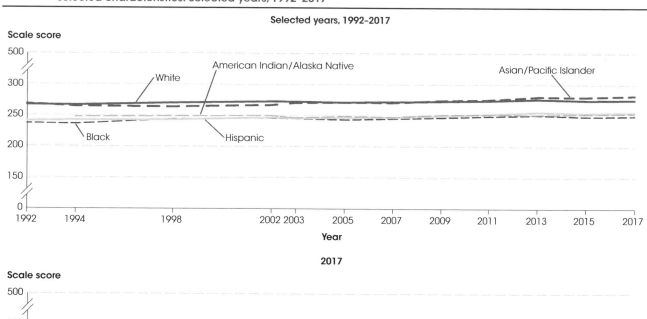

Selected years, 1992–2017

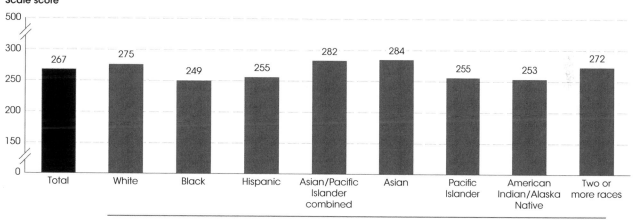

2017

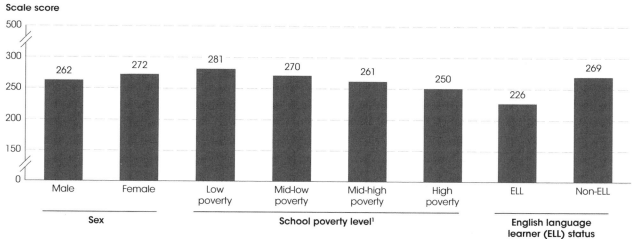

2017

¹ High-poverty schools are defined as schools where 76 to 100 percent of the students are eligible for free or reduced-price lunch (FRPL). Mid-high poverty schools are those schools where 51 to 75 percent of the students are eligible for FRPL, and mid-low poverty schools are those schools where 26 to 50 percent of the students are eligible for FRPL. Low-poverty schools are defined as schools where 25 percent or less of the students are eligible for FRPL. For more information on eligibility for FRPL and its relationship to poverty, see NCES blog post "Free or reduced price lunch: A proxy for poverty?"
NOTE: Includes public and private schools. The reading scale scores range from 0 to 500. Scale scores for American Indian/Alaska Native students were suppressed in 1992 and 1998 because reporting standards were not met (too few cases for a reliable estimate). Testing accommodations (e.g., extended time, small group testing) for children with disabilities and English language learners were not permitted in 1992 and 1994. Race categories exclude persons of Hispanic ethnicity.
SOURCE: U.S. Department of Education, National Center for Education Statistics, National Assessment of Educational Progress (NAEP), selected years, 1992–2017 Reading Assessments, NAEP Data Explorer. See *Digest of Education Statistics 2017*, tables 221.10 and 221.12.

At grade 8, the average reading scores for White (275), Black (249), Hispanic (255), and Asian/Pacific Islander (282) students in 2017 were not measurably different from the corresponding scores in 2015, but the average score for each group was higher in 2017 than in 1992 (267, 237, 241, and 268, respectively). In 2017, the average score for 8th-grade American Indian/Alaska Native students (253) was not measurably different from the scores in 2015 and 1994 (1994 was the first year data were available for 8th-grade American Indian/Alaska Native students). In 2011, NAEP began reporting separate data for Asian students, Pacific Islander students, and students of Two or more races. At grade 8, the 2017 average reading scores for Pacific Islander students (255) and students of Two or more races (272) were not measurably different from the scores in 2015 and 2011. However, while the 2017 average reading score for Asian 8th-graders (284) was not measurably different from the score in 2015, it was higher than the score in 2011 (277).

From 1992 through 2017, the average reading score for White 8th-graders was higher than the scores of their Black and Hispanic peers. Although the White-Black and White-Hispanic achievement gaps at grade 8 did not change measurably from 2015 to 2017, the White-Hispanic gap narrowed from 26 points in 1992 to 19 points in 2017. The White-Black gap in 2017 (25 points) was not measurably different from the White-Black gap in 1992.

At grade 8, the average reading scores in 2017 for both male (262) and female students (272) were not measurably different from the corresponding scores in 2015 but were higher than the scores in 1992 (254 and 267, respectively). In each year since 1992, female students have scored higher than male students at grade 8. The 2017 achievement gap between male and female 8th-grade students (10 points) was not measurably different from the male-female achievement gaps in 2015 and 1992.

In 2017, the average reading score for 8th-grade ELL students (226) was 43 points lower than the average score for their non-ELL peers (269). The average 2017 reading score for 8th-grade students in high-poverty schools (250) was lower than the average scores for 8th-grade students in mid-high poverty schools (261), mid-low poverty schools (270), and low-poverty schools (281). At grade 8, the 2017 achievement gap between students at high-poverty and low-poverty schools (31 points) was not measurably different from the corresponding achievement gap in 2015, but was smaller than the gap in 2005 (34 points).

Figure 5.   Average National Assessment of Educational Progress (NAEP) reading scale scores of 12th-grade students, by selected characteristics: Selected years, 1992–2015

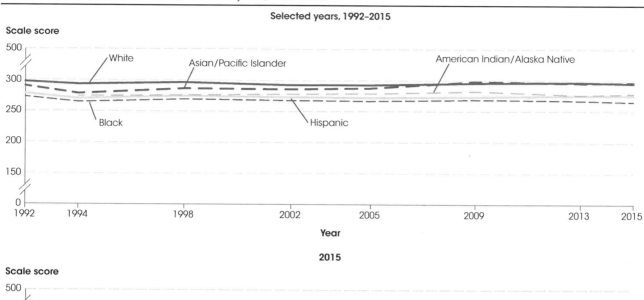

Selected years, 1992–2015

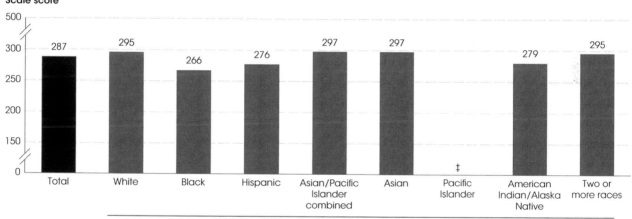

2015

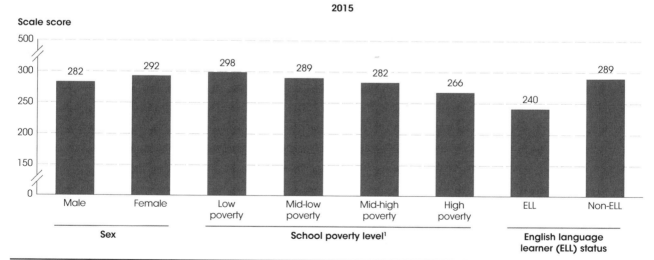

2015

‡Reporting standards not met. There were too few cases for a reliable estimate.
[1] High-poverty schools are defined as schools where 76 to 100 percent of the students are eligible for free or reduced-price lunch (FRPL). Mid-high poverty schools are those schools where 51 to 75 percent of the students are eligible for FRPL, and mid-low poverty schools are those schools where 26 to 50 percent of the students are eligible for FRPL. Low-poverty schools are defined as schools where 25 percent or less of the students are eligible for FRPL. For more information on eligibility for FRPL and its relationship to poverty, see NCES blog post "Free or reduced price lunch: A proxy for poverty?"
NOTE: Includes public and private schools. The reading scale scores range from 0 to 500. Assessment was not conducted for grade 12 in 2017. Scale scores for American Indian/Alaska Native students were suppressed in 1992, 1998, and 2002 because reporting standards were not met (too few cases for a reliable estimate). Testing accommodations (e.g., extended time, small group testing) for children with disabilities and English language learners were not permitted in 1992 and 1994. Race categories exclude persons of Hispanic ethnicity.
SOURCE: U.S. Department of Education, National Center for Education Statistics, National Assessment of Educational Progress (NAEP), selected years, 1992–2015 Reading Assessments, NAEP Data Explorer. See *Digest of Education Statistics 2017*, tables 221.10 and 221.12.

At grade 12, the average 2015 reading scores for White (295), Hispanic (276), and Asian/Pacific Islander students (297) were not measurably different from the scores in 2013 and 1992. For Black students, the 2015 average score (266) was lower than the 1992 score (273) but not measurably different from the 2013 score. The average score for American Indian/Alaska Native students in 2015 (279) was not measurably different from the scores in 2013 and 1994 (1994 was the first year data were available for 12th-grade American Indian/Alaska Native students). In 2013, NAEP began reporting separate data at the 12th-grade level for Asian students, Pacific Islander students, and students of Two or more races. The 2015 average scores for Asian students (297) and students of Two or more races (295) were not measurably different from the scores in 2013. The average score for Pacific Islanders was 289 in 2013, but was suppressed in 2015 because reporting standards were not met. The White-Black achievement gap for 12th-grade students was wider in 2015 (30 points) than in 1992 (24 points), while the White-Hispanic gap in 2015 (20 points) was not measurably different from the gap in any previous assessment year.

The 2015 average reading scores for male (282) and female (292) 12th-grade students were not measurably different from the scores in 2013 but were lower than the scores in 1992 (287 for males and 297 for females). The achievement gap between male and female students at grade 12 in 2015 (10 points) was not measurably different from the male-female achievement gaps in 2013 and 1992.

In 2015, the average reading score for 12th-grade ELL students (240) was 49 points lower than the score for their non-ELL peers (289). In addition, the average reading score for 12th-grade students in high-poverty schools (266) was lower than the average scores for 12th-grade students in mid-high poverty schools (282), mid-low poverty schools (289), and low-poverty schools (298). At grade 12, the 2015 achievement gap between students at high-poverty and low-poverty schools (32 points) was not measurably different from the corresponding achievement gap in 2005 and 2013.

NAEP results also permit state-level comparisons of the reading achievement of 4th- and 8th-grade students in public schools.[6] In 2017, the national average score for public school students at grade 4 was 221, and scores across states ranged from 207 to 236. In 19 states, average scores for 4th-grade students in public schools were higher than the national average score for 4th-grade students in public schools. Average scores for 4th-grade public school students in 16 states were not measurably different from the national average for public school students. Average scores in the District of Columbia and the remaining 15 states were lower than the national average for public school students.

At grade 8, the national average reading score for public school students in 2017 was 265, and scores across states ranged from 247 to 278. In 18 states, average scores for public school students in 2017 were higher than the national average for 8th-grade students in public schools, and in 15 states public school students had average scores that were not measurably different from the national average. Average scores in the District of Columbia and the remaining 17 states were lower than the national average for 8th-grade students in public schools.

Figure 6. Change in average National Assessment of Educational Progress (NAEP) reading scale scores of 4th- and 8th-grade public school students, by state: 2015 to 2017

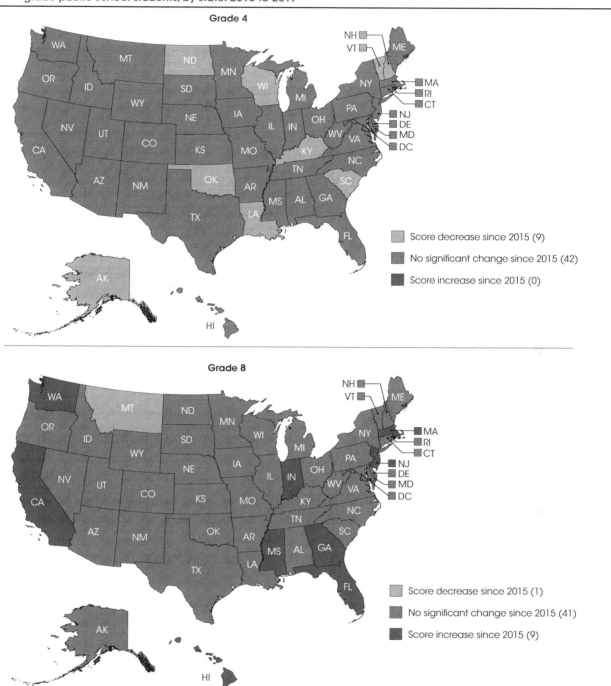

Grade 4

Score decrease since 2015 (9)

No significant change since 2015 (42)

Score increase since 2015 (0)

Grade 8

Score decrease since 2015 (1)

No significant change since 2015 (41)

Score increase since 2015 (9)

NOTE: The reading scale scores range from 0 to 500.
SOURCE: U.S. Department of Education, National Center for Education Statistics, National Assessment of Educational Progress (NAEP), 2015 and 2017 Reading Assessments, Nations Report Card (http://www.nationsreportcard.gov/). See *Digest of Education Statistics 2017*, tables 221.40 and 221.60.

While there was no measurable change from 2015 to 2017 in the average reading score for 4th-grade public school students nationally, average scores were lower in 2017 than in 2015 in nine states. The average scores in the remaining 41 states and the District of Columbia showed no measurable change from 2015 to 2017. At the 8th-grade level, the national average reading score for public school students was higher in 2017 than in 2015. It was also higher in 2017 than in 2015 in nine states, although it was lower in 2017 than in 2015 in one state (Montana). In the remaining 40 states and the District of Columbia, the average score for 8th-grade students in public schools showed no measurable change from 2015 to 2017.

Endnotes:

[1] This indicator presents data from the Main NAEP reading assessment, which is not directly comparable to the Long-Term Trend NAEP reading assessment. The Main NAEP reading assessment was first administered in 1992 and assesses student performance at grades 4, 8, and 12, while the Long-Term Trend NAEP reading assessment was first administered in 1971 and assesses student performance at ages 9, 13, and 17. In addition, the two assessments differ in the content assessed, how often the assessment is administered, and how the results are reported.
[2] NAEP reading scores for 4th-grade students in 2017 had a mean of 222 and a standard deviation (SD) of 38. NAEP reading scores for 8th-grade students in 2017 had a mean of 267 and an SD of 36. NAEP reading scores for 12th-grade students in 2015 had a mean of 287 and an SD of 41 (retrieved March 13, 2018, from the Main NAEP Data Explorer, http://nces.ed.gov/nationsreportcard/naepdata/).
[3] For more information on NAEP scores by percentile, see the Nation's Report Card website.

[4] While NAEP reported some data on students of Two or more races for earlier years, the reporting standards changed in 2011.
[5] High-poverty schools are defined as schools where 76 to 100 percent of the students are eligible for free or reduced-price lunch (FRPL). Mid-high poverty schools are those schools where 51 to 75 percent of the students are eligible for FRPL, and mid-low poverty schools are those schools where 26 to 50 percent of the students are eligible for FRPL. Low-poverty schools are defined as schools where 25 percent or less of the students are eligible for FRPL. Data disaggregated by school poverty level are presented for 2005 and later years because prior year data are not comparable.
[6] NAEP results serve as a common metric for all states and are not comparable to results from assessments administered by state education agencies.

Reference tables: *Digest of Education Statistics 2017,* tables 221.10, 221.12, 221.40, and 221.60

Related indicators and resources: Absenteeism and Achievement [*Status and Trends in the Education of Racial and Ethnic Groups*]; International Comparisons: Reading Literacy at Grade 4; International Comparisons: Science, Reading, and Mathematics Literacy of 15-Year-Old Students; Mathematics Performance; Reading Achievement [*Status and Trends in the Education of Racial and Ethnic Groups*]; Reading and Mathematics Score Trends; Science Performance; Technology and Engineering Literacy

Glossary: Achievement gap; Achievement levels, NAEP; English language learner (ELL); Public school or institution; Racial/ethnic group

This page intentionally left blank.

Mathematics Performance

The average 4th-grade mathematics score in 2017 (240) was higher than the average score in 1990 (213), but not measurably different from the average score in 2015, when the assessment was last administered. Similarly, the average 8th-grade mathematics score was higher in 2017 (283) than in 1990 (263), but not measurably different from the average score in 2015.

The National Assessment of Educational Progress (NAEP) assesses student performance in mathematics at grades 4, 8, and 12 in both public and private schools across the nation. NAEP mathematics scale scores range from 0 to 500 for grades 4 and 8 and from 0 to 300 for grade 12. NAEP achievement levels define what students should know and be able to do: *Basic* indicates partial mastery of fundamental skills, *Proficient* indicates demonstrated competency over challenging subject matter, and *Advanced* indicates superior performance beyond proficient. NAEP mathematics assessments have been administered periodically since 1990, more frequently in grades 4 and 8 than in grade 12.[1] The most recent mathematics assessments were conducted in 2017 for grades 4 and 8 and in 2015 for grade 12.[2]

Figure 1. Average National Assessment of Educational Progress (NAEP) mathematics scale scores of 4th- and 8th-grade students: Selected years, 1990–2017

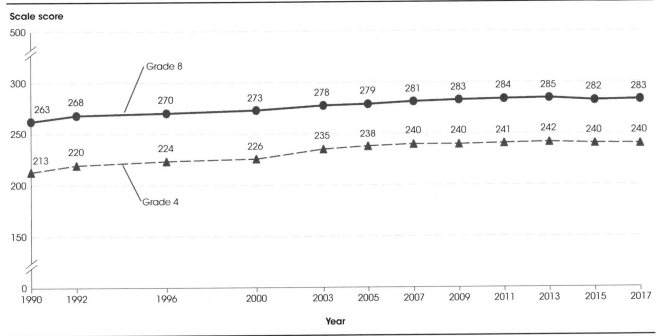

NOTE: Includes public and private schools. At grades 4 and 8, the mathematics scale scores range from 0 to 500. Testing accommodations (e.g., extended time, small group testing) for children with disabilities and English language learners were not permitted in 1990 and 1992. Grade 12 mathematics scores are not shown because they are reported on a scale of 0 to 300.
SOURCE: U.S. Department of Education, National Center for Education Statistics, National Assessment of Educational Progress (NAEP), selected years, 1990–2017 Mathematics Assessments, NAEP Data Explorer. See *Digest of Education Statistics 2017*, table 222.10.

The average 4th-grade mathematics score in 2017 (240) was not measurably different than the score in 2015, although it was higher than the score in 1990 (213). Similarly, the average 8th-grade mathematics score in 2017 (283) was not measurably different than the score in 2015, but it was higher than the score in 1990 (263). The average 12th-grade mathematics score in 2015 (152) was lower than the score in 2013 (153), but not measurably different from the score in 2005, the earliest year with comparable data.[3]

NAEP also reports scores at five selected percentiles to show the progress made by lower- (10th and 25th percentiles), middle- (50th percentile), and higher- (75th and 90th percentiles) performing students.[4] At grade 4, the mathematics scores for students at the 10th and 25th percentiles were lower in 2017 than in 2015. Also in 2017, 4th-grade mathematics scores were higher at all five selected percentiles than in 1990. At grade 8, mathematics scores for students at the 25th percentile were lower in

2017 than in 2015, and scores for students at the 75th and 90th percentiles were higher in 2017 than in 2015. In 2017, 8th-grade mathematics scores were higher at all five selected percentiles than in 1990. At grade 12, students at the 10th, 25th, and 50th percentiles scored lower in mathematics in 2015 than in 2013. In 2015, scores at all selected percentiles were not measurably different from the corresponding scores in 2005.

Figure 2. Percentage distribution of 4th-, 8th-, and 12th-grade students, by National Assessment of Educational Progress (NAEP) mathematics achievement levels: Selected years, 1990–2017

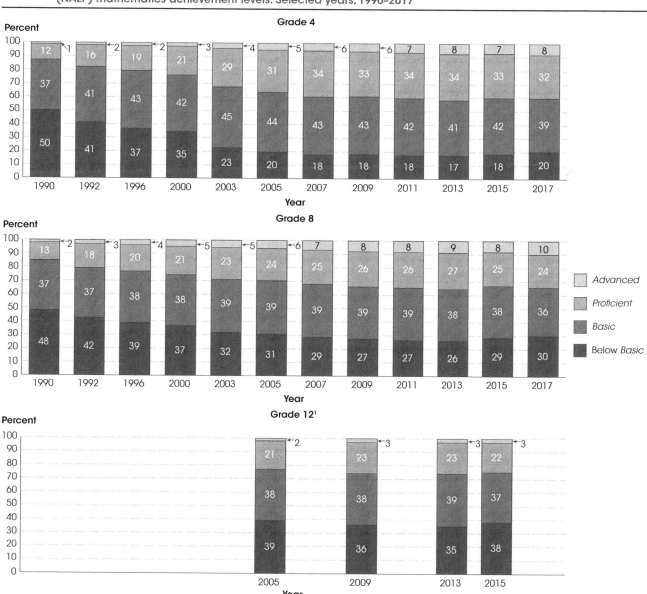

[1] In 2005, there were major changes to the framework and content of the grade 12 assessment, and, as a result, scores from 2005 and later assessment years cannot be compared with scores and results from earlier assessment years. Assessment was not conducted for grade 12 in 2007, 2011, and 2017.
NOTE: Includes public and private schools. Achievement levels define what students should know and be able to do: *Basic* indicates partial mastery of fundamental skills, *Proficient* indicates demonstrated competency over challenging subject matter, and *Advanced* indicates superior performance beyond proficient. Testing accommodations (e.g., extended time, small group testing) for children with disabilities and English language learners were not permitted in 1990 and 1992. Although rounded numbers are displayed, the figures are based on unrounded estimates. Detail may not sum to totals because of rounding.
SOURCE: U.S. Department of Education, National Center for Education Statistics, National Assessment of Educational Progress (NAEP), selected years, 1990–2017 Mathematics Assessments, NAEP Data Explorer. See *Digest of Education Statistics 2017*, table 222.12.

In 2017, some 80 percent of 4th-grade students performed at or above the *Basic* achievement level in mathematics, 40 percent performed at or above the *Proficient* level, and 8 percent performed at the *Advanced* level. While the percentage of 4th-grade students who performed at or above *Basic* in 2017 was lower than in 2015 (82 percent), it was higher than the percentage in 1990 (50 percent). The percentage of 4th-grade students who performed at or above *Proficient* in 2017 (40 percent) was not measurably different than in 2015, but it was higher than in 1990 (13 percent). Similarly, the percentage of 4th-grade students who performed at the *Advanced* level in 2017 (8 percent) was not measurably different than the percentage in 2015, but it was higher than the percentage in 1990 (1 percent).

In 2017, some 70 percent of 8th-grade students performed at or above *Basic* in mathematics, 34 percent performed at or above *Proficient*, and 10 percent performed at the *Advanced* level. The percentage of 8th-grade students who performed at or above *Basic* was lower in 2017 than in 2015 (71 percent), but was higher than the percentage in

1990 (52 percent). The percentage of 8th-grade students who performed at or above *Proficient* in 2017 (34 percent) was not measurably different than the percentage in 2015, but was higher than the percentage in 1990 (15 percent). The percentage of 8th-grade students who performed at the *Advanced* level in 2017 (10 percent) was higher than the percentages in 2015 and 1990 (8 and 2 percent, respectively).

In 2015, some 62 percent of 12th-grade students performed at or above *Basic* in mathematics, 25 percent performed at or above *Proficient*, and 3 percent performed at the *Advanced* level. The percentage of 12th-grade students who performed at or above *Basic* in 2015 was lower than the percentage in 2013 (65 percent), but not measurably different from the percentage in 2005. The percentage who performed at or above *Proficient* (25 percent) was not measurably different from the percentages in 2013 and in 2005. Similarly, the percentage of 12th-grade students who performed at the *Advanced* level in 2015 (3 percent) was not measurably different from the percentages in 2013 and 2005.

Figure 3. Average National Assessment of Educational Progress (NAEP) mathematics scale scores of 4th-grade students, by selected characteristics: Selected years, 1990–2017

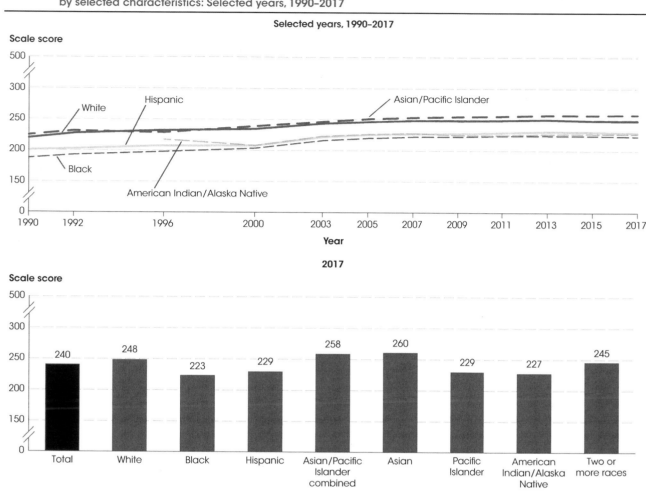

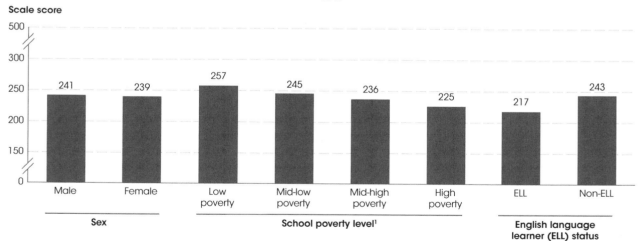

[1] High-poverty schools are defined as schools where 76 to 100 percent of the students are eligible for free or reduced-price lunch (FRPL). Mid-high poverty schools are those schools where 51 to 75 percent of the students are eligible for FRPL, and mid-low poverty schools are those schools where 26 to 50 percent of the students are eligible for FRPL. Low-poverty schools are defined as schools where 25 percent or less of the students are eligible for FRPL. For more information on eligibility for FRPL and its relationship to poverty, see NCES blog post "Free or reduced price lunch: A proxy for poverty?"
NOTE: Includes public and private schools. The mathematics scale scores range from 0 to 500. Scale scores for American Indian/Alaska Native students were suppressed in 1990 and 1992 and for Asian/Pacific Islander students in 2000 because reporting standards were not met (too few cases for a reliable estimate). Testing accommodations (e.g., extended time, small group testing) for children with disabilities and English language learners were not permitted in 1990 and 1992. Race categories exclude persons of Hispanic ethnicity.
SOURCE: U.S. Department of Education, National Center for Education Statistics, National Assessment of Educational Progress (NAEP), selected years, 1990–2017 Mathematics Assessments, NAEP Data Explorer. See Digest of Education Statistics 2017, tables 222.10 and 222.12.

At grade 4, the average mathematics scores in 2017 for White (248), Black (223), Hispanic (229), and Asian/Pacific Islander (258) students were not measurably different from the 2015 scores, but the average score for each group was higher in 2017 than in 1990 (220, 188, 200, and 225, respectively). The 2017 average score for 4th-grade American Indian/Alaska Native students (227) was not measurably different from the scores in 2015 and in 1996 (1996 was the first year data were available for 4th-grade American Indian/Alaska Native students). In 2011, NAEP began reporting separate data for Asian students, Pacific Islander students, and students of Two or more races.[5] At grade 4, the 2017 average mathematics scores for Asian students (260), Pacific Islander students (229), and students of Two or more races (245) were not measurably different from the scores in 2015 and 2011.

In 2017, and in all previous assessment years since 1990, the average mathematics score for White students in grade 4 has been higher than the scores of their Black and Hispanic peers. Although the White-Black and White-Hispanic achievement gaps did not change measurably from 2015 to 2017, the White-Black achievement gap narrowed from 32 points in 1990 to 25 points in 2017. The 4th-grade White-Hispanic achievement gap in 2017 (19 points) was not measurably different from the White-Hispanic gap in 1990.

At grade 4, the average mathematics scores for male (241) and female (239) students in 2017 were not measurably different from those in 2015 but were higher than those in 1990 (214 and 213, respectively). In 2017, the average mathematics score for male 4th-graders was 2 points higher than the average score for female students, which was not measurably different from the corresponding gaps between male and female students in 2015 and 1990.

NAEP also disaggregates scores by students' English language learner (ELL) status and by the poverty level of the school they attended.[6] In 2017, the average mathematics score for 4th-grade ELL students (217) was 26 points lower than the average score for their non-ELL peers (243). In 2017, the average mathematics score for 4th-grade students in high-poverty schools (225) was lower than the average scores for 4th-grade students in mid-high poverty schools (236), mid-low poverty schools (245), and low-poverty schools (257). At grade 4, the 2017 achievement gap between students at high-poverty and low-poverty schools (32 points) was not measurably different from the corresponding achievement gaps in 2005 and 2015.

Figure 4. Average National Assessment of Educational Progress (NAEP) mathematics scale scores of 8th-grade students, by selected characteristics: Selected years, 1990–2017

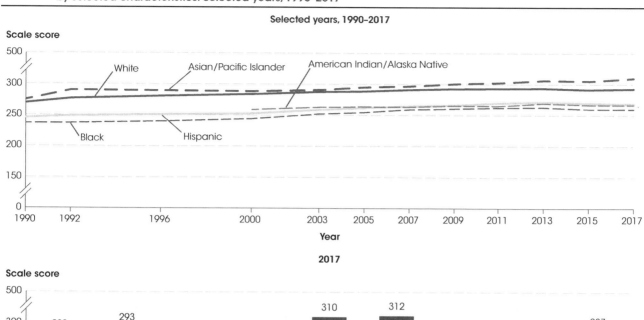

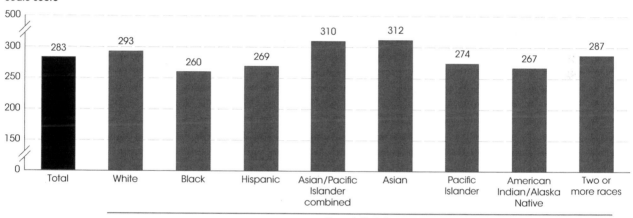

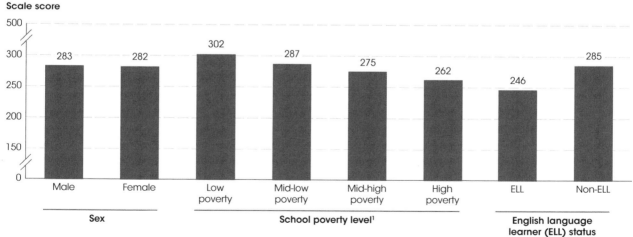

[1] High-poverty schools are defined as schools where 76 to 100 percent of the students are eligible for free or reduced-price lunch (FRPL). Mid-high poverty schools are those schools where 51 to 75 percent of the students are eligible for FRPL, and mid-low poverty schools are those schools where 26 to 50 percent of the students are eligible for FRPL. Low-poverty schools are defined as schools where 25 percent or less of the students are eligible for FRPL. For more information on eligibility for FRPL and its relationship to poverty, see NCES blog post "Free or reduced price lunch: A proxy for poverty?"
NOTE: Includes public and private schools. The mathematics scale scores range from 0 to 500. Scale scores for Asian/Pacific Islander students in 1996 and for American Indian/Alaska Native students in 1990, 1992, and 1996 were suppressed because reporting standards were not met (too few cases for a reliable estimate). Testing accommodations (e.g., extended time, small group testing) for children with disabilities and English language learners were not permitted in 1990 and 1992. Race categories exclude persons of Hispanic ethnicity.
SOURCE: U.S. Department of Education, National Center for Education Statistics, National Assessment of Educational Progress (NAEP), selected years, 1990–2017 Mathematics Assessments, NAEP Data Explorer. See *Digest of Education Statistics 2017*, tables 222.10 and 222.12.

At grade 8, the average mathematics scores for White (293), Black (260), Hispanic (269), and Asian/Pacific Islander (310) students in 2017 were not measurably different from the corresponding scores in 2015, but the average score for each group was higher in 2017 than in 1990 (270, 237, 246, and 275, respectively). In 2017, the average score for 8th-grade American Indian/Alaska Native students (267) was not measurably different from the scores in 2015 and in 2000 (2000 was the first year data were available for 8th-grade American Indian/Alaska Native students). In 2011, NAEP began reporting separate data for Asian students, Pacific Islander students, and students of Two or more races. At grade 8, the 2017 average mathematics scores for Pacific Islander students (274) and students of Two or more races (287) were not measurably different from the scores in 2015 and 2011. The average mathematics score for Asian students (312) in 2017 was higher than in 2011 (305), but not measurably different from the score in 2015.

In 2017, and in all previous assessment years since 1990, the average mathematics scores for White students in grade 8 have been higher than the scores of their Black and Hispanic peers. In 2017, the 8th-grade achievement gaps between White and Black students' average scores (32 points) and between White and Hispanic students' scores (24 points) were not measurably different from the corresponding gaps in 2015 or 1990.

At grade 8, the average mathematics scores for male (283) and female (282) students in 2017 were not measurably different from those in 2015 but were higher than those in 1990 (263 and 262, respectively). At grade 8, male students scored 1 point higher than female students in 2017. This gap was not measurably different from the gaps observed in 2015 and 1990.

In 2017, the average mathematics score for 8th-grade ELL students (246) was 40 points lower than the average score for their non-ELL peers (285). The average 2017 mathematics score for 8th-grade students in high-poverty schools (262) was lower than the average scores for students in mid-high poverty schools (275), mid-low poverty schools (287), and low-poverty schools (302). At grade 8, the 2017 achievement gap between students at high-poverty and low-poverty schools (39 points) was not measurably different from the corresponding achievement gaps in 2005 and 2015.

Figure 5. Average National Assessment of Educational Progress (NAEP) mathematics scale scores of 12th-grade students, by selected characteristics: Selected years, 2005–2015

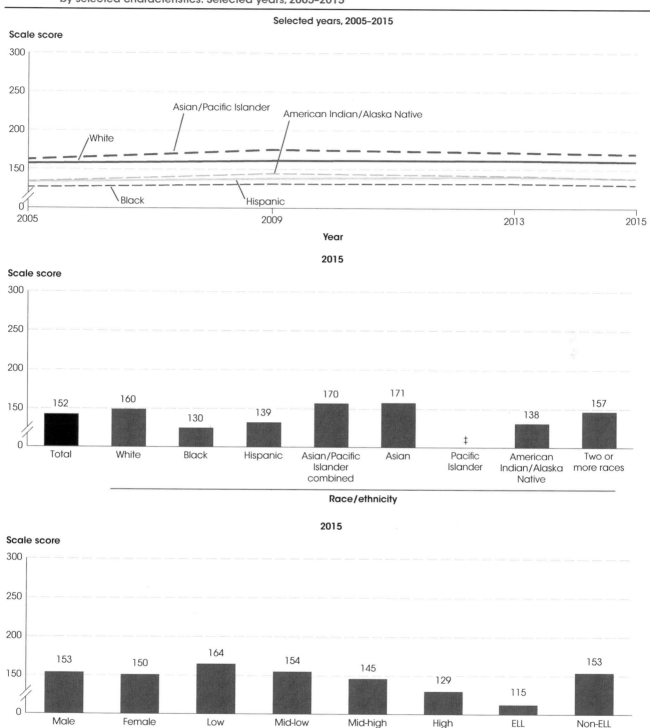

‡ Reporting standards not met. There were too few cases for a reliable estimate.

[1] High-poverty schools are defined as schools where 76 to 100 percent of the students are eligible for free or reduced-price lunch (FRPL). Mid-high poverty schools are those schools where 51 to 75 percent of the students are eligible for FRPL, and mid-low poverty schools are those schools where 26 to 50 percent of the students are eligible for FRPL. Low-poverty schools are defined as schools where 25 percent or less of the students are eligible for FRPL. For more information on eligibility for FRPL and its relationship to poverty, see NCES blog post "Free or reduced price lunch: A proxy for poverty?"

NOTE: Includes public and private schools. The mathematics scale scores range from 0 to 300. Assessment was not conducted for grade 12 in 2007, 2011, and 2017. Because of major changes to the framework and content of the grade 12 assessment, scores from 2005 and later assessment years cannot be compared with scores from earlier assessment years. Race categories exclude persons of Hispanic ethnicity.

SOURCE: U.S. Department of Education, National Center for Education Statistics, National Assessment of Educational Progress (NAEP), selected years, 2005–2015 Mathematics Assessments, NAEP Data Explorer. See *Digest of Education Statistics 2017*, tables 222.10 and 222.12.

At grade 12, the average mathematics scores for White (160), Black (130), Hispanic (139), and Asian/Pacific Islander (170) students in 2015 were not measurably different from the scores in 2013, but the average score for each group was higher in 2015 than in 2005 (157, 127, 133, and 163, respectively). The average score for American Indian/Alaska Native students in 2015 (138) was not measurably different from the 2013 and 2005 scores. In 2013, NAEP began reporting separate data at the 12th-grade level for Asian students, Pacific Islander students, and students of Two or more races. The 2015 average scores for Asian students (171) and students of Two or more races (157) were not measurably different from the scores in 2013. The average score for Pacific Islander students was 151 in 2013, but was suppressed in 2015 because reporting standards were not met. In 2015, the average mathematics score for White 12th-grade students was 30 points higher than the score for their Black peers and 22 points higher than the score for their Hispanic peers. The White-Black and White-Hispanic gaps in 2015 were not measurably different from the corresponding gaps in 2005 and 2013.

At grade 12, the average mathematics scores for male (153) and female (150) students in 2015 were lower than the scores in 2013 (155 and 152, respectively), but not measurably different from the scores in 2005. In 2015, male students scored 3 points higher than female students. This gap was not measurably different from the gaps observed in 2005 and 2013.

In 2015, the average mathematics score for 12th-grade ELL students (115) was 37 points lower than the average score for their non-ELL peers (153). In 2015, the average

mathematics score for 12th-grade students in high-poverty schools (129) was lower than the average scores for 12th-grade students in mid-high poverty schools (145), mid-low poverty schools (154), and low-poverty schools (164). The achievement gap between the students at high-poverty schools and low-poverty schools was 36 points in 2015, which was not measurably different from the gap in previous assessment years.

NAEP results also permit state-level comparisons of the mathematics achievement of 4th- and 8th-grade students in public schools.[7] At grade 4, the national average score for public school students in 2017 was 239, and scores across states ranged from 229 to 249. In 15 states, average scores for 4th-grade students in public schools were higher than the national average for 4th-grade students in public schools. In 18 states, the average mathematics score for 4th-grade public school students was not measurably different from the national average for public school students. Average scores in the District of Columbia and the remaining 17 states were lower than the national average for public school students.

At grade 8, the national average mathematics score for public school students in 2017 was 282, and average scores varied across states from 266 to 297. In 22 states, average scores for 8th-grade students in public schools were higher than the national average for 8th-grade students in public schools, and in 11 states the average scores for 8th-grade students in public schools were not measurably different from the national average. Average scores in the District of Columbia and the remaining 17 states were lower than the national average for 8th-grade students in public schools.

Figure 6. Change in average National Assessment of Educational Progress (NAEP) mathematics scale scores of 4th- and 8th-grade public school students, by state: 2015 to 2017

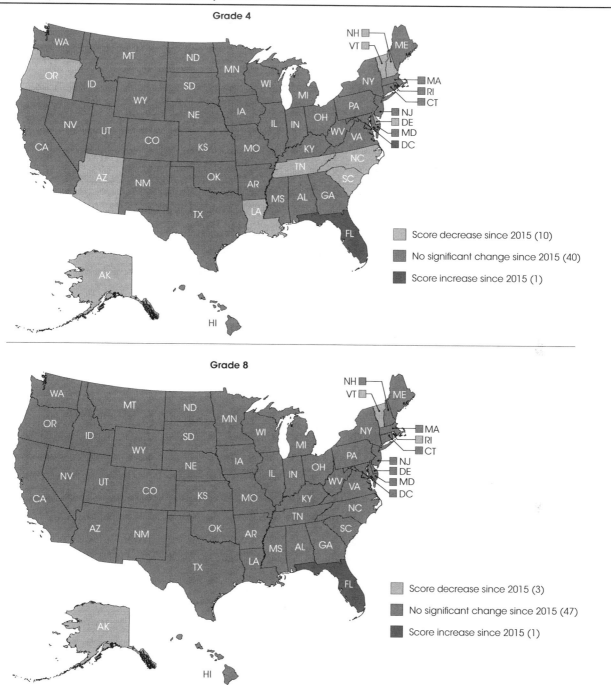

NOTE: At grades 4 and 8, the National Assessment of Educational Progress (NAEP) mathematics scale ranges from 0 to 500.
SOURCE: U.S. Department of Education, National Center for Education Statistics, National Assessment of Educational Progress (NAEP), 2015 and 2017 Mathematics Assessments, NAEP Data Explorer. See *Digest of Education Statistics 2017*, tables 222.50 and 222.60.

While there was no measurable change from 2015 to 2017 in the mathematics score for 4th-grade public school students nationally, the average score was higher in 2017 than in 2015 in one state (Florida). Average 4th-grade mathematics scores for public school students were lower in 2017 than in 2015 in 10 states. For the remaining 39 states and the District of Columbia, average scores in 2017 were not measurably different from the scores in 2015. At the 8th-grade level, the national average mathematics score for public school students in 2017 was not measurably different from the score in 2015. In one state (Florida), the average score for 8th-grade public school students was higher in 2017 than in 2015. In three states—Alaska, Rhode Island, and Vermont—the average score for 8th-grade students in public schools was lower in 2017 than in 2015. Average scores in the remaining 46 states and the District of Columbia showed no measurable change between 2015 and 2017.

Endnotes:

[1] This indicator presents data from the Main NAEP mathematics assessment, which is not directly comparable to the Long-Term Trend NAEP mathematics assessment. The Main NAEP mathematics assessment was first administered in 1990 and assesses student performance at grades 4, 8, and 12, while the Long-Term Trend NAEP mathematics assessment was first administered in 1973 and assesses student performance at ages 9, 13, and 17. In addition, the two assessments differ in the content assessed, how often the assessment is administered, and how the results are reported.

[2] NAEP mathematics scores for 4th-grade students in 2017 had a mean of 240 and a standard deviation (SD) of 31. NAEP mathematics scores for 8th-grade students in 2017 had a mean of 283 and an SD of 39. NAEP mathematics scores for 12th-grade students in 2015 had a mean of 152 and an SD of 34 (retrieved March 13, 2018, from the Main NAEP Data Explorer, http://nces.ed.gov/nationsreportcard/naepdata/).

[3] The 2005 mathematics framework for grade 12 introduced changes from the previous framework in order to reflect adjustments in curricular emphases and to ensure an appropriate balance of content. Consequently, the 12th-grade mathematics results in 2005 and subsequent years could not be compared to previous assessments, and a new trend line was established beginning in 2005.

[4] For more information on NAEP scores by percentile, see the Nation's Report Card website.

[5] While NAEP reported some data on students of Two or more races for earlier years, the reporting standards changed in 2011.

[6] High-poverty schools are defined as schools where 76 to 100 percent of the students are eligible for free or reduced-price lunch (FRPL). Mid-high poverty schools are those schools where 51 to 75 percent of the students are eligible for FRPL, and mid-low poverty schools are those schools where 26 to 50 percent of the students are eligible for FRPL. Low-poverty schools are defined as schools where 25 percent or less of the students are eligible for FRPL. Data disaggregated by school poverty level are presented for 2005 and later years because prior year data are not comparable.

[7] NAEP results serve as a common metric for all states and selected urban district and are not comparable to results from assessments administered by state education agencies.

Reference tables: *Digest of Education Statistics 2017,* tables 222.10, 222.12, 222.50, and 222.60

Related indicators and resources: Absenteeism and Achievement [*Status and Trends in the Education of Racial and Ethnic Groups*]; International Comparisons: Science, Reading, and Mathematics Literacy of 15-Year-Old Students; International Comparisons: U.S. 4th-, 8th-, and 12th-Graders' Mathematics and Science Achievement; Mathematics Achievement [*Status and Trends in the Education of Racial and Ethnic Groups*]; Reading and Mathematics Score Trends; Reading Performance; Science Performance; Technology and Engineering Literacy

Glossary: Achievement gap; Achievement levels, NAEP; English language learners (ELL); Public school or institution; Racial/ethnic group

This page intentionally left blank.

Science Performance

The percentage of 4th-grade students scoring at or above the Proficient level was higher in 2015 (38 percent) than in 2009 (34 percent), according to data from the National Assessment of Educational Progress. In addition, the percentage of 8th-grade students scoring at or above the Proficient level was higher in 2015 (34 percent) than in 2009 (30 percent). The percentage of 12th-grade students scoring at or above the Proficient level in 2015 (22 percent) was not measurably different from the percentage in 2009.

The National Assessment of Educational Progress (NAEP) assesses student performance in science at grades 4, 8, and 12 in both public and private schools across the nation. The NAEP science assessment was designed to measure students' knowledge of three content areas: physical science, life science, and Earth and space sciences. NAEP science scores range from 0 to 300 for all three grades. NAEP achievement levels define what students should know and be able to do: *Basic* indicates partial mastery of fundamental skills, and *Proficient* indicates demonstrated competency over challenging subject matter. The most recent science assessments were conducted in 2015 for grades 4, 8, and 12. Prior to 2015, grades 4 and 12 were last assessed in 2009 while grade 8 was assessed in 2011 and 2009.[1]

Figure 1. Average National Assessment of Educational Progress (NAEP) science scale scores of 4th-, 8th-, and 12th-grade students: 2009, 2011, and 2015

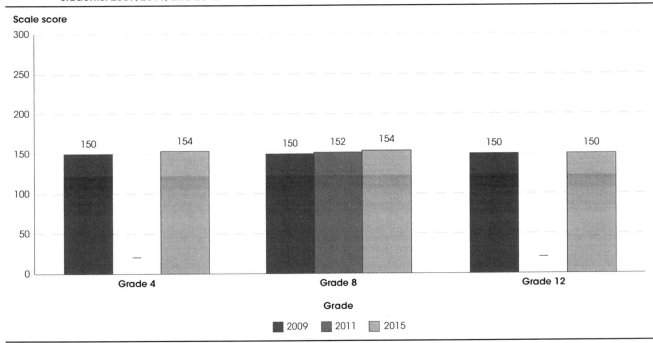

— Not available.
NOTE: Includes public and private schools. Scale ranges from 0 to 300 for all grades, but scores cannot be compared across grades. Assessment was not conducted for grades 4 and 12 in 2011.
SOURCE: U.S. Department of Education, National Center for Education Statistics, National Assessment of Educational Progress (NAEP), 2009, 2011, and 2015 Science Assessment, NAEP Data Explorer. See *Digest of Education Statistics 2016*, table 223.10.

In 2015, the average 4th-grade science score (154) was higher than the score in 2009 (150). The average 8th-grade science score in 2015 (154) was higher than the scores in both 2009 (150) and 2011 (152). The average 12th-grade science score in 2015 (150) was not measurably different from the score in 2009.

Figure 2. Percentage distribution of 4th-, 8th-, and 12th-grade students across National Assessment of Educational Progress (NAEP) science achievement levels: 2009, 2011, and 2015

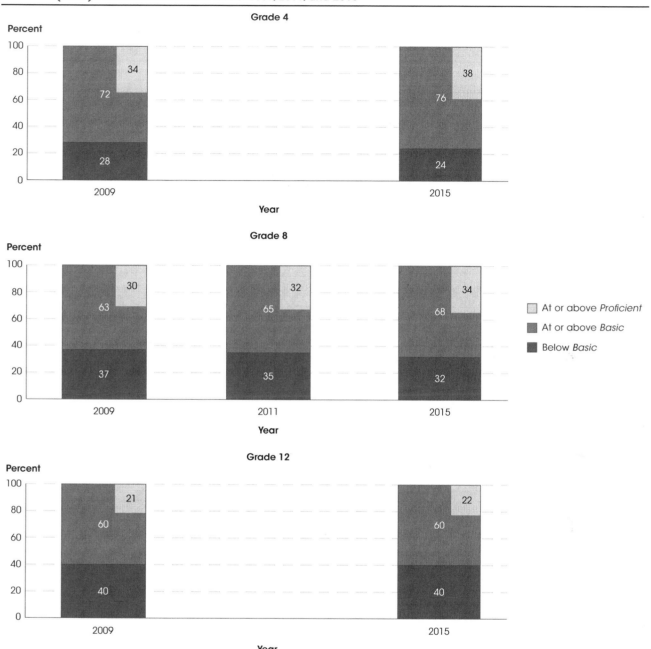

NOTE: Includes public and private schools. Achievement levels define what students should know and be able to do: *Basic* indicates partial mastery of fundamental skills, and *Proficient* indicates demonstrated competency over challenging subject matter. Assessment was not conducted for grades 4 and 12 in 2011. Detail may not sum to totals because of rounding.
SOURCE: U.S. Department of Education, National Center for Education Statistics, National Assessment of Educational Progress (NAEP), 2009, 2011, and 2015 Science Assessment, NAEP Data Explorer. See *Digest of Education Statistics 2016*, table 223.10.

In 2015, about 76 percent of 4th-grade students performed at or above the *Basic* achievement level in science, and 38 percent performed at or above the *Proficient* level. These percentages were higher than the corresponding 2009 percentages for at or above *Basic* (72 percent) and at or above *Proficient* (34 percent). Among 8th-grade students in 2015, about 68 percent performed at or above *Basic* in science, and 34 percent performed at or above *Proficient*. The percentage performing at or above *Basic*

was higher in 2015 than in both 2009 (63 percent) and 2011 (65 percent), and the percentage performing at or above *Proficient* was also higher in 2015 than in 2009 (30 percent) and 2011 (32 percent). The percentages of 12th-grade students in 2015 performing at or above *Basic* (60 percent) and at or above *Proficient* (22 percent) were not measurably different from the corresponding percentages in 2009.

Figure 3. Average National Assessment of Educational Progress (NAEP) science scale scores of 4th-, 8th-, and 12th-grade students, by race/ethnicity: 2009, 2011, and 2015

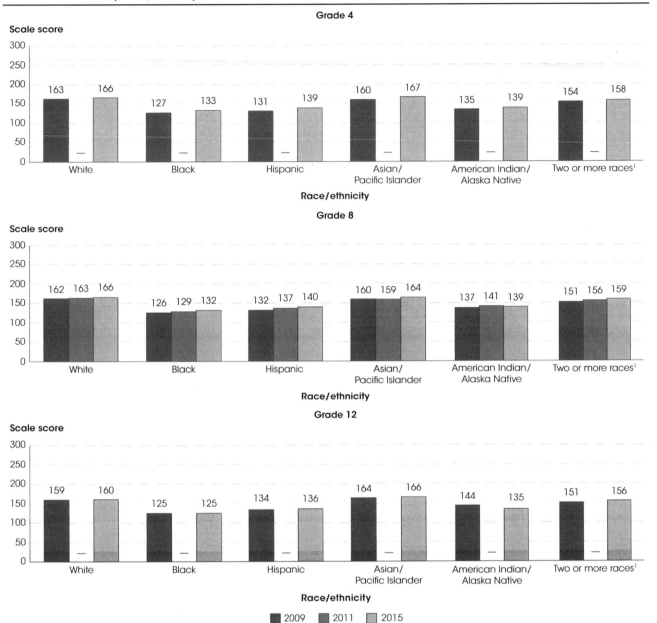

— Not available.
[1] In 2009, students in the "Two or more races" category were categorized as "Unclassified."
NOTE: Includes public and private schools. Scale ranges from 0 to 300 for all grades, but scores cannot be compared across grades. Assessment was not conducted for grades 4 and 12 in 2011. Race categories exclude persons of Hispanic ethnicity.
SOURCE: U.S. Department of Education, National Center for Education Statistics, National Assessment of Educational Progress (NAEP), 2009, 2011, and 2015 Science Assessment, NAEP Data Explorer. See *Digest of Education Statistics 2016*, table 223.10.

At grade 4, the average scores for Asian/Pacific Islander students (167), White students (166), students of Two or more races[2] (158), Hispanic students (139), American Indian/Alaska Native students (139), and Black students (133) in 2015 were higher than the corresponding scores in 2009. Starting in 2011, separate data for Asian and Pacific Islander students were collected. In 2015, the first year that data for these students were available at grade 4, the average score was 169 for Asian students and 143 for Pacific Islander students.

At grade 8, the average scores for White (166), Asian/ Pacific Islander (164), Hispanic (140), and Black students (132) in 2015 were higher than the corresponding scores in 2009 and in 2011. The 2015 average score for students of Two or more races (159) was higher than the corresponding score in 2009 but was not measurably different from the score in 2011. The 2015 average score for American Indian/Alaska Native students (139) was not measurably different from the scores in 2009 and 2011. The 2015 average score for Asian students (166) was higher than the score in 2011, while the 2015 average score for Pacific Islander students (138) was not measurably different from the score in 2011.

At grade 12, the average 2015 science scores for Asian/ Pacific Islander students (166), White students (160), students of Two or more races (156), Hispanic students (136), American Indian/Alaska Native students (135), and Black students (125) were not measurably different from the corresponding scores in 2009. The 2015 average score for Asian students was 167, while the average score for Pacific Islander students is unavailable because reporting standards were not met.

While the average science scores for White 4th- and 8th-grade students remained higher than those of their Black and Hispanic peers in 2015, racial/ethnic achievement gaps in 2015 were smaller than in 2009. At grade 4, the White-Black achievement gap was 36 points in 2009 and 33 points in 2015, and the White-Hispanic achievement gap was 32 points in 2009 and 27 points in 2015. At grade 8, the White-Black achievement gap in 2009 (36 points) was larger than in 2015 (34 points), and the White-Hispanic achievement gap was 30 points in 2009 and 26 points in 2015. However, these 2015 achievement gaps at grade 8 were not measurably different from the corresponding gaps in 2011. Additionally, while the average science scores for White 12th-grade students remained higher than those of their Black and Hispanic peers in 2015, these racial/ethnic achievement gaps did not measurably change between 2009 and 2015. At grade 12, the White-Black achievement gap (36 points) and the White-Hispanic gap (24 points) in 2015 were not measurably different from the corresponding gaps in 2009.

Figure 4. Average National Assessment of Educational Progress (NAEP) science scale scores of 4th-, 8th-, and 12th-grade students, by sex: 2009, 2011, and 2015

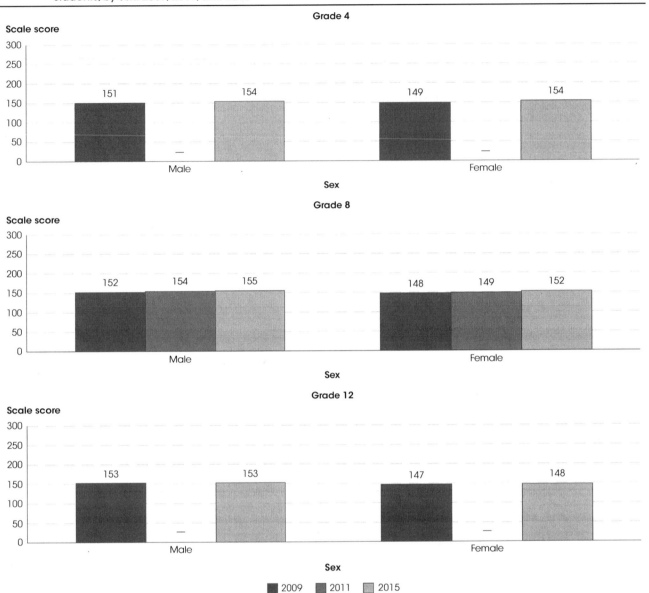

— Not available.
NOTE: Includes public and private schools. Scale ranges from 0 to 300 for all grades, but scores cannot be compared across grades. Assessment was not conducted for grades 4 and 12 in 2011.
SOURCE: U.S. Department of Education, National Center for Education Statistics, National Assessment of Educational Progress (NAEP), 2009, 2011, and 2015 Science Assessment, NAEP Data Explorer. See *Digest of Education Statistics 2016*, table 223.10.

The average science score for male 4th-grade students in 2015 (154) was higher than the score in 2009 (151). The average score for female 4th-grade students was also higher in 2015 (154) than in 2009 (149). While there was a 1-point gap between male and female 4th-grade students in 2009, there was no measurable gender gap in 2015. The average science score for male 8th-grade students in 2015 (155) was higher than the scores in 2009 (152) and 2011 (154). Similarly, for female 8th-grade students, the average score in 2015 (152) was higher than the scores in 2009 (148) and 2011 (149). In 2015, 2011,

and 2009, the average science score for male 8th-grade students was higher than that of their female peers. The 3-point score gap between male and female 8th-graders in 2015 was smaller than the gap in 2011 (5 points) but not measurably different from the gap in 2009. Average science scores in 2015 for 12th-grade male (153) and female (148) students were not measurably different from the corresponding scores in 2009. In addition, the 5-point gender gap among 12th-grade students in 2015 was not measurably different from the gap in 2009.

Since 2009, the average science scores for English language learner (ELL) 4th- and 8th-grade students were lower than their non-ELL peers' scores. At grade 4, the achievement gap between non-ELL and ELL students was larger in 2009 (39 points) than in 2015 (36 points). At grade 8, the 2015 achievement gap (46 points) was not measurably different from the gaps in 2009 and 2011. At grade 12, the average scores for non-ELL students in 2015 (152) and 2009 (151) were higher than their ELL peers' scores in those years (105 and 104, respectively). The 47-point achievement gap between non-ELL and ELL 12th-grade students in 2015 was not measurably different from the gap in 2009.

In 2015, the average science score for 4th-grade students in high-poverty schools (134) was lower than the average scores for 4th-grade students in mid-high poverty schools (151), mid-low poverty schools (161), and low-poverty schools (172).[3] At grade 8, the average 2015 science score for students in high-poverty schools (134) was lower than the average scores for students in mid-high poverty schools (150), mid-low poverty schools (161), and low-poverty schools (170). At grade 4, the 2015 achievement gap between students at high-poverty schools and low-poverty schools (38 points) was lower than the gap in 2009 (41 points). At grade 8, the 2015 achievement gap (36 points) was lower than the gap in 2009 (41 points)

but was not measurably different from the gap in 2011. At grade 12 in 2015, the average science score for students in high-poverty schools (126) was lower than the average scores for those in mid-high poverty schools (143), mid-low poverty schools (154), and low-poverty schools (165). The achievement gap between students at high-poverty schools and low-poverty schools was 39 points in 2015, which was not measurably different from the gap in 2009.

NAEP results also permit state-level comparisons of the science performance of 4th- and 8th-grade students in public schools. Forty-six states[4] participated in the NAEP science assessment in 2015, and average scores varied across the states for both grades. At grade 4, the national public school average score was 153, and state average scores ranged from 140 to 165. Twenty-two states had average scores that were higher than the national average, 15 states had average scores that were not measurably different from the national average, and 9 states had average scores that were lower than the national average. At grade 8, the 2015 national public school average score was also 153, and state average scores ranged from 140 to 166. Twenty-six states had average scores that were higher than the national average, 6 states had average scores that were not measurably different from the national average, and 14 states had scores that were lower than the national average.

Figure 5. Change in average National Assessment of Educational Progress (NAEP) science scale scores of 4th- and 8th-grade public school students, by state: 2009 and 2015

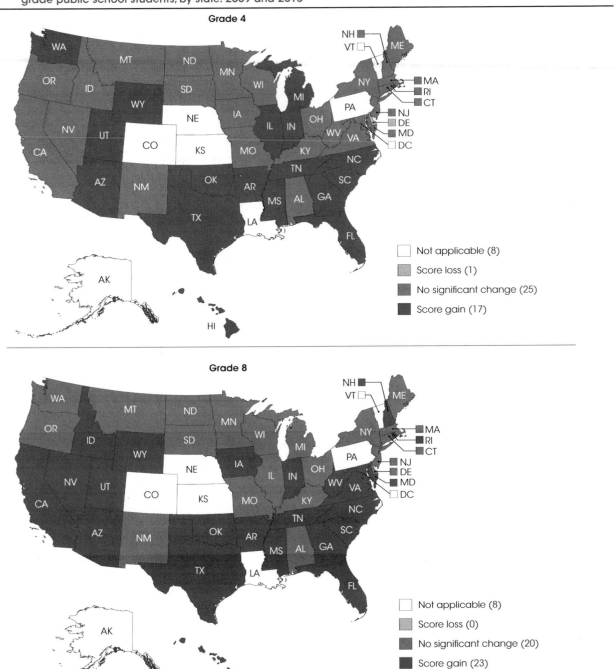

NOTE: Scale ranges from 0 to 300 for all grades, but scores cannot be compared across grades. "Gain" is defined as a significant increase from 2009 to 2015, "no change" is defined as no significant change from 2009 to 2015, and "loss" is defined as a significant decrease from 2009 to 2015.
SOURCE: U.S. Department of Education, National Center for Education Statistics, National Assessment of Educational Progress (NAEP), 2009 and 2015 Science Assessment, NAEP Data Explorer. See *Digest of Education Statistics 2016*, table 223.20.

Forty-three states participated in the NAEP science assessment in both 2009 and 2015 at grades 4 and 8.[5] The average science score for 4th-grade public school students across the nation was higher in 2015 (153) than in 2009 (149). Seventeen states had average 4th-grade scores that were also higher in 2015 than in 2009, while 25 states had average scores in 2015 that were not measurably different from their average scores in 2009. Delaware's average score for 4th-grade students was lower in 2015 (150) than in 2009 (153). The national public school average science score for 8th-grade students was also higher in 2015 (153) than in 2009 (149). Similarly, 23 states had higher average 8th-grade scores in 2015 than in 2009, while average scores for the remaining 20 states in 2015 were not measurably different from their scores in 2009. During this time, no state experienced a score loss at the 8th-grade level.

Endnotes:

[1] In 2009, a new science framework was introduced at all grade levels. A variety of factors made it necessary to create a new framework: the publication of *National Science Education Standards* (1996) and *Benchmarks for Scientific Literacy* (1993), advances in both science and cognitive research, the growth in national and international science assessments, advances in innovative assessment approaches, and the need to incorporate accommodations so that the widest possible range of students can be fairly assessed. Consequently, the science results in 2009 and subsequent years cannot be compared to previous assessments, and a new trend line was established beginning in 2009.

[2] In 2009, students in the "Two or more races" category were categorized as "Unclassified."

[3] High-poverty schools are defined as schools where 76 percent or more of students are eligible for free or reduced-price lunch (FRPL). Mid-high poverty schools are schools where 51 to 75 percent of students are eligible for FRPL, and mid-low poverty schools are schools where 26 to 50 percent of students are eligible for FRPL. Low-poverty schools are defined as schools where 25 percent or less of students are eligible for FRPL.

[4] In 2015, Alaska, Colorado, the District of Columbia, Louisiana, and Pennsylvania did not participate or did not meet the minimum participation guidelines for reporting at grades 4 and 8.

[5] 2009 NAEP science assessment results are not available for Alaska, the District of Columbia, Kansas, Nebraska, and Vermont, and 2015 results are not available for Alaska, Colorado, the District of Columbia, Louisiana, and Pennsylvania. States either did not participate or did not meet the minimum participation guidelines for reporting.

Reference tables: *Digest of Education Statistics 2016*, tables 223.10 and 223.20

Related indicators and resources: International Comparisons: Science, Reading, and Mathematics Literacy of 15-Year-Old Students; International Comparisons: U.S. 4th-, 8th-, and 12th-Graders' Mathematics and Science Achievement; Mathematics Performance; Reading Performance; Technology and Engineering Literacy Assessment

Glossary: Achievement gap; Achievement levels, NAEP; English language learners (ELL); Public school or institution; Racial/ethnic group

Public High School Graduation Rates

In school year 2015–16, the adjusted cohort graduation rate (ACGR) for public high school students was 84 percent, the highest it has been since the rate was first measured in 2010–11. In other words, more than four out of five students graduated with a regular high school diploma within 4 years of starting 9th grade. Asian/Pacific Islander students had the highest ACGR (91 percent), followed by White (88 percent), Hispanic (79 percent), Black (76 percent), and American Indian/Alaska Native (72 percent) students.

This indicator examines the percentage of public high school students who graduate on time, as measured by the adjusted cohort graduation rate (ACGR). State education agencies calculate the ACGR by identifying the "cohort" of first-time 9th-graders in a particular school year. The cohort is then adjusted by adding any students who transfer into the cohort after 9th grade and subtracting any students who transfer out, emigrate to another country, or die. The ACGR is the percentage of students in this adjusted cohort who graduate within 4 years with a regular high school diploma. The U.S. Department of Education first collected the ACGR in 2010–11.

Figure 1.   Adjusted cohort graduation rate (ACGR) for public high school students, by state: 2015–16

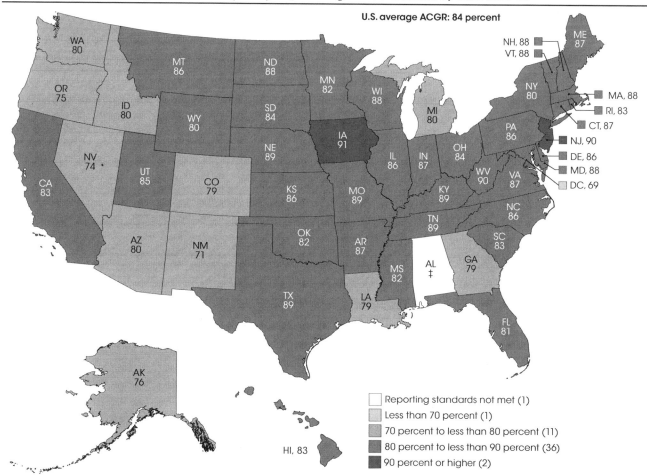

U.S. average ACGR: 84 percent

Reporting standards not met (1)

Less than 70 percent (1)

70 percent to less than 80 percent (11)

80 percent to less than 90 percent (36)

90 percent or higher (2)

‡ Reporting standards not met. The Alabama State Department of Education indicated that its ACGR data were misstated. For more information, please see the following press release issued by the state: https://www.alsde.edu/sec/comm/News%20Releases/12-08-2016%20Graduation%20Rate%20Review.pdf.
NOTE: The ACGR is the percentage of public high school freshmen who graduate with a regular diploma within 4 years of starting 9th grade. The Bureau of Indian Education and Puerto Rico were not included in the U.S. 4-year ACGR estimate. The graduation rates displayed above have been rounded to whole numbers. Categorizations are based on unrounded percentages.
SOURCE: U.S. Department of Education, Office of Elementary and Secondary Education, Consolidated State Performance Report, 2015–16. See *Digest of Education Statistics 2017*, table 219.46.

The ACGR increased over the first 6 years it was collected, from 79 percent in 2010–11 to 84 percent in 2015–16. In other words, more than four out of five 9th-graders in 2012–13 had completed high school within 4 years by 2015–16. In 2015–16, the state-level ACGRs ranged from 69 percent in the District of Columbia to 91 percent in Iowa.[1] More than two-thirds of states (36) reported graduation rates from 80 percent to less than 90 percent.[2]

Figure 2. Adjusted cohort graduation rate (ACGR) for public high school students, by race/ethnicity: 2015–16

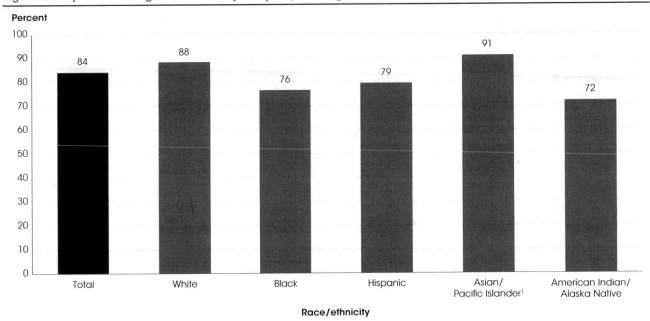

NOTE: The ACGR is the percentage of public high school freshmen who graduate with a regular diploma within 4 years of starting 9th grade. The Bureau of Indian Education and Puerto Rico were not included in the U.S. 4-year ACGR estimates. Race categories exclude persons of Hispanic ethnicity.
SOURCE: U.S. Department of Education, Office of Elementary and Secondary Education, Consolidated State Performance Report, 2015–16. See *Digest of Education Statistics 2017*, table 219.46.

In 2015–16, the ACGRs for American Indian/Alaska Native (72 percent), Black (76 percent), and Hispanic (79 percent) public high school students were below the national average of 84 percent. The ACGRs for White (88 percent) and Asian/Pacific Islander[3] (91 percent) students were above the national average. Across states, ACGRs for White students ranged from 76 percent in New Mexico to 94 percent in New Jersey, and were higher than the overall national ACGR of 84 percent in 35 states and the District of Columbia. The rates for Black students ranged from 57 percent in Nevada to 88 percent in West Virginia. Texas and West Virginia were the only two states in which the ACGR for Black students was higher than the overall national ACGR. The ACGRs for Hispanic students ranged from 65 percent in

Minnesota to 89 percent in Vermont and West Virginia, and were higher than the overall national ACGR in six states (Arkansas, Iowa, Maine, Texas, Vermont, and West Virginia). For Asian/Pacific Islander students, ACGRs ranged from 77 percent in the District of Columbia to 95 percent or higher in Maryland, New Jersey, Texas, and West Virginia,[4] and were higher than the overall national ACGR in 40 states. The ACGRs for American Indian/Alaska Native students ranged from 51 percent in South Dakota to 90 percent or higher in Delaware,[5] and were higher than the overall national ACGR in nine states (Arkansas, Connecticut, Delaware, Maine, Massachusetts, Mississippi, Missouri, Tennessee, and Texas).[6]

Figure 3. Adjusted cohort graduation rate (ACGR) of White and Black public high school students, by state: 2015–16

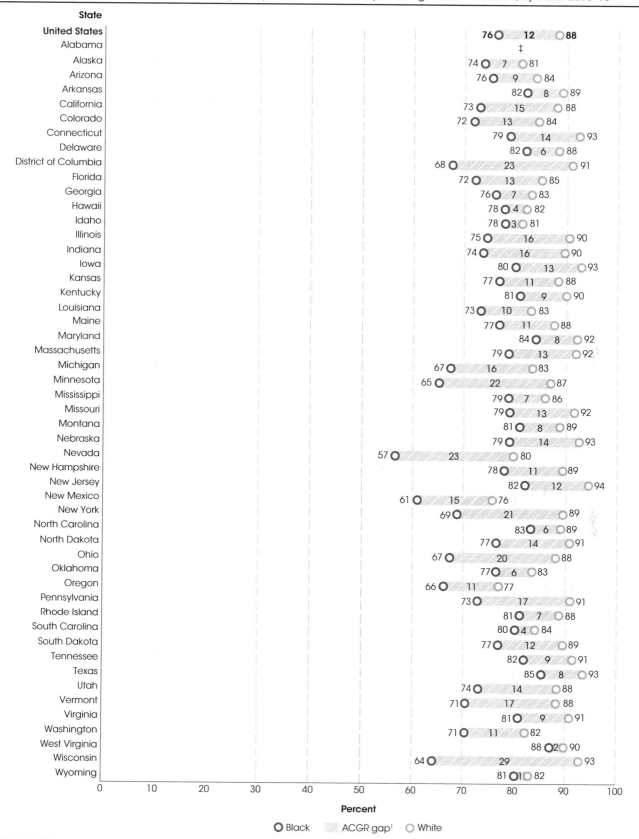

State	Black	ACGR gap[1]	White
United States	76	12	88
Alabama	‡		
Alaska	74	7	81
Arizona	76	9	84
Arkansas	82	8	89
California	73	15	88
Colorado	72	13	84
Connecticut	79	14	93
Delaware	82	6	88
District of Columbia	68	23	91
Florida	72	13	85
Georgia	76	7	83
Hawaii	78	4	82
Idaho	78	3	81
Illinois	75	16	90
Indiana	74	16	90
Iowa	80	13	93
Kansas	77	11	88
Kentucky	81	9	90
Louisiana	73	10	83
Maine	77	11	88
Maryland	84	8	92
Massachusetts	79	13	92
Michigan	67	16	83
Minnesota	65	22	87
Mississippi	79	7	86
Missouri	79	13	92
Montana	81	8	89
Nebraska	79	14	93
Nevada	57	23	80
New Hampshire	78	11	89
New Jersey	82	12	94
New Mexico	61	15	76
New York	69	21	89
North Carolina	83	6	89
North Dakota	77	14	91
Ohio	67	20	88
Oklahoma	77	6	83
Oregon	66	11	77
Pennsylvania	73	17	91
Rhode Island	81	7	88
South Carolina	80	4	84
South Dakota	77	12	89
Tennessee	82	9	91
Texas	85	8	93
Utah	74	14	88
Vermont	71	17	88
Virginia	81	9	91
Washington	71	11	82
West Virginia	88	2	90
Wisconsin	64	29	93
Wyoming	81	1	82

○ Black   ▨ ACGR gap[1]   ○ White

See notes on next page.

‡ Reporting standards not met. The Alabama State Department of Education indicated that its ACGR data were misstated. For more information, please see the following press release issued by the state: https://www.alsde.edu/sec/comm/News%20Releases/12-08-2016%20Graduation%20Rate%20Review.pdf.
[1] The graduation rate gaps were calculated using the most precise graduation rates available for public use, which include some rates rounded to one decimal place and some rates rounded to whole numbers. These gaps may vary slightly from those that would be calculated using unrounded rates.
NOTE: The ACGR is the percentage of public high school freshmen who graduate with a regular diploma within 4 years of starting 9th grade. The Bureau of Indian Education and Puerto Rico were not included in the U.S. 4-year ACGR estimate. Race categories exclude persons of Hispanic ethnicity.
SOURCE: U.S. Department of Education, Office of Elementary and Secondary Education, Consolidated State Performance Report, 2015–16. See *Digest of Education Statistics 2017*, table 219.46.

The national ACGR for White public high school students (88 percent) was 12 percentage points higher than the national ACGR for their Black peers (76 percent) in 2015–16.[7] White students had higher ACGRs than Black students in every state and the District of Columbia. The District of Columbia, Minnesota, Nevada, New York, Ohio, and Wisconsin reported the largest gaps between White and Black students. In each of these six jurisdictions, the ACGR for White students was at least 20 percentage points higher than the ACGR for Black students.

Figure 4.   Adjusted cohort graduation rate (ACGR) of White and Hispanic public high school students, by state: 2015–16

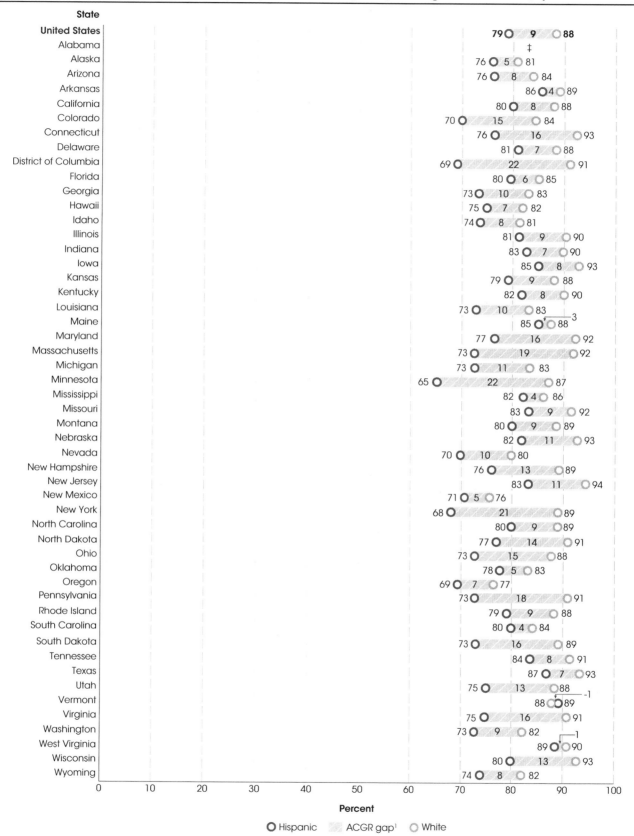

State

State	Hispanic	ACGR gap	White
United States	79	9	88
Alabama	‡		
Alaska	76	5	81
Arizona	76	8	84
Arkansas	86	4	89
California	80	8	88
Colorado	70	15	84
Connecticut	76	16	93
Delaware	81	7	88
District of Columbia	69	22	91
Florida	80	6	85
Georgia	73	10	83
Hawaii	75	7	82
Idaho	74	8	81
Illinois	81	9	90
Indiana	83	7	90
Iowa	85	8	93
Kansas	79	9	88
Kentucky	82	8	90
Louisiana	73	10	83
Maine	85		88	-3
Maryland	77	16	92
Massachusetts	73	19	92
Michigan	73	11	83
Minnesota	65	22	87
Mississippi	82	4	86
Missouri	83	9	92
Montana	80	9	89
Nebraska	82	11	93
Nevada	70	10	80
New Hampshire	76	13	89
New Jersey	83	11	94
New Mexico	71	5	76
New York	68	21	89
North Carolina	80	9	89
North Dakota	77	14	91
Ohio	73	15	88
Oklahoma	78	5	83
Oregon	69	7	77
Pennsylvania	73	18	91
Rhode Island	79	9	88
South Carolina	80	4	84
South Dakota	73	16	89
Tennessee	84	8	91
Texas	87	7	93
Utah	75	13	88
Vermont	88		89	-1
Virginia	75	16	91
Washington	73	9	82
West Virginia	89		90	-1
Wisconsin	80	13	93
Wyoming	74	8	82

Percent

○ Hispanic   ▨ ACGR gap[1]   ○ White

See notes on next page.

‡ Reporting standards not met. The Alabama State Department of Education indicated that its ACGR data were misstated. For more information, please see the following press release issued by the state: https://www.alsde.edu/sec/comm/News%20Releases/12-08-2016%20Graduation%20Rate%20Review.pdf.
[1] The graduation rate gaps were calculated using the most precise graduation rates available for public use, which include some rates rounded to one decimal place and some rates rounded to whole numbers. These gaps may vary slightly from those that would be calculated using unrounded rates.
NOTE: The ACGR is the percentage of public high school freshmen who graduate with a regular diploma within 4 years of starting 9th grade. The Bureau of Indian Education and Puerto Rico were not included in the U.S. 4-year ACGR estimate. Race categories exclude persons of Hispanic ethnicity.
SOURCE: U.S. Department of Education, Office of Elementary and Secondary Education, Consolidated State Performance Report, 2015–16. See *Digest of Education Statistics 2017*, table 219.46.

States reported similar gaps in ACGRs between White and Hispanic public high school students. The national ACGR for White students (88 percent) was 9 percentage points higher than the national ACGR for Hispanic students (79 percent) in 2015–16. The ACGRs for White students were higher than the ACGRs for Hispanic students in 48 states and the District of Columbia. The District of Columbia, Minnesota, and New York reported the largest gaps between White and Hispanic students. In each of these three jurisdictions, the ACGR for White students was at least 20 percentage points higher than the ACGR for Hispanic students. Vermont was the only state in which the ACGR for Hispanic students (89 percent) was higher than the ACGR for White students (88 percent).

Endnotes:

[1] Alabama's data, including data by racial/ethnic groups, are not included in this indicator. The Alabama State Department of Education indicated that its ACGR data were misstated. For more information, please see the following press release issued by the state: https://www.alsde.edu/sec/comm/News%20Releases/12-08-2016%20Graduation%20Rate%20Review.pdf.
[2] Based on unrounded graduation rates.
[3] Reporting practices for data on Asian and Pacific Islander students varied by state. Asian/Pacific Islander data in this indicator represent either the value reported by the state for the "Asian/Pacific Islander" group or an aggregation of separate values reported by the state for "Asian" and "Pacific Islander." "Pacific Islander" includes the "Filipino" group, which only California and Utah report separately.
[4] The ACGR for Asian/Pacific Islander students in West Virginia was greater than or equal to 95 percent. To protect student privacy, the exact value is not displayed.

[5] The ACGR for American Indian/Alaska Native students in Delaware was greater than or equal to 90 percent. To protect student privacy, the exact value is not displayed.
[6] Discussion of ACGRs for American Indian/Alaska Native students excludes data for three states (Vermont, Virginia, and West Virginia) and the District of Columbia. Data for the District of Columbia, Vermont, and West Virginia were suppressed to protect student privacy, and data for Virginia were unavailable.
[7] Percentage point gaps were calculated using the most precise graduation rates available for public use, which include some rates rounded to one decimal place and some rates rounded to whole numbers. These gaps may vary slightly from those that would be calculated using unrounded rates.

Reference tables: *Digest of Education Statistics 2017*, table 219.46

Related indicators and resources: Educational Attainment of Young Adults; High School Status Completion Rates [*Status and Trends in the Education of Racial and Ethnic Groups*]; Status Dropout Rates; *Trends in High School Dropout and Completion Rates in the United States*

Glossary: Adjusted cohort graduation rate (ACGR), Gap, High school completer, High school diploma, Public school or institution, Racial/ethnic group

This page intentionally left blank.

Status Dropout Rates

The overall status dropout rate decreased from 10.9 percent in 2000 to 6.1 percent in 2016. During this time, the Hispanic status dropout rate decreased by 19.2 percentage points, while the Black and White status dropout rates decreased by 6.9 and 1.7 percentage points, respectively. Nevertheless, in 2016 the Hispanic status dropout rate (8.6 percent) remained higher than the Black (6.2 percent) and White (5.2 percent) status dropout rates.

The *status dropout rate* represents the percentage of 16- to 24-year-olds (referred to as youth in this indicator) who are not enrolled in school and have not earned a high school credential (either a diploma or an equivalency credential such as a GED certificate). In this indicator, status dropout rates are estimated using both the Current Population Survey (CPS) and the American Community Survey (ACS). The CPS is a household survey that has been collected annually for decades, allowing for the analysis

of long-term trends, or changes over time, for the civilian, noninstitutionalized population. The ACS covers a broader population, including individuals living in households as well as individuals living in noninstitutionalized group quarters (such as college or military housing) and institutionalized group quarters (such as correctional or nursing facilities).[1] ACS data are available for fewer years than CPS data, but can provide detail on smaller demographic groups.

Figure 1. Status dropout rates of 16- to 24-year-olds, by sex: 2000 through 2016

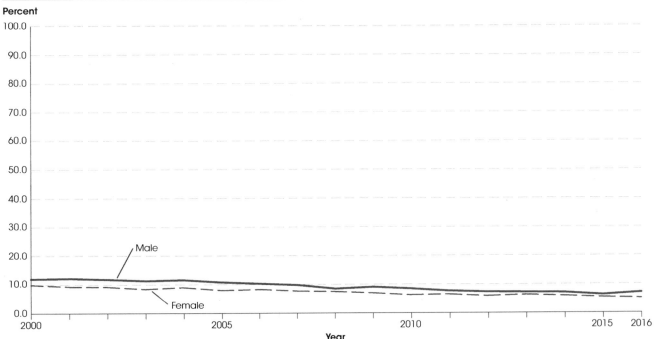

NOTE: The status dropout rate is the percentage of 16- to 24-year-olds who are not enrolled in school and have not earned a high school credential (either a diploma or an equivalency credential such as a GED certificate). Data are based on sample surveys of the civilian noninstitutionalized population, which excludes persons in the military and persons living in institutions (e.g., prisons or nursing facilities).
SOURCE: U.S. Department of Commerce, Census Bureau, Current Population Survey (CPS), October 2000 through 2016. See *Digest of Education Statistics 2017*, table 219.70.

Based on data from the CPS, the overall status dropout rate decreased from 10.9 percent in 2000 to 6.1 percent in 2016. More recently, from 2010 to 2016, the status dropout rate fell from 7.4 to 6.1 percent. Between 2000 and 2016, the male status dropout rate declined from 12.0 to 7.1 percent, and the female status dropout rate declined from 9.9 to 5.1 percent. The 2016 status dropout rate was 2.0 percentage points higher for male youth than for female youth.

Figure 2. Status dropout rates of 16- to 24-year-olds, by race/ethnicity: 2000 through 2016

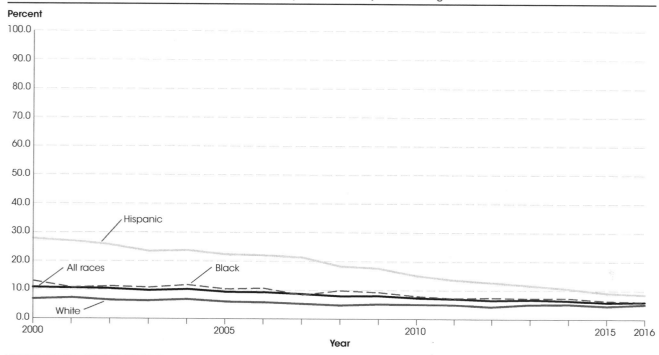

NOTE: The status dropout rate is the percentage of 16- to 24-year-olds who are not enrolled in school and have not earned a high school credential (either a diploma or an equivalency credential such as a GED certificate). Data are based on sample surveys of the civilian noninstitutionalized population, which excludes persons in the military and persons living in institutions (e.g., prisons or nursing facilities). Data for all races include other racial/ethnic categories not separately shown. Race categories exclude persons of Hispanic ethnicity.
SOURCE: U.S. Department of Commerce, Census Bureau, Current Population Survey (CPS), October 2000 through 2016. See *Digest of Education Statistics 2017*, table 219.70.

In each year from 2000 to 2016, the status dropout rates for White youth and Black youth were lower than the rate for Hispanic youth. During this time, the status dropout rate for White youth was also lower than the rate for Black youth in every year except 2016, when there was no measurable difference between the two rates. From 2000 to 2016, the status dropout rate declined from 6.9 to 5.2 percent for White youth, from 13.1 to 6.2 percent for Black youth, and from 27.8 to 8.6 percent for Hispanic youth. As a result, the gap between White and Black youth was 6.2 percentage points in 2000 but no longer statistically significant in 2016, and the gap between White and Hispanic youth narrowed from 20.9 percentage points in 2000 to 3.4 percentage points in 2016.

Figure 3.   Percentage distribution of status dropouts, by years of school completed: 2000 through 2016

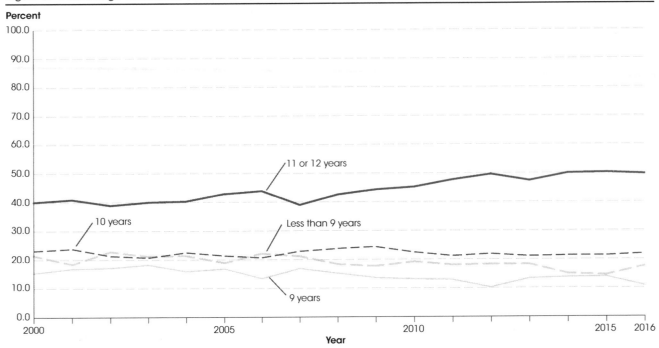

NOTE: Status dropouts are 16- to 24-year-olds who are not enrolled in school and have not earned a high school credential (either a diploma or an equivalency credential such as a GED certificate). Data are based on sample surveys of the civilian noninstitutionalized population, which excludes persons in the military and persons living in institutions (e.g., prisons or nursing facilities).
SOURCE: U.S. Department of Commerce, Census Bureau, Current Population Survey (CPS), October 2000 through 2016. See *Digest of Education Statistics 2017*, table 219.75.

The decline in the overall status dropout rate from 10.9 percent in 2000 to 6.1 percent in 2016 coincided with a shift in the distribution of years of school completed by status dropouts, as fewer status dropouts completed 9 years of schooling while more completed 11 or 12 years of schooling. The percentage of status dropouts with 9 years of schooling decreased from 15.3 percent in 2000 to 10.8 percent in 2016. Conversely, the percentage of status dropouts who had completed 11 or 12 years of schooling but did not receive a diploma or GED certificate increased from 40.0 percent in 2000 to 49.7 percent in 2016.

Based on data from the ACS, which covers a broader population than the CPS, the overall status dropout rate in 2016 was 5.8 percent. The status dropout rate was lower for individuals living in households and noninstitutionalized group quarters (5.5 percent) than for individuals living in institutionalized group quarters (33.7 percent).

According to data from the ACS, the status dropout rate varied by race/ethnicity in 2016. The status dropout rate was 2.0 percent for Asian youth, which was lower than the rates for White youth (4.5 percent) and youth of Two or more races (4.8 percent). The status dropout rates for these three groups were all lower than the rates for Pacific Islander (6.9 percent) and Black youth (7.0 percent), which were, in turn, lower than the rates for Hispanic (9.1 percent) and American Indian/Alaska Native youth (11.0 percent).

Figure 4. Status dropout rates of 16- to 24-year-olds, by race/ethnicity and nativity: 2016

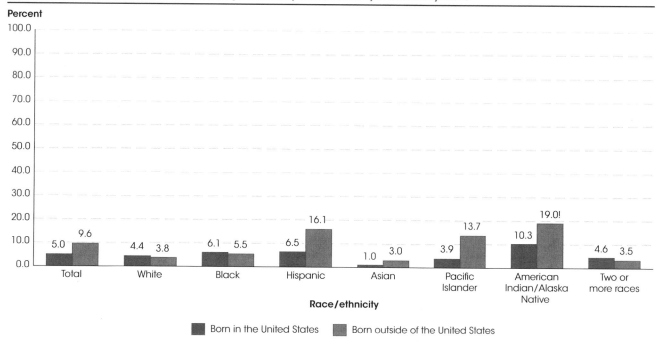

! Interpret data with caution. The coefficient of variation (CV) for this estimate is between 30 and 50 percent.
NOTE: This figure uses a different data source than figure 2; therefore, estimates are not directly comparable to the estimates in figure 2. United States refers to the 50 states, the District of Columbia, Puerto Rico, American Samoa, Guam, the U.S. Virgin Islands, and the Northern Marianas. The status dropout rate is the percentage of 16- to 24-year-olds who are not enrolled in school and have not earned a high school credential (either a diploma or an equivalency credential such as a GED certificate). Data are based on sample surveys of persons living in households and noninstitutionalized group quarters (such as college or military housing). Among those counted in noninstitutionalized group quarters in the American Community Survey, only the residents of military barracks are not counted in the civilian noninstitutionalized population in the Current Population Survey. Race categories exclude persons of Hispanic ethnicity.
SOURCE: U.S. Department of Commerce, Census Bureau, American Community Survey (ACS), 2016. See *Digest of Education Statistics 2017*, table 219.80.

Differences in status dropout rates between U.S.- and foreign-born youth[2] varied by race/ethnicity in 2016. Hispanic, Asian, and Pacific Islander youth born in the United States had lower status dropout rates than did their peers born outside of the United States. The status dropout rate was 6.5 percent for U.S.-born Hispanic youth versus 16.1 percent for foreign-born Hispanic youth. The status dropout rate was 1.0 percent for U.S.-born Asian youth versus 3.0 percent for their foreign-born peers. Similarly, the status dropout rate was 3.9 percent for U.S.-born Pacific Islander youth versus 13.7 percent for their foreign-born peers. There were no measurable differences in status dropout rates by nativity for White, Black, and American Indian/Alaska Native youth and for youth of Two or more races.

Endnotes:
[1] More specifically, institutional group quarters include adult and juvenile correctional facilities, nursing facilities, and other health care facilities. Noninstitutionalized group quarters include college and university housing, military quarters, facilities for workers and religious groups, and temporary shelters for the homeless.

[2] Includes youth living in households and noninstitutionalized group quarters. Excludes youth living in institutionalized group quarters.

Reference tables: *Digest of Education Statistics 2017*, tables 219.70, 219.75, and 219.80

Related indicators and resources: <u>Educational Attainment of Young Adults</u>; <u>High School Status Dropout Rates</u> [*Status and Trends in the Education of Racial and Ethnic Groups*]; <u>Public High School Graduation Rates</u>; <u>Snapshot: High School Status Dropout Rates for Racial/Ethnic Subgroups</u> [*Status and Trends in the Education of Racial and Ethnic Groups*]; <u>*Trends in High School Dropout and Completion Rates in the United States*</u>

Glossary: Gap, High school diploma, Household, Racial/ethnic group, Status dropout rate (Current Population Survey), Status dropout rate (American Community Survey)

Public School Revenue Sources

In school year 2014–15, elementary and secondary public school revenues totaled $664 billion in constant 2016–17 dollars. Of this total, 8 percent of revenues were from federal sources, 47 percent were from state sources, and 45 percent were from local sources.

In school year 2014–15, elementary and secondary public school revenues totaled $664 billion in constant 2016–17 dollars.[1] Of this total, 8 percent, or $56 billion, were from federal sources; 47 percent, or $309 billion, were from state sources; and 45 percent, or $299 billion, were from local sources.[2] In 2014–15, the percentages from each source differed across the states and the District of Columbia. For example, the percentages of total revenues coming from federal, state, and local sources in Illinois were 8 percent, 25 percent, and 67 percent, respectively, while the corresponding total revenues in Vermont were 6 percent, 90 percent, and 4 percent.

Total elementary and secondary public school revenues were 19 percent higher in 2014–15 than in 2000–01 ($664 billion vs. $556 billion, in constant 2016–17 dollars). During this time, total revenues rose from $556 billion in 2000–01 to $670 billion in 2007–08 and then fluctuated between 2007–08 and 2014–15. These changes were accompanied by a 7 percent increase in total elementary and secondary public school enrollment, from 47 million students in 2000–01 to 50 million students in 2014–15 (see indicator Elementary and Secondary Enrollment).

Figure 1. Revenues for public elementary and secondary schools, by revenue source: School years 2000–01 through 2014–15

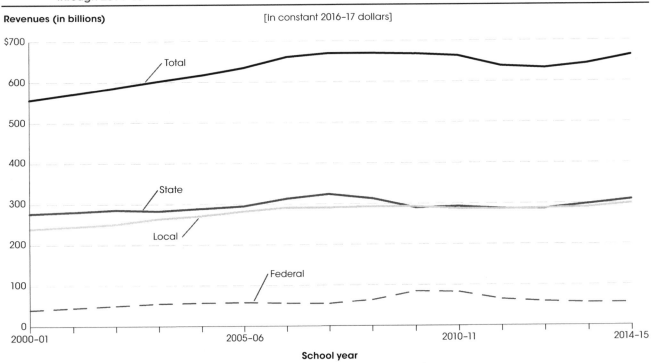

NOTE: Revenues are in constant 2016–17 dollars, adjusted using the Consumer Price Index (CPI). See *Digest of Education Statistics 2017*, table 106.70.
SOURCE: U.S. Department of Education, National Center for Education Statistics, Common Core of Data (CCD), "National Public Education Financial Survey," 2000–01 through 2014–15. See *Digest of Education Statistics 2017*, table 235.10.

Federal revenues were 111 percent higher in 2009–10, the year after the passage of the American Recovery and Reinvestment Act of 2009, than in 2000–01 ($85 billion vs. $40 billion). Federal revenues then decreased each year from 2009–10 through 2013–14 before increasing to $56 billion in 2014–15, which was 34 percent lower than in 2009–10. Local revenues increased by 25 percent, to $299 billion, from 2000–01 through 2014–15. State revenues fluctuated between $277 billion and $324 billion during this period, and were 12 percent higher in 2014–15 than in 2000–01 ($309 billion vs. $277 billion). During this period, federal revenues peaked in 2009–10 at $85 billion and state revenues peaked in 2007–08 at $324 billion. Local revenues were highest in 2014–15 at $299 billion.

Between school years 2000–01 and 2014–15, the percentage of total revenues coming from federal sources fluctuated between 7 and 13 percent, accounting for 7 percent of total revenues in 2000–01 and 8 percent in 2014–15. Local sources accounted for 45 percent of total revenues from 2011–12 through 2014–15, higher than their percentages during the 2000–01 to 2010–11 period. The percentage of total revenues coming from state sources decreased 3 percentage points between 2000–01 and 2014–15 (50 vs. 47 percent). Within the

2000–01 to 2014–15 period, the percentage of revenues coming from state sources was highest in 2000–01 (50 percent) and lowest in 2009–10 (43 percent).

More recently, from school year 2013–14 through school year 2014–15, total revenues for public elementary and secondary schools increased by $20 billion (3 percent) in constant 2016–17 dollars (from $644 billion to $664 billion). Federal revenues increased by $0.1 billion (less than 1 percent) from 2013–14 to 2014–15. State revenues increased by $11 billion (4 percent) from 2013–14 to 2014–15. Local revenues increased by $8.8 billion (3 percent), reflecting a $7.4 billion (3 percent) increase in revenues from local property taxes, a $1.8 billion (4 percent) increase in other local public revenues, and a $0.3 billion (3 percent) decrease in private revenues.[3]

In school year 2014–15, there were significant variations across the states in the percentages of public school revenues coming from state, local, and federal sources. In 23 states, at least half of education revenues came from state governments, while in 15 states and the District of Columbia at least half came from local revenues. In the remaining 12 states, no single revenue source made up more than half of education revenues.

Figure 2.   State revenues for public elementary and secondary schools as a percentage of total public school revenues, by state: School year 2014–15

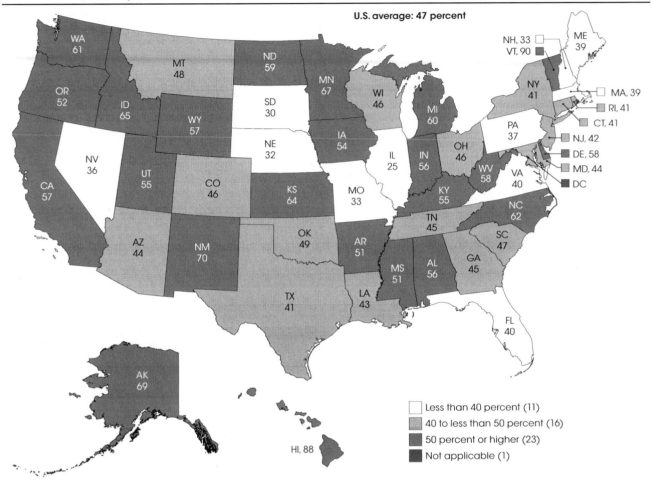

NOTE: All 50 states and the District of Columbia are included in the U.S. average, even though the District of Columbia does not receive any state revenue. The District of Columbia and Hawaii have only one school district each; therefore, the distinction between state and local revenue sources is not comparable to other states. Categorizations are based on unrounded percentages. Excludes revenues for state education agencies.
SOURCE: U.S. Department of Education, National Center for Education Statistics, Common Core of Data (CCD), "National Public Education Financial Survey," 2014–15. See *Digest of Education Statistics 2017*, table 235.20.

In school year 2014–15, the percentages of public school revenues coming from state sources were highest in Vermont and Hawaii (90 and 88 percent, respectively) and lowest in South Dakota and Illinois (30 and 25 percent, respectively). The percentages of revenues coming from federal sources were highest in South Dakota, Mississippi, and Louisiana (15 percent each), and lowest in Connecticut and New Jersey (4 percent each).

Among all states, the percentages of revenues coming from local sources were highest in Illinois and New Hampshire (67 and 61 percent, respectively), and lowest in Vermont and Hawaii (4 and 2 percent, respectively). Ninety percent of the revenues for the District of Columbia were from local sources; the remaining 10 percent were from federal sources.

Figure 3. Property tax revenues for public elementary and secondary schools as a percentage of total public school revenues, by state: School year 2014–15

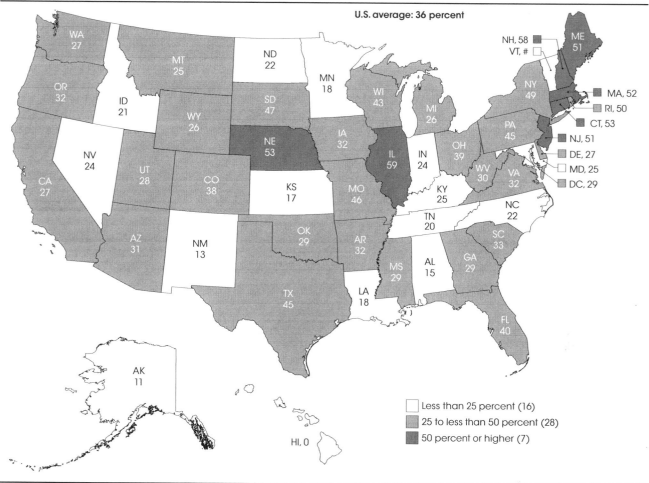

Rounds to zero.
NOTE: All 50 states and the District of Columbia are included in the U.S. average. The District of Columbia and Hawaii have only one school district each; therefore, the distinction between state and local revenue sources is not comparable to other states. Categorizations are based on unrounded percentages.
SOURCE: U.S. Department of Education, National Center for Education Statistics, Common Core of Data (CCD), "National Public Education Financial Survey," 2014–15. See *Digest of Education Statistics 2017*, table 235.20.

On a national basis in 2014–15, some $236 billion,[4] or 81 percent, of local revenues for public elementary and secondary school districts were derived from local property taxes. The percentages of total revenues from local property taxes differed by state. In 2014–15, Illinois and New Hampshire had the highest percentages of revenues from property taxes (59 and 58 percent, respectively). In Vermont, the percentage of revenues from local property taxes rounded to zero. Hawaii has only one school district, which received no funding from property taxes.

Endnotes:

[1] Revenues in this indicator are adjusted for inflation using the Consumer Price Index, or CPI. For this indicator, the CPI is adjusted to a school-year basis. The CPI is prepared by the Bureau of Labor Statistics, U.S. Department of Labor.
[2] Local revenues include revenues from such sources as local property and nonproperty taxes, investments, and student activities such as textbook sales, transportation and tuition fees, and food service revenues. Local revenues also include revenues from intermediate sources (education agencies with fundraising capabilities that operate between the state and local government levels).
[3] Private revenues consist of tuition and fees from patrons and revenues from gifts.
[4] In adjusted dollars.

Reference tables: *Digest of Education Statistics 2016,* table 203.20; *Digest of Education Statistics 2017,* tables 235.10 and 235.20

Related indicators and resources: <u>Public School Expenditures</u>

Glossary: Constant dollars, Consumer Price Index (CPI), Elementary school, Property tax, Public school or institution, Revenue, School district, Secondary school

Public School Expenditures

In 2014–15, public schools spent $11,734 per student on current expenditures, a category that includes salaries, employee benefits, purchased services, and supplies. Current expenditures per student were 15 percent higher in 2014–15 than in 2000–01, after adjusting for inflation. During this period, current expenditures per student peaked in 2008–09 at $11,914, and fluctuated between 2008–09 and 2014–15.

Total expenditures for public elementary and secondary schools in the United States in 2014–15 amounted to $668 billion, or $13,119 per public school student enrolled in the fall (in constant 2016–17 dollars).[1] Total expenditures included $11,734 per student in current expenditures, which includes salaries, employee benefits, purchased services, tuition, and supplies. Total expenditures also included $1,029 per student in capital outlay (expenditures for property and for buildings and alterations completed by school district staff or contractors) and $356 for interest on school debt.

Figure 1. Current expenditures, interest payments, and capital outlays per student in fall enrollment in public elementary and secondary schools, by type of expenditure: Selected years, 2000–01 through 2014–15

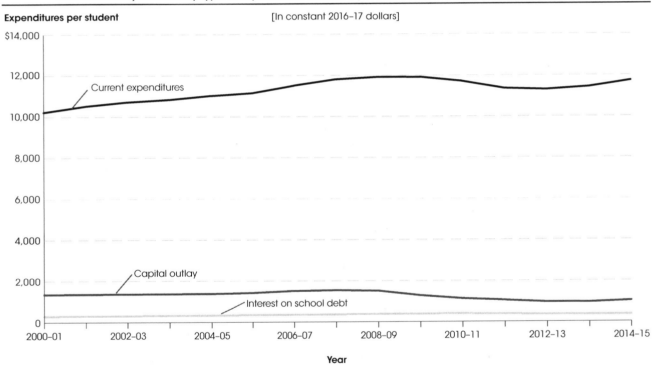

NOTE: "Current expenditures," "Capital outlay," and "Interest on school debt" are subcategories of total expenditures. Current expenditures include instruction, support services, food services, and enterprise operations (expenditures for operations funded by sales of products and services). Capital outlay includes expenditures for property and for buildings and alterations completed by school district staff or contractors. Expenditures are reported in constant 2016–17 dollars, based on the Consumer Price Index (CPI). Some data have been revised from previous figures. Excludes expenditures for state education agencies. SOURCE: U.S. Department of Education, National Center for Education Statistics, Common Core of Data (CCD), "National Public Education Financial Survey," 2000–01 through 2014–15; CCD, "State Nonfiscal Survey of Public Elementary/Secondary Education," 2005–06 through 2008–09. See *Digest of Education Statistics 2016*, table 203.20, and *Digest of Education Statistics 2017*, tables 236.10, 236.55, and 236.60.

Current expenditures per student enrolled in the fall in public elementary and secondary schools were 15 percent higher in 2014–15 than in 2000–01 ($11,734 vs. $10,228, both in constant 2016–17 dollars). Current expenditures per student increased between 2000–01 and 2008–09, peaking at $11,914 in 2008–09, and fluctuated between 2008–09 and 2014–15, reaching $11,734 in 2014–15.

Interest payments on school debt per student were 19 percent higher in 2014–15 than in 2000–01. Interest payments per student increased from $298 in 2000–01 to $398 in 2010–11, before declining to $356 in 2014–15 (all amounts in constant 2016–17 dollars). Capital outlay expenditures per student in 2014–15 ($1,029) were 24 percent lower than in 2000–01 ($1,353). Capital outlay expenditures per student were 17 percent lower in 2010–11 ($1,129) than in 2000–01 and a further 9 percent lower in 2014–15 than in 2010–11.

Figure 2. Percentage of current expenditures per student in fall enrollment in public elementary and secondary schools, by type of expenditure: 2000–01, 2010–11, and 2014–15

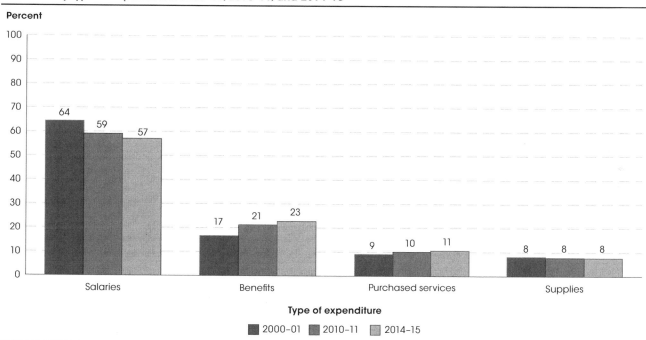

NOTE: "Salaries," "Benefits," "Purchased services," and "Supplies" are subcategories of current expenditures. Purchased services include expenditures for contracts for food, transportation, and janitorial services, and professional development for teachers. Supplies include expenditures for items ranging from books to heating oil. Two additional subcategories of expenditure, "Tuition" and "Other," are not included in this figure. Excludes expenditures for state education agencies.
SOURCE: U.S. Department of Education, National Center for Education Statistics, Common Core of Data (CCD), "National Public Education Financial Survey," 2000–01, 2010–11, and 2014–15. See *Digest of Education Statistics 2017*, table 236.60.

Current expenditures for education can be expressed in terms of the percentage of funds going toward salaries, benefits, purchased services, tuition, or supplies. On a national basis in 2014–15, approximately 80 percent of current expenditures were for salaries and benefits for staff, compared with 81 percent in 2000–01. There were, however, shifts within the distribution of salaries and benefits for staff, as the proportion of current expenditures for staff salaries decreased from 64 percent in 2000–01 to 57 percent in 2014–15, and the proportion of current expenditures for staff benefits increased from 17 to 23 percent during this period. Approximately 11 percent of current expenditures in 2014–15 were for purchased services, which include a wide variety of items, such as contracts for food, transportation, and janitorial services and for professional development for teachers. The percentage of the expenditure distribution going toward purchased services shifted only slightly from 2000–01 to 2014–15, increasing from 9 to 11 percent. Eight percent of school expenditures in 2014–15 were for supplies, ranging from books to heating oil. The percentage of current expenditures for supplies decreased less than 1 percentage point from 2000–01 to 2014–15.

Endnotes:
[1] Expenditures in this indicator are adjusted for inflation using the Consumer Price Index, or CPI. For this indicator, the CPI is adjusted to a school-year basis. The CPI is prepared by the Bureau of Labor Statistics, U.S. Department of Labor.

Reference tables: *Digest of Education Statistics 2016,* table 203.20; *Digest of Education Statistics 2017,* tables 236.10, 236.55, and 236.60

Related indicators and resources: Education Expenditures by Country; Public School Revenue Sources

Glossary: Capital outlay; Constant dollars; Consumer Price Index (CPI); Current expenditures (elementary/secondary); Elementary school; Expenditures per pupil; Expenditures, total; Interest on debt; Public school or institution; Salary; Secondary school

This page intentionally left blank.

The indicators in this chapter of *The Condition of Education* examine features of postsecondary education, many of which parallel those presented in the previous chapter on elementary and secondary education. The indicators describe enrollment, student characteristics, programs and courses of study, institutional financial resources, student costs, and degrees conferred.

Postsecondary education is characterized by diversity in both institutional and student characteristics. Postsecondary institutions vary by the types of degrees awarded, control (public or private), and whether they are operated on a nonprofit or for-profit basis. In addition, postsecondary institutions have distinctly different missions and provide students with a wide range of learning environments.

This chapter's indicators, as well as additional indicators on postsecondary education, are available at *The Condition of Education* website: http://nces.ed.gov/programs/coe.

Chapter 2

Postsecondary Education

Immediate College Enrollment Rate

The immediate college enrollment rate for high school completers increased from 63 percent in 2000 to 70 percent in 2016. The enrollment rate for those from high-income families (83 percent) was higher than the rate for those from low-income (67 percent) and middle-income families (64 percent) in 2016. The gap in enrollment rates between low- and high-income students narrowed from 30 percentage points in 2000 to 16 percentage points in 2016. The gap between low- and middle-income students was 12 percentage points in 2000, but there was no measurable gap between low- and middle-income students in 2016.

Of the 3.1 million recent high school completers[1] in 2016, some 2.2 million, or 70 percent, enrolled in college by the following October. The annual percentage of high school completers who enroll in 2- or 4-year colleges in the fall immediately following high school completion is known as the immediate college enrollment rate. The overall *immediate college enrollment rate* increased from 63 percent in 2000 to 70 percent in 2016, though the 2016 rate was not measurably different from that in 2010.

Figure 1. Percentage of high school completers who were enrolled in 2- or 4-year colleges by the October immediately following high school completion, by level of institution: 2000 through 2016

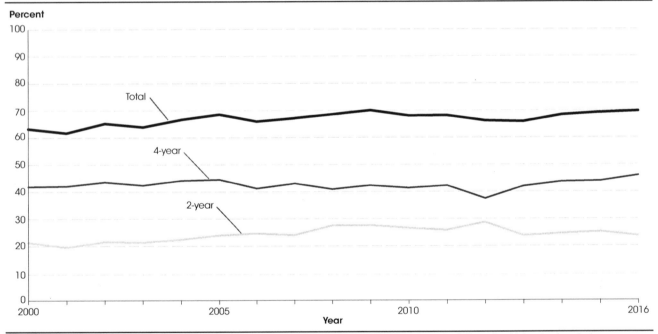

NOTE: High school completers are individuals ages 16 to 24 who graduated from high school or completed a GED or other high school equivalency credential prior to October of the calendar year.
SOURCE: U.S. Department of Commerce, Census Bureau, Current Population Survey (CPS), October Supplement, 2000 through 2016. See *Digest of Education Statistics 2017*, table 302.10.

Higher percentages of high school completers immediately enrolled in 4-year colleges than in 2-year colleges in every year from 2000 to 2016. In 2016, about 46 percent of high school completers enrolled in a 4-year college and 24 percent enrolled in a 2-year college. The immediate college enrollment rates for 4-year and for 2-year colleges in 2016 were not measurably different from 2000.

Figure 2. Percentage of high school completers who were enrolled in 2- or 4-year colleges by the October immediately following high school completion, by sex: 2000 through 2016

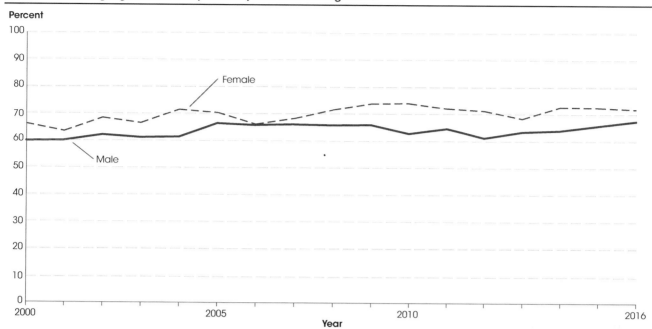

NOTE: High school completers are individuals ages 16 to 24 who graduated from high school or completed a GED or other high school equivalency credential prior to October of the calendar year.
SOURCE: U.S. Department of Commerce, Census Bureau, Current Population Survey (CPS), October Supplement, 2000 through 2016. See *Digest of Education Statistics 2017*, table 302.10.

In 2016, the overall immediate college enrollment rate for males (67 percent) was not measurably different from the rate for females (72 percent). From 2000 to 2016, the immediate college enrollment rate for males increased from 60 to 67 percent. The enrollment rate for females in 2016 was not measurably different from the rate in 2000. The immediate enrollment rates at 2-year colleges were not measurably different for males (25 percent) and females (22 percent). At 4-year colleges, the immediate college enrollment rate for females (50 percent) was higher than the rate for males (42 percent).

Figure 3. Percentage of high school completers who were enrolled in 2- or 4-year colleges by the October immediately following high school completion, by family income: 2000 through 2016

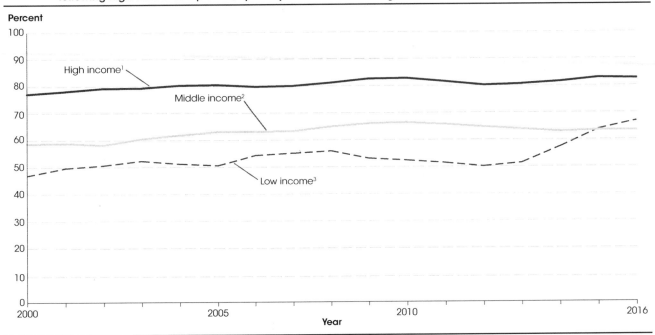

[1] High income refers to the top 20 percent of all family incomes.
[2] Middle income refers to the 60 percent in between the bottom 20 percent and the top 20 percent of all family incomes.
[3] Low income refers to the bottom 20 percent of all family incomes.
NOTE: High school completers are individuals ages 16 to 24 who graduated from high school or completed a GED or other high school equivalency credential prior to October of the calendar year. Due to some short-term data fluctuations associated with small sample sizes, percentages for income groups were calculated based on 3-year moving averages, except in 2016, when estimates were calculated based on a 2-year moving average (an average of 2015 and 2016).
SOURCE: U.S. Department of Commerce, Census Bureau, Current Population Survey (CPS), October Supplement, 2000 through 2016. See *Digest of Education Statistics 2017*, table 302.30.

In each year from 2000 to 2016, the immediate college enrollment rate for students[2] from high-income[3] families was higher than the rates for students from middle-income and low-income families.[4] In 2016, the immediate college enrollment rate for students from high-income families was 83 percent, compared with 64 percent for students from middle-income families and 67 percent for students from low-income families. In every year since 2000 except in 2015 and 2016, the enrollment rate for students from middle-income families was higher than the rate for students from low-income families.

The gap between the immediate college enrollment rates for students from high-income and low-income families narrowed between 2000 and 2016. The gap between the immediate college enrollment rates for students from high-income and low-income families was 14 percentage points smaller in 2016 (16 percentage points) than in 2000 (30 percentage points). However, the gap between the enrollment rates for students from high-income and middle-income families in 2016 (19 percentage points) was not measurably different from the gap in 2000.

Figure 4. Percentage of high school completers who were enrolled in 2- or 4-year colleges by the October immediately following high school completion, by race/ethnicity: 2000 through 2016

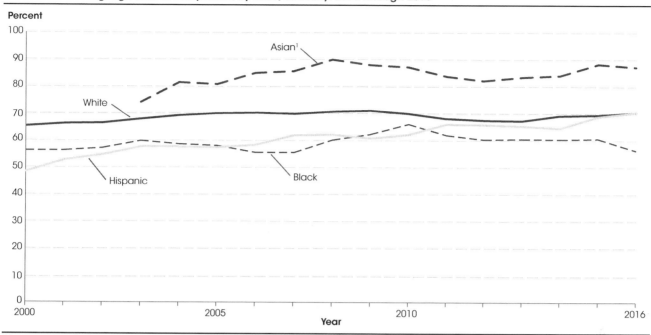

[1] The separate collection of data on Asian high school completers did not begin until 2003.
NOTE: High school completers are individuals ages 16 to 24 who graduated from high school or completed a GED or other high school equivalency credential prior to October of the calendar year. Due to some short-term data fluctuations associated with small sample sizes, percentages for racial/ethnic groups were calculated based on 3-year moving averages with the following exceptions: The percentages for 2016 were calculated based on a 2-year moving average (an average of 2015 and 2016), and the 2003 percentage for Asian high school completers was based on a 2-year moving average (an average of 2003 and 2004). From 2003 onward, data for White, Black, and Asian high school completers exclude persons identifying themselves as of Two or more races. Race categories exclude persons of Hispanic ethnicity.
SOURCE: U.S. Department of Commerce, Census Bureau, Current Population Survey (CPS), October Supplement, 2000 through 2016. See *Digest of Education Statistics 2017*, table 302.20.

The immediate college enrollment rate for White students was higher in 2016 (71 percent) than in 2000 (65 percent), as was the rate for Hispanic students (71 percent in 2016 and 49 percent in 2000). The enrollment rate for Asian students was also higher in 2016 (87 percent) than in 2003 (74 percent), when the collection of separate data on Asian students began.[5] The immediate college enrollment rate for Black students in 2016 (56 percent) was not measurably different from the rate in 2000.

The immediate college enrollment rate for White students was higher than that for Black students every year since 2000 except for 2010, when there was no measurable difference between their rates. Additionally, the immediate

college enrollment rate for White students was higher than that for Hispanic students from 2000 through 2010. In every year since 2011, there was no measurable difference between the immediate college enrollment rates for White and Hispanic students. The immediate college enrollment rate for Black students was higher than the rate for Hispanic students in 2000, not measurably different from the rate for Hispanic students in 2001 through 2014, and lower than the rate for Hispanic students in 2015 and 2016. The immediate college enrollment rate for Asian students was higher than the rates for Black students and Hispanic students every year since 2003. In addition, the enrollment rate for Asian students was higher than the rate for White students every year since 2004.

Endnotes:
[1] High school completers are individuals ages 16 to 24 who graduated from high school or completed a GED or other high school equivalency credential prior to October of the calendar year.
[2] The terms "high school completers" and "students" are used interchangeably throughout the indicator.
[3] High income refers to the top 20 percent of all family incomes, low income refers to the bottom 20 percent of all family incomes, and middle income refers to the 60 percent in between.

[4] Due to some short-term data fluctuations associated with small sample sizes, estimates for the income groups and racial/ethnic groups were calculated based on 3-year moving averages with the following exceptions: The percentages for 2016 were calculated based on a 2-year moving average (an average of 2015 and 2016), and the 2003 percentage for Asians was based on a 2-year moving average (an average of 2003 and 2004).
[5] Prior to 2003, data were collected for the combined race category of Asian/Pacific Islander.

Reference tables: *Digest of Education Statistics 2017*, tables 302.10, 302.20, and 302.30
Related indicators and resources: College Enrollment Rates; College Participation Rates [*Status and Trends in the Education of Racial and Ethnic Groups*]; Public High School Graduation Rates; Status Dropout Rates; Undergraduate Enrollment

Glossary: College, Enrollment, Gap, High school completer, Postsecondary institutions (basic classification by level), Racial/ethnic group

College Enrollment Rates

The overall college enrollment rate for young adults increased from 35 percent in 2000 to 41 percent in 2016. During this time period, the enrollment rate increased by 3 percentage points for White young adults, 6 percentage points for Black young adults, and 17 percentage points for Hispanic young adults. In 2016, the rate for White young adults (42 percent) was higher than the rate for Black young adults (36 percent), but not measurably different from the rate for Hispanic young adults (39 percent).

The college enrollment rate has increased since 2000. Different factors, such as changes in the labor market and the economy, may have contributed to this increase.[1,2] In this indicator, *college enrollment rate* is defined as the percentage of 18- to 24-year-olds (referred to as "young adults" in this indicator) enrolled as undergraduate or

graduate students in 2- or 4-year colleges. The Immediate College Enrollment Rate indicator, in contrast, presents data on the percentage of high school completers who enroll in 2- or 4-year colleges in the fall immediately following high school.

Figure 1. Enrollment rates of 18- to 24-year-olds in colleges, by level of institution: 2000 through 2016

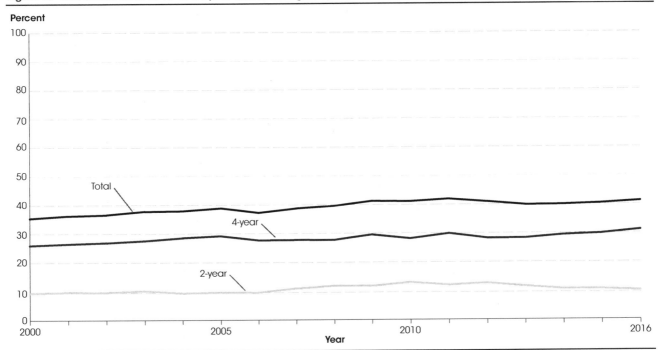

NOTE: Data are based on sample surveys of the civilian noninstitutionalized population.
SOURCE: U.S. Department of Commerce, Census Bureau, Current Population Survey (CPS), October Supplement, 2000 through 2016. See *Digest of Education Statistics 2017*, table 302.60.

The overall college enrollment rate for young adults increased from 35 percent in 2000 to 41 percent in 2016. During this period, the rate increased at 4-year institutions (from 26 to 31 percent) but did not change measurably at 2-year institutions. Over a more recent time period, the

overall college enrollment rate in 2010 was not measurably different from the rate in 2016, but the rate at 4-year institutions was lower in 2010 (28 percent) than in 2016 (31 percent), and the rate at 2-year institutions was higher in 2010 (13 percent) than in 2016 (10 percent).

Figure 2. Enrollment rates of 18- to 24-year-olds in colleges, by race/ethnicity: 2000, 2010, and 2016

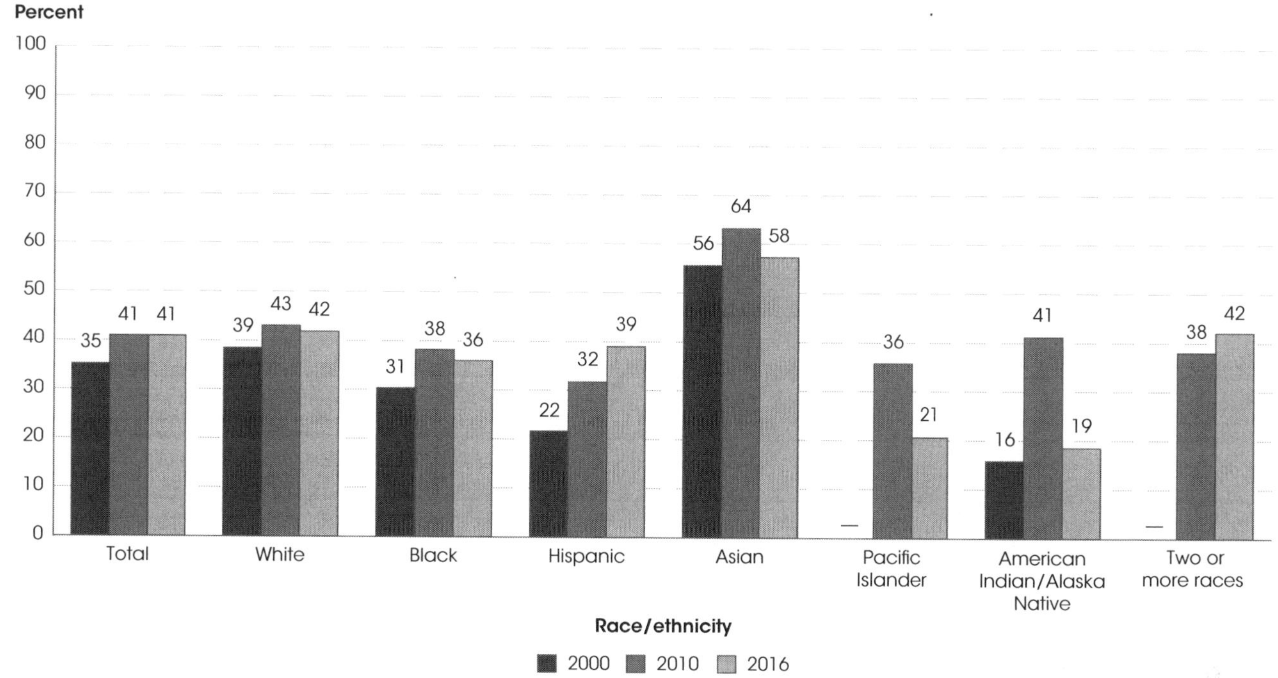

— Not available.
! Interpret data with caution. The coefficient of variation (CV) for this estimate is between 30 and 50 percent.
NOTE: Data are based on sample surveys of the civilian noninstitutionalized population. Separate data for Pacific Islanders and persons of Two or more races were not available in 2000. In 2000, data for individual race categories include persons of Two or more races. Prior to 2003, data for Asians include Pacific Islanders. Race categories exclude persons of Hispanic ethnicity.
SOURCE: U.S. Department of Commerce, Census Bureau, Current Population Survey (CPS), October Supplement, 2000, 2010, and 2016. See *Digest of Education Statistics 2017*, table 302.60.

From 2000 to 2016, college enrollment rates increased for White (from 39 to 42 percent), Black (from 31 to 36 percent), and Hispanic young adults (from 22 to 39 percent). The rates in 2016 were not measurably different from the rates in 2000 for Asian and American Indian/Alaska Native young adults.[3] More recently, college enrollment rates were higher in 2016 than in 2010 for Hispanic young adults (39 vs. 32 percent) and lower in 2016 than in 2010 for American Indian/Alaska Native young adults (19 vs. 41 percent). There was no measurable difference between the 2010 and 2016 college enrollment rates for White, Black, Asian, and Pacific Islander young adults and young adults of Two or more races.

In 2016, the college enrollment rate was higher for Asian young adults (58 percent) than for White (42 percent),

Black (36 percent), and Hispanic young adults (39 percent); and the rate for White young adults was higher than the rate for Black young adults. This pattern has held for every year since 2000. While the enrollment rate for White young adults was also higher than the rate for Hispanic young adults for every year between 2000 and 2015 (for example, 42 vs. 37 percent in 2015), there was no measurable difference between White and Hispanic enrollment rates in 2016. The 2016 enrollment rate was also higher for Asian young adults than for Pacific Islander young adults (21 percent), American Indian/Alaska Native young adults (19 percent), and young adults of Two or more races (42 percent).

Figure 3. Enrollment rates of 18- to 24-year-olds in colleges, by sex and race/ethnicity: 2000 and 2016

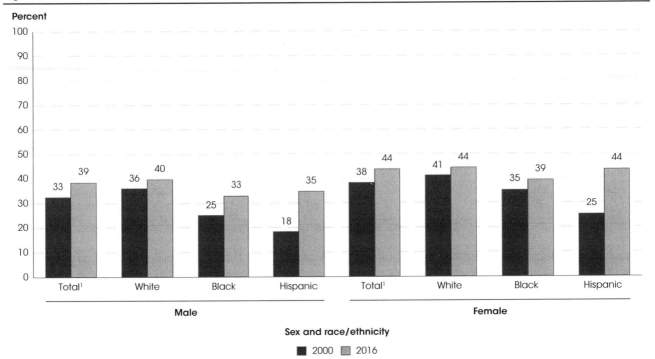

¹ Includes other racial/ethnic groups not shown separately.
NOTE: Data are based on sample surveys of the civilian noninstitutionalized population. In 2000, data for individual race categories include persons of Two or more races. Race categories exclude persons of Hispanic ethnicity.
SOURCE: U.S. Department of Commerce, Census Bureau, Current Population Survey (CPS), October Supplement, 2000 and 2016. See *Digest of Education Statistics 2017*, table 302.60.

Between 2000 and 2016, college enrollment rates increased overall for both young adult males (from 33 to 39 percent) and young adult females (from 38 to 44 percent). Among young adult males, enrollment rates were higher in 2016 than in 2000 for Whites (40 vs. 36 percent), Blacks (33 vs. 25 percent), and Hispanics (35 vs. 18 percent). Among young adult females, rates were also higher in 2016 than in 2000 for Whites (44 vs. 41 percent) and Hispanics (44 vs. 25 percent). The rate for Black young adult females in 2016 was not measurably different from the rate in 2000.

In every year since 2000, college enrollment rates for young adults were higher for females than for males. This pattern was observed for young adults overall and for White and Hispanic young adults specifically. For example, in 2016 the male-female gap in college enrollment rates was 5 percentage points for young adults overall, 5 percentage points for White young adults, and 9 percentage points for Hispanic young adults. Among Black young adults, the college enrollment rate was higher for females than for males in most years since 2000, except in 2007, 2012, 2015, and 2016, when the rates were not measurably different. While in 2000 the enrollment rate for Black females (35 percent) was 10 percentage points higher than the rate for Black males (25 percent), there was no measurable difference between the rates for Black females and Black males in 2016.

Endnotes:
¹ Fry, R. (2009). *College Enrollment Hits All-Time High, Fueled by Community College Surge.* Washington, DC: Pew Research Center. Retrieved May 3, 2017, from http://www.pewsocialtrends.org/2009/10/29/college-enrollment-hits-all-time-high-fueled-by-community-college-surge/.
² Brown, J.R., and Hoxby, C.M. (Eds.). (2014). *How the Financial Crisis and Great Recession Affected Higher Education.* Chicago: University of Chicago Press.

³ Separate data for Pacific Islanders and persons of Two or more races were not available in 2000. Prior to 2003, data for Asians include Pacific Islanders. Information from *Digest of Education Statistics 2016*, table 101.20, based on the Census Bureau Current Population Reports, indicates that 96 percent of all Asian/Pacific Islander 18- to 24-year-olds are Asian.

Reference tables: *Digest of Education Statistics 2017*, table 302.60
Related indicators and resources: College Participation Rates [*Status and Trends in the Education of Racial and Ethnic Groups*]; Immediate College Enrollment Rate; Snapshot: College Participation Rates for Racial/Ethnic Subgroups [*Status and Trends in the Education of Racial and Ethnic Groups*]; Undergraduate Enrollment

Glossary: College, Enrollment, Racial/ethnic group

This page intentionally left blank.

Indicator 2.3

Undergraduate Enrollment

Between 2000 and 2016, total undergraduate enrollment in degree-granting postsecondary institutions increased by 28 percent (from 13.2 million to 16.9 million students). By 2027, total undergraduate enrollment is projected to increase to 17.4 million students.

In fall 2016, total undergraduate enrollment in degree-granting postsecondary institutions was 16.9 million students, an increase of 28 percent from 2000, when enrollment was 13.2 million students. While total undergraduate enrollment increased by 37 percent between 2000 and 2010 (from 13.2 million to

18.1 million students), enrollment decreased by 7 percent between 2010 and 2016 (from 18.1 million to 16.9 million students). Undergraduate enrollment is projected to increase by 3 percent (from 16.9 million to 17.4 million students) between 2016 and 2027.

Figure 1. Actual and projected undergraduate enrollment in degree-granting postsecondary institutions, by sex: Fall 2000 through 2027

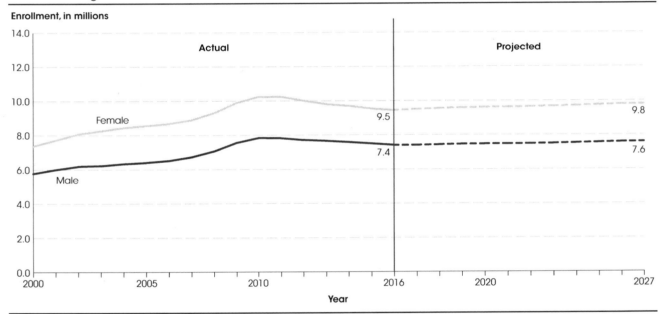

NOTE: Degree-granting institutions grant associate's or higher degrees and participate in Title IV federal financial aid programs. Projections are based on data through 2016. Some data have been revised from previously published figures.
SOURCE: U.S. Department of Education, National Center for Education Statistics, Integrated Postsecondary Education Data System (IPEDS), Spring 2001 through Spring 2017, Fall Enrollment component; and Enrollment in Degree-Granting Institutions Projection Model, 2000 through 2027. See *Digest of Education Statistics 2017*, table 303.70.

In fall 2016, female students made up 56 percent of total undergraduate enrollment (9.5 million students), and male students made up 44 percent (7.4 million students). Between 2000 and 2016, enrollment for both groups showed similar patterns of change: both female and male enrollment increased between 2000 and 2010 (by 39 percent and 36 percent, respectively) and then

decreased between 2010 and 2016 (by 8 percent and 5 percent, respectively). Between 2016 and 2027, female enrollment is projected to increase by 4 percent (from 9.5 million to 9.8 million students), and male enrollment is projected to increase by 2 percent (from 7.4 million to 7.6 million students).

Figure 2. Undergraduate enrollment in degree-granting postsecondary institutions, by race/ethnicity: Fall 2000 through 2016

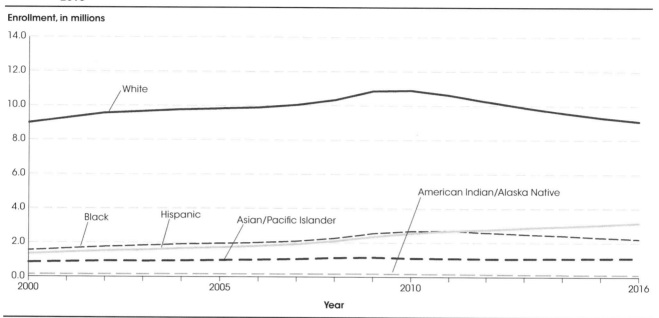

NOTE: Race categories exclude persons of Hispanic ethnicity. Degree-granting institutions grant associate's or higher degrees and participate in Title IV federal financial aid programs. Some data have been revised from previously published figures. Race/ethnicity categories exclude nonresident aliens.
SOURCE: U.S. Department of Education, National Center for Education Statistics, Integrated Postsecondary Education Data System (IPEDS), Spring 2001 through Spring 2017, Fall Enrollment component. See *Digest of Education Statistics 2005*, table 205; *Digest of Education Statistics 2009*, table 226; *Digest of Education Statistics 2015*, table 306.10; and *Digest of Education Statistics 2017*, table 306.10.

Of the 16.9 million undergraduate students in fall 2016, some 9.1 million were White, 3.2 million were Hispanic, 2.2 million were Black, 1.1 million were Asian/Pacific Islander, and 129,000 were American Indian/Alaska Native. Hispanic enrollment increased in each year between 2000 and 2016, more than doubling during this period (from 1.4 million to 3.2 million students, a 134 percent increase). In contrast, enrollment trends for other racial/ethnic groups varied over time. Between 2000 and 2010, Black enrollment increased by 73 percent (from 1.5 million to 2.7 million students), Asian/Pacific Islander enrollment increased by 29 percent (from 846,000 to 1.1 million students), American Indian/Alaska Native enrollment increased by 29 percent (from 139,000 to 179,000 students), and White enrollment increased by 21 percent (from 9.0 million to 10.9 million students). However, between 2010 and 2016, American Indian/Alaska Native enrollment decreased by 28 percent (from 179,000 to 129,000 students), Black enrollment decreased by 17 percent (from 2.7 million to 2.2 million students), White enrollment decreased by 17 percent (from 10.9 million to 9.1 million students), and Asian/Pacific Islander enrollment remained relatively unchanged (at 1.1 million students).

Figure 3. Actual and projected undergraduate enrollment in degree-granting postsecondary institutions, by attendance status: Fall 2000 through 2027

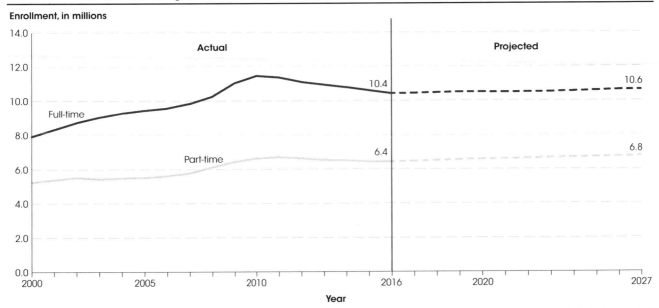

NOTE: Degree-granting institutions grant associate's or higher degrees and participate in Title IV federal financial aid programs. Projections are based on data through 2016. Some data have been revised from previously published figures.
SOURCE: U.S. Department of Education, National Center for Education Statistics, Integrated Postsecondary Education Data System (IPEDS), Spring 2001 through Spring 2017, Fall Enrollment component; and Enrollment in Degree-Granting Institutions Projection Model, 2000 through 2027. See *Digest of Education Statistics 2017*, table 303.70.

In fall 2016, there were 10.4 million full-time and 6.4 million part-time undergraduate students. Enrollment for both full- and part-time students has generally increased since 2000, particularly between 2000 and 2010, when full-time enrollment increased by 45 percent (from 7.9 million to 11.5 million students) and part-time enrollment increased by 27 percent (from 5.2 million to 6.6 million students). More recently, between 2010 and 2016, full-time enrollment decreased by 9 percent (from 11.5 million to 10.4 million students) and part-time enrollment decreased by 3 percent (from 6.6 million to 6.4 million students). Between 2016 and 2027, full-time enrollment is projected to increase by 2 percent (from 10.4 million to 10.6 million students) and part-time enrollment is projected to increase by 5 percent (from 6.4 million to 6.8 million students).

Figure 4. Undergraduate enrollment in degree-granting postsecondary institutions, by control of institution: Fall 2000 through 2016

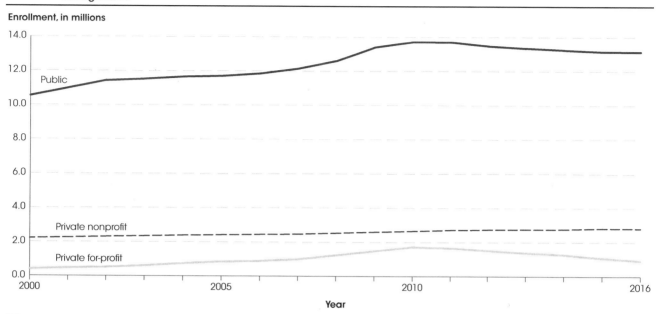

Enrollment, in millions

NOTE: Degree-granting institutions grant associate's or higher degrees and participate in Title IV federal financial aid programs. Some data have been revised from previously published figures.
SOURCE: U.S. Department of Education, National Center for Education Statistics, Integrated Postsecondary Education Data System (IPEDS), IPEDS Spring 2001 through Spring 2017, Fall Enrollment component. See *Digest of Education Statistics 2017*, table 303.70.

Between fall 2000 and fall 2016, undergraduate enrollment increased at a greater rate at private for-profit institutions (127 percent) than at private nonprofit institutions (27 percent) and public institutions (25 percent), although in 2000, undergraduate enrollment at private for-profit institutions was relatively small (at 403,000 students). From 2000 to 2010, enrollment at private for-profit institutions increased by 329 percent (from 403,000 to 1.7 million students). In comparison, enrollment increased by 30 percent at public institutions (from 10.5 million to 13.7 million students) and by

20 percent at private nonprofit institutions (from 2.2 million to 2.7 million students) during this period. However, after peaking in 2010, enrollment at private for-profit institutions decreased by 47 percent (from 1.7 million to 915,000 students) between 2010 and 2016. During this period, enrollment at public institutions decreased by 4 percent (from 13.7 million to 13.1 million students), while enrollment at private nonprofit institutions increased by 6 percent (from 2.7 million to 2.8 million students).

Figure 5. Actual and projected undergraduate enrollment in degree-granting postsecondary institutions, by level of institution: Fall 2000 through 2027

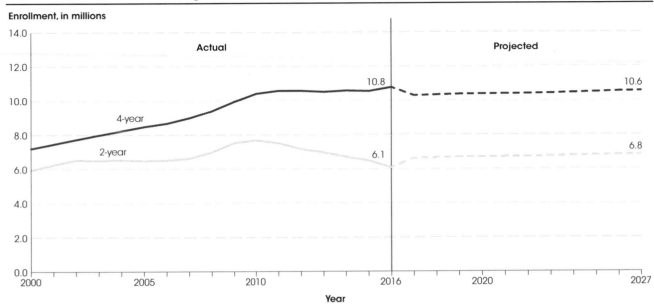

NOTE: Degree-granting institutions grant associate's or higher degrees and participate in Title IV federal financial aid programs. Projections are based on data through 2016. Some data have been revised from previously published figures.
SOURCE: U.S. Department of Education, National Center for Education Statistics, Integrated Postsecondary Education Data System (IPEDS), IPEDS Spring 2001 through Spring 2017, Fall Enrollment component; and Enrollment in Degree-Granting Institutions Projection Model, 2000 through 2027. See *Digest of Education Statistics 2017*, table 303.70.

In fall 2016, the 10.8 million students at 4-year institutions made up 64 percent of total undergraduate enrollment; the remaining 36 percent (6.1 million students) were enrolled at 2-year institutions. Between 2000 and 2010, enrollment increased by 44 percent at 4-year institutions (from 7.2 million to 10.4 million students) and by 29 percent at 2-year institutions (from 5.9 million to 7.7 million students). However, between 2010 and 2016, enrollment increased by

4 percent at 4-year institutions (from 10.4 million to 10.8 million students) and decreased by 21 percent at 2-year institutions (from 7.7 million to 6.1 million students).[1] Between 2016 and 2027, undergraduate enrollment at 2-year institutions is projected to increase by 12 percent (from 6.1 million to 6.8 million students), while enrollment at 4-year institutions is projected to be 2 percent lower in 2027 than in 2016 (10.6 million students compared with 10.8 million students).

Figure 6. Percentage of undergraduate students at degree-granting postsecondary institutions who enrolled exclusively in distance education courses, by level and control of institution: Fall 2016

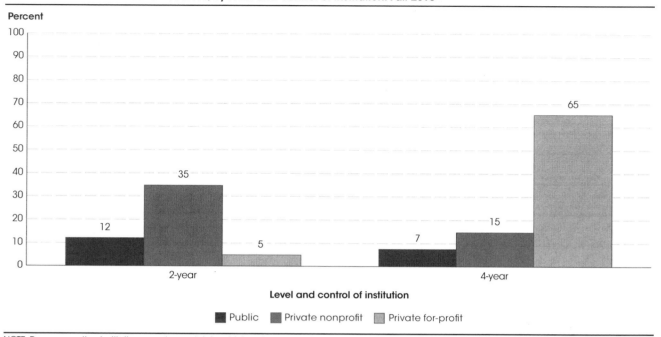

Level and control of institution

■ Public   ■ Private nonprofit   ▢ Private for-profit

NOTE: Degree-granting institutions grant associate's or higher degrees and participate in Title IV federal financial aid programs. Distance education uses one or more technologies to deliver instruction to students who are separated from the instructor as well as to support regular and substantive interaction between the student and the instructor synchronously or asynchronously. Technologies used for instruction may include the following: the Internet; one-way and two-way transmissions through open broadcasts, closed circuit, cable, microwave, broadband lines, fiber optics, satellite, or wireless communication devices; audio conferencing; and videocassettes, DVDs, and CD-ROMs, only if the videocassettes, DVDs, and CD-ROMs are used in a course in conjunction with the technologies listed above.
SOURCE: U.S. Department of Education, National Center for Education Statistics, Integrated Postsecondary Education Data System (IPEDS), Spring 2017, Fall Enrollment component. See *Digest of Education Statistics 2017*, table 311.15.

Distance education[2] courses and programs provide students with flexible learning opportunities. In fall 2016, nearly one-third of undergraduate students (5.2 million) participated in distance education, with 2.2 million students, or 13 percent of total undergraduate enrollment, exclusively taking distance education courses. Of the 2.2 million undergraduate students who exclusively took distance education courses, 1.3 million were enrolled at institutions located in the same state in which they resided, and 774,000 were enrolled at institutions in a different state.

The percentage of undergraduate students enrolled exclusively in distance education courses varied by institutional level and control. In fall 2016, the percentage of students at private for-profit institutions who exclusively

took distance education courses (52 percent) was more than three times that of students at private nonprofit institutions (15 percent) and more than five times that of students at public institutions (10 percent). In particular, the percentage of students at private for-profit 4-year institutions who exclusively took distance education courses (65 percent) is larger than the percentages of students at 2-year institutions who exclusively took distance education courses (percentages at these institutions ranged from 5 percent at private for-profit 2-year institutions to 35 percent at private nonprofit 2-year institutions) and also larger than the percentages of students at public 4-year institutions (7 percent) and private nonprofit 4-year institutions (15 percent) who exclusively took distance education courses.[3]

Endnotes:

[1] Some of the shift in enrollment patterns for 2-year and 4-year institutions between 2010 and 2016 may have been impacted by 2-year institutions beginning to offer 4-year programs, causing their classification to change. In 2016, some 499,000 undergraduate students were enrolled at 4-year institutions that in 2010 were classified as 2-year institutions.

[2] Distance education uses one or more technologies to deliver instruction to students who are separated from the instructor and to support regular and substantive interaction between the student and the instructor synchronously or asynchronously. Technologies used for instruction may include the following:

the Internet; one-way and two-way transmissions through open broadcasts, closed circuit, cable, microwave, broadband lines, fiber optics, satellite, or wireless communication devices; audio conferencing; and videocassettes, DVDs, and CD-ROMs, only if the videocassettes, DVDs, and CD-ROMs are used in a course in conjunction with the technologies listed above.

[3] The increase in comparison to fall 2015 in the percentage of students at nonprofit 2-year institutions who enrolled exclusively in distance education courses was related to one larger institution in which students primarily enroll in distance education.

Reference tables: *Digest of Education Statistics 2017*, tables 303.70, 306.10, and 311.15

Related indicators and resources: Characteristics of Degree-Granting Postsecondary Institutions; College Enrollment Rates; Differences in Postsecondary Enrollment Among Recent High School Completers [*The Condition of Education 2016 Spotlight*]; Immediate College Enrollment Rate; Postbaccalaureate Enrollment; STEM Degrees [*Status and Trends in the Education of Racial and Ethnic Groups*]; Undergraduate and Postbaccalaureate Enrollment [*Status and Trends in the Education of Racial and Ethnic Groups*]

Glossary: Control of institutions, Degree-granting institution, Distance education, Enrollment, Full-time enrollment, Part-time enrollment, Postsecondary institutions (basic classification by level), Private institution, Public school or institution, Racial/ethnic group, Undergraduate students

This page intentionally left blank.

Postbaccalaureate Enrollment

Between 2000 and 2016, total postbaccalaureate enrollment increased by 38 percent (from 2.2 million to 3.0 million students). By 2027, postbaccalaureate enrollment is projected to increase to 3.1 million students.

In fall 2016, some 3.0 million students were enrolled in postbaccalaureate degree programs. Postbaccalaureate degree programs include master's and doctoral programs, including professional doctoral programs such as law, medicine, and dentistry. Total postbaccalaureate enrollment increased by 36 percent between 2000 and 2010 (from 2.2 million to 2.9 million students) and was 1 percent higher in 2016 than in 2010 (3.0 million vs. 2.9 million students). Between 2016 and 2027, postbaccalaureate enrollment is projected to increase by 3 percent (from 3.0 million to 3.1 million students).

Figure 1.   Actual and projected postbaccalaureate enrollment in degree-granting postsecondary institutions, by sex: Fall 2000 through 2027

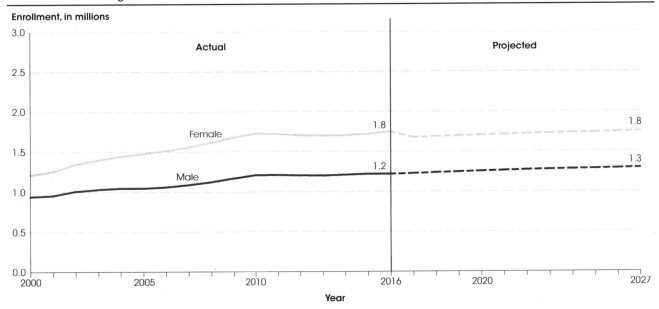

NOTE: Postbaccalaureate degree programs include master's and doctoral programs, including professional doctoral programs such as law, medicine, and dentistry. Degree-granting institutions grant associate's or higher degrees and participate in Title IV federal financial aid programs. Projections are based on data through 2016. Some data have been revised from previously published figures.
SOURCE: U.S. Department of Education, National Center for Education Statistics, Integrated Postsecondary Education Data System (IPEDS), Spring 2001 through Spring 2017, Fall Enrollment component; and Enrollment in Degree-Granting Institutions Projection Model, 2000 through 2027. See *Digest of Education Statistics 2017*, table 303.80.

In fall 2016, female students made up 59 percent of total postbaccalaureate enrollment (1.8 million students), and male students made up 41 percent (1.2 million students). Between 2000 and 2010, female enrollment increased by 42 percent, a faster increase than that observed for male enrollment (28 percent). In addition, both female and male postbaccalaureate enrollments were 1 percent higher in 2016 than in 2010. Between 2016 and 2027, however, male enrollment is projected to increase by 6 percent (from 1.2 million to 1.3 million students) whereas female enrollment is projected to remain relatively unchanged (at 1.8 million students).

Figure 2.   Postbaccalaureate enrollment in degree-granting postsecondary institutions, by race/ethnicity: Fall 2000 through 2016

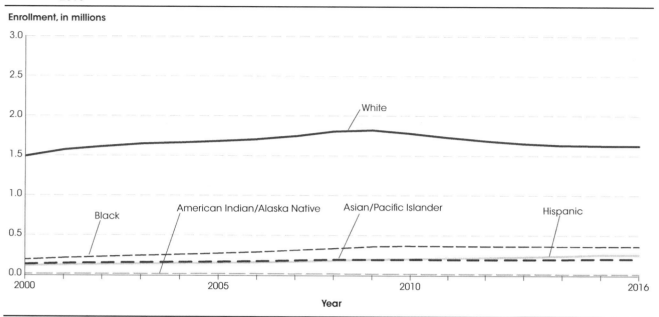

NOTE: Postbaccalaureate degree programs include master's and doctoral programs, including professional doctoral programs such as law, medicine, and dentistry. Race categories exclude persons of Hispanic ethnicity. Degree-granting institutions grant associate's or higher degrees and participate in Title IV federal financial aid programs. Some data have been revised from previously published figures. Race/ethnicity categories exclude nonresident aliens.
SOURCE: U.S. Department of Education, National Center for Education Statistics, Integrated Postsecondary Education Data System (IPEDS), IPEDS Spring 2001 through Spring 2017, Fall Enrollment component. See *Digest of Education Statistics 2005*, table 205; *Digest of Education Statistics 2009*, table 226; *Digest of Education Statistics 2015*, table 306.10; and *Digest of Education Statistics 2017*, table 306.10.

Of the 3.0 million postbaccalaureate students enrolled in fall 2016, some 1.6 million were White, 363,000 were Black, 260,000 were Hispanic, 206,000 were Asian/Pacific Islander, and 13,700 were American Indian/Alaska Native. Between 2000 and 2010, enrollments for all racial/ethnic groups increased: Black enrollment increased by 99 percent (from 181,000 to 362,000 students), Hispanic enrollment increased by 79 percent (from 111,000 to 198,000 students), Asian/Pacific Islander enrollment increased by 46 percent (from 133,000 to 194,000 students), American Indian/Alaska Native enrollment increased by 36 percent (from 12,600 to 17,100 students), and White enrollment increased by 23 percent (from 1.5 million to 1.8 million students). However, between 2010 and 2016, changes in enrollment for racial/ethnic groups varied. During this period,

White and American Indian/Alaska Native enrollment decreased by 11 percent (from 1.8 million to 1.6 million students) and 20 percent (from 17,100 to 13,700 students), respectively, while Hispanic and Asian/Pacific Islander enrollment increased by 31 percent (from 198,00 to 260,000 students) and 6 percent (from 194,000 to 206,000 students), respectively. Black enrollment remained relatively unchanged during this period (at 362,000 in 2010 and 363,000 in 2016). Overall, postbaccalaureate enrollment for each racial/ethnic group was higher in 2016 than in 2010. For example, between 2000 and 2016, enrollment doubled for Black students (from 181,000 to 363,000, an increase of 100 percent), and more than doubled for Hispanic students (from 111,000 to 260,000, an increase of 134 percent).

Figure 3. Percentage distribution of postbaccalaureate enrollment in degree-granting postsecondary institutions, by race/ethnicity: Fall 2000, fall 2010, and fall 2016

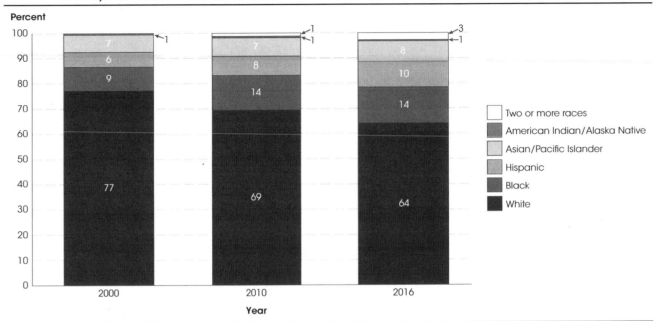

NOTE: Postbaccalaureate degree programs include master's and doctoral programs, including professional doctoral programs such as law, medicine, and dentistry. Data for students of Two or more races were unavailable for 2000. Race categories exclude persons of Hispanic ethnicity. Degree-granting institutions grant associate's or higher degrees and participate in Title IV federal financial aid programs. Race/ethnicity categories exclude nonresident aliens.
SOURCE: U.S. Department of Education, National Center for Education Statistics, Integrated Postsecondary Education Data System (IPEDS), IPEDS Spring 2017, Fall Enrollment component. See *Digest of Education Statistics 2017*, table 306.10.

The percentage distribution of postbaccalaureate students by race/ethnicity shifted between 2000, 2010, and 2016. The percentage of postbaccalaureate students who were White was lower in 2016 (64 percent) than in 2010 (69 percent) and 2000 (77 percent). The percentage of postbaccalaureate students who were Black was higher in 2010 and 2016 (14 percent in both years) than in 2000 (9 percent). The percentage who were Hispanic was higher in 2016 (10 percent) than in 2010 (8 percent) and 2000 (6 percent). In all 3 years, the percentage of postbaccalaureate students who were Asian/Pacific Islander was between 7 and 8 percent and the percentage who were American Indian/Alaska Native was 1 percent. The percentage who were of Two or more races was 3 percent in 2016 and 1 percent in 2010. Data for students of Two or more races were unavailable for 2000.

Figure 4. Actual and projected postbaccalaureate enrollment in degree-granting postsecondary institutions, by attendance status: Fall 2000 through 2027

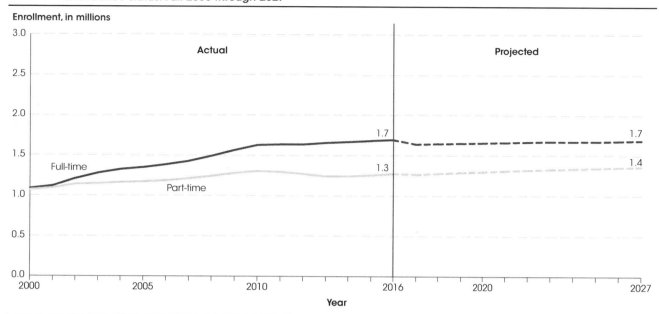

NOTE: Postbaccalaureate degree programs include master's and doctoral programs, including professional doctoral programs such as law, medicine, and dentistry. Degree-granting institutions grant associate's or higher degrees and participate in Title IV federal financial aid programs. Projections are based on data through 2016. Some data have been revised from previously published figures.
SOURCE: U.S. Department of Education, National Center for Education Statistics, Integrated Postsecondary Education Data System (IPEDS), IPEDS Spring 2001 through Spring 2017, Fall Enrollment component; and Enrollment in Degree-Granting Institutions Projection Model, 2000 through 2027. See *Digest of Education Statistics 2017*, table 303.80.

In fall 2016, there were 1.7 million full-time postbaccalaureate students and 1.3 million part-time postbaccalaureate students. Between 2000 and 2016, full-time enrollment increased at a faster rate (56 percent, from 1.1 million to 1.7 million students) than part-time enrollment (19 percent, from 1.1 million to 1.3 million students). Between 2000 and 2010, full-time enrollment increased by 50 percent (from 1.1 million to 1.6 million students), while part-time enrollment increased by 22 percent (from 1.1 million to 1.3 million students).

However, more recently, the pattern of postbaccalaureate enrollment has changed: in 2016, full-time enrollment was 4 percent higher than in 2010 (1.7 million vs. 1.6 million students), while part-time enrollment was 2 percent lower (1.31 million vs. 1.28 million students). Between 2016 and 2027, however, part-time enrollment is projected to increase by 7 percent (from 1.3 million to 1.4 million students), whereas full-time enrollment is projected to remain relatively unchanged (at 1.7 million students).

Figure 5. Postbaccalaureate enrollment in degree-granting postsecondary institutions, by control of institution: Fall 2000 through 2016

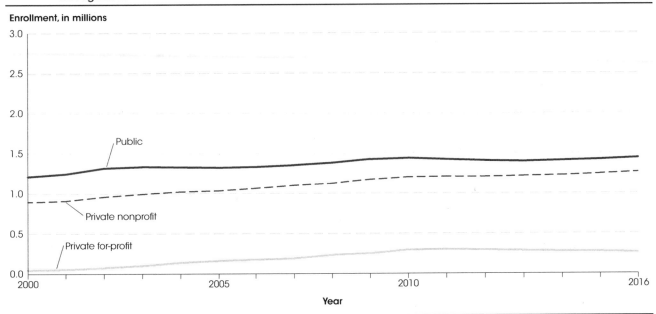

NOTE: Postbaccalaureate degree programs include master's and doctoral programs, including professional doctoral programs such as law, medicine, and dentistry. Degree-granting institutions grant associate's or higher degrees and participate in Title IV federal financial aid programs. Some data have been revised from previously published figures.
SOURCE: U.S. Department of Education, National Center for Education Statistics, Integrated Postsecondary Education Data System (IPEDS), Spring 2001 through Spring 2017, Fall Enrollment component. See *Digest of Education Statistics 2017*, table 303.80.

From fall 2000 to fall 2016, postbaccalaureate enrollment grew at a faster rate at private for-profit institutions (461 percent, from 47,200 to 265,000 students) than at private nonprofit institutions (41 percent, from 896,000 to 1.3 million students) and public institutions (19 percent, from 1.2 million to 1.4 million students). Between 2000 and 2010, postbaccalaureate enrollment increased by 528 percent (from 47,200 to 296,000 students) at private for-profit institutions, while it increased by 34 percent (from 896,000 to 1.2 million students) at private nonprofit institutions and by 19 percent (from 1.2 million to 1.4 million students) at public institutions. More recently, between 2010 and 2016, enrollment at private for-profit institutions decreased by 11 percent (from 296,000 to 265,000 students), while enrollment at private nonprofit institutions increased by 5 percent (from 1.2 million to 1.3 million students). Enrollment at public institutions remained relatively unchanged during this period (at 1.4 million students).

Figure 6. Percentage of postbaccalaureate students enrolled in degree-granting postsecondary institutions, by participation in distance education and control of institution: Fall 2016

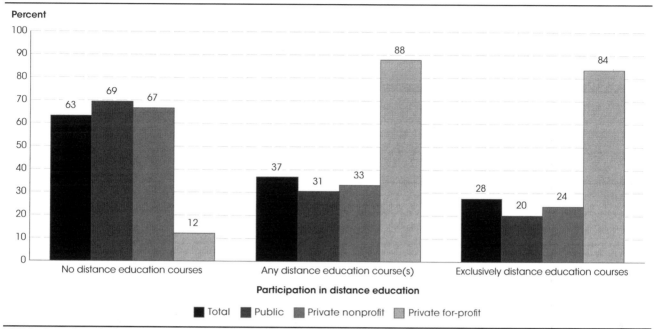

NOTE: Postbaccalaureate degree programs include master's and doctoral programs, including professional doctoral programs such as law, medicine, and dentistry. Distance education uses one or more technologies to deliver instruction to students who are separated from the instructor and to support regular and substantive interaction between the student and the instructor synchronously or asynchronously. Technologies used for instruction may include the following: the Internet; one-way and two-way transmissions through open broadcasts, closed circuit, cable, microwave, broadband lines, fiber optics, satellite, or wireless communication devices; audio conferencing; and videocassettes, DVDs, and CD-ROMs, only if the videocassettes, DVDs, and CD-ROMs are used in a course in conjunction with the technologies listed above. Degree-granting institutions grant associate's or higher degrees and participate in Title IV federal financial aid programs.
SOURCE: U.S. Department of Education, National Center for Education Statistics, Integrated Postsecondary Education Data System (IPEDS), Spring 2017, Fall Enrollment component. See *Digest of Education Statistics 2017*, table 311.15.

Distance education[1] courses and programs provide flexible learning opportunities to postbaccalaureate students. In fall 2016, more than one-third of total postbaccalaureate students (1.1 million) participated in distance education, with 819,000 students, or 28 percent of total postbaccalaureate enrollment, exclusively taking distance education courses.[2] Of the 819,000 students who exclusively took distance education courses, 350,000 were enrolled at institutions located in the same state in which they resided, and 440,000 were enrolled at institutions in a different state.

The percentage of postbaccalaureate students enrolled exclusively in distance education courses differed by institutional control. In fall 2016, the percentage of students at private for-profit institutions who exclusively took distance education courses (84 percent) was higher than that of students at private nonprofit (24 percent) and public (20 percent) institutions. The percentage of students who did not take any distance education courses was higher for those enrolled at public (69 percent) and private nonprofit (67 percent) institutions than for those at private for-profit institutions (12 percent).

Endnotes:

[1] Distance education uses one or more technologies to deliver instruction to students who are separated from the instructor and to support regular and substantive interaction between the student and the instructor synchronously or asynchronously. Technologies used for instruction may include the following: the Internet; one-way and two-way transmissions through open broadcasts, closed circuit, cable, microwave, broadband lines,

fiber optics, satellite, or wireless communication devices; audio conferencing; and videocassettes, DVDs, and CD-ROMs, only if the videocassettes, DVDs, and CD-ROMs are used in a course in conjunction with the technologies listed above.
[2] In comparison, 13 percent of undergraduate students exclusively took distance education courses. See indicator on Undergraduate Enrollment.

Reference tables: *Digest of Education Statistics 2017*, tables 303.80, 306.10, and 311.15

Related indicators and resources: Characteristics of Degree-Granting Postsecondary Institutions; Undergraduate and Postbaccalaureate Enrollment [*Status and Trends in the Education of Racial and Ethnic Groups*]; Trends in Student Loan Debt for Graduate School Completers; Undergraduate Enrollment

Glossary: Control of institutions, Distance education, Enrollment, Full-time enrollment, Part-time enrollment, Postbaccalaureate enrollment, Private institution, Public school or institution, Racial/ethnic group

Characteristics of Postsecondary Students

In fall 2015, some 77 percent of the 10.5 million undergraduate students at 4-year institutions were enrolled full time, compared with 39 percent of the 6.5 million undergraduate students at 2-year institutions.

In fall 2015,[1] there were 17.0 million undergraduate students and 2.9 million postbaccalaureate (graduate) students attending degree-granting postsecondary institutions in the United States.[2] The characteristics of students, such as their age and race or ethnicity, varied between public, private nonprofit, and private for-profit 2- and 4-year institutions in fall 2015.

Some 10.5 million undergraduate students (62 percent) attended 4-year institutions, and 6.5 million (38 percent) attended 2-year institutions. Of the undergraduate students at 4-year institutions, 8.1 million (77 percent) attended full time and 2.5 million (23 percent) attended part time. Of the undergraduate students at 2-year institutions, 2.5 million (39 percent) attended full time and 4.0 million (61 percent) attended part time.

Figure 1. Percentage of full-time undergraduate enrollment in degree-granting postsecondary institutions, by institutional level and control and student age: Fall 2015

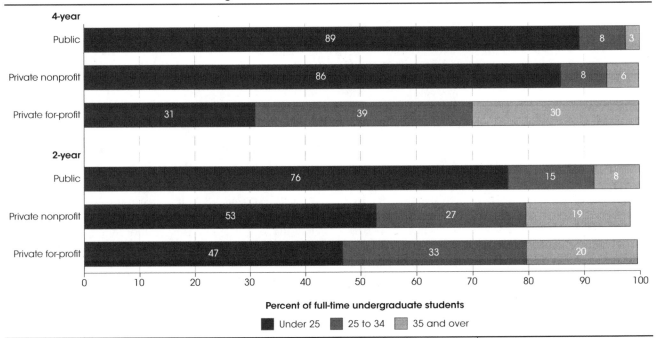

NOTE: Degree-granting institutions grant associate's or higher degrees and participate in Title IV federal financial aid programs. Detail may not sum to totals because of rounding and the exclusion of students whose ages were unknown.
SOURCE: U.S. Department of Education, National Center for Education Statistics, Integrated Postsecondary Education Data System (IPEDS), Spring 2016, Fall Enrollment component. See *Digest of Education Statistics 2016*, table 303.50.

At 4-year institutions, the percentage of full-time undergraduate students in fall 2015 who were under age 25 was higher at public institutions (89 percent) and private nonprofit institutions (86 percent) than at private for-profit institutions (31 percent). At both public and private nonprofit 4-year institutions, 8 percent of full-time undergraduate students were ages 25 to 34. In contrast, at private for-profit 4-year institutions, undergraduate students age 25 to 34 made up the largest age group of those enrolled full time (39 percent).

In 2015, the percentage of full-time undergraduates who were under age 25 was higher at public 2-year institutions (76 percent) than at private nonprofit (53 percent) and for-profit 2-year institutions (47 percent). On the other hand, lower percentages of full-time undergraduates were ages 35 and over at public 2-year institutions (8 percent) compared to private nonprofit (19 percent) and private for-profit (20 percent) 2-year institutions.

Figure 2.   Percentage of part-time undergraduate enrollment in degree-granting postsecondary institutions, by institutional level and control and student age: Fall 2015

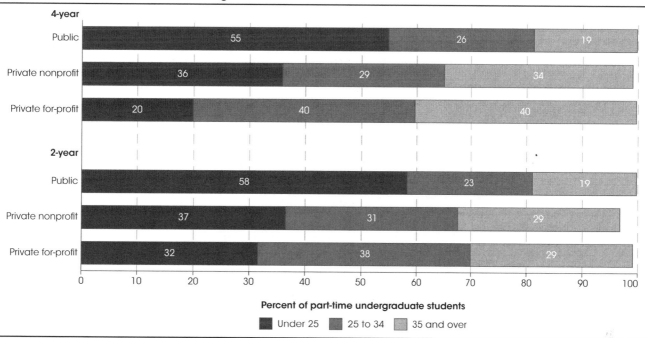

NOTE: Degree-granting institutions grant associate's or higher degrees and participate in Title IV federal financial aid programs. Detail may not sum to totals because of rounding and the exclusion of students whose ages were unknown.
SOURCE: U.S. Department of Education, National Center for Education Statistics, Integrated Postsecondary Education Data System (IPEDS), Spring 2016, Fall Enrollment component. See *Digest of Education Statistics 2016*, table 303.50.

At 4-year institutions, the percentage of part-time undergraduate students in fall 2015 who were under age 25 was higher at public institutions (55 percent) than at private nonprofit (36 percent) and for-profit institutions (20 percent). The percentage of part-time undergraduates who were ages 25 to 34 was lower at public (26 percent) and private nonprofit institutions (29 percent) than at for-profit institutions (40 percent). The percentage of part-time undergraduates who were ages 35 and over was lower at public institutions (19 percent) than at private nonprofit (34 percent) and private for-profit institutions (40 percent).

At 2-year institutions, the percentage of part-time students in fall 2015 who were under age 25 was higher at public institutions (58 percent) than at private nonprofit (37 percent) and private for-profit institutions (32 percent). The percentage of part-time students who were ages 25 to 34 was lower at public institutions (23 percent) than at private nonprofit (31 percent) and private for-profit institutions (38 percent). Similarly, the percentage of part-time students who were ages 35 and over was lower at public institutions (19 percent) than at private nonprofit and private for-profit institutions (29 percent each).

Figure 3. Percentage distribution of U.S. resident undergraduate enrollment in degree-granting postsecondary institutions, by institutional level and control and student race/ethnicity: Fall 2016

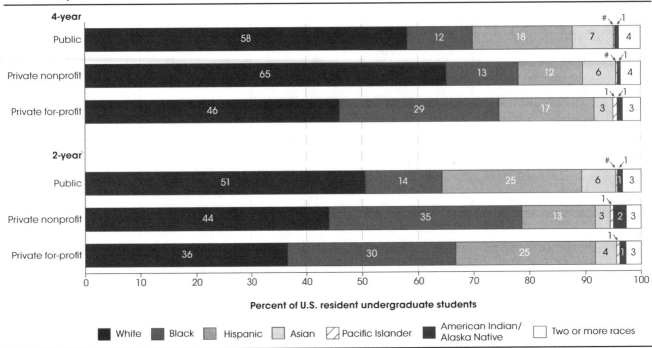

Percent of U.S. resident undergraduate students

Legend: ■ White ■ Black ■ Hispanic □ Asian ⬚ Pacific Islander ■ American Indian/Alaska Native □ Two or more races

Rounds to zero.
NOTE: Degree-granting institutions grant associate's or higher degrees and participate in Title IV federal financial aid programs. Race categories exclude persons of Hispanic ethnicity. Detail may not sum to totals because of rounding.
SOURCE: U.S. Department of Education, National Center for Education Statistics, Integrated Postsecondary Education Data System (IPEDS), Spring 2017, Fall Enrollment component. See *Digest of Education Statistics 2017*, table 306.50.

The distribution of U.S. resident undergraduate students (full and part time) by racial and ethnic groups varied among public, private nonprofit, and private for-profit institutions and between 2- and 4-year institutions.[3] Sixty-five percent of undergraduate students at private nonprofit 4-year institutions in 2016 were White, which was higher than the percentages of White students at public 4-year institutions (58 percent) and at private for-profit 4-year institutions (46 percent). The percentage of students at private for-profit 4-year institutions who were Black (29 percent) was more than twice as high as the percentages at private nonprofit (13 percent) and public 4-year institutions (12 percent). The percentages of students at public 4-year institutions and private for-profit 4-year institutions who were Hispanic (18 and 17 percent, respectively) were higher than the percentage at private nonprofit 4-year institutions (12 percent). The percentages of undergraduate students at public 4-year institutions and

private nonprofit 4-year institutions who were Asian (7 and 6 percent, respectively) were higher than the percentage at private for-profit 4-year institutions (3 percent).

In fall 2016, the percentages of both White and Asian U.S. resident undergraduate students at public 2-year institutions (51 and 6 percent, respectively) were higher than the corresponding percentages at private nonprofit 2-year institutions (44 and 3 percent, respectively) and at private for-profit 2-year institutions (36 and 4 percent, respectively). In contrast, the percentage of students at private nonprofit 2-year institutions who were Black (35 percent) was higher than the corresponding percentages at private for-profit 2-year institutions and public 2-year institutions (30 and 14 percent, respectively). A higher percentage of students at public and private for-profit 2-year institutions were Hispanic (both 25 percent) than at private nonprofit 2-year institutions (13 percent).

Figure 4. Percentage of full-time and part-time postbaccalaureate enrollment in degree-granting postsecondary institutions, by attendance status, institutional control, and student age: Fall 2015

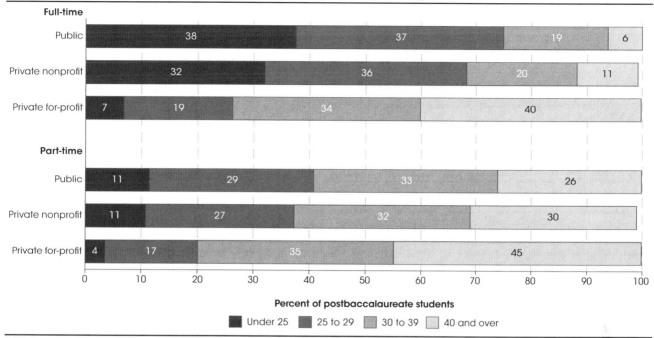

NOTE: Degree-granting institutions grant associate's or higher degrees and participate in Title IV federal financial aid programs. Detail may not sum to totals because of rounding and the exclusion of students whose ages were unknown.
SOURCE: U.S. Department of Education, National Center for Education Statistics, Integrated Postsecondary Education Data System (IPEDS), Spring 2016, Fall Enrollment component. See *Digest of Education Statistics 2016*, table 303.50.

In fall 2015, some 48 percent of all graduate students attended public institutions, 42 percent attended private nonprofit institutions, and 9 percent attended private for-profit institutions. The majority of full-time graduate students at public institutions were under age 30 (38 percent were under age 25 and 37 percent were ages 25 to 29); the same was true at private nonprofit institutions, where 32 percent were under age 25 and 36 percent were ages

25 to 29. In contrast, the majority of full-time graduate students at private for-profit institutions were older: 34 percent were ages 30 to 39 and 40 percent were ages 40 and over. Among part-time graduate students, 80 percent of students at private for-profit institutions were ages 30 and over, as were 62 percent at private nonprofit institutions and 59 percent at public institutions.

Figure 5. Percentage distribution of U.S. resident postbaccalaureate enrollment in degree-granting postsecondary institutions, by institutional control and student race/ethnicity: Fall 2016

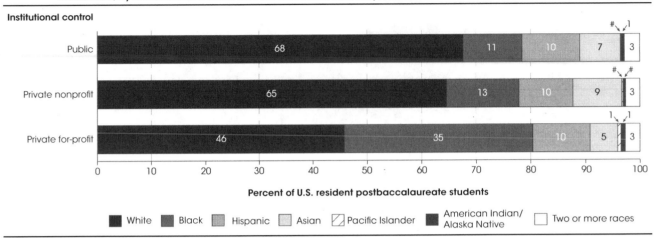

Institutional control

Percent of U.S. resident postbaccalaureate students

■ White   ■ Black   ■ Hispanic   ▢ Asian   ▨ Pacific Islander   ■ American Indian/ Alaska Native   ▢ Two or more races

Rounds to zero.
NOTE: Degree-granting institutions grant associate's or higher degrees and participate in Title IV federal financial aid programs. Race categories exclude persons of Hispanic ethnicity. Detail may not sum to totals because of rounding.
SOURCE: U.S. Department of Education, National Center for Education Statistics, Integrated Postsecondary Education Data System (IPEDS), Spring 2017, Fall Enrollment component. See *Digest of Education Statistics 2017*, table 306.50.

In fall 2016, approximately two-thirds of U.S. resident graduate students at both public and private nonprofit institutions were White, compared with less than one-half of students at private for-profit institutions. The percentage of graduate students who were Black was more than twice as high at private for-profit institutions (35 percent) as at private nonprofit institutions (13 percent) and public institutions (11 percent). Hispanic students accounted for 10 percent of graduate enrollment at each type of institution—public, private nonprofit, and private for-profit. Asian students accounted for 9 percent of graduate enrollment at private nonprofit institutions, 7 percent at public institutions, and 5 percent at private for-profit institutions.

Endnotes:

[1] 2015 is the most recent year available for enrollment data by age group. 2016 is the most recent year available for enrollment data by racial/ethnic group.
[2] For more information on how postsecondary enrollment has changed over time, see indicators Undergraduate Enrollment and Postbaccalaureate Enrollment.

[3] Throughout this indicator, comparisons by race/ethnicity exclude nonresident alien students.

Reference tables: *Digest of Education Statistics 2016*, tables 303.50 and 306.50; *Digest of Education Statistics 2017*, table 306.50
Related indicators and resources: Postbaccalaureate Enrollment; Undergraduate Enrollment

Glossary: College, Control of institutions, Enrollment, Full-time enrollment, Part-time enrollment, Postbaccalaureate enrollment, Postsecondary institutions (basic classification by level), Private institution, Public school or institution, Racial/ethnic group, Undergraduate students

This page intentionally left blank.

Characteristics of Degree-Granting Postsecondary Institutions

In academic year 2016–17, some 27 percent of 4-year institutions had open admissions policies (accepted all applicants), an additional 27 percent accepted three-quarters or more of their applicants, 32 percent accepted from one-half to less than three-quarters of their applicants, and 14 percent accepted less than one-half of their applicants.

In academic year 2016–17, there were 3,895 degree-granting institutions in the United States with first-year undergraduates: 2,395 were 4-year institutions offering programs at the bachelor's or higher degree level and 1,500 were 2-year institutions offering associate's degrees and other certificates. Some of the differences in characteristics of 2-year and 4-year institutions may be related to their differing institutional missions. The instructional missions of 2-year institutions generally focus on providing a range of career-oriented programs at the certificate and associate's degree levels and preparing students for transfer to 4-year institutions. Four-year

institutions tend to have a broad range of instructional programs at the undergraduate and graduate levels. Some 4-year institutions have a strong research focus. Degree-granting institutions may be governed by publicly appointed or elected officials, with major support from public funds (public control), or by privately elected or appointed officials, with major support from private sources (private control). Private institutions may be operated on a nonprofit or for-profit basis. All institutions in this analysis enroll first-year undergraduates in degree-granting programs.

Figure 1. Number of degree-granting institutions with first-year undergraduates, by level and control of institution: Academic years 2000–01, 2012–13, and 2016–17

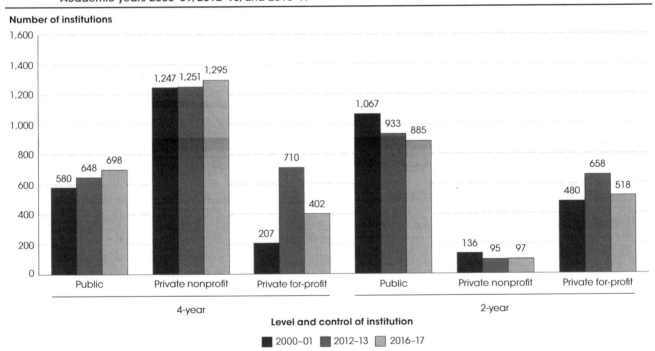

NOTE: Degree-granting institutions grant associate's or higher degrees and participate in Title IV federal financial aid programs. Excludes institutions not enrolling any first-time degree/certificate-seeking undergraduates.
SOURCE: U.S. Department of Education, National Center for Education Statistics, Integrated Postsecondary Education Data System (IPEDS), Fall 2000 and Fall 2012, Institutional Characteristics component; and Winter 2016–17, Admissions component. See *Digest of Education Statistics 2013*, table 305.30; and *Digest of Education Statistics 2017*, table 305.30.

In 2016–17, the number of public 4-year institutions (698) was 20 percent higher than in 2000–01 (580), and the number of private nonprofit 4-year institutions (1,295) was 4 percent higher than in 2000–01 (1,247). In contrast, there was fluctuation in the number of private for-profit 4-year institutions. Between 2000–01 and 2012–13, the number of private for-profit 4-year institutions more than tripled, from 207 to 710. After peaking in 2012–13, the number of private for-profit 4-year institutions declined by more than 40 percent to 402 in 2016–17. The number of private for-profit 4-year institutions in 2016–17 (402) was 94 percent higher than in 2000–01 (207).

The number of public 2-year institutions declined from 1,067 in 2000–01 to 933 in 2012–13 and subsequently to 885 in 2016–17. The number of private nonprofit 2-year institutions decreased from 136 in 2000–01 to 95 in 2012–13 and then fluctuated to 97 in 2016–17. The number of private for-profit 2-year institutions also fluctuated during this period, but not as widely as the number of private for-profit 4-year institutions. Between 2000–01 and 2012–13, the number of private for-profit 2-year institutions increased 37 percent from 480 to 658, and then declined 21 percent to 518 in 2016–17.

Figure 2. Percentage distribution of application acceptance rates at degree-granting institutions with first-year undergraduates, by level and control of institution: Academic year 2016–17

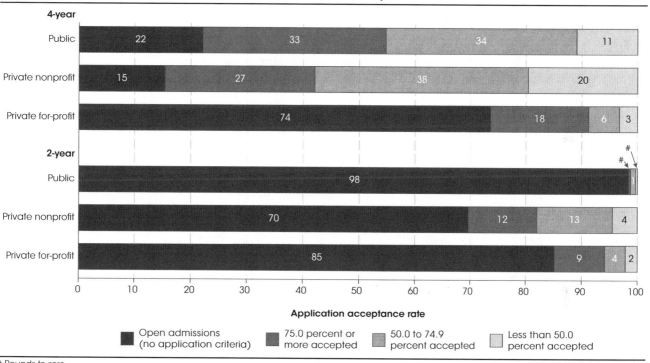

Rounds to zero.
NOTE: Degree-granting institutions grant associate's or higher degrees and participate in Title IV federal financial aid programs. Excludes institutions not enrolling any first-time degree/certificate-seeking undergraduates. Although rounded numbers are displayed, the figures are based on unrounded estimates. Detail may not sum to totals because of rounding.
SOURCE: U.S. Department of Education, National Center for Education Statistics, Integrated Postsecondary Education Data System (IPEDS), Winter 2016–17, Admissions component. See *Digest of Education Statistics 2017*, table 305.40.

Admissions policies varied among public, private nonprofit, and private for-profit institutions at both the 2-year and 4-year levels in 2016–17. For example, the percentage of 4-year institutions that had open admissions policies (i.e., accepted all applicants) ranged from 74 percent at private for-profit institutions to 22 percent at public institutions and 15 percent at private nonprofit institutions. Accordingly, a lower percentage of private for-profit 4-year institutions (3 percent) accepted less than one-half of their applicants than did private nonprofit (20 percent) and public (11 percent) 4-year institutions.

Most 2-year institutions (92 percent) had open admissions policies in 2016–17. Some 98 percent of public 2-year institutions and 85 percent of private for-profit 2-year institutions had open admissions policies, compared with 70 percent of private nonprofit 2-year institutions. A higher percentage of private nonprofit 2-year institutions were selective than public and private for-profit 2-year institutions. Four percent of private nonprofit 2-year institutions accepted less than one-half of their applicants, compared to less than 1 percent of public 2-year institutions and 2 percent of private for-profit 2-year institutions.

Figure 3. Number of 4-year degree-granting institutions, by classification and control of institution: Fall 2016

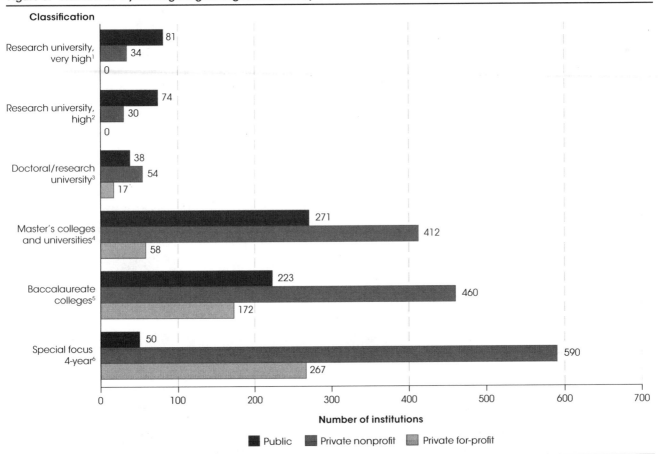

¹ Research universities with a very high level of research activity.
² Research universities with a high level of research activity.
³ Institutions that award at least 20 research/scholarship doctor's degrees per year but did not have a high level of research activity.
⁴ Institutions that award at least 50 master's degrees and fewer than 20 doctor's degrees per year.
⁵ Institutions that primarily emphasize undergraduate education. In addition to institutions that primarily award bachelor's degrees, also includes institutions classified as 4-year in the IPEDS system, but classified as 2-year baccalaureate/associate's colleges in the Carnegie Classification system because they primarily award associate's degrees.
⁶ Institutions that award degrees primarily in single fields of study, such as medicine, business, fine arts, theology, and engineering.
NOTE: Institutions with no enrollment reported separately from the enrollment of an associated main campus are excluded. Degree-granting institutions grant associate's or higher degrees and participate in Title IV federal financial aid programs. Relative levels of research activity for research universities were determined by an analysis of research and development expenditures, science and engineering research staffing, and doctoral degrees conferred, by field. Further information on the research index ranking may be obtained from http://carnegieclassifications.iu.edu/.
SOURCE: U.S. Department of Education, National Center for Education Statistics, Integrated Postsecondary Education Data System (IPEDS), Spring 2017, Fall Enrollment component. See *Digest of Education Statistics 2017*, table 317.40.

Another way to classify institutions beyond level (2-year vs. 4-year) and control (public vs. private) is by Carnegie Classification, which takes into account such considerations as the types of degrees offered, as well as institutional mission. Institutions that confer 4-year or higher degrees are classified in four broad categories: doctoral and research universities (institutions that award at least 20 research/scholarship doctor's degrees per year); master's colleges and universities (institutions that award at least 50 master's and fewer than 20 doctor's degrees per year); baccalaureate colleges¹ (institutions that have at least one baccalaureate degree program and primarily emphasize undergraduate education); and special focus 4-year institutions (those that award degrees primarily in single fields or related fields of study, such as medicine,

business, fine arts, theology, and engineering, at both the undergraduate and graduate levels).

In 2016–17, there were more than twice as many baccalaureate colleges (855) and master's colleges and universities (741) as doctoral universities (328). Doctoral universities are further classified into one of three categories based on level of research activity. Among the 328 doctoral universities, 219 were classified as research institutions with a very high (115) or high (104) level of research activity. The remaining 109 institutions awarded at least 20 doctor's degrees per year, but did not have a high level of research activity. There were 907 special focus 4-year institutions in 2016–17.

Among public 4-year institutions, there were more doctoral (193), master's (271), and baccalaureate institutions (223) than special focus institutions (50) in 2016–17. Among private nonprofit and private for-profit institutions, on the other hand, the number of special focus institutions was higher than the number of doctoral, master's, and baccalaureate institutions. Among private nonprofit 4-year institutions, there were 590 special focus, 118 doctoral, 412 master's, and 460 baccalaureate institutions; among private for-profit 4-year institutions, there were 267 special focus, 17 doctoral, 58 master's, and 172 baccalaureate institutions.

Figure 4. Number of 2-year degree-granting institutions, by classification and control of institution: Fall 2016

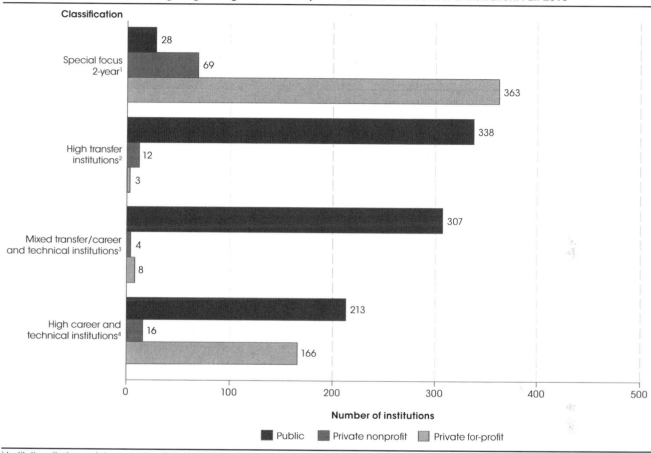

[1] Institutions that award degrees primarily in single fields of study, such as medicine, business, fine arts, theology, and engineering.
[2] Institutions that award less than 30 percent of their awards in career and technical programs.
[3] Institutions that award 30 to 49 percent of their awards in career and technical programs.
[4] Institutions that award 50 percent or more of their awards in career and technical programs.
NOTE: Degree-granting institutions grant associate's or higher degrees and participate in Title IV federal financial aid programs.
SOURCE: U.S. Department of Education, National Center for Education Statistics, Integrated Postsecondary Education Data System (IPEDS), Spring 2017, Fall Enrollment component. See *Digest of Education Statistics 2017*, table 317.40.

Two-year institutions that conferred associate's degrees as the highest degree-level offering are further divided into subcategories according to program focus (i.e., high transfer, high career and technical, mixed transfer/career and technical, and special focus 2-year). Most public institutions were categorized as high transfer (338 institutions), mixed transfer/career and technical (307 institutions) or high career and technical institutions (213 institutions). Only 28 public 2-year institutions were classified as special focus institutions. In contrast, roughly two-thirds of private nonprofit and private for-profit institutions were classified as special focus institutions. Among private nonprofit institutions, there were 69 special focus institutions, 12 high transfer institutions, 4 mixed transfer/career and technical institutions, and 16 high career and technical institutions. Among private for-profit institutions, there were 363 special focus institutions, 3 high transfer institutions, 8 mixed transfer/career and technical institutions, and 166 high career and technical institutions.

Historically Black colleges and universities (HBCUs) are degree-granting institutions established prior to 1964 with the principal mission of educating Black Americans. In 2016–17, there were 102 4-year and 2-year degree-granting HBCUs in operation—51 were public institutions and 51 were private nonprofit institutions. Other institutions serving specific populations in 2016 included 38 colleges and universities identified by the Women's College Coalition as women's colleges and 35 tribal colleges, which are members of the American Indian Higher Education Consortium. With few exceptions, tribal colleges are tribally controlled and located on reservations. About three-quarters of the 35 tribally controlled institutions in operation in 2016–17 were public institutions.

In addition, for fiscal year 2016 the U.S. Department of Education categorized 415 institutions as eligible Hispanic-Serving Institutions. These institutions are eligible to apply for a number of grant programs through the Hispanic-Serving Institutions Division in the Department's Office of Postsecondary Education. Eligible institutions meet various program criteria and have at least 25 percent Hispanic student enrollment.[2]

Endnotes:

[1] In addition to institutions that primarily award bachelor's degrees, also includes institutions classified as 4-year in the IPEDS system, but classified as 2-year baccalaureate/associate's colleges in the Carnegie Classification system because they primarily award associate's degrees.

[2] For more information on Hispanic-Serving Institutions, including a list of eligible Hispanic-Serving Institutions for fiscal year 2016, please see https://www2.ed.gov/about/offices/list/ope/idues/hsidivision.html.

Reference tables: *Digest of Education Statistics 2013,* table 305.30; *Digest of Education Statistics 2017,* tables 305.30, 305.40, 312.30, 312.50, 313.10, and 317.40

Related indicators and resources: Characteristics of Postsecondary Faculty; Postbaccalaureate Enrollment; Postsecondary Institution Expenses; Postsecondary Institution Revenues; Undergraduate Enrollment

Glossary: Associate's degree, Bachelor's degree, Control of institutions, Degree-granting institution, Doctor's degree, Historically Black colleges and universities, Master's degree, Postsecondary education, Postsecondary institutions (basic classification by level), Private institution, Public school or institution, Undergraduate students

This page intentionally left blank.

Characteristics of Postsecondary Faculty

From fall 1999 to fall 2016, the number of faculty in degree-granting postsecondary institutions increased by 51 percent (from 1.0 to 1.5 million). The number of full-time faculty increased by 38 percent over this period, while the number of part-time faculty increased by 74 percent between 1999 and 2011, and then decreased by 4 percent between 2011 and 2016.

In fall 2016, of the 1.5 million faculty in degree-granting postsecondary institutions, 53 percent were full time and 47 percent were part time. Faculty include professors, associate professors, assistant professors, instructors, lecturers, assisting professors, adjunct professors, and interim professors.

Figure 1. Number of faculty in degree-granting postsecondary institutions, by employment status: Selected years, fall 1999 through fall 2016

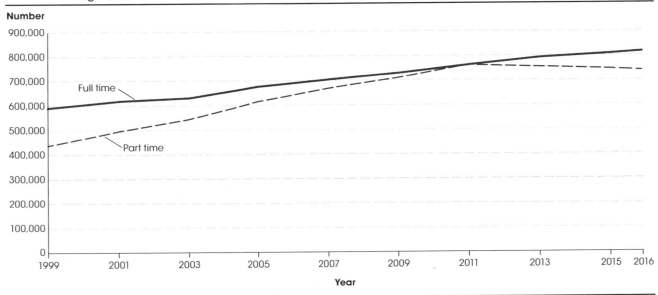

NOTE: Includes faculty members with the title of professor, associate professor, assistant professor, instructor, lecturer, assisting professor, adjunct professor, or interim professor (or the equivalent). Excludes graduate students with titles such as graduate or teaching fellow who assist senior faculty. Degree-granting institutions grant associate's or higher degrees and participate in Title IV federal financial aid programs. Beginning in 2007, includes institutions with fewer than 15 full-time employees; these institutions did not report staff data prior to 2007. Some data have been revised from previously published figures. SOURCE: U.S. Department of Education, National Center for Education Statistics, Integrated Postsecondary Education Data System (IPEDS), "Fall Staff Survey" (IPEDS-S:99); IPEDS Winter 2001–02 through Winter 2004–05, Fall Staff survey; IPEDS Winter 2005–06 through Winter 2011–12, Human Resources component, Fall Staff section; and IPEDS Spring 2013 through Spring 2017, Human Resources component. See *Digest of Education Statistics 2017,* table 315.10.

From fall 1999 to fall 2016, the total number of faculty in degree-granting postsecondary institutions increased by 51 percent (from 1.0 to 1.5 million). The number of full-time faculty increased by 38 percent (from 591,000 to 816,000) from fall 1999 to fall 2016, an increase of 29 percent from fall 1999 to fall 2011 and 7 percent from fall 2011 to fall 2016. In comparison, the number of part-time faculty increased by 74 percent (from 437,000 to 762,000) between 1999 and 2011, and then decreased by 4 percent (from 762,000 to 733,000) between 2011 and 2016. As a result of the faster increase in the number of part-time faculty, the percentage of all faculty who were part time increased from 43 to 47 percent between 1999 and 2016. The percentage of all faculty who were female increased from 41 percent in 1999 to 49 percent in 2016.

Although the number of faculty increased in degree-granting public, private nonprofit, and private for-profit postsecondary institutions between fall 1999 and fall 2016, the percentage increases in faculty were much smaller in public institutions and private nonprofit institutions than in private for-profit institutions. Over this period, the number of faculty increased by 37 percent (from 713,000 to 977,000) in public institutions, by 68 percent (from 285,000 to 477,000) in private nonprofit institutions, and by 218 percent (from 30,000 to 95,000) in private for-profit institutions. Despite the faster growth in the number of faculty in private for-profit institutions over this period, only 6 percent of all faculty were employed by private for-profit institutions in 2016, while 63 percent were employed by public institutions and 31 percent by private nonprofit institutions.

The ratio of full-time-equivalent (FTE) students to faculty in degree-granting postsecondary institutions was 14:1 in 2016. The FTE student-to-faculty ratio was higher in private for-profit institutions (21:1) and public 2-year institutions (19:1) than in public 4-year institutions (14:1) and private nonprofit 4-year institutions (10:1).[1] For more information about how student enrollments have changed over time, see the indicator Undergraduate Enrollment.

Figure 2. Percentage distribution of full-time faculty in degree-granting postsecondary institutions, by academic rank, race/ethnicity, and sex: Fall 2016

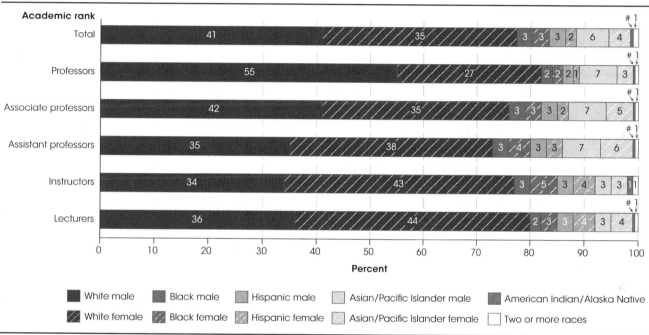

Rounds to zero.
NOTE: Sex breakouts excluded for faculty who were American Indian/Alaska Native and of Two or more races because the percentages were 1 percent or less. Degree-granting institutions grant associate's or higher degrees and participate in Title IV federal financial aid programs. Race categories exclude persons of Hispanic ethnicity. Estimates are based on full-time faculty whose race/ethnicity was known. Detail may not sum to 100 percent due to rounding. Although rounded numbers are displayed, figures are based on unrounded percentages.
SOURCE: U.S. Department of Education, National Center for Education Statistics, Integrated Postsecondary Education Data System (IPEDS), IPEDS Spring 2017, Human Resources component. See Digest of Education Statistics 2017, table 315.20.

Of all full-time faculty in degree-granting postsecondary institutions in fall 2016, 41 percent were White males; 35 percent were White females; 6 percent were Asian/Pacific Islander males; 4 percent were Asian/Pacific Islander females; 3 percent each were Black males, Black females, and Hispanic males; and 2 percent were Hispanic females.[2] Those who were American Indian/Alaska Native and those who were of Two or more races each made up 1 percent or less of full-time faculty in these institutions.

The racial and ethnic and sex distribution of faculty varied by academic rank. For example, among full-time professors, 55 percent were White males, 27 percent were White females, 7 percent were Asian/Pacific Islander males, and 3 percent were Asian/Pacific Islander females. Black males, Black females, and Hispanic males each accounted for 2 percent of full-time professors. The following groups each made up 1 percent or less of the total number of full-time professors: Hispanic females, American Indian/Alaska Native individuals, and individuals of Two or more races. In comparison, among full-time assistant professors, 35 percent were White males, 38 percent were White females, 7 percent were Asian/Pacific Islander males, 6 percent were Asian/Pacific Islander females, and 4 percent were Black females. Black males, Hispanic males, and Hispanic females each accounted for 3 percent of full-time assistant professors, while American Indian/Alaska Native individuals and individuals of Two or more races each made up 1 percent or less of the total number of full-time assistant professors.

Figure 3. Average salary of full-time instructional faculty on 9-month contracts in degree-granting postsecondary institutions, by academic rank: Selected years, 1999–2000 through 2016–17

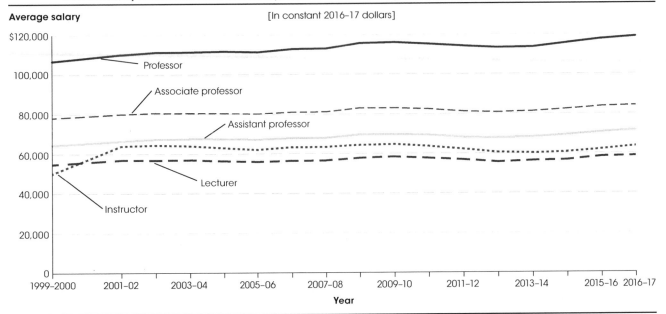

NOTE: Data for academic year 2000–01 are not available. Degree-granting institutions grant associate's or higher degrees and participate in Title IV federal financial aid programs. Beginning in 2007, includes institutions with fewer than 15 full-time employees; these institutions did not report staff data prior to 2007. Data exclude instructional faculty at medical schools. Salaries are reported in constant 2016–17 dollars, based on the Consumer Price Index (CPI). Some data have been revised from previously published figures.
SOURCE: U.S. Department of Education, National Center for Education Statistics, Integrated Postsecondary Education Data System (IPEDS), "Salaries, Tenure, and Fringe Benefits of Full-Time Instructional Faculty Survey" (IPEDS-SA:1999–2000); IPEDS Winter 2001–02 through Winter 2004–05, Salaries survey; IPEDS Winter 2005–06 through Winter 2011–12, Human Resources component, Salaries section; and IPEDS Spring 2013 through Spring 2017, Human Resources component. See *Digest of Education Statistics 2017*, table 316.10.

In academic year 2016–17, the average salary for full-time instructional faculty on 9-month contracts in degree-granting postsecondary institutions was $84,600. Average salaries ranged from $58,700 for lecturers to $118,900 for professors. The average salary for all full-time instructional faculty increased by 4 percent between 1999–2000 and 2009–10 (from $80,100 to $83,500) and was 1 percent higher in 2016–17 ($84,600) than in 2009–10 (salaries are expressed in constant 2016–17 dollars). A similar pattern was observed for faculty at most individual academic ranks. The increase in average salary between 1999–2000 and 2009–10 was 9 percent for professors (from $106,700 to $116,100), 6 percent for associate professors (from $78,200 to $83,000), 8 percent for assistant professors (from $64,500 to $69,700), and 7 percent for lecturers (from $54,700 to $58,400). The average salary for most academic ranks showed smaller changes between 2009–10 and 2016–17 than between 1999–2000 and 2009–10. The average salary was 3 percent higher for assistant professors, 2 percent higher for professors, and 1 percent higher for associate professors and for lecturers in 2016–17 than

in 2009–10. Instructors, however, showed a different pattern, with an average salary that was 28 percent higher in 2001–02 ($63,900) than in 1999–2000 ($50,100) but that showed no clear trend between 2001–02 and 2016–17, when the average salary for instructors was $63,600.

Average faculty salaries also varied by sex. The average salary for all full-time instructional faculty in degree-granting postsecondary institutions was higher for males than for females in every year from 1999–2000 to 2016–17. In academic year 2016–17, the average salary was $91,900 for males and $76,100 for females. Between 1999–2000 and 2016–17, the average salary increased by 7 percent for males and by 8 percent for females. The inflation-adjusted salary gap between male and female instructional faculty overall was slightly lower in 2016–17 than in 1999–2000 ($15,800 vs. $15,900). The male-female salary gap among professors, however, increased between 1999–2000 and 2016–17 (from $13,500 to $18,400).

Figure 4. Average salary of full-time instructional faculty on 9-month contracts in degree-granting postsecondary institutions, by control and level of institution: 2016–17

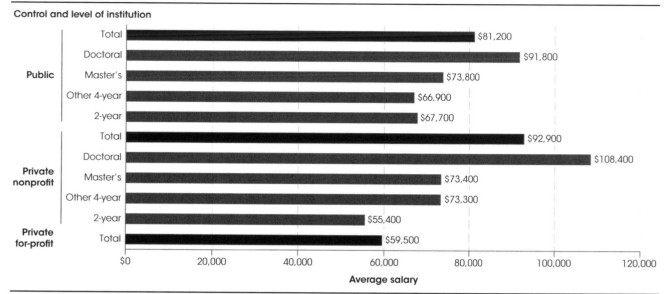

NOTE: Doctoral institutions include institutions that awarded 20 or more doctor's degrees during the previous academic year. Master's institutions include institutions that awarded 20 or more master's degrees, but less than 20 doctor's degrees, during the previous academic year. Data exclude instructional faculty at medical schools. Degree-granting postsecondary institutions grant associate's or higher degrees and participate in Title IV federal financial aid programs. Salaries are reported in constant 2016–17 dollars, based on the Consumer Price Index (CPI).
SOURCE: U.S. Department of Education, National Center for Education Statistics, Integrated Postsecondary Education Data System (IPEDS), IPEDS Spring 2017, Human Resources component. See *Digest of Education Statistics 2017*, table 316.20.

Faculty salaries also varied according to control and level of degree-granting postsecondary institutions. In academic year 2016–17, the average salary for full-time instructional faculty in private nonprofit institutions ($92,900) was higher than the average salaries for full-time instructional faculty in public institutions ($81,200) and in private for-profit institutions ($59,500). Among the specific types of private nonprofit institutions and public institutions, average salaries for instructional faculty were highest in private nonprofit doctoral institutions ($108,400) and public doctoral institutions ($91,800). Average salaries were lowest for instructional faculty in private nonprofit 2-year institutions ($55,400), public 4-year institutions other than doctoral and master's degree-granting institutions ($66,900), and public 2-year institutions ($67,700). Average salaries for instructional faculty were 3 percent higher in 2016–17 than in 1999–2000 in public institutions ($81,200 vs. $78,900), 11 percent higher in private nonprofit institutions ($92,900 vs. $83,400), and 41 percent higher in private for-profit institutions ($59,500 vs. $42,300).

In academic year 2016–17, approximately 54 percent of degree-granting postsecondary institutions had tenure systems. A tenure system guarantees that, after completing a probationary period, a professor will not be terminated without just cause. The percentage of institutions with tenure systems ranged from 1 percent at private for-profit institutions to almost 100 percent at public doctoral institutions. Of full-time faculty at institutions with tenure systems, 46 percent had tenure in 2016–17, down from 54 percent in 1999–2000. At public institutions with tenure systems, the percentage of full-time faculty with tenure decreased by 8 percentage points over this period; at private nonprofit institutions, the percentage decreased by 6 percentage points; and at private for-profit institutions, the percentage decreased by 60 percentage points. At institutions with tenure systems, the percentage of full-time instructional faculty with tenure was higher for males than for females. In 2016–17, some 55 percent of males had tenure, compared with 42 percent of females.

Endnotes:

[1] The ratios are calculated by dividing the number of FTE undergraduate and graduate students by the number of FTE faculty (including instructional, research, and public service faculty).

[2] Percentages are based on full-time faculty whose race/ethnicity was known.

Reference tables: *Digest of Education Statistics 2017*, tables 314.10, 314.50, 314.60, 315.10, 315.20, 316.10, 316.20, and 316.80

Related indicators and resources: Characteristics of Degree-Granting Postsecondary Institutions; Characteristics of Postsecondary Students

Glossary: Constant dollars, Control of institution, Degree-granting institution, Doctor's degree, Gap, Postsecondary education, Postsecondary institutions (basic classification by level), Private institution, Public school or institution, Racial/ethnic group, Salary

Undergraduate Degree Fields

In 2015–16, over two-thirds of the 1.0 million associate's degrees conferred by postsecondary institutions were concentrated in three fields of study: liberal arts and sciences, general studies, and humanities (381,000 degrees); health professions and related programs (191,000 degrees); and business (128,000 degrees). Of the 1.9 million bachelor's degrees conferred in 2015–16, over half were concentrated in six fields of study: business (372,000 degrees), health professions and related programs (229,000 degrees), social sciences and history (161,000 degrees), psychology (117,000 degrees), biological and biomedical sciences (114,000 degrees), and engineering (107,000 degrees).

In academic year 2015–16, postsecondary institutions conferred 1.0 million associate's degrees. Over two-thirds (70 percent) of these degrees were concentrated in three fields of study: liberal arts and sciences, general studies, and humanities (38 percent, or 381,000 degrees); health professions and related programs (19 percent, or 191,000 degrees); and business[1] (13 percent, or 128,000 degrees). The three next largest percentages

of associate's degrees conferred in 2015–16 were in the following fields: homeland security, law enforcement, and firefighting (4 percent, or 39,900 degrees); computer and information sciences and support services (3 percent, or 30,600 degrees); and multi/interdisciplinary studies[2] (3 percent, or 30,500 degrees). Overall, 79,900 associate's degrees (8 percent) were conferred in science, technology, engineering, and mathematics (STEM)[3] fields in 2015–16.

Figure 1. Number of associate's degrees conferred by postsecondary institutions in selected fields of study: Academic years 2000–01 through 2015–16

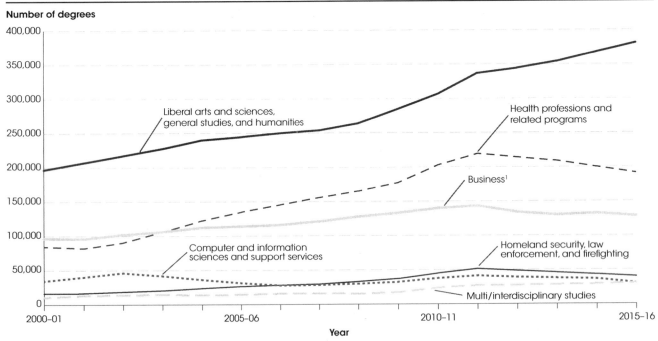

Between 2000–01 and 2015–16, the number of associate's degrees conferred increased by 74 percent, from 579,000 to 1.0 million. Over this time period, the number of associate's degrees conferred in liberal arts and sciences, general studies, and humanities increased by 94 percent, from 197,000 degrees in 2000–01 to 381,000 degrees in 2015–16. The number of associate's degrees conferred in health professions and related programs increased by 159 percent, from 84,700 degrees in 2000–01 to 219,000 degrees in 2011–12, and then decreased by 13 percent between 2011–12 and 2015–16 (191,000 associate's degrees were conferred in health professions and related programs in 2015–16). The number of associate's degrees conferred in business increased by 48 percent, from 96,800 degrees in 2000–01 to 143,000 degrees in 2011–12, and showed no clear trend between 2011–12 and 2015–16 (128,000 associate's degrees were conferred in business in 2015–16). Among other fields in which at least 10,000 associate's degrees were conferred in 2015–16, the number of degrees conferred more than doubled between 2000–01 and 2015–16 in the following fields: homeland security, law enforcement, and firefighting (from 16,400 to 39,900, an increase of 143 percent); multi/interdisciplinary studies (from 10,400 to 30,500, an increase of 192 percent); social sciences and history (from 5,100 to 20,100, an increase of 291 percent); and psychology (from 1,600 to 10,600, an increase of 582 percent).

Figure 2. Percentage of associate's degrees awarded in science, technology, and mathematics (STEM) fields, by race/ethnicity: Academic year 2015–16

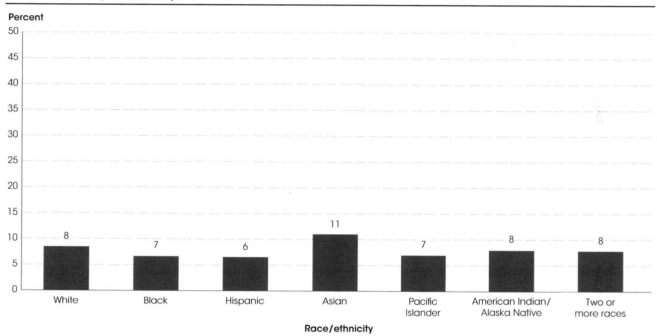

NOTE: STEM fields include biological and biomedical sciences, computer and information sciences, engineering and engineering technologies, mathematics and statistics, and physical sciences and science technologies. Data are for degree-granting postsecondary institutions participating in Title IV federal financial aid programs. Race categories exclude persons of Hispanic ethnicity. Although rounded numbers are displayed, the figures are based on unrounded estimates.
SOURCE: U.S. Department of Education, National Center for Education Statistics, Integrated Postsecondary Education Data System (IPEDS), Fall 2016, Completions component. See *Digest of Education Statistics 2017*, tables 318.45 and 321.30.

Liberal arts and sciences, general studies, and humanities; health professions and related programs; and business were the top three associate's degree fields of study for all racial/ethnic groups in 2015–16. The percentage of associate's degrees conferred in STEM fields varied by race/ethnicity. Eleven percent of associate's degrees conferred to Asian graduates were in a STEM field, which was higher than the percentage for graduates who were White (8 percent), American Indian/Alaska Native (8 percent), of Two or more races (8 percent), Pacific Islander (7 percent), Black (7 percent), and Hispanic (6 percent).

Postsecondary institutions conferred approximately 1.9 million bachelor's degrees in 2015–16. Over half were concentrated in six fields of study: business (19 percent, or 372,000 degrees), health professions and related programs (12 percent, or 229,000 degrees), social sciences and history (8 percent, or 161,000 degrees), psychology (6 percent, or 117,000 degrees), biological and biomedical sciences (6 percent, or 114,000 degrees), and engineering (6 percent, or 107,000 degrees). The fields in which the next largest percentages of bachelor's degrees were conferred in 2015–16 were visual and performing arts (5 percent, or 93,000 degrees); communication, journalism, and related programs (5 percent, or 92,600 degrees); and education (5 percent, or 87,200 degrees). Overall, 355,000 bachelor's degrees (18 percent) were conferred in STEM fields.

Figure 3. Number of bachelor's degrees conferred by postsecondary institutions in selected fields of study: Academic years 2000–01 through 2015–16

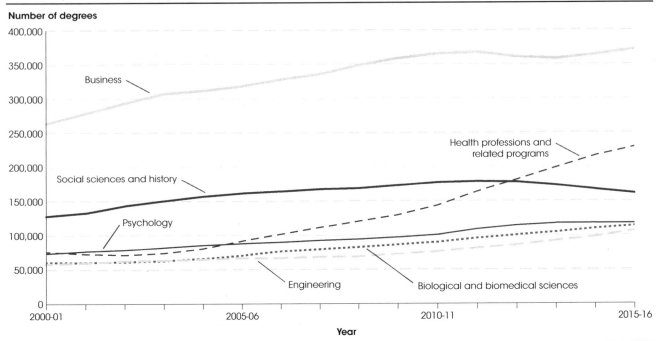

NOTE: The fields shown are the six programs in which the largest number of bachelor's degrees were conferred in 2015–16. Data are for postsecondary institutions participating in Title IV federal financial aid programs. Data have been adjusted where necessary to conform to the 2009–10 Classification of Instructional Programs. Some data have been revised from previously published figures.
SOURCE: U.S. Department of Education, National Center for Education Statistics, Integrated Postsecondary Education Data System (IPEDS), Fall 2001 through Fall 2016, Completions component. See *Digest of Education Statistics 2012*, table 313; and *Digest of Education Statistics 2017*, table 322.10.

Between 2000–01 and 2015–16, the number of bachelor's degrees conferred increased by 54 percent, from 1.2 million to 1.9 million. Over this time period, the number of bachelor's degrees conferred in business increased by 39 percent, from 264,000 in 2000–01 to 367,000 in 2011–12, and showed no clear trend between 2011–12 and 2015–16 (372,000 degrees were conferred in business in 2015–16). The number of bachelor's degrees conferred in health professions and related programs increased by 201 percent between 2000–01 and 2015–16, from 75,900 to 229,000. During the same period, the number of bachelor's degrees conferred in social sciences and history increased by 39 percent, from 128,000 in 2000–01 to 179,000 in 2011–12, and then decreased by 10 percent to 161,000 in 2015–16. Among other fields in which more than 10,000 bachelor's degrees were conferred in 2015–16, the number of degrees conferred more than doubled between 2000–01 and 2015–16 in each of the following fields: homeland security, law enforcement, and firefighting (from 25,200 to 61,200, an increase of 143 percent); parks, recreation, leisure, and fitness studies (from 17,900 to 50,900, an increase of 184 percent); and mathematics and statistics (from 11,200 to 22,800, an increase of 104 percent).

Figure 4. Percentage of bachelor's degrees awarded in science, technology, and mathematics (STEM) fields, by race/ethnicity: Academic year 2015–16

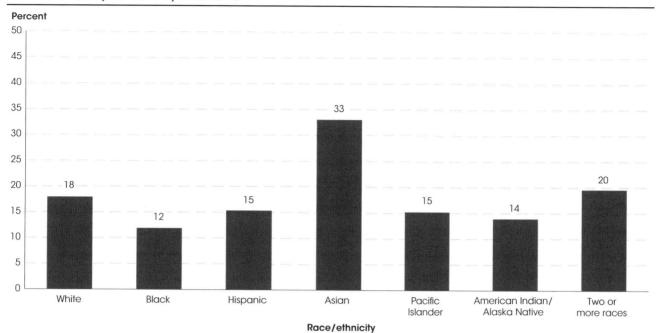

NOTE: STEM fields include biological and biomedical sciences, computer and information sciences, engineering and engineering technologies, mathematics and statistics, and physical sciences and science technologies. Data are for postsecondary institutions participating in Title IV federal financial aid programs. Race categories exclude persons of Hispanic ethnicity. Although rounded numbers are displayed, the figures are based on unrounded estimates.
SOURCE: U.S. Department of Education, National Center for Education Statistics, Integrated Postsecondary Education Data System (IPEDS), Fall 2016, Completions component. See *Digest of Education Statistics 2017*, tables 318.45 and 322.30.

Within each racial/ethnic group, business was the most common field of study for bachelor's degrees conferred in 2015–16. As with associate's degrees, the percentage of bachelor's degrees that were conferred in STEM fields varied by race/ethnicity. One-third (33 percent) of bachelor's degrees conferred to Asian graduates were in a STEM field, which was higher than the percentage for graduates who were of Two or more races (20 percent), White (18 percent), Hispanic (15 percent), Pacific Islander (15 percent), American Indian/Alaska Native (14 percent), and Black (12 percent).

Figure 5. Percentage distribution of associate's and bachelor's degrees conferred by postsecondary institutions in largest fields of study, by sex: Academic year 2015–16

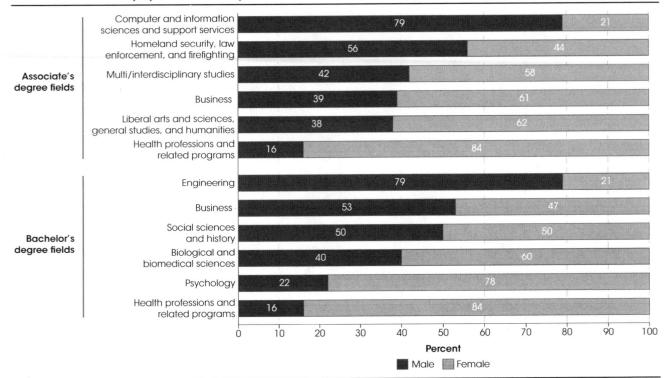

NOTE: Data are for postsecondary institutions participating in Title IV federal financial aid programs. The "business" field of study includes business, management, marketing, and related support services, as well as personal and culinary services.
SOURCE: U.S. Department of Education, National Center for Education Statistics, Integrated Postsecondary Education Data System (IPEDS), Fall 2016, Completions component. See *Digest of Education Statistics 2017*, tables 321.10, 322.40, and 322.50.

In 2015–16, females earned 616,000 associate's degrees, representing 61 percent of all associate's degrees conferred. Males were conferred the remaining 39 percent (392,000 degrees). Of the six fields in which the most associate's degrees were conferred in 2015–16, females were conferred the majority of degrees in four: health professions and related programs; liberal arts and sciences, general studies, and humanities; business; and multi/interdisciplinary studies (84 percent, 62 percent, 61 percent, and 58 percent, respectively). Males earned the majority of associate's degrees conferred in computer and information sciences and support services (79 percent) and in homeland security, law enforcement, and firefighting (56 percent).

In 2015–16, females earned 1.1 million bachelor's degrees, representing 57 percent of all bachelor's degrees conferred. Males were conferred the remaining 43 percent (0.8 million degrees). Of the six fields in which the most bachelor's degrees were conferred in 2015–16, females earned the majority of degrees in three: health professions and related programs, psychology, and biological and biomedical sciences (84 percent, 78 percent, and 60 percent, respectively). Bachelor's degrees conferred in social sciences and history were almost equally divided between males and females (50 percent each). Males earned the majority of degrees conferred in engineering and business (79 and 53 percent of degrees, respectively).

Endnotes:

[1] Personal and culinary services have been added to the definition of "business" for associate's degree data in order to be consistent with the definition of "business" for bachelor's degree data. Thus, for all data in this indicator, "business" is defined as business, management, marketing and related support services, as well as personal and culinary services.

[2] Instructional programs that derive from two or more distinct programs to provide a cross-cutting focus on a subject concentration that is not subsumed under a single discipline or occupational field. Examples include biological and physical sciences, peace studies and conflict resolution, systems science and theory, and mathematics and computer science.

[3] STEM fields include biological and biomedical sciences, computer and information sciences, engineering and engineering technologies, mathematics and statistics, and physical sciences and science technologies. Construction trades and mechanic and repair technologies/technicians are categorized as engineering technologies in some tables to faciliate trend comparisons, but are not included as STEM fields in this indicator.

Reference tables: *Digest of Education Statistics 2012*, tables 312 and 313; *Digest of Education Statistics 2017*, tables 318.45, 321.10, 321.30, 322.10, 322.30, 322.40, and 322.50

Related indicators and resources: Employment Outcomes of Bachelor's Degree Recipients [*web-only*]; Graduate Degree Fields; Post-College Employment Outcomes by Field of Study and Race/Ethnicity [*The Condition of Education 2016 Spotlight*]; Postsecondary Certificates and Degrees Conferred; Undergraduate and Graduate Degree Fields [*Status and Trends in the Education of Racial and Ethnic Groups*]

Glossary: Associate's degree, Bachelor's degree, Classification of Instructional Programs (CIP), Racial/ethnic group, STEM fields

Graduate Degree Fields

In 2015–16, over half of the 786,000 master's degrees conferred were concentrated in three fields of study: business (187,000 degrees), education (146,000 degrees), and health professions and related programs (110,000 degrees). Of the 178,000 doctor's degrees conferred, almost two-thirds were concentrated in two fields: health professions and related programs (73,700 degrees) and legal professions and studies (37,000 degrees).

In academic year 2015–16, postsecondary institutions conferred 786,000 master's degrees. Over half of the master's degrees conferred in 2015–16 were concentrated in three fields of study: business (24 percent, or 187,000 degrees), education (19 percent, or 146,000 degrees), and health professions and related programs (14 percent, or 110,000 degrees). The fields in which the next largest

percentages of master's degrees were conferred were engineering (7 percent, or 51,600 degrees) and public administration and social services (6 percent, or 46,800 degrees). Overall, 129,000 master's degrees (16 percent) were conferred in science, technology, engineering, and mathematics (STEM)[1] fields in 2015–16.

Figure 1. Number of master's degrees conferred by postsecondary institutions in selected fields of study: Academic years 2000–01 through 2015–16

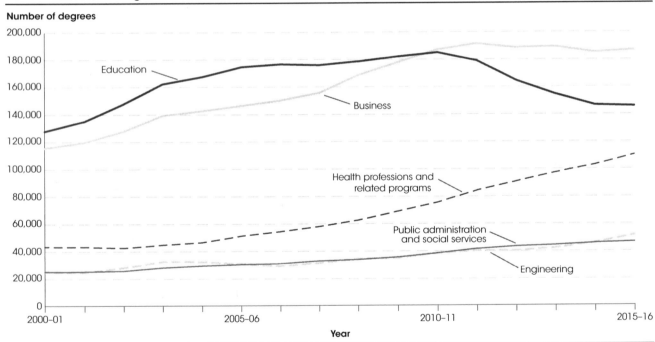

NOTE: The fields shown are the five programs in which the largest numbers of master's degrees were conferred in 2015–16. Data are for postsecondary institutions participating in Title IV federal financial aid programs. Data have been adjusted where necessary to conform to the 2009–10 Classification of Instructional Programs.
SOURCE: U.S. Department of Education, National Center for Education Statistics, Integrated Postsecondary Education Data System (IPEDS), Fall 2001 through Fall 2016, Completions component. See *Digest of Education Statistics 2012*, table 314; *Digest of Education Statistics 2017*, table 323.10.

Between 2000–01 and 2015–16 the number of master's degrees conferred increased by 66 percent, from 474,000 to 786,000. During this period the number of master's degrees conferred in business rose by 66 percent from 116,000 degrees in 2000–01 to 192,000 degrees in 2011–12, and showed no clear trend between 2011–12 and 2015–16 (187,000 master's degrees were conferred in business in 2015–16). In 2010–11, business surpassed education as the field in which the largest number of master's degrees were conferred and has remained the largest field in each subsequent year. The number of master's degrees conferred in education rose by 45 percent from 128,000 degrees in 2000–01 to 185,000 degrees in 2010–11, and then fell by 21 percent to 146,000 degrees

in 2015–16. In each of the three next largest fields of study, the number of degrees conferred increased between 2000–01 and 2015–16: health professions and related programs (by 153 percent, from 43,600 to 110,000), engineering (by 105 percent, from 25,200 to 51,600), and public administration and social services (by 85 percent, from 25,300 to 46,800). Among other degree fields in which at least 10,000 master's degrees were conferred in 2015–16, the number of degrees conferred more than doubled between 2000–01 and 2015–16 in computer and information sciences (from 16,900 to 40,100, an increase of 137 percent) and biological and biomedical sciences (from 7,000 to 15,700, an increase of 124 percent).

Figure 2. Percentage of master's degrees awarded in science, technology, and mathematics (STEM) fields, by race/ethnicity: Academic year 2015–16

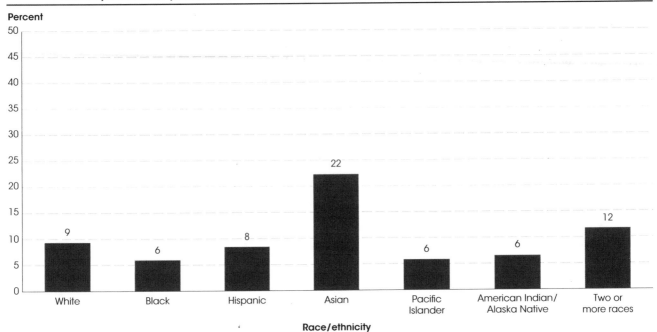

NOTE: STEM fields include biological and biomedical sciences, computer and information sciences, engineering and engineering technologies, mathematics and statistics, and physical sciences and science technologies. Data are for postsecondary institutions participating in Title IV federal financial aid programs. Race categories exclude persons of Hispanic ethnicity. Although rounded numbers are displayed, the figures are based on unrounded estimates.
SOURCE: U.S. Department of Education, National Center for Education Statistics, Integrated Postsecondary Education Data System (IPEDS), Fall 2016, Completions component. See *Digest of Education Statistics 2017*, tables 318.45 and 323.30.

In 2015–16, the three fields in which the most master's degrees were conferred—business, education, and health professions and related programs—were the same for all racial/ethnic groups, although the rank order of these fields differed across groups. The percentage of master's degrees conferred in STEM fields varied by race/ethnicity in 2015–16. Some 22 percent of master's degrees conferred

to Asian graduates were in a STEM field, which was higher than the percentages for graduates who were of Two or more races (12 percent), White (9 percent), Hispanic (8 percent), American Indian/Alaska Native (6 percent), Black (6 percent), and Pacific Islander (6 percent).

Figure 3.   Percentage distribution of master's degrees conferred by postsecondary institutions in largest fields of study, by sex: Academic year 2015–16

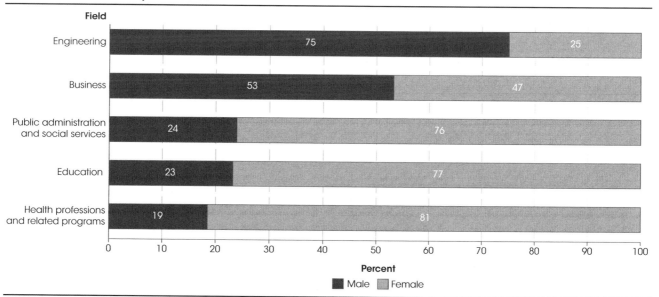

NOTE: Data are for postsecondary institutions participating in Title IV federal financial aid programs.
SOURCE: U.S. Department of Education, National Center for Education Statistics, Integrated Postsecondary Education Data System (IPEDS), Fall 2016, Completions component. See *Digest of Education Statistics 2017*, tables 323.40 and 323.50.

In 2015–16, females earned 465,000 master's degrees, representing 59 percent of all master's degrees conferred. Males earned the remaining 41 percent (320,000 degrees). Of the five fields in which the most master's degrees were conferred in 2015–16, females earned the majority of degrees in health professions and related programs; education; and public administration and social services (81 percent, 77 percent, and 76 percent, respectively). Males earned the majority of degrees conferred in business and engineering (53 percent and 75 percent, respectively).

Of the 178,000 doctor's degrees conferred by postsecondary institutions in 2015–16, almost two-thirds were concentrated in two fields of study: health professions and related programs (41 percent, or 73,700 degrees) and legal professions and studies (21 percent, or 37,000 degrees). The three fields in which the next largest percentages of doctor's degrees were conferred were education (7 percent, or 11,800 degrees), engineering (6 percent, or 10,200 degrees), and biological and biomedical sciences (4 percent, or 7,900 degrees). For the purposes of this analysis, doctor's degrees include Ph.D., Ed.D., and comparable degrees at the doctoral level, as well as first-professional degrees such as M.D., D.D.S., and J.D. degrees.

Figure 4. Number of doctor's degrees conferred by postsecondary institutions in selected fields of study: Academic years 2000–01 through 2015–16

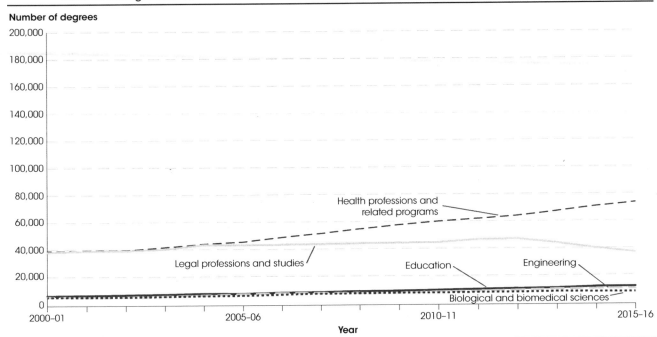

NOTE: Doctor's degrees include Ph.D., Ed.D., and comparable degrees at the doctoral level, as well as such degrees as M.D., D.D.S., and law degrees that were formerly classified as first-professional degrees. The fields shown are the five programs in which the largest numbers of doctor's degrees were conferred in 2015–16. Data are for postsecondary institutions participating in Title IV federal financial aid programs. Data have been adjusted where necessary to conform to the 2009-10 Classification of Instructional Programs.
SOURCE: U.S. Department of Education, National Center for Education Statistics, Integrated Postsecondary Education Data System (IPEDS), Fall 2001 through Fall 2016, Completions component. See *Digest of Education Statistics 2012*, table 315; *Digest of Education Statistics 2017*, table 324.10.

Between 2000–01 and 2015–16, the number of doctor's degrees conferred increased by 49 percent, from 120,000 to 178,000. Over this time period, the number of doctor's degrees conferred in health professions and related programs increased by 89 percent, from 39,000 in 2000–01 to 73,700 in 2015–16. The number of doctor's degrees conferred in legal professions increased by 24 percent from 38,200 in 2000–01 to 47,200 in 2012–13 and fell in each subsequent year, to 37,000 in 2015–16. Between 2000–01 and 2015–16, the number of doctor's degrees conferred increased in each of the next three largest fields: education (by 88 percent, from 6,300 to 11,800), engineering (by 86 percent, from 5,500 to 10,200), and biological and biomedical sciences (by 51 percent, from 5,200 to 7,900).

Figure 5. Percentage of doctor's degrees awarded in science, technology, and mathematics (STEM) fields, by race/ethnicity: Academic year 2015–16

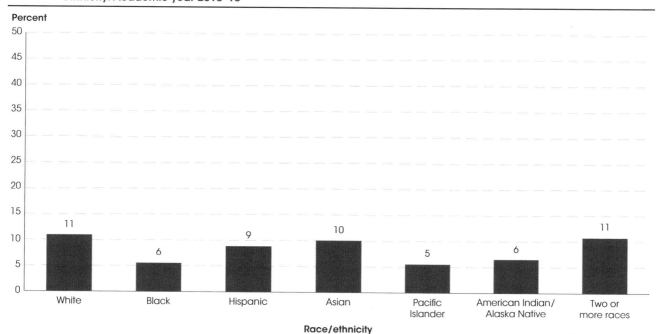

NOTE: STEM fields include biological and biomedical sciences, computer and information sciences, engineering and engineering technologies, mathematics and statistics, and physical sciences and science technologies. Data are for postsecondary institutions participating in Title IV federal financial aid programs. Race categories exclude persons of Hispanic ethnicity. Although rounded numbers are displayed, the figures are based on unrounded estimates.
SOURCE: U.S. Department of Education, National Center for Education Statistics, Integrated Postsecondary Education Data System (IPEDS), Fall 2016, Completions component. See *Digest of Education Statistics 2017*, tables 318.45 and 324.25.

In 2015–16, the two fields in which the most doctor's degrees were conferred—health professions and related programs, and legal professions and studies—were the same for all racial/ethnic groups, although the rank order of these fields differed across groups. As with master's degrees, the percentage of doctor's degrees conferred in STEM fields varied among racial/ethnic groups.

Some 11 percent of doctor's degrees conferred to White graduates and graduates of Two or more races were in a STEM field, which was higher than the percentages for Asian (10 percent), Hispanic (9 percent), American Indian/Alaska Native (6 percent), Black (6 percent), and Pacific Islander graduates (5 percent).

Endnotes:
[1] STEM fields include biological and biomedical sciences, computer and information sciences, engineering and engineering technologies, mathematics and statistics, and physical sciences and science technologies.

Reference tables: *Digest of Education Statistics 2012*, tables 314 and 315; *Digest of Education Statistics 2017*, tables 318.45, 323.10, 323.20, 323.30, 323.40, 323.50, 324.10, 324.20, and 324.25

Related indicators and resources: Postsecondary Certificates and Degrees Conferred; Undergraduate and Graduate Degree Fields [*Status and Trends in the Education of Racial and Ethnic Groups*]; Undergraduate Degree Fields; Trends in Student Loan Debt for Graduate School Completers [*The Condition of Education 2018 Spotlight*]

Glossary: Classification of Instructional Programs (CIP), Doctor's degree, Master's degree, Racial/ethnic group, STEM fields

Undergraduate Retention and Graduation Rates

About 60 percent of students who began seeking a bachelor's degree at a 4-year institution in fall 2010 completed that degree within 6 years; the 6-year graduation rate was higher for females than for males (63 vs. 57 percent).

Retention rates measure the percentage of first-time, full-time undergraduate students who return to the same institution the following fall, and graduation rates measure the percentage of first-time, full-time undergraduate students who complete their program at the same institution within a specified period of time.

This indicator examines how retention and graduation rates vary among different types of postsecondary institutions. It also examines how graduation rates have changed over time and how they differ between male and female students.

Figure 1. Percentage of first-time, full-time degree-seeking undergraduates retained at 4-year degree-granting institutions, by control of institution and acceptance rate: 2015 to 2016

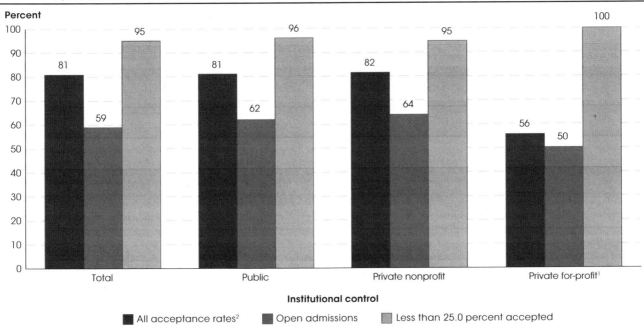

[1] The 100 percent retention rate for private for-profit institutions with acceptance rates of less than 25.0 percent is calculated from an adjusted cohort of eight students.
[2] Includes institutions that have an open admissions policy, institutions that have various applicant acceptance rates, and institutions for which no acceptance rate information is available.
NOTE: Data are for 4-year degree-granting postsecondary institutions participating in Title IV federal financial aid programs. Retained first-time undergraduates are those who returned to the institutions to continue their studies the following fall. Although rounded numbers are displayed, the figures are based on unrounded estimates.
SOURCE: U.S. Department of Education, National Center for Education Statistics, Integrated Postsecondary Education Data System (IPEDS), Spring 2017, Fall Enrollment component; and Fall 2015, Institutional Characteristics component. See *Digest of Education Statistics 2017*, table 326.30.

For first-time, full-time degree-seeking students who enrolled at 4-year degree-granting institutions in fall 2015, the retention rate (i.e., the percentage of students returning the following fall) was 81 percent. Retention rates were higher at institutions that were more selective (i.e., those with lower admission acceptance rates), regardless of institutional control (public, private nonprofit, or private for-profit). At public 4-year institutions overall, the retention rate was 81 percent. At the least selective public institutions (i.e., those with open admissions), the retention rate was 62 percent,

and at the most selective public institutions (i.e., those that accept less than 25 percent of applicants), the retention rate was 96 percent. Similarly, the retention rate for private nonprofit 4-year institutions overall was 82 percent, ranging from 64 percent at institutions with open admissions to 95 percent at institutions that accept less than 25 percent of applicants. The retention rate for private for-profit 4-year institutions overall was 56 percent, ranging from 50 percent at institutions with open admissions to 100 percent at institutions that accept less than 25 percent of applicants.[1]

Figure 2. Percentage of first-time, full-time degree-seeking undergraduates retained at 2-year degree-granting institutions, by control of institution: 2015 to 2016

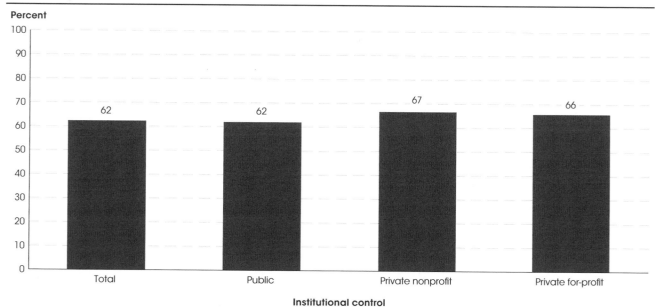

NOTE: Data are for 2-year degree-granting postsecondary institutions participating in Title IV federal financial aid programs. Returning students data for 2-year institutions include returning students, plus students who completed their program. Although rounded numbers are displayed, the figures are based on unrounded estimates.
SOURCE: U.S. Department of Education, National Center for Education Statistics, Integrated Postsecondary Education Data System (IPEDS), Spring 2017, Fall Enrollment component. See *Digest of Education Statistics 2017*, table 326.30.

At 2-year institutions, the overall retention rate for first-time, full-time students was 62 percent. The retention rates for private nonprofit and private for-profit 2-year institutions (67 and 66 percent, respectively) were higher than the rate for public institutions (62 percent).

The 1990 Student Right-to-Know Act requires postsecondary institutions to report the percentage of students who complete their program within 150 percent of the normal time for completion (e.g., within 6 years for students pursuing a bachelor's degree). The graduation rates in this indicator are based on this measure. Students who transfer without completing a degree are counted as noncompleters in the calculation of these rates regardless of whether they complete a degree at another institution.

Figure 3.   Graduation rate within 150 percent of normal time (within 6 years) for degree completion from first institution attended for first-time, full-time bachelor's degree-seeking students at 4-year postsecondary institutions, by control of institution and sex: Cohort entry year 2010

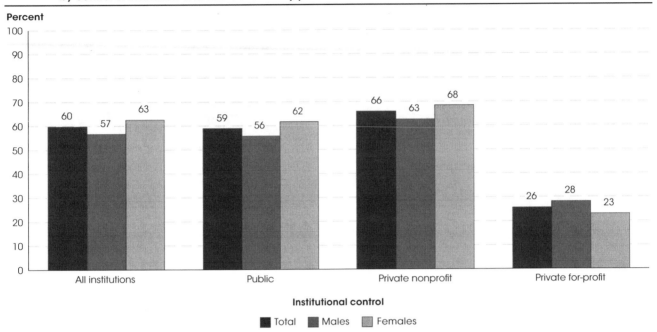

NOTE: Data are for 4-year degree-granting postsecondary institutions participating in Title IV federal financial aid programs. Graduation rates include students receiving bachelor's degrees from their initial institution of attendance only. Although rounded numbers are displayed, the figures are based on unrounded estimates.
SOURCE: U.S. Department of Education, National Center for Education Statistics, Integrated Postsecondary Education Data System (IPEDS), Winter 2016–17, Graduation Rates component. See *Digest of Education Statistics 2017*, table 326.10.

The 6-year graduation rate (150 percent graduation rate) for first-time, full-time undergraduate students who began seeking a bachelor's degree at a 4-year degree-granting institution in fall 2010 was 60 percent. That is, by 2016 some 60 percent of students had completed a bachelor's degree at the same institution where they started in 2010. The 6-year graduation rate was 59 percent at public institutions, 66 percent at private nonprofit institutions,

and 26 percent at private for-profit institutions. The 6-year graduation rate was 63 percent for females and 57 percent for males; it was higher for females than for males at both public (62 vs. 56 percent) and private nonprofit (68 vs. 63 percent) institutions. However, at private for-profit institutions, males had a higher 6-year graduation rate than females (28 vs. 23 percent).

Figure 4. Graduation rate within 150 percent of normal time (within 6 years) for degree completion from first institution attended for first-time, full-time bachelor's degree-seeking students at 4-year postsecondary institutions, by acceptance rate of institution: Cohort entry year 2010

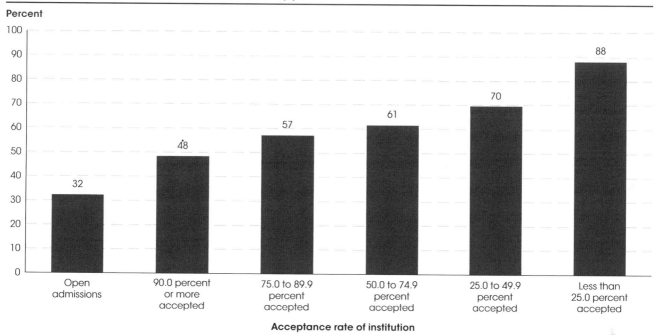

NOTE: Data are for 4-year degree-granting postsecondary institutions participating in Title IV federal financial aid programs. Graduation rates include students receiving bachelor's degrees from their initial institution of attendance only.
SOURCE: U.S. Department of Education, National Center for Education Statistics, Integrated Postsecondary Education Data System (IPEDS), Winter 2016–17, Graduation Rates component, and Fall 2010, Institutional Characteristics component. See *Digest of Education Statistics 2017*, table 326.10.

Six-year graduation rates for first-time, full-time students who began seeking a bachelor's degree in fall 2010 varied according to institutional selectivity. In particular, 6-year graduation rates were highest at institutions that were the most selective (i.e., those that accepted less than 25 percent of applicants) and were lowest at institutions that were the least selective (i.e., those that had open admissions policies). For example, at 4-year institutions with open admissions policies, 32 percent of students completed a bachelor's degree within 6 years. At 4-year institutions where the acceptance rate was less than 25 percent of applicants, the 6-year graduation rate was 88 percent.

Between 2011 and 2016, the overall 6-year graduation rate for first-time, full-time students who began seeking

a bachelor's degree at 4-year degree-granting institutions increased by 1 percentage point, from 59 percent (for students who began their studies in 2005 and graduated within 6 years) to 60 percent (for students who began their studies in 2010 and graduated within 6 years). During this period, 6-year graduation rates were higher in 2016 than in 2011 at public institutions (59 vs. 57 percent) and private nonprofit institutions (66 vs. 65 percent), but lower in 2016 than in 2011 at private for-profit institutions (26 vs. 29 percent). In addition, the 6-year graduation rate was 2 percentage points higher in 2016 (63 percent) than in 2011 (61 percent) for females and was 1 percentage point higher in 2016 (57 percent) than in 2011 (56 percent) for males.

Figure 5. Graduation rate within 150 percent of normal time for degree completion from first institution attended for first-time, full-time degree/certificate-seeking students at 2-year postsecondary institutions, by control of institution and sex: Cohort entry year 2013

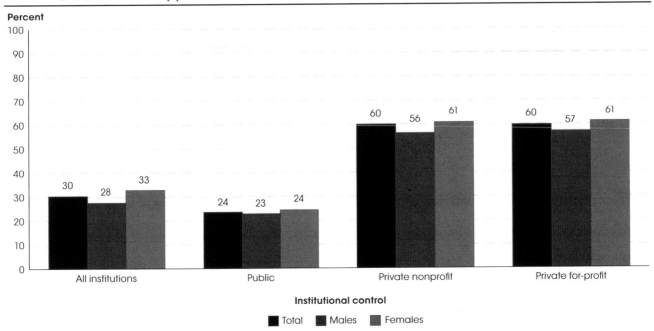

NOTE: Data are for 2-year degree-granting postsecondary institutions participating in Title IV federal financial aid programs. Graduation rates include students receiving associate's degrees or certificates from their initial institution of attendance only. An example of completing a credential within 150 percent of the normal time is completing a 2-year degree within 3 years. Although rounded numbers are displayed, the figures are based on unrounded estimates.
SOURCE: U.S. Department of Education, National Center for Education Statistics, Integrated Postsecondary Education Data System (IPEDS), Winter 2016–17, Graduation Rates component. See *Digest of Education Statistics 2017*, table 326.20.

At 2-year degree-granting institutions overall, 30 percent of first-time, full-time undergraduate students who began seeking a certificate or associate's degree in fall 2013 attained it within 150 percent of the normal time required for completion of these programs (an example of completing a credential within 150 percent of the normal time is completing a 2-year degree within 3 years). The graduation rate was 24 percent at public 2-year institutions and 60 percent at both private nonprofit and private for-profit 2-year institutions. At 2-year institutions overall, as well as at public, private nonprofit, and private for-profit 2-year institutions, the graduation rates were higher for females than for males. At private for-profit 2-year institutions, for example, 61 percent of females versus 57 percent of males who began pursuing a certificate or associate's degree in 2013 completed it within 150 percent of the normal time required for completion.

Endnotes:
[1] The 100 percent retention rate for private for-profit institutions is calculated from an adjusted cohort of eight students.

Reference tables: *Digest of Education Statistics 2017*, tables 326.10, 326.20, and 326.30
Related indicators and resources: Educational Attainment of Young Adults; First-Time Postsecondary Students' Persistence After 3 Years [*The Condition of Education 2017 Spotlight*]; Postsecondary Graduation Rates [*Status and Trends in the Education of Racial and Ethnic Groups*]

Glossary: Associate's degree, Bachelor's degree, Certificate, Degree-granting institution, Full-time enrollment, Open admissions, Postsecondary education, Postsecondary institutions (basic classification by level), Private institution, Public school or institution, Retention rate, Undergraduate students

This page intentionally left blank.

Postsecondary Certificates and Degrees Conferred

The number of postsecondary certificates and degrees conferred at each award level increased between 2000–01 and 2015–16. The number of certificates below the associate's level conferred during this period increased by 70 percent. The number of degrees conferred during this period increased by 74 percent at the associate's level, by 54 percent at the bachelor's level, by 66 percent at the master's level, and by 49 percent at the doctor's level.

In academic year 2015–16, postsecondary institutions conferred 939,000 certificates[1] below the associate's level, 1.0 million associate's degrees, 1.9 million bachelor's degrees, 786,000 master's degrees, and 178,000 doctor's degrees. The number of postsecondary certificates and degrees conferred at each award level increased between 2000–01 and 2015–16.

Figure 1. Number of certificates and degrees conferred by postsecondary institutions: Academic years 2000–01 through 2015–16

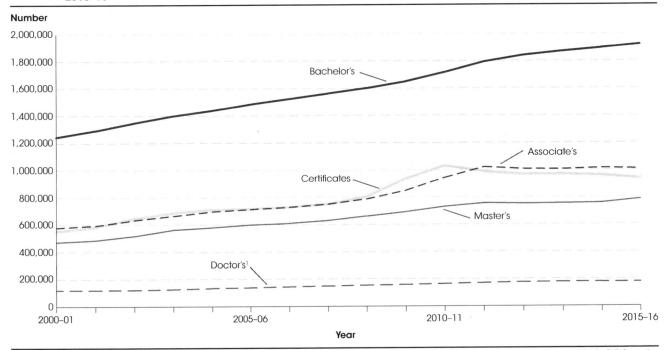

[1] Includes Ph.D., Ed.D., and comparable degrees at the doctoral level. Includes most degrees formerly classified as first-professional, such as M.D., D.D.S., and law degrees.
NOTE: Data are for postsecondary institutions participating in Title IV federal financial aid programs. Data for associate's degrees and higher awards are for degree-granting institutions. Data for certificates are for certificates below the associate's degree level. Some data have been revised from previously published figures.
SOURCE: U.S. Department of Education, National Center for Education Statistics, Integrated Postsecondary Education Data System (IPEDS), Fall 2001 through Fall 2016, Completions component. See *Digest of Education Statistics 2017*, table 318.40.

The number of certificates conferred below the associate's level increased by 87 percent between 2000–01 and 2010–11, from 553,000 to 1.0 million. The number of certificates conferred then decreased by 9 percent to 939,000 in 2015–16. In contrast, the number of associate's degrees conferred peaked one year later in 2011–12. Between 2000–01 and 2011–12 the number of associate's degrees increased by 77 percent, from 579,000 to 1.0 million. The number of associate's degrees conferred then fluctuated and was 1 percent lower in 2015–16 than in 2011–12. The number of bachelor's degrees conferred rose each year

between 2000–01 and 2015–16, increasing by 54 percent (from 1.2 million to 1.9 million) during this period.

Between 2000–01 and 2011–12 the number of master's degrees conferred increased by 60 percent, from 474,000 to 756,000, but showed no clear trend between 2011–12 and 2015–16, when 786,000 master's degrees were conferred. The number of doctor's degrees conferred increased by 49 percent (from 120,000 to 178,000) between 2000–01 and 2015–16.

Figure 2.   Percentage distribution of certificates and associate's degrees conferred by postsecondary institutions, by control of institution: Academic years 2000–01 and 2015–16

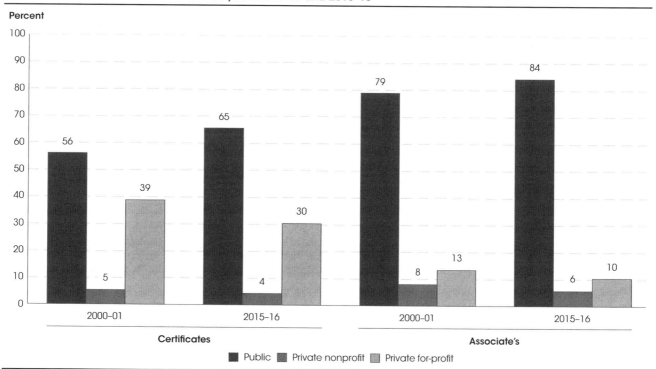

NOTE: Data are for postsecondary institutions participating in Title IV federal financial aid programs. Data for associate's degrees are from degree-granting institutions. Data for certificates are for certificates below the associate's degree level. Detail may not sum to totals because of rounding.
SOURCE: U.S. Department of Education, National Center for Education Statistics, Integrated Postsecondary Education Data System (IPEDS), Fall 2001 and Fall 2016, Completions component. See *Digest of Education Statistics 2017*, table 318.40.

From 2000–01 to 2015–16, the number of certificates below the associate's level conferred by public institutions increased by 99 percent (from 310,000 to 615,000). The number of certificates conferred by private nonprofit institutions was 37 percent higher in 2015–16 (40,000) than in 2000–01 (29,000), but showed no clear trend during this period. The number conferred by private for-profit institutions increased by 33 percent (from 214,000 in 2000–01 to 284,000 in 2015–16). Over this period, the proportion of certificates conferred by public institutions increased from 56 to 65 percent, while the proportion of certificates conferred by private nonprofit institutions decreased from 5 to 4 percent. The proportion conferred by private for-profit institutions was lower in 2015–16 (30 percent) than in 2000–01 (39 percent).

Likewise, from 2000–01 to 2015–16, the number of associate's degrees conferred increased by 86 percent at public institutions (from 456,000 to 848,000), by 24 percent at private nonprofit institutions (from 46,000 to 57,000), and by 35 percent at private for-profit institutions (from 77,000 to 104,000). The proportion of associate's degrees conferred by public institutions was higher in 2015–16 (84 percent) than in 2000–01 (79 percent). By contrast, the proportion of all associate's degrees conferred by private nonprofit institutions was lower in 2015–16 (6 percent) than in 2000–01 (8 percent), as was the proportion conferred by private for-profit institutions (10 percent in 2015–16 vs. 13 percent in 2000–01).

Figure 3. Percentage distribution of bachelor's, master's, and doctor's degrees conferred by postsecondary institutions, by control of institution: Academic years 2000–01 and 2015–16

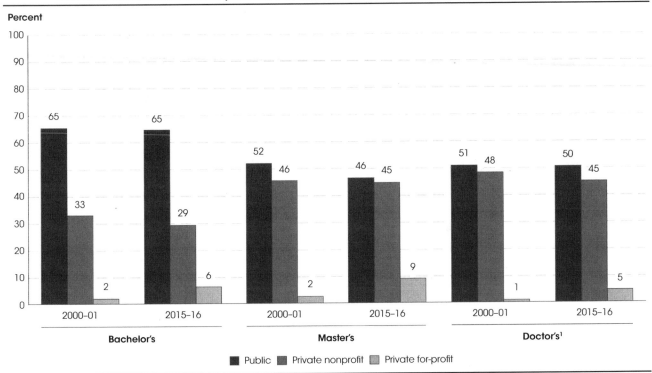

[1] Includes Ph.D., Ed.D., and comparable degrees at the doctoral level. Includes most degrees formerly classified as first-professional, such as M.D., D.D.S., and law degrees.
NOTE: Data are for degree-granting postsecondary institutions participating in Title IV federal financial aid programs.
SOURCE: U.S. Department of Education, National Center for Education Statistics, Integrated Postsecondary Education Data System (IPEDS), Fall 2001 and Fall 2016, Completions component. See *Digest of Education Statistics 2017*, table 318.40.

From 2000–01 to 2015–16, the number of bachelor's degrees conferred by public institutions increased by 53 percent (from 812,000 to 1.2 million), the number conferred by private nonprofit institutions increased by 37 percent (from 409,000 to 561,000), and the number conferred by private for-profit institutions increased by 419 percent (from 23,000 to 120,000). While the proportion of all bachelor's degrees conferred by public institutions was 65 percent in both 2000–01 and 2015–16, the proportion conferred by private nonprofit institutions decreased over that period (from 33 to 29 percent) and the proportion conferred by private for-profit institutions increased (from 2 to 6 percent).

The number of master's degrees conferred increased from 2000–01 to 2015–16, by 48 percent at public institutions (from 246,000 to 365,000), by 63 percent at private nonprofit institutions (from 216,000 to 351,000), and by 505 percent at private for-profit institutions (from 12,000 to 70,000). Over this period, the proportion of all master's degrees conferred by public institutions decreased (from 52 to 46 percent), as did the proportion conferred by private nonprofit institutions (from 46 to 45 percent). In contrast, the proportion of all master's degrees conferred by private for-profit institutions increased (from 2 to 9 percent).

From 2000–01 to 2015–16, the number of doctor's degrees conferred increased by 48 percent at public institutions (from 61,000 to 90,000), by 39 percent at private nonprofit institutions (from 58,000 to 80,000), and by 671 percent at private for-profit institutions (from 1,000 to 8,000). Over this period, the proportion of doctor's degrees conferred decreased at public institutions (from 51 to 50 percent) and at private nonprofit institutions (from 48 to 45 percent). At private for-profit institutions, however, the proportion conferred increased (from 1 to 5 percent).

Endnotes:
[1] A formal award certifying the satisfactory completion of a postsecondary education program.

Reference tables: *Digest of Education Statistics 2017*, table 318.40
Related indicators and resources: Degrees Awarded [*Status and Trends in the Education of Racial and Ethnic Groups*]; Graduate Degree Fields; Trends in Student Loan Debt for Graduate School Completers [*The Condition of Education 2018 Spotlight*]; Undergraduate Degree Fields

Glossary: Associate's degree, Bachelor's degree, Certificate, Control of institution, Doctor's degree, Master's degree, Private institution, Public school or institution

This page intentionally left blank.

Price of Attending an Undergraduate Institution

In 2015–16, the average net price of attendance (total cost minus grant and scholarship aid) at 4-year institutions for first-time, full-time undergraduate students at public institutions was $13,400, compared with $26,200 at private nonprofit institutions and $22,300 at private for-profit institutions (in constant 2016–17 dollars).

The total cost of attending a postsecondary institution includes the sum of published tuition and required fees (the lower of in-district or in-state for public institutions), books and supplies, and the weighted average cost for room, board, and other expenses. In academic year 2016–17, the total cost of attendance for first-time, full-time undergraduate students[1] differed by institutional control (public,[2] private nonprofit, or private for-profit) and institution level (2- year or 4-year). In addition, the total cost of attendance varied by student living arrangement (on campus; off campus, living with family; and off campus, not living with family).

Figure 1. Average total cost of attending degree-granting institutions for first-time, full-time undergraduate students, by level and control of institution and student living arrangement: Academic year 2016–17

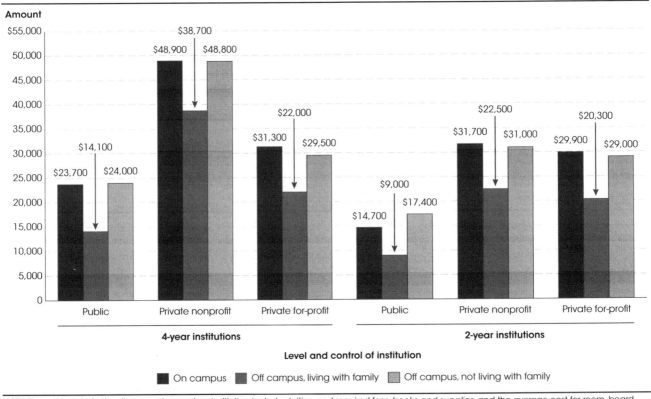

NOTE: The total cost of attending a postsecondary institution includes tuition and required fees, books and supplies, and the average cost for room, board, and other expenses. Tuition and fees at public institutions are the lower of either in-district or in-state tuition and fees. Excludes students who have already attended another postsecondary institution or who began their studies on a part-time basis. Data are weighted by the number of students at the institution who were awarded Title IV aid. Title IV aid includes grant aid, work-study aid, and loan aid.
SOURCE: U.S. Department of Education, National Center for Education Statistics, Integrated Postsecondary Education Data System (IPEDS), Winter 2016–17, Student Financial Aid component; and Fall 2016, Institutional Characteristics component. See *Digest of Education Statistics 2017*, table 330.40.

In academic year 2016–17, the average total cost of attendance for students living on campus was higher at private nonprofit institutions than at private for-profit institutions, and it was higher at private for-profit institutions than at public institutions. The average total cost of attendance for students living on campus ranged from $14,700 at public 2-year institutions to $48,900 at private nonprofit 4-year institutions. At every institutional control category and level, the average total cost of attendance was lowest for students living with family. For example, at public 2-year institutions, the average total cost of attendance was $9,000 for students living with family, compared with $14,700 for students living on campus and $17,400 for students living off campus but not with family.

Figure 2. Average tuition and fees of degree-granting institutions for first-time, full-time undergraduate students, by level and control of institution: Academic years 2010–11 and 2016–17

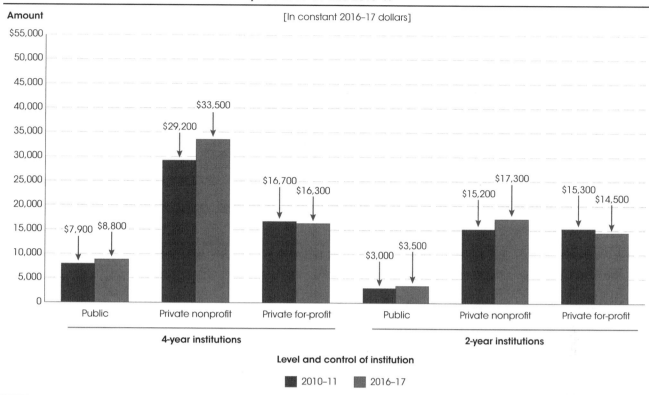

NOTE: Tuition and fees at public institutions are the lower of either in-district or in-state tuition and fees. Excludes students who have already attended another postsecondary institution or who began their studies on a part-time basis. Data are weighted by the number of students at the institution who were awarded Title IV aid. Title IV aid includes grant aid, work-study aid, and loan aid. Constant dollars based on the Consumer Price Index, prepared by the Bureau of Labor Statistics, U.S. Department of Labor, adjusted to an academic-year basis.
SOURCE: U.S. Department of Education, National Center for Education Statistics, Integrated Postsecondary Education Data System (IPEDS), Spring 2011 and Winter 2016–17, Student Financial Aid component; and Fall 2010 through Fall 2016, Institutional Characteristics component. See *Digest of Education Statistics 2017*, table 330.40.

Average tuition and fees were higher in 2016–17 than in 2010–11 for first-time, full-time undergraduates at public and private nonprofit 4-year institutions (in constant 2016–17 dollars). At public 4-year institutions, average tuition and fees were $8,800 in 2016–17, 12 percent higher than they were in 2010–11 ($7,900). At private nonprofit 4-year institutions, average tuition and fees were $33,500 in 2016–17, 15 percent higher than they were in 2010–11 ($29,200). At private for-profit 4-year institutions, in contrast, average tuition and fees in 2016–17 ($16,300) were 2 percent lower than in 2010–11 ($16,700).

The pattern in average tuition and fees at 2-year institutions was generally similar to the pattern at 4-year institutions. Average tuition and fees were 17 percent higher in 2016–17 than in 2010–11 at public 2-year institutions ($3,500 vs $3,000) and 14 percent higher in 2016–17 than in 2010–11 at private nonprofit 2-year institution ($17,300 vs. $15,200). In contrast, average tuition and fees were 6 percent lower in 2016–17 than in 2010–11 at private for-profit 2-year institutions ($14,500 vs. $15,300).

Many students and their families pay less than the full price of attendance because they receive financial aid

to help cover expenses. The primary types of financial aid are grant and scholarship aid, which do not have to be repaid, and loans, which must be repaid. Grant and scholarship aid may be awarded on the basis of financial need, merit, or both, and may include tuition aid from employers. In academic year 2015–16, the average amount of grant and scholarship aid[3] (in constant 2016–17 dollars) for first-time, full-time undergraduate students awarded Title IV aid[4] was higher for students at private nonprofit institutions than for those at public and private for-profit institutions. Students at private nonprofit 4-year institutions received an average of $21,300 in grant and scholarship aid, compared with $7,300 at public and $6,100 at private for-profit 4-year institutions.

The net price of attendance is the estimate of the actual amount of money that students and their families need to pay in a given year to cover educational expenses. Net price is calculated here as the total cost of attendance minus grant and scholarship aid. Net price provides an indication of what the actual financial burden is upon students and their families.

In 2015–16, among 4-year institutions, the average net price of attendance (in constant 2016–17 dollars) for first-time, full-time undergraduate students awarded Title IV aid was lower for students at public institutions ($13,400) than for those at both private nonprofit ($26,200) and private for-profit ($22,300) institutions. Similarly, the average net price at 2-year institutions in 2015–16 was lowest at public institutions ($7,200) and higher at private nonprofit and private for-profit institutions (both $20,800).

Figure 3. Average total cost, grant and scholarship aid, and net price for first-time, full-time degree/certificate-seeking undergraduate students paying in-state tuition and awarded aid at public 4-year institutions, by family income level: Academic year 2015–16

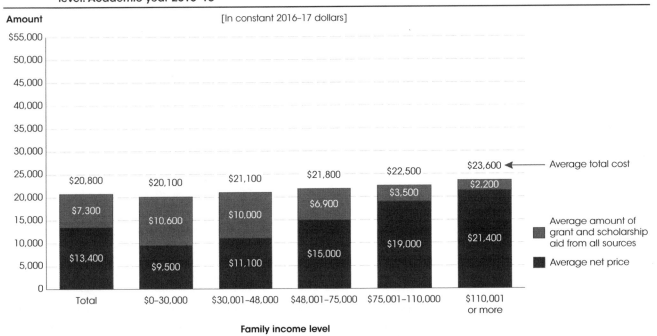

NOTE: Excludes students who previously attended another postsecondary institution or who began their studies on a part-time basis. Net price is calculated here as the average total cost of attendance minus average grant and scholarship aid. Includes only first-time, full-time students who paid the in-state or in-district tuition rate and who were awarded Title IV aid. Excludes students who were not awarded any Title IV aid. Title IV aid includes grant aid, work-study aid, and loan aid. Grant and scholarship aid consists of federal Title IV grants, as well as other grant or scholarship aid from the federal government, state or local governments, or institutional sources. Data are weighted by the number of students at the institution who were awarded Title IV aid. Totals include students for whom income data were not available. Constant dollars based on the Consumer Price Index, prepared by the Bureau of Labor Statistics, U.S. Department of Labor, adjusted to an academic-year basis. Detail may not sum to totals because of rounding.
SOURCE: U.S. Department of Education, National Center for Education Statistics, Integrated Postsecondary Education Data System (IPEDS), Winter 2016–17, Student Financial Aid component. See *Digest of Education Statistics 2017*, table 331.30.

The average amount of grant and scholarship aid awarded and the net price paid (in constant 2016–17 dollars) differed by students' family income level. In general, the lower the income, the greater the average amount of grant and scholarship aid awarded. For example, at public 4-year institutions, the average amount of grant and scholarship aid awarded to first-time, full-time undergraduate students paying in-state tuition in 2015–16 was highest for those with family incomes of $30,000 or less ($10,600 in aid) and lowest for those with family incomes of $110,001 or more ($2,200 in aid). Accordingly, at public 4-year institutions, the lowest average net price ($9,500) was for students with family incomes of $30,000 or less, and the highest average net price ($21,400) was for those with family incomes of $110,001 or more.

Figure 4. Average total cost, grant and scholarship aid, and net price for first-time, full-time degree/certificate-seeking undergraduate students awarded aid at private nonprofit 4-year institutions, by family income level: Academic year 2015–16

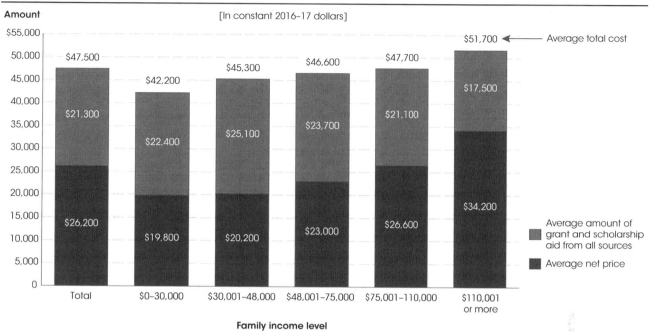

NOTE: Excludes students who previously attended another postsecondary institution or who began their studies on a part-time basis. Net price is calculated here as the average total cost of attendance minus average grant and scholarship aid. Includes only first-time, full-time students who were awarded Title IV aid. Excludes students who were not awarded any Title IV aid. Title IV aid includes grant aid, work-study aid, and loan aid. Grant and scholarship aid consists of federal Title IV grants, as well as other grant or scholarship aid from the federal government, state or local governments, or institutional sources. Data are weighted by the number of students at the institution who were awarded Title IV aid. Totals include students for whom income data were not available. Constant dollars based on the Consumer Price Index, prepared by the Bureau of Labor Statistics, U.S. Department of Labor, adjusted to an academic-year basis. Detail may not sum to totals because of rounding.
SOURCE: U.S. Department of Education, National Center for Education Statistics, Integrated Postsecondary Education Data System (IPEDS), Winter 2016–17, Student Financial Aid component. See *Digest of Education Statistics 2017*, table 331.30.

The pattern of average net price increasing with family income was also observed at private nonprofit 4-year institutions in 2015–16. However, the average amount of grant and scholarship aid awarded (in constant 2016–17 dollars) followed a different pattern. It was highest for students with family incomes between $30,001 and $48,000 ($25,100 in aid), followed by those with family incomes between $48,001 and $75,000 ($23,700 in aid),

those with family incomes of $30,000 or less ($22,400 in aid), those with family incomes between $75,001 and $110,000 ($21,100 in aid), and those with family incomes of $110,001 or more ($17,500 in aid). The lowest average net price ($19,800) was paid by students with family incomes of $30,000 or less, and the highest average net price ($34,200) was paid by those with family incomes of $110,001 or more.

Figure 5. Average total cost, grant and scholarship aid, and net price for first-time, full-time degree/certificate-seeking undergraduate students awarded aid at private for-profit 4-year institutions, by family income level: Academic year 2015–16

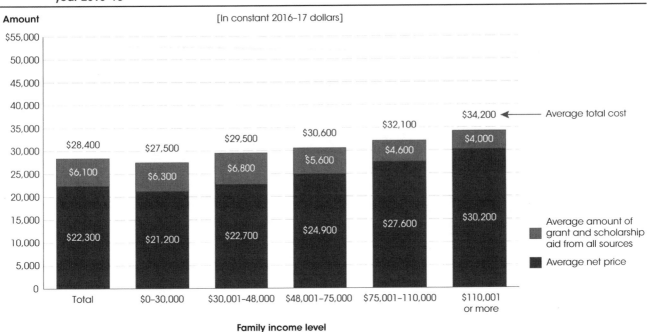

NOTE: Excludes students who previously attended another postsecondary institution or who began their studies on a part-time basis. Net price is calculated here as the average total cost of attendance minus average grant and scholarship aid. Includes only first-time, full-time students who were awarded Title IV aid. Excludes students who were not awarded any Title IV aid. Title IV aid includes grant aid, work-study aid, and loan aid. Grant and scholarship aid consists of federal Title IV grants, as well as other grant or scholarship aid from the federal government, state or local governments, or institutional sources. Data are weighted by the number of students at the institution who were awarded Title IV aid. Totals include students for whom income data were not available. Constant dollars based on the Consumer Price Index, prepared by the Bureau of Labor Statistics, U.S. Department of Labor, adjusted to an academic-year basis. Detail may not sum to totals because of rounding.
SOURCE: U.S. Department of Education, National Center for Education Statistics, Integrated Postsecondary Education Data System (IPEDS), Winter 2016–17, Student Financial Aid component. See *Digest of Education Statistics 2017*, table 331.30.

At private for-profit 4-year institutions, the average amount of grant and scholarship aid awarded (in constant 2016–17 dollars) also followed a different pattern from that of public 4-year institutions. The average amount of grant and scholarship aid awarded to first-time, full-time undergraduate students in 2015–16 at private for-profit 4-year institutions was highest for those with family incomes between $30,001 and $48,000 ($6,800 in aid), second highest for those with family income levels of $30,000 or less ($6,300 in aid), and lowest for those with family incomes of $110,001 or more ($4,000 in aid). The lowest average net price ($21,200) was paid by students with family incomes of $30,000 or less, and the highest average net price ($30,200) was paid by those with family incomes of $110,001 or more.

Looking at the average amount of grant and scholarship aid awarded and the average net price of attendance (in constant 2016–17 dollars) within each income level shows a range across public, private nonprofit, and private for-

profit institutions in 2015–16. At most family income levels, the average amount of grant and scholarship aid was highest for students attending private nonprofit 4-year institutions and lowest for students at private for-profit 4-year institutions. Additionally, at each family income level except the highest level ($110,001 or more), the average net price was highest for students attending private for-profit 4-year institutions and lowest for students attending public 4-year institutions. For example, the average amount of grant and scholarship aid (in constant 2016–17 dollars) awarded to students with family incomes between $30,001 and $48,000 who attended 4-year institutions was highest at private nonprofit institutions ($25,100), followed by public institutions ($10,000) and private for-profit institutions ($6,800). The average net price of attending a private for-profit 4-year institution ($22,700) at this family income level was higher than the price of attending a private nonprofit ($20,200) or a public 4-year ($11,100) institution.

Endnotes:

[1] Includes only students who are seeking a degree or certificate.
[2] All data for public institutions only include students who paid the in-state or in-district tuition and fees.
[3] Average amounts of grant and scholarship aid include federal Title IV grants, as well as other grant or scholarship aid from the federal government, state or local governments, or institutional sources.
[4] Title IV aid includes grant aid, work-study aid, and loan aid. Data for net price and grant and scholarship aid only include students who were awarded Title IV aid.

Reference tables: *Digest of Education Statistics 2017*, tables 330.40 and 331.30

Related indicators and resources: Financing Postsecondary Education in the United States [*The Condition of Education 2013 Spotlight*]; Loans for Undergraduate Students; Sources of Financial Aid

Glossary: Constant dollars, Control of institutions, Financial aid, Full-time enrollment, Postsecondary institutions (basic classification by level), Private institution, Public school or institution, Title IV eligible institution, Tuition and fees, Undergraduate students

Loans for Undergraduate Students

In 2015–16, the average annual undergraduate student loan amount of $7,100 was 2 percent lower than the 2010–11 average of $7,300 (in constant 2016–17 dollars). Less than half (46 percent) of first-time, full-time undergraduate students were awarded loan aid in 2015–16, a 4 percentage point decrease from 2010–11 (50 percent).

To help offset the cost of attending a postsecondary institution, Title IV of the Higher Education Act of 1965 authorized several student financial assistance programs— namely, federal grants, loans, and Work-Study. The largest federal loan program is the William D. Ford Federal Direct Loan Program, established in 2010, for which the federal government is the lender. Interest on the loans provided

under the Direct Loan Program may be subsidized, based on need, while the recipient is in school. Other types of student loans include institutional loans and private loans. Most loans are payable over 10 years, beginning 6 months after the student does one of the following: graduates, drops below half-time enrollment, or withdraws from the academic program.

Figure 1. Average undergraduate tuition and fees for full-time students at degree-granting postsecondary institutions, by level and control of institution: 2010–11 through 2015–16

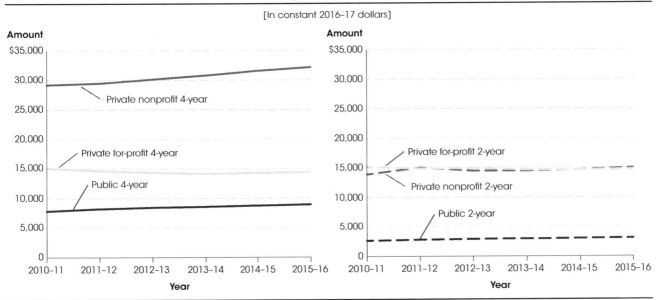

NOTE: Degree-granting institutions grant associate's or higher degrees and participate in Title IV federal financial aid programs. Some data have been revised from previously published figures. For public institutions, in-state tuition and required fees are used. Tuition and fees are weighted by the number of full-time-equivalent undergraduates. Constant dollars are based on the Consumer Price Index, prepared by the Bureau of Labor Statistics, U.S. Department of Labor, adjusted to an academic-year basis.
SOURCE: U.S. Department of Education, National Center for Education Statistics, Integrated Postsecondary Education Data System (IPEDS), Fall 2010 through Fall 2015, Institutional Characteristics component. See *Digest of Education Statistics 2017*, table 330.10.

Between academic years 2010–11 and 2015–16, average undergraduate tuition and fees for full-time students across all degree-granting postsecondary institutions increased by 15 percent, from $10,500 to $12,100.[1] Among 4-year institutions, the largest percentage increase in tuition and fees between 2010–11 and 2015–16 was at public institutions (14 percent, from $7,800 to $8,900); however, the largest dollar amount increase was at private nonprofit institutions (a $3,000 increase, from $29,200 to $32,200). By contrast, tuition and fees at private for-profit 4-year institutions were 4 percent lower in 2015–16 ($14,400) than in 2010–11 ($15,100).

As at 4-year institutions, the largest percentage increase in tuition and fees among 2-year institutions during this period was at public institutions (15 percent, from $2,700 to $3,100). Tuition and fees at private nonprofit 2-year institutions were 8 percent higher in 2015–16 than in 2010–11 ($15,000 vs. $13,900). By contrast, tuition and fees at private for-profit 2-year institutions decreased 3 percent between 2010–11 ($15,100) and 2015–16 ($14,700).

Figure 2. Percentage of first-time, full-time students awarded loan aid at degree-granting postsecondary institutions, by level and control of institution: 2010–11 through 2015–16

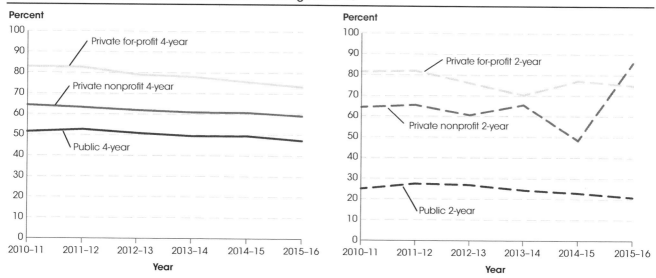

NOTE: Degree-granting institutions grant associate's or higher degrees and participate in Title IV federal financial aid programs. Some data have been revised from previously published figures. Includes only loans made directly to students; does not include Parent Loans for Undergraduate Students (PLUS) and other loans made directly to parents.
SOURCE: U.S. Department of Education, National Center for Education Statistics, Integrated Postsecondary Education Data System (IPEDS), Winter 2011–12 through Winter 2016–17, Student Financial Aid component. See *Digest of Education Statistics 2017*, table 331.20.

Less than half (46 percent) of first-time, full-time undergraduate students were awarded loan aid in 2015–16, a 4 percentage point decrease from 2010–11 (50 percent).[2] Among 4-year institutions, the largest decrease in the percentage of students awarded loan aid was at private for-profit institutions (10 percentage points), from 83 percent in 2010–11 to 73 percent in 2015–16. At public 4-year institutions, the percentage of undergraduates awarded loans decreased 4 percentage points, from 51 percent in 2010–11 to 47 percent in 2015–16. Likewise, at private nonprofit 4-year institutions, the percentage of undergraduates awarded loans decreased by

5 percentage points from 2010–11 (64 percent) to 2015–16 (59 percent). Among 2-year institutions, the percentage of students awarded loans was about 4 percentage points lower in 2015–16 than in 2010–11 at public institutions (21 vs. 25 percent). Likewise, at private for-profit 2-year institutions, the percentage of undergraduates awarded loans was 7 percentage points lower in 2015–16 (75 percent) than in 2010–11 (82 percent). In contrast, the percentage of undergraduates awarded loans at private nonprofit 2-year institutions was about 21 percentage points higher in 2015–16 (86 percent) than in 2010–11 (64 percent).

Figure 3. Average annual loan amounts for first-time, full-time students awarded loan aid at degree-granting postsecondary institutions, by level and control of institution: 2010–11 through 2015–16

[In constant 2016–17 dollars]

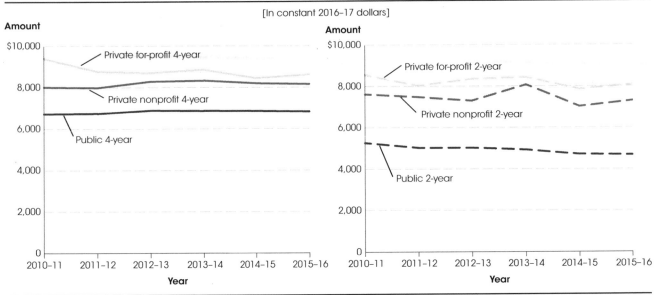

NOTE: Degree-granting institutions grant associate's or higher degrees and participate in Title IV federal financial aid programs. Some data have been revised from previously published figures. Includes only loans made directly to students; does not include Parent Loans for Undergraduate Students (PLUS) and other loans made directly to parents. Constant dollars are based on the Consumer Price Index, prepared by the Bureau of Labor Statistics, U.S. Department of Labor, adjusted to an academic-year basis.
SOURCE: U.S. Department of Education, National Center for Education Statistics, Integrated Postsecondary Education Data System (IPEDS), Winter 2011–12 through Winter 2016–17, Student Financial Aid component. See *Digest of Education Statistics 2017*, table 331.20.

Overall, the average loan amount that undergraduate students were awarded in 2015–16 was 2 percent lower than in 2010–11. Average annual student loan amounts for first-time, full-time degree/certificate-seeking undergraduate students awarded loan aid were $7,100 in 2015–16 and $7,300 in 2010–11.[1] At public 4-year and private nonprofit 4-year institutions, average loan amounts were 2 percent higher in 2015–16 than in 2010–11 ($6,800 vs. $6,700 at public 4-year institutions and $8,200 vs. $8,000 at private nonprofit 4-year institutions). In contrast, at private for-profit 4-year institutions, average loan amounts were 8 percent lower in 2015–16 ($8,600) than in 2010–11 ($9,400). At public 2-year institutions,

loan amounts were 11 percent lower (the largest percentage decrease) in 2015–16 ($4,700) than in 2010–11 ($5,300). The average annual loan amount was 4 percent lower at private nonprofit 2-year institutions in 2015–16 ($7,300) than it was in 2010–11 ($7,600) and 6 percent lower at private for-profit 2-year institutions ($8,100 in 2015–16 vs. $8,600 in 2010–11). In 2015–16, the average annual student loan amount for students at private for-profit 4-year institutions ($8,600) was higher than the amount for students at all other categories of institutions (public, private nonprofit, and private for-profit 2-year institutions and public and private nonprofit 4-year institutions).

Endnotes:
[1] Dollar amounts are expressed in constant 2016–17 dollars.

[2] Includes only loans made directly to students. Does not include Parent Loans for Undergraduate Students (PLUS) and other loans made directly to parents.

Reference tables: *Digest of Education Statistics 2017*, tables 330.10 and 331.20
Related indicators and resources: Financing Postsecondary Education in the United States [*The Condition of Education 2013 Spotlight*]; Price of Attending an Undergraduate Institution; Sources of Financial Aid; Trends in Student Loan Debt for Graduate School Completers [*The Condition of Education 2018 Spotlight*]

Glossary: Certificate, College, Constant dollars, Control of institutions, Direct Loan Program, Full-time enrollment, Postsecondary institutions (basic classification by level), Private institution, Public school or institution, Title IV eligible institution, Tuition and fees, Undergraduate students

This page intentionally left blank.

Sources of Financial Aid

The percentage of first-time, full-time degree/certificate-seeking undergraduate students at 4-year postsecondary institutions awarded financial aid was higher in 2015–16 (85 percent) than in 2000–01 (75 percent).

Grants and loans are the major forms of federal financial aid for first-time, full-time degree/certificate-seeking undergraduate students. The largest federal grant program available to undergraduate students is the Pell Grant program. In order to qualify for a Pell Grant, a student must demonstrate financial need. Some federal loan programs are available to all students and some are based on financial need. Other sources of financial aid include state and local governments, institutions, and private sources, as well as private loans. The forms of financial aid discussed in this indicator are only those provided directly to students. For example, student loans include only loans made directly to students; they do not include Parent Loans for Undergraduate Students (PLUS) and other loans made directly to parents.

Figure 1. Percentage of first-time, full-time undergraduate students awarded financial aid at 4-year degree-granting postsecondary institutions, by control of institution: Academic years 2000–01, 2005–06, 2010–11, and 2015–16

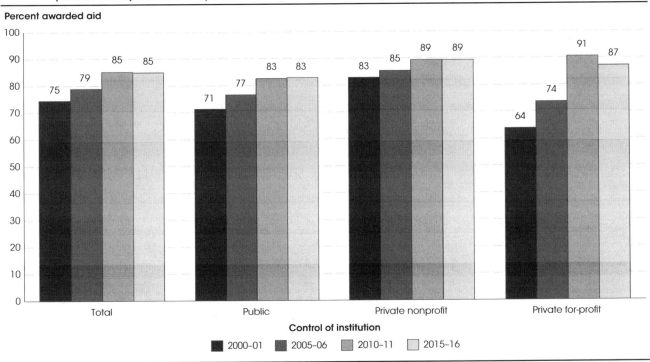

Percent awarded aid

NOTE: Degree-granting institutions grant associate's or higher degrees and participate in Title IV federal financial aid programs. Some data have been revised from previously published figures. Student financial aid includes any federal and private loans to students and federal, state/local, and institutional grants. Student loans include only loans made directly to students; they do not include Parent Loans for Undergraduate Students (PLUS) and other loans made directly to parents. For academic years 2000–01 and 2005–06, the percentage represents students receiving aid, rather than students awarded aid. Students receiving aid are those who were not only awarded aid, but also accepted it. Some data have been revised from previously published figures. Although rounded numbers are displayed, the figures are based on unrounded estimates.
SOURCE: U.S. Department of Education, National Center for Education Statistics, Integrated Postsecondary Education Data System (IPEDS), Spring 2002, Spring 2007, Winter 2011–12, and Winter 2016–17, Student Financial Aid component. See *Digest of Education Statistics 2017*, table 331.20.

At 4-year degree-granting postsecondary institutions, the percentage of first-time, full-time degree/certificate-seeking undergraduate students who were awarded financial aid was higher in academic year 2015–16 (85 percent) than in 2000–01 (75 percent).[1] The pattern of higher percentages of students being awarded aid in 2015–16 than in 2000–01 was observed for public (83 vs. 71 percent), private nonprofit (89 vs. 83 percent), and private for-profit (87 vs. 64 percent) 4-year institutions. Over a more recent time period, similar percentages of students overall were awarded aid in 2010–11 and 2015–16 (85 percent in both years). This pattern was also observed for public (83 percent in both 2010–11 and 2015–16) and private nonprofit (89 percent in both years) 4-year institutions. At private for-profit 4-year institutions, in contrast, the percentage of students awarded financial aid was lower in 2015–16 (87 percent) than in 2010–11 (91 percent).

Figure 2. Percentage of first-time, full-time undergraduate students awarded financial aid at 2-year degree-granting postsecondary institutions, by control of institution: Academic years 2000–01, 2005–06, 2010–11, and 2015–16

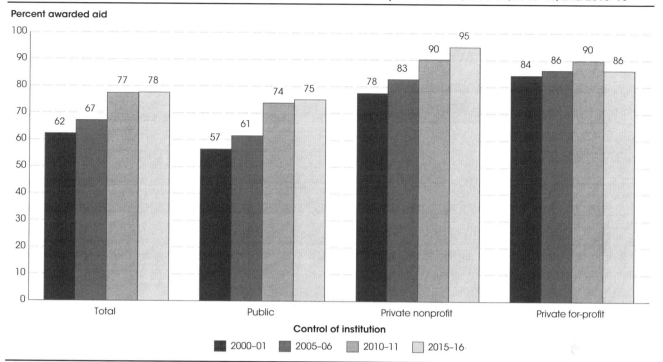

NOTE: Degree-granting institutions grant associate's or higher degrees and participate in Title IV federal financial aid programs. Some data have been revised from previously published figures. Student financial aid includes any federal and private loans to students and federal, state/local, and institutional grants. Student loans include only loans made directly to students; they do not include Parent Loans for Undergraduate Students (PLUS) and other loans made directly to parents. For academic years 2000–01 and 2005–06, the percentage represents students receiving aid, rather than students awarded aid. Students receiving aid are those who were not only awarded aid, but also accepted it. Some data have been revised from previously published figures.
SOURCE: U.S. Department of Education, National Center for Education Statistics, Integrated Postsecondary Education Data System (IPEDS), Spring 2002, Spring 2007, Winter 2011–12, and Winter 2016–17, Student Financial Aid component. See *Digest of Education Statistics 2017*, table 331.20.

At 2-year degree-granting postsecondary institutions, the percentage of first-time, full-time degree/certificate-seeking undergraduate students who were awarded financial aid was higher in 2015–16 (78 percent) than in 2000–01 (62 percent). This pattern was also observed at public 2-year institutions (where 75 percent of students were awarded aid in 2015–16 vs. 57 percent in 2000–01),

and at private nonprofit 2-year institutions (where 95 percent of students were awarded aid in 2015–16 vs. 78 percent in 2000–01). At private for-profit 2-year institutions, the percentage of students awarded aid was lower in both 2015–16 (86 percent) and 2000–01 (84 percent) than in 2010–11 (90 percent).

Figure 3. Percentage of first-time, full-time undergraduate students awarded financial aid at 4-year degree-granting postsecondary institutions, by type of financial aid and control of institution: Academic year 2015–16

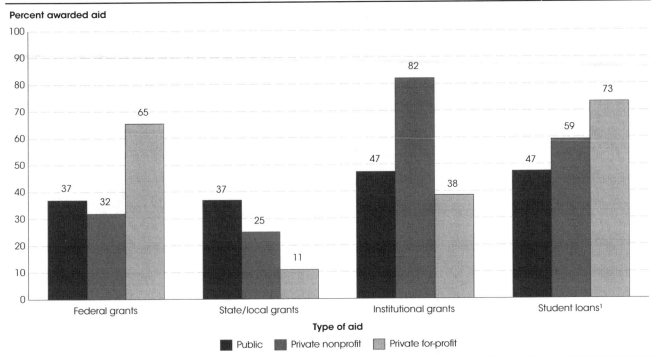

Percent awarded aid

¹ Student loans include only loans made directly to students; they do not include Parent Loans for Undergraduate Students (PLUS) and other loans made directly to parents.
NOTE: Degree-granting institutions grant associate's or higher degrees and participate in Title IV federal financial aid programs. Student financial aid includes any federal and private loans to students and federal, state/local, and institutional grants.
SOURCE: U.S. Department of Education, National Center for Education Statistics, Integrated Postsecondary Education Data System (IPEDS), Winter 2016–17, Student Financial Aid component. See *Digest of Education Statistics 2017*, table 331.20.

The percentage of first-time, full-time degree/certificate-seeking undergraduate students at 4-year institutions who were awarded specific types of financial aid varied according to institution control. In academic year 2015–16, the percentage of students awarded federal grants at 4-year institutions was higher at private for-profit institutions (65 percent) than at public institutions (37 percent) and private nonprofit institutions (32 percent). The percentage of students at 4-year institutions awarded state or local grants was higher at public institutions (37 percent) than at private nonprofit

institutions (25 percent) and private for-profit institutions (11 percent). The percentage of students awarded institutional grants at 4-year institutions was higher at private nonprofit institutions (82 percent) than at public institutions (47 percent) and private for-profit institutions (38 percent). The percentage of students awarded student loans at 4-year institutions was highest at private for-profit institutions (73 percent), compared with 59 percent at private nonprofit institutions and 47 percent at public institutions.

Figure 4. Percentage of first-time, full-time undergraduate students awarded financial aid at 2-year degree-granting postsecondary institutions, by type of financial aid and control of institution: Academic year 2015–16

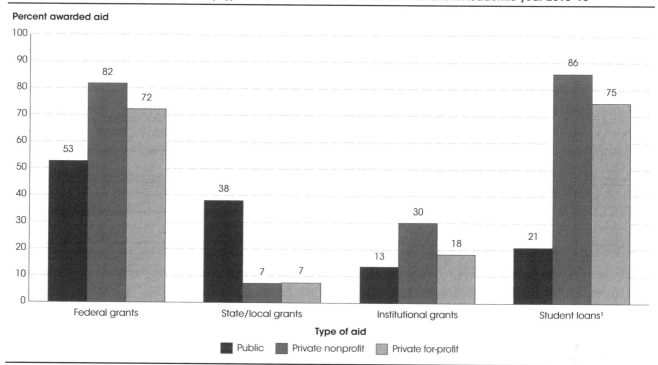

Percent awarded aid

¹ Student loans include only loans made directly to students; they do not include Parent Loans for Undergraduate Students (PLUS) and other loans made directly to parents.
NOTE: Degree-granting institutions grant associate's or higher degrees and participate in Title IV federal financial aid programs. Student financial aid includes any federal and private loans to students and federal, state/local, and institutional grants. Although rounded numbers are displayed, the figures are based on unrounded estimates.
SOURCE: U.S. Department of Education, National Center for Education Statistics, Integrated Postsecondary Education Data System (IPEDS), Winter 2016–17, Student Financial Aid component. See *Digest of Education Statistics 2017*, table 331.20.

The percentage of first-time, full-time degree/certificate-seeking undergraduate students who were awarded specific types of financial aid also varied according to institution control at 2-year institutions. In academic year 2015–16, the percentage of students awarded federal grants at 2-year institutions was higher at private nonprofit institutions (82 percent) and private for-profit institutions (72 percent) than at public institutions (53 percent). The percentage of students at public 2-year institutions who were awarded state or local grants (38 percent) was five times higher

than the percentage at private nonprofit 2-year institutions and private for-profit 2-year institutions (both 7 percent). About 30 percent of students at private nonprofit 2-year institutions were awarded institutional grants, compared with 18 percent of students at private for-profit institutions and 13 percent of students at public institutions. The percentages of students at 2-year institutions awarded student loans were higher at private nonprofit institutions (86 percent) and private for-profit institutions (75 percent) than at public institutions (21 percent).

Figure 5. Average amount of financial aid awarded to first-time, full-time undergraduate students awarded financial aid at 4-year degree-granting postsecondary institutions, by type of financial aid and control of institution: Academic year 2015–16

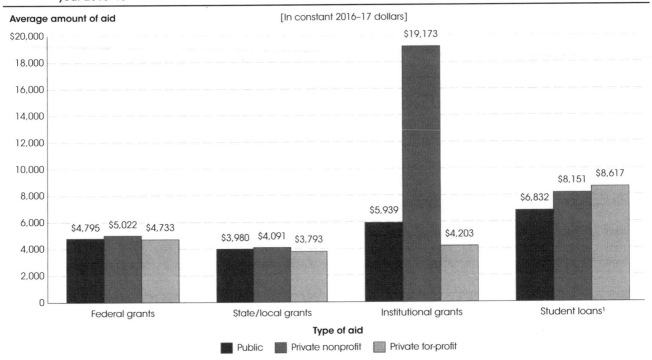

[1] Student loans include only loans made directly to students; they do not include Parent Loans for Undergraduate Students (PLUS) and other loans made directly to parents.

NOTE: Degree-granting institutions grant associate's or higher degrees and participate in Title IV federal financial aid programs. Student financial aid includes any federal and private loans to students and federal, state/local, and institutional grants. Award amounts are in constant 2016–17 dollars, based on the Consumer Price Index (CPI).

SOURCE: U.S. Department of Education, National Center for Education Statistics, Integrated Postsecondary Education Data System (IPEDS), Winter 2016–17, Student Financial Aid component. See *Digest of Education Statistics 2017*, table 331.20.

Across 4-year institutions, the average federal grant award in academic year 2015–16 ranged from $4,733 at private for-profit institutions to $5,022 at private nonprofit institutions. The average state or local grant award ranged from $3,793 at private for-profit institutions to $4,091 at private nonprofit institutions (reported in constant 2016–17 dollars). There were larger differences by institution control in average institutional grant awards. The average institutional grant award at private nonprofit institutions ($19,173) was more than three times higher than at public institutions ($5,939) and private for-profit institutions ($4,203). The average student loan amount was higher at private for-profit institutions ($8,617) and private nonprofit institutions ($8,151) than at public institutions ($6,832).

Figure 6. Average amount of financial aid awarded to first-time, full-time undergraduate students awarded financial aid at 2-year degree-granting postsecondary institutions, by type of financial aid and control of institution: Academic year 2015–16

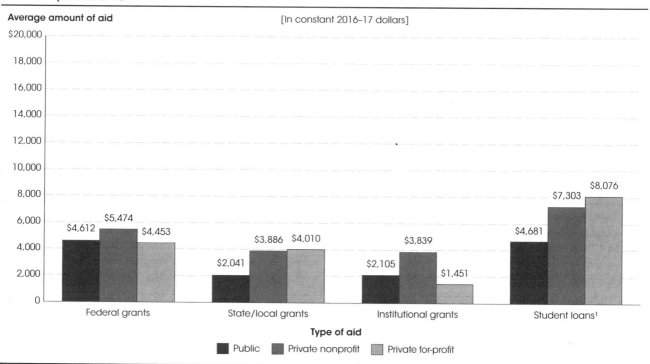

[1] Student loans include only loans made directly to students; they do not include Parent Loans for Undergraduate Students (PLUS) and other loans made directly to parents.
NOTE: Degree-granting institutions grant associate's or higher degrees and participate in Title IV federal financial aid programs. Student financial aid includes any federal and private loans to students and federal, state/local, and institutional grants. Award amounts are in constant 2016–17 dollars, based on the Consumer Price Index (CPI).
SOURCE: U.S. Department of Education, National Center for Education Statistics, Integrated Postsecondary Education Data System (IPEDS), Winter 2016–17, Student Financial Aid component. See *Digest of Education Statistics 2017*, table 331.20.

Across 2-year institutions, the average federal grant award in academic year 2015–16 ranged from $4,453 at private for-profit institutions to $5,474 at private nonprofit institutions (reported in constant 2016–17 dollars). There were larger differences by institution control among the other award types. The average state or local grant award was higher at private for-profit institutions ($4,010) and private nonprofit institutions ($3,886) than at public

institutions ($2,041). The average institutional grant award was higher at private nonprofit institutions ($3,839) than at public institutions ($2,105) and private for-profit institutions ($1,451). Similar to 4-year institutions, the average student loan amount at 2-year institutions in 2015–16 was higher at private for-profit ($8,076) and private nonprofit ($7,303) institutions than at public institutions ($4,681).

Endnotes:

[1] Student financial aid includes any federal and private loans to students and federal, state/local, and institutional grants. For academic years 2000–01 and 2005–06, the percentage of students with financial aid was reported as the percentage of students

who "received aid." Starting with academic year 2010–11, postsecondary institutions reported the same data as the percentage of students who "were awarded aid," to better reflect that some students were awarded aid but did not receive it.

Reference tables: *Digest of Education Statistics 2017*, table 331.20
Related indicators and resources: Financial Aid [*Status and Trends in the Education of Racial and Ethnic Groups*]; Financing Postsecondary Education in the United States [*The Condition of Education 2013 Spotlight*]; Loans for Undergraduate Students; Price of Attending an Undergraduate Institution; Trends in Student Loan Debt for Graduate School Completers [*The Condition of Education 2018 Spotlight*]

Glossary: Certificate, Constant dollars, Control of institutions, Degree-granting institutions, Financial aid, Full-time enrollment, Postsecondary institutions (basic classification by level), Private institution, Public school or institution, Undergraduate students

Postsecondary Institution Revenues

Between 2010–11 and 2015–16, revenues from tuition and fees per full-time-equivalent (FTE) student increased by 23 percent at public institutions (from $6,003 to $7,380 in constant 2016–17 dollars) and by 7 percent at private nonprofit institutions (from $20,071 to $21,394). At private for-profit institutions, revenues from tuition and fees per FTE student were 5 percent lower in 2015–16 than in 2010–11 ($15,806 vs. $16,698).

In 2015–16, total revenues at degree-granting postsecondary institutions in the United States were $564 billion (in current dollars). Total revenues were $364 billion at public institutions, $183 billion at private nonprofit institutions, and $17 billion at private for-profit institutions.

Figure 1.   Percentage distribution of total revenues at degree-granting postsecondary institutions, by institutional control and source of funds: 2015–16

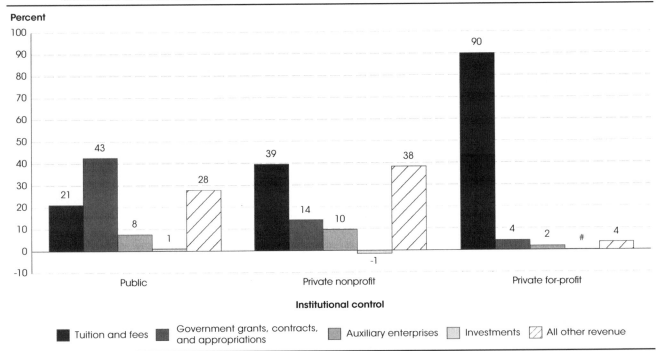

Rounds to zero.
NOTE: Government grants, contracts, and appropriations include revenues from federal, state, and local governments. Private grants and contracts are included in the local government revenue category at public institutions. All other revenue includes gifts, capital or private grants and contracts, hospital revenue, sales and services of educational activities, and other revenue. Revenue data are not directly comparable across institutional control categories because Pell Grants are included in the federal grant revenues at public institutions but tend to be included in tuition and fees and auxiliary enterprise revenues at private nonprofit and private for-profit institutions. Revenues from tuition and fees are net of discounts and allowances. Degree-granting institutions grant associate's or higher degrees and participate in Title IV federal financial aid programs. Detail may not sum to totals because of rounding.
SOURCE: U.S. Department of Education, National Center for Education Statistics, Integrated Postsecondary Education Data System (IPEDS), Spring 2017, Finance component. See *Digest of Education Statistics 2017*, tables 333.10, 333.40, and 333.55.

The primary sources of revenue for degree-granting institutions were tuition and fees; investments;[1] and government grants, contracts, and appropriations. The percentages from these revenue sources varied by institutional control (i.e., public, private nonprofit, and private for-profit). In 2015–16, public institutions received 43 percent of their overall revenues from government sources (which include federal, state, and local government[2] grants, contracts, and appropriations). In 2015–16, student tuition and fees constituted the largest percentage of total revenues at private nonprofit institutions and private for-profit institutions (39 and 90 percent, respectively).

It is important to note that public and private institutions report financial information according to the accounting standards that govern institution types. Pell Grants are included in federal grant revenues at public institutions but tend to be included in tuition and fees and auxiliary enterprise revenues at private nonprofit and private for-profit institutions. Thus, some categories of revenue data are not directly comparable across public, private nonprofit, and private for-profit institutions.

Figure 2. Revenues from tuition and fees per full-time-equivalent (FTE) student for degree-granting postsecondary institutions, by institutional control: 2010–11 and 2015–16

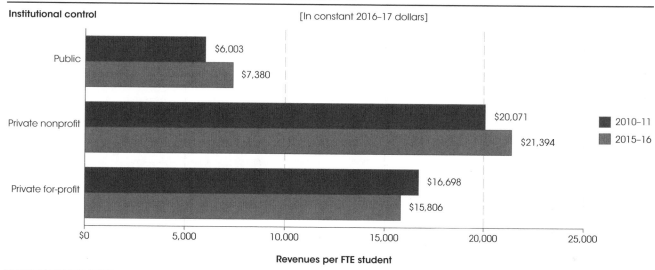

NOTE: Full-time-equivalent (FTE) student enrollment includes full-time students plus the full-time equivalent of part-time students. Revenues per FTE student are reported in constant 2016–17 dollars, based on the Consumer Price Index (CPI) adjusted to a school-year basis. Revenue data are not directly comparable across institutional control categories because Pell Grants are included in the federal grant revenues at public institutions but tend to be included in tuition and fees and auxiliary enterprise revenues at private nonprofit and private for-profit institutions. Revenues from tuition and fees are net of discounts and allowances. Degree-granting institutions grant associate's or higher degrees and participate in Title IV federal financial aid programs. Some data have been revised from previously published figures.
SOURCE: U.S. Department of Education, National Center for Education Statistics, Integrated Postsecondary Education Data System (IPEDS), Spring 2012 and Spring 2017, Finance component; and Spring 2011 and 2016, Fall Enrollment component. See *Digest of Education Statistics 2017*, tables 333.10, 333.40, and 333.55.

Between 2010–11 and 2015–16, the percentage change in revenues from tuition and fees per full-time-equivalent (FTE) student varied by institutional control. Revenues per FTE student are presented in constant 2016–17 dollars, based on the Consumer Price Index (CPI). During this period, tuition and fee revenues per FTE student increased at both public and private nonprofit institutions. The largest increase in revenues from tuition and fees per FTE student was at public institutions, where they increased by 23 percent (from $6,003 to $7,380), more than three times the percentage increase at private nonprofit institutions (7 percent, from $20,071 to $21,394). Although revenues from tuition and fees remained the primary revenue source at private for-profit institutions, revenues from tuition and fees per FTE student were 5 percent lower in 2015–16 ($15,806) than in 2010–11 ($16,698).

Figure 3. Revenues from government grants, contracts, and appropriations per full-time-equivalent (FTE) student for degree-granting postsecondary institutions, by source of funds and institutional control: 2010–11 and 2015–16

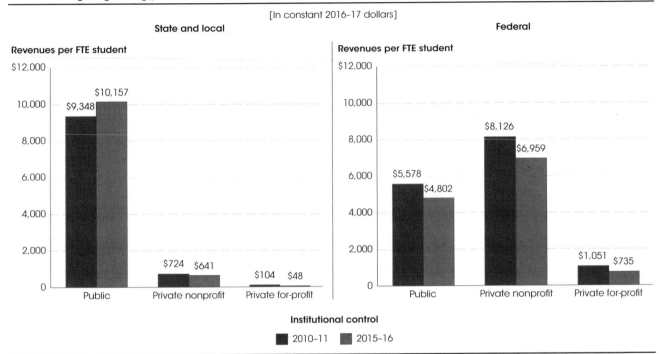

[In constant 2016–17 dollars]

NOTE: Full-time-equivalent (FTE) student enrollment includes full-time students plus the full-time equivalent of part-time students. Revenues per FTE student are reported in constant 2016–17 dollars, based on the Consumer Price Index (CPI) adjusted to a school-year basis. Private grants and contracts are included in the local government revenue category at public institutions. Revenue data are not comparable across institutional control categories because Pell Grants are included in the federal grant revenues at public institutions but tend to be included in tuition and fees and auxiliary enterprise revenues at private nonprofit and private for-profit institutions. Degree-granting institutions grant associate's or higher degrees and participate in Title IV federal financial aid programs. Some data have been revised from previously published figures.
SOURCE: U.S. Department of Education, National Center for Education Statistics, Integrated Postsecondary Education Data System (IPEDS), Spring 2012 and Spring 2017, Finance component; and Spring 2011 and 2016, Fall Enrollment component. See *Digest of Education Statistics 2017*, tables 333.10, 333.40, and 333.55.

Total revenues per FTE student from federal, state, and local government sources between 2010–11 and 2015–16 varied by institutional control. Revenues per FTE student from government sources were 32 percent lower in 2015–16 ($783) than in 2010–11 ($1,155) at private for-profit institutions and 14 percent lower in 2015–16 ($7,600) than in 2010–11 ($8,849) at private nonprofit institutions. At public institutions, revenues per FTE student from these sources were similar in 2015–16 ($14,959) and in 2010–11 ($14,926).

Revenues per FTE student from federal government sources alone were lower in 2015–16 than in 2010–11 across all institutional control categories. The largest percentage change was at private for-profit institutions, where federal revenues per FTE student fell by 30 percent (from $1,051 to $735). At both private nonprofit and

public institutions, federal revenues per FTE student decreased by 14 percent during this period (from $8,126 to $6,959 at private nonprofit institutions and $5,578 to $4,802 at public institutions).

The percentage change in state and local government revenues per FTE student varied by institutional control. Revenues per FTE student from these sources were 9 percent higher in 2015–16 ($10,157) than in 2010–11 ($9,348) at public institutions but 11 percent lower in 2015–16 ($641) than in 2010–11 ($724) at private nonprofit institutions. At private for-profit institutions, revenues per FTE student from state and local government sources decreased by 54 percent during this period (from $104 to $48) but accounted for only a small percentage (less than one-half of 1 percent) of total revenues.

Endnotes:
[1] Investments/investment returns are aggregate amounts of dividends, interest, royalties, rent, and gains or losses from both fair value adjustments and trades of the institution's investment and/or endowment.

[2] Private grants and contracts are included in local government revenues at public institutions.

Reference tables: *Digest of Education Statistics 2017*, tables 333.10, 333.40, and 333.55

Related indicators and resources: Postsecondary Institution Expenses

Glossary: Constant dollars, Consumer Price Index (CPI), Control of institutions, Degree-granting institution, Full-time-equivalent (FTE) enrollment, Private institution, Public school or institution, Revenue, Tuition and fees

This page intentionally left blank.

Postsecondary Institution Expenses

In 2015–16, instruction expenses per full-time-equivalent (FTE) student (in constant 2016–17 dollars) was the largest expense category at public institutions ($10,422) and private nonprofit institutions ($17,860). At private for-profit institutions, the combined category of student services, academic support, and institutional support expenses per FTE student was the largest expense category ($10,398).

In 2015–16, postsecondary institutions in the United States spent $559 billion (in current dollars). Total expenses were $355 billion at public institutions, $189 billion at private nonprofit institutions, and $16 billion at private for-profit institutions. Some data may not be comparable across institutions by control categories (i.e., public, private nonprofit, and private for-profit) because of differences in accounting standards. Comparisons by institutional level (i.e., between 2-year and 4-year institutions) may also be limited because of different institutional missions. The instructional missions of 2-year institutions generally focus on student instruction and related activities that include providing a range of career-oriented programs at the certificate

and associate's degree levels, and preparing students for transfer to 4-year institutions. Four-year institutions tend to have a broad range of instructional programs at the undergraduate level, leading to bachelor's degrees. Many 4-year institutions offer graduate-level programs as well. Research activities, on-campus student housing, teaching hospitals, and auxiliary enterprises can also have a substantial impact on the financial structure of 4-year institutions. In this indicator, expenses are grouped into the following broad categories: instruction, research, public service, academic support, student services, institutional support, scholarships and fellowships, auxiliary enterprises, hospitals, independent operations, and other.[1]

Figure 1. Percentage of total expenses at degree-granting postsecondary institutions, by control of institution and purpose of selected expenses: 2015–16

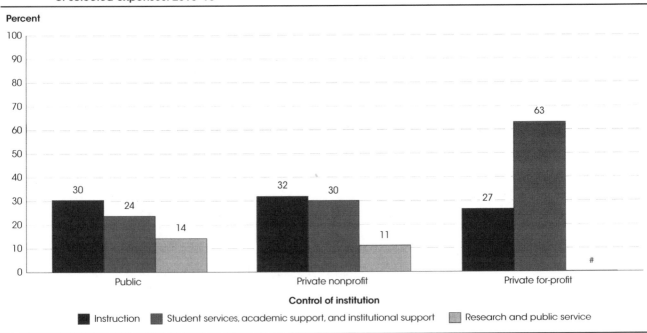

Rounds to zero.
NOTE: Degree-granting institutions grant associate's or higher degrees and participate in Title IV federal financial aid programs.
SOURCE: U.S. Department of Education, National Center for Education Statistics, Integrated Postsecondary Education Data System (IPEDS), Spring 2017, Finance component. See *Digest of Education Statistics 2017*, tables 334.10, 334.30, and 334.50.

Instruction, including faculty salaries and benefits, was the largest single expense category at public and private nonprofit postsecondary institutions in 2015–16, accounting for 30 percent of total expenses at public institutions and 32 percent of total expenses at private nonprofit institutions. At private for-profit institutions, the largest single expense category was the combined category of student services, academic support, and institutional support, which includes expenses associated with noninstructional activities, such as admissions, student activities, libraries, and administrative and executive activities. At private for-profit institutions, these expenses accounted for 63 percent of total spending. By comparison, student services, academic support, and institutional support made up 24 percent of total expenses at public institutions and 30 percent of total expenses at private nonprofit institutions.

Combined expenses for research and public service (such as expenses for public broadcasting and community services) constituted 14 percent of total expenses at public institutions, hospital expenses accounted for 13 percent, and auxiliary enterprises (e.g., self-supporting operations,

such as residence halls) constituted 9 percent of total expenses in 2015–16. At private nonprofit institutions, combined expenses for research and public service constituted 11 percent of total expenses, as did hospital expenses; auxiliary enterprises constituted 9 percent of total expenses. At private for-profit institutions, combined expenses for research and public service accounted for less than 1 percent of total expenses and auxiliary enterprises accounted for 2 percent of total expenses.

In 2015–16, the percentage of total expenses going toward instruction varied by institutional control and level. At public and private for-profit institutions, 2-year institutions spent a greater share of their total expenses on instruction than did 4-year institutions. Instruction expenses accounted for 42 percent of total expenses at public 2-year institutions, compared with 28 percent at public 4-year institutions. Instruction expenses accounted for 31 percent of total expenses at private for-profit 2-year institutions, compared with 25 percent at private for-profit 4-year institutions. At private nonprofit institutions, instruction accounted for 32 percent of total expenses at 4-year institutions and 31 percent at 2-year institutions.

Figure 2. Expenses per full-time-equivalent (FTE) student at 4-year degree-granting postsecondary institutions, by purpose of selected expenses and control of institution: 2015–16

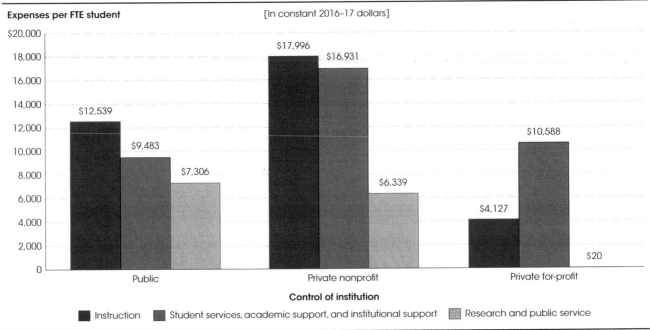

NOTE: Full-time-equivalent (FTE) students include full-time students plus the full-time equivalent of part-time students. Expenses per FTE student are reported in constant 2016–17 dollars, based on the Consumer Price Index (CPI) adjusted to a school-year basis. Degree-granting institutions grant associate's or higher degrees and participate in Title IV federal financial aid programs.
SOURCE: U.S. Department of Education, National Center for Education Statistics, Integrated Postsecondary Education Data System (IPEDS), Spring 2017, Finance component; and Spring 2016, Fall Enrollment component. See *Digest of Education Statistics 2017*, tables 334.10, 334.30, and 334.50.

In 2015–16, total expenses per full-time-equivalent (FTE) student were higher at private nonprofit 4-year postsecondary institutions ($56,401) than at public 4-year institutions ($44,009) and private for-profit 4-year institutions ($16,208). Expenses per FTE student in this indicator are adjusted for inflation using constant 2016–17 dollars, based on the Consumer Price Index (CPI). For instructional costs, private nonprofit 4-year institutions spent 44 percent more per FTE student ($17,996) than public 4-year institutions ($12,539) and 336 percent more than private for-profit 4-year institutions ($4,127). Similarly, for the combined expenses of student services, academic support, and institutional support, private

nonprofit 4-year institutions spent $16,931 per FTE student, which was 79 percent higher than the amount spent at public 4-year institutions ($9,483 per FTE student) and 60 percent higher than the amount spent at private for-profit 4-year institutions ($10,588 per FTE student). Expenses per FTE student for research and public service were much higher at public ($7,306) and private nonprofit 4-year institutions ($6,339) than at private for-profit 4-year institutions ($20). Among 2-year institutions, private nonprofit institutions and public institutions spent more per FTE student on instruction ($6,646 and $6,322, respectively) than did private for-profit institutions ($5,374).

Figure 3. Expenses per full-time-equivalent (FTE) student for instruction at degree-granting postsecondary institutions, by level and control of institution: 2010–11 and 2015–16

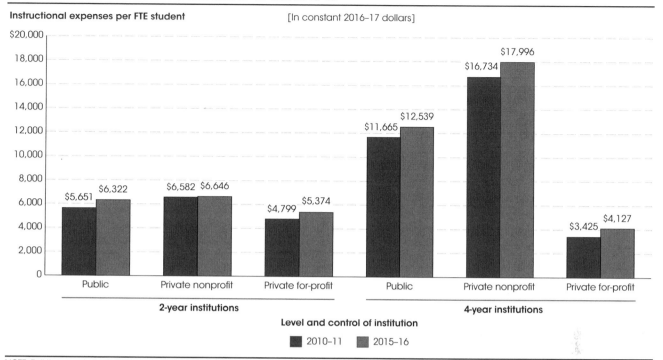

Instructional expenses per FTE student   [In constant 2016–17 dollars]

NOTE: Full-time-equivalent (FTE) students include full-time students plus the full-time equivalent of part-time students. Expenses per FTE student are reported in constant 2016-17 dollars, based on the Consumer Price Index (CPI) adjusted to a school-year basis. Degree-granting institutions grant associate's or higher degrees and participate in Title IV federal financial aid programs.
SOURCE: U.S. Department of Education, National Center for Education Statistics, Integrated Postsecondary Education Data System (IPEDS), Spring 2012 and Spring 2017, Finance component; and Spring 2011 and Spring 2016, Fall Enrollment component. See *Digest of Education Statistics 2017*, tables 334.10, 334.30, and 334.50.

Changes in inflation-adjusted instruction expenses per FTE student between 2010–11 and 2015–16 varied by postsecondary institution control and level. Among 2-year institutions, instruction expenses per FTE student increased by 12 percent at both public and private for-profit institutions (from $5,651 to $6,322 and from $4,799 to $5,374, respectively). At private nonprofit 2-year institutions, instruction expenses per FTE student were 1 percent higher in 2015–16 than in 2010–11 ($6,646 vs. $6,582). Among 4-year institutions, instruction expenses per FTE student were higher in 2015–16 than in 2010–11 at public ($12,539 vs. $11,665, an increase of 7 percent), private nonprofit ($17,996 vs $16,734, an increase of 8 percent), and private for-profit institutions ($4,127 vs. $3,425, an increase of 20 percent).

Endnotes:
[1] For private for-profit institutions, hospital expenses are included in the "other" category.

Reference tables: *Digest of Education Statistics 2017*, tables 334.10, 334.30, and 334.50
Related indicators and resources: Education Expenditures by Country; Postsecondary Institution Revenues

Glossary: Constant dollars, Consumer Price Index (CPI), Control of institutions, Full-time-equivalent (FTE) enrollment, Postsecondary education, Postsecondary institutions (basic classification by level), Private institution, Public school or institution, Tuition and fees

The indicators in this chapter of *The Condition of Education* describe population characteristics and economic outcomes for the United States. Individuals' levels of educational attainment are related to median earnings and other labor outcomes, such as unemployment rates.

Chapter 3

Population Characteristics and Economic Outcomes

Population Characteristics

Economic Outcomes

Educational Attainment of Young Adults

Educational attainment rates for 25- to 29-year-olds increased at all levels between 2000 and 2017. During this time, the percentage who had completed high school increased from 88 to 92 percent, the percentage with an associate's or higher degree increased from 38 to 46 percent, the percentage with a bachelor's or higher degree increased from 29 to 36 percent, and the percentage with a master's or higher degree increased from 5 to 9 percent.

Educational attainment refers to the highest level of education completed (defined here as a high school diploma or equivalency certificate, an associate's degree, a bachelor's degree, or a master's or higher degree). Between 2000 and 2017, educational attainment rates among 25- to 29-year-olds increased at each attainment level. During this time, the percentage who had received at least a high school diploma or its equivalent increased from 88 to 92 percent, the percentage with an associate's or higher degree increased from 38 to 46 percent, the percentage with a bachelor's or higher degree increased from 29 to 36 percent, and the percentage with a master's or higher degree increased from 5 to 9 percent.

Figure 1. Percentage of 25- to 29-year-olds, by educational attainment and sex: 2000 and 2017

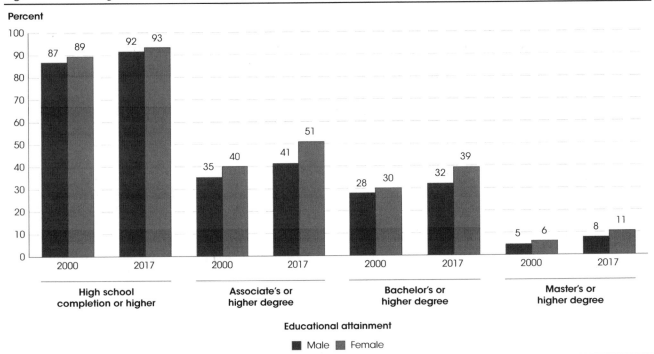

NOTE: High school completion includes those persons who graduated from high school with a diploma as well as those who completed high school through equivalency programs, such as a GED program.
SOURCE: U.S. Department of Commerce, Census Bureau, Current Population Survey (CPS), Annual Social and Economic Supplement, 2000 and 2017. See *Digest of Education Statistics 2017*, table 104.20.

Between 2000 and 2017, attainment rates increased for both female and male 25- to 29-year-olds across all education levels. Attainment rates for 25- to 29-year-olds were generally higher for females than for males during this period. Between 2000 and 2017, the difference between the attainment rates for 25- to 29-year-old females and males (also referred to in this indicator as the gender gap) did not vary measurably at the high school completion or higher and master's or higher degree attainment levels; however, the gender gap did widen at the associate's or higher degree and bachelor's or higher degree attainment levels. Among 25- to 29-year-olds who had completed an associate's or higher degree, the gender gap widened from 5 percentage points in 2000 to 10 percentage points in 2017. Similarly, among 25- to 29-year-olds who had completed a bachelor's or higher degree, the gender gap widened from 2 percentage points in 2000 to 7 percentage points in 2017.

Figure 2. Percentage of 25- to 29-year-olds with at least a high school diploma or its equivalent, by race/ethnicity: 2000 through 2017

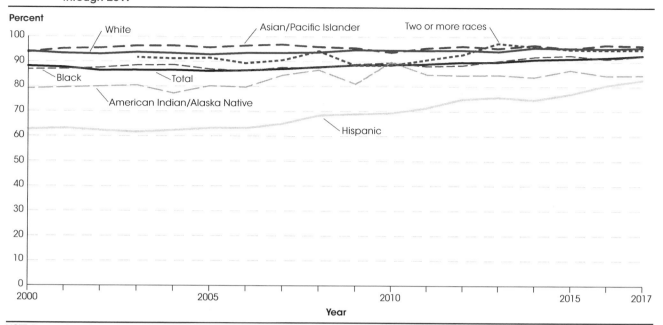

NOTE: Race categories exclude persons of Hispanic ethnicity. Separate data on persons of Two or more races were not available prior to 2003. Data on American Indian/Alaska Natives were not available in 2001 and 2002.
SOURCE: U.S. Department of Commerce, Census Bureau, Current Population Survey (CPS), Annual Social and Economic Supplement, selected years, 2000 through 2017. See *Digest of Education Statistics 2011*, table 8, and *Digest of Education Statistics 2014, 2016,* and *2017,* table 104.20.

Between 2000 and 2017, the percentage of 25- to 29-year-olds who had received at least a high school diploma or its equivalent increased for those who were White (from 94 to 96 percent), Black (from 87 to 92 percent), and Hispanic (from 63 to 83 percent). However, the percentages of Asian/Pacific Islander and American Indian/Alaska Native 25- to 29-year-olds with at least a high school diploma or its equivalent in 2017 (96 percent and 85 percent, respectively) were not measurably different from the corresponding percentages in 2000. In addition, the percentage of 25- to 29-year-olds of Two or more races who had received a high school diploma or its equivalent in 2017 (95 percent) was not measurably different from the percentage who had attained this

education level in 2003, the first year for which data on persons of Two or more races were available.

Between 2000 and 2017, the percentage of White 25- to 29-year-olds who had received at least a high school diploma or its equivalent remained higher than the percentages of Black and Hispanic 25- to 29-year-olds who had attained this education level. However, the White-Black attainment gap at this attainment level narrowed from 7 to 3 percentage points over this period. In addition, the White-Hispanic gap at this attainment level narrowed from 31 to 13 percentage points, primarily due to the increase in the percentage of Hispanic 25- to 29-year-olds who had completed high school.

Figure 3. Percentage of 25- to 29-year-olds with an associate's or higher degree, by race/ethnicity: 2000 through 2017

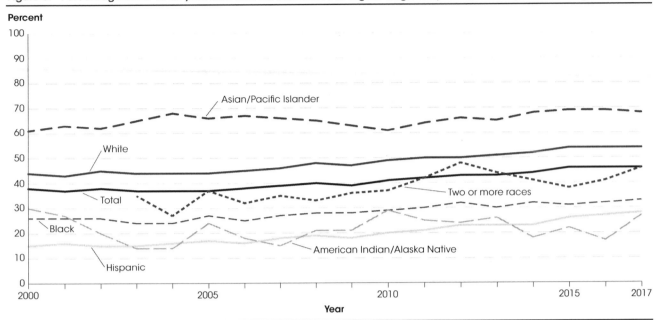

NOTE: Race categories exclude persons of Hispanic ethnicity. Prior to 2003, separate data on persons of Two or more races were not available.
SOURCE: U.S. Department of Commerce, Census Bureau, Current Population Survey (CPS), Annual Social and Economic Supplement, 2000 through 2017. See *Digest of Education Statistics 2015*, table 104.65, and *Digest of Education Statistics 2017*, table 104.20.

From 2000 to 2017, the percentage of 25- to 29-year-olds who had attained an associate's or higher degree increased for those who were White (from 44 to 54 percent), Black (from 26 to 33 percent), Hispanic (from 15 to 28 percent), and Asian/Pacific Islander (from 61 to 68 percent). The percentage of American Indian/Alaska Native 25- to 29-year-olds (27 percent) who had attained an associate's or higher degree in 2017 was not measurably different from the percentage attaining this education level in 2000. Similarly, the percentage of 25- to 29-year-olds of Two or more races in 2017 with an associate's or higher

degree (46 percent) was not measurably different from the corresponding percentage in 2003.

The gap between the percentages of White and Black 25- to 29-year-olds who had attained an associate's or higher degree in 2017 (21 percent) was not measurably different from the corresponding gap in 2000. Similarly, the gap between the percentages of White and Hispanic 25- to 29-year-olds with an associate's or higher degree in 2017 (26 percent) was not measurably different from the corresponding gap in 2000.

Figure 4. Percentage of 25- to 29-year-olds with a bachelor's or higher degree, by race/ethnicity: Selected years, 2000 through 2017

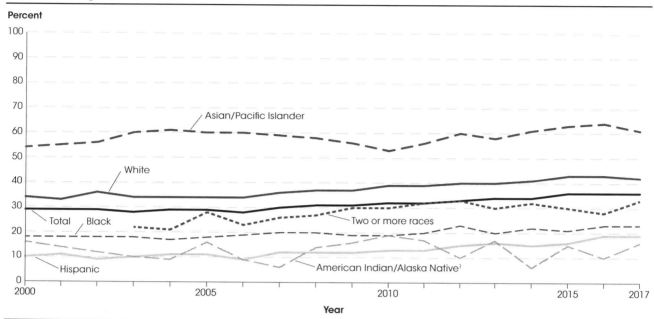

[1] Interpret data for 2003, 2004, 2006, 2007, 2014, and 2017 with caution. The coefficients of variation (CVs) for these estimates are between 30 and 50 percent.
NOTE: Race categories exclude persons of Hispanic ethnicity. Separate data on persons of Two or more races were not available prior to 2003. Data on American Indians/Alaska Natives were not available in 2001 and 2002.
SOURCE: U.S. Department of Commerce, Census Bureau, Current Population Survey (CPS), Annual Social and Economic Supplement, selected years, 2000 through 2017. See *Digest of Education Statistics 2011*, table 8, and *Digest of Education Statistics 2014, 2016*, and *2017*, table 104.20.

From 2000 to 2017, the percentage of 25- to 29-year-olds who had attained a bachelor's or higher degree increased for those who were White (from 34 to 42 percent), Black (from 18 to 23 percent), and Hispanic (from 10 to 19 percent). Similarly, the percentage of 25- to 29-year-olds of Two or more races who had attained a bachelor's or higher degree increased from 2003 to 2017 (from 22 to 33 percent). However, the percentage of Asian/Pacific Islander 25- to 29-year-olds who had attained a bachelor's or higher degree in 2017 (61 percent) was not measurably different from the percentage in 2000, and the percentage of their American Indian/Alaska Native peers who had attained a bachelor's or higher degree in 2017 (16 percent) was not measurably different from the percentage in 2000.

The gap between the percentages of White and Black 25- to 29-year-olds who had attained a bachelor's or higher degree in 2017 (19 percent) was not measurably different from the corresponding gap in 2000; similarly, the gap between the percentages of White and Hispanic 25- to 29-year-olds who had attained a bachelor's or

higher degree in 2017 (24 percent) was not measurably different from the corresponding gap in 2000.

From 2000 to 2017, the percentage of 25- to 29-year-olds who had attained a master's or higher degree increased for those who were White (from 6 to 10 percent), Hispanic (from 2 to 4 percent), and Asian/Pacific Islander (from 16 to 25 percent). The percentage of Black 25- to 29-year-olds who had attained a master's or higher degree in 2017 (5 percent) was not measurably different from the percentage in 2000. Similarly, the percentage of 25- to 29-year-olds of Two or more races with a master's or higher degree in 2017 (5 percent) was not measurably different from the percentage in 2003.[1]

The gap between the percentages of White and Black 25- to 29-year-olds who had attained a master's or higher degree widened from 2 to 5 percentage points between 2000 and 2017. The White-Hispanic gap at the master's or higher degree attainment level also widened during this time, from 4 to 6 percentage points.

Endnotes:

[1] American Indian/Alaska Native students who had attained a master's or higher degree are not included in this comparison because sample sizes were too small to provide a reliable estimate in 2000.

Reference tables: *Digest of Education Statistics 2011*, table 8; *Digest of Education Statistics 2015*, table 104.65; *Digest of Education Statistics 2014, 2016,* and *2017*, table 104.20

Related indicators and resources: Disability Rates and Employment Status by Educational Attainment [*The Condition of Education 2017 Spotlight*]; Educational Attainment [*Status and Trends in the Education of Racial and Ethnic Groups*]; International Educational Attainment; Snapshot: Attainment of a Bachelor's or Higher Degree for Racial/Ethnic Subgroups [*Status and Trends in the Education of Racial and Ethnic Groups*]; Trends in Employment Rates by Educational Attainment [*The Condition of Education 2013 Spotlight*]

Glossary: Associate's degree, Bachelor's degree, Educational attainment (Current Population Survey), Gap, High school completer, High school diploma, Master's degree, Postsecondary education, Racial/ethnic group

This page intentionally left blank.

Youth Neither Enrolled in School nor Working

In 2016, some 17 percent of 20- to 24-year-olds were neither enrolled in school nor working, compared to 12 percent of 18- and 19-year-olds and 5 percent of 16- and 17-year-olds. In each age group, the percentage who were neither in school nor working was higher for those in poor households than for those in nonpoor households. For example, among 20- to 24-year-olds in 2016, some 31 percent of those in poor households were neither in school nor working, compared to 13 percent of those in nonpoor households.

Schooling and work are considered core activities in the transition from childhood to adulthood. Youth who are detached from these core activities, particularly if they are detached for several years, may have difficulty building a work history that contributes to future employability and higher wages.[1] Youth who are neither enrolled in school nor working[2] may be detached from these activities for several reasons. They may be seeking educational opportunities or work but are unable to find them. They may have left the workforce or school temporarily or permanently, for personal, family, or financial reasons.

This indicator examines rates of being neither in school nor working for 16- to 24-year-olds[3] (also referred to as "youth" in this indicator), including comparisons between younger and older youth within this age range. The indicator presents data across three years: 2006, 2011, and 2016. The 2006 data provide information on outcomes prior to the recession experienced by the U.S. economy between December 2007 and June 2009.[4] The 2011 data represent the period shortly after the recession ended, and the 2016 data provide the most recently available data.

Figure 1. Percentage of youth ages 16 to 24 who were neither enrolled in school nor working, by age group: 2006, 2011, and 2016

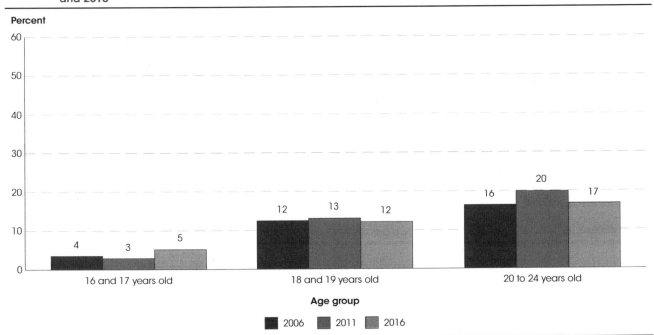

SOURCE: U.S. Department of Commerce, Census Bureau, Current Population Survey (CPS), Annual Social and Economic Supplement, 2006, 2011, and 2016. See *Digest of Education Statistics 2016*, table 501.30.

In 2016, the percentage of youth neither in school nor working was higher for older youth than for younger youth. Specifically, 17 percent of 20- to 24-year-olds were neither in school nor working, compared to 12 percent of 18- and 19-year-olds and 5 percent of 16- and 17-year-olds. Among 16- and 17-year-olds, the percentage neither in school nor working was higher in 2016 (5 percent) than in 2006 (4 percent) and 2011 (3 percent). Among 18- and 19-year-olds, there were no measurable differences in the percentage neither in school nor working across 2006, 2011, and 2016. The percentage of 20- to 24-year-olds neither in school nor working was lower in 2016 (17 percent) than in 2011 (20 percent), but not measurably different than in 2006.

Figure 2.   Percentage of youth ages 16 to 24 who were neither enrolled in school nor working, by race/ethnicity and age group: 2016

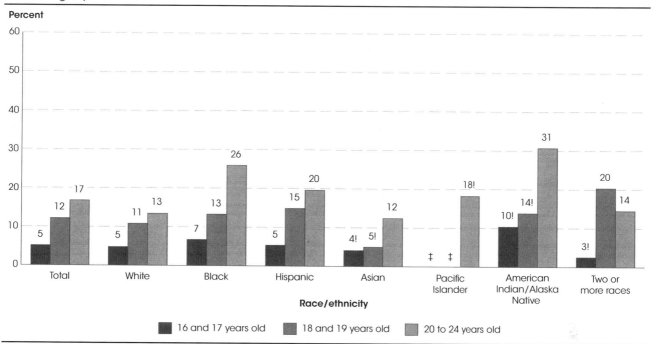

! Interpret data with caution. The coefficient of variation (CV) for this estimate is between 30 and 50 percent.
‡ Reporting standards not met. Either there are too few cases for a reliable estimate or the coefficient of variation (CV) is 50 percent or greater.
NOTE: Race categories exclude persons of Hispanic ethnicity.
SOURCE: U.S. Department of Commerce, Census Bureau, Current Population Survey (CPS), Annual Social and Economic Supplement, 2016. See *Digest of Education Statistics 2016*, table 501.30.

The percentage of youth who were neither in school nor working varied by race/ethnicity in 2016. For example, the percentage of 20- to 24-year-olds neither in school nor working was higher for American Indian/Alaska Native, Black, and Hispanic youth (31, 26, and 20 percent, respectively) than for their White and Asian peers (13 and 12 percent, respectively). In addition, the percentage neither in school nor working was higher for Black and American Indian/Alaska Native 20- to 24-year-olds than for their peers of Two or more races (14 percent), while the percentage for Pacific Islander 20- to 24-year-olds (18 percent) was not measurably different from that of any other racial/ethnic group.

Among 18- and 19-year-olds, the percentage neither in school nor working was higher for Hispanic youth

(15 percent) than for White youth (11 percent), and the percentages for both groups were higher than the percentage for Asian youth (5 percent). The percentage for Black 18- and 19-year-olds (13 percent) was higher than the percentage for Asian 18- and 19-year-olds, but not measurably different from the percentages for White and Hispanic youth in the same age range. Among 16- and 17-year-olds, the percentage neither in school nor working was higher for Hispanic (5 percent) and Black youth (7 percent) than for youth of Two or more races (3 percent), but there were no other measurable differences among racial/ethnic groups (excluding Pacific Islander youth, for whom reliable estimates were not available).

Figure 3.   Percentage of youth ages 16 to 24 who were neither enrolled in school nor working, by age group and family poverty status: 2016

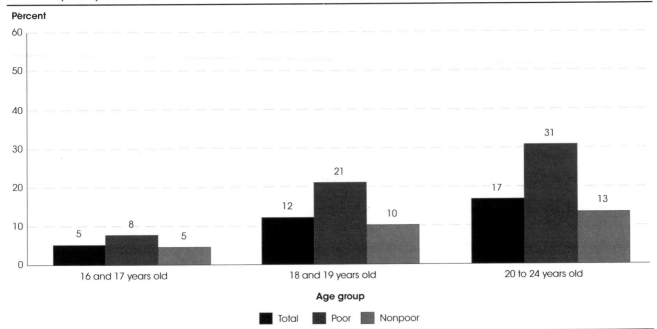

NOTE: Poor is defined to include families below the poverty threshold, and nonpoor is defined to include families at or above the poverty threshold. For information about how the Census Bureau determines who is in poverty, see http://www.census.gov/topics/income-poverty/poverty/guidance/poverty-measures.html.
SOURCE: U.S. Department of Commerce, Census Bureau, Current Population Survey (CPS), Annual Social and Economic Supplement, 2016. See *Digest of Education Statistics 2016*, table 501.30:

In 2016, the percentage of youth in each age group who were neither in school nor working was higher for youth in poor households than for youth in nonpoor households. For the purposes of this indicator, poor is defined to include families below the Census-defined poverty threshold, and nonpoor is defined to include families at or above the poverty threshold.[5] For example, 31 percent of poor 20- to 24-year-olds were neither in school nor working compared with 13 percent of nonpoor 20- to 24-year-olds. Similar patterns were observed in 2006 and 2011.

Figure 4. Percentage of youth ages 20 to 24 who were neither enrolled in school nor working, by race/ethnicity and family poverty status: 2016

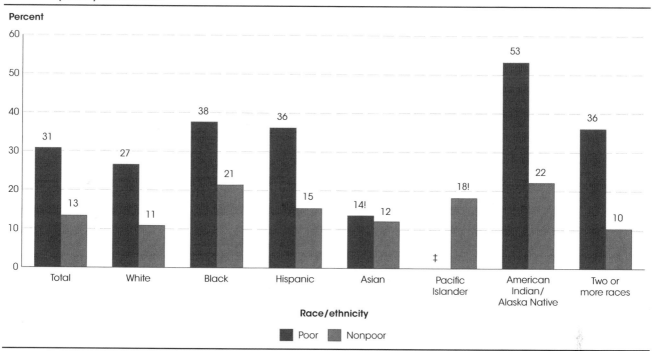

! Interpret data with caution. The coefficient of variation (CV) for this estimate is between 30 and 50 percent.
‡ Reporting standards not met. Either there are too few cases for a reliable estimate or the coefficient of variation (CV) is 50 percent or greater.
NOTE: Poor is defined to include families below the poverty threshold, and nonpoor is defined to include families at or above the poverty threshold. For information about how the Census Bureau determines who is in poverty, see http://www.census.gov/topics/income-poverty/poverty/guidance/poverty-measures.html. Race categories exclude persons of Hispanic ethnicity.
SOURCE: U.S. Department of Commerce, Census Bureau, Current Population Survey (CPS), Annual Social and Economic Supplement, 2016. See *Digest of Education Statistics 2016*, table 501.30.

Across all racial/ethnic groups except Asian and Pacific Islanders, the percentage of 20- to 24-year-olds who were neither in school nor working was higher for those in poor households than for those in nonpoor households. For Asian 20- to 24-year-olds, there was no measurable difference between the percentages for those in poor and nonpoor households. Reliable estimates were not available for Pacific Islander 20- to 24-year-olds. The gap between the percentages of poor and nonpoor 20- to 24-year-olds who were neither in school nor working ranged from 16 percentage points for White and Black youth to 31 percentage points for American Indian/Alaska Native youth.

Figure 5. Percentage of youth ages 20 to 24 who were neither enrolled in school nor working, by educational attainment: 2006, 2011, and 2016

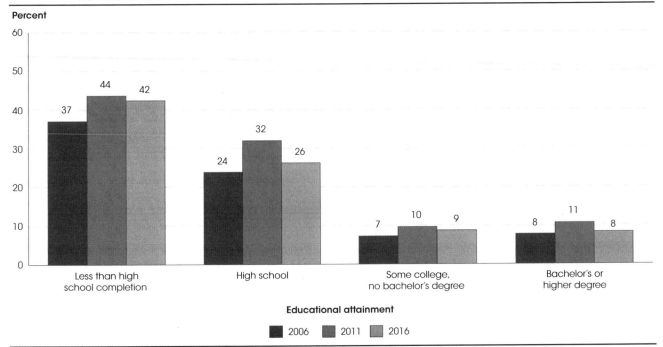

NOTE: High school completion includes equivalency credentials, such as the GED credential. Some college, no bachelor's degree includes persons with no college degree as well as those with an associate's degree.
SOURCE: U.S. Department of Commerce, Census Bureau, Current Population Survey (CPS), Annual Social and Economic Supplement, 2006, 2011, and 2016. See *Digest of Education Statistics 2016*, table 501.30.

In 2016, the percentage of 20- to 24-year-olds neither in school nor working was generally higher for those with lower levels of educational attainment than for those with higher levels of educational attainment. The percentage neither in school nor working was higher for 20- to 24-year-olds who had not completed high school (42 percent) than for those who had completed high school (26 percent), and the percentages for both groups were higher than the percentages for those with some college (9 percent) and those with a bachelor's degree or higher (8 percent).

Among 20- to 24-year-olds who had not completed high school, the percentage neither in school nor working was 42 percent in 2016, compared with 44 percent in 2011 and 37 percent in 2006. Meanwhile, among 20- to 24-year-olds with a bachelor's degree or higher, the percentage neither in school nor working was 8 percent in 2016, which was not measurably different from the percentages in 2006 or 2011. However, the percentage for the same group in 2011 (11 percent) was higher than the percentage in 2006 (8 percent).

Figure 6. Percentage of youth ages 20 to 24 who were neither enrolled in school nor working, by educational attainment and sex: 2016

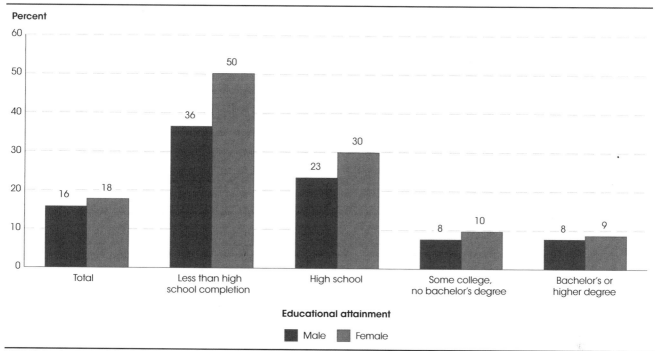

NOTE: High school completion includes equivalency credentials, such as the GED credential. Some college, no bachelor's degree includes persons with no college degree as well as those with an associate's degree.
SOURCE: U.S. Department of Commerce, Census Bureau, Current Population Survey (CPS), Annual Social and Economic Supplement, 2016. See *Digest of Education Statistics 2016*, table 501.30.

In 2016, the percentage of 20- to 24-year-olds who were neither in school nor working was higher for females (18 percent) than for males (16 percent). This gap ranged from 14 percentage points for 20- to 24-year-olds who had not completed high school to 2 percentage points for those with some college. Among 20- to 24-year-olds with a bachelor's degree, there was no measurable difference between the percentages of males and females who were neither in school nor working.

Endnotes:
[1] Fernandes-Alcantara, A. (2015). *Disconnected Youth: A Look at 16- to 24-Year-Olds Who Are Not Working or in School* (CRS Report No. R40535). Washington, DC: Congressional Research Service. Retrieved February 7, 2017, from http://www.fas.org/sgp/crs/misc/R40535.pdf.
[2] Referred to as "youth neither in school or working" in this indicator.
[3] Prior editions of this indicator presented data on 18- to 24-year-olds. This edition has been expanded to include data on 16- and 17-year-olds, allowing for a discussion of differences between younger and older youth.
[4] National Bureau of Economic Research. (2010). *U.S. Business Cycle Expansions and Contractions*. Retrieved January 23, 2018, from http://www.nber.org/cycles.html.
[5] For information about how the Census Bureau determines who is in poverty, see http://www.census.gov/topics/income-poverty/poverty/guidance/poverty-measures.html.

Reference tables: *Digest of Education Statistics 2016*, table 501.30
Related indicators and resources: College Enrollment Rates; Employment and Unemployment Rates by Educational Attainment; Immediate College Enrollment Rate; Youth and Young Adults Neither Enrolled in School nor Working [*Status and Trends in the Education of Racial and Ethnic Groups*]

Glossary: Bachelor's degree, College, Educational attainment (Current Population Survey), Enrollment, Gap, High school completer, Household, Poverty (official measure), Racial/ethnic group

Annual Earnings of Young Adults

In 2016, the median earnings of young adults with a bachelor's degree ($50,000) were 57 percent higher than those of young adult high school completers ($31,800). The median earnings of young adult high school completers were 26 percent higher than those of young adults who did not complete high school ($25,400).

This indicator examines the annual earnings of young adults ages 25–34 employed full time, year round (i.e., worked 35 or more hours per week for 50 or more weeks per year). Many people in this age group recently exited formal education and may be entering the workforce for the first time or transitioning from part-time to full-time work. In 2016, some 73 percent of young adults ages 25–34 who were in the labor force[1] worked full time,

year round. The percentage of young adults in the labor force working full time, year round was generally higher for those with higher levels of educational attainment. For example, 79 percent of young adults with a bachelor's degree worked full time, year round in 2016, compared with 69 percent of young adult high school completers (those with only a high school diploma or an equivalency credential such as a GED certificate).

Figure 1. Percentage of the labor force ages 25–34 who worked full time, year round, by educational attainment: 2000–2016

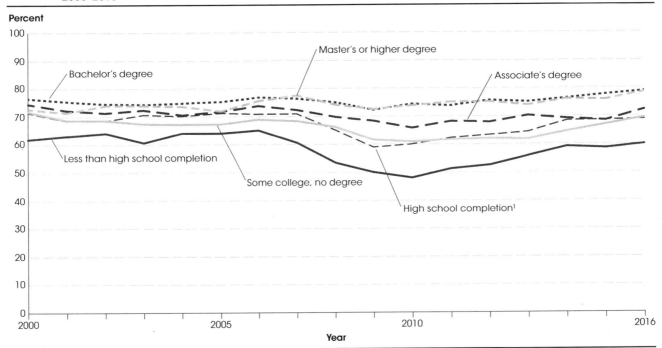

[1] Includes equivalency credentials, such as the GED credential.
NOTE: Data are based on sample surveys of the noninstitutionalized population, which excludes persons living in institutions (e.g., prisons or nursing facilities) and military barracks. *Full-time, year-round* workers are those who worked 35 or more hours per week for 50 or more weeks per year. The *labor force* refers to the population who reported working or looking for work in the given year.
SOURCE: U.S. Department of Commerce, Census Bureau, Current Population Survey (CPS), "Annual Social and Economic Supplement," 2001–2017; and previously unpublished tabulations. See *Digest of Education Statistics 2017*, table 502.30.

Changes over time in the percentage of young adults in the labor force who worked full time, year round varied by level of educational attainment. Among young adult high school completers who were in the labor force, a lower percentage worked full time, year round in 2016 (69 percent) than in 2000 (71 percent). In contrast, the corresponding percentage for those with a bachelor's

degree was higher in 2016 (79 percent) than in 2000 (77 percent). In addition, the percentage of young adult labor force participants who worked full time, year round increased among those with a master's or higher degree (from 73 percent in 2000 to 79 percent in 2016). At the following educational attainment levels, there was no measurable difference between 2000 and 2016 in the percentage of young adult labor force participants who worked full time, year round: those without a high school diploma or an equivalent credential such as a GED, those with some college but no degree, and those with an associate's degree (60 percent, 69 percent, and 72 percent, respectively, in 2016).

More recently, between 2010 and 2016, the percentages of young adult labor force participants working full time, year round increased for every level of educational attainment. For example, during this period the percentage for young adult high school completers who worked full time, year round increased from 60 to 69 percent, and the corresponding percentage for young adults with a bachelor's degree increased from 74 to 79 percent.

Figure 2. Median annual earnings of full-time, year-round workers ages 25–34, by educational attainment: 2016

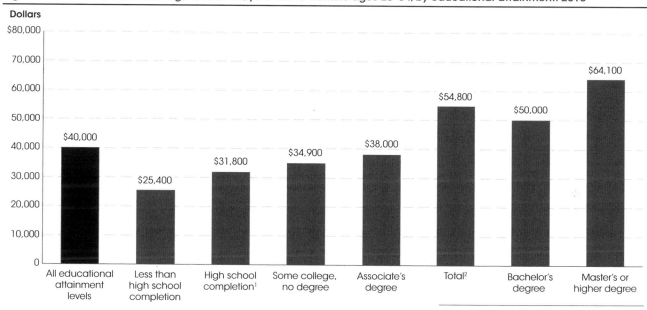

¹ Includes equivalency credentials, such as the GED credential.
² Represents median annual earnings of full-time, year-round workers ages 25–34 with a bachelor's or higher degree.
NOTE: Data are based on sample surveys of the noninstitutionalized population, which excludes persons living in institutions (e.g., prisons or nursing facilities) and military barracks. *Full-time, year-round* workers are those who worked 35 or more hours per week for 50 or more weeks per year.
SOURCE: U.S. Department of Commerce, Census Bureau, Current Population Survey (CPS), "Annual Social and Economic Supplement," 2017. See *Digest of Education Statistics 2017*, table 502.30.

For young adults ages 25–34 who worked full time, year round, higher educational attainment was associated with higher median earnings; this pattern was consistent from 2000 through 2016. For example, in 2016 the median earnings of young adults with a master's or higher degree were $64,100, some 28 percent higher than those of young adults with a bachelor's degree ($50,000). In the same year, the median earnings of young adults with a bachelor's degree were 57 percent higher than those

of young adult high school completers ($31,800). In addition, in 2016, the median earnings of young adult high school completers were 26 percent higher than those of young adults who did not complete high school ($25,400). This pattern of higher earnings associated with higher levels of educational attainment also held for both male and female young adults as well as for White, Black, Hispanic, and Asian young adults.

Figure 3. Median annual earnings of full-time, year-round workers ages 25–34, by educational attainment: 2000–2016

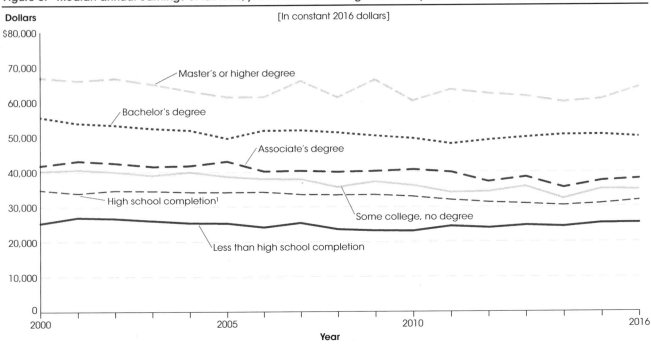

[1] Includes equivalency credentials, such as the GED credential.
NOTE: Data are based on sample surveys of the noninstitutionalized population, which excludes persons living in institutions (e.g., prisons or nursing facilities) and military barracks. *Full-time, year-round* workers are those who worked 35 or more hours per week for 50 or more weeks per year. Earnings are presented in constant 2016 dollars, based on the Consumer Price Index (CPI), to eliminate inflationary factors and to allow for direct comparison across years.
SOURCE: U.S. Department of Commerce, Census Bureau, Current Population Survey (CPS), "Annual Social and Economic Supplement," 2001–2017; and previously unpublished tabulations. See *Digest of Education Statistics 2017*, table 502.30.

The median earnings (in constant 2016 dollars)[2] of young adults who worked full time, year round declined from 2000 to 2016 at most educational attainment levels, except for those who did not complete high school and those with a master's or higher degree, both of whom saw no measurable change in median earnings between these two years. During this period, the median earnings of young adult high school completers declined from $34,800 to $31,800 (a 9 percent decrease), and the median earnings of those with some college but no degree declined from $40,200 to $34,900 (a 13 percent decrease). In addition, the median earnings of young adults with an associate's degree declined from $41,800 to $38,000 (a 9 percent decrease), and the median earnings of young adults with a bachelor's degree declined from $55,600 to $50,000 (a 10 percent decrease).

The difference in median earnings between young adult high school completers and those who did not complete high school narrowed between 2000 and 2016. In 2000, the median earnings of young adult high school completers were $9,600 higher than the median earnings of those who did not complete high school; in 2016, this difference was $6,500. In addition, the difference in median earnings between young adults with a bachelor's degree and high school completers was smaller in 2016 ($18,200) than in 2000 ($20,800). The difference in median earnings between young adults with a master's or higher degree and those with a bachelor's degree did not change measurably during this period.

Figure 4. Median annual earnings of full-time, year-round workers ages 25–34, by educational attainment and sex: 2016

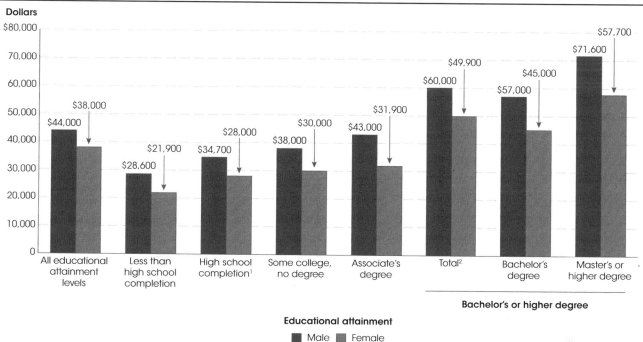

¹ Includes equivalency credentials, such as the GED credential.
² Represents median annual earnings of full-time, year-round workers ages 25–34 with a bachelor's or higher degree.
NOTE: Data are based on sample surveys of the noninstitutionalized population, which excludes persons living in institutions (e.g., prisons or nursing facilities) and military barracks. *Full-time, year-round workers* are those who worked 35 or more hours per week for 50 or more weeks per year.
SOURCE: U.S. Department of Commerce, Census Bureau, Current Population Survey (CPS), "Annual Social and Economic Supplement," 2017. See *Digest of Education Statistics 2017*, table 502.30.

In 2016, the median earnings of young adult males who worked full time, year round were higher than the corresponding median earnings of young adult females at every level of educational attainment. For example, the median earnings of young adult males with an associate's degree were $43,000 in 2016, while those of their female counterparts were $31,900. The median earnings of young adult male high school completers were $34,700, compared with $28,000 for their female counterparts.

The median earnings of White young adults who worked full time, year round exceeded the corresponding median earnings of Black and Hispanic young adults at most attainment levels in 2016, except for those with a master's or higher degree, where there were no measurable differences in median earnings between White ($61,100), Black ($59,700), and Hispanic ($55,700) young adults. In addition, the median earnings of White young adults ($50,000) with a bachelor's degree were not measurably different from those of their Black counterparts ($45,800). Among those with a bachelor's degree and those with a master's or higher degree, Asian young adults had higher median earnings than their White, Black, and Hispanic peers. For example, the median earnings in 2016 for young adults with a bachelor's degree were $59,700 for Asian young adults, $50,000 for White young adults, $45,800 for Black young adults, and $44,700 for Hispanic young adults.

Endnotes:

¹ The labor force consists of all civilians who are employed or seeking employment.

² Constant dollars based on the Consumer Price Index, prepared by the Bureau of Labor Statistics, U.S. Department of Labor.

Reference tables: *Digest of Education Statistics 2017*, table 502.30
Related indicators and resources: Employment and Earnings [*Status and Trends in the Education of Racial and Ethnic Groups*]; Employment and Unemployment Rates by Educational Attainment; Employment Outcomes of Bachelor's Degree Recipients; Post-College Employment Outcomes by Field of Study and Race/Ethnicity [*The Condition of Education 2016 Spotlight*]

Glossary: Associate's degree, Bachelor's degree, Constant dollars, Consumer Price Index (CPI), Educational attainment (Current Population Survey), High school completer, High school diploma, Master's degree, Median earnings, Racial/ethnic group

Employment and Unemployment Rates by Educational Attainment

In 2017, the employment rate was higher for young adults with higher levels of educational attainment than for those with lower levels of educational attainment. For example, the employment rate was 86 percent for young adults with a bachelor's or higher degree and 57 percent for those who had not completed high school.

Focusing on 25- to 34-year-olds (referred to here as "young adults"), this indicator examines recent trends in two distinct yet related measures of labor market conditions: the employment rate and the unemployment rate. The *employment rate* (also known as the employment to population ratio) is the number of persons in a given group who are employed as a percentage of the civilian population in that group. The *unemployment rate* is the percentage of persons in the civilian labor force (i.e., all civilians who are employed or seeking employment) who are not working and who made specific efforts to find employment sometime during the prior 4 weeks.

Figure 1. Employment rates of 25- to 34-year-olds, by sex and educational attainment: 2017

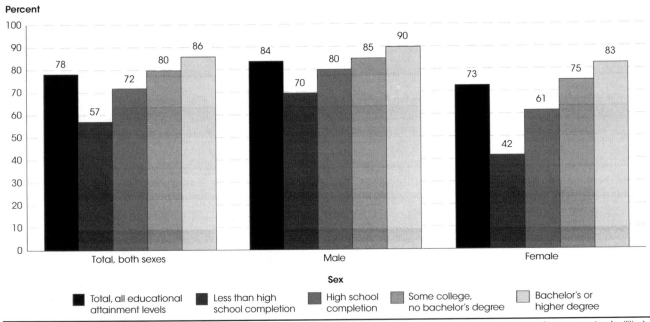

NOTE: Data are based on sample surveys of the noninstitutionalized population, which excludes persons living in institutions (e.g., prisons or nursing facilities); this figure includes data only on the civilian population (excludes all military personnel). The employment rate, or employment to population ratio, is the number of persons in each group who are employed as a percentage of the civilian population in that group. "Some college, no bachelor's degree" includes persons with an associate's degree. "High school completion" includes equivalency credentials, such as the GED.
SOURCE: U.S. Department of Commerce, Census Bureau, Current Population Survey (CPS), Annual Social and Economic Supplement, March 2017. See *Digest of Education Statistics 2017*, tables 501.50, 501.60, and 501.70.

In 2017, the employment rate was higher for those with higher levels of educational attainment. For example, the employment rate was highest for young adults with a bachelor's or higher degree (86 percent). The employment rate for young adults with some college[1] (80 percent) was higher than the rate for those who had completed high school[2] (72 percent), which was, in turn, higher than the employment rate for those who had not completed high school (57 percent). The same pattern was observed among

both young adult males and young adult females. For example, the employment rate for young adult females was highest for those with a bachelor's or higher degree (83 percent) and lowest for those who had not completed high school (42 percent).

Employment rates were higher for young adult males than for young adult females in 2017, overall and at all levels of educational attainment. Specifically, the employment rate for young adult males was higher than the rate for young adult females overall (84 vs. 73 percent) and among those with a bachelor's or higher degree (90 vs. 83 percent), those with some college (85 vs. 75 percent), those who had completed high school (80 vs. 61 percent), and those who had not completed high school (70 vs. 42 percent). The difference in employment rates between young adult males and females (also referred to in this indicator as the gender gap) was generally narrower at higher levels of educational attainment. For instance, the gender gap was 7 percentage points for those with a bachelor's or higher degree. In comparison, the gender gap was 18 percentage points for those who had completed high school and 28 percentage points for those who had not completed high school.

Figure 2. Employment rates of 25- to 34-year-olds, by educational attainment: Selected years, 2000 through 2017

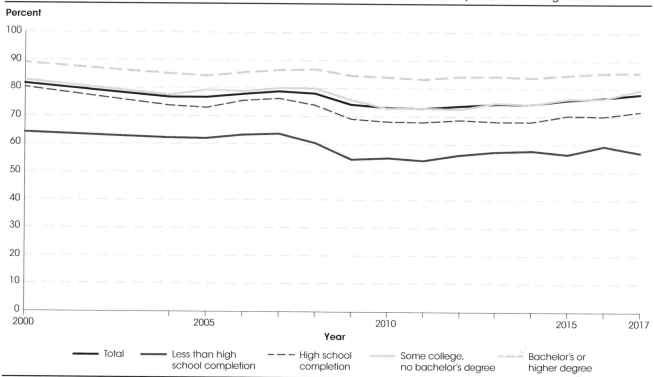

NOTE: Data are based on sample surveys of the noninstitutionalized population, which excludes persons living in institutions (e.g., prisons or nursing facilities); this figure includes data only on the civilian population (excludes all military personnel). The employment rate, or employment to population ratio, is the number of persons in each group who are employed as a percentage of the civilian population in that group. "Some college, no bachelor's degree" includes persons with an associate's degree. "High school completion" includes equivalency credentials, such as the GED.
SOURCE: U.S. Department of Commerce, Census Bureau, Current Population Survey (CPS), Annual Social and Economic Supplement, selected years, March 2000 through 2017. See Digest of Education Statistics 2013, 2014, 2016, and 2017, table 501.50.

From December 2007 through June 2009, the U.S. economy experienced a recession.[3] For young adults overall, the employment rate was lower in 2010 (73 percent), immediately after the recession, than in 2000 (82 percent), prior to the recession. The employment rate then increased from 2010 to 2017, to 78 percent, but this rate was still lower than the rate in 2000. During these years, the same patterns in employment rates were observed for young adults with a bachelor's or higher degree, for those with some college, and for those who had completed high school. However, for young adults who had not completed high school, the employment rate in 2017 (57 percent) was not measurably different from the rate in 2010 but was lower than the rate in 2000 (64 percent).

Figure 3. Unemployment rates of 25- to 34-year-olds, by sex and educational attainment: 2017

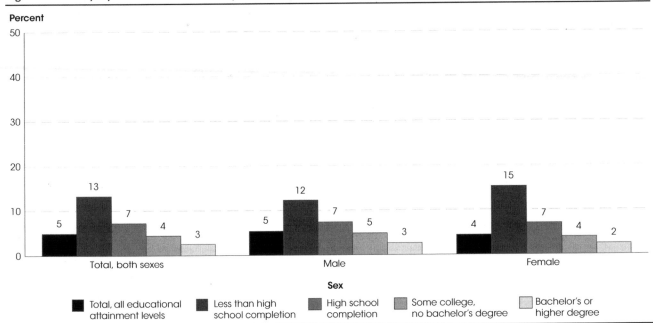

NOTE: Data are based on sample surveys of the noninstitutionalized population, which excludes persons living in institutions (e.g., prisons or nursing facilities); this figure includes data only on the civilian population (excludes all military personnel). The unemployment rate is the percentage of persons in the civilian labor force who are not working and who made specific efforts to find employment sometime during the prior 4 weeks. The civilian labor force consists of all civilians who are employed or seeking employment. "Some college, no bachelor's degree" includes persons with an associate's degree. "High school completion" includes equivalency credentials, such as the GED.
SOURCE: U.S. Department of Commerce, Census Bureau, Current Population Survey (CPS), Annual Social and Economic Supplement, March 2017. See *Digest of Education Statistics 2017*, tables 501.80, 501.85, and 501.90.

The unemployment rate in 2017 was lower for those with higher levels of educational attainment. For example, the unemployment rate was lowest for those with a bachelor's or higher degree (3 percent). The unemployment rate was lower for young adults with some college (4 percent) than for those who had completed high school (7 percent), which was, in turn, lower than the rate for those who had not completed high school (13 percent). This pattern was observed for both young adult males and females. For example, the unemployment rate for young adult males

was lowest for those with a bachelor's or higher degree (3 percent) and highest for those who had not completed high school (12 percent).

In 2017, the unemployment rate for young adults overall was higher for males than for females (5 vs. 4 percent). However, there were no measurable differences between the unemployment rates of young adult males and females at any individual level of educational attainment.

Figure 4. Unemployment rates of 25- to 34-year-olds, by educational attainment: Selected years, 2000 through 2017

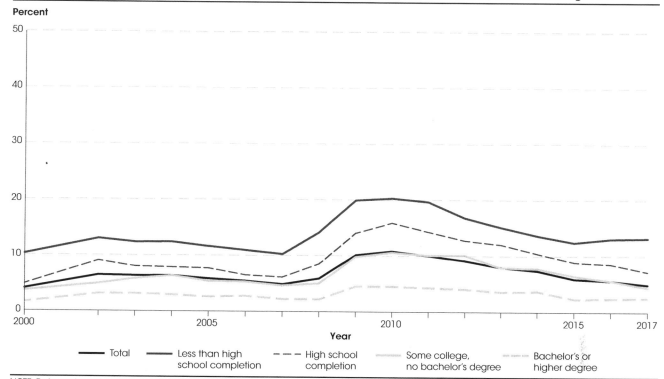

NOTE: Data are based on sample surveys of the noninstitutionalized population, which excludes persons living in institutions (e.g., prisons or nursing facilities); this figure includes data only on the civilian population (excludes all military personnel). The unemployment rate is the percentage of persons in the civilian labor force who are not working and who made specific efforts to find employment sometime during the prior 4 weeks. The civilian labor force consists of all civilians who are employed or seeking employment. "Some college, no bachelor's degree" includes persons with an associate's degree. "High school completion" includes equivalency credentials, such as the GED.
SOURCE: U.S. Department of Commerce, Census Bureau, Current Population Survey (CPS), Annual Social and Economic Supplement, selected years, March 2000 through 2017. See *Digest of Education Statistics 2013* and *2017*, table 501.80.

For young adults overall, the unemployment rate was higher in 2010 (11 percent), immediately after the recession, than in 2000 (4 percent), prior to the recession. The unemployment rate then decreased from 2010 to 2017, to 5 percent, but this rate was still higher than the rate in 2000. During these years, the same patterns in unemployment rates were observed for young adults with a bachelor's or higher degree and for those who had completed high school. For young adults with some college and for those who had not completed high school, the unemployment rates in 2010 were also higher than in 2000, and the rates decreased from 2010 to 2017; however, the rates in 2017 were not measurably different from the rates in 2000.

Endnotes:

[1] In this indicator, "some college" includes those with an associate's degree, and those who have attended college but have not obtained a bachelor's degree.
[2] Includes equivalency credentials, such as the GED.

[3] National Bureau of Economic Research. (2010). *U.S. Business Cycle Expansions and Contractions.* Retrieved January 23, 2018, from http://www.nber.org/cycles.html.

Reference tables: *Digest of Education Statistics 2017,* tables 501.50, 501.60, 501.70, 501.80, 501.85, and 501.90

Related indicators and resources: Annual Earnings of Young Adults; Disability Rates and Employment Status by Educational Attainment [*The Condition of Education 2017 Spotlight*]; Employment Outcomes of Bachelor's Degree Recipients; Post-College Employment Outcomes by Field of Study and Race/Ethnicity [*The Condition of Education 2016 Spotlight*]; Trends in Employment Rates by Educational Attainment [*The Condition of Education 2013 Spotlight*]

Glossary: Bachelor's degree, College, Educational attainment (Current Population Survey), Employment status, High school completer

The indicators in this chapter of *The Condition of Education* compare the United States education system to the education systems in other countries. The indicators examine educational attainment, education expenditures, and student performance on international assessments in reading, mathematics, and science. The indicators focus on comparison to other countries in the Organization for Economic Cooperation and Development (OECD), and include supplemental data from other countries when available.

This chapter's indicators are available at *The Condition of Education* website: http://nces.ed.gov/programs/coe.

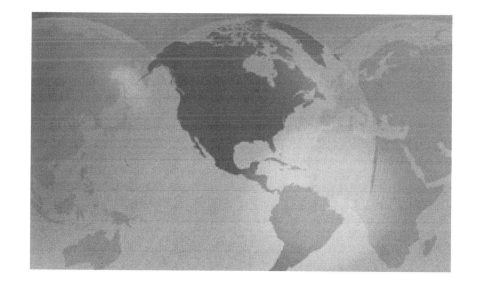

Chapter 4

International Comparisons

Indicator 4.1

International Comparisons: Reading Literacy at Grade 4

In 2016, the United States, along with 15 other education systems, participated in the new ePIRLS assessment of students' comprehension of online information. The average online informational reading score for fourth-grade students in the United States (557) was higher than the ePIRLS scale centerpoint (500). Only three education systems (Singapore, Norway, and Ireland) scored higher than the United States.

The Progress in International Reading Literacy Study (PIRLS) is an international comparative assessment that evaluates reading literacy at grade 4. The assessment is coordinated by the TIMSS[1] and PIRLS International Study Center at Boston College with the support of the International Association for the Evaluation of Educational Achievement (IEA). PIRLS has been administered every 5 years since 2001. In 2016, there were 58 education systems that had PIRLS reading literacy data at grade 4.[2] These 58 education systems included both countries and other benchmarking education systems (portions of a country, nation, kingdom, emirate, or other non-national entity).[3] Sixteen of these education systems, including the United States, also administered ePIRLS, a new computer-based extension of PIRLS designed to assess students' comprehension of online information.

Figure 1.   Average reading scale scores of fourth-grade students on PIRLS, by education system: 2016

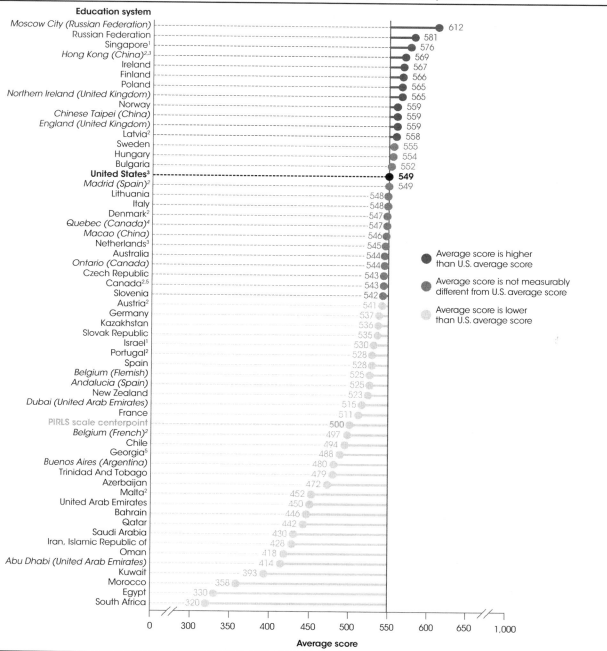

In 2016, the average reading literacy score for fourth-grade students in the United States (549) was higher than the PIRLS scale centerpoint (500).[4] The U.S. average score was higher than the average scores of 30 education systems (over half of the participating education systems) and not measurably different from the average scores of 15 education systems. The United States scored lower than 12 education systems: Moscow City (Russian Federation), the Russian Federation, Singapore, Hong Kong (China), Ireland, Finland, Poland, Northern Ireland (United Kingdom), Norway, Chinese Taipei (China), England (United Kingdom), and Latvia.

Figure 2. Percentage of fourth-grade students performing at selected PIRLS international benchmarks in reading, by education system: 2016

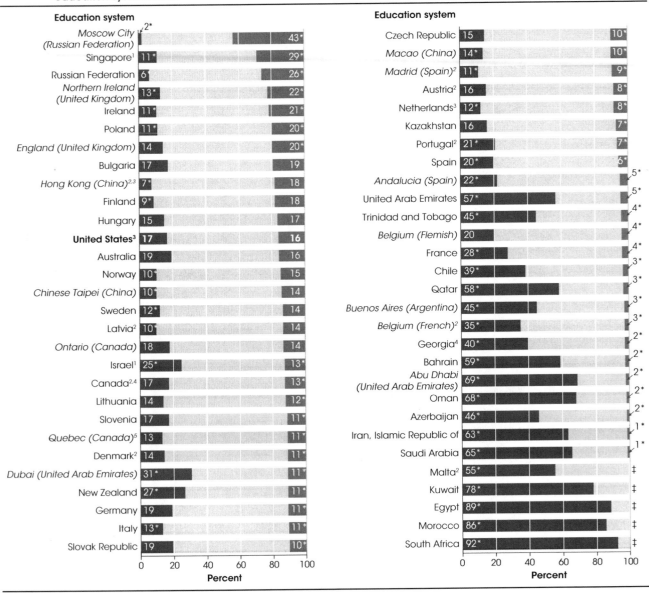

■ Low or below
▨ Advanced
* *p* < .05. Significantly different from the U.S. percentage.
‡ Reporting standards not met (too few cases for a reliable estimate).
[1] National Defined Population covers less than 90 percent of the National Target Population (but at least 77 percent).
[2] National Defined Population covers 90 to 95 percent of the National Target Population.
[3] Met guidelines for sample participation rates only after replacement schools were included.
[4] National Target Population does not include all of the International Target Population.
[5] Did not satisfy guidelines for sample participation rates.
NOTE: Education systems are ordered by the percentage of students reaching the *Advanced* international benchmark. Although rounded numbers are displayed, the figures are based on unrounded estimates. The PIRLS scores are reported on a scale from 0 to 1,000. PIRLS describes achievement along the reading achievement scale: *Low* (400), *Intermediate* (475), *High* (550), and *Advanced* (625). The score cut-points were selected to be as close as possible to the 25th, 50th, 75th, and 90th percentiles. Each successive point, or benchmark, is associated with the knowledge and skills that students successfully demonstrate at each level. Italics indicate participants identified as a non-national entity that represents a portion of a country. Education systems that did not administer PIRLS at the target grade are not shown. For more information about individual countries and assessment methodology, please see *Methods and Procedures in PIRLS 2016* (https://timssandpirls.bc.edu/publications/pirls/2016-methods.html).
SOURCE: International Association for the Evaluation of Educational Achievement (IEA), Progress in International Reading Literacy Study (PIRLS), 2016. See *Digest of Education Statistics 2017*, table 602.10.

PIRLS describes achievement at four international benchmarks along the reading achievement scale: *Low* (400), *Intermediate* (475), *High* (550), and *Advanced* (625). In 2016, about 16 percent of U.S. fourth-graders reached the *Advanced* benchmark. The percentages of students reaching this benchmark ranged from 1 percent in Saudi Arabia and in the Islamic Republic of Iran to 43 percent in Moscow City (Russian Federation). Seven education systems (Moscow City [Russian Federation], Singapore, the Russian Federation, Northern Ireland [United Kingdom], Ireland, Poland, and England [United Kingdom]) had a higher percentage of fourth-graders who reached the *Advanced* benchmark than the United States did.

Figure 3. Average online informational reading scale scores of fourth-grade students on ePIRLS, by education system: 2016

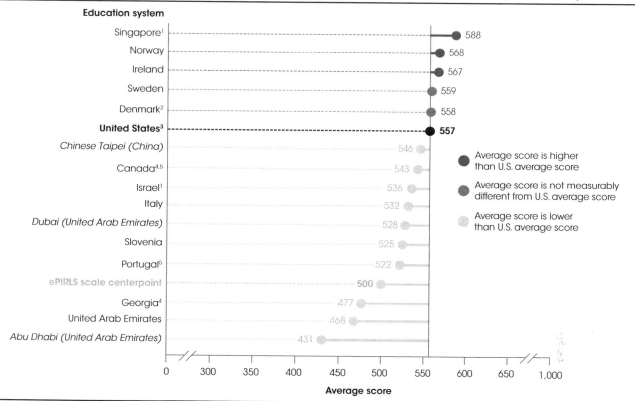

[1] National Defined Population covers less than 90 percent of the National Target Population (but at least 77 percent).
[2] Did not satisfy guidelines for sample participation rates.
[3] Met guidelines for sample participation rates only after replacement schools were included.
[4] National Target Population does not include all of the International Target Population.
[5] National Defined Population covers 90 to 95 percent of the National Target Population.
NOTE: Education systems are ordered by ePIRLS average scale score. Italics indicate participants identified as a non-national entity that represents a portion of a country. The ePIRLS scores are reported on a scale from 0 to 1,000, with the scale centerpoint set at 500 and the standard deviation set at 100. For more information about individual countries and assessment methodology, please see *Methods and Procedures in PIRLS 2016* (https://timssandpirls.bc.edu/publications/pirls/2016-methods.html).
SOURCE: International Association for the Evaluation of Educational Achievement (IEA), Progress in International Reading Literacy Study (PIRLS), 2016. See *Digest of Education Statistics 2017*, table 602.15.

In 2016, the United States, along with 15 other education systems, participated in the new ePIRLS assessment of students' comprehension of online information. The average online informational reading score for fourth-grade students in the United States (557) was higher than the ePIRLS scale centerpoint (500). The U.S. average score was higher than the average scores of 10 education systems and not measurably different from the average scores of 2 education systems. Only three education systems (Singapore, Norway, and Ireland) scored higher than the United States.

Figure 4. Percentage of fourth-grade students performing at selected ePIRLS international benchmarks in online informational reading, by education system: 2016

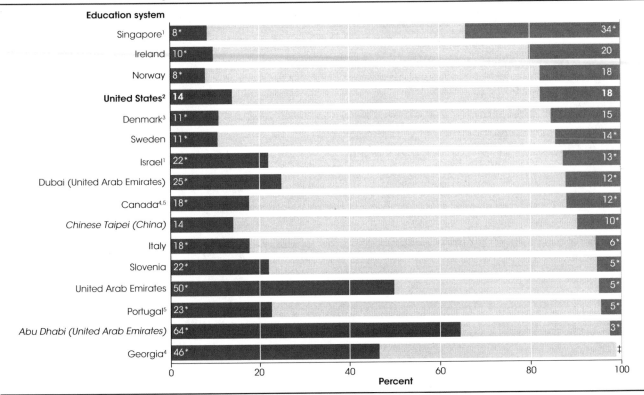

- ■ Low or below
- ■ Advanced
- * *p* < .05. Significantly different from the U.S. percentage.
- ‡ Reporting standards not met (too few cases for a reliable estimate).
- ¹ National Defined Population covers less than 90 percent of the National Target Population (but at least 77 percent).
- ² Met guidelines for sample participation rates only after replacement schools were included.
- ³ Did not satisfy guidelines for sample participation rates.
- ⁴ National Target Population does not include all of the International Target Population.
- ⁵ National Defined Population covers 90 to 95 percent of the National Target Population.

NOTE: Education systems are ordered by the percentage of students reaching the *Advanced* international benchmark. Although rounded numbers are displayed, the figures are based on unrounded estimates. The ePIRLS scores are reported on a scale from 0 to 1,000. ePIRLS describes achievement at four international benchmarks along the reading achievement scale: *Low* (400), *Intermediate* (475), *High* (550), and *Advanced* (625). The score cut-points were selected to be as close as possible to the 25th, 50th, 75th, and 90th percentiles. Each successive point, or benchmark, is associated with the knowledge and skills that students successfully demonstrate at each level. Italics indicate participants identified as a non-national entity that represents a portion of a country. For more information about individual countries and assessment methodology, please see *Methods and Procedures in PIRLS 2016* (https://timssandpirls.bc.edu/publications/pirls/2016-methods.html).

SOURCE: International Association for the Evaluation of Educational Achievement (IEA), Progress in International Reading Literacy Study (PIRLS), 2016. See *Digest of Education Statistics 2017*, table 602.15.

Similar to PIRLS, ePIRLS also describes achievement at four international benchmarks along the reading achievement scale: *Low* (400), *Intermediate* (475), *High* (550), and *Advanced* (625). In 2016, about 18 percent of U.S. fourth-graders reached the *Advanced* benchmark. The percentages of students reaching this benchmark ranged from 3 percent in Abu Dhabi (United Arab Emirates) to 34 percent in Singapore. Singapore was the only education system with a higher percentage of fourth-graders who reached the *Advanced* benchmark than in the United States. Ireland, Norway, and Denmark had percentages of fourth-graders who reached the *Advanced* benchmark that were not measurably different from the percentage in the United States.

Endnotes:

[1] The Trends in International Mathematics and Science Study (TIMSS) assesses mathematics and science knowledge and skills at grades 4 and 8. For more information on TIMSS, see indicator International Comparisons: U.S. 4th-, 8th-, and 12th-Graders' Mathematics and Science Achievement.

[2] PIRLS was administered in 61 education systems. However, three education systems did not administer PIRLS at the target grade and are not included in this indicator.

[3] The IEA differentiates between IEA members, referred to always as "countries," and "benchmarking participants." IEA member countries include both "countries," which are complete, independent political entities, and "other education systems," or non-national entities (e.g., England, the Flemish community of Belgium). Non-national entities that are not IEA member countries (e.g., Abu Dhabi [United Arab Emirates], Ontario [Canada]) are designated as "benchmarking participants." These benchmarking systems are able to participate in PIRLS even though they may not be members of the IEA. For convenience, the generic term "education systems" is used when summarizing across results.

[4] PIRLS and ePIRLS scores are reported on a scale from 0 to 1,000, with the scale centerpoint set at 500 and the standard deviation set at 100. The scale centerpoint represents the mean of the overall PIRLS achievement distribution in 2001. The PIRLS scale is the same in each administration; thus a value of 500 in 2016 equals 500 in 2001.

Reference tables: *Digest of Education Statistics 2017*, tables 602.10 and 602.15

Related indicators and resources: International Comparisons: Science, Reading, and Mathematics Literacy of 15-Year-Old Students; International Comparisons: U.S. 4th-, 8th-, and 12th-Graders' Mathematics and Science Achievement; Reading Performance

Glossary: N/A

International Comparisons: U.S. 4th-, 8th-, and 12th-Graders' Mathematics and Science Achievement

According to the 2015 Trends in International Mathematics and Science Study (TIMSS), the United States was among the top 15 education systems in science (out of 54) at grade 4 and among the top 17 education systems in science (out of 43) at grade 8. In mathematics, the United States was among the top 20 education systems at grade 4 and top 19 education systems at grade 8.

The Trends in International Mathematics and Science Study (TIMSS) is an international comparative assessment that evaluates mathematics and science knowledge and skills at grades 4 and 8. The TIMSS program also includes TIMSS Advanced, an international comparative study that measures the advanced mathematics and physics achievement of students in their final year of secondary school who are taking or have taken advanced courses. These assessments are coordinated by the TIMSS & PIRLS[1] International Study Center at Boston College, under the auspices of the International Association for the Evaluation of Educational Achievement (IEA), an international organization of national research institutions and government agencies.

In 2015, TIMSS mathematics and science data were collected by 54 education systems at 4th grade and 43 education systems at 8th grade.[2] TIMSS Advanced data were also collected by nine education systems from students in the final year of their secondary schools (in the U.S., 12th-graders). Education systems include countries (complete, independent, and political entities) and other benchmarking education systems (portions of a country, nation, kingdom, or emirate, and other non-national entities).[3] In addition to participating in the U.S. national sample, Florida participated individually as a state at the 4th and 8th grades.

Figure 1. Average TIMSS mathematics assessment scale scores of 4th-grade students, by education system: 2015

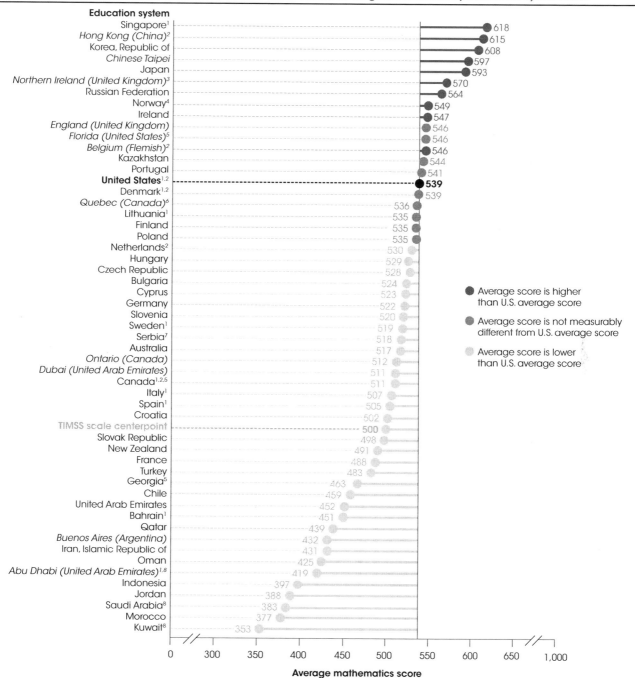

¹ National Defined Population covers 90 to 95 percent of the National Target Population, as defined by TIMSS.
² Met guidelines for sample participation rates only after replacement schools were included.
³ Nearly satisfied guidelines for sample participation rates after replacement schools were included.
⁴ Norway collected data from students in their fifth year of schooling rather than in grade 4 because year 1 in Norway is considered the equivalent of kindergarten rather than the first year of primary school.
⁵ National Target Population does not include all of the International Target Population, as defined by TIMSS.
⁶ Did not satisfy guidelines for sample participation rates.
⁷ National Defined Population covers less than 90 percent of the National Target Population (but at least 77 percent), as defined by TIMSS.
⁸ Reservations about reliability because the percentage of students with achievement too low for estimation exceeds 15 percent but does not exceed 25 percent.
NOTE: Education systems are ordered by average score. Education systems that are not countries are shown in italics. Participants that did not administer TIMSS at the target grade are not shown; see the international report for their results (http://timssandpirls.bc.edu/timss2015/international-results/). U.S. state data are based on public school students only. The TIMSS scale centerpoint is set at 500 points and represents the mean of the overall achievement distribution in 1995. The TIMSS scale is the same in each administration; thus, a value of 500 in 2015 equals 500 in 1995. For more information on the International and National Target Populations, see https://nces.ed.gov/timss/timss15technotes_intlreqs.asp.
SOURCE: International Association for the Evaluation of Educational Achievement (IEA), Trends in International Mathematics and Science Study (TIMSS), 2015. See Digest of Education Statistics 2016, table 602.20.

At grade 4, the U.S. average mathematics score (539) in 2015 was higher than the TIMSS scale centerpoint (500).[4] Ten education systems[5] had higher average mathematics scores than the United States, 9 had scores that were not measurably different, and 34 education systems had lower average scores. The 10 education systems with average mathematics scores above the U.S. score were Belgium (Flemish), Chinese Taipei, Hong Kong (China), Ireland, Japan, Northern Ireland (Great Britain), Norway, the Republic of Korea, the Russian Federation, and Singapore. Florida's average mathematics score was not measurably different from the U.S. national average.

At grade 4, the U.S. average science score (546) in 2015 was also higher than the TIMSS scale centerpoint of 500. Seven education systems had higher average science scores than the United States, 7 had scores that were not measurably different, and 38 education systems had lower average scores. The 7 education systems with average science scores above the U.S. score were Chinese Taipei, Finland, Japan, Hong Kong (China), the Republic of Korea, the Russian Federation, and Singapore. Florida's average science score was not measurably different from the U.S. national average.

Figure 2. Average TIMSS science assessment scale scores of 4th-grade students, by education system: 2015

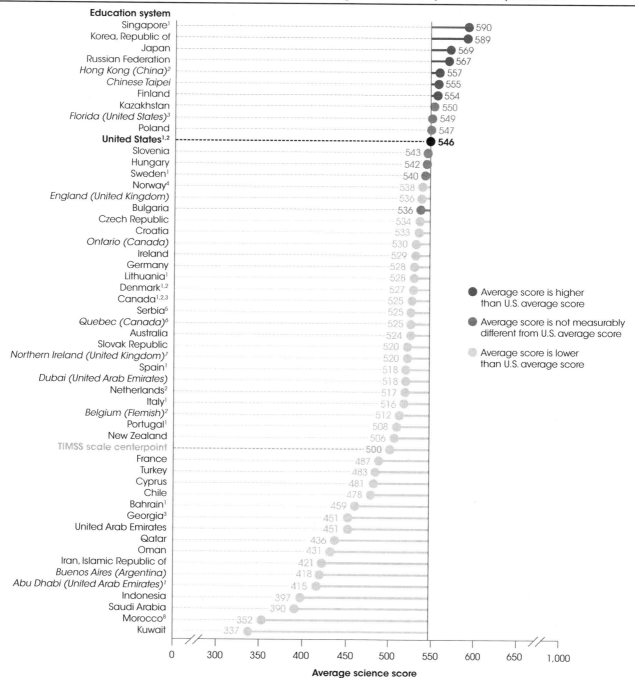

Education system

Education system	Score
Singapore[1]	590
Korea, Republic of	589
Japan	569
Russian Federation	567
Hong Kong (China)[2]	557
Chinese Taipei	555
Finland	554
Kazakhstan	550
Florida (United States)[3]	549
Poland	547
United States[1,2]	**546**
Slovenia	543
Hungary	542
Sweden[1]	540
Norway[4]	538
England (United Kingdom)	536
Bulgaria	536
Czech Republic	534
Croatia	533
Ontario (Canada)	530
Ireland	529
Germany	528
Lithuania[1]	528
Denmark[1,2]	527
Canada[1,2,3]	525
Serbia[5]	525
Quebec (Canada)[6]	525
Australia	524
Slovak Republic	520
Northern Ireland (United Kingdom)[7]	520
Spain[1]	518
Dubai (United Arab Emirates)	518
Netherlands[2]	517
Italy[1]	516
Belgium (Flemish)[2]	512
Portugal[1]	508
New Zealand	506
TIMSS scale centerpoint	500
France	487
Turkey	483
Cyprus	481
Chile	478
Bahrain[1]	459
Georgia[3]	451
United Arab Emirates	451
Qatar	436
Oman	431
Iran, Islamic Republic of	421
Buenos Aires (Argentina)	418
Abu Dhabi (United Arab Emirates)[1]	415
Indonesia	397
Saudi Arabia	390
Morocco[8]	352
Kuwait	337

● Average score is higher than U.S. average score

● Average score is not measurably different from U.S. average score

● Average score is lower than U.S. average score

Average science score

[1] National Defined Population covers 90 to 95 percent of the National Target Population, as defined by TIMSS.
[2] Met guidelines for sample participation rates only after replacement schools were included.
[3] National Target Population does not include all of the International Target Population, as defined by TIMSS.
[4] Norway collected data from students in their fifth year of schooling rather than in grade 4 because year 1 in Norway is considered the equivalent of kindergarten rather than the first year of primary school.
[5] National Defined Population covers less than 90 percent of the National Target Population (but at least 77 percent), as defined by TIMSS.
[6] Did not satisfy guidelines for sample participation rates.
[7] Nearly satisfied guidelines for sample participation rates after replacement schools were included.
[8] Reservations about reliability because the percentage of students with achievement too low for estimation exceeds 15 percent but does not exceed 25 percent.
NOTE: Education systems are ordered by average score. Education systems that are not countries are shown in italics. Participants that did not administer TIMSS at the target grade are not shown; see the international report for their results (http://timssandpirls.bc.edu/timss2015/international-results/). U.S. state data are based on public school students only. The TIMSS scale centerpoint is set at 500 points and represents the mean of the overall achievement distribution in 1995. The TIMSS scale is the same in each administration; thus, a value of 500 in 2015 equals 500 in 1995. For more information on the International and National Target Populations, see https://nces.ed.gov/timss/timss15technotes_intlreqs.asp.
SOURCE: International Association for the Evaluation of Educational Achievement (IEA), Trends in International Mathematics and Science Study (TIMSS), 2015. See *Digest of Education Statistics 2016*, table 602.20.

Figure 3. Average TIMSS mathematics assessment scale scores of 8th-grade students, by education system: 2015

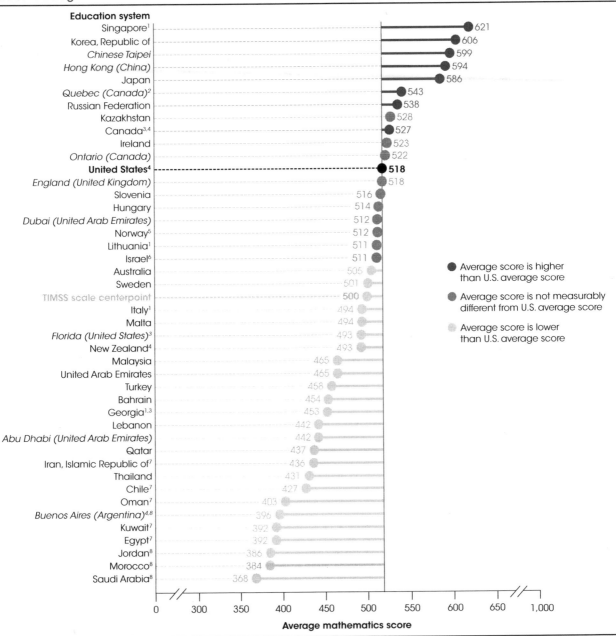

[1] National Defined Population covers 90 to 95 percent of the National Target Population, as defined by TIMSS.
[2] Did not satisfy guidelines for sample participation rates.
[3] National Target Population does not include all of the International Target Population, as defined by TIMSS.
[4] Met guidelines for sample participation rates only after replacement schools were included.
[5] Norway collected data from students in their fifth year of schooling rather than in grade 4 because year 1 in Norway is considered the equivalent of kindergarten rather than the first year of primary school.
[6] National Defined Population covers less than 90 percent of the National Target Population (but at least 77 percent), as defined by TIMSS.
[7] Reservations about reliability because the percentage of students with achievement too low for estimation exceeds 15 percent but does not exceed 25 percent.
[8] Reservations about reliability because the percentage of students with achievement too low for estimation exceeds 25 percent.
NOTE: Education systems are ordered by average score. Education systems that are not countries are shown in italics. Participants that did not administer TIMSS at the target grade are not shown; see the international report for their results (http://timssandpirls.bc.edu/timss2015/international-results/). U.S. state data are based on public school students only. The TIMSS scale centerpoint is set at 500 points and represents the mean of the overall achievement distribution in 1995. The TIMSS scale is the same in each administration; thus, a value of 500 in 2015 equals 500 in 1995. For more information on the International and National Target Populations, see https://nces.ed.gov/timss/timss15technotes_intlreqs.asp.
SOURCE: International Association for the Evaluation of Educational Achievement (IEA), Trends in International Mathematics and Science Study (TIMSS), 2015.
See *Digest of Education Statistics 2016*, table 602.30.

At grade 8, the U.S. average mathematics score (518) in 2015 was higher than the TIMSS scale centerpoint of 500. Eight education systems had higher average mathematics scores than the United States, 10 had scores that were not measurably different, and 24 education systems had lower average scores. The 8 education systems with average mathematics scores above the U.S. score were Canada, Chinese Taipei, Hong Kong (China), Japan, Quebec (Canada), the Republic of Korea, the Russian Federation, and Singapore. Florida's average mathematics score was below the U.S. national average.

Figure 4. Average TIMSS science assessment scale scores of 8th-grade students, by education system: 2015

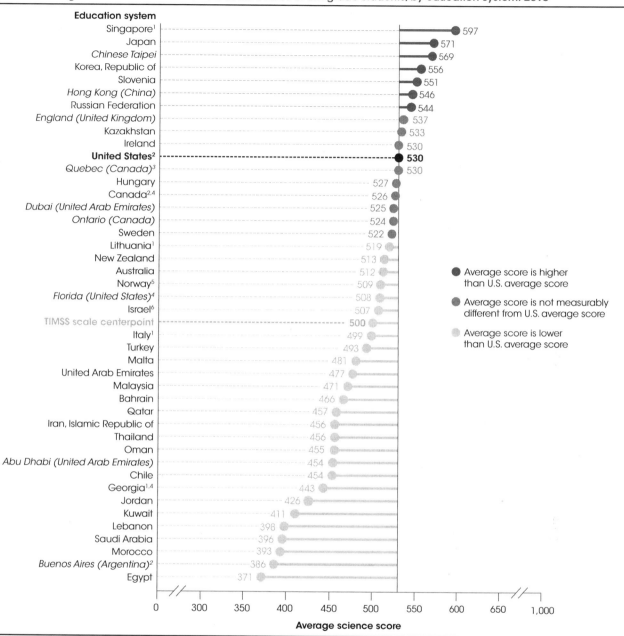

NOTE: Education systems are ordered by average score. Education systems that are not countries are shown in italics. Participants that did not administer TIMSS at the target grade are not shown; see the international report for their results (http://timssandpirls.bc.edu/timss2015/international-results/). U.S. state data are based on public school students only. The TIMSS scale centerpoint is set at 500 points and represents the mean of the overall achievement distribution in 1995. The TIMSS scale is the same in each administration; thus, a value of 500 in 2015 equals 500 in 1995. For more information on the International and National Target Populations, see https://nces.ed.gov/timss/timss15technotes_intlreqs.asp.

[1] National Defined Population covers 90 to 95 percent of the National Target Population, as defined by TIMSS.
[2] Met guidelines for sample participation rates only after replacement schools were included.
[3] Did not satisfy guidelines for sample participation rates.
[4] National Target Population does not include all of the International Target Population, as defined by TIMSS.
[5] Norway collected data from students in their fifth year of schooling rather than in grade 4 because year 1 in Norway is considered the equivalent of kindergarten rather than the first year of primary school.
[6] National Defined Population covers less than 90 percent of the National Target Population (but at least 77 percent), as defined by TIMSS.
SOURCE: International Association for the Evaluation of Educational Achievement (IEA), Trends in International Mathematics and Science Study (TIMSS), 2015. See *Digest of Education Statistics 2016*, table 602.30.

At grade 8, the U.S. average science score (530) in 2015 was higher than the TIMSS scale centerpoint of 500. Seven education systems had higher average science scores than the United States, 9 had scores that were not measurably different, and 26 education systems had lower average scores. The seven education systems with average science scores above the U.S. score were Chinese Taipei, Hong Kong (China), Japan, the Republic of Korea, the Russian Federation, Singapore, and Slovenia. Florida's average science score was below the U.S. national average.

Figure 5. Average advanced mathematics scores and coverage index of TIMSS Advanced students, by education system: 2015

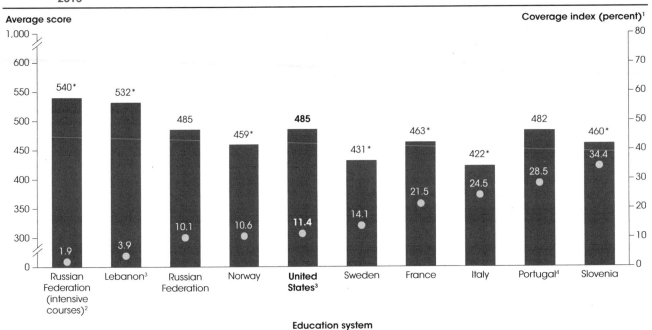

* *p* < .05. Significantly different from the U.S. percentage.
[1] The advanced mathematics coverage index is the percentage of the corresponding age cohort covered by students in their final year of secondary school who have taken or are taking advanced mathematics courses. The corresponding age cohort is determined for education systems individually. In the United States, the corresponding age cohort is considered 18-year-olds. For additional details, see the Technical Notes available at http://nces.ed.gov/timss/timss15technotes.asp.
[2] Intensive courses are advanced mathematics courses that involve 6 or more hours per week. Results for students in these courses are reported separately from the results for other students from the Russian Federation taking courses that involve 4.5 hours per week.
[3] Did not satisfy guidelines for sample participation rates.
[4] Met guidelines for sample participation rates only after replacement schools were included.
NOTE: Education systems are ordered by the advanced mathematics coverage index. The TIMSS Advanced scale centerpoint is set at 500 points and represents the mean of the overall achievement distribution in 1995. The TIMSS Advanced scale is the same in each administration; thus, a value of 500 in 2015 equals 500 in 1995.
SOURCE: International Association for the Evaluation of Educational Achievement (IEA), Trends in International Mathematics and Science Study (TIMSS) Advanced, 2015. See *Digest of Education Statistics 2016*, table 602.35.

The TIMSS Advanced assessment measures the advanced mathematics and physics achievement of students in their final year of secondary school who are taking or have taken advanced courses. In TIMSS Advanced, the U.S. average advanced mathematics score (485) in 2015 was lower than the TIMSS Advanced scale centerpoint (500). Two education systems had higher average advanced mathematics scores than the United States, two (Portugal and the Russian Federation) had scores that were not measurably different, and five education systems had lower average scores. The education systems with higher average advanced mathematics scores than the United States were Lebanon and the Russian Federation's intensive track (i.e., advanced students taking 6 or more hours of advanced mathematics per week).[6] Such comparisons, however, should take into account the "coverage index," which represents the percentage of students eligible to take the advanced mathematics assessment. The advanced mathematics coverage index ranged from 1.9 percent for the Russian Federation's intensive track to 34.4 percent in Slovenia.

Figure 6.   Average physics scores and coverage index of TIMSS Advanced students, by education system: 2015

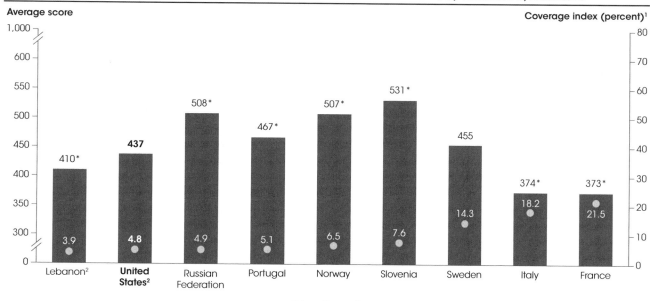

* *p* < .05. Significantly different from the U.S. percentage.
[1] The physics coverage index is the percentage of the corresponding age cohort covered by students in their final year of secondary school who have taken or are taking physics courses. The corresponding age cohort is determined for education systems individually. In the United States, the corresponding age cohort is considered 18-year-olds. For additional details, see the Technical Notes available at http://nces.ed.gov/timss/timss15technotes.asp.
[2] Did not satisfy guidelines for sample participation rates.
NOTE: Education systems are ordered by the advanced physics coverage index. The TIMSS Advanced scale centerpoint is set at 500 points and represents the mean of the overall achievement distribution in 1995. The TIMSS Advanced scale is the same in each administration; thus, a value of 500 in 2015 equals 500 in 1995.
SOURCE: International Association for the Evaluation of Educational Achievement (IEA), Trends in International Mathematics and Science Study (TIMSS) Advanced, 2015. See *Digest of Education Statistics 2016*, table 602.35.

In TIMSS Advanced, the U.S. average physics score (437) in 2015 was lower than the TIMSS Advanced scale centerpoint (500). Four education systems had higher average physics scores than the United States, one (Sweden) had a score that was not measurably different, and three education systems had lower average scores. The education systems with higher average advanced science scores than the United States were Norway, Portugal, the Russian Federation, and Slovenia. The physics coverage index ranged from 3.9 percent in Lebanon to 21.5 percent in France.

Endnotes:

[1] The Progress in International Reading Literacy Study (PIRLS) evaluates reading literacy at grade 4. For more information on PIRLS, see indicator <u>International Comparisons: Reading Literacy at Grade 4</u>.

[2] Armenia, which participated at both grades, is not included in these counts or the results reported in this indicator because their data are not comparable for trend analyses.

[3] Benchmarking systems are able to participate in TIMSS even though they may not be members of the IEA. Participating allows them the opportunity to assess their students' achievement and to evaluate their curricula in an international context.

[4] TIMSS and TIMSS Advanced scores are reported on a scale from 0 to 1,000, with a scale centerpoint set at 500 and the standard deviation set at 100. The TIMSS scale centerpoint represents the mean of the overall achievement distribution in 1995. The TIMSS scale is the same in each administration; thus, a value of 500 in 2015 equals 500 in 1995 when that was the international average.

[5] The IEA differentiates between IEA members, referred to always as "countries" and "benchmarking participants." IEA member countries include both "countries," which are complete, independent political entities and "other education systems," or non-national entities (e.g., England, the Flemish community of Belgium). Non-national entities that are not IEA member countries (i.e., Florida, Abu Dhabi) are designated as "benchmarking participants." For convenience, the generic term "education systems" is used when summarizing across results.

[6] The Russian Federation tested two samples in advanced mathematics in 2015. Results for students in the intensive mathematics courses of 6 or more hours per week are reported separately from the results for the Russian Federation's advanced students taking courses of only 4.5 hours per week.

Reference tables: *Digest of Education Statistics 2016*, tables 602.20, 602.30, and 602.35

Related indicators and resources: <u>International Comparisons: Reading Literacy at Grade 4</u>; <u>International Comparisons: Science, Reading and Mathematics Literacy of 15-Year-Old Students</u>; <u>Mathematics Performance</u>; <u>Science Performance</u>

Glossary: N/A

This page intentionally left blank.

International Comparisons: Science, Reading, and Mathematics Literacy of 15-Year-Old Students

In 2015, there were 18 education systems with higher average science literacy scores for 15-year-olds than the United States, 14 with higher reading literacy scores, and 36 with higher mathematics literacy scores.

The Program for International Student Assessment (PISA), coordinated by the Organization for Economic Cooperation and Development (OECD), has measured the performance of 15-year-old students in science, reading, and mathematics literacy every 3 years since 2000. In 2015, PISA was administered in 73[1] countries and education systems,[2] including all 35 member countries of the OECD. In addition to participating in the U.S. national sample, Massachusetts and North Carolina participated individually as states. Puerto Rico also participated in the PISA assessment, but was not included in the U.S. national results. The samples of schools and students for all education systems and Puerto Rico

included both public and private schools, while the samples of schools and students for Massachusetts and North Carolina were from public schools only.

PISA 2015 results are reported by average scale score (from 0 to 1,000) as well as by the percentage of students reaching particular proficiency levels. Proficiency results are presented in terms of the percentages of students reaching proficiency level 5 and above (i.e., percentages of top performers) and the percentages of students performing below proficiency level 2. Proficiency level 2 is considered a baseline of proficiency by the OECD (i.e., percentages of low performers).

Table 1. Average scores of 15-year-old students on the Program for International Student Assessment (PISA) science literacy scale, by education system: 2015

Education system	Average score		Education system	Average score	
OECD average	**493**		Iceland	473	▼
Singapore	556	⬤	Israel	467	▼
Japan	538	⬤	*Malta*	465	▼
Estonia	534	⬤	Slovak Republic	461	▼
Chinese Taipei	532	⬤	Greece	455	▼
Finland	531	⬤	Chile	447	▼
Macau (China)	529	⬤	*Bulgaria*	446	▼
Canada	528	⬤	*United Arab Emirates*	437	▼
Vietnam	525	⬤	*Uruguay*	435	▼
Hong Kong (China)	523	⬤	*Romania*	435	▼
B-S-J-G (China)[1]	518	⬤	*Cyprus*	433	▼
Korea, Republic of	516	⬤	*Moldova, Republic of*	428	▼
New Zealand	513	⬤	*Albania*	427	▼
Slovenia	513	⬤	Turkey	425	▼
Australia	510	⬤	*Trinidad and Tobago*	425	▼
United Kingdom	509	⬤	*Thailand*	421	▼
German	509	⬤	*Costa Rica*	420	▼
Netherlands	509	⬤	*Qatar*	418	▼
Switzerland	506	⬤	*Colombia*	416	▼
Ireland	503		Mexico	416	▼
Belgium	502		*Montenegro, Republic of*	411	▼
Denmark	502		*Georgia*	411	▼
Poland	501		*Jordan*	409	▼
Portugal	501		*Indonesia*	403	▼
Norway	498		*Brazil*	401	▼
United States	**496**		*Peru*	397	▼
Austria	495		*Lebanon*	386	▼
France	495		*Tunisia*	386	▼
Sweden	493		*Macedonia, Republic of*	384	▼
Czech Republic	493		*Kosovo*	378	▼
Spain	493		*Algeria*	376	▼
Latvia	490		*Dominican Republic*	332	▼
Russian Federation	487	▼			
Luxembourg	483	▼			
Italy	481	▼			
Hungary	477	▼	**U.S. states and territories**		
Lithuania	475	▼	*Massachusetts*	529	⬤
Croatia	475	▼	*North Carolina*	502	
Buenos Aires (Argentina)	475	▼	*Puerto Rico*	403	▼

⬤ Average score is higher than U.S. average score.
▼ Average score is lower than U.S. average score.
[1] B-S-J-G (China) refers to the four PISA participating China provinces: Beijing, Shanghai, Jiangsu, and Guangdong.
NOTE: Education systems are ordered by 2015 average score. The OECD average is the average of the national averages of the OECD member countries, with each country weighted equally. Scores are reported on a scale from 0 to 1,000. All average scores reported as higher or lower than the U.S. average score are different at a .05 level of statistical significance. Italics indicate non-OECD countries and education systems. Results for Massachusetts and North Carolina are for public school students only. Although Argentina, Kazakhstan, and Malaysia participated in PISA 2015, technical problems with their samples prevent results from being discussed in this report.
SOURCE: Organization for Economic Cooperation and Development (OECD), Program for International Student Assessment (PISA), 2015. See *Digest of Education Statistics 2016,* table 602.70.

In 2015, average science literacy scores ranged from 332 in the Dominican Republic to 556 in Singapore. The U.S. average science score (496) was not measurably different from the OECD average (493). Eighteen education systems and Massachusetts had higher average science scores than the United States, and 12 systems and North Carolina had scores that were not measurably different

from the U.S. average score. Massachusetts's average score (529) was higher than both the U.S. and OECD averages, North Carolina's average score (502) was not measurably different from the U.S. and OECD averages, and Puerto Rico's average score (403) was lower than both the U.S. and OECD averages.

Figure 1. Percentage of 15-year-old students performing on the Program for International Student Assessment (PISA) science literacy scale, by selected proficiency levels and education system: 2015

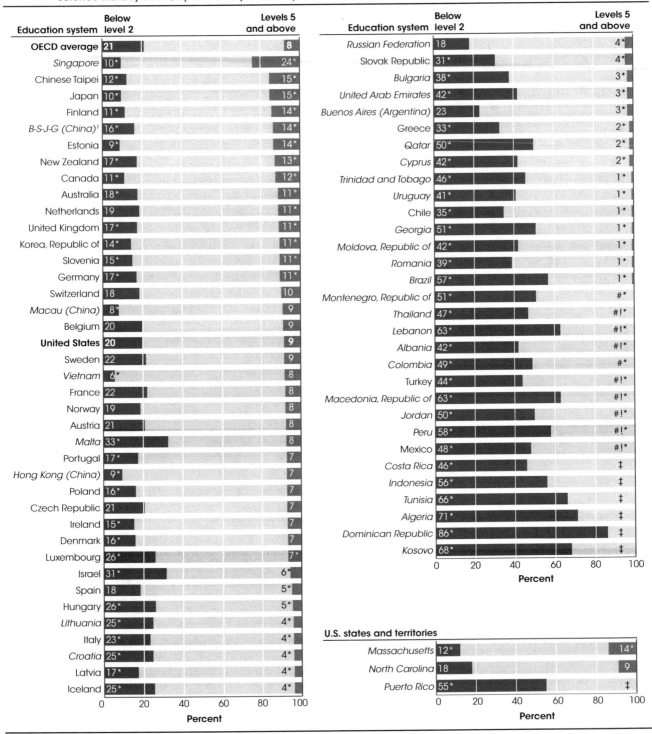

■ Below level 2
■ Levels 5 and above
Rounds to zero.
! Interpret data with caution. The coefficient of variation (CV) for this estimate is between 30 and 50 percent.
‡ Reporting standards not met. The coefficient of variation (CV) for this estimate is 50 percent or greater.
* p < .05. Significantly different from the U.S. percentage.
[1] B-S-J-G (China) refers to the four PISA participating China provinces: Beijing, Shanghai, Jiangsu, and Guangdong.
NOTE: Education systems are ordered by percentage of 15-year-olds in levels 5 and above. To reach a particular proficiency level, students must correctly answer a majority of items at that level. Students were classified into science proficiency levels according to their scores. Cut scores for each proficiency level can be found in table A-1 available at http://nces.ed.gov/surveys/pisa/PISA2015/index.asp. The OECD average is the average of the national percentages of the OECD member countries, with each country weighted equally. Italics indicate non-OECD countries and education systems. Results for Massachusetts and North Carolina are for public school students only. Although Argentina, Kazakhstan, and Malaysia participated in PISA 2015, technical problems with their samples prevent results from being discussed in this report.
SOURCE: Organization for Economic Cooperation and Development (OECD), Program for International Student Assessment (PISA), 2015. See Digest of Education Statistics 2016, table 602.70.

PISA reports science literacy in terms of seven proficiency levels, with level 1b being the lowest and level 6 being the highest. Students performing at levels 5 and 6 can apply scientific knowledge in a variety of complex real-life situations. The percentage of U.S. top performers on the science literacy scale (9 percent) was not measurably different from the OECD average (8 percent). Percentages of top performers ranged from near 0 percent in 10 education systems to 24 percent in Singapore. Fourteen education systems and Massachusetts (14 percent) had percentages of top performers higher than the United States in science literacy, while North Carolina had a percentage that was not measurably different (9 percent) than the United States.

The percentage of U.S. students who scored below proficiency level 2 in science literacy (20 percent) was not measurably different from the OECD average (21 percent). Percentages of low performers ranged from 6 percent in Vietnam to 86 percent in the Dominican Republic. Twenty-one education systems and Massachusetts (12 percent) had lower percentages of low performers in science literacy than the United States. The percentage of low performers in North Carolina (18 percent) was not measurably different from the U.S. percentage, while the percentage in Puerto Rico (55 percent) was higher.

Table 2. Average scores of 15-year-old students on the Program for International Student Assessment (PISA) reading literacy scale, by education system: 2015

Education system	Average score		Education system	Average score	
OECD average	493		Lithuania	472	▼
Singapore	535	⬥	Hungary	470	▼
Hong Kong (China)	527	⬥	Greece	467	▼
Canada	527	⬥	Chile	459	▼
Finland	526	⬥	Slovak Republic	453	▼
Ireland	521	⬥	Malta	447	▼
Estonia	519	⬥	Cyprus	443	▼
Korea, Republic of	517	⬥	Uruguay	437	▼
Japan	516	⬥	Romania	434	▼
Norway	513	⬥	United Arab Emirates	434	▼
New Zealand	509	⬥	Bulgaria	432	▼
Germany	509	⬥	Turkey	428	▼
Macau (China)	509	⬥	Costa Rica	427	▼
Poland	506	⬥	Trinidad and Tobago	427	▼
Slovenia	505	⬥	Montenegro, Republic of	427	▼
Netherlands	503		Colombia	425	▼
Australia	503		Mexico	423	▼
Sweden	500		Moldova, Republic of	416	▼
Denmark	500		Thailand	409	▼
France	499		Jordan	408	▼
Belgium	499		Brazil	407	▼
Portugal	498		Albania	405	▼
United Kingdom	498		Qatar	402	▼
Chinese Taipei	497		George	401	▼
United States	497		Peru	398	▼
Spain	496		Indonesia	397	▼
Russian Federation	495		Tunisia	361	▼
B-S-J-G (China)[1]	494		Dominican Republic	358	▼
Switzerland	492		Macedonia, Republic of	352	▼
Latvia	488	▼	Algeria	350	▼
Czech Republic	487	▼	Kosovo	347	▼
Croatia	487	▼	Lebanon	347	▼
Vietnam	487	▼			
Austria	485	▼			
Italy	485	▼			
Iceland	482	▼	**U.S. states and territories**		
Luxembourg	481	▼	Massachusetts	527	⬥
Israel	479	▼	North Carolina	500	
Buenos Aires (Argentina)	475	▼	Puerto Rico	410	▼

⬥ Average score is higher than U.S. average score.
▼ Average score is lower than U.S. average score.
[1] B-S-J-G (China) refers to the four PISA participating China provinces: Beijing, Shanghai, Jiangsu, and Guangdong.
NOTE: Education systems are ordered by 2015 average score. The OECD average is the average of the national averages of the OECD member countries, with each country weighted equally. Scores are reported on a scale from 0 to 1,000. All average scores reported as higher or lower than the U.S. average score are different at a .05 level of statistical significance. Italics indicate non-OECD countries and education systems. Results for Massachusetts and North Carolina are for public school students only. Although Argentina, Kazakhstan, and Malaysia participated in PISA 2015, technical problems with their samples prevent results from being discussed in this report.
SOURCE: Organization for Economic Cooperation and Development (OECD), Program for International Student Assessment (PISA), 2015. See *Digest of Education Statistics 2016*, table 602.50.

In reading literacy, average scores ranged from 347 in Lebanon to 535 in Singapore. The U.S. average score (497) was not measurably different from the OECD average (493). Fourteen education systems had higher average reading scores than the United States, and 13 education systems had scores that were not measurably different from the U.S. score. Massachusetts's average score (527) was higher than the U.S. average, North Carolina's (500) was not measurably different, and Puerto Rico's (410) was lower.

Figure 2.   Percentage of 15-year-old students performing on the Program for International Student Assessment (PISA) reading literacy scale, by selected proficiency levels and education system: 2015

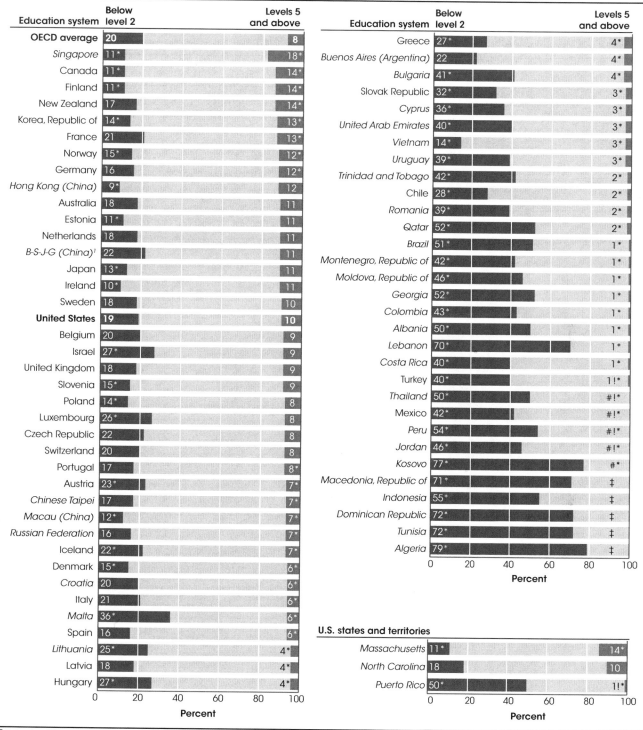

Below level 2
Levels 5 and above
Rounds to zero.
! Interpret data with caution. The coefficient of variation (CV) for this estimate is between 30 and 50 percent.
‡ Reporting standards not met. The coefficient of variation (CV) for this estimate is 50 percent or greater.
* p < .05. Significantly different from the U.S. percentage.
¹ B-S-J-G (China) refers to the four PISA participating China provinces: Beijing, Shanghai, Jiangsu, and Guangdong.
NOTE: Education systems are ordered by percentage of 15-year-olds in levels 5 and above. To reach a particular proficiency level, students must correctly answer a majority of items at that level. Students were classified into science proficiency levels according to their scores. Cut scores for each proficiency level can be found in table A-1 available at http://nces.ed.gov/surveys/pisa/PISA2015/index.asp. The OECD average is the average of the national percentages of the OECD member countries, with each country weighted equally. Italics indicate non-OECD countries and education systems. Results for Massachusetts and North Carolina are for public school students only. Although Argentina, Kazakhstan, and Malaysia participated in PISA 2015, technical problems with their samples prevent results from being discussed in this report.
SOURCE: Organization for Economic Cooperation and Development (OECD), Program for International Student Assessment (PISA), 2015. See Digest of Education Statistics 2016, table 602.50.

As with science literacy, PISA reports reading literacy by seven proficiency levels, with level 1b being the lowest and level 6 being the highest. At levels 5 and 6, students have mastered sophisticated reading skills required to interpret and evaluate deeply embedded or abstract text. The percentage of U.S. top performers (levels 5 and above) on the reading literacy scale (10 percent) was not measurably different from the OECD average (8 percent). Percentages of top performers ranged from near 0 percent in five education systems to 18 percent in Singapore. Eight education systems had higher percentages of top performers in reading literacy than the United States. Massachusetts had a higher percentage of top performers (14 percent) than the United States, North Carolina had a percentage (10 percent) that was not measurably different, and Puerto Rico had a lower percentage (1 percent).

The percentage of U.S. students who were low performers in reading literacy (19 percent) was not measurably different from the OECD average (20 percent). Percentages of low performers ranged from 9 percent in Hong Kong (China) to 79 percent in Algeria. Fourteen education systems had lower percentages of low performers in reading literacy than the United States. Massachusetts had a lower percentage (11 percent) than the United States, North Carolina had a percentage that was not measurably different (18 percent), and Puerto Rico had a higher percentage (50 percent).

Table 3.   Average scores of 15-year-old students on the Program for International Student Assessment (PISA) mathematics literacy scale, by education system: 2015

Education system	Average score		Education system	Average score	
OECD average	**490**	⬥	Israel	470	
Singapore	564	⬥	**United States**	**470**	
Hong Kong (China)	548	⬥	*Croatia*	464	
Macau (China)	544	⬥	*Buenos Aires (Argentina)*	456	
Chinese Taipei	542	⬥	Greece	454	▼
Japan	532	⬥	*Romania*	444	▼
B-S-J-G (China)[1]	531	⬥	*Bulgaria*	441	▼
Korea, Republic of	524	⬥	*Cyprus*	437	▼
Switzerland	521	⬥	*United Arab Emirates*	427	▼
Estonia	520	⬥	Chile	423	▼
Canada	516	⬥	Turkey	420	▼
Netherlands	512	⬥	*Moldova, Republic of*	420	▼
Denmark	511	⬥	*Uruguay*	418	▼
Finland	511	⬥	*Montenegro, Republic of*	418	▼
Slovenia	510	⬥	*Trinidad and Tobago*	417	▼
Belgium	507	⬥	*Thailand*	415	▼
Germany	506	⬥	*Albania*	413	▼
Poland	504	⬥	Mexico	408	▼
Ireland	504	⬥	*Georgia*	404	▼
Norway	502	⬥	*Qatar*	402	▼
Austria	497	⬥	*Costa Rica*	400	▼
New Zealand	495	⬥	*Lebanon*	396	▼
Vietnam	495	⬥	*Colombia*	390	▼
Russian Federation	494	⬥	Peru	387	▼
Sweden	494	⬥	*Indonesia*	386	▼
Australia	494	⬥	*Jordan*	380	▼
France	493	⬥	*Brazil*	377	▼
United Kingdom	492	⬥	*Macedonia, Republic of*	371	▼
Czech Republic	492	⬥	*Tunisia*	367	▼
Portugal	492	⬥	*Kosovo*	362	▼
Italy	490	⬥	*Algeria*	360	▼
Iceland	488	⬥	*Dominican Republic*	328	▼
Spain	486	⬥			
Luxembourg	486	⬥			
Latvia	482	⬥	**U.S. states and territories**		
Malta	479	⬥	*Massachusetts*	500	⬥
Lithuania	478	⬥	*North Carolina*	471	
Hungary	477		*Puerto Rico*	378	▼
Slovak Republic	475				

⬥ Average score is higher than U.S. average score.
▼ Average score is lower than U.S. average score.
[1] B-S-J-G (China) refers to the four PISA participating China provinces: Beijing, Shanghai, Jiangsu, and Guangdong.
NOTE: Education systems are ordered by 2015 average score. The OECD average is the average of the national averages of the OECD member countries, with each country weighted equally. Scores are reported on a scale from 0 to 1,000. All average scores reported as higher or lower than the U.S. average score are different at a .05 level of statistical significance. Italics indicate non-OECD countries and education systems. Results for Massachusetts and North Carolina are for public school students only. Although Argentina, Kazakhstan, and Malaysia participated in PISA 2015, technical problems with their samples prevent results from being discussed in this report.
SOURCE: Organization for Economic Cooperation and Development (OECD), Program for International Student Assessment (PISA), 2015. See *Digest of Education Statistics 2016*, table 602.60.

Average scores in mathematics literacy in 2015 ranged from 328 in the Dominican Republic to 564 in Singapore. The U.S. average mathematics score (470) was lower than the OECD average (490). Thirty-six education systems had higher average mathematics scores than the United States, and five had scores not measurably different from the U.S. average. Massachusetts's average score (500) was higher than the U.S. average, North Carolina's (471) was not measurably different, and Puerto Rico's (378) was lower.

Figure 3. Percentage of 15-year-old students performing on the Program for International Student Assessment (PISA) mathematics literacy scale, by selected proficiency levels and education system: 2015

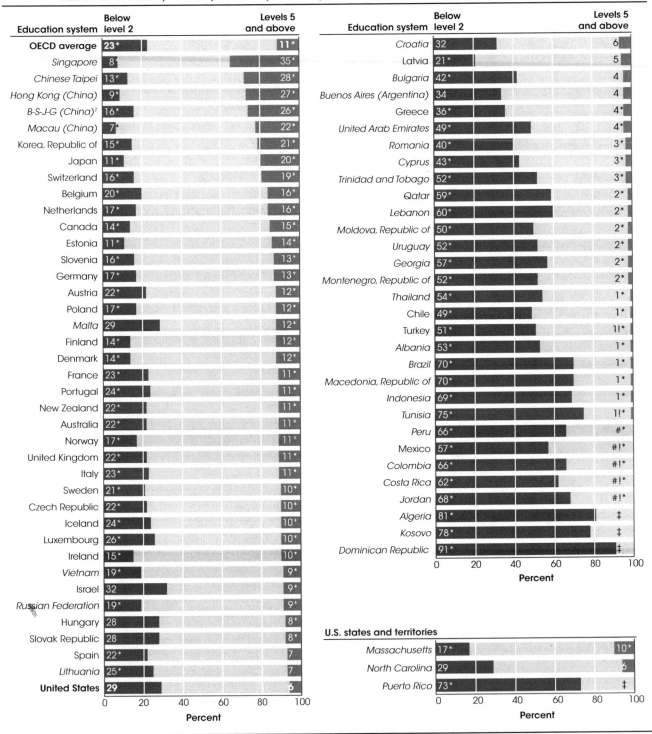

Education system	Below level 2	Levels 5 and above
OECD average	23*	11*
Singapore	8*	35*
Chinese Taipei	13*	28*
Hong Kong (China)	9*	27*
B-S-J-G (China)¹	16*	26*
Macau (China)	7*	22*
Korea, Republic of	15*	21*
Japan	11*	20*
Switzerland	16*	19*
Belgium	20*	16*
Netherlands	17*	16*
Canada	14*	15*
Estonia	11*	14*
Slovenia	16*	13*
Germany	17*	13*
Austria	22*	12*
Poland	17*	12*
Malta	29	12*
Finland	14*	12*
Denmark	14*	12*
France	23*	11*
Portugal	24*	11*
New Zealand	22*	11*
Australia	22*	11*
Norway	17*	11*
United Kingdom	22*	11*
Italy	23*	11*
Sweden	21*	10*
Czech Republic	22*	10*
Iceland	24*	10*
Luxembourg	26*	10*
Ireland	15*	10*
Vietnam	19*	9*
Israel	32	9*
Russian Federation	19*	9*
Hungary	28	8*
Slovak Republic	28	8*
Spain	22*	7
Lithuania	25*	7
United States	29	6

Education system	Below level 2	Levels 5 and above
Croatia	32	6
Latvia	21*	5
Bulgaria	42*	4
Buenos Aires (Argentina)	34	4
Greece	36*	4*
United Arab Emirates	49*	4*
Romania	40*	3*
Cyprus	43*	3*
Trinidad and Tobago	52*	3*
Qatar	59*	2*
Lebanon	60*	2*
Moldova, Republic of	50*	2*
Uruguay	52*	2*
Georgia	57*	2*
Montenegro, Republic of	52*	2*
Thailand	54*	1*
Chile	49*	1*
Turkey	51*	1!*
Albania	53*	1*
Brazil	70*	1*
Macedonia, Republic of	70*	1*
Indonesia	69*	1*
Tunisia	75*	1!*
Peru	66*	#*
Mexico	57*	#!*
Colombia	66*	#!*
Costa Rica	62*	#!*
Jordan	68*	#!*
Algeria	81*	‡
Kosovo	78*	‡
Dominican Republic	91*	‡

U.S. states and territories

Education system	Below level 2	Levels 5 and above
Massachusetts	17*	10*
North Carolina	29	6
Puerto Rico	73*	‡

■ Below level 2
■ Levels 5 and above
\# Rounds to zero.
! Interpret data with caution. The coefficient of variation (CV) for this estimate is between 30 and 50 percent.
‡ Reporting standards not met. The coefficient of variation (CV) for this estimate is 50 percent or greater.
* $p < .05$. Significantly different from the U.S. percentage.
¹ B-S-J-G (China) refers to the four PISA participating China provinces: Beijing, Shanghai, Jiangsu, and Guangdong.
NOTE: Education systems are ordered by percentage of 15-year-olds in levels 5 and above. To reach a particular proficiency level, students must correctly answer a majority of items at that level. Students were classified into mathematics proficiency levels according to their scores. Cut scores for each proficiency level can be found in table A-1 at https://nces.ed.gov/surveys/pisa/PISA2015/index.asp. The OECD average is the average of the national percentages of the OECD member countries, with each country weighted equally. Italics indicate non-OECD countries and education systems. Results for Massachusetts and North Carolina are for public school students only. Although Argentina, Kazakhstan, and Malaysia participated in PISA 2015, technical problems with their samples prevent results from being discussed in this report.
SOURCE: Organization for Economic Cooperation and Development (OECD), Program for International Student Assessment (PISA), 2015. See *Digest of Education Statistics 2016*, table 602.60.

PISA reports mathematics literacy in terms of six proficiency levels, with level 1 being the lowest and level 6 being the highest. Students scoring at proficiency levels 5 and above are considered to be top performers since they have demonstrated advanced mathematical thinking and reasoning skills required to solve problems of greater complexity. The percentage of top performers in the United States (6 percent) was lower than the OECD average (11 percent). Percentages of top performers ranged from near 0 percent in five education systems to 35 percent in Singapore. Thirty-six education systems and Massachusetts (10 percent) had higher percentages of top performers in mathematics literacy than the United States. North Carolina had a percentage of top performers (6 percent) not measurably different from the U.S. percentage.

The percentage of 15-year-olds in the United States who score below proficiency level 2 in mathematics literacy (29 percent) was higher than the OECD average (23 percent). Percentages of low performers ranged from 7 percent in Macau (China) to 91 percent in the Dominican Republic. Thirty-five education systems and Massachusetts (17 percent) had lower percentages of low performers in mathematics literacy than the United States. The percentage of low performers in North Carolina (29 percent) was not measurably different from the U.S. percentage, while the percentage in Puerto Rico (73 percent) was higher.

Endnotes:

[1] Although Argentina, Kazakhstan, and Malaysia participated in PISA 2015, technical problems with their samples prevent results from being discussed; therefore, results are presented for 70 education systems.

[2] For the purposes of this indicator, "education systems" refers to all entities participating in PISA, including countries as well as subnational entities (e.g., cities or provinces). Massachusetts, North Carolina, and Puerto Rico are treated separately in this indicator and are not included in counts of education systems.

Reference tables: *Digest of Education Statistics 2016*, tables 602.50, 602.60, and 602.70

Related indicators and resources: International Comparisons: Reading Literacy at Grade 4; International Comparisons: U.S. 4th-, 8th-, and 12th-Graders' Mathematics and Science Achievement; Mathematics Performance; Reading Performance; Science Performance

Glossary: Organization for Economic Cooperation and Development (OECD)

Education Expenditures by Country

In 2014, the United States spent $12,300 per full-time-equivalent (FTE) student on elementary and secondary education, which was 29 percent higher than the OECD average of $9,600. At the postsecondary level, the United States spent $29,700 per FTE student, which was 81 percent higher than the OECD average of $16,400.

This indicator uses material from the Organization for Economic Cooperation and Development (OECD) to compare countries' expenditures on education using two measures: *expenditures by public and private education institutions per full-time-equivalent (FTE) student* and *total government and private expenditures on education institutions as a percentage of gross domestic product (GDP).* The OECD is an organization of 35 countries that collects and publishes an array of data on its member countries. Education expenditures are from public revenue sources (governments) and private revenue sources and include current and capital expenditures. Private sources include payments from households for school-based expenses such as tuition, transportation fees, book rentals, and food services, as well as public funding via subsidies to households, private fees for education services, and other private spending that goes through the educational institution. The *total government and private expenditures on education institutions as a percentage of GDP* measure allows for a comparison of countries' expenditures relative to their ability to finance education. Purchasing power parity (PPP) indexes are used to convert other currencies into U.S. dollars. Monetary amounts are in constant 2016 dollars based on national Consumer Price Indexes.[1]

Expenditures per FTE student at the elementary/ secondary level varied widely across OECD countries[2] in 2014, ranging from $3,200 in Mexico to $15,000 in Norway. The United States spent $12,300 per FTE student at the elementary/secondary level, which was 29 percent higher than the average of $9,600 for OECD member countries reporting data.

Expenditures per FTE student at the postsecondary level also varied across OECD countries in 2014, ranging from $8,500 in Chile to $29,700 in the United States. Expenditures per FTE student at the postsecondary level in the United States were 81 percent higher than the OECD average of $16,400.

Figure 1. Expenditures and percentage change in expenditures per full-time-equivalent (FTE) student for elementary and secondary education from 2005 to 2014, by Organization for Economic Cooperation and Development (OECD) country

[In constant 2016 U.S. dollars]

OECD country	2005	2014	Percent change, 2005 to 2014
Norway	$12,600	$15,000	19
Switzerland[1,2]	10,900	14,900	36
Austria	11,500	13,700	19
United States[3]	**12,000**	**12,300**	**3**
Belgium	9,000	12,200	36
United Kingdom	8,900	12,100	36
Denmark	10,700	11,400	6
Sweden	8,900	11,100	25
Iceland	15,800	11,000	-30
Germany	8,200	10,900	33
Netherlands	8,300	10,800	30
Canada[3,4]	9,300	10,700	15
Republic of Korea	7,300	10,200	41
Japan	7,600	10,000	32
France	8,500	10,000	17
Finland	7,900	9,800	24
Australia	9,400	9,700	3
OECD average[5]	**8,300**	**9,600**	**15**
Ireland	7,200	9,200	27
New Zealand	7,100	9,100	29
Slovenia	8,600	9,000	4
Italy[1,3]	8,700	8,800	#
Portugal[1,3]	6,600	7,800	18
Spain	7,700	7,700	1
Czech Republic	5,100	7,000	37
Estonia	5,300	7,000	32
Israel	6,100	6,700	9
Poland[1]	3,900	6,600	68
Slovak Republic[2]	3,400	6,300	86
Hungary[1]	5,900	5,600	-4
Chile	3,100	4,500	47
Mexico	3,100	3,200	4

-50 -40 -30 -20 -10 0 10 20 30 40 50 60 70 80 90 100 110 120 130

Percentage change in expenditures per FTE student

Rounds to zero.

[1] Education expenditures include public institutions only in one or both data years (2005 and 2014).

[2] Occupation-specific education corresponding to that offered at the vocational associate's degree level in the United States is included in elementary and secondary education instead of in higher education in one or both data years (2005 and 2014).

[3] Education expenditures exclude postsecondary non-higher-education in one or both data years (2005 and 2014).

[4] Elementary and secondary education expenditures include preprimary education (for children ages 3 and older) in one or both data years (2005 and 2014).

[5] Refers to the mean of the data values for all reporting Organization for Economic Cooperation and Development (OECD) countries, to which each country reporting data contributes equally. The average includes all current OECD countries for which a given year's data are available, even if they were not members of OECD in that year.

NOTE: Data for Luxembourg, a country with one of the highest annual expenditures per FTE student, are excluded from the figure because of anomalies in that country's gross domestic product (GDP) per capita data (large revenues from international finance institutions in Luxembourg distort the wealth of the country's population). Data for Greece, Latvia, and Turkey are excluded because data on expenditures were not available for either 2005 or 2014. Expenditures for International Standard Classification of Education (ISCED) level 4 (postsecondary non-higher-education) are included in elementary and secondary education unless otherwise noted. Data adjusted to U.S. dollars using the purchasing power parity (PPP) index. Constant dollars based on national Consumer Price Indexes available on the OECD database cited in the source note below. Although rounded numbers are displayed, the figures are based on unrounded estimates.

SOURCE: Organization for Economic Cooperation and Development (OECD), *Education at a Glance 2017*; and Online Education Database, retrieved December 1, 2017, from http://stats.oecd.org/Index.aspx. See *Digest of Education Statistics 2017*, table 605.10.

Across OECD countries, expenditures per FTE student at the elementary/secondary level were generally higher in 2014 than in 2005. However, countries with the highest expenditures per FTE student at the elementary/secondary level in 2014 generally also had high expenditures in 2005, and countries with the lowest expenditures per FTE student at this level in 2014 generally also had among the lowest expenditures in 2005. In 2014, OECD average expenditures per FTE student at the elementary/secondary level were $9,600, compared with $8,300 in 2005. Of the 31 OECD countries with expenditures per FTE student data available in both years, the average expenditures per FTE student at the elementary/secondary level were higher in 2014 than in 2005 in 29 countries, including the United States. In the United States, annual expenditures per FTE were 3 percent higher in 2014, when they were $12,300, than in 2005, when they were $12,000. Of countries with expenditures per FTE student that were higher in 2014 than in 2005, the percentage increases ranged from a low of less than 1 percent in Italy to a high of 86 percent in the Slovak Republic. Only two countries (Iceland and Hungary) had expenditures per FTE student at the elementary/secondary level that were lower in 2014 than in 2005.

Figure 2. Expenditures and percentage change in expenditures per full-time-equivalent (FTE) student for postsecondary education from 2005 to 2014, by Organization for Economic Cooperation and Development (OECD) country

[In constant 2016 U.S. dollars]

OECD country	2005	2014	Percent change, 2005 to 2014
United States	$29,900	$29,700	-1
Switzerland[1,2]	22,200	27,400	23
United Kingdom	17,400	24,700	42
Sweden	18,000	24,300	35
Norway	19,600	22,200	13
Canada[1,3]	27,400	21,900	-20
Netherlands	16,400	19,300	18
Australia	19,200	18,500	-3
Japan[4]	12,700	18,100	43
Finland	14,700	17,900	22
Germany	14,500	17,300	20
Austria	18,100	17,200	-5
Belgium	14,700	17,000	16
Denmark[1,4]	17,800	16,700	-7
France	12,500	16,500	31
OECD average[5]	13,900	16,400	18
New Zealand	12,800	15,200	19
Ireland	11,800	14,100	20
Israel	13,200	12,800	-3
Spain	12,100	12,400	3
Estonia	5,500	12,300	126
Slovenia	10,500	12,000	15
Portugal[1,4]	10,300	11,900	16
Iceland[4]	16,900	11,800	-30
Italy[1]	9,500	11,500	21
Slovak Republic[1,2]	7,200	11,200	55
Czech Republic	8,300	10,600	28
Republic of Korea	9,800	9,700	-1
Poland[1]	6,900	9,600	38
Mexico	9,800	9,500	-3
Hungary[1]	9,100	8,700	-4
Chile	10,100	8,500	-16

-50 -40 -30 -20 -10 0 10 20 30 40 50 60 70 80 90 100 110 120 130

Percentage change in expenditures per FTE student

[1] Education expenditures include public institutions only in one or both data years (2005 and 2014).
[2] Occupation-specific education corresponding to that offered at the vocational associate's degree level in the United States is included in elementary and secondary education instead of in higher education in one or both data years (2005 and 2014).
[3] Data for 2005 exclude occupation-specific education corresponding to that offered at the vocational associate's degree level in the United States.
[4] Postsecondary non-higher-education included in both secondary and higher education in one or both data years (2005 and 2014).
[5] Refers to the mean of the data values for all reporting Organization for Economic Cooperation and Development (OECD) countries, to which each country reporting data contributes equally. The average includes all current OECD countries for which a given year's data are available, even if they were not members of OECD in that year.
NOTE: Data for Luxembourg, a country with one of the highest annual expenditures per FTE student, are excluded from the figure because of anomalies in that country's gross domestic product (GDP) per capita data (large revenues from international finance institutions in Luxembourg distort the wealth of the country's population). Data for Greece, Latvia, and Turkey are excluded because data on expenditures were not available for either 2005 or 2014. Data adjusted to U.S. dollars using the purchasing power parity (PPP) index. Constant dollars based on national Consumer Price Indexes available on the OECD database cited in the source note below. Although rounded numbers are displayed, the figures are based on unrounded estimates.
SOURCE: Organization for Economic Cooperation and Development (OECD), *Education at a Glance 2017*; and Online Education Database, retrieved December 1, 2017, from http://stats.oecd.org/Index.aspx. See *Digest of Education Statistics 2017*, table 605.10.

Compared with the elementary/secondary level, there were more OECD countries where postsecondary expenditures per FTE student were lower in 2014 than in 2005. In 2014, OECD average expenditures per FTE student at the postsecondary level were $16,400, compared with $13,900 in 2005. Of the 31 OECD countries with expenditures per FTE student data available in both years, expenditures per FTE student at the postsecondary level were higher in 2014 than in 2005 in 20 countries. Of those 20 countries, the percentage increase in expenditures per

FTE student ranged from a low of 3 percent in Spain to a high of 126 percent in Estonia. Conversely, there were 11 countries, including the United States, where average expenditures per FTE student at the postsecondary level were lower in 2014 than in 2005. In the United States, expenditures per FTE student in 2014 were $29,700, less than 1 percent lower than in 2005 (when they were $29,900). However, the United States had the highest expenditures per FTE student of any OECD country in both 2005 and 2014 at the postsecondary level.

Figure 3. Expenditures per full-time-equivalent (FTE) student for elementary and secondary education in selected Organization for Economic Cooperation and Development (OECD) countries, by gross domestic product (GDP) per capita: 2014

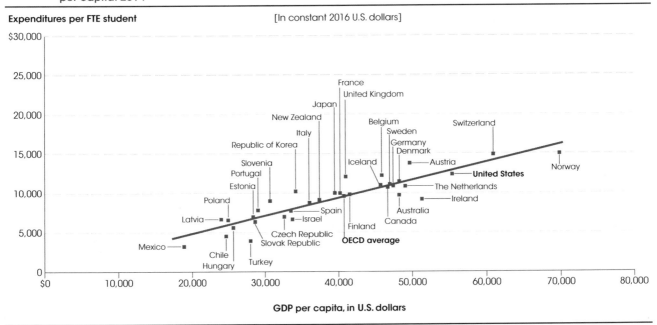

Linear relationship between spending and country wealth for 33 OECD countries reporting data (elementary/secondary): r² = .82; slope = 0.23; intercept = 322.
NOTE: Data for Luxembourg are excluded from the figure because of anomalies in that country's gross domestic product (GDP) per capita data (large revenues from international finance institutions in Luxembourg distort the wealth of the country's population). Data for Greece are excluded because data on expenditures were not available in 2014. Expenditures for International Standard Classification of Education (ISCED) level 4 (postsecondary non-higher-education) are included in elementary and secondary education unless otherwise noted. Data on expenditures for Canada and Italy do not include postsecondary non-higher-education. Data on expenditures for Canada include preprimary education. Data on expenditures for Switzerland include public institutions only and include occupation-specific education corresponding to that offered at the vocational associate's degree level in the United States. Data adjusted to U.S. dollars using the purchasing power parity (PPP) index. Constant dollars based on national Consumer Price Indexes available on the OECD database cited in the source note below.
SOURCE: Organization for Economic Cooperation and Development (OECD), Education at a Glance 2017; and Online Education Database, retrieved December 1, 2017, from http://stats.oecd.org/Index.aspx. See Digest of Education Statistics 2017, table 605.10.

A country's wealth (defined as GDP per capita) is positively associated with its education expenditures per FTE student at the elementary/secondary and postsecondary levels. In 2014, of the 15 countries with a GDP per capita greater than the OECD average, 14 countries also had elementary/secondary education expenditures per FTE student that were higher than the OECD average. These 14 countries were Norway, Switzerland, the United States, Austria, the Netherlands, Denmark, Australia, Germany, Sweden, Canada, Belgium, Iceland, Finland, and the United Kingdom. The exception was Ireland, which had lower elementary/secondary expenditures per FTE student than the OECD average ($9,200 vs. $9,600).

Of the 18 countries with a GDP per capita lower than the OECD average, 15 countries also had elementary/secondary education expenditures per FTE student that were lower than the OECD average. These 15 countries were New Zealand, Italy, Israel, Spain, the Czech Republic, Slovenia, Portugal, the Slovak Republic, Estonia, Turkey, Hungary, Poland, Chile, Latvia, and Mexico. The exceptions were France, Japan, and the Republic of Korea, which had expenditures per FTE student at the elementary/secondary level that were higher than the OECD average.

Figure 4. Expenditures per full-time-equivalent (FTE) student for postsecondary education in selected Organization for Economic Cooperation and Development (OECD) countries, by gross domestic product (GDP) per capita: 2014

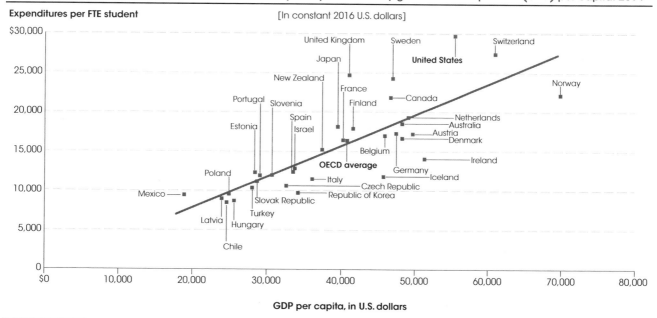

Expenditures per FTE student   [In constant 2016 U.S. dollars]

GDP per capita, in U.S. dollars

Linear relationship between spending and country wealth for 33 OECD countries reporting data (postsecondary): r^2 = .65; slope = 0.39; intercept = 28. NOTE: Data for Luxembourg are excluded from the figure because of anomalies in that country's gross domestic product (GDP) per capita data (large revenues from international finance institutions in Luxembourg distort the wealth of the country's population). Data for Greece are excluded because data on expenditures were not available in 2014. Expenditures for International Standard Classification of Education (ISCED) level 4 (postsecondary non-higher-education) are excluded from postsecondary education unless otherwise noted. Data on expenditures for Japan and Portugal include postsecondary non-higher-education. Data on expenditures for Canada, Denmark, the Slovak Republic, and Switzerland include public institutions only. Data on expenditures for Switzerland exclude occupation-specific education corresponding to that offered at the vocational associate's degree level in the United States. Data adjusted to U.S. dollars using the purchasing power parity (PPP) index. Constant dollars based on national Consumer Price Indexes available on the OECD database cited in the source note below.
SOURCE: Organization for Economic Cooperation and Development (OECD), *Education at a Glance 2017*; and Online Education Database, retrieved December 1, 2017, from http://stats.oecd.org/Index.aspx. See *Digest of Education Statistics 2017*, table 605.10.

At the postsecondary level, 13 of the 15 countries with a GDP per capita that was higher than the OECD average also had education expenditures per FTE student that were higher than the OECD average. The two exceptions were Ireland and Iceland, both of which had lower expenditures per FTE student at the postsecondary level ($14,100 and $11,800, respectively) than the OECD average ($16,400). Of the 18 countries with a lower GDP per capita than the OECD average, 16 countries had education expenditures per FTE student that were lower than the OECD average at the postsecondary level. The two exceptions were Japan and France; both countries reported higher postsecondary expenditures per FTE student ($18,100 and $16,500, respectively) than the OECD average.

Figure 5. Government and private expenditures on education institutions as a percentage of gross domestic product (GDP) for Organization for Economic Cooperation and Development (OECD) countries with the three highest and lowest percentages of expenditures for all institutions, by level of education: 2014

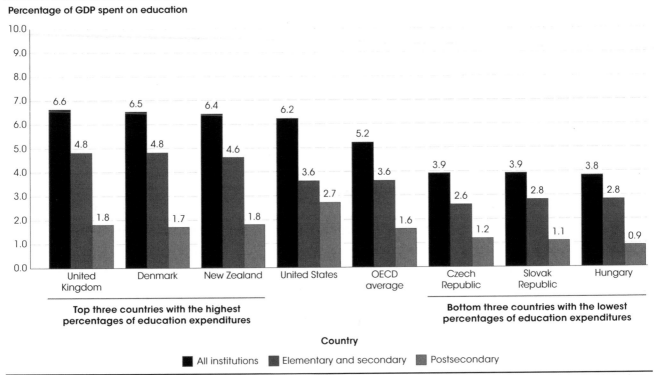

Percentage of GDP spent on education

Top three countries with the highest percentages of education expenditures

Bottom three countries with the lowest percentages of education expenditures

Country

■ All institutions   ■ Elementary and secondary   ■ Postsecondary

NOTE: Expenditures for International Standard Classification of Education (ISCED) level 4 (postsecondary non-higher-education) are included in elementary and secondary education. Although rounded numbers are displayed, the figures are based on unrounded estimates.
SOURCE: Organization for Economic Cooperation and Development (OECD), Online Education Database, retrieved December 1, 2017, from http://stats. oecd.org/Index.aspx. See *Digest of Education Statistics 2017*, table 605.20.

Among the 32 OECD countries reporting data in 2014, there were 18 countries that spent a higher percentage of GDP on total government and private expenditures on education institutions than the OECD average of 5.2 percent. The United Kingdom reported the highest total education expenditures as a percentage of GDP (6.6 percent), followed by Denmark (6.5 percent), New Zealand (6.4 percent), the Republic of Korea (6.3 percent), and the United States (6.2 percent). Conversely, 14 countries spent a percentage of GDP on total education expenditures that was lower than the OECD average. Hungary reported the lowest total education expenditures as a percentage of GDP (3.8 percent), followed by the Slovak Republic (3.9 percent) and the Czech Republic (3.9 percent).

In terms of countries' total government and private expenditures on education institutions by education level in 2014, the percentage of GDP that the United States spent on elementary and secondary education

(3.6 percent) was slightly lower than the OECD average. Sixteen other countries also spent a percentage of GDP on elementary and secondary education that was lower than the OECD average. In contrast, 15 countries spent more on elementary and secondary education as a percentage of GDP than the OECD average, and 9 of the 15 countries spent 4.0 percent or more of GDP. Elementary and secondary education as a percentage of GDP was highest in the United Kingdom (4.8 percent).

At the postsecondary level, total government and private expenditures on education institutions as a percentage of GDP by the United States (2.7 percent) were higher than the OECD average (1.6 percent) and were higher than those of all other OECD countries reporting data. In addition to the United States, only three other countries spent 2.0 percent or more of GDP on postsecondary education: Canada (2.6 percent), Chile (2.3 percent), and the Republic of Korea (2.3 percent).

Endnotes:

[1] National Consumer Price Indexes are available at the OECD Online Education Database (http://stats.oecd.org/index.aspx).

[2] Greece and Luxembourg are excluded from all analyses. Expenditure data at the elementary/secondary and postsecondary levels were not available in 2014 for Greece. For Luxembourg, data on education expenditures were available in 2014 but are excluded because of anomalies in the country's GDP per capita data (large revenues from international finance institutions in Luxembourg distort the wealth of the country's population).

Reference tables: *Digest of Education Statistics 2017*, tables 605.10 and 605.20

Related indicators and resources: International Educational Attainment; Public School Expenditures

Glossary: Constant dollars, Consumer Price Index (CPI), Elementary school, Expenditures per pupil, Full-time-equivalent (FTE) enrollment, Gross domestic product (GDP), International Standard Classification of Education (ISCED), Organization for Economic Cooperation and Development (OECD), Postsecondary education, Purchasing Power Parity (PPP) indexes, Secondary school

International Educational Attainment

Across OECD countries, the average percentage of the adult population with any postsecondary degree was 36 percent in 2016, an increase of 14 percentage points from 2000. During the same period, the percentage of U.S. adults with any postsecondary degree increased 9 percentage points to 46 percent.

The Organization for Economic Cooperation and Development (OECD) is an organization of 35 countries whose purpose is to promote trade and economic growth. The OECD also collects and publishes an array of data on its member countries. This indicator uses OECD data to compare educational attainment across countries using two measures: *high school completion* and *attainment of any postsecondary degree*.[1] Among the 32 countries[2] for which the OECD reported 2016 data, the percentages of the adult populations (ages 25 to 64) who had completed high school ranged from under 40 percent in Mexico and Turkey to 90 percent or more in the United States,

Canada, Poland, the Slovak Republic, and the Czech Republic.[3] Nineteen countries reported that more than 80 percent of their adult populations had completed high school in 2016. Additionally, of the 33 countries[4] for which the OECD reported 2016 data on postsecondary attainment rates, the percentages of adults earning any postsecondary degree[5] ranged from under 20 percent in Mexico, Italy, and Turkey to more than 50 percent in Japan and Canada. Twenty-three countries reported that more than 30 percent of their adult populations had earned any postsecondary degree in 2016.

Figure 1.   Percentage of the population 25 to 64 years old who had completed high school in Organization for Economic Cooperation and Development (OECD) countries: 2000 and 2016

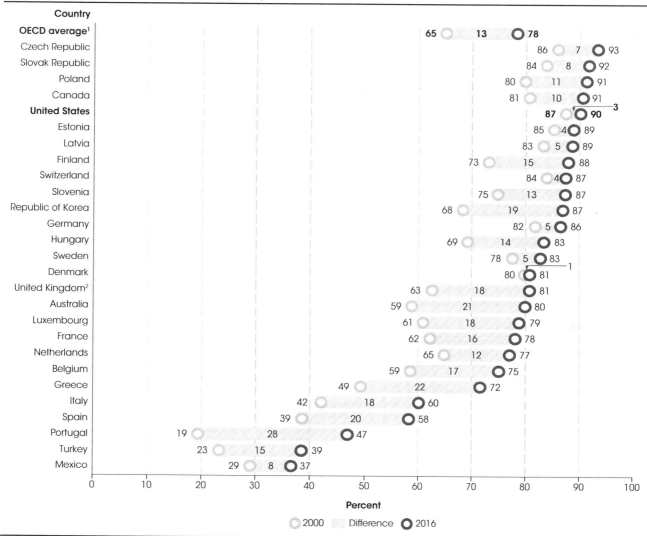

In each of the 27 countries[6] for which the OECD reported data on high school completion rates in both 2000 and 2016, the percentage of 25- to 64-year-olds who had completed a high school education was higher in 2016 than in 2000. The OECD average percentage[7] of the adult population with a high school education rose from 65 percent in 2000 to 78 percent in 2016. Meanwhile,

the percentage of adults in the United States who had completed high school rose from 87 to 90 percent during this period. For 25- to 34-year-olds, the OECD average percentage with a high school education rose from 75 to 84 percent during this period, while the corresponding percentage for U.S. 25- to 34-year-olds increased from 88 to 91 percent.

Figure 2. Percentage of the population 25 to 64 years old who had attained any postsecondary degree in Organization for Economic Cooperation and Development (OECD) countries: 2000 and 2016

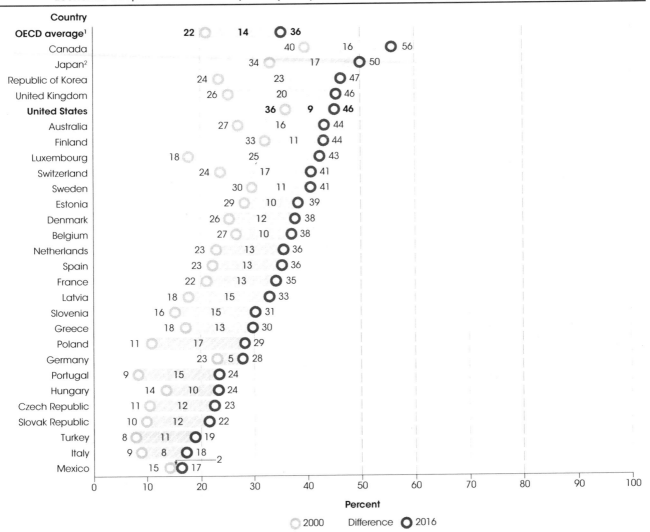

○ 2000   Difference   ◉ 2016

¹ Refers to the mean of the data values for all reporting OECD countries, to which each country reporting data contributes equally. The average includes all current OECD countries for which a given year's data are available, even if they were not members of the OECD in that year. Countries not shown in this figure may be included in the OECD average.
² Data for both years include some upper secondary and postsecondary nontertiary awards (i.e., awards that are below the associate's degree level).
NOTE: Of the 35 OECD countries, 28 are included in this figure. Austria, Chile, Iceland, Ireland, Israel, New Zealand, and Norway are excluded from this figure because data are not available for these countries for either 2000 or 2016. Data in this figure include all tertiary (postsecondary) degrees, which correspond to all degrees at the associate's level and above in the United States. The International Standard Classification of Education (ISCED) was revised in 2011. The previous version, ISCED 1997, was used to calculate all data for 2000. ISCED 2011 was used to calculate all data for 2016 and may not be directly comparable to ISCED 1997. Under ISCED 2011, tertiary degrees are classified at the following levels: level 5 (corresponding to an associate's degree in the United States), level 6 (a bachelor's or equivalent degree), level 7 (a master's or equivalent degree), and level 8 (a doctor's or equivalent degree). Some data have been revised from previously published figures. Although rounded numbers are displayed, the figures are based on unrounded estimates.
SOURCE: Organization for Economic Cooperation and Development (OECD), Online Education Database, retrieved October 20, 2017, from http://stats.oecd.org/Index.aspx. See Digest of Education Statistics 2017, table 603.20.

Similarly, in each of the 28 countries[8] for which the OECD reported data on postsecondary attainment rates in both 2000 and 2016, the percentage of 25- to 64-year-olds who had earned any postsecondary degree was higher in 2016 than in 2000. During this period, the OECD average percentage of the adult population with any postsecondary degree increased by 14 percentage points to 36 percent in 2016, while the corresponding percentage for U.S. adults increased by 9 percentage points to 46 percent.

For 25- to 34-year-olds, the OECD average percentage with any postsecondary degree rose from 26 percent

in 2000 to 43 percent in 2016. The corresponding percentage for 25- to 34-year-olds in the United States rose from 38 to 48 percent. As a result of the relatively larger increases in postsecondary degree attainment among the 25- to 34-year-old populations in most OECD countries, the postsecondary attainment gap between the United States and the OECD average decreased between 2000 and 2016. In 2000, the rate of attainment of any postsecondary degree among 25- to 34-year-olds in the United States was 12 percentage points higher than the OECD average; by 2016, this gap had decreased to 4 percentage points.

Figure 3. Percentage of the population who had completed high school in Organization for Economic Cooperation and Development (OECD) countries, by selected age groups: 2016

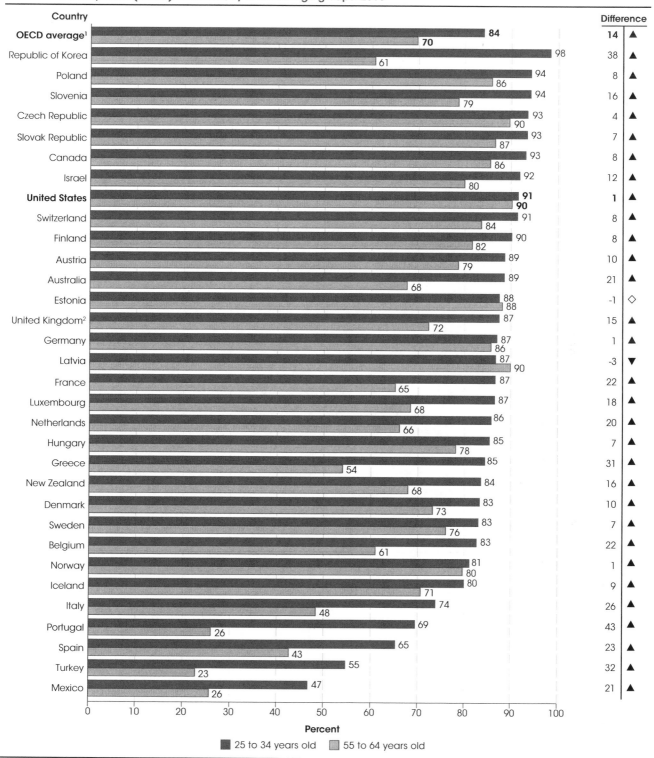

▲ The percentage of 25- to 34-year-olds who had completed high school is higher than the percentage of 55- to 64-year-olds who had completed high school.

▼ The percentage of 25- to 34-year-olds who had completed high school is lower than the percentage of 55- to 64-year-olds who had completed high school.

◇ The percentages of 25- to 34-year-olds and 55- to 64-year-olds who had completed high school are not measurably different.

[1] Refers to the mean of the data values for all reporting OECD countries, to which each country reporting data contributes equally. The average includes all current OECD countries for which a given year's data are available, even if they were not members of the OECD in that year.

[2] Data include some persons who have completed a sufficient number of certain types of programs, any one of which individually would be classified as a program that only partially completes the high school (or upper secondary) level of education.

NOTE: Of the 35 OECD countries, 32 are included in this figure. Chile, Ireland, and Japan are excluded because 2016 data on high school completion rates are not available for these countries. Except where otherwise noted, data in this table refer to degrees classified under the International Standard Classification of Education (ISCED) 2011 as completing level 3 (upper secondary education). Some data have been revised from previously published figures. Although rounded numbers are displayed, the figures are based on unrounded estimates.

SOURCE: Organization for Economic Cooperation and Development (OECD), Online Education Database, retrieved September 28, 2017, from http://stats.oecd.org/Index.aspx. See *Digest of Education Statistics 2017*, table 603.10.

In nearly all of the 32 countries for which the OECD reported 2016 data on high school completion rates, higher percentages of 25- to 34-year-olds than of 55- to 64-year-olds had completed high school. Across OECD countries, the average high school completion percentage was higher for 25- to 34-year-olds (84 percent) than for 55- to 64-year-olds (70 percent). The exceptions were Latvia, where the high school completion rate for 55- to 64-year-olds was 3 percentage points higher than the high school completion rate for 25- to 34-year-olds, and

Estonia, where the high school completion percentages for these two age groups were not measurably different from each other (both 88 percent). In 26 countries, including the United States, more than 80 percent of 25- to 34-year-olds had completed high school in 2016. In comparison, the percentage of 55- to 64-year-olds who had completed high school was more than 80 percent in 10 countries (Finland, Switzerland, Canada, Germany, Poland, the Slovak Republic, Estonia, the Czech Republic, Latvia, and the United States).

Figure 4.   Percentage of the population who had attained any postsecondary degree in Organization for Economic Cooperation and Development (OECD) countries, by selected age groups: 2016

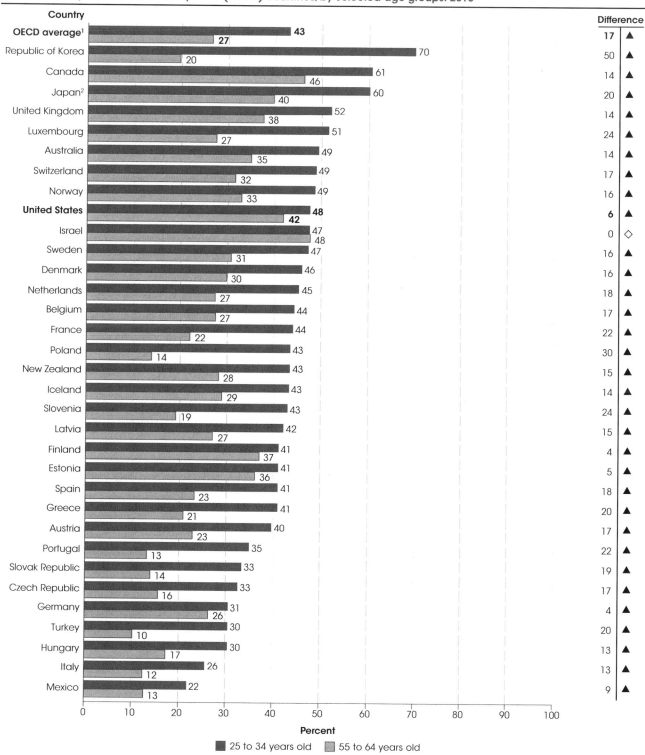

▲ The percentage of 25- to 34-year-olds with any postsecondary degree is higher than the percentage of 55- to 64-year-olds with any postsecondary degree.
◇ The percentages of 25- to 34-year-olds and 55- to 64-year-olds who had attained any postsecondary degree are not measurably different.
[1] Refers to the mean of the data values for all reporting OECD countries, to which each country reporting data contributes equally. The average includes all current OECD countries for which a given year's data are available, even if they were not members of the OECD in that year.
[2] Data include some upper secondary and postsecondary nontertiary awards (i.e., awards that are below the associate's degree level).
NOTE: Of the 35 OECD countries, 33 are included in this figure. Chile and Ireland are excluded from the figure because data are not available for these countries for 2016. All data in this figure were calculated using the International Standard Classification of Education (ISCED) 2011 classification of tertiary (postsecondary) degrees. Under ISCED 2011, tertiary degrees are classified at the following levels: level 5 (corresponding to an associate's degree in the United States), level 6 (a bachelor's or equivalent degree), level 7 (a master's or equivalent degree), and level 8 (a doctor's or equivalent degree). Some data have been revised from previously published figures. Although rounded numbers are displayed, the figures are based on unrounded estimates.
SOURCE: Organization for Economic Cooperation and Development (OECD), Online Education Database, retrieved October 20, 2017, from http://stats.oecd.org/Index.aspx. See *Digest of Education Statistics 2017*, table 603.20.

Similarly, postsecondary attainment rates were higher among 25- to 34-year-olds than among 55- to 64-year-olds in nearly all of the 33 countries for which the OECD reported 2016 data. The exception was Israel, where the postsecondary degree attainment rates for 25- to 34-year-olds and 55- to 64-year-olds were not measurably different. Across OECD countries, on average, 43 percent of 25- to 34-year-olds had earned any postsecondary degree in 2016 compared with 27 percent of 55- to 64-year-olds. In the United States, 48 percent of 25- to 34-year-olds and 42 percent of 55- to 64-year-olds had earned any postsecondary degree. Canada (46 percent) and Israel (48 percent) were the only other countries where more than 40 percent of 55- to 64-year-olds had earned any postsecondary degree. In comparison, there were 23 countries in which more than 40 percent of 25- to 34-year-olds had earned any postsecondary degree.

Figure 5. Percentage of the population 25 to 34 years old who had attained a postsecondary degree in Organization for Economic Cooperation and Development (OECD) countries, by highest degree attained: 2016

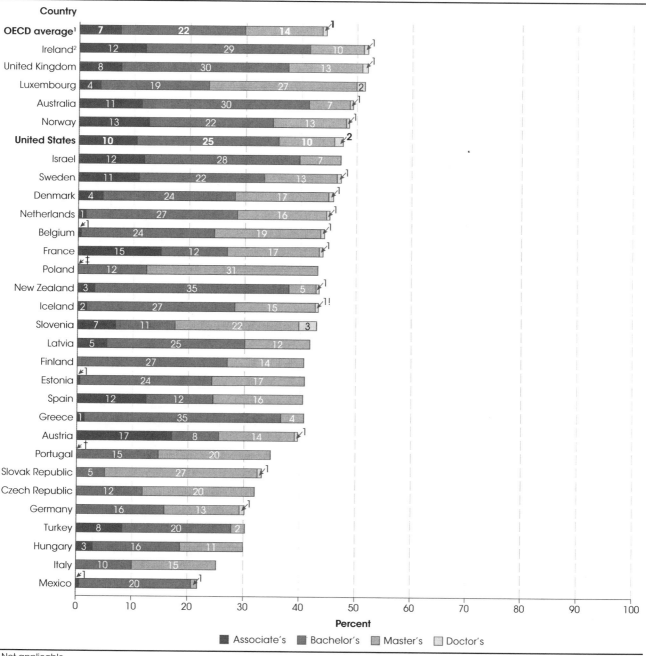

† Not applicable.
! Interpret data with caution. The coefficient of variation (CV) for this estimate is between 30 and 50 percent.
‡ Reporting standards not met. Either there are too few cases for a reliable estimate or the coefficient of variation (CV) is 50 percent or greater.
[1] Refers to the mean of the data values for all reporting OECD countries, to which each country reporting data contributes equally. The average includes all current OECD countries for which a given year's data are available, even if they were not members of the OECD in that year. Countries not shown in this figure may be included in the OECD average.
[2] Data are from 2015.
NOTE: Of the 35 OECD countries, 30 are included in this figure. Data for Canada, Chile, Japan, the Republic of Korea, and Switzerland are excluded from the figure because separate data are not available for all attainment levels. All data in this figure were calculated using the International Standard Classification of Education (ISCED) 2011 classification of tertiary (postsecondary) degrees. Under ISCED 2011, tertiary degrees are classified at the following levels: level 5 (corresponding to an associate's degree in the United States), level 6 (bachelor's or equivalent degree), level 7 (master's or equivalent degree), and level 8 (doctor's or equivalent degree). Categories not shown round to zero unless otherwise noted. Although rounded numbers are displayed, the figures are based on unrounded estimates.
SOURCE: Organization for Economic Cooperation and Development (OECD), Online Education Database, retrieved October 20, 2017, from http://stats.oecd.org/Index.aspx. See *Digest of Education Statistics 2017*, table 603.30.

The percentage of 25- to 34-year-olds who had attained specific postsecondary degrees (e.g., associate's degrees, bachelor's degrees, master's degrees, and doctor's degrees) varied across OECD countries in 2016. Among the 30 countries[9] for which the OECD reported 2016 data for all attainment levels, the percentage of 25- to 34-year-olds whose highest degree attained was an associate's degree ranged from less than 1 percent in

Italy, Finland, the Czech Republic, the Slovak Republic, Germany, Belgium, Estonia, and Mexico to 17 percent in Austria. The percentage of 25- to 34-year-olds whose highest degree attained was an associate's degree in the United States (10 percent) was higher than the OECD average (7 percent). Meanwhile, the percentage of 25- to 34-year-olds whose highest degree attained was a bachelor's degree ranged from 5 percent in the Slovak Republic to 35 percent in New Zealand and Greece, while the percentage whose highest degree attained was a master's degree ranged from about 1 percent in Mexico to 31 percent in Poland. In the United States, the percentage of 25- to 34-year-olds whose highest degree attained was a bachelor's degree (25 percent) was higher than the OECD average (22 percent). In contrast, the percentage of U.S. 25- to 34-year-olds whose highest degree attained was a master's degree (10 percent) was lower than the OECD average (14 percent). The percentage of 25- to 34-year-olds attaining doctor's degrees did not vary as widely across OECD countries; with the exception of the United States and Luxembourg (both about 2 percent) and Slovenia (3 percent), all countries reported that 1 percent or less of 25- to 34-year-olds had attained this level of education.

Endnotes:

[1] Attainment data in this indicator refer to comparable levels of degrees, as classified by the International Standard Classification of Education (ISCED). ISCED was revised in 2011. The previous version, ISCED 1997, was used to calculate data for all years prior to 2014. ISCED 2011 was used to calculate data for 2014 and later years and may not be directly comparable to ISCED 1997.

[2] Chile, Ireland, and Japan are excluded because 2016 data on high school completion rates are not available for these countries.

[3] Data in this section refer to degrees classified as ISCED 2011 level 3, which generally corresponds to high school completion in the United States, with some exceptions.

[4] Chile and Ireland are excluded because 2016 data on postsecondary attainment rates are not available for these countries.

[5] Postsecondary degrees correspond to all degrees at the associate's degree or higher level in the United States. Under ISCED 2011, postsecondary degrees are classified at the following levels: level 5 (corresponding to an associate's degree in the United States), level 6 (a bachelor's or equivalent degree), level 7 (a master's or equivalent degree), and level 8 (a doctor's or equivalent degree).

[6] Austria, Chile, Iceland, Ireland, Israel, Japan, New Zealand, and Norway are excluded because data are not available for these countries for either 2000 or 2016.

[7] Refers to the mean of the data values for all reporting Organization for Economic Cooperation and Development (OECD) countries, to which each country reporting data contributes equally. The average includes all current OECD countries for which a given year's data are available, even if they were not members of the OECD in that year. Countries excluded from analyses in this indicator may be included in the OECD average.

[8] Austria, Chile, Iceland, Ireland, Israel, New Zealand, and Norway are excluded because data are not available for these countries for either 2000 or 2016.

[9] Canada, Chile, Japan, the Republic of Korea, and Switzerland are excluded from this analysis because separate data are not available for all attainment levels for these countries.

Reference tables: *Digest of Education Statistics 2017*, tables 603.10, 603.20, and 603.30

Related indicators and resources: Educational Attainment of Young Adults; Education Expenditures by Country; International Comparisons: Reading Literacy at Grade 4; International Comparisons: Science, Reading, and Mathematics Literacy of 15-Year-Old Students; International Comparisons: U.S. 4th-, 8th-, and 12th-Graders' Mathematics and Science Achievement

Glossary: Associate's degree, Bachelor's degree, Doctor's degree, Educational attainment, Gap, High school completer, International Standard Classification of Education (ISCED), Master's degree, Organization for Economic Cooperation and Development (OECD), Postsecondary education

Guide to Sources

National Center for Education Statistics (NCES)

Common Core of Data

The Common Core of Data (CCD) is NCES's primary database on public elementary and secondary education in the United States. It is a comprehensive, annual, national statistical database of all public elementary and secondary schools and school districts containing data designed to be comparable across all states. This database can be used to select samples for other NCES surveys and provide basic information and descriptive statistics on public elementary and secondary schools and schooling in general.

The CCD collects statistical information annually from approximately 100,000 public elementary and secondary schools and approximately 18,000 public school districts (including supervisory unions and regional education service agencies) in the 50 states, the District of Columbia, Department of Defense (DoD) dependents schools, the Bureau of Indian Education (BIE), Puerto Rico, American Samoa, Guam, the Northern Mariana Islands, and the U.S. Virgin Islands. Three categories of information are collected in the CCD survey: general descriptive information on schools and school districts, data on students and staff, and fiscal data. The general school and district descriptive information includes name, address, phone number, and type of locale; the data on students and staff include selected demographic characteristics; and the fiscal data pertain to revenues and current expenditures.

The ED*Facts* data collection system is the primary collection tool for the CCD. NCES works collaboratively with the Department of Education's Performance Information Management Service to develop the CCD collection procedures and data definitions. Coordinators from state education agencies (SEAs) submit the CCD data at different levels (school, agency, and state) to the ED*Facts* collection system. Prior to submitting CCD files to ED*Facts*, SEAs must collect and compile information from their respective local education agencies (LEAs) through established administrative records systems within their state or jurisdiction.

Once SEAs have completed their submissions, the CCD survey staff analyzes and verifies the data for quality assurance. Even though the CCD is a universe collection and thus not subject to sampling errors, nonsampling errors can occur. The two potential sources of nonsampling errors are nonresponse and inaccurate reporting. NCES attempts to minimize nonsampling errors through the use of annual training of SEA coordinators, extensive quality reviews, and survey editing procedures. In addition, each year SEAs are given the opportunity to revise their state-level aggregates from the previous survey cycle.

The CCD survey consists of five components: The Public Elementary/Secondary School Universe Survey, the Local Education Agency (School District) Universe Survey, the State Nonfiscal Survey of Public Elementary/Secondary Education, the National Public Education Financial Survey (NPEFS), and the School District Finance Survey (F-33).

Public Elementary/Secondary School Universe Survey

The Public Elementary/Secondary School Universe Survey includes all public schools providing education services to prekindergarten (preK), kindergarten, grades 1–13, and ungraded students. For school year (SY) 2015–16, the survey included records for each public elementary and secondary school in the 50 states, the District of Columbia, the DoD dependents schools (overseas and domestic), the Bureau of Indian Education (BIE), Puerto Rico, American Samoa, the Northern Mariana Islands, Guam, and the U.S. Virgin Islands.

The Public Elementary/Secondary School Universe Survey includes data for the following variables: NCES school ID number, state school ID number, name of the school, name of the agency that operates the school, mailing address, physical location address, phone number, school type, operational status, locale code, latitude, longitude, county number, county name, full-time-equivalent (FTE) classroom teacher count, low/high grade span offered, congressional district code, school level, students eligible for free lunch, students eligible for reduced-price lunch, total students eligible for free and reduced-price lunch, and student totals and detail (by grade, by race/ethnicity, and by sex). The survey also contains flags indicating whether a school is Title I eligible, schoolwide Title I eligible, a magnet school, a charter school, a shared-time school, or a BIE school, as well as which grades are offered at the school.

Local Education Agency (School District) Universe Survey

The coverage of the Local Education Agency Universe Survey includes all school districts and administrative units providing education services to prekindergarten, kindergarten, grades 1–13, and ungraded students. The Local Education Agency Universe Survey includes records for the 50 states, the District of Columbia, Puerto Rico, the Bureau of Indian Education (BIE), American Samoa, Guam, the Northern Mariana Islands, the U.S. Virgin Islands, and the DoD dependents schools (overseas and domestic).

The Local Education Agency Universe Survey includes the following variables: NCES agency ID number, state agency ID number, agency name, phone number, mailing address, physical location address, agency type code, supervisory union number, American National Standards Institute (ANSI) state and county code, county name, core based statistical area (CBSA), metropolitan/micropolitan code, metropolitan status code, locale code, congressional district, operational status code, BIE agency status, low/high grade span offered, agency charter status, number of schools, number of full-time-equivalent teachers, number of ungraded students, number of preK–13 students, number of special education/Individualized Education Program students, number of English language learner students, instructional staff fields, support staff fields, and LEA charter status.

State Nonfiscal Survey of Public Elementary/ Secondary Education

The State Nonfiscal Survey of Public Elementary/Secondary Education for the 2015–16 school year provides state-level, aggregate information about students and staff in public elementary and secondary education. It includes data from the 50 states, the District of Columbia, Puerto Rico, the U.S. Virgin Islands, the Northern Mariana Islands, Guam, and American Samoa. The DoD dependents schools (overseas and domestic) and the BIE are also included in the survey universe. This survey covers public school student membership by grade, race/ethnicity, and state or jurisdiction and covers number of staff in public schools by category and state or jurisdiction. Beginning with the 2006–07 school year, the number of diploma recipients and other high school completers are no longer included in the State Nonfiscal Survey of Public Elementary/Secondary Education File. These data are now published in the public-use CCD State Dropout and Completion Data File.

National Public Education Financial Survey

The purpose of the National Public Education Financial Survey (NPEFS) is to provide district, state, and federal policymakers, researchers, and other interested users with descriptive information about revenues and expenditures for public elementary and secondary education. The data collected are useful to (1) chief officers of state education agencies; (2) policymakers in the executive and legislative branches of federal and state governments; (3) education policy and public policy researchers; and (4) the public, journalists, and others.

Data for NPEFS are collected from state education agencies (SEAs) in the 50 states, the District of Columbia, Puerto Rico, American Samoa, Guam, the Northern Mariana Islands, and the U.S. Virgin Islands. The data file is organized by state or jurisdiction and contains revenue data by funding source; expenditure data by function (the activity being supported by the expenditure) and object (the category of expenditure); average daily attendance data; and total student membership data from the CCD State Nonfiscal Survey of Public Elementary/Secondary Education.

School District Finance Survey

The purpose of the School District Finance Survey (F-33) is to provide finance data for all local education agencies (LEAs) that provide free public elementary and secondary education in the United States. National and state totals are not included (national- and state-level figures are presented, however, in the National Public Education Financial Survey).

NCES partners with the U.S. Census Bureau in the collection of school district finance data. The Census Bureau distributes Census Form F-33, Annual Survey of School System Finances, to all SEAs, and representatives from the SEAs collect and edit data from their LEAs and submit data to the Census Bureau. The Census Bureau then produces two data files: one for distribution and reporting by NCES and the other for distribution and reporting by the Census Bureau. The files include variables for revenues by source, expenditures by function and object, indebtedness, assets, and student membership counts, as well as identification variables.

Further information on the nonfiscal CCD data may be obtained from

Mark Glander
Elementary and Secondary Branch
Adminstrative Data Division
National Center for Education Statistics
550 12th Street SW
Washington, DC 20202
mark.glander@ed.gov
http://nces.ed.gov/ccd

Further information on the fiscal CCD data may be obtained from

Stephen Cornman
Elementary and Secondary Branch
Administrative Data Division
National Center for Education Statistics
550 12th Street SW
Washington, DC 20202
stephen.cornman@ed.gov
http://nces.ed.gov/ccd

EDFacts

EDFacts is a centralized data collection through which state education agencies submit preK–12 education data to the U.S. Department of Education (ED). All data in EDFacts are organized into "data groups" and reported to ED using defined file specifications. Depending on the data group, state education agencies may submit aggregate counts for the state as a whole or detailed counts for individual schools or school districts. EDFacts does not collect student-level records. The entities that are required to report EDFacts data vary by data group but may include the 50 states, the District of Columbia, the Department of Defense (DoD) dependents schools, the Bureau of Indian Education, Puerto Rico, American Samoa, Guam, the Northern Mariana Islands, and the U.S. Virgin Islands. More information about ED*Facts* file specifications and data groups can be found at http://www.ed.gov/EDFacts.

ED*Facts* is a universe collection and is not subject to sampling error, but nonsampling errors such as nonresponse and inaccurate reporting may occur. The U.S. Department of Education attempts to minimize nonsampling errors by training data submission coordinators and reviewing the quality of state data submissions. However, anomalies may still be present in the data.

Differences in state data collection systems may limit the comparability of ED*Facts* data across states and across time. To build ED*Facts* files, state education agencies rely on data that were reported by their schools and school districts. The systems used to collect these data are evolving rapidly and differ from state to state.

In some cases, ED*Facts* data may not align with data reported on state education agency websites. States may update their websites on schedules different from those they use to report data to ED. Furthermore, ED may use methods for protecting the privacy of individuals represented within the data that could be different from the methods used by an individual state.

ED*Facts* data on homeless students enrolled in public schools are collected in data group 655 within file 118. ED*Facts* data on English language learners enrolled in public schools are collected in data group 678 within file 141. ED*Facts* four-year adjusted cohort graduation rate (ACGR) data are collected in data group 695 within file 150 and in data group 696 within file 151. ED*Facts* collects these data groups on behalf of the Office of Elementary and Secondary Education.

For more information about ED*Facts*, please contact

ED*Facts*
Elementary/Secondary Branch
Adminstrative Data Division
National Center for Education Statistics
550 12th Street SW
Washington, DC 20202
EDFacts@ed.gov
http://www.ed.gov/EDFacts

Fast Response Survey System

The Fast Response Survey System (FRSS) was established in 1975 to collect issue-oriented data quickly, with a minimal burden on respondents. The FRSS, whose surveys collect and report data on key education issues at the elementary and secondary levels, was designed to meet the data needs of Department of Education analysts, planners, and decisionmakers when information could not be collected quickly through NCES's large recurring surveys. Findings from FRSS surveys have been included in congressional reports, testimony to congressional subcommittees, NCES reports, and other Department of Education reports. The findings are also often used by state and local education officials.

Data collected through FRSS surveys are representative at the national level, drawing from a sample that is appropriate for each study. The FRSS collects data from state education agencies and national samples of other educational organizations and participants, including local education agencies, public and private elementary and secondary schools, elementary and secondary school teachers and principals, and public libraries and school libraries. To ensure a minimal burden on respondents, the surveys are generally limited to three pages of questions, with a response burden of about 30 minutes per respondent. Sample sizes are relatively small (usually about 1,000 to 1,500 respondents per survey) so that data collection can be completed quickly.

Further information on the FRSS may be obtained from

John Ralph
Annual Reports and Information Staff
National Center for Education Statistics
550 12th Street SW
Washington, DC 20202
john.ralph@ed.gov
http://nces.ed.gov/surveys/frss

School Safety and Discipline

The FRSS survey "School Safety and Discipline: 2013–14" (FRSS 106, 2014) collected nationally representative data on public school safety and discipline for the 2013–14 school year. The topics covered included specific safety and discipline plans and practices, training for classroom teachers and aides related to school safety and discipline issues, security personnel, frequency of specific discipline problems, and number of incidents of various offenses.

The survey was mailed to approximately 1,600 regular public schools in the 50 states and the District of Columbia. Recipients were informed that the survey was designed to be completed by the person most knowledgeable about safety and discipline at the school. The unweighted survey response rate was 86 percent, and the weighted response rate using the initial base weights was 85 percent. The survey weights were adjusted for questionnaire nonresponse, and the data were then weighted to yield national estimates that represent all eligible regular public schools in the United States. The report *Public School Safety and Discipline: 2013–14* (NCES 2015-051) presents selected findings from the survey.

Further information on this FRSS survey may be obtained from

John Ralph
Annual Reports and Information Staff
National Center for Education Statistics
550 12th Street SW
Washington, DC 20202
john.ralph@ed.gov
http://nces.ed.gov/surveys/frss

Integrated Postsecondary Education Data System

The Integrated Postsecondary Education Data System (IPEDS) surveys over 7,300 postsecondary institutions, including universities and colleges, as well as institutions offering technical and vocational education beyond the high school level. IPEDS, an annual universe collection that began in 1986, replaced the Higher Education General Information Survey (HEGIS).

IPEDS consists of interrelated survey components that provide information on postsecondary institutions, student enrollment, programs offered, degrees and certificates conferred, and both the human and financial resources involved in the provision of institutionally based postsecondary education. Prior to 2000, the IPEDS survey had the following subject-matter components: Graduation Rates; Fall Enrollment; Institutional Characteristics; Completions; Salaries, Tenure, and Fringe Benefits of Full-Time Faculty; Fall Staff; Finance; and Academic Libraries (in 2000, the Academic Libraries component became a survey separate from IPEDS). Since 2000, IPEDS survey components occurring in a particular collection year have been organized into three seasonal collection periods: fall, winter, and spring. The Institutional Characteristics and Completions components first took place during the fall 2000 collection; the Employees by Assigned Position (EAP), Salaries, and Fall Staff components first took place during the winter 2001–02 collection; and the Enrollment, Student Financial Aid, Finance, and Graduation Rates components first took place during the spring 2001 collection. In the winter 2005–06 data collection, the EAP, Fall Staff, and Salaries components were merged into the Human Resources component. During the 2007–08 collection year, the Enrollment component was broken into two separate components: 12-Month Enrollment (taking place in the fall collection) and Fall Enrollment (taking place in the spring collection). In the 2011–12 IPEDS data collection year, the Student Financial Aid component was moved to the winter data collection to aid in the timing of the net price of attendance calculations displayed on the College Navigator (http://nces.ed.gov/collegenavigator). In the 2012–13 IPEDS data collection year, the Human Resources component was moved from the winter data collection to the spring data collection, and in the 2013–14 data collection year, the Graduation

Rates and Graduation Rates 200 Percent components were moved from the spring data collection to the winter data collection. In the 2014–15 data collection year, a new component (Admissions) was added to IPEDS and a former IPEDS component (Academic Libraries) was reintegrated into IPEDS. The Admissions component, created out of admissions data contained in the fall collection's Institutional Characteristics component, was made a part of the winter collection. The Academic Libraries component, after having been conducted as a survey independent of IPEDS between 2000 and 2012, was reintegrated into IPEDS as part of the spring collection.

Beginning in 2008–09, the first-professional degree category was combined with the doctor's degree category. However, some degrees formerly identified as first-professional that take more than 2 full-time-equivalent academic years to complete, such as those in Theology (M.Div, M.H.L./Rav), are included in the master's degree category. Doctor's degrees were broken out into three distinct categories: research/scholarship, professional practice, and other doctor's degrees.

IPEDS race/ethnicity data collection also changed in 2008–09. The "Asian" race category is now separate from a "Native Hawaiian or Other Pacific Islander" category, and a new category of "Two or more races" has been added.

The degree-granting institutions portion of IPEDS is a census of colleges that award associate's or higher degrees and are eligible to participate in Title IV financial aid programs. Prior to 1993, data from technical and vocational institutions were collected through a sample survey. Beginning in 1993, all data are gathered in a census of all postsecondary institutions. Beginning in 1997, the survey was restricted to institutions participating in Title IV programs.

The classification of institutions offering college and university education changed as of 1996. Prior to 1996, institutions that had courses leading to an associate's or higher degree or that had courses accepted for credit toward those degrees were considered higher education institutions. Higher education institutions were accredited by an agency or association that was recognized by the U.S. Department of Education or were recognized directly by the Secretary of Education. The newer standard includes institutions that award associate's or higher degrees and that are eligible to participate in Title IV federal financial aid programs. Tables that contain any data according to this standard are titled "degree-granting" institutions. Time-series tables may contain data from both series, and they are noted accordingly. The impact of this change on data collected in 1996 was not large. For example, tables on faculty salaries and benefits were only affected to a very small extent. Also, degrees awarded at the bachelor's level or higher were not heavily affected. The largest impact was on private 2-year college enrollment. In contrast, most of the data on public 4-year colleges were affected to a minimal extent. The impact on enrollment in public 2-year colleges was noticeable in certain states, such as Arizona, Arkansas, Georgia, Louisiana, and Washington, but was relatively small at the national level. Overall, total enrollment for all institutions was about one-half of 1 percent higher in 1996 for degree-granting institutions than for higher education institutions.

Prior to the establishment of IPEDS in 1986, HEGIS acquired and maintained statistical data on the characteristics and operations of higher education institutions. Implemented in 1966, HEGIS was an annual universe survey of institutions accredited at the college level by an agency recognized by the Secretary of the U.S. Department of Education. These institutions were listed in NCES's *Education Directory, Colleges and Universities*.

HEGIS surveys collected information on institutional characteristics, faculty salaries, finances, enrollment, and degrees. Since these surveys, like IPEDS, were distributed to all higher education institutions, the data presented are not subject to sampling error. However, they are subject to nonsampling error, the sources of which varied with the survey instrument.

The NCES Taskforce for IPEDS Redesign recognized that there were issues related to the consistency of data definitions as well as the accuracy, reliability, and validity of other quality measures within and across surveys. The IPEDS redesign in 2000 provided institution-specific web-based data forms. While the new system shortened data processing time and provided better data consistency, it did not address the accuracy of the data provided by institutions.

Beginning in 2003–04 with the Prior Year Data Revision System, prior-year data have been available to institutions entering current data. This allows institutions to make changes to their prior-year entries either by adjusting the data or by providing missing data. These revisions allow the evaluation of the data's accuracy by looking at the changes made.

NCES conducted a study (NCES 2005-175) of the 2002–03 data that were revised in 2003–04 to determine the accuracy of the imputations, track the institutions that submitted revised data, and analyze the revised data they submitted. When institutions made changes to their data, it was assumed that the revised data were the "true" data. The data were analyzed for the number and type of institutions making changes, the type of changes, the magnitude of the changes, and the impact on published data.

Because NCES imputes for missing data, imputation procedures were also addressed by the Redesign Taskforce. For the 2003–04 assessment, differences between revised values and values that were imputed in the original files were compared (i.e., revised value minus imputed value). These differences were then used to provide an assessment

of the effectiveness of imputation procedures. The size of the differences also provides an indication of the accuracy of imputation procedures. To assess the overall impact of changes on aggregate IPEDS estimates, published tables for each component were reconstructed using the revised 2002–03 data. These reconstructed tables were then compared to the published tables to determine the magnitude of aggregate bias and the direction of this bias.

Since the 2000–01 data collection year, IPEDS data collections have been web-based. Data have been provided by "keyholders," institutional representatives appointed by campus chief executives, who are responsible for ensuring that survey data submitted by the institution are correct and complete. Because Title IV institutions are the primary focus of IPEDS and because these institutions are required to respond to IPEDS, response rates for Title IV institutions have been high (data on specific components are cited below). More details on the accuracy and reliability of IPEDS data can be found in the *Integrated Postsecondary Education Data System Data Quality Study* (NCES 2005-175).

Further information on IPEDS may be obtained from

Richard Reeves
Postsecondary Branch
Administrative Data Division
National Center for Education Statistics
550 12th Street SW
Washington, DC 20202
richard.reeves@ed.gov
http://nces.ed.gov/ipeds

Fall (12-Month Enrollment)

The 12-month period during which data are collected is July 1 through June 30. Data are collected by race/ethnicity, gender, and level of study (undergraduate or postbaccalaureate) and include unduplicated headcounts and instructional activity (contact or credit hours). These data are also used to calculate a full-time-equivalent (FTE) enrollment based on instructional activity. FTE enrollment is useful for gauging the size of the educational enterprise at the institution. Prior to the 2007–08 IPEDS data collection, the data collected in the 12-Month Enrollment component were part of the Fall Enrollment component, which is conducted during the spring data collection period. However, to improve the timeliness of the data, a separate 12-Month Enrollment survey component was developed in 2007. These data are now collected in the fall for the previous academic year. The response rate for the 12-Month Enrollment component of the fall 2016 data collection was nearly 100 percent. Data from 5 of 6,756 Title IV institutions that were expected to respond to this component contained item nonresponse, and these missing items were imputed.

Further information on the IPEDS 12-Month Enrollment component may be obtained from

Aida Aliyeva
Postsecondary Branch
Administrative Data Division
National Center for Education Statistics
550 12th Street SW
Washington, DC 20202
aaliyeva@air.org
http://nces.ed.gov/ipeds

Fall (Completions)

This survey was part of the HEGIS series throughout its existence. However, the degree classification taxonomy was revised in 1970–71, 1982–83, 1991–92, 2002–03, and 2009–10. Collection of degree data has been maintained through IPEDS.

The nonresponse rate does not appear to be a significant source of nonsampling error for this survey. The response rate over the years has been high; for the fall 2016 Completions component, it rounded to 100 percent. Because of the high response rate, there was no need to conduct a nonresponse bias analysis. Imputation methods for the fall 2016 IPEDS Completions component are discussed in the *2016–17 Integrated Postsecondary Education Data System (IPEDS) Methodology Report* (NCES 2017-078).

The *Integrated Postsecondary Education Data System Data Quality Study* (NCES 2005-175) indicated that most Title IV institutions supplying revised data on completions in 2003–04 were able to supply missing data for the prior year. The small differences between imputed data for the prior year and the revised actual data supplied by the institution indicated that the imputed values produced by NCES were acceptable.

Further information on the IPEDS Completions component may be obtained from

Christopher Cody
Postsecondary Branch
Administrative Data Division
National Center for Education Statistics
550 12th Street SW
Washington, DC 20202
christopher.cody@ed.gov
http://nces.ed.gov/ipeds

Fall (Institutional Characteristics)

This survey collects the basic information necessary to classify institutions, including control, level, and types of programs offered, as well as information on tuition, fees, and room and board charges. Beginning in 2000, the survey collected institutional pricing data from

institutions with first-time, full-time, degree/certificate-seeking undergraduate students. Unduplicated full-year enrollment counts and instructional activity are now collected in the 12-Month Enrollment survey. Beginning in 2008–09, the student financial aid data collected include greater detail. The overall unweighted response rate was 100.0 percent for Title IV degree-granting institutions for 2009 data.

In the fall 2016 data collection, the response rate for Title IV entities on the Institutional Characteristics component rounded to 100 percent: Of the 6,834 Title IV entities that were expected to respond, only 1 response was missing.

The *Integrated Postsecondary Education Data System Data Quality Study* (NCES 2005-175) looked at tuition and price in Title IV institutions. Only 8 percent of institutions in 2002–03 and 2003–04 reported the same data to IPEDS and Thomson Peterson—a company providing information about institutions based on the institutions' voluntary data submissions—consistently across all selected data items. Differences in wordings or survey items may account for some of these inconsistencies.

Further information on the IPEDS Institutional Characteristics component may be obtained from

Moussa Ezzeddine
Christopher Cody
Postsecondary Branch
Administrative Data Division
National Center for Education Statistics
550 12th Street SW
Washington, DC 20202
moussa.ezzeddine@ed.gov
christopher.cody@ed.gov
http://nces.ed.gov/ipeds

Winter (Student Financial Aid)

This component was part of the spring data collection from IPEDS data collection years 2000–01 to 2010–11, but it moved to the winter data collection starting with the 2011–12 IPEDS data collection year. This move assists with the timing of the net price of attendance calculations displayed on College Navigator (http://nces.ed.gov/collegenavigator).

Financial aid data are collected for undergraduate students. Data are collected regarding federal grants, state and local government grants, institutional grants, and loans. The collected data include the number of students receiving each type of financial assistance and the average amount of aid received by type of aid. Beginning in 2008–09, student financial aid data collected includes greater detail on types of aid offered.

In the winter 2016–17 data collection, the Student Financial Aid component collected data about financial aid awarded to undergraduate students, with particular emphasis on full-time, first-time degree/certificate-seeking undergraduate students awarded financial aid for the 2015–16 academic year. In addition, the component collected data on undergraduate and graduate students receiving benefits for veterans and members of the military service. Finally, student counts and awarded aid amounts were collected to calculate the net price of attendance for two subsets of full-time, first-time degree/certificate-seeking undergraduate students: those awarded any grant aid, and those awarded Title IV aid. The response rate for the Student Financial Aid component in 2016–17 rounded to 100 percent: Of the 6,682 Title IV institutions that were expected to respond, responses were missing for 10 institutions.

Further information on the IPEDS Student Financial Aid component may be obtained from

Bao Le
Postsecondary Branch
Administrative Data Division
National Center for Education Statistics
550 12th Street SW
Washington, DC 20202
bao.le@ed.gov
http://nces.ed.gov/ipeds

Winter (Graduation Rates and Graduation Rates 200 Percent)

In IPEDS data collection years 2012–13 and earlier, the Graduation Rates and Graduation Rates 200 Percent components were collected during the spring collection. In the IPEDS 2013–14 data collection year, however, the Graduation Rates and Graduation Rates 200 Percent collections were moved to the winter data collection.

The 2016–17 Graduation Rates component collected counts of full-time, first-time degree/certificate-seeking undergraduate students beginning their postsecondary education in the specified cohort year and their completion status as of 150 percent of normal program completion time at the same institution where the students started. If 150 percent of normal program completion time extended beyond August 31, 2016, the counts as of that date were collected. Four-year institutions used 2010 as the cohort year, while less-than-4-year institutions used 2013 as the cohort year. Of the 5,995 institutions that were expected to respond to the Graduation Rates component, responses were missing for 11 institutions, resulting in a response rate that rounded to 100 percent.

The 2016–17 Graduation Rates 200 Percent component was designed to combine information reported in a prior collection via the Graduation Rates component with current information about the same cohort of students. From previously collected data, the following

counts were obtained: the number of students entering the institution as full-time, first-time degree/certificate-seeking students in a cohort year; the number of students in this cohort completing within 100 and 150 percent of normal program completion time; and the number of cohort exclusions (such as students who left for military service). Then the number of additional cohort exclusions and additional program completers between 151 and 200 percent of normal program completion time was collected. Four-year institutions reported on bachelor's or equivalent degree-seeking students and used cohort year 2008 as the reference period, while less-than-4-year institutions reported on all students in the cohort and used cohort year 2012 as the reference period. Of the 5,594 institutions that were expected to respond to the Graduation Rates 200 Percent component, responses were missing for 10 institutions, resulting in a response rate that rounded to 100 percent.

Further information on the IPEDS Graduation Rates and Graduation Rates 200 Percent components may be obtained from

Andrew Mary
Postsecondary Branch
Administrative Data Division
National Center for Education Statistics
550 12th Street SW
Washington, DC 20202
andrew.mary@ed.gov
http://nces.ed.gov/ipeds/

Winter (Admissions)

In the 2014–15 survey year, an Admissions component was added to the winter data collection. This component was created out of the admissions data that had previously been a part of the fall Institutional Characteristics component. Situating these data in a new component in the winter collection enables all institutions to report data for the most recent fall period.

The Admissions component collects information about the selection process for entering first-time degree/certificate-seeking undergraduate students. Data obtained from institutions include admissions considerations (e.g., secondary school records, admission test scores), the number of first-time degree/certificate-seeking undergraduate students who applied, the number admitted, and the number enrolled. Admissions data were collected only from institutions that do not have an open admissions policy for entering first-time students. Data collected for the IPEDS winter 2016–17 Admissions component relate to individuals applying to be admitted during the fall of the 2016–17 academic year (the fall 2016 reporting period). Of the 2,045 Title IV institutions that were expected to respond to the Admissions component, responses were missing for 2 institutions.

Further information on the IPEDS Admissions component may be obtained from

Moussa Ezzeddine
Postsecondary Branch
Administrative Data Division
National Center for Education Statistics
550 12th Street SW
Washington, DC 20202
moussa.ezzeddine@ed.gov
http://nces.ed.gov/ipeds

Spring (Fall Enrollment)

This survey has been part of the HEGIS and IPEDS series since 1966. Response rates have been relatively high, generally exceeding 85 percent. Beginning in 2000, with web-based data collection, higher response rates were attained. In the spring 2017 data collection, the Fall Enrollment component covered fall 2016. Of the 6,742 institutions that were expected to respond, 6,734 provided data, for a response rate that rounded to 100 percent. Data collection procedures for the Fall Enrollment component of the spring 2017 data collection are presented in *Enrollment and Employees in Postsecondary Institutions, Fall 2016; and Financial Statistics and Academic Libraries, Fiscal Year 2016: First Look (Provisional Data)* (NCES 2018-002).

Beginning with the fall 1986 survey and the introduction of IPEDS (see above), the survey was redesigned. The survey allows (in alternating years) for the collection of age and residence data. Beginning in 2000, the survey collected instructional activity and unduplicated headcount data, which are needed to compute a standardized, full-time-equivalent (FTE) enrollment statistic for the entire academic year. As of 2007–08, the timeliness of the instructional activity data has been improved by collecting these data in the fall as part of the 12-Month Enrollment component instead of in the spring as part of the Fall Enrollment component.

The *Integrated Postsecondary Education Data System Data Quality Study* (NCES 2005-175) showed that public institutions made the majority of changes to enrollment data during the 2004 revision period. The majority of changes were made to unduplicated headcount data, with the net differences between the original data and the revised data being about 1 percent. Part-time students in general and enrollment in private not-for-profit institutions were often underestimated. The fewest changes by institutions were to Classification of Instructional Programs (CIP) code data. (The CIP is a taxonomic coding scheme that contains titles and descriptions of primarily postsecondary instructional programs.)

Further information on the IPEDS Fall Enrollment component may be obtained from

Aida Aliyeva
Postsecondary Branch
Administrative Data Division
National Center for Education Statistics
550 12th Street SW
Washington, DC 20202
aaliyeva@air.org
http://nces.ed.gov/ipeds

Spring (Finance)

This survey was part of the HEGIS series and has been continued under IPEDS. Substantial changes were made in the financial survey instruments in fiscal year (FY) 1976, FY 1982, FY 1987, FY 1997, and FY 2002. While these changes were significant, a considerable effort has been made to present only comparable information on trends and to note inconsistencies. The FY 1976 survey instrument contained numerous revisions to earlier survey forms, which made direct comparisons of line items very difficult. Beginning in FY 1982, Pell Grant data were collected in the categories of federal restricted grant and contract revenues and restricted scholarship and fellowship expenditures. The introduction of IPEDS in the FY 1987 survey included several important changes to the survey instrument and data processing procedures. Beginning in FY 1997, data for private institutions were collected using new financial concepts consistent with Financial Accounting Standards Board (FASB) reporting standards, which provide a more comprehensive view of college finance activities. The data for public institutions continued to be collected using the older survey form. The data for public and private institutions were no longer comparable and, as a result, no longer presented together in analysis tables. In FY 2001, public institutions had the option of either continuing to report using Government Accounting Standards Board (GASB) standards or using the new FASB reporting standards. Beginning in FY 2002, public institutions could use either the original GASB standards, the FASB standards, or the new GASB Statement 35 standards (GASB35).

Possible sources of nonsampling error in the financial statistics include nonresponse, imputation, and misclassification. The unweighted response rate has been about 85 to 90 percent for most years these data appeared in NCES reports; however, in more recent years, response rates have been much higher because Title IV institutions are required to respond. Since 2002, the IPEDS data collection has been a full-scale web-based collection, which has improved the quality and timeliness of the data. For example, the ability of IPEDS to tailor online data entry forms for each institution based on characteristics such as institutional control, level of institution, and calendar system and the institutions' ability to submit their data online are aspects of full-scale web-based collections that have improved response.

The response rate for the FY 2016 Finance component was nearly 100 percent: Of the 6,825 institutions and administrative offices that were expected to respond, 6,816 provided data. Data collection procedures for the FY 2016 component are discussed in *Enrollment and Employees in Postsecondary Institutions, Fall 2016; and Financial Statistics and Academic Libraries, Fiscal Year 2016: First Look (Provisional Data)* (NCES 2018-002).

The *Integrated Postsecondary Education Data System Data Quality Study* (NCES 2005-175) found that only a small percentage (2.9 percent, or 168) of postsecondary institutions either revised 2002–03 data or submitted data for items they previously left unreported. Though relatively few institutions made changes, the changes made were relatively large—greater than 10 percent of the original data. With a few exceptions, these changes, large as they were, did not greatly affect the aggregate totals.

Further information on the IPEDS Finance component may be obtained from

Bao Le
Postsecondary Branch
Administrative Data Division
National Center for Education Statistics
550 12th Street SW
Washington, DC 20202
bao.le@ed.gov
http://nces.ed.gov/ipeds

Spring (Human Resources)

The Human Resources component was part of the IPEDS winter data collection from data collection years 2000–01 to 2011–12. For the 2012–13 data collection year, the Human Resources component was moved to the spring 2013 data collection, in order to give institutions more time to prepare their survey responses (the spring and winter collections begin on the same date, but the reporting deadline for the spring collection is several weeks later than the reporting deadline for the winter collection).

IPEDS Collection Years 2012–13 and Later

In 2012–13, new occupational categories replaced the primary function/occupational activity categories previously used in the IPEDS Human Resources component. This change was required in order to align the IPEDS Human Resources categories with the 2010 Standard Occupational Classification (SOC) system. In tandem with the change in 2012–13 from using primary

function/occupational activity categories to using the new occupational categories, the sections making up the IPEDS Human Resources component (which previously had been Employees by Assigned Position, Fall Staff, and Salaries) were changed to Full-Time Instructional Staff, Full-time Noninstructional Staff, Salaries, Part-Time Staff, and New Hires.

The webpage "Archived Changes—Changes to IPEDS Data Collections, 2012–13" (https://nces.ed.gov/ipeds/InsidePages/ArchivedChanges?year=2012-13) provides information on the redesigned IPEDS Human Resources component. "Resources for Implementing Changes to the IPEDS Human Resources (HR) Survey Component Due to Updated 2010 Standard Occupational Classification (SOC) System" (https://nces.ed.gov/ipeds/Section/resources_soc) is a webpage containing additional information, including notes comparing the new classifications with the old ("Comparison of New IPEDS Occupational Categories with Previous Categories"), a crosswalk from the new IPEDS occupational categories to the 2010 SOC occupational categories ("New IPEDS Occupational Categories and 2010 SOC"), answers to frequently asked questions, and a link to current IPEDS Human Resources survey screens.

Of the 6,819 institutions and administrative offices that were expected to respond to the spring 2017 Human Resources component, 6,811 provided data, for a response rate that rounded to 100 percent. Data collection procedures for this component are presented in *Enrollment and Employees in Postsecondary Institutions, Fall 2016; and Financial Statistics and Academic Libraries, Fiscal Year 2016: First Look (Provisional Data)* (NCES 2018-002).

IPEDS Collection Years Prior to 2012–13

In collection years before 2001–02, IPEDS conducted a Fall Staff survey and a Salaries survey; in the 2001–02 collection year, the Employees by Assigned Position survey was added to IPEDS. In the 2005–06 collection year, these three surveys became sections of the IPEDS "Human Resources" component.

Data gathered by the Employees by Assigned Position section categorized all employees by full- or part-time status, faculty status, and primary function/occupational activity. Institutions with M.D. or D.O. programs were required to report their medical school employees separately. A response to the EAP was required of all 6,858 Title IV institutions and administrative offices in the United States and other jurisdictions for winter 2008–09, and 6,845, or 99.8 percent unweighted, responded. Of the 6,970 Title IV institutions and administrative offices required to respond to the winter 2009–10 EAP, 6,964, or 99.9 percent, responded. And of the 7,256 Title IV institutions and administrative offices required to respond to the EAP for winter 2010–11, 7,252, or 99.9 percent, responded.

The main functions/occupational activities of the EAP section were primarily instruction, instruction combined with research and/or public service, primarily research, primarily public service, executive/administrative/managerial, other professionals (support/service), graduate assistants, technical and paraprofessionals, clerical and secretarial, skilled crafts, and service/maintenance.

All full-time instructional faculty classified in the EAP full-time nonmedical school part as either (1) primarily instruction or (2) instruction combined with research and/or public service were included in the Salaries section, unless they were exempt.

The Fall Staff section categorized all staff on the institution's payroll as of November 1 of the collection year by employment status (full time or part time), primary function/occupational activity, gender, and race/ethnicity. These data elements were collected from degree-granting and non-degree-granting institutions; however, additional data elements were collected from degree-granting institutions and related administrative offices with 15 or more full-time staff. These elements include faculty status, contract length/teaching period, academic rank, salary class intervals, and newly hired full-time permanent staff.

The Fall Staff section, which was required only in odd-numbered reporting years, was not required during the 2008–09 Human Resources data collection. However, of the 6,858 Title IV institutions and administrative offices in the United States and other jurisdictions, 3,295, or 48.0 percent unweighted, did provide data in the Fall Staff section that year. During the 2009–10 Human Resources data collection, when all 6,970 Title IV institutions and administrative offices were required to respond to the Fall Staff section, 6,964, or 99.9 percent, did so. A response to the Fall Staff section of the 2010–11 Human Resources collection was optional, and 3,364 Title IV institutions and administrative offices responded that year (a response rate of 46.3 percent).

The *Integrated Postsecondary Education Data System Data Quality Study* (NCES 2005-175) found that for 2003–04 employee data items, changes were made by 1.2 percent (77) of the institutions that responded. For all institutions making changes, the changes resulted in different employee counts. For both institutional and aggregate differences, however, the changes had little impact on the original employee count submissions. A large number of institutions reported different staff data to IPEDS and Thomson Peterson; however, the magnitude of the differences was small—usually no more than 17 faculty members for any faculty variable.

The Salaries section collected data for full-time instructional faculty (except those in medical schools in the EAP section, described above) on the institution's payroll as of November 1 of the collection year by contract length/teaching period, gender, and academic rank. The reporting of data by faculty status in the Salaries section was required from 4-year degree-granting institutions and above only. Salary outlays and fringe benefits were also collected for full-time instructional staff on 9/10- and 11/12-month contracts/teaching periods. This section was applicable to degree-granting institutions unless exempt.

Between 1966–67 and 1985–86, this survey differed from other HEGIS surveys in that imputations were not made for nonrespondents. Thus, there is some possibility that the salary averages presented in this report may differ from the results of a complete enumeration of all colleges and universities. Beginning with the surveys for 1987–88, the IPEDS data tabulation procedures included imputations for survey nonrespondents. The unweighted response rate for the 2008–09 Salaries survey section was 99.9 percent. The response rate for the 2009–10 Salaries section was 100.0 percent (4,453 of the 4,455 required institutions responded), and the response rate for 2010–11 was 99.9 percent (4,561 of the 4,565 required institutions responded). Imputation methods for the 2010–11 Salaries survey section are discussed in *Employees in Postsecondary Institutions, Fall 2010, and Salaries of Full-Time Instructional Staff, 2010–11* (NCES 2012-276).

Although data from this survey are not subject to sampling error, sources of nonsampling error may include computational errors and misclassification in reporting and processing. The electronic reporting system does allow corrections to prior-year reported or missing data, and this should help alleviate these problems. Also, NCES reviews individual institutions' data for internal and longitudinal consistency and contacts institutions to check inconsistent data.

The *Integrated Postsecondary Education Data System Data Quality Study* (NCES 2005-175) found that only 1.3 percent of the responding Title IV institutions in 2003–04 made changes to their salaries data. The differences between the imputed data and the revised data were small and found to have little impact on the published data.

Further information on the Human Resources component may be obtained from

Christopher Cody
Postsecondary Branch
Administrative Data Division
National Center for Education Statistics
550 12th Street SW
Washington, DC 20202
christopher.cody@ed.gov
http://nces.ed.gov/ipeds

National Assessment of Educational Progress

The National Assessment of Educational Progress (NAEP) is a series of cross-sectional studies initially implemented in 1969 to assess the educational achievement of U.S. students and monitor changes in those achievements. In the main national NAEP, a nationally representative sample of students is assessed at grades 4, 8, and 12 in various academic subjects. The assessment is based on frameworks developed by the National Assessment Governing Board (NAGB). It includes both multiple-choice items and constructed-response items (those requiring written answers). Results are reported in two ways: by average score and by achievement level. Average scores are reported for the nation, for participating states and jurisdictions, and for subgroups of the population. Percentages of students performing at or above three achievement levels (*Basic*, *Proficient*, and *Advanced*) are also reported for these groups.

Main NAEP Assessments

From 1990 until 2001, main NAEP was conducted for states and other jurisdictions that chose to participate. In 2002, under the provisions of the No Child Left Behind Act of 2001, all states began to participate in main NAEP, and an aggregate of all state samples replaced the separate national sample. (School district-level assessments—under the Trial Urban District Assessment [TUDA] program—also began in 2002.)

Results are available for the mathematics assessments administered in 2000, 2003, 2005, 2007, 2009, 2011, 2013, 2015, and 2017. In 2005, NAGB called for the development of a new mathematics framework. The revisions made to the mathematics framework for the 2005 assessment were intended to reflect recent curricular emphases and better assess the specific objectives for students at each grade level.

The revised mathematics framework focuses on two dimensions: mathematical content and cognitive demand. By considering these two dimensions for each item in the assessment, the framework ensures that NAEP assesses an appropriate balance of content, as well as a variety of ways of knowing and doing mathematics.

Since the 2005 changes to the mathematics framework were minimal for grades 4 and 8, comparisons over time can be made between assessments conducted before and after the framework's implementation for these grades. The changes that the 2005 framework made to the grade 12 assessment, however, were too drastic to allow grade 12 results from before and after implementation to be directly compared. These changes included adding more questions on algebra, data analysis, and probability to reflect changes in high school mathematics standards and coursework; merging the measurement and geometry content areas; and changing the reporting scale from 0–500 to 0–300. For more information

regarding the 2005 mathematics framework revisions, see http://nces.ed.gov/nationsreportcard/mathematics/frameworkcomparison.asp.

Results are available for the reading assessments administered in 2000, 2002, 2003, 2005, 2007, 2009, 2011, 2013, 2015, and 2017. In 2009, a new framework was developed for the 4th-, 8th-, and 12th-grade NAEP reading assessments.

Both a content alignment study and a reading trend, or bridge, study were conducted to determine if the new reading assessment was comparable to the prior assessment. Overall, the results of the special analyses suggested that the assessments were similar in terms of their item and scale characteristics and the results they produced for important demographic groups of students. Thus, it was determined that the results of the 2009 reading assessment could still be compared to those from earlier assessment years, thereby maintaining the trend lines first established in 1992. For more information regarding the 2009 reading framework revisions, see http://nces.ed.gov/nationsreportcard/reading/whatmeasure.asp.

In spring 2013, NAEP released results from the NAEP 2012 economics assessment in *The Nation's Report Card: Economics 2012* (NCES 2013-453). First administered in 2006, the NAEP economics assessment measures 12th-graders' understanding of a wide range of topics in three main content areas: market economy, national economy, and international economy. The 2012 assessment is based on a nationally representative sample of nearly 11,000 students in the 12th grade.

In *The Nation's Report Card: A First Look—2013 Mathematics and Reading* (NCES 2014-451), NAEP released the results of the 2013 mathematics and reading assessments. Results can also be accessed using the interactive graphics and downloadable data available at the online Nation's Report Card website (http://nationsreportcard.gov/reading_math_2013/#/).

The Nation's Report Card: A First Look—2013 Mathematics and Reading Trial Urban District Assessment (NCES 2014-466) provides the results of the 2013 mathematics and reading TUDA, which measured the reading and mathematics progress of 4th- and 8th-graders from 21 urban school districts. Results from the 2013 mathematics and reading TUDA can also be accessed using the interactive graphics and downloadable data available at the online TUDA website (http://nationsreportcard.gov/reading_math_tuda_2013/#/).

The online interactive report *The Nation's Report Card: 2014 U.S. History, Geography, and Civics at Grade 8* (NCES 2015-112) provides grade 8 results for the 2014 NAEP U.S. history, geography, and civics assessments. Trend results for previous assessment years in these three subjects, as well as information on school and student participation rates and sample tasks and student responses, are also presented.

In 2014, the first administration of the NAEP Technology and Engineering Literacy (TEL) Assessment asked 8th-graders to respond to questions aimed at assessing their knowledge and skill in understanding technological principles, solving technology and engineering-related problems, and using technology to communicate and collaborate. The online report *The Nation's Report Card: Technology and Engineering Literacy* (NCES 2016-119) presents national results for 8th-graders on the TEL assessment.

The Nation's Report Card: 2015 Mathematics and Reading Assessments (NCES 2015-136) is an online interactive report that presents national and state results for 4th- and 8th-graders on the NAEP 2015 mathematics and reading assessments. The report also presents TUDA results in mathematics and reading for 4th- and 8th-graders. The online interactive report *The Nation's Report Card: 2015 Mathematics and Reading at Grade 12* (NCES 2016-018) presents grade 12 results from the NAEP 2015 mathematics and reading assessments.

Results from the 2015 NAEP science assessment are presented in the online report *The Nation's Report Card: 2015 Science at Grades 4, 8, and 12* (NCES 2016-162). The assessment measures the knowledge of 4th-, 8th-, and 12th-graders in the content areas of physical science, life science, and Earth and space sciences, as well as their understanding of four science practices (identifying science principles, using science principles, using scientific inquiry, and using technological design). National results are reported for grades 4, 8, and 12, and results from 46 participating states and one jurisdiction are reported for grades 4 and 8. Since a new NAEP science framework was introduced in 2009, results from the 2015 science assessment can be compared to results from the 2009 and 2011 science assessments, but cannot be compared to the science assessments conducted prior to 2009.

NAEP is in the process of transitioning from paper-based assessments to technology-based assessments; consequently, data are needed regarding students' access to and familiarity with technology, at home and at school. The Computer Access and Familiarity Study (CAFS) is designed to fulfill this need. CAFS was conducted as part of the main administration of the 2015 NAEP. A subset of the grade 4, 8, and 12 students who took the main NAEP were chosen to take the additional CAFS questionnaire. The main 2015 NAEP was administered in a paper-and-pencil format to some students and a digital-based format to others, and CAFS participants were given questionnaires in the same format as their NAEP questionnaires.

The online Highlights report *2017 NAEP Mathematics and Reading Assessments: Highlighted Results at Grades 4 and 8 for the Nation, States, and Districts* (NCES 2018-037) presents an overview of results from the NAEP 2017 mathematics and reading reports. Highlighted results include key findings for the nation, states/jurisdictions, and 27 districts that participated in the Trial Urban District Assessment (TUDA) in mathematics and reading at grades 4 and 8.

NAEP Long-Term Trend Assessments

In addition to conducting the main assessments, NAEP also conducts the long-term trend assessments. Long-term trend assessments provide an opportunity to observe educational progress in reading and mathematics of 9-, 13-, and 17-year-olds since the early 1970s. The long-term trend reading assessment measures students' reading comprehension skills using an array of passages that vary by text types and length. The assessment was designed to measure students' ability to locate specific information in the text provided; make inferences across a passage to provide an explanation; and identify the main idea in the text.

The NAEP long-term trend assessment in mathematics measures knowledge of mathematical facts; ability to carry out computations using paper and pencil; knowledge of basic formulas, such as those applied in geometric settings; and ability to apply mathematics to skills of daily life, such as those involving time and money.

The Nation's Report Card: Trends in Academic Progress 2012 (NCES 2013-456) provides the results of 12 long-term trend reading assessments dating back to 1971 and 11 long-term trend mathematics assessments dating back to 1973.

Further information on NAEP may be obtained from

Daniel McGrath
Reporting and Dissemination Branch
Assessments Division
National Center for Education Statistics
550 12th Street SW
Washington, DC 20202
daniel.mcgrath@ed.gov
http://nces.ed.gov/nationsreportcard

National Household Education Surveys Program

The National Household Education Surveys Program (NHES) is a data collection system that is designed to address a wide range of education-related issues. Surveys have been conducted in 1991, 1993, 1995, 1996, 1999, 2001, 2003, 2005, 2007, 2012, and 2016. NHES targets specific populations for detailed data collection. It is intended to provide more detailed data on the topics and populations of interest than are collected through supplements to other household surveys.

The topics addressed by NHES:1991 were early childhood education and adult education. About 60,000 households were screened for NHES:1991. In the Early Childhood

Education Survey, about 14,000 parents/guardians of 3- to 8-year-olds completed interviews about their children's early educational experiences. Included in this component were participation in nonparental care/education; care arrangements and school; and family, household, and child characteristics. In the NHES:1991 Adult Education Survey, about 9,800 people 16 years of age and over, identified as having participated in an adult education activity in the previous 12 months, were questioned about their activities. Data were collected on programs and up to four courses, including the subject matter, duration, sponsorship, purpose, and cost. Information on the household and the adult's background and current employment was also collected.

In NHES:1993, nearly 64,000 households were screened. Approximately 11,000 parents of 3- to 7-year-olds completed interviews for the School Readiness Survey. Topics included the developmental characteristics of preschoolers; school adjustment and teacher feedback to parents for kindergartners and primary students; center-based program participation; early school experiences; home activities with family members; and health status. In the School Safety and Discipline Survey, about 12,700 parents of children in grades 3 to 12 and about 6,500 youth in grades 6 to 12 were interviewed about their school experiences. Topics included the school learning environment, discipline policy, safety at school, victimization, the availability and use of alcohol/drugs, and alcohol/drug education. Peer norms for behavior in school and substance use were also included in this topical component. Extensive family and household background information was collected, as well as characteristics of the school attended by the child.

In NHES:1995, the Early Childhood Program Participation Survey and the Adult Education Survey were similar to those fielded in 1991. In the Early Childhood component, about 14,000 parents of children from birth to 3rd grade were interviewed out of 16,000 sampled, for a completion rate of 90.4 percent. In the Adult Education Survey, about 24,000 adults were sampled and 82.3 percent (20,000) completed the interview.

NHES:1996 covered parent and family involvement in education and civic involvement. Data on homeschooling and school choice also were collected. The 1996 survey screened about 56,000 households. For the Parent and Family Involvement in Education Survey, nearly 21,000 parents of children in grades 3 to 12 were interviewed. For the Civic Involvement Survey, about 8,000 youth in grades 6 to 12, about 9,000 parents, and about 2,000 adults were interviewed. The 1996 survey also addressed public library use. Adults in almost 55,000 households were interviewed to support state-level estimates of household public library use.

NHES:1999 collected end-of-decade estimates of key indicators from the surveys conducted throughout the 1990s. Approximately 60,000 households were screened for a total of about 31,000 interviews with parents of

children from birth through grade 12 (including about 6,900 infants, toddlers, and preschoolers) and adults age 16 or older not enrolled in grade 12 or below. Key indicators included participation of children in nonparental care and early childhood programs, school experiences, parent/family involvement in education at home and at school, youth community service activities, plans for future education, and adult participation in educational activities and community service.

NHES:2001 included two surveys that were largely repeats of similar surveys included in earlier NHES collections. The Early Childhood Program Participation Survey was similar in content to the Early Childhood Program Participation Survey fielded as part of NHES:1995, and the Adult Education and Lifelong Learning Survey was similar in content to the Adult Education Survey of NHES:1995. The Before- and After-School Programs and Activities Survey, while containing items fielded in earlier NHES collections, had a number of new items that collected information about what school-age children were doing during the time they spent in child care or in other activities, what parents were looking for in care arrangements and activities, and parent evaluations of care arrangements and activities. Parents of approximately 6,700 children from birth through age 6 who were not yet in kindergarten completed Early Childhood Program Participation Survey interviews. Nearly 10,900 adults completed Adult Education and Lifelong Learning Survey interviews, and parents of nearly 9,600 children in kindergarten through grade 8 completed Before- and After-School Programs and Activities Survey interviews.

NHES:2003 included two surveys: the Parent and Family Involvement in Education Survey and the Adult Education for Work-Related Reasons Survey (the first administration). Whereas previous adult education surveys were more general in scope, this survey had a narrower focus on occupation-related adult education programs. It collected in-depth information about training and education in which adults participated specifically for work-related reasons, either to prepare for work or a career or to maintain or improve work-related skills and knowledge they already had. The Parent and Family Involvement Survey expanded on the first survey fielded on this topic in 1996. In 2003, screeners were completed with 32,050 households. About 12,700 of the 16,000 sampled adults completed the Adult Education for Work-Related Reasons Survey, for a weighted response rate of 76 percent. For the Parent and Family Involvement in Education Survey, interviews were completed by the parents of about 12,400 of the 14,900 sampled children in kindergarten through grade 12, yielding a weighted unit response rate of 83 percent.

NHES:2005 included surveys that covered adult education, early childhood program participation, and after-school programs and activities. Data were collected from about 8,900 adults for the Adult Education Survey, from parents of about 7,200 children for the Early Childhood Program Participation Survey, and from parents of nearly 11,700 children for the After-School Programs and Activities Survey. These surveys were substantially similar to the surveys conducted in 2001, with the exceptions that the Adult Education Survey addressed a new topic—informal learning activities for personal interest—and the Early Childhood Program Participation Survey and After-School Programs and Activities Survey did not collect information about before-school care for school-age children.

NHES:2007 fielded the Parent and Family Involvement in Education Survey and the School Readiness Survey. These surveys were similar in design and content to surveys included in the 2003 and 1993 collections, respectively. New features added to the Parent and Family Involvement Survey were questions about supplemental education services provided by schools and school districts (including use of and satisfaction with such services), as well as questions that would efficiently identify the school attended by the sampled students. New features added to the School Readiness Survey were questions that collected details about TV programs watched by the sampled children. For the Parent and Family Involvement Survey, interviews were completed with parents of 10,680 sampled children in kindergarten through grade 12, including 10,370 students enrolled in public or private schools and 310 homeschooled children. For the School Readiness Survey, interviews were completed with parents of 2,630 sampled children ages 3 to 6 and not yet in kindergarten. Parents who were interviewed about children in kindergarten through 2nd grade for the Parent and Family Involvement Survey were also asked some questions about these children's school readiness.

The 2007 and earlier administrations of NHES used a random-digit-dial sample of landline phones and computer-assisted telephone interviewing to conduct interviews. However, due to declining response rates for all telephone surveys and the increase in households that only or mostly use a cell phone instead of a landline, the data collection method was changed to an address-based sample survey for NHES:2012. Because of this change in survey mode, readers should use caution when comparing NHES:2012 estimates to those of prior NHES administrations.

NHES:2012 included the Parent and Family Involvement in Education Survey and the Early Childhood Program Participation Survey. The Parent and Family Involvement in Education Survey gathered data on students age 20 or younger who were enrolled in kindergarten through grade 12 or who were homeschooled at equivalent grade levels. Survey questions that pertained to students enrolled in kindergarten through grade 12 requested information on various aspects of parent involvement in education (such as help with homework, family activities, and parent involvement at school) and survey questions pertaining to homeschooled students requested information on the student's homeschooling experiences, the sources of the curriculum, and the reasons for homeschooling.

The 2012 Parent and Family Involvement in Education Survey questionnaires were completed for 17,563 (397 homeschooled and 17,166 enrolled) children, for a weighted unit response rate of 78.4 percent. The overall estimated unit response rate (the product of the screener unit response rate of 73.8 percent and the Parent and Family Involvement in Education Survey unit response rate) was 57.8 percent.

The 2012 Early Childhood Program Participation Survey collected data on the early care and education arrangements and early learning of children from birth through the age of 5 who were not yet enrolled in kindergarten. Questionnaires were completed for 7,893 children, for a weighted unit response rate of 78.7 percent. The overall estimated weighted unit response rate (the product of the screener weighted unit response rate of 73.8 percent and the Early Childhood Program Participation Survey unit weighted response rate) was 58.1 percent.

NHES:2016 used a nationally representative address-based sample covering the 50 states and the District of Columbia. The 2016 administration included a screener survey questionnaire that identified households with children or youth under age 20 and adults ages 16 to 65. A total of 206,000 households were selected based on this screener, and the screener response rate was 66.4 percent. All sampled households received initial contact by mail. Although the majority of respondents completed paper questionnaires, a small sample of cases was part of a web experiment with mailed invitations to complete the survey online.

The 2016 Parent and Family Involvement in Education Survey, like its predecessor in 2012, gathered data about students age 20 or under who were enrolled in kindergarten through grade 12 or who were being homeschooled for the equivalent grades. The 2016 survey's questions also covered aspects of parental involvement in education similar to those in the 2012 survey. The total number of completed questionnaires in the 2016 survey was 14,075 (13,523 enrolled and 552 homeschooled children), representing a population of 53.2 million students either homeschooled or enrolled in a public or private school in 2015–16. The survey's weighted unit response rate was 74.3 percent, and the overall response rate was 49.3 percent.

The 2016 Early Childhood Program Participation Survey collected data about children from birth through age 6 who were not yet enrolled in kindergarten. The survey asked about children's participation in relative care, nonrelative care, and center-based care arrangements. It also requested information such as the main reason for choosing care, factors that were important to parents when choosing a care arrangement, the primary barriers to finding satisfactory care, activities the family does with the child, and what the child is learning. Questionnaires were completed for 5,844 children, for a weighted unit response rate of 73.4 percent and an overall estimated weighted unit response rate of 48.7 percent.

Data for the 2016 Parent and Family Involvement in Education Survey are available in *Parent and Family Involvement in Education: Results From the National Household Education Surveys Program of 2016* (NCES 2017-102); data for the 2016 Early Childhood Program Participation Survey are available in *Early Childhood Program Participation, Results From the National Household Education Surveys Program of 2016* (NCES 2017-101).

Further information on NHES may be obtained from

Sarah Grady
Andrew Zukerberg
Sample Surveys Division
National Center for Education Statistics
550 12th Street SW
Washington, DC 20202
sarah.grady@ed.gov
andrew.zukerberg@ed.gov
http://nces.ed.gov/nhes

National Postsecondary Student Aid Study

The National Postsecondary Student Aid Study (NPSAS) is a comprehensive nationwide study of how students and their families pay for postsecondary education. Data gathered from the study are used to help guide future federal student financial aid policy. The study covers nationally representative samples of undergraduates, graduates, and first-professional students in the 50 states, the District of Columbia, and Puerto Rico, including students attending less-than-2-year institutions, community colleges, and 4-year colleges and universities. Participants include students who do not receive aid and those who do receive financial aid. Since NPSAS identifies nationally representative samples of student subpopulations of interest to policymakers and obtains baseline data for longitudinal study of these subpopulations, data from the study provide the base-year sample for the Beginning Postsecondary Students (BPS) longitudinal study and the Baccalaureate and Beyond (B&B) longitudinal study.

Originally, NPSAS was conducted every 3 years. Beginning with the 1999–2000 study (NPSAS:2000), NPSAS has been conducted every 4 years. NPSAS:08 included a new set of instrument items to obtain baseline measures of the awareness of two new federal grants introduced in 2006: the Academic Competitiveness Grant (ACG) and the National Science and Mathematics Access to Retain Talent (SMART) grant.

The first NPSAS (NPSAS:87) was conducted during the 1986–87 school year. Data were gathered from about 1,100 colleges, universities, and other postsecondary institutions; 60,000 students; and 14,000 parents. These data provided information on the cost of postsecondary education, the distribution of financial aid, and the characteristics of both aided and nonaided students and their families.

For NPSAS:93, information on 77,000 undergraduates and graduate students enrolled during the school year was collected at 1,000 postsecondary institutions. The sample included students who were enrolled at any time between July 1, 1992, and June 30, 1993. About 66,000 students and a subsample of their parents were interviewed by telephone. NPSAS:96 contained information on more than 48,000 undergraduate and graduate students from about 1,000 postsecondary institutions who were enrolled at any time during the 1995–96 school year. NPSAS:2000 included nearly 62,000 students (50,000 undergraduates and almost 12,000 graduate students) from 1,000 postsecondary institutions. NPSAS:04 collected data on about 80,000 undergraduates and 11,000 graduate students from 1,400 postsecondary institutions. For NPSAS:08, about 114,000 undergraduate students and 14,000 graduate students who were enrolled in postsecondary education during the 2007–08 school year were selected from more than 1,730 postsecondary institutions.

NPSAS:12 sampled about 95,000 undergraduates and 16,000 graduate students from approximately 1,500 postsecondary institutions. Public access to the data is available online through PowerStats (http://nces.ed.gov/datalab/).

NPSAS:16 sampled about 89,000 undergraduate and 24,000 graduate students attending approximately 1,800 Title IV eligible postsecondary institutions in the 50 states, the District of Columbia, and Puerto Rico. The sample represents approximately 20 million undergraduate and 4 million graduate students enrolled in postsecondary education at Title IV eligible institutions at any time between July 1, 2015, and June 30, 2016.

Further information on NPSAS may be obtained from

Aurora D'Amico
Tracy Hunt-White
Longitudinal Surveys Branch
Sample Surveys Division
National Center for Education Statistics
550 12th Street SW
Washington, DC 20202
aurora.damico@ed.gov
tracy.hunt-white@ed.gov
http://nces.ed.gov/npsas

National Teacher and Principal Survey (NTPS)

The National Teacher and Principal Survey is a set of related questionnaires that collect descriptive data on the context of elementary and secondary education. Data reported by schools, principals, and teachers provide a variety of statistics on the condition of education in the United States that may be used by policymakers and the general public. The NTPS covers a wide range of topics, including teacher demand, teacher and principal characteristics, teachers' and principals' perceptions of school climate and problems in their schools, teacher and principal compensation, district hiring and retention practices, general conditions in schools, and basic characteristics of the student population.

The NTPS was first conducted during the 2015–16 school year. The survey is a redesign of the Schools and Staffing Survey (SASS), which was conducted from the 1987–88 school year to the 2011–12 school year. Although the NTPS maintains the SASS survey's focus on schools, teachers, and administrators, the NTPS has a different structure and sample than SASS. In addition, whereas SASS operated on a 4-year survey cycle, the NTPS operates on a 2-year survey cycle.

The school sample for the 2015–16 NTPS was based on an adjusted public school universe file from the 2013–14 Common Core of Data (CCD), a database of all the nation's public school districts and public schools. The NTPS definition of a school is the same as the SASS definition of a school—an institution or part of an institution that provides classroom instruction to students, has one or more teachers to provide instruction, serves students in one or more of grades 1–12 or the ungraded equivalent, and is located in one or more buildings apart from a private home.

The 2015–16 NTPS universe of schools is confined to the 50 states plus the District of Columbia. It excludes the Department of Defense dependents schools overseas, schools in U.S. territories overseas, and CCD schools that do not offer teacher-provided classroom instruction in grades 1–12 or the ungraded equivalent. Bureau of Indian Education schools are included in the NTPS universe, but these schools were not oversampled and the data do not support separate BIE estimates.

The NTPS includes three key components: school questionnaires, principal questionnaires, and teacher questionnaires. NTPS data are collected by the U.S. Census Bureau through a mail questionnaire with telephone and in-person field follow-up. The school and principal questionnaires were sent to sampled schools, and the teacher questionnaire was sent to a sample of teachers working at sampled schools. The NTPS school sample consisted of about 8,300 public schools; the principal sample consisted of about 8,300 public school principals; and the teacher sample consisted of about 40,000 public school teachers.

The school questionnaire asks knowledgeable school staff members about grades offered, student attendance and enrollment, staffing patterns, teaching vacancies, programs and services offered, curriculum, and community service requirements. In addition, basic information is collected about the school year, including the beginning time of students' school days and the length of the school year. The weighted unit response rate for the 2015–16 school survey was 72.5 percent.

The principal questionnaire collects information about principal/school head demographic characteristics, training, experience, salary, goals for the school, and judgments about school working conditions and climate. Information is also obtained on professional development opportunities for teachers and principals, teacher performance, barriers to dismissal of underperforming teachers, school climate and safety, parent/guardian participation in school events, and attitudes about educational goals and school governance. The weighted unit response rate for the 2015–16 principal survey was 71.8 percent.

The teacher questionnaire collects data from teachers about their current teaching assignment, workload, education history, and perceptions and attitudes about teaching. Questions are also asked about teacher preparation, induction, organization of classes, computers, and professional development. The weighted response rate for the 2015–16 teacher survey was 67.8 percent.

Further information about the NTPS is available in *User's Manual for the 2015–16 National Teacher and Principal Survey, Volumes 1–4* (NCES 2017-131 through NCES 2017-134).

For additional information about the NTPS program, please contact

Maura Spiegelman
Cross-Sectional Surveys Branch
Sample Surveys Division
National Center for Education Statistics
550 12th Street SW
Washington, DC 20202
maura.spiegelman@ed.gov
http://nces.ed.gov/surveys/ntps

Private School Universe Survey

The purposes of the Private School Universe Survey (PSS) data collection activities are (1) to build an accurate and complete list of private schools to serve as a sampling frame for NCES sample surveys of private schools and (2) to report data on the total number of private schools, teachers, and students in the survey universe. Begun in 1989, the PSS has been conducted every 2 years, and data for the 1989–90, 1991–92, 1993–94, 1995–96, 1997–98, 1999–2000, 2001–02, 2003–04, 2005–06, 2007–08, 2009–10, 2011–12, 2013–14, and 2015–16 school years have been released. The First Look report *Characteristics of Private Schools in the United States: Results From the 2015–16 Private School Universe Survey* (NCES 2017-073) presents selected findings from the 2015–16 PSS.

The PSS produces data similar to that of the Common Core of Data for public schools, and can be used for public-private comparisons. The data are useful for a variety of policy- and research-relevant issues, such as the growth of religiously affiliated schools, the number of private high school graduates, the length of the school year for various private schools, and the number of private school students and teachers.

The target population for this universe survey is all private schools in the United States that meet the PSS criteria of a private school (i.e., the private school is an institution that provides instruction for any of grades K through 12, has one or more teachers to give instruction, is not administered by a public agency, and is not operated in a private home).

The survey universe is composed of schools identified from a variety of sources. The main source is a list frame initially developed for the 1989–90 PSS. The list is updated regularly by matching it with lists provided by nationwide private school associations, state departments of education, and other national guides and sources that list private schools. The other source is an area frame search in approximately 124 geographic areas, conducted by the U.S. Census Bureau.

Of the 40,302 schools included in the 2009–10 sample, 10,229 were found ineligible for the survey. Those not responding numbered 1,856, and those responding numbered 28,217. The unweighted response rate for the 2009–10 PSS survey was 93.8 percent.

Of the 39,325 schools included in the 2011–12 sample, 10,030 cases were considered as out-of-scope (not eligible for the PSS). A total of 26,983 private schools completed a PSS interview (15.8 percent completed online), while 2,312 schools refused to participate, resulting in an unweighted response rate of 92.1 percent.

There were 40,298 schools in the 2013–14 sample; of these, 10,659 were considered as out-of-scope (not eligible for the PSS). A total of 24,566 private schools completed a PSS interview (34.1 percent completed online), while 5,073 schools refused to participate, resulting in an unweighted response rate of 82.9 percent.

The 2015–16 PSS included 42,389 schools, of which 12,754 were considered as out-of-scope (not eligible for the PSS). A total of 22,428 private schools completed a PSS interview and 7,207 schools failed to respond, which resulted in an unweighted response rate of 75.7 percent.

Further information on the PSS may be obtained from

Steve Broughman
Cross-Sectional Surveys Branch
Sample Surveys Division
National Center for Education Statistics
550 12th Street SW
Washington, DC 20202
stephen.broughman@ed.gov
http://nces.ed.gov/surveys/pss

Projections of Education Statistics

Since 1964, NCES has published projections of key statistics for elementary and secondary schools and higher education institutions. The latest report is *Projections of Education Statistics to 2026* (NCES 2018-019). The *Projections of Education Statistics* series uses projection models for elementary and secondary enrollment, high school graduates, elementary and secondary teachers, expenditures for public elementary and secondary education, enrollment in postsecondary degree-granting institutions, and postsecondary degrees conferred to develop national and state projections. These models are described more fully in the report's appendix on projection methodology.

Differences between the reported and projected values are, of course, almost inevitable. An evaluation of past projections revealed that, at the elementary and secondary level, projections of public school enrollments have been quite accurate: mean absolute percentage differences for enrollment in public schools ranged from 0.3 to 1.2 percent for projections from 1 to 5 years in the future, while those for teachers in public schools were 3.1 percent or less. At the higher education level, projections of enrollment have been fairly accurate: mean absolute percentage differences were 5.9 percent or less for projections from 1 to 5 years into the future.

Further information on *Projections of Education Statistics* may be obtained from

William Hussar
Annual Reports and Information Staff
National Center for Education Statistics
550 12th Street SW
Washington, DC 20202
william.hussar@ed.gov
https://nces.ed.gov/pubs2018/2018019.pdf

School Survey on Crime and Safety (SSOCS)

The School Survey on Crime and Safety (SSOCS) is the only recurring federal survey that collects detailed information on the incidence, frequency, seriousness, and nature of violence affecting students and school personnel, as well as other indicators of school safety from the schools' perspective. SSOCS is conducted by the National Center for Education Statistics (NCES) within the U.S. Department of Education and collected by the U.S. Census Bureau. Data from this collection can be used to examine the relationship between school characteristics and violent and serious violent crimes in primary, middle, high, and combined schools. In addition, data from SSOCS can be used to assess what crime prevention programs, practices, and policies are used by schools. SSOCS has been conducted in school years 1999–2000, 2003–04, 2005–06, 2007–08, 2009–10, and 2015–16.

The sampling frame for SSOCS:2016 was constructed from the 2013–14 Public Elementary/Secondary School Universe data file of the Common Core of Data (CCD), an annual collection of data on all public K–12 schools and school districts. The SSOCS sampling frame was restricted to regular public schools (including charter schools) in the United States and the District of Columbia. Other types of schools from the CCD Public Elementary/Secondary School Universe file were excluded from the SSOCS sampling frame. For instance, schools in Puerto Rico, American Samoa, the Commonwealth of the Northern Mariana Islands, Guam, and the U.S. Virgin Islands, as well as Department of Defense dependents schools and Bureau of Indian Education schools, were excluded. Also excluded were special education, alternative, vocational, virtual, newly closed, ungraded, and home schools, and schools with the highest grade of kindergarten or lower.

The SSOCS:2016 universe totaled 83,600 schools. From this total, 3,553 schools were selected for participation in the survey. The sample was stratified by instructional level, type of locale (urbanicity), and enrollment size. The sample of schools in each instructional level was allocated to each of the 16 cells formed by the cross-classification of the four categories of enrollment size and four types of locale. The target number of responding schools allocated to each of the 16 cells was proportional to the sum of the square roots of the total student enrollment over all schools in the cell. The target respondent count within each stratum was then inflated to account for anticipated nonresponse; this inflated count was the sample size for the stratum.

Data collection began in February 2016 and ended in early July 2016. Questionnaire packets were mailed to the principals of the sampled schools, who were asked to complete the survey or have it completed by the person at the school who is most knowledgeable about school crime and policies for providing a safe school environment. A total of 2,092 public schools submitted usable questionnaires, resulting in an overall weighted unit response rate of 62.9 percent.

Further information about SSOCS may be obtained from

Rachel Hansen
Cross-Sectional Surveys Branch
Sample Surveys Division
National Center for Education Statistics
550 12th Street SW
Washington, DC 20202
(202) 245-7082
rachel.hansen@ed.gov
http://nces.ed.gov/surveys/ssocs/

Other Department of Education Agencies

Office of Special Education Programs

Annual Report to Congress on the Implementation of the Individuals with Disabilities Education Act

The Individuals with Disabilities Education Act (IDEA) is a law ensuring services to children with disabilities throughout the nation. IDEA governs how states and public agencies provide early intervention, special education, and related services to more than 6.8 million eligible infants, toddlers, children, and youth with disabilities.

IDEA, formerly the Education of the Handicapped Act (EHA), requires the Secretary of Education to transmit, on an annual basis, a report to Congress describing the progress made in serving the nation's children with disabilities. This annual report contains information on children served by public schools under the provisions of Part B of IDEA and on children served in state-operated programs for persons with disabilities under Chapter I of the Elementary and Secondary Education Act.

Statistics on children receiving special education and related services in various settings, and school personnel providing such services, are reported in an annual submission of data to the Office of Special Education Programs (OSEP) by the 50 states, the District of Columbia, the Bureau of Indian Education schools, Puerto Rico, American Samoa, Guam, the Northern Mariana Islands, the U.S. Virgin Islands, the Federated States of Micronesia, the Republic of Palau, and the Republic of the Marshall Islands. The child count information is based on the number of children with disabilities receiving special education and related services on December 1 of each year. Count information is available from http://www.ideadata.org.

Since all participants in programs for persons with disabilities are reported to OSEP, the data are not subject to sampling error. However, nonsampling error can arise from a variety of sources. Some states only produce counts of students receiving special education services by disability category because Part B of the EHA requires it. In those states that typically produce counts of students receiving special education services by disability category without regard to EHA requirements, definitions and labeling practices vary.

Further information on this annual report to Congress may be obtained from

Office of Special Education Programs
Office of Special Education and Rehabilitative Services
U.S. Department of Education
400 Maryland Avenue SW
Washington, DC 20202-7100
https://www.ed.gov/about/reports/annual/osep/index.html
https://sites.ed.gov/idea/
http://www.ideadata.org

Other Governmental Agencies and Programs

Bureau of Labor Statistics

Consumer Price Indexes

The Consumer Price Index (CPI) represents changes in prices of all goods and services purchased for consumption by urban households. Indexes are available for two population groups: a CPI for All Urban Consumers (CPI-U) and a CPI for Urban Wage Earners and Clerical Workers (CPI-W). Unless otherwise specified, data in this report are adjusted for inflation using the CPI-U. These values are generally adjusted to a school-year basis by averaging the July through June figures. Price indexes are available for the United States, the four Census regions, size of city, cross-classifications of regions and size classes, and 26 local areas. The major uses of the CPI include as an economic indicator, as a deflator of other economic series, and as a means of adjusting income.

Also available is the Consumer Price Index research series using current methods (CPI-U-RS), which presents an estimate of the CPI-U from 1978 to the present that incorporates most of the improvements that the Bureau of Labor Statistics has made over that time span into the entire series. The historical price index series of the CPI-U does not reflect these changes, though these changes do make the present and future CPI more accurate. The limitations of the CPI-U-RS include considerable uncertainty surrounding the magnitude of the adjustments and the several improvements in the CPI that have not been incorporated into the CPI-U-RS for various reasons. Nonetheless, the CPI-U-RS can serve as a valuable proxy for researchers needing a historical estimate of inflation using current methods. This series has not been used in NCES tables.

Further information on consumer price indexes may be obtained from

Bureau of Labor Statistics
U.S. Department of Labor
2 Massachusetts Avenue NE
Washington, DC 20212
http://www.bls.gov/cpi

Employment and Unemployment Surveys

Statistics on the employment and unemployment status of the population and related data are compiled by the Bureau of Labor Statistics (BLS) using data from the Current Population Survey (CPS) (see below) and other surveys. The CPS, a monthly household survey conducted by the U.S. Census Bureau for the Bureau of Labor Statistics, provides a comprehensive body of information on the employment and unemployment experience of the nation's population, classified by age, sex, race, and various other characteristics.

Further information on unemployment surveys may be obtained from

Bureau of Labor Statistics
U.S. Department of Labor
2 Massachusetts Avenue NE
Washington, DC 20212
cpsinfo@bls.gov
http://www.bls.gov/bls/employment.htm

Census Bureau

American Community Survey

The Census Bureau introduced the American Community Survey (ACS) in 1996. Fully implemented in 2005, it provides a large monthly sample of demographic, socioeconomic, and housing data comparable in content to the Long Forms of the Decennial Census up to and including the 2000 long form. Aggregated over time, these data serve as a replacement for the Long Form of the Decennial Census. The survey includes questions mandated by federal law, federal regulations, and court decisions.

Since 2011, the survey has been mailed to approximately 295,000 addresses in the United States and Puerto Rico each month, or about 3.5 million addresses annually. A larger proportion of addresses in small governmental units (e.g., American Indian reservations, small counties, and towns) also receive the survey. The monthly sample size is designed to approximate the ratio used in the 2000 Census, which requires more intensive distribution in these areas. The ACS covers the U.S. resident population, which includes the entire civilian, noninstitutionalized population; incarcerated persons; institutionalized persons; and the active duty military who are in the United States. In 2006, the ACS began interviewing residents in group quarter facilities. Institutionalized group quarters include adult and juvenile correctional facilities, nursing facilities, and other health care facilities. Noninstitutionalized group quarters include college and university housing, military barracks, and other noninstitutional facilities such as workers and religious group quarters and temporary shelters for the homeless.

National-level data from the ACS are available from 2000 onward. The ACS produces 1-year estimates for jurisdictions with populations of 65,000 and over and 5-year estimates for jurisdictions with smaller populations. The 1-year estimates for 2016 used data collected between January 1, 2016, and December 31, 2016, and the 5-year estimates for 2012–2016 used data collected between January 1, 2012, and December 31, 2016. The ACS produced 3-year estimates (for jurisdictions with populations of 20,000 or over) for the periods 2005–2007, 2006–2008, 2007–2009, 2008–2010, 2009–2011, 2010–2012, and 2011–2013. Three-year estimates for these periods will continue to be available to data users, but no further 3-year estimates will be produced.

Further information about the ACS is available at http://www.census.gov/acs/www/.

Census of Population—Education in the United States

Some NCES tables are based on a part of the decennial census that consisted of questions asked of a 1 in 6 sample of people and housing units in the United States. This sample was asked more detailed questions about income, occupation, and housing costs, as well as questions about general demographic information. This decennial census "long form" has been discontinued and has been replaced by the American Community Survey (ACS).

School enrollment. People classified as enrolled in school reported attending a "regular" public or private school or college. They were asked whether the institution they attended was public or private and what level of school they were enrolled in.

Educational attainment. Data for educational attainment were tabulated for people ages 15 and over and classified according to the highest grade completed or the highest degree received. Instructions were also given to include the level of the previous grade attended or the highest degree received for people currently enrolled in school.

Poverty status. To determine poverty status, answers to income questions were used to make comparisons to the appropriate poverty threshold. All people except those who were institutionalized, people in military group quarters and college dormitories, and unrelated people under age 15 were considered. If the total income of each family or unrelated individual in the sample was below the corresponding cutoff, that family or individual was classified as "below the poverty level."

Further information on the 1990 and 2000 Census of Population may be obtained from

Population Division
Census Bureau
U.S. Department of Commerce
4600 Silver Hill Road
Washington, DC 20233
http://www.census.gov/main/www/cen1990.html
http://www.census.gov/main/www/cen2000.html

Current Population Survey

The Current Population Survey (CPS) is a monthly survey of about 54,000 households conducted by the U.S. Census Bureau for the Bureau of Labor Statistics. The CPS is the primary source of labor force statistics on the U.S. population. In addition, supplemental questionnaires are used to provide further information about the U.S. population. The March supplement (also known as the Annual Social and Economic [ASEC] supplement) contains detailed questions on topics such as income, employment, and educational attainment; additional questions, such as items on disabilities, have also been included. In the July supplement, items on computer and internet use are the principal focus. The October supplement also contains some questions about computer and internet use, but most of its questions relate to school enrollment and school characteristics.

CPS samples are initially selected based on results from the decennial census and are periodically updated to reflect new housing construction. The current sample design for the main CPS, last revised in July 2015, includes about 74,000 households. Each month, about 54,000 of the 74,000 households are interviewed. Information is obtained each month from those in the household who are 15 years of age and over, and demographic data are collected for children 0–14 years of age. In addition, supplemental questions regarding school enrollment are asked about eligible household members age 3 and over in the October CPS supplement.

In January 1992, the CPS educational attainment variable was changed. The "Highest grade attended" and "Year completed" questions were replaced by the question "What is the highest level of school . . . has completed or the highest degree . . . has received?" Thus, for example, while the old questions elicited data for those who completed more than 4 years of high school, the new question elicited data for those who were high school completers, i.e., those who graduated from high school with a diploma as well as those who completed high school through equivalency programs, such as a GED program.

A major redesign of the CPS was implemented in January 1994 to improve the quality of the data collected. Survey questions were revised, new questions were added, and computer-assisted interviewing methods were used for the survey data collection. Further information about the redesign is available in *Current Population Survey, October 1995: (School Enrollment Supplement) Technical Documentation* at http://www.census.gov/prod/techdoc/cps/cpsoct95.pdf.

Caution should be used when comparing data from 1994 through 2001 with data from 1993 and earlier. Data from 1994 through 2001 reflect 1990 census-based population controls, while data from 1993 and earlier reflect 1980 or earlier census-based population controls. Changes in population controls generally have relatively little impact on summary measures such as means, medians, and percentage distributions; they can, however, have a significant impact on population counts. For example, use of the 1990 census-based population controls resulted in about a 1 percent increase in the civilian noninstitutional population and in the number of families and households. Thus, estimates of levels for data collected in 1994 and later years will differ from those for earlier years by more than what could be attributed to actual changes in the population. These differences could be disproportionately greater for certain subpopulation groups than for the total population.

Beginning in 2003, the race/ethnicity questions were expanded. Information on people of Two or more races were included, and the Asian and Pacific Islander race category was split into two categories—Asian and Native Hawaiian or Other Pacific Islander. In addition, questions were reworded to make it clear that self-reported data on race/ethnicity should reflect the race/ethnicity with which the responder identifies, rather than what may be written in official documentation.

The estimation procedure employed for monthly CPS data involves inflating weighted sample results to independent estimates of characteristics of the civilian noninstitutional population in the United States by age, sex, and race. These independent estimates are based on statistics from decennial censuses; statistics on births, deaths, immigration, and emigration; and statistics on the population in the armed services. Generalized standard error tables are provided in the Current Population Reports; methods for deriving standard errors can be found within the CPS technical documentation at http://www.census.gov/programs-surveys/cps/technical-documentation/complete.html. The CPS data are subject to both nonsampling and sampling errors.

Standard errors were estimated using the generalized variance function prior to 2005 for March CPS data and prior to 2010 for October CPS data. The generalized variance function is a simple model that expresses the variance as a function of the expected value of a survey estimate. Standard errors were estimated using replicate weight methodology beginning in 2005 for March CPS data and beginning in 2010 for October CPS data. Those interested in using CPS household-level supplement replicate weights to calculate variances may refer to *Estimating Current Population Survey (CPS) Household-Level Supplement Variances Using Replicate Weights* at http://thedataweb.rm.census.gov/pub/cps/supps/HH-level_Use_of_the_Public_Use_Replicate_Weight_File.doc.

Further information on the CPS may be obtained from

Education and Social Stratification Branch
Population Division
Census Bureau
U.S. Department of Commerce
4600 Silver Hill Road
Washington, DC 20233
http://www.census.gov/cps

Computer and Internet Use

The Current Population Survey (CPS) has been conducting supplemental data collections regarding computer use since 1984. In 1997, these supplemental data collections were expanded to include data on internet access. More recently, data regarding computer and internet use were collected in October 2010, July 2011, October 2012, July 2013, and July 2015.

In the July 2011, 2013, and 2015 supplements, the sole focus was on computer and internet use. In the October 2010 and 2012 supplements questions on school enrollment were the principal focus, and questions on computer and internet use were less prominent. Measurable differences in estimates taken from these supplements across years could reflect actual changes in the population; however, differences could also reflect seasonal variations in data collection or differences between the content of the July and October supplements. Therefore, caution should be used when making year-to-year comparisons of CPS computer and internet use estimates.

The most recent computer and internet use supplement, conducted in July 2015, collected household information from all eligible CPS households, as well as information from individual household members age 3 and over. Information was collected about the household's computer and internet use and the household member's use of the Internet from any location in the past year. Additionally, information was gathered regarding a randomly selected household respondent's use of the Internet.

For the July 2015 basic CPS, the household-level nonresponse rate was 13.0 percent. The person-level nonresponse rate for the computer and internet use supplement was an additional 23.0 percent. Since one rate is a person-level rate and the other a household-level rate, the rates cannot be combined to derive an overall rate.

Further information on the CPS Computer and Internet Use Supplement may be obtained from

Education and Social Stratification Branch
Census Bureau
U.S. Department of Commerce
4600 Silver Hill Road
Washington, DC 20233
http://census.gov/topics/population/computer-internet.html

Dropouts

Each October, the Current Population Survey (CPS) includes supplemental questions on the enrollment status of the population age 3 years and over as part of the monthly basic survey on labor force participation. In addition to gathering the information on school enrollment, with the limitations on accuracy as noted below under "School Enrollment," the survey data permit calculations of dropout rates. Both status and event dropout rates are tabulated from the October CPS. Event rates describe the proportion of students who leave school each year without completing a high school program. Status rates provide cumulative data on dropouts among all young adults within a specified age range. Status rates are higher than event rates because they include all dropouts ages 16 through 24, regardless of when they last attended school.

In addition to other survey limitations, dropout rates may be affected by survey coverage and exclusion of the institutionalized population. The incarcerated population has grown rapidly and has a high dropout rate. Dropout rates for the total population might be higher than those for the noninstitutionalized population if the prison and jail populations were included in the dropout rate calculations. On the other hand, if military personnel, who tend to be high school graduates, were included, it might offset some or all of the impact from the theoretical inclusion of the jail and prison populations.

Another area of concern with tabulations involving young people in household surveys is the relatively low coverage ratio compared to older age groups. CPS undercoverage results from missed housing units and missed people within sample households. Overall CPS undercoverage for October 2016 is estimated to be about 11 percent. CPS coverage varies with age, sex, and race. Generally, coverage is larger for females than for males and larger for non-Blacks than for Blacks. This differential coverage is a general problem for most household-based surveys. Further information on CPS methodology may be found in the technical documentation at http://www.census.gov/cps.

Further information on the calculation of dropouts and dropout rates may be obtained from the *Trends in High School Dropout and Completion Rates in the United States* report at https://nces.ed.gov/programs/dropout/index.asp or by contacting

Joel McFarland
Annual Reports and Information Staff
National Center for Education Statistics
550 12th Street SW
Washington, DC 20202
joel.mcfarland@ed.gov

Educational Attainment

Reports documenting educational attainment are produced by the Census Bureau using the March Current Population Survey (CPS) supplement (Annual Social and Economic supplement [ASEC]). Currently, the ASEC supplement consists of approximately 70,000 interviewed households. Both recent and earlier editions

of *Educational Attainment in the United States* may be downloaded at https://www.census.gov/topics/education/educational-attainment/data/tables.All.html.

In addition to the general constraints of CPS, some data indicate that the respondents have a tendency to overestimate the educational level of members of their household. Some inaccuracy is due to a lack of the respondent's knowledge of the exact educational attainment of each household member and the hesitancy to acknowledge anything less than a high school education.

Further information on educational attainment data from CPS may be obtained from

Education and Social Stratification Branch
Census Bureau
U.S. Department of Commerce
4600 Silver Hill Road
Washington, DC 20233
https://www.census.gov/topics/education/educational-attainment/data.html

School Enrollment

Each October, the Current Population Survey (CPS) includes supplemental questions on the enrollment status of the population age 3 years and over. Currently, the October supplement consists of approximately 54,000 interviewed households, the same households interviewed in the basic Current Population Survey. The main sources of nonsampling variability in the responses to the supplement are those inherent in the survey instrument. The question of current enrollment may not be answered accurately for various reasons. Some respondents may not know current grade information for every student in the household, a problem especially prevalent for households with members in college or in nursery school. Confusion over college credits or hours taken by a student may make it difficult to determine the year in which the student is enrolled. Problems may occur with the definition of nursery school (a group or class organized to provide educational experiences for children) where respondents' interpretations of "educational experiences" vary.

For the October 2016 basic CPS, the household-level nonresponse rate was 12.7 percent. The person-level nonresponse rate for the school enrollment supplement was an additional 8.0 percent. Since the basic CPS nonresponse rate is a household-level rate and the school enrollment supplement nonresponse rate is a person-level rate, these rates cannot be combined to derive an overall nonresponse rate. Nonresponding households may have fewer persons than interviewed ones, so combining these rates may lead to an overestimate of the true overall nonresponse rate for persons for the school enrollment supplement.

Although the principal focus of the October supplement is school enrollment, in some years the supplement has included additional questions on other topics. In 2010 and 2012, for example, the October supplement included additional questions on computer and internet use.

Further information on CPS methodology may be obtained from http://www.census.gov/cps.

Further information on the CPS School Enrollment Supplement may be obtained from

Education and Social Stratification Branch
Census Bureau
U.S. Department of Commerce
4600 Silver Hill Road
Washington, DC 20233
https://www.census.gov/topics/education/school-enrollment.html

Decennial Census, Population Estimates, and Population Projections

The decennial census is a universe survey mandated by the U.S. Constitution. It is a questionnaire sent to every household in the country, and it is composed of seven questions about the household and its members (name, sex, age, relationship, Hispanic origin, race, and whether the housing unit is owned or rented). The Census Bureau also produces annual estimates of the resident population by demographic characteristics (age, sex, race, and Hispanic origin) for the nation, states, and counties, as well as national and state projections for the resident population. The reference date for population estimates is July 1 of the given year. With each new issue of July 1 estimates, the Census Bureau revises estimates for each year back to the last census. Previously published estimates are superseded and archived.

Census respondents self-report race and ethnicity. The race questions on the 1990 and 2000 censuses differed in some significant ways. In 1990, the respondent was instructed to select the one race "that the respondent considers himself/herself to be," whereas in 2000, the respondent could select one or more races that the person considered himself or herself to be. American Indian, Eskimo, and Aleut were three separate race categories in 1990; in 2000, the American Indian and Alaska Native categories were combined, with an option to write in a tribal affiliation. This write-in option was provided only for the American Indian category in 1990. There was a combined Asian and Pacific Islander race category in 1990, but the groups were separated into two categories in 2000.

The census question on ethnicity asks whether the respondent is of Hispanic origin, regardless of the race option(s) selected; thus, persons of Hispanic origin may be of any race. In the 2000 census, respondents were first asked, "Is this person Spanish/Hispanic/Latino?" and then given the following options: No, not Spanish/Hispanic/Latino; Yes, Puerto Rican; Yes, Mexican, Mexican American, Chicano; Yes, Cuban; and Yes, other Spanish/Hispanic/Latino (with space to print the specific group). In the 2010 census, respondents were asked "Is this person of Hispanic, Latino, or Spanish origin?" The options given were No, not of Hispanic, Latino, or Spanish origin; Yes, Mexican, Mexican Am., Chicano; Yes, Puerto Rican; Yes, Cuban; and Yes, another Hispanic, Latino, or Spanish origin—along with instructions to print "Argentinean, Colombian, Dominican, Nicaraguan, Salvadoran, Spaniard, and so on" in a specific box.

The 2000 and 2010 censuses each asked the respondent "What is this person's race?" and allowed the respondent to select one or more options. The options provided were largely the same in both the 2000 and 2010 censuses: White; Black, African American, or Negro; American Indian or Alaska Native (with space to print the name of enrolled or principal tribe); Asian Indian; Japanese; Native Hawaiian; Chinese; Korean; Guamanian or Chamorro; Filipino; Vietnamese; Samoan; Other Asian; Other Pacific Islander; and Some other race. The last three options included space to print the specific race. Two significant differences between the 2000 and 2010 census questions on race were that no race examples were provided for the "Other Asian" and "Other Pacific Islander" responses in 2000, whereas the race examples of "Hmong, Laotian, Thai, Pakistani, Cambodian, and so on" and "Fijian, Tongan, and so on," were provided for the "Other Asian" and "Other Pacific Islander" responses, respectively, in 2010.

The census population estimates program modified the enumerated population from the 2010 census to produce the population estimates base for 2010 and onward. As part of the modification, the Census Bureau recoded the "Some other race" responses from the 2010 census to one or more of the five OMB race categories used in the estimates program (for more information, see http://www.census.gov/programs-surveys/popest/technical-documentation/methodology.html).

Further information on the decennial census may be obtained from http://www.census.gov.

Department of Justice

Bureau of Justice Statistics

A division of the U.S. Department of Justice Office of Justice Programs, the Bureau of Justice Statistics (BJS) collects, analyzes, publishes, and disseminates statistical information on crime, criminal offenders, victims of crime, and the operations of the justice system at all levels of government and internationally. It also provides technical and financial support to state governments for development of criminal justice statistics and information systems on crime and justice.

For information on the BJS, see https://www.bjs.gov/.

National Crime Victimization Survey

The National Crime Victimization Survey (NCVS), administered for the U.S. Bureau of Justice Statistics (BJS) by the U.S. Census Bureau, is the nation's primary source of information on crime and the victims of crime. Initiated in 1972 and redesigned in 1992 and 2016, the NCVS collects detailed information on the frequency and nature of the crimes of rape, sexual assault, robbery, aggravated and simple assault, theft, household burglary, and motor vehicle theft experienced by Americans and American households each year. The survey measures both crimes reported to the police and crimes not reported to the police.

NCVS estimates presented may differ from those in previous published reports. This is because a small number of victimizations, referred to as series victimizations, are included using a new counting strategy. High-frequency repeat victimizations, or series victimizations, are six or more similar but separate victimizations that occur with such frequency that the victim is unable to recall each individual event or describe each event in detail. As part of ongoing research efforts associated with the redesign of the NCVS, BJS investigated ways to include high-frequency repeat victimizations, or series victimizations, in estimates of criminal victimization. Including series victimizations results in more accurate estimates of victimization. BJS has decided to include series victimizations using the victim's estimates of the number of times the victimizations occurred over the past 6 months, capping the number of victimizations within each series at a maximum of 10. This strategy for counting series victimizations balances the desire to estimate national rates and account for the experiences of persons who have been subjected to repeat victimizations against the desire to minimize the estimation errors that can occur when repeat victimizations are reported. Including series victimizations in national rates results in rather large increases in the level of violent victimization; however, trends in violence are generally similar regardless of whether series victimizations are included. For more information on the new counting strategy and supporting research, see *Methods for Counting High-Frequency Repeat Victimizations in the National Crime Victimization Survey* at https://www.bjs.gov/content/pub/pdf/mchfrv.pdf.

Readers should note that in 2003, in accordance with changes to the Office of Management and Budget's standards for the classification of federal data on race and ethnicity, the NCVS item on race/ethnicity was modified. A question on Hispanic origin is now followed by a new question on race. The new question about race allows the respondent to choose more than one race and delineates Asian as a separate category from Native Hawaiian or Other Pacific Islander. An analysis conducted by the Demographic Surveys Division at the U.S. Census Bureau showed that the new race question had very little impact on the aggregate racial distribution of the NCVS respondents, with one exception: There was a 1.6 percentage point decrease in the percentage of respondents who reported themselves as White. Due to changes in race/ethnicity categories, comparisons of race/ethnicity across years should be made with caution.

There were changes in the sample design and survey methodology in the 2006 NCVS that may have affected survey estimates. Caution should be used when comparing the 2006 estimates to estimates of other years. Data from 2007 onward are comparable to earlier years. Analyses of the 2007 estimates indicate that the program changes made in 2006 had relatively small effects on NCVS estimates. For more information on the 2006 NCVS data, see *Criminal Victimization, 2006*, at https://www.bjs.gov/content/pub/pdf/cv06.pdf; the NCVS 2006 technical notes, at https://www.bjs.gov/content/pub/pdf/cv06tn.pdf; and *Criminal Victimization, 2007*, at https://bjs.gov/content/pub/pdf/cv07.pdf.

The NCVS sample was redesigned in 2016 in order to account for changes in the U.S. population identified through the 2010 Decennial Census and to make it possible to produce state- and local-level victimization estimates for the largest 22 states and specific metropolitan areas within those states. Because of this redesign, 2016 victimization data are not comparable to data from 2015 and prior years. For more information on the 2016 NCVS data, see *Criminal Victimization, 2016*, at https://www.bjs.gov/content/pub/pdf/cv16.pdf, and the technical notes, at https://www.bjs.gov/content/pub/pdf/ncvstd16.pdf.

The number of NCVS-eligible households in the sample in 2016 was about 134,690. Households were selected using a stratified, multistage cluster design. In the first stage, the primary sampling units (PSUs), consisting of counties or groups of counties, were selected. In the second stage, smaller areas, called Enumeration Districts (EDs), were selected from each sampled PSU. Finally, from selected EDs, clusters of four households, called segments, were selected for interview. At each stage, the selection was done proportionate to population size in order to create a self-weighting sample. The final sample was augmented to account for households constructed after the decennial census. Within each sampled household, the U.S. Census Bureau interviewer attempts to interview all household members age 12 and over to determine whether they had been victimized by the measured crimes during the 6 months preceding the interview.

The first NCVS interview with a housing unit is conducted in person. Subsequent interviews are conducted by telephone, if possible. Households remain in the sample for 3 years and are interviewed seven times at 6-month intervals. Since the survey's inception, the initial interview at each sample unit has been used only to bound future interviews to establish a time frame to avoid duplication of crimes uncovered in these subsequent interviews. Beginning in 2006, data from the initial interview have been adjusted to account for the effects of bounding and have been included in the survey estimates. After a household has been interviewed its seventh time, it is replaced by a new sample household. In 2016, the household response rate was about 78 percent and the completion rate for persons within households was about 84 percent. Weights were developed to permit estimates for the total U.S. population 12 years and older.

Further information on the NCVS may be obtained from

Rachel E. Morgan
Victimization Statistics Branch
Bureau of Justice Statistics
rachel.morgan@usdoj.gov
http://www.bjs.gov/

Other Organization Sources

International Association for the Evaluation of Educational Achievement

The International Association for the Evaluation of Educational Achievement (IEA) is composed of governmental research centers and national research institutions around the world whose aim is to investigate education problems common among countries. Since its inception in 1958, the IEA has conducted more than 30 research studies of cross-national achievement. The regular cycle of studies encompasses learning in basic school subjects. Examples are the Trends in International Mathematics and Science Study (TIMSS) and the Progress in International Reading Literacy Study (PIRLS). IEA projects also include studies of particular interest to IEA members, such as the TIMSS 1999 Video Study of Mathematics and Science Teaching, the Civic Education Study, and studies on information technology in education.

The international bodies that coordinate international assessments vary in the labels they apply to participating education systems, most of which are countries. IEA differentiates between IEA members, which IEA refers to as "countries" in all cases, and "benchmarking participants." IEA members include countries such as the United States and Ireland, as well as subnational entities such as England and Scotland (which are both part of the United Kingdom), the Flemish community of Belgium, and Hong Kong (a Special Administrative

Region of China). IEA benchmarking participants are all subnational entities and include Canadian provinces, U.S. states, and Dubai in the United Arab Emirates (among others). Benchmarking participants, like the participating countries, are given the opportunity to assess the comparative international standing of their students' achievement and to view their curriculum and instruction in an international context.

Some IEA studies, such as TIMSS and PIRLS, include an assessment portion, as well as contextual questionnaires for collecting information about students' home and school experiences. The TIMSS and PIRLS scales, including the scale averages and standard deviations, are designed to remain constant from assessment to assessment so that education systems (including countries and subnational education systems) can compare their scores over time as well as compare their scores directly with the scores of other education systems. Although each scale was created to have a mean of 500 and a standard deviation of 100, the subject matter and the level of difficulty of items necessarily differ by grade, subject, and domain/dimension. Therefore, direct comparisons between scores across grades, subjects, and different domain/dimension types should not be made.

Further information on the International Association for the Evaluation of Educational Achievement may be obtained from http://www.iea.nl.

Trends in International Mathematics and Science Study

The Trends in International Mathematics and Science Study (TIMSS, formerly known as the Third International Mathematics and Science Study) provides data on the mathematics and science achievement of U.S. 4th- and 8th-graders compared with that of their peers in other countries. TIMSS collects information through mathematics and science assessments and questionnaires. The questionnaires request information to help provide a context for student performance. They focus on such topics as students' attitudes and beliefs about learning mathematics and science, what students do as part of their mathematics and science lessons, students' completion of homework, and their lives both in and outside of school; teachers' perceptions of their preparedness for teaching mathematics and science, teaching assignments, class size and organization, instructional content and practices, collaboration with other teachers, and participation in professional development activities; and principals' viewpoints on policy and budget responsibilities, curriculum and instruction issues, and student behavior. The questionnaires also elicit information on the organization of schools and courses. The assessments and questionnaires are designed to specifications in a guiding framework. The TIMSS framework describes the mathematics and science content to be assessed and provides grade-specific objectives, an overview of the assessment design, and guidelines for item development.

TIMSS is on a 4-year cycle. Data collections occurred in 1995, 1999 (8th grade only), 2003, 2007, 2011, and 2015. TIMSS 2015 consisted of assessments in 4th-grade mathematics; numeracy (a less difficult version of 4th-grade mathematics, newly developed for 2015); 8th-grade mathematics; 4th-grade science; and 8th-grade science. In addition, TIMSS 2015 included the third administration of TIMSS Advanced since 1995. TIMSS Advanced is an international comparative study that measures the advanced mathematics and physics achievement of students in their final year of secondary school (the equivalent of 12th grade in the United States) who are taking or have taken advanced courses. The TIMSS 2015 survey also collected policy-relevant information about students, curriculum emphasis, technology use, and teacher preparation and training.

Progress in International Reading Literacy Study

The Progress in International Reading Literacy Study (PIRLS) provides data on the reading literacy of U.S. 4th-graders compared with that of their peers in other countries. PIRLS is on a 5-year cycle: PIRLS data collections have been conducted in 2001, 2006, 2011, and 2016. In 2016, a total of 58 education systems, including both IEA members and IEA benchmarking participants, participated in the survey. Sixteen of the education systems participating in PIRLS also participated in ePIRLS, an innovative, computer-based assessment of online reading designed to measure students' approaches to informational reading in an online environment.

PIRLS collects information through a reading literacy assessment and questionnaires that help to provide a context for student performance. Questionnaires are administered to collect information about students' home and school experiences in learning to read. A student questionnaire addresses students' attitudes toward reading and their reading habits. In addition, questionnaires are given to students' teachers and school principals in order to gather information about students' school experiences in developing reading literacy. In countries other than the United States, a parent questionnaire is also administered. The assessments and questionnaires are designed to specifications in a guiding framework. The PIRLS framework describes the reading content to be assessed and provides objectives specific to 4th grade, an overview of the assessment design, and guidelines for item development.

TIMSS and PIRLS Sampling and Response Rates

2016 PIRLS

As is done in all participating countries and other education systems, representative samples of students in the United States are selected. The sample design that was employed by PIRLS in 2016 is generally referred to as a two-stage stratified cluster sample. In the first stage of sampling, individual schools were selected with a probability proportionate to size (PPS) approach, which means that the probability is proportional to the estimated number of students enrolled in the target grade. In the second stage of sampling, intact classrooms were selected within sampled schools.

PIRLS guidelines call for a minimum of 150 schools to be sampled, with a minimum of 4,000 students assessed. The basic sample design of one classroom per school was designed to yield a total sample of approximately 4,500 students per population. About 4,400 U.S. students participated in PIRLS in 2016, joining 319,000 other student participants around the world. Accommodations were not provided for students with disabilities or students who were unable to read or speak the language of the test. These students were excluded from the sample. The IEA requirement is that the overall exclusion rate, which includes exclusions of schools and students, should not exceed more than 5 percent of the national desired target population.

In order to minimize the potential for response biases, the IEA developed participation or response rate standards that apply to all participating education systems and govern whether or not an education system's data are included in the TIMSS or PIRLS international datasets and the way in which its statistics are presented in the international reports. These standards were set using composites of response rates at the school, classroom, and student and teacher levels. Response rates were calculated with and without the inclusion of substitute schools that were selected to replace schools refusing to participate. In the 2016 PIRLS administered in the United States, the unweighted school response rate was 76 percent, and the weighted school response rate was 75 percent. All schools selected for PIRLS were also asked to participate in ePIRLS. The unweighted school response rate for ePIRLS in the final sample with replacement schools was 89.0 percent and the weighted response rate was 89.1 percent. The weighted and unweighted student response rates for PIRLS were both 94 percent. The weighted and unweighted student response rates for ePIRLS were both 90 percent.

2015 TIMSS and TIMSS Advanced

TIMSS 2015 was administered between March and May of 2015 in the United States. The U.S. sample was randomly selected and weighted to be representative of the nation. In order to reliably and accurately represent the performance of each country, international guidelines required that countries sample at least 150 schools and at least 4,000 students per grade (countries with small class sizes of fewer than 30 students per school were directed to consider sampling more schools, more classrooms per school, or both, to meet the minimum target of 4,000 tested students). In the United States, a total of 250 schools and 10,029 students participated in the grade 4 TIMSS survey, and 246 schools and 10,221 students participated in the grade 8 TIMSS (these figures do not include the participation of the state of Florida as a subnational education system, which was separate from and additional to its participation in the U.S. national sample).

TIMSS Advanced, also administered between March and May of 2015 in the United States, required participating countries and other education systems to draw probability samples of students in their final year of secondary school—ISCED Level 3—who were taking or had taken courses in advanced mathematics or who were taking or had taken courses in physics. International guidelines for TIMSS Advanced called for a minimum of 120 schools to be sampled, with a minimum of 3,600 students assessed per subject. In the United States, a total of 241 schools and 2,954 students participated in advanced mathematics, and 165 schools and 2,932 students participated in physics.

In TIMSS 2015, the weighted school response rate for the United States was 77 percent for grade 4 before the use of substitute schools (schools substituted for originally sampled schools that refused to participate) and 85 percent with the inclusion of substitute schools. For grade 8, the weighted school response rate before the use of substitute schools was 78 percent, and it was 84 percent with the inclusion of substitute schools. The weighted student response rate was 96 percent for grade 4 and 94 percent for grade 8.

In TIMSS Advanced 2015, the weighted school response rate for the United States for advanced mathematics was 72 percent before the use of substitute schools and 76 percent with the inclusion of substitute schools. The weighted school response rate for the United States for physics was 65 percent before the use of substitute schools and 68 percent with the inclusion of substitute schools. The weighted student response rate was 87 percent for advanced mathematics and 85 percent for physics. Student response rates are based on a combined total of students from both sampled and substitute schools.

Further information on the TIMSS study may be obtained from

Stephen Provasnik
International Assessment Branch
Assessments Division
National Center for Education Statistics
550 12th Street SW
Washington, DC 20202
(202) 245-6442
stephen.provasnik@ed.gov
http://nces.ed.gov/timss
http://www.iea.nl/timss

Further information on the PIRLS study may be obtained from

Sheila Thompson
International Assessment Branch
Assessments Division
National Center for Education Statistics
550 12th Street SW
Washington, DC 20202
(202) 245-8330
sheila.thompson@ed.gov
http://nces.ed.gov/surveys/pirls/
http://www.iea.nl/pirls

Organization for Economic Cooperation and Development

The Organization for Economic Cooperation and Development (OECD) publishes analyses of national policies and survey data in education, training, and economics in OECD and partner countries. Newer studies include student survey data on financial literacy and on digital literacy.

Education at a Glance

To highlight current education issues and create a set of comparative education indicators that represent key features of education systems, OECD initiated the Indicators of Education Systems (INES) project and charged the Centre for Educational Research and Innovation (CERI) with developing the cross-national indicators for it. The development of these indicators involved representatives of the OECD countries and the OECD Secretariat. Improvements in data quality and comparability among OECD countries have resulted from the country-to-country interaction sponsored through the INES project. The most recent publication in this series is *Education at a Glance 2017: OECD Indicators.*

Education at a Glance 2017 features data on the 35 OECD countries (Australia, Austria, Belgium, Canada, Chile, the Czech Republic, Denmark, Estonia, Finland, France, Germany, Greece, Hungary, Iceland, Ireland, Israel, Italy, Japan, the Republic of Korea, Latvia, Luxembourg, Mexico, the Netherlands, New Zealand, Norway, Poland, Portugal, the Slovak Republic, Slovenia, Spain, Sweden, Switzerland, Turkey, the United Kingdom, and the United States) and a number of partner countries, including Argentina, Brazil, China, Colombia, Costa Rica, India, Indonesia, Lithuania, the Russian Federation, Saudi Arabia, and South Africa.

The *OECD Handbook for Internationally Comparative Education Statistics: Concepts, Standards, Definitions, and Classifications* provides countries with specific guidance on how to prepare information for OECD education surveys; facilitates countries' understanding of OECD indicators and their use in policy analysis; and provides a reference for collecting and assimilating educational data. Chapter 6 of the *OECD Handbook for Internationally Comparative Education Statistics* contains a discussion of data quality issues. Users should examine footnotes carefully to recognize some of the data limitations.

Further information on international education statistics may be obtained from

Andreas Schleicher
Director for the Directorate of Education and Skills
 and Special Advisor on Education Policy
 to the OECD's Secretary General
OECD Directorate for Education and Skills
2, rue André Pascal
75775 Paris CEDEX 16
France
andreas.schleicher@oecd.org
http://www.oecd.org

Online Education Database (OECD.Stat)

OECD.Stat is the statistical online platform of the OECD; it allows users to access OECD's databases for OECD member countries and selected nonmember countries. A user can build tables using selected variables and customizable table layouts, extract and download data, and view metadata on methodology and sources.

Data for educational attainment, as published in the International Educational Attainment indicator, are pulled directly from OECD.Stat. (Information on these data can be found in chapter A, indicator A1 of annex 3 in *Education at a Glance 2017* and accessed at http://www.oecd.org/education/skills-beyond-school/EAG2017-Annex-3.pdf.) However, to support statistical testing, standard errors for some countries had to be estimated and therefore may differ from those published on OECD.Stat.

NCES calculated standard errors for all data years for the United States. Standard errors for 2016 for Canada, the Republic of Korea, the Netherlands, Poland, Slovenia, and Turkey, as well as standard errors for the 2016 postsecondary educational attainment data for Japan, were estimated by NCES using a simple random sample assumption. These standard errors are likely to be lower than standard errors that take into account complex sample designs. Lastly, NCES estimated the standard errors for the OECD average using the sum of squares technique.

OECD.Stat can be accessed at http://stats.oecd.org. A user's guide for OECD.Stat can be accessed at https://stats.oecd.org/Content/themes/OECD/static/help/WBOS%20User%20Guide%20(EN).pdf.

Program for International Student Assessment

The Program for International Student Assessment (PISA) is a system of international assessments organized by the Organization for Economic Cooperation and Development (OECD), an intergovernmental organization of industrialized countries, that focuses on 15-year-olds' capabilities in reading literacy, mathematics literacy, and science literacy. PISA also includes measures of general, or cross-curricular, competencies such as learning strategies. PISA emphasizes functional skills that students have acquired as they near the end of compulsory schooling.

PISA is a 2-hour exam. Assessment items include a combination of multiple-choice questions and open-ended questions that require students to develop their own response. PISA scores are reported on a scale that ranges from 0 to 1,000, with the OECD mean set at 500 and a standard deviation set at 100. In 2015, literacy in science, reading, and mathematics were assessed through a computer-based assessment in the majority of countries, including the United States. Education systems could also participate in optional pencil-and-paper financial literacy assessments and computer-based mathematics and reading assessments. In each education system, the assessment is translated into the primary language of instruction; in the United States, all materials are written in English.

Forty-three education systems participated in the 2000 PISA; 41 education systems participated in 2003; 57 (30 OECD member countries and 27 nonmember countries or education systems) participated in 2006; and 65 (34 OECD member countries and 31 nonmember countries or education systems) participated in 2009. (An additional nine education systems administered the 2009 PISA in 2010.) In PISA 2012, 65 education systems (34 OECD member countries and 31 nonmember countries or education systems), as well as the U.S. states of Connecticut, Florida, and Massachusetts, participated. In the 2015 PISA, 73 education systems (35 OECD member countries and 31 nonmember countries or education systems), as well as the states of Massachusetts and North Carolina and the territory of Puerto Rico, participated.

To implement PISA, each of the participating education systems scientifically draws a nationally representative sample of 15-year-olds, regardless of grade level. In the PISA 2015 national sample for the United States, about 5,700 students from 177 public and private schools were represented. Massachusetts, North Carolina, and Puerto Rico also participated in PISA 2015 as separate education systems. In Massachusetts, about 1,400 students from 48 public schools participated; in North Carolina, about 1,900 students from 54 public schools participated; and in Puerto Rico, about 1,400 students in 47 public and private schools participated.

The intent of PISA reporting is to provide an overall description of performance in reading literacy, mathematics literacy, and science literacy every 3 years, and to provide a more detailed look at each domain in the years when it is the major focus. These cycles will allow education systems to compare changes in trends for each of the three subject areas over time. In the first cycle, PISA 2000, reading literacy was the major focus, occupying roughly two-thirds of assessment time. For 2003, PISA focused on mathematics literacy as well as the ability of students to solve problems in real-life settings. In 2006, PISA focused on science literacy; in 2009, it focused on reading literacy again; and in 2012, it focused on mathematics literacy. PISA 2015 focused on science, as it did in 2006.

Further information on PISA may be obtained from

Patrick Gonzales
International Assessment Branch
Assessments Division
National Center for Education Statistics
550 12th Street SW
Washington, DC 20202
patrick.gonzales@ed.gov
http://nces.ed.gov/surveys/pisa

This page intentionally left blank.

Glossary

A

Achievement gap See Gap.

Achievement levels, NAEP Specific achievement levels for each subject area and grade to provide a context for interpreting student performance. At this time they are being used on a trial basis.

> **Basic**—denotes partial mastery of the knowledge and skills that are fundamental for *proficient* work at a given grade.

> **Proficient**—represents solid academic performance. Students reaching this level have demonstrated competency over challenging subject matter.

> **Advanced**—signifies superior performance.

Adjusted Cohort Graduation Rate (ACGR) The number of students who graduate in 4 years with a regular high school diploma divided by the number of students who form the adjusted cohort for the graduating class. From the beginning of 9th grade (or the earliest high school grade), students who are entering that grade for the first time form a cohort that is "adjusted" by adding any students who subsequently transfer into the cohort and subtracting any students who subsequently transfer out, emigrate to another country, or die.

Associate's degree A degree granted for the successful completion of a sub-baccalaureate program of studies, usually requiring at least 2 years (or equivalent) of full-time college-level study. This includes degrees granted in a cooperative or work-study program.

B

Bachelor's degree A degree granted for the successful completion of a baccalaureate program of studies, usually requiring at least 4 years (or equivalent) of full-time college-level study. This includes degrees granted in a cooperative or work-study program.

C

Capital outlay Funds for the acquisition of land and buildings; building construction, remodeling, and additions; the initial installation or extension of service systems and other built-in equipment; and site improvement. The category also encompasses architectural and engineering services including the development of blueprints.

Catholic school A private school over which a Roman Catholic church group exercises some control or provides some form of subsidy. Catholic schools for the most part include those operated or supported by a parish, a group of parishes, a diocese, or a Catholic religious order.

Certificate A formal award certifying the satisfactory completion of a postsecondary education program. Certificates can be awarded at any level of postsecondary education and include awards below the associate's degree level.

Charter school See Public charter school.

Classification of Instructional Programs (CIP) The CIP is a taxonomic coding scheme that contains titles and descriptions of primarily postsecondary instructional programs. It was developed to facilitate NCES' collection and reporting of postsecondary degree completions by major field of study using standard classifications that capture the majority of reportable program activity. It was originally published in 1980 and was revised in 1985, 1990, 2000, and 2010.

College A postsecondary school that offers general or liberal arts education, usually leading to an associate's, bachelor's, master's, or doctor's degree. Junior colleges and community colleges are included under this terminology.

Combined school A school that encompasses instruction at both the elementary and the secondary levels; includes schools starting with grade 6 or below and ending with grade 9 or above.

Constant dollars Dollar amounts that have been adjusted by means of price and cost indexes to eliminate inflationary factors and allow direct comparison across years.

Consumer Price Index (CPI) This price index measures the average change in the cost of a fixed market basket of goods and services purchased by consumers. Indexes vary for specific areas or regions, periods of time, major groups of consumer expenditures, and population groups. The CPI reflects spending patterns for two population groups: (1) all urban consumers and urban wage earners and (2) clerical workers. CPIs are calculated for both the calendar year and the school year using the U.S. All Items CPI for All Urban Consumers (CPI-U). The calendar year CPI is the same as the annual CPI-U. The school year CPI is calculated by adding the monthly CPI-U figures, beginning with July of the first year and ending with June of the following year, and then dividing that figure by 12.

Control of institutions A classification of institutions of elementary/secondary or postsecondary education by whether the institution is operated by publicly elected or appointed officials and derives its primary support from public funds (public control) or is operated by privately elected or appointed officials and derives its major source of funds from private sources (private control).

Current expenditures (elementary/secondary) The expenditures for operating local public schools, excluding capital outlay and interest on school debt. These expenditures include such items as salaries for school personnel, benefits, student transportation, school books and materials, and energy costs. Beginning in 1980–81, expenditures for state administration are excluded.

Instruction expenditures Includes expenditures for activities related to the interaction between teacher and students. Includes salaries and benefits for teachers and instructional aides, textbooks, supplies, and purchased services such as instruction via television, webinars, and other online instruction. Also included are tuition expenditures to other local education agencies.

Administration expenditures Includes expenditures for school administration (i.e., the office of the principal, full-time department chairpersons, and graduation expenses), general administration (the superintendent and board of education and their immediate staff), and other support services expenditures.

Transportation Includes expenditures for vehicle operation, monitoring, and vehicle servicing and maintenance.

Food services Includes all expenditures associated with providing food to students and staff in a school or school district. The services include preparing and serving regular and incidental meals or snacks in connection with school activities, as well as the delivery of food to schools.

Enterprise operations Includes expenditures for activities that are financed, at least in part, by user charges, similar to a private business. These include operations funded by sales of products or services, together with amounts for direct program support made by state education agencies for local school districts.

D

Degree-granting institutions Postsecondary institutions that are eligible for Title IV federal financial aid programs and grant an associate's or higher degree. For an institution to be eligible to participate in Title IV financial aid programs it must offer a program of at least 300 clock hours in length, have accreditation recognized by the U.S. Department of Education, have been in business for at least 2 years, and have signed a participation agreement with the Department.

Direct Loan Program The William D. Ford Federal Direct Loan (Direct Loan) Program, established in 2010, is the largest federal student loan program. Direct Loans can be awarded to undergraduate students, either with the interest subsidized (based on need) or unsubsidized; to parents of undergraduate students; or to graduate students. The U.S. Department of Education is the lender for these loans.

Disabilities, children with Those children evaluated as having any of the following impairments and who, by reason thereof, receive special education and related services under the Individuals with Disabilities Education Act (IDEA) according to an Individualized Education Program (IEP), Individualized Family Service Plan (IFSP), or a services plan. There are local variations in the determination of disability conditions, and not all states use all reporting categories.

Autism Having a developmental disability significantly affecting verbal and nonverbal communication and social interaction, generally evident before age 3, that adversely affects educational performance. Other characteristics often associated with autism are engagement in repetitive activities and stereotyped movements, resistance to environmental change or change in daily routines, and unusual responses to sensory experiences. A child is not considered autistic if the child's educational performance is adversely affected primarily because of an emotional disturbance.

Deaf-blindness Having concomitant hearing and visual impairments which cause such severe communication and other developmental and educational problems that the student cannot be accommodated in special education programs solely for deaf or blind students.

Developmental delay Having developmental delays, as defined at the state level, and as measured by appropriate diagnostic instruments and procedures in one or more of the following cognitive areas: physical development, cognitive development, communication development, social or emotional development, or adaptive development. Applies only to 3- through 9-year-old children.

Emotional disturbance Exhibiting one or more of the following characteristics over a long period of time, to a marked degree, and adversely affecting educational performance: an inability to learn which cannot be explained by intellectual, sensory, or health factors; an inability to build or maintain satisfactory interpersonal relationships with peers and teachers; inappropriate types of behavior or feelings under normal circumstances; a general pervasive mood of unhappiness or depression; or a tendency to develop physical symptoms or fears associated with personal or school problems. This term does not include children who are socially maladjusted, unless they also display one or more of the listed characteristics.

Hearing impairment Having a hearing impairment, whether permanent or fluctuating, which adversely affects the student's educational performance, but which is not included under the definition of "deaf" in this section.

Intellectual disability Having significantly subaverage general intellectual functioning, existing concurrently with defects in adaptive behavior and manifested during the developmental period, which adversely affects the child's educational performance.

Multiple disabilities Having concomitant impairments (such as intellectually disabled-blind, intellectually disabled-orthopedically impaired, etc.), the combination of which causes such severe educational problems that the student cannot be accommodated in special education programs solely for one of the impairments. Term does not include deaf-blind students.

Orthopedic impairment Having a severe orthopedic impairment which adversely affects a student's educational performance. The term includes impairment resulting from congenital anomaly, disease, or other causes.

Other health impairment Having limited strength, vitality, or alertness due to chronic or acute health problems, such as a heart condition, tuberculosis, rheumatic fever, nephritis, asthma, sickle cell anemia, hemophilia, epilepsy, lead poisoning, leukemia, or diabetes, which adversely affect the student's educational performance.

Specific learning disability Having a disorder in one or more of the basic psychological processes involved in understanding or in using spoken or written language, which may manifest itself in an imperfect ability to listen, think, speak, read, write, spell, or do mathematical calculations. The term includes such conditions as perceptual disabilities, brain injury, minimal brain dysfunction, dyslexia, and developmental aphasia. The term does not include children who have learning problems which are primarily the result of visual, hearing, motor, or intellectual disabilities, or of environmental, cultural, or economic disadvantage.

Speech or language impairment Having a communication disorder, such as stuttering, impaired articulation, language impairment, or voice impairment, which adversely affects the student's educational performance.

Traumatic brain injury Having an acquired injury to the brain caused by an external physical force, resulting in total or partial functional disability or psychosocial impairment or both, that adversely affects the student's educational performance. The term applies to open or closed head injuries resulting in impairments in one or more areas, such as cognition; language; memory; attention; reasoning; abstract thinking; judgment; problem-solving; sensory, perceptual, and motor abilities; psychosocial behavior; physical functions; information processing; and speech. The term does not apply to brain injuries that are congenital or degenerative or to brain injuries induced by birth trauma.

Visual impairment Having a visual impairment which, even with correction, adversely affects the student's educational performance. The term includes partially seeing and blind children.

Distance education Education that uses one or more technologies to deliver instruction to students who are separated from the instructor and to support regular and substantive interaction between the students and the instructor synchronously or asynchronously. Technologies used for instruction may include the following: Internet; one-way and two-way transmissions through open broadcasts, closed circuit, cable, microwave, broadband lines, fiber optics, and satellite or wireless communication devices; audio conferencing; and DVDs and CD-ROMs, if used in a course in conjunction with the technologies listed above.

Doctor's degree The highest award a student can earn for graduate study. Includes such degrees as the Doctor of Education (Ed.D.); the Doctor of Juridical Science (S.J.D.); the Doctor of Public Health (Dr.P.H.); and the Doctor of Philosophy (Ph.D.) in any field, such as agronomy, food technology, education, engineering, public administration, ophthalmology, or radiology. The doctor's degree classification encompasses three main subcategories—research/scholarship degrees, professional practice degrees, and other degrees—which are described below.

Doctor's degree—research/scholarship A Ph.D. or other doctor's degree that requires advanced work beyond the master's level, including the preparation and defense of a dissertation based on original research, or the planning and execution of an original project demonstrating substantial artistic or scholarly achievement. Examples of this type of degree may include the following and others, as designated by the awarding institution: the Ed.D. (in education), D.M.A. (in musical arts), D.B.A. (in business administration), D.Sc. (in science), D.A. (in arts), or D.M (in medicine).

Doctor's degree—professional practice A doctor's degree that is conferred upon completion of a program providing the knowledge and skills for the recognition, credential, or license required for professional practice. The degree is awarded after a period of study such that the total time to the degree, including both preprofessional and professional preparation, equals at least 6 full-time-equivalent academic years. Some doctor's degrees of this type were formerly classified as first-professional degrees. Examples of this type of degree may include the following and others, as designated by the awarding institution: the D.C. or D.C.M. (in chiropractic); D.D.S. or D.M.D. (in dentistry); L.L.B. or J.D. (in law); M.D. (in medicine); O.D. (in optometry); D.O. (in osteopathic medicine); Pharm.D. (in pharmacy); D.P.M., Pod.D., or D.P. (in podiatry); or D.V.M. (in veterinary medicine).

Doctor's degree—other A doctor's degree that does not meet the definition of either a doctor's degree—research/scholarship or a doctor's degree—professional practice.

E

Education specialist/professional diploma A certificate of advanced graduate studies that advance educators in their instructional and leadership skills beyond a master's degree level of competence.

Educational attainment The highest grade of regular school attended and completed.

Educational attainment (Current Population Survey) This measure uses March CPS data to estimate the percentage of civilian, noninstitutionalized people who have achieved certain levels of educational attainment. Estimates of educational attainment do not differentiate between those who graduated from public schools, those who graduated from private schools, and those who earned a GED; these estimates also include individuals who earned their credential or completed their highest level of education outside of the United States.

1972–1991 During this period, an individual's educational attainment was considered to be his or her last fully completed year of school. Individuals who completed 12 years of schooling were deemed to be high school graduates, as were those who began but did not complete the first year of college. Respondents who completed 16 or more years of schooling were counted as college graduates.

1992–present Beginning in 1992, CPS asked respondents to report their highest level of school completed or their highest degree received. This change means that some data collected before 1992 are not strictly comparable with data collected from 1992 onward and that care must be taken when making comparisons across years. The revised survey question emphasizes credentials received rather than the last grade level attended or completed. The new categories include the following:

- High school graduate, high school diploma, or the equivalent (e.g., GED)

- Some college but no degree

- Associate's degree in college, occupational/vocational program

- Associate's degree in college, academic program (e.g., A.A., A.S., A.A.S.)

- Bachelor's degree (e.g., B.A., A.B., B.S.)

- Master's degree (e.g., M.A., M.S., M.Eng., M.Ed., M.S.W., M.B.A.)

- Professional school degree (e.g., M.D., D.D.S., D.V.M., LL.B., J.D.)

- Doctor's degree (e.g., Ph.D., Ed.D.)

Elementary school A school classified as elementary by state and local practice and composed of any span of grades not above grade 8.

Employment status A classification of individuals as employed (either full or part time), unemployed (looking for work or on layoff), or not in the labor force (due to being retired, having unpaid employment, or some other reason).

English language learner (ELL) An individual who, due to any of the reasons listed below, has sufficient difficulty speaking, reading, writing, or understanding the English language to be denied the opportunity to learn successfully in classrooms where the language of instruction is English or to participate fully in the larger U.S. society. Such an individual (1) was not born in the United States or has a native language other than English; (2) comes from environments where a language other than English is dominant; or (3) is an American Indian or Alaska Native and comes from environments where a language other than English has had a significant impact on the individual's level of English language proficiency.

Enrollment The total number of students registered in a given school unit at a given time, generally in the fall of a year. At the postsecondary level, separate counts are also available for full-time and part-time students, as well as full-time-equivalent enrollment. See also Full-time enrollment, Full-time-equivalent (FTE) enrollment, and Part-time enrollment.

Expenditures per pupil Charges incurred for a particular period of time divided by a student unit of measure, such as average daily attendance or fall enrollment.

Expenditures, total For elementary/secondary schools, these include all charges for current outlays plus capital outlays and interest on school debt. For degree-granting institutions, these include current outlays plus capital outlays. For government, these include charges net of recoveries and other correcting transactions other than for retirement of debt, investment in securities, extension of credit, or as agency transactions. Government expenditures include only external transactions, such as the provision of perquisites or other payments in kind. Aggregates for groups of governments exclude intergovernmental transactions among the governments.

F

Financial aid Grants, loans, assistantships, scholarships, fellowships, tuition waivers, tuition discounts, veteran's benefits, employer aid (tuition reimbursement), and other monies (other than from relatives or friends) provided to students to help them meet expenses. Except where designated, includes Title IV subsidized and unsubsidized loans made directly to students.

For-profit institution See Private institution.

Free or reduced-price lunch See National School Lunch Program.

Full-time enrollment The number of students enrolled in postsecondary education courses with total credit load equal to at least 75 percent of the normal full-time course load. At the undergraduate level, full-time enrollment typically includes students who have a credit load of 12 or more semester or quarter credits. At the postbaccalaureate level, full-time enrollment includes students who typically have a credit load of 9 or more semester or quarter credits, as well as other students who are considered full time by their institutions.

Full-time-equivalent (FTE) enrollment For postsecondary institutions, enrollment of full-time students, plus the full-time equivalent of part-time students. The full-time equivalent of the part-time students is estimated using different factors depending on the type and control of institution and level of student.

G

Gap Occurs when an outcome—for example, average test score or level of educational attainment—is higher for one group than for another group, and the difference between the two groups' outcomes is statistically significant.

Geographic region One of the four regions of the United States used by the U.S. Census Bureau, as follows:

Northeast
Connecticut (CT)
Maine (ME)
Massachusetts (MA)
New Hampshire (NH)
New Jersey (NJ)
New York (NY)
Pennsylvania (PA)
Rhode Island (RI)
Vermont (VT)

Midwest
Illinois (IL)
Indiana (IN)
Iowa (IA)
Kansas (KS)
Michigan (MI)
Minnesota (MN)
Missouri (MO)
Nebraska (NE)
North Dakota (ND)
Ohio (OH)
South Dakota (SD)
Wisconsin (WI)

South
Alabama (AL)
Arkansas (AR)
Delaware (DE)
District of Columbia (DC)
Florida (FL)
Georgia (GA)
Kentucky (KY)
Louisiana (LA)
Maryland (MD)
Mississippi (MS)
North Carolina (NC)
Oklahoma (OK)
South Carolina (SC)
Tennessee (TN)
Texas (TX)
Virginia (VA)
West Virginia (WV)

West
Alaska (AK)
Arizona (AZ)
California (CA)
Colorado (CO)
Hawaii (HI)
Idaho (ID)
Montana (MT)
Nevada (NV)
New Mexico (NM)
Oregon (OR)
Utah (UT)
Washington (WA)
Wyoming (WY)

Gross domestic product (GDP) The total national output of goods and services valued at market prices. GDP can be viewed in terms of expenditure categories which include purchases of goods and services by consumers and government, gross private domestic investment, and net exports of goods and services. The goods and services included are largely those bought for final use (excluding illegal transactions) in the market economy. A number of inclusions, however, represent imputed values, the most important of which is rental value of owner-occupied housing.

H

High school completer An individual who has been awarded a high school diploma or an equivalent credential, including a GED certificate.

High school diploma A formal document regulated by the state certifying the successful completion of a prescribed secondary school program of studies. In some states or communities, high school diplomas are differentiated by type, such as an academic diploma, a general diploma, or a vocational diploma.

Historically black colleges and universities Accredited higher education institutions established prior to 1964 with the principal mission of educating black Americans. Federal regulations (20 USC 1061 [2]) allow for certain exceptions of the founding date.

Household All the people who occupy a housing unit. A house, an apartment, a mobile home, a group of rooms, or a single room is regarded as a housing unit when it is occupied or intended for occupancy as separate living quarters, that is, when the occupants do not live and eat with any other people in the structure, and there is direct access from the outside or through a common hall.

I

Individuals with Disabilities Education Act (IDEA) IDEA is a federal law enacted in 1990 and reauthorized in 1997 and 2004. IDEA requires services to children with disabilities throughout the nation. IDEA governs how states and public agencies provide early intervention, special education, and related services to eligible infants, toddlers, children, and youth with disabilities. Infants and toddlers with disabilities (birth-age 2) and their families receive early intervention services under IDEA, Part C. Children and youth (ages 3–21) receive special education and related services under IDEA, Part B.

Interest on debt Includes expenditures for long-term debt service interest payments (i.e., those longer than 1 year).

International Standard Classification of Education (ISCED) Used to compare educational systems in different countries. ISCED is the standard used by many countries to report education statistics to the United Nations Educational, Scientific, and Cultural Organization (UNESCO) and the Organization for Economic Cooperation and Development (OECD). ISCED was revised in 2011.

ISCED 2011 ISCED 2011 divides educational systems into the following nine categories, based on eight levels of education.

ISCED Level 0 Education preceding the first level (early childhood education) includes early childhood programs that target children below the age of entry into primary education.

ISCED Level 01 Early childhood educational development programs are generally designed for children younger than 3 years.

ISCED Level 02 Preprimary education preceding the first level usually begins at age 3, 4, or 5 (sometimes earlier) and lasts from 1 to 3 years, when it is provided. In the United States, this level includes nursery school and kindergarten.

ISCED Level 1 Education at the first level (primary or elementary education) usually begins at age 5, 6, or 7 and continues for about 4 to 6 years. For the United States, the first level starts with 1st grade and ends with 6th grade.

ISCED Level 2 Education at the second level (lower secondary education) typically begins at about age 11 or 12 and continues for about 2 to 6 years. For the United States, the second level starts with 7th grade and typically ends with 9th grade. Education at the lower secondary level continues the basic programs of the first level, although teaching is typically more subject focused, often using more specialized teachers who conduct classes in their field of specialization. The main criterion for distinguishing lower secondary education from primary education is whether programs begin to be organized in a more subject-oriented pattern, using more specialized teachers conducting classes in their field of specialization. If there is no clear breakpoint for this organizational change, lower secondary education is considered to begin at the end of 6 years of primary education. In countries with no clear division between lower secondary and upper secondary education, and where lower secondary education lasts for more than 3 years, only the first 3 years following primary education are counted as lower secondary education.

ISCED Level 3 Education at the third level (upper secondary education) typically begins at age 15 or 16 and lasts for approximately 3 years. In the United States, the third level starts with 10th grade and ends with 12th grade. Upper secondary education is the final stage of secondary education in most OECD countries. Instruction is often organized along subject-matter lines, in contrast to the lower secondary level, and teachers typically must have a higher level, or more subject-specific, qualification. There are substantial differences in the typical duration of programs both across and between countries, ranging from 2 to 5 years of schooling. The main criteria for classifications are (1) national boundaries between lower and upper secondary education and (2) admission into educational programs, which usually requires the completion of lower secondary education or a combination of basic education and life experience that demonstrates the ability to handle the subject matter in upper secondary schools. Includes programs designed to review the content of third level programs, such as preparatory courses for tertiary education entrance examinations, and programs leading to a qualification equivalent to upper secondary general education.

ISCED Level 4 Education at the fourth level (postsecondary non-tertiary education) straddles the boundary between secondary and postsecondary education. This program of study, which is primarily vocational in nature, is generally taken after the completion of secondary school and typically lasts from 6 months to 2 years. Although the content of these programs may not be significantly more advanced than upper secondary programs, these programs serve to broaden the knowledge of participants who have already gained an upper secondary qualification.

ISCED Level 5 Education at the fifth level (short-cycle tertiary education) is noticeably more complex than in upper secondary programs giving access to this level. Content at the fifth level is usually practically-based, occupationally specific, and prepare students to enter the labor market. However, the fifth level may also provide a pathway to other tertiary education programs (the sixth or seventh level). Short cycle-tertiary programs last for at least 2 years, and usually for no more than 3. In the United States, this level includes associate's degrees.

ISCED Level 6 Education at the sixth level (bachelor's or equivalent level) is longer and usually more theoretically oriented than programs at the fifth level, but may include practical components. Entry into these programs normally requires the completion of a third or fourth level program. They typically have a duration of 3 to 4 years of full-time study. Programs at the sixth level do not necessarily require the preparation of a substantive thesis or dissertation.

ISCED Level 7 Education at the seventh level (master's or equivalent level) has significantly more complex and specialized content than programs at the sixth level. The content at the seventh level is often designed to provide participants with advanced academic and/or professional knowledge, skills, and competencies, leading to a second degree or equivalent qualification. Programs at this level may have a substantial research component but do not yet lead to the award of a doctoral qualification. In the United States, this level includes professional degrees such as J.D., M.D., and D.D.S., as well as master degrees.

ISCED Level 8 Education at the eighth level (doctoral or equivalent level) is provided in graduate and professional schools that generally require a university degree or diploma as a minimum condition for admission. Programs at this level lead to the award of an advanced, postgraduate degree, such as a Ph.D. The theoretical duration of these programs is 3 years of full-time enrollment in most countries (for a cumulative total of at least 7 years at the tertiary level), although the length of the actual enrollment is often longer. Programs at this level are devoted to advanced study and original research.

ISCED 1997 ISCED 1997 divides educational systems into the following seven categories, based on six levels of education.

ISCED Level 0 Education preceding the first level (early childhood education) usually begins at age 3, 4, or 5 (sometimes earlier) and lasts from 1 to 3 years, when it is provided. In the United States, this level includes nursery school and kindergarten.

ISCED Level 1 Education at the first level (primary or elementary education) usually begins at age 5, 6, or 7 and continues for about 4 to 6 years. For the United States, the first level starts with 1st grade and ends with 6th grade.

ISCED Level 2 Education at the second level (lower secondary education) typically begins at about age 11 or 12 and continues for about 2 to 6 years. For the United States, the second level starts with 7th grade and typically ends with 9th grade. Education at the lower secondary level continues the basic programs of the first level, although teaching is typically more subject focused, often using more specialized teachers who conduct classes in their field of specialization. The main criterion for distinguishing lower secondary education from primary education is whether programs begin to be organized in a more subject-oriented pattern, using more specialized teachers conducting classes in their field of specialization. If there is no clear breakpoint for this organizational change, lower secondary education is considered to begin at the end of 6 years of primary education. In countries with no clear division between lower secondary and upper secondary education, and where lower secondary education lasts for more than 3 years, only the first 3 years following primary education are counted as lower secondary education.

ISCED Level 3 Education at the third level (upper secondary education) typically begins at age 15 or 16 and lasts for approximately 3 years. In the United States, the third level starts with 10th grade and ends with 12th grade. Upper secondary education is the final stage of secondary education in most OECD countries. Instruction is often organized along subject-matter lines, in contrast to the lower secondary level, and teachers typically must have a higher level, or more subject-specific, qualification. There are substantial differences in the typical duration of programs both across and between countries, ranging from 2 to 5 years of schooling. The main criteria for classifications are (1) national boundaries between lower and upper secondary education and (2) admission into educational programs, which usually requires the completion of lower secondary education or a combination of basic education and life experience that demonstrates the ability to handle the subject matter in upper secondary schools.

ISCED Level 4 Education at the fourth level (postsecondary non-tertiary education) straddles the boundary between secondary and postsecondary education. This program of study, which is primarily vocational in nature, is generally taken after the completion of secondary school and typically lasts from 6 months to 2 years. Although the content of these programs may not be significantly more advanced than upper secondary programs, these programs serve to broaden the knowledge of participants who have already gained an upper secondary qualification.

ISCED Level 5 Education at the fifth level (first stage of tertiary education) includes programs with more advanced content than those offered at the two previous levels. Entry into programs at the fifth level normally requires successful completion of either of the two previous levels.

ISCED Level 5A Tertiary-type A programs provide an education that is largely theoretical and is intended to provide sufficient qualifications for gaining entry into advanced research programs and professions with high skill requirements. Entry into these programs normally requires the successful completion of an upper secondary education; admission is competitive in most cases. The minimum cumulative theoretical duration at this level is 3 years of full-time enrollment. In the United States, tertiary-type A programs include first university programs that last approximately 4 years and lead to the award of a bachelor's degree and second university programs that lead to a master's degree or a first-professional degree such as an M.D., a J.D., or a D.V.M.

ISCED Level 5B Tertiary-type B programs are typically shorter than tertiary-type A programs and focus on practical, technical, or occupational skills for direct entry into the labor market, although they may cover some theoretical foundations in the respective programs. They have a minimum duration of 2 years of full-time enrollment at the tertiary level. In the United States, such programs are often provided at community colleges and lead to an associate's degree.

ISCED Level 6 Education at the sixth level (advanced research qualification) is provided in graduate and professional schools that generally require a university degree or diploma as a minimum condition for admission. Programs at this level lead to the award of an advanced, postgraduate degree, such as a Ph.D. The theoretical duration of these programs is 3 years of full-time enrollment in most countries (for a cumulative total of at least 7 years at levels five and six), although the length of the actual enrollment is often longer. Programs at this level are devoted to advanced study and original research.

L

Locale codes A classification system to describe a type of location. The "Metro-Centric" locale codes, developed in the 1980s, classified all schools and school districts based on their county's proximity to a Metropolitan Statistical Area (MSA) and their specific location's population size and density. In 2006, the "Urban-Centric" locale codes were introduced. These locale codes are based on an address's proximity to an urbanized area. For more information see https://nces.ed.gov/programs/edge/docs/EDGE_NCES_LOCALE_2015.pdf.

Pre-2006 Metro-Centric Locale Codes

Large City: A central city of a consolidated metropolitan statistical area (CMSA) or MSA, with the city having a population greater than or equal to 250,000.

Mid-Size City: A central city of a CMSA or MSA, with the city having a population less than 250,000.

Urban Fringe of a Large City: Any territory within a CMSA or MSA of a Large City and defined as urban by the Census Bureau.

Urban Fringe of a Mid-Size City: Any territory within a CMSA or MSA of a Mid-Size City and defined as urban by the Census Bureau.

Large Town: An incorporated place or Census-designated place with a population greater than or equal to 25,000 and located outside a CMSA or MSA.

Small Town: An incorporated place or Census-designated place with a population less than 25,000 and greater than or equal to 2,500 and located outside a CMSA or MSA.

Rural, Outside MSA: Any territory designated as rural by the Census Bureau that is outside a CMSA or MSA of a Large or Mid-Size City.

Rural, Inside MSA: Any territory designated as rural by the Census Bureau that is within a CMSA or MSA of a Large or Mid-Size City.

2006 Urban-Centric Locale Codes

City, Large: Territory inside an urbanized area and inside a principal city with population of 250,000 or more.

City, Midsize: Territory inside an urbanized area and inside a principal city with population less than 250,000 and greater than or equal to 100,000.

City, Small: Territory inside an urbanized area and inside a principal city with population less than 100,000.

Suburb, Large: Territory outside a principal city and inside an urbanized area with population of 250,000 or more.

Suburb, Midsize: Territory outside a principal city and inside an urbanized area with population less than 250,000 and greater than or equal to 100,000.

Suburb, Small: Territory outside a principal city and inside an urbanized area with population less than 100,000.

Town, Fringe: Territory inside an urban cluster that is less than or equal to 10 miles from an urbanized area.

Town, Distant: Territory inside an urban cluster that is more than 10 miles and less than or equal to 35 miles from an urbanized area.

Town, Remote: Territory inside an urban cluster that is more than 35 miles from an urbanized area.

Rural, Fringe: Census-defined rural territory that is less than or equal to 5 miles from an urbanized area, as well as rural territory that is less than or equal to 2.5 miles from an urban cluster.

Rural, Distant: Census-defined rural territory that is more than 5 miles but less than or equal to 25 miles from an urbanized area, as well as rural territory that is more than 2.5 miles but less than or equal to 10 miles from an urban cluster.

Rural, Remote: Census-defined rural territory that is more than 25 miles from an urbanized area and is also more than 10 miles from an urban cluster.

M

Master's degree A degree awarded for successful completion of a program generally requiring 1 or 2 years of full-time college-level study beyond the bachelor's degree. One type of master's degree, including the Master of Arts degree, or M.A., and the Master of Science degree, or M.S., is awarded in the liberal arts and sciences for advanced scholarship in a subject field or discipline and demonstrated ability to perform scholarly research. A second type of master's degree is awarded for the completion of a professionally oriented program, for example, an M.Ed. in education, an M.B.A. in business administration, an M.F.A. in fine arts, an M.M. in music, an M.S.W. in social work, and an M.P.A. in public administration. Some master's degrees—such as divinity degrees (M.Div. or M.H.L./Rav), which were formerly classified as "first-professional"—may require more than 2 years of full-time study beyond the bachelor's degree.

Median earnings The amount which divides the income distribution into two equal groups, half having income above that amount and half having income below that amount. Earnings include all wage and salary income. Unlike mean earnings, median earnings either do not change or change very little in response to extreme observations.

N

National School Lunch Program Established by President Truman in 1946, the program is a federally assisted meal program operated in public and private nonprofit schools and residential child care centers. To be eligible for free lunch, a student must be from a household with an income at or below 130 percent of the federal poverty guideline; to be eligible for reduced-price lunch, a student must be from a household with an income between 130 percent and 185 percent of the federal poverty guideline.

Nonprofit institution See Private institution.

Nonsectarian school Nonsectarian schools do not have a religious orientation or purpose and are categorized as regular, special program emphasis, or special education schools. See also Regular school.

O

Organization for Economic Cooperation and Development (OECD) An intergovernmental organization of industrialized countries that serves as a forum for member countries to cooperate in research and policy development on social and economic topics of common interest. In addition to member countries, partner countries contribute to the OECD's work in a sustained and comprehensive manner.

Open admissions Admission policy whereby the school will accept any student who applies.

Other religious school Other religious schools have a religious orientation or purpose, but are not Roman Catholic. Other religious schools are categorized according to religious association membership as Conservative Christian, other affiliated, or unaffiliated.

P

Part-time enrollment The number of students enrolled in postsecondary education courses with a total credit load less than 75 percent of the normal full-time credit load. At the undergraduate level, part-time enrollment typically includes students who have a credit load of less than 12 semester or quarter credits. At the postbaccalaureate level, part-time enrollment typically includes students who have a credit load of less than 9 semester or quarter credits.

Postbaccalaureate certificate An award that requires completion of an organized program of study beyond a bachelor's degree. It is designed for persons who have completed a baccalaureate degree, but does not meet the requirements of a master's degree. Even though teacher preparation certificate programs may require a bachelor's degree for admission, they are considered sub-baccalaureate undergraduate programs, and students in these programs are undergraduate students.

Postbaccalaureate enrollment The number of students working towards advanced degrees and of students enrolled in graduate-level classes but not enrolled in degree programs.

Postsecondary education The provision of formal instructional programs with a curriculum designed primarily for students who have completed the requirements for a high school diploma or equivalent. This includes programs of an academic, vocational, and continuing professional education purpose, and excludes avocational and adult basic education programs.

Postsecondary institutions (basic classification by level)

4-year institution An institution offering at least a 4-year program of college-level studies wholly or principally creditable toward a baccalaureate degree.

2-year institution An institution offering at least a 2-year program of college-level studies which terminates in an associate degree or is principally creditable toward a baccalaureate degree. Data prior to 1996 include some institutions that have a less-than-2-year program, but were designated as institutions of higher education in the Higher Education General Information Survey.

Less-than-2-year institution An institution that offers programs of less than 2 years' duration below the baccalaureate level. Includes occupational and vocational schools with programs that do not exceed 1,800 contact hours.

Poverty (official measure) The U.S. Census Bureau uses a set of money income thresholds that vary by family size and composition. A family, along with each individual in it, is considered poor if the family's total income is less than that family's threshold. The poverty thresholds do not vary geographically and are adjusted annually for inflation using the Consumer Price Index. The official poverty definition counts money income before taxes and does not include capital gains and noncash benefits (such as public housing, Medicaid, and food stamps).

Prekindergarten Preprimary education for children typically ages 3–4 who have not yet entered kindergarten. It may offer a program of general education or special education and may be part of a collaborative effort with Head Start.

Preschool An instructional program enrolling children generally younger than 5 years of age and organized to provide children with educational experiences under professionally qualified teachers during the year or years immediately preceding kindergarten (or prior to entry into elementary school when there is no kindergarten). See also Prekindergarten.

Private institution An institution that is controlled by an individual or agency other than a state, a subdivision of a state, or the federal government, which is usually supported primarily by other than public funds, and the operation of whose program rests with other than publicly elected or appointed officials.

Private nonprofit institution An institution in which the individual(s) or agency in control receives no compensation other than wages, rent, or other expenses for the assumption of risk. These include both independent nonprofit institutions and those affiliated with a religious organization.

Private for-profit institution An institution in which the individual(s) or agency in control receives compensation other than wages, rent, or other expenses for the assumption of risk (e.g., proprietary schools).

Private school Private elementary/secondary schools surveyed by the Private School Universe Survey (PSS) are assigned to one of three major categories (Catholic, other religious, or nonsectarian) and, within each major category, one of three subcategories based on the school's religious affiliation provided by respondents.

Catholic Schools categorized according to governance, provided by Catholic school respondents, into parochial, diocesan, and private schools.

Other religious Schools that have a religious orientation or purpose but are not Roman Catholic. Other religious schools are categorized according to religious association membership, provided by respondents, into Conservative Christian, other affiliated, and unaffiliated schools. Conservative Christian schools are those "Other religious" schools with membership in at least one of four associations: Accelerated Christian Education, American Association of Christian Schools, Association of Christian Schools International, and Oral Roberts University Education Fellowship. Affiliated schools are those "Other religious" schools not classified as Conservative Christian with membership in at least 1 of 11 associations—Association of Christian Teachers and Schools, Christian Schools International, Evangelical Lutheran Education Association, Friends Council on Education, General Conference of the Seventh-Day Adventist Church, Islamic School League of America, National Association of Episcopal Schools, National Christian School Association, National Society for Hebrew Day Schools, Solomon Schechter Day Schools, and Southern Baptist Association of Christian Schools—or indicating membership in "other religious school associations." Unaffiliated schools are those "Other religious" schools that have a religious orientation or purpose but are not classified as Conservative Christian or affiliated.

Nonsectarian Schools that do not have a religious orientation or purpose and are categorized according to program emphasis, provided by respondents, into regular, special emphasis, and special education schools. Regular schools are those that have a regular elementary/secondary or early childhood program emphasis. Special emphasis schools are those that have a Montessori, vocational/technical, alternative, or special program emphasis. Special education schools are those that have a special education program emphasis.

Property tax The sum of money collected from a tax levied against the value of property.

Public charter school A school providing free public elementary and/or secondary education to eligible students under a specific charter granted by the state legislature or other authority, and designated by such authority to be a charter school.

Public school or institution A school or institution controlled and operated by publicly elected or appointed officials and deriving its primary support from public funds.

Purchasing Power Parity (PPP) indexes PPP exchange rates, or indexes, are the currency exchange rates that equalize the purchasing power of different currencies, meaning that when a given sum of money is converted into different currencies at the PPP exchange rates, it will buy the same basket of goods and services in all countries. PPP indexes are the rates of currency conversion that eliminate the difference in price levels among countries. Thus, when expenditures on gross domestic product (GDP) for different countries are converted into a common currency by means of PPP indexes, they are expressed at the same set of international prices, so that comparisons among countries reflect only differences in the volume of goods and services purchased.

R

Racial/ethnic group Classification indicating general racial or ethnic heritage. Race/ethnicity data are based on the *Hispanic* ethnic category and the race categories listed below (five single-race categories, plus the *Two or more races* category). Race categories exclude persons of Hispanic ethnicity unless otherwise noted.

> **White** A person having origins in any of the original peoples of Europe, the Middle East, or North Africa.

> **Black or African American** A person having origins in any of the black racial groups of Africa. Used interchangeably with the shortened term *Black*.

> **Hispanic or Latino** A person of Cuban, Mexican, Puerto Rican, South or Central American, or other Spanish culture or origin, regardless of race. Used interchangeably with the shortened term *Hispanic*.

> **Asian** A person having origins in any of the original peoples of the Far East, Southeast Asia, or the Indian subcontinent, including, for example, Cambodia, China, India, Japan, Korea, Malaysia, Pakistan, the Philippine Islands, Thailand, and Vietnam. Prior to 2010–11, the Common Core of Data (CCD) combined Asian and Pacific Islander categories.

> **Native Hawaiian or Other Pacific Islander** A person having origins in any of the original peoples of Hawaii, Guam, Samoa, or other Pacific Islands. Prior to 2010–11, the Common Core of Data (CCD) combined Asian and Pacific Islander categories. Used interchangeably with the shortened term *Pacific Islander*.

> **American Indian or Alaska Native** A person having origins in any of the original peoples of North and South America (including Central America), and who maintains tribal affiliation or community attachment.

> **Two or more races** A person identifying himself or herself as of two or more of the following race groups: White, Black, Asian, Native Hawaiian or Other Pacific Islander, or American Indian or Alaska Native. Some, but not all, reporting districts use this category. "Two or more races" was introduced in the 2000 Census and became a regular category for data collection in the Current Population Survey in 2003. The category is sometimes excluded from a historical series of data with constant categories. It is sometimes included within the category "Other."

Regular school A public elementary/secondary or charter school providing instruction and education services that does not focus primarily on special education, vocational/technical education, or alternative education.

Retention rate A measure of the rate at which students persist in their educational program at an institution, expressed as a percentage. For four-year institutions, this is the percentage of first-time bachelor's (or equivalent) degree-seeking undergraduates from the previous fall who are again enrolled in the current fall. For all other institutions, this is the percentage of first-time degree/certificate-seeking students from the previous fall who either re-enrolled or successfully completed their program by the current fall.

Revenue All funds received from external sources, net of refunds, and correcting transactions. Noncash transactions, such as receipt of services, commodities, or other receipts in kind are excluded, as are funds received from the issuance of debt, liquidation of investments, and nonroutine sale of property.

S

Salary The total amount regularly paid or stipulated to be paid to an individual, before deductions, for personal services rendered while on the payroll of a business or organization.

School district An education agency at the local level that exists primarily to operate public schools or to contract for public school services. Synonyms are "local basic administrative unit" and "local education agency."

Secondary school A school comprising any span of grades beginning with the next grade following an elementary or middle school (usually 7, 8, or 9) and ending with or below grade 12. Both junior high schools and senior high schools are included.

Status dropout rate (American Community Survey) Similar to the status dropout rate (Current Population Survey), except that institutionalized persons, incarcerated persons, and active duty military personnel living in barracks in the United States may be included in this calculation.

Status dropout rate (Current Population Survey) The percentage of civilian, noninstitutionalized young people ages 16–24 who are not in school and have not earned a high school credential (either a diploma or equivalency credential such as a GED certificate). The numerator of the status dropout rate for a given year is the number of individuals ages 16–24 who, as of October of that year, have not completed a high school credential and are not currently enrolled in school. The denominator is the total number of individuals ages 16–24 in the United States in October of that year. Status dropout rates count the following individuals as dropouts: those who never attended school and immigrants who did not complete the equivalent of a high school education in their home country.

STEM fields Science, Technology, Engineering, and Mathematics (STEM) fields of study that are considered to be of particular relevance to advanced societies. For the purposes of *The Condition of Education 2018*, STEM fields include biological and biomedical sciences, computer and information sciences, engineering and engineering technologies, mathematics and statistics, and physical sciences and science technologies. STEM occupations include computer scientists and mathematicians; engineers and architects; life, physical, and social scientists; medical professionals; and managers of STEM activities.

Student membership Student membership is an annual headcount of students enrolled in school on October 1 or the school day closest to that date. The Common Core of Data (CCD) allows a student to be reported for only a single school or agency. For example, a vocational school (identified as a "shared time" school) may provide classes for students from a number of districts and show no membership.

T

Title IV eligible institution A postsecondary institution that meets the criteria for participating in federal student financial aid programs. An eligible institution must be any of the following: (1) an institution of higher education (with public or private, nonprofit control), (2) a proprietary institution (with private for-profit control), and (3) a postsecondary vocational institution (with public or private, nonprofit control). In addition, it must have acceptable legal authorization, acceptable accreditation and admission standards, eligible academic program(s), administrative capability, and financial responsibility.

Traditional public school Publicly funded schools other than public charter schools. See also Public school or institution and Public charter school.

Tuition and fees A payment or charge for instruction or compensation for services, privileges, or the use of equipment, books, or other goods. Tuition may be charged per term, per course, or per credit.

U

Undergraduate students Students registered at an institution of postsecondary education who are working in a baccalaureate degree program or other formal program below the baccalaureate, such as an associate's degree, vocational, or technical program.